P9-CKS-429

CYCLING AUSTRALIA

Nicola Wells
Ian Connellan
Peter Hines
Lesley Hodgson
Neil Irvine
Catherine Palmer

LONELY PLANET PUBLICATIONS
Melbourne • Oakland • London • Paris

INDONESIA

EAST
TIMOR

TIMOR   SEA

Arafura
Sea

Melville
Island

Bathurst
Island

Darwin

ARNHEM
LAND

To Christmas &
Cocos (Keeling) Islands

A1

Katherine

Mataranka

INDIAN

OCEAN

THE
KIMBERLEY

Wyndham Kununurra

Lake
Argyle

Daly Waters

Derby

Halls
Creek

NORTHERN

Broome

Fitzroy
Crossing

A1

Tanami

TERRITORY

GREAT
SANDY
DESERT

Tennant Creek

Port Hedland

Desert

A87

Dampier

Marble Bar

Macdonnell   Ranges

Onslow

Exmouth

THE PILBARA

Tom Price

Newman

Alice Springs

GIBSON

Tropic of Capricorn

A1

DESERT

Uluru
(Ayers Rock)

Carnarvon

A95

Shark
Bay

WESTERN

Denham

Meekatharra

SOUTH

GREAT
VICTORIA
DESERT

Coober Pedy

INDIAN

Mt Magnet

AUSTRALIA

OCEAN

Geraldton

NULLARBOR   PLAIN

Kalgoorlie

Eucla

Ceduna

A94

Perth

Norseman

A1

GREAT

Penong

Fremantle

AUSTRALIAN

Esperance

BIGHT

Bunbury

A1

Cape
Leeuwin

Albany

SOUTH AUSTRALIA
Get off the beaten track on the
Mawson Trail in the premier
wine-growing region of the
Barossa or enjoy pounding surf
beaches and gorgeous coastal
towns on the Fleurieu Peninsula.

0   250   500km

0   125   250mi

1:21,500,000

WESTERN AUSTRALIA
Relaxed cycling past
Australia's best wild flower
displays, rare forest giants,
Margaret River wineries, quiet
towns and the Southern Ocean's
wild, rocky coast.

SOUTHERN   OCEAN

ELEVATION

1500m

1000m

500m

200m

0

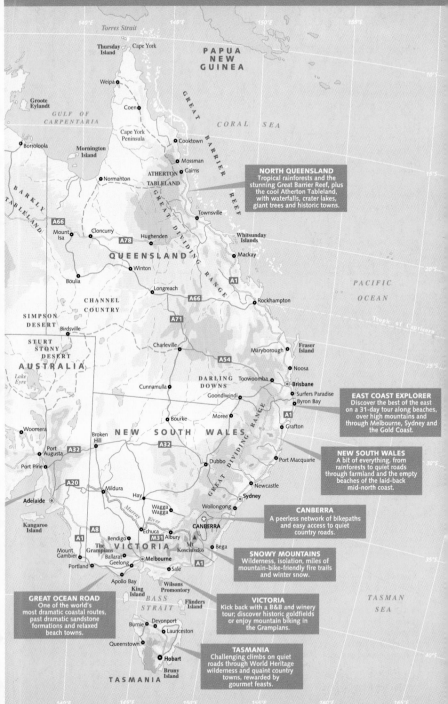

NORTH QUEENSLAND
Tropical rainforests and the stunning Great Barrier Reef, plus the cool Atherton Tableland, with waterfalls, crater lakes, giant trees and historic towns.

EAST COAST EXPLORER
Discover the best of the east on a 31-day tour along beaches, over high mountains and through Melbourne, Sydney and the Gold Coast.

NEW SOUTH WALES
A bit of everything, from rainforests to quiet roads through farmland and the empty beaches of the laid-back mid-north coast.

CANBERRA
A peerless network of bikepaths and easy access to quiet country roads.

SNOWY MOUNTAINS
Wilderness, isolation, miles of mountain-bike-friendly fire trails and winter snow.

GREAT OCEAN ROAD
One of the world's most dramatic coastal routes, past dramatic sandstone formations and relaxed beach towns.

VICTORIA
Kick back with a B&B and winery tour; discover historic goldfields or enjoy mountain biking in the Grampians.

TASMANIA
Challenging climbs on quiet roads through World Heritage wilderness and quaint country towns, rewarded by gourmet feasts.

Cycling Australia
1st edition – April 2001

Published by
Lonely Planet Publications Pty Ltd ABN 36 005 607 983
90 Maribyrnong St, Footscray, Victoria 3011, Australia

Lonely Planet Offices
Australia Locked Bag 1, Footscray, Victoria 3011
USA 150 Linden St, Oakland, CA 94607
UK 10a Spring Place, London NW5 3BH
France 1 rue du Dahomey, 75011 Paris

Photographs
Most of the images in this guide are available for licensing from
Lonely Planet Images (e lpi@lonelyplanet.com.au)

Main front cover photograph
The road to Kata Tjuta (the Olgas), NT (Richard I'Anson)

Small front cover photograph
Sign in Nelson Bay, NSW (Ian Connellan)

Back cover photographs (from left to right)
Cyclists in the Tour Down Under, Adelaide, SA (Russell Mountford)
Mountain biking in Western Australia (Trevor Creighton)
Tandem touring with a child, NSW (Peter Hines)

ISBN 1 86450 166 9

Printed by SNP SPrint (M) Sdn Bhd
Printed in Malaysia

Although the authors and Lonely Planet try to make the information as accurate as possible, we accept no responsibility for any loss, injury or inconvenience sustained by anyone using this book.

Contents

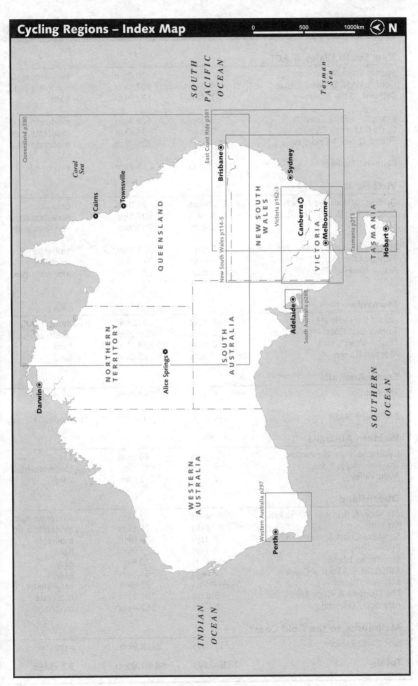

0   500   1000km   N

SOUTH PACIFIC OCEAN

Tasman Sea

Queensland p330

Coral Sea

East Coast Ride p381

⦿ Brisbane

⦿ Sydney

⦿ Cairns

⦿ Townsville

QUEENSLAND

Victoria p162-3

NEW SOUTH WALES

New South Wales p114-5

Canberra ✛

⦿ Melbourne

VICTORIA

TASMANIA

Tasmania p213

⦿ Hobart

NORTHERN TERRITORY

SOUTH AUSTRALIA

⦿ Adelaide

South Australia p268

⦿ Alice Springs

⦿ Darwin

SOUTHERN OCEAN

WESTERN AUSTRALIA

Western Australia p297

⦿ Perth

INDIAN OCEAN

The Rides	Duration	Distance	Difficulty
New South Wales & ACT			
Sydney Olympic Explorer	2–3 hours	30.0km	easy-moderate
Gold & Wine Country Circuit	4 days	307.5km	moderate-hard
Bathurst to the Blueys	2 days	132.9km	hard
Kosciuszko High Country	3 days	128.4km	moderate-hard
Coffs & Dorrigo Circuit	2 days	136.6km	moderate-hard
Thunderbolts & Bucketts	4 days	281.4km	moderate-hard
Canberra Explorer	2½–3 hours	35.7km	easy-moderate
Victoria			
Cycling to/from the Airport	1½–2½ hours	25.0km	easy
Central Gold & Spa Country	5 days	307.1km	easy-moderate
The Grampians	3 days	207.9km	easy-moderate
The Great Ocean Road	5 days	281.4km	moderate
Riches of the North-East	4 days	221.1km	moderate
Across the High Country	3 days	237.8km	moderate-hard
Tasmania			
Across the Central Plateau	6 days	384.2km	moderate-hard
Tassie's East Coast	6 days	438.2km	moderate-hard
Tassie's West Coast	10 days	669.5km	hard
Meehan Range	2½–3½ hours	25.0km	hard
South Australia			
The Fleurieu	5 days	289.0km	moderate
Barossa Heritage	6 days	301.4km	moderate
Western Australia			
Cycling to/from the Airport	1–2 hours	26.6km	easy
Tall Trees & High Seas	9 days	611.4km	moderate-hard
Avon Valley	3 days	272.0km	hard
Queensland			
Mt Nebo & Brisbane Forest Park	3–5 hours	52.1km	moderate-hard
Mt Mee	4–7½ hours	75.9km	moderate-hard
Sunshine Coast & Hinterland	3 days	135.0km	moderate
Border Loop	5 days	338.9km	hard
Stradbroke Island	3–5 hours	46.8km	easy
Mt Stuart & Alligator Creek	2 days	64.6km	easy
Magnetic Island	1½–2½ hours	22.6km	easy-moderate
The Daintree & Cape Tribulation	3 days	181.7km	moderate
Atherton Tableland	5 days	252.4km	moderate
Melbourne to the Gold Coast			
East Coast Explorer	31 days	2319.9km	hard
Totals	**138 days**	**8840.0km**	**32 rides**

Features	Page

The Authors

Nicola Wells

Nicola lives in Melbourne and grew up in regional Victoria. She rode a bike while living in Sweden, aged 12, and rediscovered cycling at university, where she became passionate about bicycling's environmental, social and health benefits. It is still her main transport, preserver of sanity and preferred mode for travel.

With an honours degree in ecology, she has had various writing and research-based jobs; worked for Bicycle Victoria; and done a stint in a bike shop. She has also co-authored Lonely Planet's *Cycling New Zealand* and *Cycling Britain*. Her other passions include classical music, especially choral singing (which, she regrets, is not terribly compatible with cycle touring) and food (which is). She has a particular weakness for good coffee.

Ian Connellan

Ian grew up in Sydney and currently lives there with his family; he spent several years ski-and-cycle bumming in Australia, the USA and Europe after completing university studies in literature, history and professional writing. Since the late 1980s he has worked as a writer and editor on magazines and books. This is his second book for Lonely Planet.

Peter Hines

Peter grew up riding the suburbs of Brisbane on a three-speed dragster, long after they were decidedly uncool. Despite the fashion accident he kept riding, and the bike is still his principal transport. An organised tour in north Queensland in 1993 showed him the open road and he has been exploring it ever since. Peter has cycled in New Zealand, Thailand, the UK, France and throughout Australia. He loves hammering down a dirt track in the Australian bush, but knows too the enchantment of freewheeling down a quiet, English country lane. Peter is married with a tandem, seven single bikes and a unicycle.

Lesley Hodgson

Lesley has been cycle touring in Victoria for nearly 20 years and there isn't much of the state she hasn't ridden to, through, up or down. Lesley is a physical geographer with a passionate interest in geomorphology, a subject which she is able to indulge on her many cycling forays. Her favourite holidays involve getting away from it all on a fully laden mountain bike and exploring Victoria's high country.

Neil Irvine

Neil has been a cycling journalist for much of his working life, founding *Australian Cyclist* magazine in 1989 and remaining its editor until 1998, a career punctuated by cycle tours abroad with his features editor and wife, Alethea.

Neil has toured extensively – by road bike, mountain bike and tandem – in Australia, North America, and Europe (and more recently as a Lonely Planet author, in New Zealand, France and Tasmania).

His interests and experience include lobbying for better cycling conditions at local, state and national level. With his very supportive wife, he has shared a love of the challenges of distance and mountains, in combination where possible. Lately his riding has been more gentle, with a child-seat or trailer on the back, as he introduces his young children, Alexander and Laura, to the pleasures of cycling.

Catherine Palmer

Born in Adelaide, South Australia, Catherine has worked in a number of jobs, including researcher, university lecturer and ethnographer. Having worked for Lonely Planet on *Cycling France*, Catherine gets to cycle somewhat closer to home for the South Australia chapter of this guide.

FROM THE AUTHORS

Nicola Wells I'm grateful to the many who responded to my pestering with grace and camaraderie – including Damien Grundy, Andrew Jones from the Fat Tyre Flyers, Ron Shepherd (a bicycle historian who should go down in the annals himself), Terry Lindley from Bike West, Justin from Mallard Cycles, Bruce from Fleet Cycles, Ian and Richard from Christie Cycles, staff at Albany's Great Southern Bicycle Company, Gary from the Black Cockatoo, Simon from Margaret River Lodge, Walter from Northbridge YHA, Neville from Augusta YHA, Albany YHA, Albany Backpackers, Kylie Smith, and the staff at many visitor centres.

I'm particularly appreciative of the support of friends and family (thanks, for various bits of assistance – and generally, to Mum and Dad, Alison, Tim, Ann, Rosie, Lynden, Brian, Jim and Gwynneth, and to the long-suffering Jen, Stuey and Paul). Special thanks to John Cleary for a western home base, taxi service and fun. Finally, the fraternalism of my colleagues – thanks especially to Ian, Lesley and Darren – have kept the fun times rolling through the uphill bits.

Ian Connellan Ian Connellan thanks in-housers at LP – in particular Darren Elder – and fellow East Coast Explorer authors Nicola Wells and Peter Hines for their support and patience when family matters displaced schedules. The love and grand homecoming parties from Jane, Tess and Adam make all the pedalling worthwhile.

In the Snowy Mountains, Barry Dennis helped with route planning (and came for the ride) while Julie Bourke, Ross Dunstan and Cheryl Hamilton kicked in with food and lodgings. Sue Webber and Trevor Creighton served advice and croissants in Canberra; Lloyd and Angelique Mason administered dinner and local insight at Coffs Harbour. In Thunderbolt country, Matt and Jodie Cawood offered peerless route advice and hospitality at the Armidale end, and Linda and Gary German a welcome home-cooked meal in Gloucester.

Patient locals from Nimmitabel to Nowendoc answered questions with humour and kindness, and special thanks goes to the honest souls in friendly Walcha who found and returned my wallet.

On practical matters, the bag medics at Wilderness Equipment in Fremantle, WA, resuscitated my aging but brilliant Supertour panniers, while the crew at Bike Addiction in Fairlight, Sydney, extracted smooth running from a bicycle well past its prime.

Peter Hines Thanks to Dan Ellis for tips, a bed, and a cold beer at the end of the day in Townsville. Thanks too to long-suffering Bill and Ailsa Armbrust for sharing their local knowledge and rescuing me once again when Cairns had its 'No Vacancy' sign out. Joan Bryan and Deniss Reeves gave me great support during the Southeast Queensland work as did my parents Mike and Judy Hines. Special thanks to Sally Dillon for being a great partner throughout.

Lesley Hodgson I would like to thank the Melbourne Bicycle Touring Club for introducing me to cycle touring, and various members for providing heaps of advice about the best routes. Thanks to Richard for putting up with my absences (wishing he was there), to Ron Shepherd for information on Melbourne's cycling history and to my trusty green Cannondale for getting me around.

Neil Irvine Particular thanks must go to Stephen Jay of Bicycle Tasmania for his friendliness, his helpfulness and the enthusiasm with which he supplied advice and information about his state.

My gratitude, as always, goes to my wife, Alethea, for her understanding about my prolonged absences from home, and for entertaining Alexander while both accompanied me for part of my research in Tasmania. Thanks to my parents, Bob and Dulcie, and to Alethea's parents, Bill and Mary, who all helped keep the household running while I was away and during the long writing process.

It is a source of great sadness that Alethea's father, Bill Morison, former Challis Professor of Law at the University of Sydney, died as I wrote the Tasmania chapter. Bill and Mary enjoyed cycle touring together in Wales after WWII, riding heavy old single-gear clunkers with Bill often pushing Mary up the hills. I feel there is a strong parallel with Alethea's and my life (though the one needing pushing, in our case, was towing a child trailer with a chubby three-year-old on board).

Catherine Palmer Many people provided help and advice on pedaling in South Australia, and special thanks are due to the following: Craig and Celia Fielke for a much appreciated bed and bath in the Barossa, Ian and Sophie for a welcomed cuppa in the Hills, and everybody at Europa Bookshop for letting me repeatedly raid their shelves. Once again, my biggest thank you is saved for David Johnson, whose companionship, support and willingness to lead into the wind made my trip a special one.

Maps & Profiles

Most rides described in this book have an accompanying map that shows the route, services provided in towns en route as well as any attractions and possible side trips. These maps are oriented left to right in the direction of travel; a north point is located in the top right corner of each map. The maps are intended to stand alone but could be used together with one of the commercial maps recommended in the Planning section for each ride.

We provide a profile, or elevation chart, when there is a significant level of climbing and/or descending on a day's ride; most of the time these charts are included on the corresponding map but where space does not permit they accompany the text for that day. These charts are approximate and should be used as a guide only.

MAP LEGEND

Note: not all symbols displayed below appear in this book

CUE SHEET SYMBOLS

Continue Straight	Veer Left	Caution or Hazard	Alternative Route
Right Turn	Return Trip	Traffic Lights	
Veer Right	Point of Interest	Roundabout (Traffic Circle)	
Left Turn	Mountain/Hill Climb	Side Trip	

RIDE MAP SYMBOLS

Airport	Information
Bike Shop	Lookout
Cafe, Takeaway or Pub Food	Point of Interest
Camping	Point of Interest on Ride
Hostel	Restaurant
Hotel, Motel, B&B	Store, Supermarket

CITY MAP SYMBOLS

Church
Embassy
Gallery, Museum
Hospital
Post Office

POPULATION

✪CAPITAL National Capital	●LARGE Medium City
◉CAPITAL State Capital	●Town Village Town

Town Town on Ride
Urban Area

ROUTES & TRANSPORT

M1 Freeway, Tunnel	Train Line, Train Station
A30 Primary Road	Metro, Metro Station
A45 Main Road	Tramway, Bus Terminal
B4530 Secondary Road	Bikepath/Track
Unsealed Road	Chairlift
Lane (one-way)	Ferry

CYCLING ROUTES

Main Route
Alternative Route
Side Trip
Previous/Next Day
Route Direction

HYDROGRAPHIC FEATURES

Coastline, River, Creek	Spring, Rapids
Canal	Swamp
Lake	Waterfalls

GEOGRAPHIC FEATURES

Cave
Cliff, Escarpment
Mountain
Pass, Saddle

AREA FEATURES

Building	Beach
National Park, Forest	Mall, Market

BOUNDARIES

International
State

Cue Sheets

Route directions in this book are given in a series of brief 'cues', which tell you at what kilometre mark to change direction and point out features en route. The cues are placed on the route map, most of the time with a profile, or elevation chart. Together these provide all the primary directions for each route in one convenient reference. The only other thing you need is a cycle computer.

To make the cue sheets as brief and simple to understand as possible, we've developed a series of symbols (see the Map Legend on p9) and the following rule:

Once your route is following a particular road, continue on that road until the cue sheet tells you otherwise.

Follow the road first mentioned in the cue sheet even though it may cross a highway, shrink to a lane, change name (we generally only include the first name, and sometimes the last), wind, duck and climb its way across the country. Rely on us to tell you when to turn off it.

Because the cue sheets rely on an accurate odometer reading we suggest you disconnect your cycle computer (pop it out of the housing or turn the magnet away from the fork-mounted sensor) whenever you deviate from the main route.

Cue Sheet Example

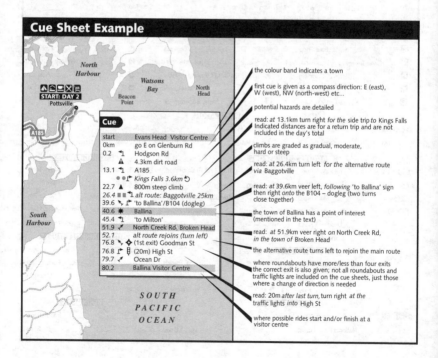

the colour band indicates a town

first cue is given as a compass direction: E (east), W (west), NW (north-west) etc...

potential hazards are detailed

read: *at* 13.1km turn right *for the* side trip *to* Kings Falls Indicated distances are for a return trip and are not included in the day's total

climbs are graded as gradual, moderate, hard or steep

read: *at* 26.4km turn left *for the* alternative route *via* Baggotville

read: *at* 39.6km veer left, *following* 'to Ballina' sign then right *onto* the B104 – dogleg (two turns close together)

the town of Ballina has a point of interest (mentioned in the text)

read: *at* 51.9km veer right *on* North Creek Rd, *in the town of* Broken Head

the alternative route turns left to rejoin the main route

where roundabouts have more/less than four exits the correct exit is also given; not all roundabouts and traffic lights are included on the cue sheets, just those where a change of direction is needed

read: 20m *after last turn,* turn right *at the* traffic lights *into* High St

where possible rides start and/or finish at a visitor centre

Foreword

HOW TO USE A LONELY PLANET GUIDEBOOK

The best way to use a Lonely Planet guidebook is any way you choose. At Lonely Planet we believe the most memorable travel experiences are often those that are unexpected, and the finest discoveries are those you make yourself. Guidebooks are not intended to be used as if they provide a detailed set of infallible instructions!

Contents All Lonely Planet guidebooks follow roughly the same format, including the cycling guides. The Facts about the Destination chapters give background information ranging from history to weather. Facts for the Cyclist gives practical information on the destination. Health & Safety covers medical advice and road rules. Basic bicycle maintenance is addressed in Your Bicycle. Getting There & Away gives a brief starting point for researching travel to/from the destination. Getting Around gives an overview of the transport options when you arrive.

The peculiar demands of each destination determine how subsequent chapters are broken up, but some things remain constant. We always start each ride with background and getting to/from the ride information. Each day's ride is summarised and the highlights en route detailed in the text, and locations noted on the map and cue sheets. A selection of the best sights and places to stay and eat in each start and end town are also detailed.

Heading Hierarchy Lonely Planet headings are used in a strict hierarchical structure that can be visualised as a set of Russian dolls. Each heading (and its following text) is encompassed by any preceding heading that is higher on the hierarchical ladder.

Entry Points We do not assume guidebooks will be read from beginning to end, but that people will dip into them. The traditional entry points are the list of contents and the index. In addition, the cycling guides also have a table of rides and a map index illustrating the regional chapter break-up.

There is also a colour map that shows highlights. These highlights are dealt with in greater detail in the Facts for the Cyclist chapter, along with planning questions and suggested itineraries. Each chapter covering a geographical region also begins with a map showing all the rides for that region. Once you find something of interest turn to the index or table of rides.

ABOUT LONELY PLANET GUIDEBOOKS

The process of creating new editions begins with the letters, postcards and emails received from travellers. This correspondence often includes suggestions, criticisms and comments about the current editions. Interesting excerpts are immediately passed on via newsletters and the Web site, and everything goes to our authors to be verified when they're researching on the road. We're keen to get more feedback from organisations or individuals who represent communities visited by travellers.

Lonely Planet gathers information for everyone who's curious about the planet – and especially for those who explore it first-hand. Through guidebooks, phrasebooks, activity guides, maps, literature, newsletters, image library, TV series and Web site we act as an information exchange for a worldwide community of travellers.

Research Authors aim to gather sufficient practical information to enable travellers to make informed choices and to make the mechanics of a journey run smoothly. They also research historical and cultural background to help enrich the travel experience and allow travellers to understand and respond appropriately to cultural and environmental issues.

Authors don't stay in every hotel because that would mean spending a couple of weeks in each medium-sized city and, no, they don't eat at every restaurant because that would mean stretching belts beyond capacity. They do visit hotels and restaurants to check standards and prices, but feedback based on readers' direct experiences can be very helpful.

Many of our authors work undercover, others aren't so secretive. None of them accept freebies in exchange for positive write-ups. And none of our guidebooks contain any advertising.

Production Authors submit their raw manuscripts and maps to offices in Australia, USA, UK or France. Editors and cartographers – all experienced travellers themselves – then begin the process of assembling the pieces. When the book finally hits the shops, some things are already out of date, we start getting feedback from readers and the process begins again...

WARNING & REQUEST

Things change – prices go up; schedules change; bad dirt roads get paved and decent ones get washed out; good places go bad and bad places go bankrupt – nothing stays the same. So, if you find things better or worse, recently opened or long since closed, please tell us and help make the next edition even more accurate and useful. We genuinely value all the feedback we receive. A well-travelled team reads and acknowledges every letter, postcard and email and ensures that every morsel of information finds its way to the appropriate authors, editors and cartographers for verification.

Everyone who writes to us will find their name in the next edition of the appropriate guidebook. They will also receive the latest issue of *Planet Talk*, our quarterly printed newsletter, or *Comet*, our monthly email newsletter. Subscriptions to both newsletters are free. The very best contributions will be rewarded with a free guidebook.

Excerpts from your correspondence may appear in new editions of Lonely Planet guidebooks, the Lonely Planet Web site, *Planet Talk* or *Comet*, so please let us know if you *don't* want your letter published or your name acknowledged.

Send all correspondence to the Lonely Planet office closest to you:

Australia: Locked Bag 1, Footscray, Victoria 3011
USA: 150 Linden St, Oakland, CA 94607
UK: 10A Spring Place, London NW5 3BH
France: 1 rue du Dahomey, 75011 Paris

Or email us at: e talk2us@lonelyplanet.com.au

For news, views and updates see our Web site: www.lonelyplanet.com

Introduction

Australia at first glance wouldn't appear to be given to easy cycle touring. All but narrow corridors of the interior is crossed only by dirt roads and tracks, and water is usually absent. Subtract the vast outback, however, and you're left with a patch of earth the size of several European countries combined, where cycling is an unabashed joy. Feel the salty breeze at your back while you cycle along some of the world's most spectacular coastline; whiz along winding mountain roads through tall, cool eucalypt forests; follow a gourmet trail; or explore historic gold-mining towns.

The great majority of Australians live in the south-east, most within a few hours' drive of the coast, in an arc extending from Adelaide, in South Australia, through Victoria, Tasmania and New South Wales to south-eastern Queensland. In the south-east you'll find Australia's best coastal route (the Great Ocean Road, in Victoria), its highest mountains, its mightiest river (the Murray), its largest cities (Sydney and Melbourne) and

most of its arable land. Apart from several days' cycling in south-western Western Australia and a few in tropical Queensland, this book's rides are concentrated in this area.

The Australian climate provides the best news of all for intending cycle tourers: it's possible – and enjoyable – to ride in many parts of the country for most of the year.

It's pointless, if not impossible, to suggest the best state, or region, in which to plan an Australian bicycle tour. Many local tourers would point you towards Tasmania, where light vehicle traffic, short distances (by Australian standards) between towns and numbingly wild and beautiful landscapes combine. There's more traffic on major roads in New South Wales and Victoria and, especially west of the Great Dividing Range, longer hauls between town. But diverse scenery – especially the stunning and accessible coastlines – make both states ideal touring destinations (although the length of the climbs here and there may surprise!). Queensland, Western Australia

Australia

and South Australia each have unique charm for cyclists, not the least of which is their smaller but lively capital cities, thin population densities and correspondingly quiet roads. Additionally, Queensland has its islands and tropical coast; South Australia its wine country, weathered landscapes and isolated coast fronting the vast Southern Ocean; and Western Australia its stunning south-east forests and sand plains, home to one of the world's greatest diversities of floral species.

To help you choose what part of the country is for you, this book maps and details a selection of the best rides in the country, broken into chapters by state. The tours range from a few hours to several days, to suit all ability levels. Plus, an entire chapter is devoted to a long-distance tour up the east coast of Australia, from Melbourne to the Gold Coast; do the entire 31 days, or dip into parts of it. We offer a wealth of suggestions to help smooth your trip: a background to Australia and its cycle-touring scene; tips on transporting your bike; inside knowledge on the best places to stay, taste wine and regional gourmet foods en route; and advice on fixing your bike and staying healthy on tour.

Cycle touring in Australia will open your eyes to vistas that defy superlatives, wide starry skies and easy-going people. You'll have many chances to learn about some of the world's oldest human cultures – those of Australia's diverse Aboriginal peoples. And you'll see that there's much more to this land than just the flat Outback and sparkling beaches.

Facts about Australia

HISTORY

60,000–50,000 years ago – Aboriginal people thought to have arrived from South-East Asia.

1600s–1640s – Dutch sailors reach Australia's west and east coasts. Abel Tasman names present-day Tasmania Van Diemen's Land; the Dutch East India Company explores further in 1642, seeking riches and fertile land.

1688 & 1698 – Englishman William Dampier investigates ashore at Western Australia's Shark Bay, his reports influencing the European idea of a primitive, godless land.

1770 – English explorer Lt James Cook, on a scientific expedition to the 'Great South Land', charts the east coast. Landing in Botany Bay, he notes the coast's fertility, encounters Aborigines, and claims the land for Britain, renaming it New South Wales.

1786 – Botany Bay is announced as a convict settlement, to solve Britain's overcrowded gaol problem. The New South Wales Aboriginal population was subsequently estimated to have been 300,000 to one million, however, the continent is considered by Europeans to be *terra nullius* – a land belonging to no-one.

1778 – The First Fleet reaches Botany Bay, under Captain Arthur Phillip, the colony's first governor. On the 11 ships are 750 convicts, 400 sailors, four companies of marines and two years' worth of livestock and supplies.

1790–91 – The Second and Third Fleets arrive in Botany Bay; the European population is now around 4000.

1802 – Matthew Flinders circumnavigates Australia.

1803 – First settlement in Van Diemen's Land, near present-day Hobart.

1804 – Settlers are authorised to shoot Aborigines.

1808 – The now rich and powerful officers of the New South Wales Corps rebel against Governor Bligh in the Rum Rebellion (the officers encouraged convicts to work for them in return for rum). Lt Col Lachlan Macquarie is sent from London to clean up the mess, and governs until 1821.

1813 – The explorers Blaxland, Wentworth and Lawson cross the Blue Mountains, breaking the 'barrier' to the great interior.

1824 – Explorers Hume and Hovell begin the first overland journey south, discovering the Murray River and Port Phillip Bay (at present-day Melbourne).

1829–37 – Settlements are established at Perth, Melbourne and Adelaide.

1851 – Gold is discovered – an event which, over the next 50 years, changes the face of the young nation, especially in Victoria. Miners flock to Australia.

1852–68 – Transportation of convicts is abolished, 168,000 convicts having arrived.

1860s–1911 – Legislation is passed restricting Aboriginal people's right to own property and seek employment. Aboriginal missions and reserves are established.

1890 – Australia's first political party – later called the Australian Labor Party (ALP) – is formed.

1886 – The first of the famous Austral Wheel Races is held at the Melbourne Cricket Ground. The event becomes hugely popular, with the final day of the 1901 meet attracting 32,000 spectators.

1901 – Federation: Australia's separate colonies become a nation, but alliance to Britain remains.

1902 – Women, nationally, are given the vote (South Australian women have been voting since 1894).

1914–18 – WWI: Australian troops are sent to fight for Britain; about 500 are killed by Turks at the Battle of Gallipoli.

1918 – In the Northern Territory, the *Aborigines Ordinance* officially allows the state to remove half-caste children from Aboriginal mothers and place them in foster homes or childcare institutions (the practice has already occurred for 30 years and continues until the 1970s). Those taken become known as the Stolen Generation.

1928 – Australian cyclist Hubert Opperman breaks the world 24-hour record (covering 904km) in Paris, then cycles for another 79 minutes to break the world 1000km record.

Early 1930s – The Great Depression: the prices of wool and wheat – Australia's mainstays – plunge.

1939 – Robert Gordon Menzies becomes Prime Minister (PM). Two years later, he's forced by his own party to resign and subsequently forms the Liberal Party.

1939–45 – WWII: Australian troops fight alongside British troops in Europe. Australia focuses on national security after the Japanese attack the USA at Pearl Harbour. The Japanese also bomb Darwin and Broome; Australian troops fight the Japanese in Papua New Guinea. The USA defeats Japan in the Battle of the Coral Sea; Australia's allegiance begins to shift from Britain to the USA.

1947–68 – More than 800,000 non-British Europeans migrate to Australia in the post-war immigration program, 'Populate or Perish'. Living standards improve rapidly with increased demand for Australian raw materials.

1949 – Menzies regains office as PM, and governs for 16 years.

1951 – The government formally adopts an assimilation policy for Aboriginal people, aiming to force Aborigines to adapt to European culture by controlling where they live and who they marry. Australia supports the USA in the Korean War, and becomes a signatory to the treaties of ANZUS (Australia, New Zealand and the United States) and the anti-communist South-East Asia Treaty Organisation (SEATO).

1950s – Australia provides aid to South-East Asian nations under the Colombo Plan of 1950, to try to prevent the spread of communism.

1956 – Melbourne hosts the XVI Olympic Games.

1965 – Menzies commits troops to support the USA in the Vietnam War, despite public anti-war demonstrations.

1967 – Federal referendum is held: 92% of non-Indigenous Australians vote to give Aborigines and Torres Strait Islanders citizen status.

1972 – The ALP comes to power for the first time in 25 years, under Gough Whitlam. He withdraws troops from Vietnam and introduces a range of social reforms. The assimilation policy is replaced by one of self-determination, granting Aborigines access to their land and allowing participation in decision-making.

1975 – The Whitlam government is dismissed by the Governor General, following talk of mismanagement and a hostile senate. Liberal Opposition Leader Malcolm Fraser leads a caretaker government and wins the ensuing election.

1981 – Phil Anderson becomes the first Australian to wear the leader's yellow jersey in the Tour de France, a feat he repeats in 1982, when he also becomes the first Australian to win a stage (he wins another stage in 1991).

1983 – The ALP returns to power under Bob Hawke.

1991 – Paul Keating (formerly Hawke's treasurer) replaces Hawke as PM during Labor's third term in office. Keating shifts Australia's focus from Britain and the USA towards the Asia-Pacific region. Australia is in recession, with a huge wool stockpile.

1992 – Mabo: the High Court rejects the notion of terra nullius, recognising that a principle of native title existed before the arrival of the British.

1993 – The *Native Title Act* defines the principle of native title, but restricts its application to land which no-one else owns.

1996 – John Howard is elected PM, heading the conservative Liberal-National Coalition.

1997 – The *Bringing them Home* report reveals the extent of the practice of removing Aboriginal children from their families. However, John Howard refuses to make an official apology.

1999 – A Federal referendum on whether Australia should become a republic is held. The 'No' vote wins.

2000 – Hundreds of thousands of people walk in demonstrations around the country to support reconciliation with Aboriginal people. The XXVII Olympic Games are held in Sydney.

History of Cycling in Australia

Around the world, bicycles were the height of fashion in the late 19th century. Boneshakers, then penny farthings (then known simply as 'high bicycles'), became popular and, in the 1890s, the 'safety bicycle' came into vogue.

At the time, Australia was one of the richest nations in the world, having built its fortune on gold, wool and wheat. People were quick to embrace anything new. Victoria was particularly wealthy and cycling was most popular there.

Melbourne, with its wide, relatively flat streets and favourable climate, became – and remains – Australia's bicycle capital.

Bicycle Belles

In the 1890s, cycling became just the thing for fashionable ladies to include at their parties, and many took up bicycle touring.

Mrs EA Maddock (at right), a famous long-distance cyclist, was the first woman to ride from Sydney to Brisbane and, in 1894, cycled from Sydney to Melbourne in nine days. Incredibly, she did so in a corset, long skirt, puffed sleeves and straw boater, believing that, even on a bicycle, ladies should look like ladies.

Dress was indeed an issue. The restrictiveness of traditional dress caused enormous frustration. Some women changed to 'rational dress': loose trousers (knickerbockers or bloomers) or divided skirts, but many persisted with skirts for fear of public ridicule.

NATIONAL LIBRARY OF AUSTRALIA

Velocipedes were first introduced to Melbourne in 1865. Smoother and faster than the early 'boneshakers', penny farthings were imported from 1875.

Bicycles for the Masses After trains, bicycles were the fastest transport in the world. Apart from the incredible personal mobility now possible, racing caused tremendous excitement. However, although penny farthings were popular with daring young men in the 1880s, they were tricky to ride and dangerous: one could easily be catapulted over the handlebars – and it was such a long way to fall!

It wasn't until the arrival of the pneumatic-tyred 'safety' bicycle in 1890 that cycling really took off. In Australia, and around the world, there was a bicycle 'boom' in the 1890s. The safety bike was a bike for everyone: comfortable, easy, efficient and much safer than the penny farthing.

The other popular feature of the safety was its diminishing price tag. Initially only for the wealthy, by mid-decade, they were more affordable. In 1897, more than 150 brands were available. Along with imports (which, at the height of the craze, could not keep up with demand) there were many local manufacturers – one of the largest, Dux Cycle Co in Melbourne, employed 150 workers. Bikes became so common that jokes were made about buying them from the corner store.

The craze had considerable social impact; as in the USA and Europe, elements of society found cycling confronting. They said it caused havoc on the streets; the clergy considered it an evil pastime – particularly if it was undertaken on Sunday. Then there was the issue of women cycling: it was said by opponents to be promiscuous or even potentially damaging to a woman's feminine health. Yet the bicycle gave women new independence, and they took to the vehicle with a passion (see the boxed text 'Bicycle Belles' opposite).

A Working Vehicle The use of bicycles soon spread to rural areas, where, rather than being a plaything for the rich and fashionable, they became a tool for workers (the rural wealthy stuck with their costly horses and many of them despised and ridiculed bicycles).

On Western Australia's (WA) goldfields in the 1890s, cycle-messenger services were important for communication between towns; and bikes were extremely popular for transport. Elsewhere, shearers and other itinerant workers cycled hundreds of kilometres on rough roads between jobs, and used bikes for sheep mustering and boundary riding. In Melbourne, the General Post Office began using bicycles for mail collection.

A 'Coolgardie nugget' on his way to the gold fields from Sydney, 1895.

Before motor cars, bicycles were the fastest way to travel around rural Australia: they were far more efficient than walking – even pushing a loaded bike was preferable to carrying a heavy swag (bed roll). Weight was a marketing point: lightweight bicycles were important, since they were easier to push through sand or lift over fences; bikes typically weighed around 24–29lb (11–13kg).

Over distance, cyclists were – to the chagrin of horsemen – considerably faster than horses and could even beat trains (in 1937, champion cyclist Hubert Opperman rode 251 miles from Albany to Perth in 12 hours, 38 minutes; the train was almost three hours behind; see the boxed text 'Sir Hubert Opperman' overleaf).

The Birth of Cycle Touring Cycle touring became popular in the 1890s. The bicycle effectively opened up the country, allowing distance to be covered faster than ever.

Incredible transcontinental journeys were made.

Long-distance journeys between the eastern cities were already common when Percy Armstrong made the first north to south continental crossing in 1893. He covered the Sydney-to-Melbourne leg in just over four days – despite having to walk sections of rough roads – averaging 138 miles (222km) per day on a single-geared bike! From mid-decade, more and more overland rides were undertaken. Arthur Richardson was the first cyclist to cross the Nullarbor in 1896, and to ride around Australia in 1899–1900.

The overlanders were tough: they travelled without maps or roads; they received food and directions from Outback stations (remote homesteads); they dealt with thirst, hunger and breakdowns. Successful overland journeys captured public imagination and became useful marketing tools for bicycle and tyre companies. Australia became known as the long-distance cycling centre of the world.

Along with the epic transcontinental journeys, bicycle touring was gaining popularity in the eastern states as a recreational activity.

The hotel industry was boosted by cycle tourists' need for food and resting places at regular intervals. And it was cycling that led to the first road maps being produced, by keen cyclists such as Victorian George Broadbent and Joseph Pearson, from New South Wales (NSW).

Touring in the Australian Alps became popular with Melbourne and Sydney cyclists. In 1897, the *Austral Wheel* published a special supplement, the *Austral Wheel Guide to the Victorian Alps*, detailing routes, accommodation and road conditions, and advertising accommodation and eating establishments. By 1898 the experiences of many cyclists in the Australian Alps led to the publication of detailed alpine touring guides – the area was well travelled by the time cars arrived.

Bicycle Racing Bicycle racing has been popular in Australia from the early years of cycling. On a per-capita basis, Australia has been, arguably, the most successful nation in the world – perhaps because of its ideal cycling conditions: the countryside is largely flat, dry and rideable year-round (see the boxed text 'Olympic Cycling' later in this chapter).

In the 1890s, bike racing was a big business. Races such as the Austral Wheel Race, held at the Melbourne Cricket Ground since 1886, drew huge crowds – 32,000 on the last day of the 1901 meet (3% of the state's population!). Some of the more popular

Bicycle racing at the Melbourne Cricket Ground drew thousands of people and was big news in the media of the day (*Illustrated Australian News*, 7 September 1869).

Sir Hubert Opperman

Hubert Opperman, known and loved as 'Oppy', was a cycling legend. Riding in the 1920s and '30s, he set dozens of Australian and world records, some of which remain unbroken. In 1988, he was listed as one of Australia's 10 all-time top athletes.

Early on, Oppy developed a partnership with Bruce Small, owner of Melbourne bicycle company Malvern Star. Bruce Small recognised Oppy, then 17, as a potential champion and realised the benefits of associating Oppy with his brand. He became Oppy's manager, friend and mentor – and Malvern Star became an Australian icon.

Oppy was a man of amazing strength and stamina: he was successful in track, road and motor-paced events, but ultra-endurance events were his forte. Following a string of Australian successes in his early 20s, he captained a small Australasian team in the 1928 Tour de France. After the Tour, in which he finished 18th, Oppy went on to ride the Bol d'Or Classic 24-hour track event in Paris.

As the starting favourite, he evidently had the punters worried: both his bike chains had been tampered with, and snapped during the race. While they were being repaired, Oppy borrowed a heavy roadster and kept riding. Back on his own bike – and 17 laps behind – he went on to win the race by 53km and break the world record (covering 904km in 24 hours). Bruce Small – and the ebullient crowd – pressed him to go on for the 1000km record, which he broke, 79 minutes later.

The French loved Oppy. He made a habit of relieving himself while riding to save time; at the Bol D'Or, this was in front of a huge crowd. Oppy's pissing in the wind made front-page news in France – and only added to his popularity. In 1931, he returned to France, where he won the Paris-Brest-Paris race in 59 hours, smashing the record.

He went on to break more and more long-distance records, including Britain's Land's End to John o'Groats (1934 and 1937), and the 4402km Fremantle to Sydney – which he covered in less than 14 days.

If Oppy rode like the wind, he ate like a horse. According to the *Miroir des Sports*, his intake during the two-day Paris-Brest-Paris was: 24 eggs, 24 bananas, 10 cutlets, two large beefsteaks, one whole chicken, 2kg peaches, 1kg raisins, 3L of black coffee, 6L of lemonade and 6L of milk.

Oppy remained in the spotlight after he retired from racing, as a federal politician (1949–66); and as high commissioner to Malta (1967–72). He was knighted in 1968 and, in 1977, his autobiography, *Pedals, Politics and People*, was published.

On his 90th birthday, Oppy finally got off his bike, donating it to the Oppy museum in Rochester (his home town) at its opening ceremony. He died in 1996, aged 91. A tribute to his achievements, the Audax Fleche Opperman, is held in Victoria every October: teams of three to five cyclists ride 360km or more in 24 hours, converging on Rochester.

AUSTRALIA'S GREATEST WHEELMAN

HUBERT OPPERMAN ('OPPY')
The World's Greatest Cyclist.

You'd be better on a *Malvern Star*

THE AUSTRALIAN CYCLING HISTORY RESOURCE CENTRE COLLECTION

road races included Australia's longest-established road race, the Melbourne to Warrnambool, first held in 1895; and the Goulburn to Sydney ride in NSW, which began in 1902. The generous prize money offered in Australia (£250 at the 1894 Austral) attracted professional cyclists from around the world. Gambling was common and the ensuing corruption eventually led to a decline in track racing.

Australian cyclists first rode in the Tour de France in 1912. Hubert Opperman captained teams in 1928 and 1931. His fame in the 1930s saw a resurgence in racing's popularity. During WWII, it declined again as cyclists enlisted to fight.

20th-Century Cycling Although the public remained enamoured of overland cyclists and champions such as Hubert Opperman, the popularity of bikes for transport declined generally after the turn of the 20th century. As Australians had embraced the new transportation technology in the 1890s, so they took to motor vehicles. After WWII, bikes all but disappeared and Australia developed one of the highest rates of car ownership in the world.

Recreational cycling made a resurgence in the 1970s, following the boom in the

Olympic Cycling

Although only small, Australia is one of the top nations in the all-time Olympic medal tally, ahead of countries such as the United States. Olympic Games achievements include:

1932 – Dunc Gray becomes the first Australian to win an Olympic gold medal in a cycling event, winning the 1000m track event in LA.

1952 – Russell Mockridge wins two gold medals at Helsinki – individually in the 1000m time trial and in the tandem event with Lionel Cox.

1956 – Tandemists Tony Marchant and Ian Browne win gold in Melbourne.

1984 – The 4000m mens team pursuit wins gold in LA.

1992 – Kathy Watt wins gold (and silver) in Barcelona.

2000 – Madison duo Scott McGrory and Brett Aitken win gold in Sydney; Australia wins six cycling medals.

USA. Bicycle-touring clubs were formed around Australia. One of the first, the Melbourne Bicycle Touring Club, established in 1973, remains active.

Bicycles, by then, were the (not overly comfortable) 10-speed racers, which were geared too high for touring. By the early '80s, mountain bikes arrived in Australia. Like the safety bike almost a century before, the mountain bike appealed to the masses because it was more comfortable and easier to ride than its predecessor (see the boxed text 'Mountain Biking in Australia' in the Facts for the Cyclist chapter).

In 1984, Bicycle Victoria held the Great Victorian Bike Ride: a supported, nine-day ride across the state, with 2000 participants. It was so successful it became an annual event, with numbers peaking at 6300 in 1991. Other state cycling organisations copied the idea.

More than a century after the first bicycling boom of the 1890s, cycling still survives in Australia, despite the predominance of motor vehicles. Cycling remains a small, but significant, mode of travel, used for 2% of all trips in Australia. Major cities are gradually building a network of bikepaths and bikelanes to encourage cycling. In 1999, a new race, the Tour Down Under, was established (see the boxed text in the South Australia chapter); mountain biking continues to gain popularity; and, in certain areas, the use of bikes for transport is slowly increasing.

GEOGRAPHY

Australia is the world's sixth largest country. Its 7,682,300 sq km (about the same as mainland USA) constitutes approximately 5% of the world's land surface. Lying between the Indian and Pacific Oceans, Australia is about 4000km from east to west and 3200km from north to south, with a 36,735km coast.

This island continent's landscape – much of it inhospitable – has gradually evolved over millions of years. It is one of the most stable land masses, having been largely free of earth-moving activity for about 100 million years.

From the east coast a narrow, fertile strip merges into the greatly eroded Great Dividing Range. Mt Kosciuszko (2228m), in NSW, is Australia's highest peak.

West of the range the country becomes increasingly flat and dry. The endless flatness is broken only by salt lakes, occasional mysterious rock protuberances like Uluru (Ayers Rock) and Kata Tjuta (the Olgas).

The extreme north of Australia is a tropical area within the monsoon belt, encouraging rainforest growth. Its latitude is the Southern-Hemisphere equivalent of Thailand and Central America.

With a similar latitude to southern Italy and northern California, the small southern states, Victoria and Tasmania, are, in contrast to most of the continent, relatively green and hilly. The World Heritage-listed south-west region of Tasmania is considered one of the world's last great wilderness areas.

The west of Australia consists mainly of a broad plateau. In the far south-west a modest mountain range and fertile coastal strip heralds the Indian Ocean, but in north-central WA, the dry country runs right to the sea.

GEOLOGY

Australia was, 180 million years ago, part of the supercontinent Gondwana, along with Africa, South America, Antarctica and India. It became a separate continent about 60 million years ago when it broke away from Antarctica. Since then it has been drifting north – currently at about 55mm per year.

Australia can be broadly divided into three regions: the Eastern Uplands, the Interior Lowlands and the Western Plateau. The Eastern Uplands rise sharply from the east coast and slope more gently westward to the Interior Lowlands. Generally referred to as the Great Divide, the most prominent feature is the escarpment that runs from just north of Cairns south to the Victoria–NSW border.

The escarpment's formation is still debated, but is widely agreed to have resulted from a series of tectonic movements. Thought to have uplifted around 90 million years ago, it is geologically much younger than a lot of the continent. The Interior Lowlands are the flat, weathered, low-lying Mesozoic and Cainozoic sediments of the continent's central east. The Western Plateau, roughly encompassing the land north and west of Adelaide, is geologically ancient. Its basement metamorphic and igneous rocks range in age from 570 million to 3.7 billion years. Its oldest rock formations – in WA's Pilbara region – contain crystals that formed 4.3 billion years ago, making them part of the earth's original crust.

Most of the interior was dry land between 250 and 140 million years ago, after which a major rise in sea level created an inland sea covering a third of the continent. Marine siltstones from this period contain precious opal, now mined at several places, including Coober Pedy in South Australia (SA) and White Cliffs in NSW. Another inundation occurred 10 to 15 million years ago, creating the limestone deposits that today make up the Nullarbor Plain.

The Great Artesian Basin, one of the world's largest ground-water resources, underlies about 20% of the continent. Much of eastern inland Australia is almost totally reliant on it for water.

CLIMATE

You have a splendid climate, a climate that enables the cyclist to wheel every month in the year.
Canadian bicycle salesman in Melbourne,
Austral Wheel, June 1898.

He was right, but there are, nevertheless, distinct seasons – and they're opposite to those in Europe and North America. The height of summer is in January while the depths of winter are in July.

Southern Australia has a temperate, Mediterranean climate, with four seasons. Only in the section straddling the NSW border with Victoria, and in Tasmania, are the mountains high enough to have winter snow. Tasmania is the coldest state: even around Christmas, it can be bitterly cold and snowing in the mountains, while Hobart's average maximum temperature in January is only 22°C.

Heading north, the climate becomes warmer and more tropical. In Queensland and the rest of northern Australia, the climate is hotter and wetter from around November/ December to April/May, the monsoon season (cyclone season is from January to March). Brisbane's coldest month is July, when the average minimum and maximum temperatures are 9° and 20°C.

The climate of the coastal region east (and south, in Victoria) of the Great Divide is milder and wetter than the more stable interior, which has hotter, drier summers and colder winters. Similarly, in WA, the narrow coastal strip in the far south-west is lush and green, while the huge inland mass is largely arid.

As one of the driest continents, much of Australia's coastal strip does not receive huge amounts of rain. Melbourne's annual rainfall averages 661mm; Adelaide is drier still, averaging 551mm. Adelaide summers can be blisteringly hot and dry (January's average maximum temperature is 30°C). Summer is similarly hot and dry in Perth. Queensland's dry season, May to November, is when Victorians traditionally head north to the beach. Northern Australia is the exception: Cairns' average annual rainfall is 2007mm, most of which falls between December and April.

A great influence on rainfall in eastern Australia is El Niño, a warming of the surface of the southern Pacific Ocean and the subsequent change in winds and currents. It occurs on average every four to five years, resulting in drought in eastern Australia. El Niño's reverse, La Niña, produces heavy rain.

Prevailing winds in Australian coastal regions are the sea breezes, which come in as the day heats up. Expect westerlies on the west coast; east or south-easterlies on the east; and southerlies in the south. These breezes are generally stronger in spring, summer and autumn and are reinforced along the east coast at lower latitudes by east to south-easterly trade winds. In the north, trade winds are replaced by moist north-westerly winds in the monsoon season. In the south, summer northerlies are cyclists' bane – they're usually strong, hot, dry and exhausting.

See the Bureau of Meteorology's Web site ⬚ www.bom.gov.au for daily wind charts and regional weather forecasts.

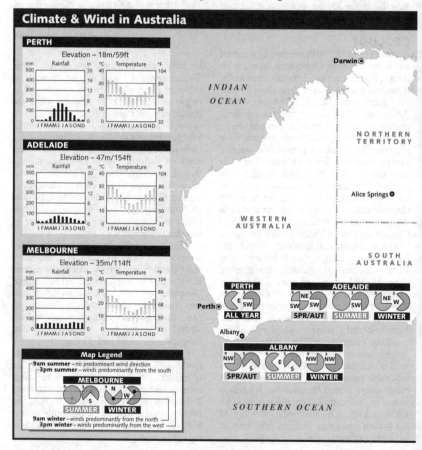

Climate & Wind in Australia

ECOLOGY & ENVIRONMENT

The typical image of Australia, of a mostly dry and harsh landscape, is largely true. But the continent supports an astonishing range of ecosystems, from arid desert to tropical rainforest, beach and coral reefs to snowy mountains.

Eucalypt forest is widespread around the edges of the continent, particularly in the east and far south-west. It can vary enormously according to climate, soil and species.

While humans have been living in, and changing, the physical environment in Australia for at least 50,000 years (Aborigines modified their environment through use of fire), it is in the 200 years since European settlement that the most dramatic changes have taken place.

Early on, the British cleared land for agriculture, grazing or timber. With the gold rush from 1851, miners dug up anything in the hope of striking it lucky, while hundreds of kilometres of forests were razed to build mine shafts and to fuel mining machinery.

Australia had set its foundations on an economy based largely on primary production and mineral resources. In 1860, the land – which had evolved without cloven-hoofed animals – supported 20 million sheep. These, along with cattle, destroyed water holes and ruined habitats that had sustained native animals and Indigenous people for thousands of years. The result has been the loss or severe altering of 70% of all native vegetation, including the total loss of 40% of forest area and 75% of rainforests in 200 years.

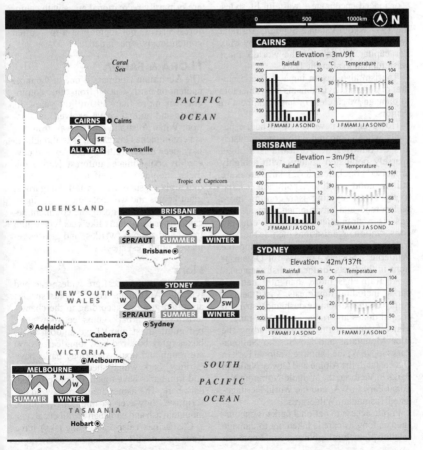

Land clearing continues at an alarming rate, leading to increased soil salinity, degradation of inland waterways and erosion. Compounding the problem is the proliferation of introduced plants and animals: these compete with indigenous species for resources, are predatory, or carry disease. Although Australia is one of the 12 most biologically diverse countries in the world, rapid change has led to many species becoming extinct or severely vulnerable.

Even now, Australian governments rarely treat environmental issues as priorities. The prevailing attitude, fuelled by mining and timber lobby groups, is that environmentally sustainable practices will lead to higher unemployment and lowered business productivity. All too often, policies fail to discourage – or indeed encourage – wasteful lifestyles, including production of greenhouse gases (at the 1997 Kyoto Climate Summit, Australia won the right to *increase* emissions by 8%). Per capita, Australia is the world's most wasteful nation after the USA.

Tourism also has an impact: fragile natural or cultural environments are vulnerable to damage by careless or large numbers of visitors.

However, the news is not all bad, especially when compared with many industrialised countries. As Australia is a huge, sparsely populated country with a highly urbanised population (88%), large areas are still in good condition, pollution is relatively low, recycling is becoming more widespread and environmental awareness has risen dramatically. Non-government conservation organisations include the Australian Conservation Foundation and the Wilderness Society (see Useful Organisations in the Facts for the Cyclist chapter).

Australia has more than 500 national parks, including rainforests, vast tracts of empty Outback (remote bushland), strips of coastal dunes and rugged mountain ranges. Many feature in this book, including the Blue Mountains and Kosciuszko National Parks in NSW; the Daintree National Park in Queensland; the Alpine and Otway National Parks in Victoria; the Walpole-Nornalup National Park in WA; and the World Heritage-listed Tasmanian Wilderness.

Public access to national parks is encouraged as long as care is taken not to damage or alter the natural environment. Approach roads, camping grounds (many with toilets and showers), walking tracks and information centres are often provided.

Thirteen areas in Australia are included on the World Heritage List. They include Queensland's Great Barrier Reef, far north Wet Tropics and Fraser Island; Kakadu and Uluru–Kata Tjuta National Parks in the Northern Territory (NT); the Tasmanian Wilderness (the Franklin–Gordon Wild Rivers and Cradle Mountain–Lake St Clair National Parks); and the Central Eastern Rainforest Reserves (15 reserves covering 1000 sq km in the eastern highlands of NSW).

Afforded a lower conservation status than national parks, state-owned state forests have fewer regulations. Often, these are primarily recreational areas with camping grounds, walking trails and signposted forest drives, but logging is also – often contentiously – permitted.

FLORA & FAUNA

The Australian landmass is one of the most ancient on earth. Cut off from other continents for more than 50 million years, its plants and animals have evolved in isolation. When Australia broke away from the supercontinent Gondwana, it is thought to have been much wetter than today and covered by cool-climate rainforest. Native animals included 'megafauna' – gigantic marsupials, such as 3m-tall kangaroos, giant koalas and wombats and huge, flightless birds. Drifting north, the continent became drier and plants like eucalypts (gum trees) and acacias (wattles) and grasses replaced rainforest species.

Flora

Eucalypts (gum trees) are widespread and typically Australian. The 500-plus species are often grouped according to the characteristics of their bark: gums (eg, snow gum, red gum, ghost gum) have smooth bark; boxes (grey box, red box, long-leafed box) are rough and textured; stringy barks have 'stringy' bark which sheds in long strips; and iron barks have tough, deeply crinkled, dark bark. The names are not always so descriptive, however jarrah, karri, tingle, mountain ash and coolabah are all eucalypts.

Casuarinas (also called sheoaks) have weeping, needle-like leaves; some look almost like conifers. The species range from stunted shrubs to tall trees. Australia has some native conifers – Norfolk Island Pines are popular beachfront trees – but, unlike areas of the northern hemisphere, they are rarely dominant. (Stands of conifers are most likely plantation *Pinus radiata*).

Australia has more than 600 acacia species, ranging from shrubs to tall trees. These nitrogen-fixing plants generally flower in a blaze of yellow in late winter and spring. *Acacia pycnantha* (golden wattle) is Australia's floral emblem.

Flowering plants are one of the delights of the Australian landscape. WA is especially famous for its show of spring wild flowers, but there are plenty to be found elsewhere. Flowering shrubs, orchids and other wild flowers can be found in spring – heathlands and heathy woodlands are especially rich. Flowering, understorey shrubs include banksias, grevilleas, callistemons (bottle brushes) and waratahs.

Fauna

Australia's most distinctive animals are marsupials and monotremes. The marsupials – including kangaroos, wallabies, possums and koalas – give birth to partially developed young which then suckle in a pouch. The truly fantastic monotremes are the world's only two egg-laying mammals – the semi-aquatic platypus with duck-like bill, webbed feet, fur and a beaver-like tail; and the ant-eating echidna, covered with fur and protective, sharp spines. If you're lucky (and quiet) you might spot an echidna foraging in the bush.

Kangaroos, wallabies and possums are common in forest and rural areas at dusk and dawn; brush-tail possums are also found in many southern city parks. Slow, solid wombats are fairly easy to spot in south-eastern forested areas – sadly, often as roadkill.

Koalas, most often seen as grey lumps high in a tree, feed only on the leaves of certain types of eucalypt. They're found along the east coast and have been reintroduced to SA. Other marsupials include carnivorous quolls – native cats – and Tasmanian devils. Other Australian mammals include native rats, bats and the dingo – a native dog.

Of Australia's 750 bird species, some of the more visible (or audible) include: the large (2m-high), flightless emu; the laughing kookaburra; magpies (enjoy their carolling at dawn, but beware of territorial swooping in spring); wedge-tailed eagles; a variety of noisy, colourful parrots; and white (sulphur-crested) cockatoos and pink galahs.

Though Australia has a number of poisonous snakes, most are very shy and the fear surrounding them is unjustified (in fact, very few people die from snakebite). If you see a snake sunning itself, simply wait for it to move, taking care not to block its path. Lizards, such as bearded dragons, frilled lizards, blue-tongues and goannas, also tend to hang out on country roads. Treat spiders with caution, especially venomous redbacks (small and glossy black with a red splash) and the Sydney funnel-web (a largish, black, ground-dwelling spider).

Marine mammals such as the humpback and southern right whales are visible in Australian waters during winter as they migrate north.

Endangered Species

Since European colonisation, 17 species of mammal have become extinct (the thylacine or Tasmanian tiger is one of the more famous – see the boxed text 'Nannup Tiger' in the Western Australia chapter) and at least 30 more are endangered. Introduced species have had enormous impact on native flora and fauna. Foxes and cats kill small mammals and birds (and have no predators); rabbits denude vast areas; others compete for habitat or introduce disease. Similarly, introduced plants such as lantana threaten to choke out native species in some areas.

GOVERNMENT & POLITICS

Australia is a federation of six states and two territories. Under the Constitution, effective since 1901 when the colonies joined to form the Commonwealth of Australia, the Federal Government is mainly responsible for the national economy and Reserve Bank, customs and excise, immigration, defence and foreign policy. The state governments are chiefly responsible for health, education, housing, transport and justice.

Australia has a parliamentary system of government based on that of the UK, and the state and federal structures are broadly similar. In Federal Parliament, the lower house is the House of Representatives and the upper house, the Senate. The party that holds the greatest number of lower-house seats forms the government. The House of Representatives has 148 members, divided among the states on a population basis, with (at least) triennial elections. Voting is by secret ballot and is compulsory for people 18 years of age and over. The Senate has 12 senators from each state, and two each from the Australian Capital Territory (ACT) and the NT. State senators serve six-year terms, territory senators only three. The Federal Government is run by a prime minister; the state governments, by a premier; the ACT and NT, by a chief minister.

Federal Parliament is based in Canberra, the nation's capital. The state parliaments are in each state capital.

Australia is a monarchy, but although Britain's king or queen is also Australia's, Australia is fully autonomous. The British sovereign is represented by the governor general as well as by state governors.

The main political groups are the Australian Labor Party (ALP) and the Liberal and National Parties, which are in coalition at federal level and in some states. The Australian Democrats have largely carried the flag for the 'green' movement and have been successful in recent times. Although the 1998 election gave a majority to the Coalition in the House of Representatives, the balance of power is held in the Senate by the Democrats.

ECONOMY

Australia is a relatively affluent and industrialised nation, but much of its wealth still comes from agriculture and mining. It has a small domestic market and its manufacturing sector is comparatively weak. For much of Australia's history it has been argued that manufacturing industries need tariff protection from imports to ensure their survival.

Today, however, tariff protection is on the way out and efforts are being made to increase Australia's international competitiveness. This has become more important as prices of traditional primary exports have become more volatile. During the 1980s and early '90s, the governing Labor Party sought to restrain the growth of real wages with the assistance of the Australian Council of Trade Unions (ACTU), to make Australian products more competitive overseas. This Accord, as it was known, ended with the

1996 election of the conservative Howard government.

The relative contribution to GDP (Gross Domestic Product) from goods-producing industries declined during the 1980s and '90s, along with an increase in the contribution from service industries. By the century's end, the proportion of people employed in manufacturing and service sectors was 17% and 40%, respectively.

The tourism industry is an increasingly important source of income, with the numbers of visitors to Australia rising each year.

Agriculture, formerly the cornerstone of the Australian economy, today accounts for about 4% of GDP; mining contributes about the same and manufacturing around 14%. Services account for nearly 60% of GDP, with wholesale and retail trade (17%) representing the largest component.

Major commodity exports include coal, non-monetary gold, iron ore, meat, wheat and wool. Services account for about 18% of total export earnings (notably transport and travel services).

Japan is Australia's biggest trading partner, but the economies of China, Korea and Vietnam are becoming increasingly important. Regionally, Australia has initiated the Asia-Pacific Economic Cooperation (APEC) group, a body aimed at furthering the economic interests of the Pacific nations. APEC countries (including the USA and New Zealand) account for over 70% of exports, and just under 70% of imports.

The Australian economy is growing at around 4% per year and inflation is around 2% per year.

POPULATION & PEOPLE

Australia's population is about 18.8 million. The most populous states are NSW (6.4 million) and Victoria (4.7 million), which also have the two largest cities: Sydney (four million) and Melbourne (3.3 million). The population is concentrated along the east coast from Adelaide to Cairns and in a similar, but much smaller, coastal region in the south-western corner of WA. The centre of Australia is very sparsely populated.

In the 1996 census 386,000 people identified themselves as Indigenous (Aborigines or Torres Strait Islanders). Torres Strait Islanders, primarily a Melanesian people, are indigenous to the islands of the Torres Strait between Cape York and Papua New Guinea.

Until WWII most non-Indigenous Australians were of British and Irish descent but that has changed dramatically. Heavy migration from Europe has created major Greek and Italian populations, also adding Germans, Dutch, Maltese, Yugoslavs, Lebanese, Turks and other groups.

More recently Australia has had large influxes of Asians, particularly Vietnamese after the Vietnam War. On the whole they have been well accepted and 'multiculturalism' is a popular concept in Australia.

ARTS
Music
Australia's large urban population supports a vibrant classical music culture. Every state and territory has its own symphony orchestra. Many other ensembles and a national opera company exist, particularly in Sydney and Melbourne. Classical music visits the bush in regional tours and special events.

Australia's participation in popular music since the 1950s has been a mix of good, indifferent, lousy, parochial and excellent. The 1970s saw music with a distinctly Australian flavour emerge, with bands such as Skyhooks leading the way. INXS, Midnight Oil and Men at Work followed in the '80s.

These days, the local scene is flooded with talent. You Am I, silverchair, Powderfinger and Regurgitator are some big names, while the new bands and performers producing live and recorded music are too numerous to list. Triple J radio broadcasts all over Australia and is a good place to catch new music. Killing Heidi, Savage Garden and The Living End all had big success on the charts recently.

The last decade or so has also seen huge success for Aboriginal music and performers. Yothu Yindi gained mainstream success with their song, 'Treaty', and the band's lead singer, Mandawuy Yunupingu, was named Australian of the Year in 1993.

Other Aboriginal musicians include Archie Roach, Bart Willoughby, Blekbala Mujik, Christine Anu (from the Torres Strait Islands), Coloured Stone, Kev Carmody, Ruby Hunter, the Sunrise Band, and the bands that started it all but no longer exist, No Fixed Address and Warumpi Band.

White country music owes much to Irish heritage and American country influences, often with a liberal sprinkling of dry Outback humour. Look for Slim Dusty, Ted Egan, John Williamson, Lee Kernaghan, Neil Murray, Kasey Chambers, Gondwanaland and Smokey Dawson, among others.

Australian folk music is derived from English, Irish and Scottish roots. Fiddles, banjos and tin whistles feature prominently in bush bands.

Literature
'The bush' inspired many popular ballads and stories which, although in vogue at the turn of the 20th century, have an enduring quality. The most famous exponents of the ballad were AB 'Banjo' Paterson and Henry Lawson.

Paterson grew up in the bush and became one of Australia's most important poets. A film was based on *The Man From Snowy River*; also well known is the satirical *Mulga Bill's Bicycle*. But Paterson is probably best remembered as the author of Australia's 'unofficial' national anthem, *Waltzing Matilda*.

His contemporary, Henry Lawson, was more of a social commentator and less of a humorist. His short stories of bush life are his greatest legacy.

Early Outback novels include DH Lawrence's *Kangaroo* (1923) and Nevil Shute's *A Town Like Alice* (1950). Katharine Susannah Prichard produced a string of novels with Outback themes and political comment. Xavier Herbert's *Capricornia* (1938) stands as one of the great epics of Outback Australia. A great nonfiction piece is Mary Durack's family chronicle, *Kings in Grass Castles* (1959), about white settlement of the Kimberley ranges. Nobel Prize-winner Patrick White used the Outback as the backdrop for a number of his monumental works.

Miles Franklin was one of Australia's early feminists. *My Brilliant Career* brought her widespread fame and criticism. Today the Miles Franklin Award is Australia's most prestigious.

Appropriately, many contemporary novelists write within an urban context. Peter Carey is one of Australia's most successful writers. His novels include *Bliss* (1981), *Oscar and Lucinda* and *The True History of the Kelly Gang* (2000).

Richard Flanagan's *The Sound of One Hand Clapping* (1997), set in Tasmania, is destined to become a classic. Tim Winton superbly evokes coastal WA, notably in best-seller *Cloudstreet* (1991).

Thomas Keneally tackles oppression in *The Chant of Jimmy Blacksmith* (1972) and the Booker Prize-winning *Schindler's Ark* (1982), on which Spielberg based the film *Schindler's List*.

Thea Astley is a lesser-known, yet fine writer. *It's Raining in Mango* (1987) expresses her outrage at the treatment of Aboriginal people. A sense of outrage is also apparent in *Snake Dreaming*, the powerful three-volume autobiography of Roberta Sykes, one of Australia's most well-known Aboriginal activists.

Elizabeth Jolley is well known as a short-story writer and novelist with a keen eye for the eccentric, while David Malouf has won just about every award in Australian literature. His works include *An Imaginary Life* (1978), *Fly Away Peter* (1981) and *Remembering Babylon*. Christopher Koch has explored Australia's relationship with Asia. *The Year of Living Dangerously* (1978) is probably his best-known work.

Architecture

Australia's European settlers arrived with memories of Georgian grandeur, but a lack of materials meant most early houses were almost caricatures of the real thing. One of the first concessions to the climate became a feature of Australian houses – a wide verandah to keep inner rooms dark and cool.

The gold rush in the second half of the 19th century saw a spate of grand Victorian-style buildings in most major towns.

By 1901, when the colonies combined to form a new nation, a simpler, more 'Australian' style evolved, now known as Federation style. Built between about 1890 and 1920, Federation houses typically feature red-brick walls and an orange-tiled roof with terracotta decoration. The rising-sun motif on their gable ends symbolised the dawn of a new age for Australia.

Differing climates led to interesting regional variations. In the tropical north the style known as the Queenslander evolved – elevated houses to allow plenty of ventilation.

The immigration boom that followed WWII led to urban sprawl – cities and towns expanded rapidly, 'brick veneer' (brick exterior on a timber frame) became the dominant medium, and remains so today.

Modern Australian architecture struggles to maintain a distinctive style, with overseas trends dominating big projects. Some notable contemporary public buildings are: the Convention Centre at Sydney's Darling Harbour, designed by Phillip Cox; the Melbourne Museum, designed by Denton Corker Marshall; the Cultural Centre at Uluru-Kata Tjuta National Park in central Australia; and Brambuk Aboriginal Cultural Centre at the Grampians in Victoria – the latter two designed in consultation with traditional owners.

Painting

In the 1880s a group of young Melbourne artists, now referred to as the Heidelberg School, developed the first distinctively Australian style of watercolour painting, capturing the qualities of Australian life and the bush. A contemporary movement developed in Sydney. Both groups were influenced by France's plein-air painters, whose work with natural light led to impressionism. The main artists were Louis Abrahams, Julian Ashton, Charles Conder, Frederick McCubbin, Tom Roberts, Arthur Streeton, Jane Sutherland and, later, Walter Withers. Their works can be found in most major galleries.

In the 1940s, under the patronage of Melbourne's John and Sunday Reed, a new generation of artists redefined the direction of Australian art. The group included some of Australia's most famous contemporary artists, such as Sir Sidney Nolan and Arthur Boyd. More recently the work of Fred Williams, John Olsen and Brett Whiteley has made an impression on the international art world.

Aboriginal Art

Art has always been an integral part of Aboriginal life, the initial forms of artistic expression being rock carvings, body painting and ground designs. Aboriginal art has changed significantly in the last few decades, with artists finding contemporary ways to express and preserve ancient Dreaming values.

While the dot paintings of the central deserts are among the more readily identifiable and probably most popular form of contemporary Aboriginal art, a huge range of material is being produced: bark paintings from Arnhem Land; wood carving and silk-screen printing from the Tiwi Islands;

batik printing and wood carving from central Australia; didjeridus and more.

Aboriginal art and craft has become increasingly popular, especially with tourists, which has created employment opportunities for Aboriginal people. Unfortunately, many so-called Aboriginal designs on souvenirs are either ripped off from Aboriginal people or just plain fake. There have even been embarrassing incidents where respected galleries have been duped. The best place to buy is either directly from Aboriginal communities or through galleries and shops owned and operated by communities.

Cinema

Australia's film industry began as early as 1896, a year after the Lumiere brothers opened the world's first cinema in Paris. Maurice Sestier, one of the Lumieres' photographers, came to Australia and made the first films in the streets of Sydney and at the Melbourne Cup.

Cinema historians regard an Australian film, *Soldiers of the Cross* (1901), as the world's first 'real' movie. The next significant Australian film, *The Story of the Kelly Gang*, was screened in 1907, and by 1911 the industry was flourishing.

In the 1930s, film companies such as Cinesound sprang up. Cinesound made 17 feature films between 1931 and 1940, many based on Australian history or literature – a highlight being Charles Chauvel's *Forty Thousand Horsemen*. Famous early Australian actors include Errol Flynn and Chips Rafferty.

A renaissance of Australian cinema during the 1970s produced successful films such as *Picnic at Hanging Rock*, *Sunday Too Far Away*, *Caddie* and *The Devil's Playground*.

Since then, Australian actors and directors (Mel Gibson, Nicole Kidman, Peter Weir and Gillian Armstrong to name a few) have gained international recognition. Films such as *Gallipoli*, *The Year of Living Dangerously*, *Mad Max*, *Crocodile Dundee*, *The Year My Voice Broke*, *Strictly Ballroom*, *The Adventures of Priscilla – Queen of the Desert*, *Babe*, *The Castle* and *Shine* have entertained and impressed audiences worldwide.

Love and Other Catastrophes by Emma-Kate Croghan and *Two Hands* by Gregor Jordan are examples of recent work by Australian writer-directors.

Aboriginal Culture Today

Colonisation and dispossession from our traditional lands has impacted upon the traditional culture of Aboriginal societies across Australia, damaging some groups more than others. Some Aboriginal peoples living in remote regions have been able to retain their traditional lands, and land-related aspects of their traditional culture. This is often because of their remoteness and the fact that no-one has yet wanted their lands for development or exploration.

However traditional culture is not only being maintained in remote, northern Aboriginal communities. In the south – including the more settled and densely populated cities and rural towns – languages are spoken, kinship obligations are met, traditional customs are observed and Aboriginal people are caring for their country. It is here that culture and tradition takes on a more contemporary form, where Aboriginal culture coexists with the changed environment.

Aboriginal peoples, like other cultures, embrace different walks of life: from academic professions in big-city universities to teaching the law in traditional communities; from nursing in a modern hospital to gathering bush medicines in a remote community.

While our population comprises a very small minority group (2% of the whole population) we have survived as culturally distinct peoples against the brutal colonisation of our territories. In our struggle to survive assimilation, many of our people have retained connections to our culture and are still living on the lands of our ancestors. We have retained many of our traditional customs and many of our ancient ceremonies are being revived throughout Australia.

Aboriginal culture moves in the cycles of the past, present, and future: 'always was, always will be'. We are culturally diverse. We are living both a traditional life and a modern one; maintaining traditional cultural beliefs in the middle of populated cities as well as by remote billabongs in the Northern Territory.

Dr Irene Watson

INDIGENOUS CULTURE
Traditional Society

Traditionally, Aboriginal people lived in extended family groups or clans, with members often descending from a common ancestral being. Many Aboriginal communities were seminomadic, others sedentary, one of the deciding factors being the availability of food and water. Communities also travelled to visit sacred places to carry out rituals.

Aboriginal people neither cultivated crops nor domesticated livestock, although some Torres Strait Islanders did. Their only major modification of the landscape was selective burning to encourage new growth, which attracted game animals to an area. Dingoes were domesticated in some societies to help hunt and to guard the camp.

Aboriginal people also traded raw materials (ochre and hardwood, for example) and manufactured goods. Trade items such as some stones or shells were rare and had great ritual significance. Along the networks which developed, large numbers of people would meet for 'exchange ceremonies', where not only goods but also songs and dances were passed on.

Aboriginal beliefs, sophisticated cultural life and laws are intrinsically connected with the land. Religious beliefs centre on the continuing existence of the creator spirit beings of the Dreaming. These beings, which took different forms, created all the features of the natural world and were the ancestors of all living things.

The ancestors eventually returned to the sleep from which they'd awoken at the dawn of time. Here their spirits remain as eternal forces that breathe life into the newborn and influence natural events. Each ancestor's spiritual energy flows along the path it travelled during the Dreaming and is strongest at the points where it left physical evidence of its activities, such as a tree, hill or claypan. These features are sacred sites.

Some sacred sites are believed to be dangerous and entry is prohibited under traditional Aboriginal law. One site in northern Australia was believed to cause sores to break out all over the body of any visitor – the area has a dangerously high level of natural radiation.

The importance of sacred sites is now more widely recognised among the non-Aboriginal community, and state governments have legislated to protect these sites. However, their presence can still lead to headline-grabbing controversy when they stand in the way of development.

LANGUAGE

While English is the main language of Australia, languages other than English are in common use, as you'd expect in a country with such a diverse ethnic mix. The 1996 census found 240 languages other than English were being spoken at home, in 15% of Australian households; almost 50 of them were indigenous languages.

At the time of European settlement it is thought Australia had around 250 separate Indigenous languages comprising about 700 dialects. Today, only around 30 are regularly spoken and being taught to children.

The most commonly used non-English languages are – in order – Italian, Greek, Cantonese, Arabic and Vietnamese. Languages rapidly growing in use are Mandarin, Vietnamese and Cantonese, while those most in decline include Dutch, German, Italian and Greek.

Australian English

Any visitor from abroad who thinks Australian is simply a weird variant of English/American will soon have a few surprises.

The meaning of some words in Australia is completely different from that in other English-speaking countries; some commonly used words have been shortened almost beyond recognition. Others are derived from Aboriginal languages, or from the slang used by early convict settlers.

There is a slight regional variation in the Australian accent, while the difference between city and country is a matter of the length and breadth of the drawl. If you want to pass for a local, speak slightly nasally; use diphthongs over pure vowels; shorten any word of more than two syllables and then add a vowel to the end of it, making anything you can into a diminutive (mosquitoes become 'mozzies', barbecue becomes 'barbie', even the Hell's Angels become mere 'bikies'); and pepper your speech with as many expletives as possible. Lonely Planet publishes an *Australian phrasebook*, an introduction to both Australian English and Aboriginal languages; the glossary at the end of this book may also help.

Facts for the Cyclist

HIGHLIGHTS

Australia is famous for its beaches and coastal scenery (it's the world's largest island, so has plenty of these). It's also the flattest continent – but don't be fooled – there's still lots of yahooing downhills and some tough climbs. The friendly people and wild natural areas are prime attractions for many – and there are dozens of others. Here are some highlights, from wine to wild flowers.

Best Coastal Scenery

It's not called the 'Great' Ocean Rd for nothing: this truly is one of the 'must sees' of Australia. The road snakes between Victoria's southern coast (looking out to famous rock formations) and the rugged Otway Ranges.

After more beaches? The East Coast Explorer looks over the Tasman Sea and South Pacific Ocean for about half of its 31 days, visiting classic Australian beach towns and featuring water-hugging sections, such as Day 16 between Shellharbour and Stanwell Park. The Fleurieu ride is another beachy ride– Port Willunga and the Ngarridjeri Way bikepath are highlights. On the other side of the country, ride Hwy One beside lovely beaches on The Daintree & Cape Tribulation ride. In Western Australia, the Tall Trees & High Seas ride passes close to some of the less populous and more beautiful sections of the Australian coastline.

Best Mountain Scenery

Stunning, seemingly endless, views over wilderness, from Pilot Lookout and Dead Horse Gap, are worthy rewards on Day 3 of the Kosciuszko High Country mountain-bike ride. The Across the High Country ride offers more fabulous views of this great wild area.

The temperate rainforests featured on the Coffs & Dorrigo Circuit are World-Heritage listed, as is the much-photographed Cradle Mountain on Tassie's West Coast ride.

Bathurst to the Blueys offers lovely vistas of the Blue Mountains and Kanangra-Boyd National Parks. Cycle Queensland's highest road and enjoy the panorama from Millaa Millaa lookout on the Atherton Tableland ride; or view the country's southern end from Hobart's Mt Wellington summit.

Best Mountain Cycling

Popular with cycle tourists since the 1890s, the Australian Alps remain a challenging and rewarding destination, offering solitude and wonderful wilderness. Try the Across the High Country ride, Days 7 to 9 of the East Coast Explorer or the Kosciuszko High Country mountain-bike ride.

There's more great cycling in the most mountainous state, Tasmania; a highlight is crossing the wilderness ranges between Queenstown and Derwent Bridge on Tassie's West Coast ride.

Best Descent

Check your brakes before blasting down the 950m Brown Mtn descent on Day 11 of the East Coast Explorer ride; count the 260 sweeping bends on the 800m drop down the Gillies Hwy on Day 5 of the Atherton Tableland ride. Both are more than 19km long.

The smooth 400m-in-8km descent on Day 3 of the Thunderbolts & Bucketts ride is fine fun; while the wild, steep and twisting back road into Jenolan Caves (Bathurst to the Blueys ride) drops 540m in 6.9km.

For the ultimate downhill thrill, grab some body armour and head for the Cannonball downhill run at Thredbo (see the Kosciuszko High Country mountain-bike ride).

Best Ascent

The 12.4km (500m) climb into the ranges behind Coffs Harbour on the Coffs & Dorrigo Circuit rises at a perfect gradient – get a rhythm happening and enjoy the wonderful forest scenery. The Canungra & Green Mountains Side Trip (Border Loop ride) is similar: the 750m climb is rarely at more than a 3% gradient. But for a solid, steady climb, you can't beat the 770m-in-15.7km rise from Jacobs River on Day 9 of the East Coast Explorer – the wild views keep unfolding as you wind up the unsealed road through Kosciuszko National Park.

For sheer length and pain, the 19.2km climb (rising more than 1km vertically) on Day 3 of the Kosciuszko High Country mountain-bike ride is probably without parallel in Australia – and the 1km descent midway only adds to the pain.

Best Long-Distance Ride

If distance is your thing, you can't go past the East Coast Explorer – 31 days of riding from Melbourne to the Gold Coast, via Sydney. Enjoy more than 2320km of some of the best cycle touring to be had along Australia's east coast.

Most Remote

Wide open spaces and distance are synonymous with Australia. Although rides in this book are concentrated around the continent's populous coastal fringes, there are, nevertheless, some pretty quiet moments. Some of them include: Days 7 to 9 and 11 of the East Coast Explorer, through the Snowy River wilderness and desolate Monaro country; the Kosciuszko High Country mountain-bike ride; the forested Days 6 and 7 of the Tall Trees & High Seas ride; and the stark central plateau of the Across the Central Plateau ride.

Best Wildlife Spotting

Apart from kangaroos, wallabies, possums, snakes, lizards and birds, which can be seen in bushland virtually anywhere, look for koalas on Day 1 of the Central Gold & Spa Country ride; and Days 1, 20, 22 and 29 of the East Coast Explorer.

The east and south coasts also provide plenty of opportunities to see dolphins and (in season) whales. Drop into Hamelin Bay (Tall Trees & High Seas ride) to see the friendly stingrays; and take an after-dark walk near Russell Falls in Mt Field National Park on Tassie's West Coast ride to see possums, bandicoots and, with luck, a Tasmanian devil. The rides through the Australian Alps also provide good opportunities for critter-watching.

Best Wild Flower Spotting

South-west Western Australia (WA) is famous for its spring wild flowers. Especially good are Days 1 and 3 of the Avon Valley ride, and Caves Rd on the Tall Trees & High Seas ride.

Spring is also an excellent time to cycle The Grampians, while you'll see alpine wild flowers aplenty in January on the Kosciuszko High Country mountain-bike ride. Late winter is best in the coastal heathlands of New South Wales' (NSW) mid-north (East Coast Explorer).

Best 'Historical' Tour

Gold was enormously significant in Australia's early development. From the 1850s to '90s, scores of gold towns sprang up. Some of the better preserved are featured on the Central Gold & Spa Country and Riches of the North-East rides, the Gold & Wine Country Circuit and the Avon Valley ride.

The best rides for exploring Aboriginal history are Thunderbolts & Bucketts and The Grampians. For a comprehensive convict experience, visit Port Arthur on the Across the Central Plateau ride.

Best 'Winery Tour'

Australia has many excellent wine-growing areas. Visit some of the best on the Barossa Heritage and The Fleurieu rides. Margaret River, on the Tall Trees & High Seas ride, has an excellent reputation. Rutherglen, on the Riches of the North-East ride, is known particularly for its ports and muscats; also recommended is the Mudgee region (Gold & Wine Country Circuit).

SUGGESTED ITINERARIES

Australia is a *big* place. Unless you've got a year or two, it's better to cover a few specific areas, than try to do the whole country. Where to go depends on when you're planning to cycle (see When to Cycle under Planning later in this chapter) and how long you've got. Here are a few suggestions.

One Week

Choose The Great Ocean Road; Tassie's East Coast ride; or (if you're fit) the Gold & Wine Country Circuit plus the Bathurst to the Blueys ride.

Two Weeks

Don't try to cover more than one state! In summer, do the Tassie's East Coast ride, a three-day circuit to Cradle Mountain, plus Across the Central Plateau from Deloraine.

For a busy spring fortnight in WA, follow the Tall Trees & High Seas ride with the Avon Valley ride; or do the Barossa Heritage and The Fleurieu rides in South Australia (SA) at a more leisurely pace.

The ambitious could cram in Victoria's Central Gold & Spa Country, linking to The Grampians – dropping Day 3 and instead heading south (over two days) to ride the Great Ocean Rd. Alternatively, start with the Great Ocean Rd, link with the East Coast Explorer at Torquay/Queenscliff and follow it to Sale (from where trains head to Melbourne), spending extra days exploring Wilsons Prom (see the boxed text, 'Cycling Wilsons Promontory' in the Melbourne to the Gold Coast chapter).

In NSW, ride the Sydney to Coffs Harbour section of the East Coast Explorer (Days 18–25); bus to Armidale (or ride Coffs to Armidale via Day 1 of the Coffs & Dorrigo Circuit); then finish with the Thunderbolts & Bucketts ride to Dungog, from where trains run back to Sydney.

In winter, warm up in Queensland with the Mt Nebo & Brisbane Forest Park ride, plus the Mt Mee ride, before catching the train south for the tough Border Loop; spend extra days doing side trips or at the beach.

One Month

For lovers of food and wild mountains, start with Victoria's Riches of the North-East ride in late summer, then shed any accumulated kilos with the strenuous Across the High Country tour, followed by the East Coast Explorer between Bairnsdale and Sydney (Days 6–17) – dallying at Jindabyne (Day 9) for the Kosciuszko High Country mountain-bike ride.

Another Victorian option is the Central Gold & Spa Country ride, followed by The Grampians and The Great Ocean Road rides; catch the train from Melbourne to Wangaratta for the Riches of the North-East ride, followed by Across the High Country.

In Tasmania, start with the Across the Central Plateau ride, followed by Tassie's East Coast and Tassie's West Coast rides; including the side trips for each, plus day rides on Mt Wellington (Hobart) and Meehan Range (mountain-bike ride).

Follow the 'Two Weeks' suggestion for NSW, adding to it the Gold & Wine Country Circuit plus Bathurst to the Blueys, and spend extra days exploring Sydney and the Blue Mountains. Alternatively, ride the East Coast Explorer from Sydney to Brisbane, with the Coffs & Dorrigo Circuit as a side trip, followed by the Border Loop; spend extra days around Sydney and Brisbane.

Spend two weeks riding in and around Brisbane, before heading north to Townsville (for the Magnetic Island and Mt Stuart & Alligator Creek rides) and Cairns (for

The Daintree & Cape Tribulation and Atherton Tableland rides).

Two Months

There's more scope for cycling in two or more states here: you might choose to cover all the rides in Tasmania and Victoria, for example; or start in WA, heading east by plane, bus or train to SA, followed by rides in Victoria or Tasmania (or Queensland, depending on your budget...).

The East Coast Explorer (in the Melbourne to the Gold Coast chapter) is highly recommended – either preceded with Victorian, SA or Tasmanian rides (do Tasmania in late summer then head up the east coast in autumn); followed by Queensland rides; or punctuated by side trips in NSW.

PLANNING
When to Cycle

The trick to enjoying a cycling trip in Australia is to be in the right place at the right time. Tackle WA's Avon Valley in February and you'll wonder – if your brain hasn't fried in the 40°C heat – how it was ever described as 'lush'; go instead in cooler September when it's transformed by greenness and flowers.

Summer is a good time for Tasmania, the high country of Victoria and southern NSW, and even the far south of WA, but anywhere else it's really too hot for comfort. For most of southern Australia, spring and autumn are the best seasons for cycling.

Further north, the warmer months are accompanied by high humidity, and monsoonal rainfall in north Queensland. Queensland is best between July and October. Winter cycling in northern NSW is pleasant along the coast, but gets cold on the tablelands inland.

Also consider other tourists. Forget any dreams of deserted beaches in January – you probably won't even find an empty tent site. Christmas school holidays (from mid-December to late January), long weekends and Easter are good times to avoid Victoria's Great Ocean Rd, Tasmania's east (and, to a lesser extent, west) coast, Queensland's Sunshine Coast, the beach generally, plus Sydney's Blue Mountains and other national parks. Easter is particularly busy in national parks and places like central Victoria and WA's Avon Valley.

Following is a general guide for where to be, when; check the Climate and Planning sections in the regional chapters for more detailed information.

December to early March Tasmania, High Country in Victoria and southern NSW
March to May Victoria, SA, WA, southern and mid-NSW
June to July Queensland, especially the north
August to September Northern NSW, Queensland; and, for wild flowers, WA
October to November NSW, SA, Victoria, WA

Maps

Most state automobile clubs produce excellent touring maps (with scales of around 1:200,000 to 1:350,000), which include road names and many tourist features, but not topographical information. They're inexpensive (typically around $3 to $5) and often free to members of an affiliated motoring organisation – if your organisation has reciprocal rights bring membership identification.

Natmap topographic maps, by Government publisher Auslig, are available in various scales: the 1:250,000 series (best for road touring) covers the whole country. Most of Australia is also covered by 1:100,000 maps, and smaller-scale maps cover populated areas or popular recreational areas. Most don't detail road names. Sheets ($7.70 each) are available from map shops, government information agencies, some outdoor shops and tourist bureaus, or by credit-card phone or email order (☎ 02-6201 4300 or ☎ 1800-800 173, ⓔ mapsales@auslig.gov.au).

Bike maps are available for some capital cities – see the regional chapters for details.

What to Bring

Keep the amount of gear you take to a minimum – every gram is noticeable on hills. That said, it's important to carry adequate weather protection. Cyclists planning to camp or use hostels will need more gear than those staying exclusively in self-contained accommodation. See also the Your Bicycle chapter for a list of tools and spares, bike-related equipment and advice on how to set your bike up for touring. The Health & Safety chapter includes a first-aid kit list.

Clothing Ideally, pack clothes that are light and dry quickly. Clothes that you can wear on or off the bike, such as a plain black thermal top, help keep your load to a minimum.

On the Bike Wear padded bike shorts or 'knicks', designed to be worn without underwear to prevent chafing. If you don't like Lycra, you can get 'shy shorts' – ordinary-looking shorts with sewn-in lightweight knicks. In colder weather, wear Lycra tights over your knicks or padded thermal 'longs'. Another option are Lycra leg warmers, which are easily removed when things warm up.

Don't underestimate the seriousness of sunburn in Australia (see Medical Problems & Treatment in the Health & Safety chapter). Long sleeves provide the best protection, though you need something light and breathable to avoid overheating. Some cycling tops are made from synthetic fabrics such as CoolMax and Intercool, designed to keep you cool. Silk is another alternative. Cotton is cool, but dries slowly, making it useless in the cold and wet. Choose bright or light-coloured clothing, which is cooler and maximises your visibility.

Sunglasses are essential to minimise exposure to UV radiation and to shield your

THIS BOOK CONTAINS A VERY ACCURATE
——— DESCRIPTION and ———

Route Map

of

27 Specially Selected Trips

within a

Radius of 50 Miles of Sydney.

Carefully Compiled by **J. PEARSON,**
The well-known Tourist
and Author of
THE CYCLISTS, MOTORISTS
and TRAVELLERS GUIDE
to NEW SOUTH WALES.

PUBLISHED BY

H. E. C. ROBINSON,

DRAFTSMAN AND MAP PUBLISHER,

41 PHILLIP STREET, SYDNEY.

Touring maps were first produced for cyclists, then for motorists once cars were invented.

eyes from insects and prevent them from drying out in the wind. Peaked helmet covers provide a little sun protection. A bandanna is useful to soak up sweat.

Be aware of the danger of exposure, especially during cooler months or in places like Tasmania or the east coast's alpine area, where the weather can change rapidly. Layering (wearing several thin layers of clothing) is the most practical way to dress in cooler weather. Start with a lightweight cycling or polypropylene top, followed by a warmer insulating layer, such as a thin synthetic fleece jacket (these are lightweight and dry quickly) and a rainproof jacket. Fine-wool thermal wear is an excellent alternative to synthetic fibres, as it stays warm when wet and is made nonitchy.

Some excellent waterproof, yet 'breathable' cycling jackets are available. Gore-Tex is probably the best-known fabric used for jackets; other fabrics such as Activent are compact, lightweight and excellent for light rain, but not for a steady downpour.

Wear fingerless cycling gloves: the padded palms reduce the impact of jarring on your hands (which can lead to nerve damage); they also prevent sunburn and protect your hands in case of a fall.

In cold weather, you may also need full-finger gloves (either thin polypropylene gloves, which can be worn with cycling gloves, or more wind- and rain-resistant ones). You can also buy thermal socks and neoprene booties to go over your shoes, so you can feel your toes on those cold mornings. A close-fitting beanie (winter hat) worn under your helmet will help keep you warm.

Helmets are compulsory in Australia; see Mandatory Equipment in the Health & Safety chapter.

Cycling shoes are ideal footwear (or, next best, stiff-soled ordinary shoes). Stiff soles transfer the power from your pedal stroke directly to the pedal. Spongy-soled running shoes are inefficient and may leave your feet sore. Many Australian touring cyclists swear by cycling sandals – stiff-soled sandals with room for a pedal cleat. They're cool in summer and dry quickly in the rain; just make sure you put sunscreen on your feet.

Off the Bike The clothing you carry for off the bike depends on the type of accommodation you're planning on using.

Campers need adequate clothing to protect against the cold, particularly in the southern and mountainous areas outside summer. Pack thermal underwear (tops and bottoms), a change of socks and underwear, a warm top and hat, and gloves.

Cold-weather gear is also important, but less critical, if you're staying indoors. Australians are pretty relaxed, so casual clothes are fine, though you may want to pack something better if you plan on eating in smart restaurants.

Take a separate pair of shoes for when you're off the bike. In summer, you can probably get away with sandals.

Bring a broad-brimmed hat to wear once you remove your helmet.

Camping Equipment Most budget accommodation (hostels, caravan parks) in Australia does not supply bedding to guests (some hire it), so it's prudent to carry a sleeping bag, even if you're not camping.

If you're planning to camp, you'll need a lightweight waterproof tent, sleeping mat, warm sleeping bag, torch (flashlight) or bike light, cooking and eating utensils and water containers; and maybe a portable stove and fuel container. A day-pack could be handy for excursions.

It's illegal to carry fuel on aircraft, but it's readily available in Australia. White gas (known as Shellite or white spirits), methylated spirits and kerosene are sold at petrol stations, hardware shops and most supermarkets. Gas cartridges can be purchased at outdoor supply shops in larger centres.

Buying & Hiring Locally Most Australian bike shops are independent businesses. Some department store-like chains, such as Wheels in Motion, exist in larger centres. These may be useful for parts but, generally speaking, service is better at a good small shop. See the regional chapters for lists of good bike shops.

Buying Bike shops – if they exist – in small towns may be combined with lawn-mowing businesses or toy shops and are best not relied upon for obscure or top-end parts.

Mountain and road-racing bikes dominate most shop floors; hybrid bikes are also readily available. Traditional touring bikes are not common, except in specialist shops; Cannondale and, to a lesser extent, Trek and

Equipment Check List

This list is a general guide to the things you might take on a bike tour. Your list will vary depending on the kind of cycling you want to do, whether you're roughing it in a tent or planning on luxury accommodation, and on the time of year. Don't forget to take on board enough water and food to see you safely between towns.

Bike Clothing
- [ ] cycling gloves
- [ ] cycling shoes and socks
- [ ] cycling tights or leg-warmers
- [ ] helmet and visor
- [ ] long-sleeved shirt or cycling jersey
- [ ] padded cycling shorts (knicks)
- [ ] sunglasses
- [ ] thermal undershirt and arm-warmers
- [ ] T-shirt or short-sleeved cycling jersey
- [ ] visibility vest
- [ ] waterproof jacket & pants
- [ ] windproof jacket or vest

Off-Bike Clothing
- [ ] change of clothing
- [ ] spare shoes or sandals
- [ ] swimming costume
- [ ] sunhat
- [ ] fleece jacket
- [ ] thermal underwear
- [ ] underwear and spare socks
- [ ] warm hat and gloves

Equipment
- [ ] bike lights (rear and front) with spare batteries (see torch)
- [ ] elastic cord
- [ ] camera and spare film
- [ ] cycle computer
- [ ] day-pack
- [ ] first-aid kit* and toiletries
- [ ] sewing/mending kit (for everything)
- [ ] panniers and waterproof liners
- [ ] pocket knife (with corkscrew)
- [ ] sleeping sheet
- [ ] small handlebar bag and/or map case
- [ ] small towel
- [ ] tool kit, pump and spares*
- [ ] torch (flashlight) with spare batteries and globe – some double as (front) bike lights
- [ ] water containers
- [ ] water purification tablets, iodine or filter

Adventure clothing's come a long way since this advertisement, dated 4 April 1895.

Camping
- [ ] cooking, eating and drinking utensils
- [ ] clothesline
- [ ] dishwashing items
- [ ] portable stove and fuel
- [ ] insulating mat
- [ ] matches or lighter and candle
- [ ] sleeping bag
- [ ] tent
- [ ] toilet paper and toilet trowel

* see the 'First-Aid Kit' boxed text in the Health & Safety chapter; and the 'Spares & Tool Kit' boxed text in the Your Bicycle chapter.

Norco are the main off-the-shelf brands. Some shops also custom build them.

A few city shops offer a 'buy back' scheme, whereby you can sell your bike back to the shop you bought it from after your trip, for up to 50% of the purchase price, although this is not as common in Australia as some countries. It *can* be cheaper than hiring and is generally a better option than the second-hand market. The buy-back schemes apply to bikes only, not to panniers and other equipment.

For a decent hybrid or rigid mountain bike you'll need to pay around $800 to $1200, though you can get a cheap one for around $500. Panniers cost from around $150 to $380 a pair. Some excellent Australian panniers are available; good brands include Wilderness Equipment, Summit Gear, Quipment and Avance. Brands such as the German Ortlieb are also available. Christie Cycles (☎ 03-9818 4011, ℮ chrisc yc@ozemail.com.au), 80 Burwood Rd, Hawthorn, Melbourne have one of the best ranges in Australia – ask for their mail-order catalogue. A good pannier rack costs around $75. Other equipment, including gloves, lock, pump, combination tool, chain lube, helmet, knicks and cycling top will set you back another $250 to $500.

Few shops have good second-hand bikes. Try the latest issue of *Australian Cyclist* magazine (see the Newspapers & Magazines section in this chapter) or the classifieds pages on Web sites such as Aussie Cycling Links (🖳 www.jub.com.au/cycling/) or Bicycling Australia (🖳 www.bicyclingaus tralia.com). Try also the weekly *Trading Post* newspaper, published regionally.

Camping and outdoor equipment is readily available in Australia, particularly in large cities, and of high quality. Along with some good independent retailers are reputable local chains such as Mountain Designs and Paddy Pallin. Good Australian brands include Wilderness Equipment, Summit Gear, One Planet, Mountain Designs and Paddy Pallin. Also recommended is New Zealand's Macpac. Australian cycle-clothing brands include Netti and Body Torque. Cycling jackets are also made by Mont, Mountain Designs and Wilderness Equipment.

Hiring It can be surprisingly difficult to hire a decent bike, particularly outside the main cities. Even rarer are hire bikes fitted with front and rear racks and panniers. Expect to pay around $100 per week for standard, rigid-fork mountain bikes or hybrids (front suspension is sometimes available). Longer-term hire is usually cheaper. Regional chapters include details of where to hire.

TOURIST OFFICES
Tourist Offices in Australia

Within Australia, tourist information is handled by various state and local offices. Each state and territory's tourist office is detailed in the rides chapters. Apart from main offices in the capital cities, they often have regional offices in major tourist centres and also in other states.

As well as supplying brochures, price lists, maps and other information, state offices will often book transport, tours and accommodation. Unfortunately, few maintain information desks at airports, and many city offices only open normal business hours (see the Business Hours section later in the chapter). The main tourist offices are:

Australian Capital Territory
Canberra Visitor Centre (☎ 02-6205 0044, 🖳 www.canberratourism.com.au) 330 Northbourne Ave (PO Box 673), Dickson, ACT 2602.
New South Wales
NSW Tourism Centre (☎ 13 2077, 🖳 www .tourism.nsw.gov.au) 106 George St, The Rocks, NSW 2000.
Northern Territory
Northern Territory Holiday Centre (☎ 1800-621 336, 🖳 www.nttc.com.au) 67 Stuart Hwy North, Alice Springs, NT 0871.
Queensland
Queensland Travel Centre (☎ 07-3874 2800 or ☎ 13 1801, 🖳 www.queensland-travel-centre .com.au) 243 Edward St, Brisbane, Queensland 4001.
South Australia
South Australian Travel Centre (☎ 08-8303 2033 or ☎ 1300-366 770, 🖳 www.tourism .sa.gov.au) 18 King William St, Adelaide, SA 5001.
Tasmania
Tasmanian Travel & Information Centre (☎ 03-6230 8233) cnr Davey & Elizabeth Sts, Hobart, Tasmania 7000.
Tourism Tasmania (☎ 03-6230 8253 or ☎ 1800-806 846, 🖳 www.tourism.tas.gov.au) 22 Elizabeth St, Hobart, Tasmania 7001.
Victoria
Victoria Visitor Information Centre: (☎ 13 2842, 🖳 www.visitvictoria.com) Melbourne

Town Hall, Swanston St, Melbourne, Victoria 3001.
RACV Travel Centre: (☎ 1800 337 743) 360 Bourke St, Melbourne, Victoria 3000.
Western Australia
Western Australian Tourist Centre: (☎ 08-9481 0190 or ☎ 1300-361 351, 🖳 www.westernaustralia.net) Forrest Place, Perth, WA 6000.

A step down from the state tourist offices are the local or regional visitor centres, which exist in almost every major town. These are often staffed by volunteers and, in many cases, are excellent, with much local information not readily available from the state offices. See Business Hours later in this chapter for opening hours.

Tourist Offices Abroad

The Australian Tourist Commission (ATC) is the government body intended to inform potential visitors about the country. It's strictly an external operator. In Australia, tourist promotion is handled by state and regional tourist offices.

ATC offices overseas have a useful, free, magazine-style booklet called *Australian Travellers Guide*, which has some handy info for potential visitors. The same information is available on the ATC Web site (🖳 www.australia.com), which also contains 'Fact Sheets' on topics such as bushwalking, fishing, disabled travel and national parks; look in the Special Interests section.

VISAS & DOCUMENTS

Photocopy important documents (passport, credit cards, travel insurance, air/bus/train tickets, driving licence etc); leave a copy with someone at home and keep another with you, separate from the originals.

Passport & Visas

All visitors to Australia need a valid passport; and all except New Zealanders require a visa before they travel. Check the Department of Immigration and Multicultural Affairs' Web site (🖳 www.immi.gov.au) for predeparture information. It includes *An Australian Government Guide to Visiting Australia*. The hot links section of Lonely Planet's Web site (🖳 www.lonelyplanet.com) also has up-to-date visa information.

Visa application forms are available from either Australian diplomatic missions overseas or travel agents, and you can apply by mail or in person. Several types of visa exist depending on the reason for your visit. When applying for a visa, you need to present your passport and a passport photo, as well as sign an undertaking that you have an onward or return ticket and 'sufficient funds' to support yourself during your stay.

Tourist visas ($50) are issued by Australian diplomatic missions abroad; they are valid for a stay of up to six months. The visa is valid for use within 12 months of the date of issue and can be used to enter and leave Australia several times within that 12 months.

A long-stay (multiple-entry, four-year) visa allows stays of up to six months on each visit and also costs $50.

Electronic Travel Authority (ETA) can be used instead of a visa for visits of up to three months. The advantages are that it's free and is obtained at the same time as making travel arrangements, through an International Air Transport Association (IATA)-registered travel agent abroad. The agent makes the application direct and issues the traveller with an ETA slip. So far, ETA is available to passport holders of the UK, the USA, most European and Scandinavian countries, Malaysia, Singapore, Japan and Korea.

Visa Extensions Visitors are allowed a maximum stay of one year, including extensions. Visa extensions are made through Department of Immigration and Multicultural Affairs offices in Australia (☎ 13 1881, 🖳 www.immi.gov.au); apply two or three weeks before your visa expires. An application fee of $145 applies, but beware – even if they turn down your application they still keep your money.

Travel Insurance

Residents of the UK, New Zealand, the Netherlands, Sweden and Italy are entitled to free or subsidised medical and hospital treatment under Australia's national insurance scheme; see Medical Cover in the Health & Safety chapter.

A travel-insurance policy to cover theft, loss and medical problems is a good idea. Some policies offer a range of medical-expense options; the higher ones are chiefly for countries such as the USA, which have extremely high medical costs. A wide variety of policies are available, so read the small print. Most cover loss of baggage; sickness; accidental injury or death; and cancellation costs in the event that your trip is cancelled due to accident, illness or death of yourself or a family member.

Some policies specifically exclude 'dangerous activities', which can include scuba diving, motorcycling, even trekking, so check carefully what it says about cycling and any other activities you might undertake in Australia.

You may prefer a policy which pays doctors or hospitals directly rather than your having to pay on the spot and claim later. If you have to claim later obtain and keep all documentation – bills and medical certificates, or police reports. Some policies ask you to call (reverse charges) a centre in your home country where your problem is immediately assessed.

Check the policy covers ambulances or an emergency flight home.

Other Documents

You can generally use your own foreign driving licence in Australia, as long as it is in English (if it's not, you must carry a certified translation). Confusingly, some states prefer that you have an International Licence, which must be supported by your home licence. To avoid potential hassles we suggest you carry both.

Proof of automobile association membership may enable you to receive reciprocal benefits from Australian state auto associations, including cheaper or free touring maps.

For transport discounts carry an International Student Identity Card (ISIC), a senior or pension card or Youth Hostel Association/VIP membership card.

EMBASSIES & CONSULATES
Australian Embassies & Consulates

The Department of Foreign Affairs and Trade has a full list of Australian diplomatic missions overseas at its Web site (💻 www.dfat.gov.au). Australian embassies abroad include:

Canada (☎ 613-236 0841, 💻 www.ahc-ottowa.org) Suite 710, 50 O'Connor St, Ottawa, Ontario K1P 6L2.

France (☎ 01-4059 3300, 💻 www.austgov.fr) 4 rue Jean Rey, 75724 Cedex 15, Paris.

Germany (☎ 030-880 0880, 💻 www.australian-embassy.de) Friedrichstrasse 200, Berlin 10117.

Ireland (☎ 01-676 1517, 💻 www.australianembassy.ie) Fitzwilton House, Wilton Terrace, Dublin 2.

Japan (☎ 03-5232 4111, 💻 www.australia.or.jp) 2-1-14 Mita, Minato-Ku, Tokyo 108.

Netherlands (☎ 070-310 8200, 💻 www.australian-embassy.nl) Carnegielaan 4, 2517 KH The Hague.

New Zealand (☎ 04-473 6411) 72–78 Hobson St, Thorndon, Wellington.

South Africa (☎ 012-342 3781) 292 Orient St, Arcadia, Pretoria 0083.

UK (☎ 0171-379 4334, 💻 www.australia.org.uk) Australia House, The Strand, London WC2B 4LA.

USA (☎ 202-797 3000, 💻 www.austemb.org/) 1601 Massachusetts Ave NW, Washington DC 20036.

Embassies & Consulates in Australia

The principal diplomatic representations to Australia are in Canberra. There are also representatives in other major cities, particularly from countries with a strong connection with Australia like the USA, the UK or New Zealand.

Big cities like Sydney and Melbourne have nearly as many consular offices as Canberra, although visa applications are usually handled in Canberra. Here is a selective list (look under Consulates & Legations in the *Yellow Pages* telephone book or Web site 💻 www.yellowpages.com.au for more):

Canada (☎ 02-6270 4000) Commonwealth Ave, Yarralumla, ACT 2600.

France (☎ 02-6216 0100) 6 Perth Ave, Yarralumla, ACT 2600.

Germany (☎ 02-6270 1911) 119 Empire Circuit, Yarralumla, ACT 2600.

Ireland (☎ 02-6273 3022) 20 Arkana St, Yarralumla, ACT 2600.

Japan (☎ 02-6273 3244) 112 Empire Circuit, Yarralumla, ACT 2600.

Netherlands (☎ 02-6273 3111) 120 Empire Circuit, Yarralumla, ACT 2600.

New Zealand (☎ 02-6270 4211) Commonwealth Ave, Canberra, ACT 2600.

South Africa (☎ 02-6273 2424) cnr State Circle & Rhodes Place, Yarralumla, ACT 2600.

UK (☎ 02-6270 6666) Commonwealth Ave, Yarralumla, ACT 2600.

USA (☎ 02-6214 5600) 21 Moonah Place, Yarralumla, ACT 2600.

CUSTOMS

Most articles can be brought into Australia free of duty if they are for personal use. There's also a duty-free, per-person quota of 1125mL of alcohol, 250 cigarettes and dutiable goods up to the value of A$400.

However, strict laws prohibit or restrict the entry of drugs (*don't* bring them), steroids, weapons, protected wildlife and animal or plant products. Australia has escaped many of the agricultural pests and diseases prevalent in other parts of the world and authorities are keen to keep things that way. You'll be asked to declare all goods of animal or vegetable origin – food, wooden spoons, straw hats, the lot – and show them to an official. Sniffer dogs are routinely used and failure to declare can mean a fine or prosecution. (There are also restrictions on taking fruit and vegetables between states.)

Quarantine officials may also inspect bikes and camping equipment; make sure they're clean. Remember, too, that fuel or gas for camping stoves is prohibited on aeroplanes.

MONEY
Currency

Australia's currency is the Australian dollar, which comprises 100 cents. There are 5c, 10c, 20c, 50c, $1 and $2 coins, and $5, $10, $20, $50 and $100 notes.

Although the smallest coin in circulation is 5c, prices are still marked in single cents, and the bill is rounded to the nearest 5c.

There are no notable restrictions on importing or exporting travellers cheques. Cash amounts in excess of the equivalent of A$5000 (in any currency) must be declared on arrival or departure.

In this book, unless otherwise stated, all prices are given in Australian dollars.

Exchange Rates

The Australian dollar fluctuates quite markedly against the US dollar, but is generally around US$0.55 to $0.70.

country	unit		dollar
Canada	C$1	=	A$1.20
France	10FF	=	A$2.50
Germany	DM1	=	A$0.84
Euro	€1	=	A$1.64
Japan	¥100	=	A$1.63
New Zealand	NZ$1	=	A$0.78
United Kingdom	UK£1	=	A$2.71
United States	US$1	=	A$1.84

Exchanging Money

Cash Changing foreign money or travellers cheques is usually no problem at banks or licensed moneychangers such as Thomas Cook or American Express (found only in major cities or at airports). Moneychangers' rates are usually less competitive than those of the banks.

Travellers Cheques If your stay is limited, then travellers cheques are straightforward and generally enjoy a better exchange rate than foreign cash in Australia.

American Express, Thomas Cook and other well known international brands of travellers cheques are widely used. While a passport is usually adequate for identification, it's wise to carry additional identification. Fees for changing foreign currency travellers cheques vary from bank to bank and from year to year.

Consider buying Australian dollar travellers cheques, which can be exchanged immediately with the bank teller without being converted from a foreign currency and incurring commissions, fees and exchange-rate fluctuations.

Credit Cards Credit cards are an alternative to carrying large numbers of travellers cheques. Visa and MasterCard especially, Diners Club and American Express (Amex) are widely accepted in Australia.

Cash advances from credit cards are available over the counter and from many automated teller machines (ATMs).

Credit cards can be used to make phone calls in special public telephones, found in most towns (minimum call fees apply). A credit card also makes it easier to rent a car for part of your trip.

They also provide an easy way to get emergency cash – arrange for someone at home to deposit money into your credit card account, which you can then withdraw as a cash advance. If your credit card is linked to a savings account, you may also be able to use phone-banking facilities to transfer money yourself.

Bank Accounts & ATMs

If you're in Australia longer than a month or so, it may be worth opening a bank account which includes a cash card. Westpac, ANZ, National and Commonwealth banks are found nationwide. However, with the trend towards electronic banking, branch numbers are shrinking. Small country towns are particularly hard hit and banking services are frequently carried out from within another business; Commonwealth Bank services are available at selected post offices.

ATMs, available in most (but not all) Australian towns, can be used day or night, and most will accept cards from other banks. There is a limit on how much you can withdraw (usually $400 per day; some banks allow more). Some banks allow ATM access to overseas savings accounts, via networks such as Cirrus or Visa. Arrange access to the network with your bank before you go.

A great many businesses, including supermarkets, service stations, outdoor-gear shops and restaurants, are linked into the Eftpos (Electronic Funds Transfer at Point Of Sale) system. Here you can use your bank cash card (or, in many cases, credit card) to pay for purchases, and can often withdraw cash. Some small towns don't have an ATM, although there's usually at least one business with the Eftpos system.

Opening an account at an Australian bank is easy for overseas visitors provided they do it within six weeks of arrival. You simply present your passport. After six weeks a more complicated system applies.

Security

While some country areas are relatively crime-free, increasing drug use and decreased social spending have contributed to a rise in begging and petty theft in some cities. Don't leave money or valuables sitting in a pannier pocket or handlebar bag. Take particular care also in tourist areas.

Costs

See also Taxes & Refunds in this section.

Compared with the USA, Canada and European countries, Australia tends to have more expensive manufactured goods, but cheaper, high-quality fresh food. Prepared foods tend to cost more than in the USA. You can get a takeaway meal from around $5; a main meal in a cafe or mid-priced restaurant generally costs around $12 to $20.

Accommodation, too, is very reasonably priced. Dorm beds in backpacker hostels cost around $15 to $22, though you won't

find them everywhere. However, most places have a caravan park, with camp sites for around $14 for two people and on-site caravans from around $35. Country hotels may also have backpacker beds; otherwise, rooms generally start at around $25 per person. Standard motels cost around $55 to $75 for two people, while B&Bs tend towards the upper end of the price bracket with doubles from $70.

Transport can be expensive because of the great distances: an airfare from Sydney or Melbourne to Perth, for example, costs around $500 to $800. From Melbourne to Tasmania, it's $225 to fly; $175 by fast-cat ferry. A train from Sydney to Melbourne or Brisbane costs around $110. See the Getting Around chapter for more travel prices.

Some standard costs include:

item	cost
1kg bananas	$3.00
glass of beer in a pub	$2.50
loaf of bread	$2.50
chocolate bar	$1.30
cup of coffee	$2.50
double scoop of ice cream	$3.50
good-quality bicycle tube	$10.00

Tipping

In Australia tipping isn't entrenched. It's only customary to tip in more expensive restaurants and only then if you feel it's necessary. If the service has been especially good and you decide to leave a tip, 10% of the bill is the usual amount. Taxi drivers don't expect tips (of course, they don't hurl it back at you if you decide to leave the change).

Taxes & Refunds

The GST (Goods and Services Tax) was introduced in July 2000. While the cost of a wide range of goods (including unprocessed food) has fallen, many services (including accommodation, transport and prepared food) may have increased in price, by anything up to 10%, since this book was researched. Shelf prices include the GST – there is no add-on, such as occurs in the USA.

International air and sea travel to/from Australia is GST-free, as is domestic air travel when purchased outside Australia by nonresidents.

Overseas visitors are entitled to GST refunds on goods purchased not more than

30 days before departure. The refund is available for goods with a single tax invoice totalling $300 or more; and can be collected by presenting the goods and an invoice to Tourist Refund Scheme (TRS) booths at international airports. For more information, contact Customs (☎ 1300 363 263) or check the TRS section of the Web site (🖥 www .customs.gov.au).

POST & COMMUNICATIONS
Post
The postal service is relatively efficient and reasonably cheap. It costs 45c to send a standard letter or postcard within Australia; airmail letters cost $1.00/1.50 to Asia Pacific regions/other destinations. And postcards/aerograms cost $1.00/0.80 to anywhere.

Parcels to Europe and the USA, via seamail, cost $14/26 for 1/2kg. Airmail rates are considerably more expensive.

Stamps are available at post offices and postal agencies (operated from newsagencies, which have longer hours). Call ☎ 13 1318 Australia-wide for postal enquiries.

All post offices hold mail for visitors; some GPOs (General Post Offices – main city post offices) have busy poste restante sections.

Telephone
Local calls are untimed, and cost 40c from public phones, 25c (or less) from private phones. Long-distance (ie, to more than about 50km away), or STD, calls are timed and are charged at different rates, depending on the distance and the time you call (different providers offer various rates but, generally, STD calls are cheaper outside business hours).

Australia has four area-code regions: see the boxed text 'Useful Numbers'. Some cross-pollination occurs around state borders, eg, some towns in north-eastern Victoria use ☎ 02. The codes are only needed if you're dialling from a different region. All local numbers have eight digits.

Payphones accept coins and/or phone cards. Telstra phonecards are charged at a minimum rate of 40c per call (more for long-distance calls); there's also a wide range of local and international phonecards, with various rates. Generally, these are best value for international, rather than local, calls. Check the call charges carefully.

Many payphones also accept credit cards (although minimum charges apply).

Australia has embraced mobile phones (cell phones). There are two separate mobile networks: digital and the digitally-based CDMA. Ask the carrier you use in your home country whether your mobile phone will work in Australia. While these two networks service more than 90% of the population, vast tracts (inland) of the country are not covered at all – check the service providers' coverage maps before signing up. The main mobile operators are the mostly government-owned Telstra, and two private companies Optus and Vodafone.

International Calls To call Australia from abroad, dial the international access code for the country you're in, followed by 61, the area code (omit the initial '0') and the local number.

International calls from Australia are among the cheapest you'll find anywhere; it's worth checking for special deals – call ☎ 12 552.

The Country Direct service gives callers in Australia direct access to operators in nearly 60 countries, for reverse-charge (collect) or credit-card calls. For a list of participating countries, check any *White Pages* telephone book.

Useful Numbers

Directory assistance	☎ 1223
Emergency	☎ 000
International pricing and codes info	☎ 12 552

General Prefixes

☎ 1800	free call
☎ 13 or ☎ 1300	local-call cost
☎ 190	information calls (per-minute charges)
☎ 04XX	mobile phones
☎ 0011	international access code

State Prefixes

☎ 02	NSW and ACT
☎ 03	Victoria and Tasmania
☎ 08	SA, WA and the NT
☎ 07	Queensland

eKno Communication Service

Lonely Planet's eKno global communication service provides low-cost international calls – for local calls you're usually better off with a local phonecard. The eKno service also offers free messaging services, email, travel information and an online travel vault, where you can securely store all your important documents. Join online at ⌨ www.ekno.lonelyplanet.com, where you will find the local-access numbers for the 24-hour customer-service centre. Once you have joined, always check the eKno Web site for the latest access numbers for each country and updates on new features.

Fax

Post offices and many small businesses offer fax services. The charge to send a fax is from about $2 per page. Receiving a fax costs around $1 per page.

Email

Cybercafes are popping up in tourist areas everywhere and many hostels have coin-operated Internet machines. Most public libraries have Internet access – it's normally free but you have to book. Not all will allow you to access email.

The Tasmanian and WA governments have set up internet-access centres in towns across their states. Tasmanian centres are called On-line Access Centres (⌨ www.tco.asn.au); in rural WA, they're known as telecentres.

The most convenient (and often the only) way to send and receive email is to open an account with one of the free Web-based email services, such as Yahoo! Mail, Hotmail or Rocket Mail.

INTERNET RESOURCES

The World Wide Web is a rich resource for travellers. At the Lonely Planet Web site (⌨ www.lonelyplanet.com) you'll find succinct summaries on travelling to Australia, postcards from other travellers and the Thorn Tree bulletin board, where you can ask questions before you go or dispense advice when you get back. You can also find travel news and updates to many of our most popular guidebooks, and the sub-WWWay section links you to the most useful travel resources elsewhere on the Web.

In addition to other sites listed throughout this chapter, try these useful Australian sites:

Aussie Cycling Links (⌨ www.jub.com.au/cycling/) As its name suggests, this site is a great starting point; it includes links to clubs, chat rooms, information and an Australian on-line cycling book store.

The Aussie Index (⌨ www.aussie.com.au) This is a fairly comprehensive list of Australian companies, educational institutions and government departments that maintain Web sites.

Australia Focussed Bicycle Resource (⌨ www.bicycles.net.au) Find a list of links to cycling organisations, the bicycle section of amazon.com online book shop and more.

Bicycle Fish (⌨ www.cobweb.com.au/~gloria/index.html) This down-to-earth site on bicycle travel in Australia includes a bicycle-travellers message board, information on work opportunities such as harvesting, and tips for cycle-camping in the desert.

Bureau of Meteorology (⌨ www.bom.gov.au) This site includes information such as wind maps and weather forecasts.

Guide to Australia (⌨ www.csu.edu.au/education/australia.html) Maintained by the Charles Sturt University in NSW, this is a mine of information, with links to Australian government departments, weather information, books, maps etc.

The Bicycle Federation of Australia (⌨ www.bfa.asn.au/) The BFA is the national association of major bicycle advocacy groups. Its Web site details campaigns and links to state member groups.

The Bicycle Industry Traders Association & Retail Cycle Traders Association Web site (⌨ www.bikeoz.com) Go here for a list of RCTA member bike shops.

BOOKS

The Arts section in the Facts about Australia chapter discusses Australian literature in general. Australian capital cities have some excellent independent book stores; large chains include Collins and Dymocks. Many towns also have second-hand bookshops. Public libraries are also useful.

Lonely Planet

For more detail than is provided in this guide, Lonely Planet has an *Australia* guide as well as individual guides to each state, *Melbourne* and *Sydney* city guides and *Out to Eat* restaurant guides to Melbourne and Sydney. *Watching Wildlife Australia* is an all-in-one guide to finding, identifying and understanding Australian wildlife.

Sean & David's Long Drive, a hilarious, offbeat road book by Sean Condon, is part of Lonely Planet's travel-literature series.

Also look for *Bushwalking in Australia, Outback Australia, Islands of Australia's Great Barrier Reef,* and diving guides *Australia's Great Barrier Reef, Victoria Australia* and *Australia: Southeast Coast & Tasmania.*

With contributions from more than 60 Indigenous people, *Aboriginal Australia & the Torres Strait Islands* is a guide to experiencing Australia's 50,000-year-old Indigenous cultures.

Cycling

Keiren Ryan's *Off Road Cycling Adventures* is a great book for mountain biking around Melbourne (available from good Melbourne bike stores or via the Web site ▫ www.orca.net.au). If you're heading into the outback, Bob Craine's 1997 *Cycling Northern Australia* is worth a look. *Railtrails of Victoria* by Fiona Colquhoun et al details 25 trails for cycling.

Now out of print (but available at good libraries), *The Bicycle and the Bush* (1980), by Jim Fitzpatrick, is a very readable, fascinating work on Australian cycling history. Keith Dunstan's *Confessions of a Bicycle Nut* is entertaining, as are accounts of journeys by early overland cyclists; you should find Francis Birtles' *Lonely Lands* (out of print) at large public libraries.

Other Guidebooks

A different type of guidebook is Aussie surf star Nat Young's *Surfing Australia's East Coast* – it's slim, cheap and comprehensive. He's also written the *Surfing & Sailboard Guide to Australia.*

Travel

Travel accounts include *Tracks*, by Robyn Davidson, who walked from Alice Springs to the WA coast with her camels; Tony Horwitz's entertaining hitchhiking account, *One for the Road*; or *The Ribbon and the Ragged Square*, by Linda Christmas, an intelligent, sober account of an investigatory trip by an English *Guardian* journalist.

History & Politics

Respected Australian historian, the late Manning Clark, has provided a good, accessible introduction to Australian history in *A Short History of Australia*. Another is *The Fatal Shore*, Robert Hughes' best-selling account of the convict era.

John Pilger's *A Secret Country* vividly addresses Australia's historical roots and its shabby treatment of Aboriginal people.

The Australian Aborigines by Kenneth Maddock is a good cultural summary. The award-winning *Triumph of the Nomads*, by Geoffrey Blainey, convincingly demolishes the myth that Aborigines were 'primitive'. Richard Broome's *Aboriginal Australians* is a sympathetic historical account of what's happened to the original Australians since Europeans arrived. *The Other Side of the Frontier*, by Henry Reynolds, gives an Aboriginal view of the European arrival.

NEWSPAPERS & MAGAZINES

Most of Australia's bicycle magazines focus on racing or mountain biking. The bi-monthly *Australian Cyclist* is an exception: its coverage includes touring, commuting, personality stories, and bicycle advocacy. *Bicycling Australia* (monthly) covers road, track, mountain biking and racing, as does the sporadic *Freewheel*; *Australian Mountain Bike* (bimonthly) caters to recreational and competitive sorts; *Ride* (quarterly) covers racing (road, track, mountain biking), while *Totally Bitumen* is exclusively devoted to road racing.

Good outdoor magazines include *Wild* and *Outdoor Australia*, published quarterly, and *Rock* (monthly).

Each major city has an important daily newspaper; and often a tabloid too. The *Sydney Morning Herald* and Melbourne *Age* are two of the most important. The *Australian* is the only national daily.

Widely available weekly magazines include the Australian *Time*; the combined Australian *Bulletin* and *Newsweek*; *Business Review Weekly*; and the British *Guardian Weekly*, good for international news.

WEATHER FORECASTS

Regional weather forecasts are broadcast on most radio stations following the news (usually on the hour). For more comprehensive information, the Telstra Dial-it Weather Information Service (☎ 1196) provides regional forecasts from the Bureau of Meteorology.

RADIO & TV

The national, government-run TV and radio network is the Australian Broadcasting Corporation (ABC). It broadcasts Radio

National (world news, current affairs, other topics); Classic FM; Triple J, the youth FM station (independent music); and ABC TV.

There's a host of regional commercial radio stations, both AM and FM. Capital cities receive the commercial TV networks (Seven, Nine and Ten); and many country areas generally have a regional commercial TV station. SBS, a government-sponsored multicultural station, beams to capital cities and main regional centres. It covers the Tour de France and large Australian races.

Pay TV is beginning to take off in Australia, with the major players (Optus Vision and Murdoch's Foxtel) jockeying for position and market share. Austar is the only provider outside the metropolitan areas.

PHOTOGRAPHY & VIDEO

Big cities have plenty of good camera shops. Print film is available almost everywhere (slide film more reliably so in cities) and prices are similar to other western countries. A roll of 36-exposure Kodachrome 64 or Fujichrome 100 slide film costs around $26, including developing – less if you buy it in quantity.

Australian light is intense, so 100 ASA film is usually adequate; photos are generally better taken early or late in the day. Keep film cool where possible, especially after exposure, and packaged to keep out dust and damp.

Be polite (and ask) when photographing people. Note that many Aboriginal people don't like being photographed, even from a distance.

Australia uses the PAL video system.

TIME

Australia is divided into three time zones: WA, eight hours ahead of GMT/UTC, is in the Western Standard Time zone; SA and the Northern Territory (NT), 9½ hours ahead, go by Central Standard Time; and NSW, Australian Capital Territory (ACT), Victoria, Tasmania, and Queensland, in the Eastern Standard Time zone, are 10 hours ahead of GMT/UTC. When it's noon in Perth, it's 1.30pm in Adelaide and 2pm in Sydney; it's 8pm the previous day in Los Angeles, 11pm in New York and 4am in London.

Things get confusing during 'daylight saving' – for which clocks are put forward an hour – in NSW, ACT, Victoria, Tasmania and SA. It operates from the end of October (start of October in Tasmania) to the end of March.

ELECTRICITY

The standard is 220–240V AC and 50Hz with three-pin (flat) plugs.

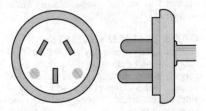

Apart from in fancy hotels, it's difficult to find converters for US-flat or European-round two-pin plugs (eg, for shavers). Adaptors for British plugs can be found in good hardware shops, chemists and travel agents.

WEIGHTS & MEASURES

Australia uses the metric system. Distance is measured in metres (m) or kilometres (km); speed limits are in kilometres per hour (km/h). Colloquially, distance is often quoted as the time it takes to get there (which invariably means by car). Liquids are sold by the litre (L), fruit and vegetables by the kilogram (kg). A conversion table is at the back of this book.

LAUNDRY

Most reasonable-sized towns have a laundrette. Opening hours vary: many open 7am to 7pm or later; others keep standard business hours. Almost all hostels and caravan parks have laundries, as do many motels. Coin-operated machines typically cost around $2.40 for a wash (detergent extra); dryers generally cost 20c for five minutes.

WOMEN CYCLISTS

Australia is generally a safe place for women travellers and plenty of women cycle alone with very few hassles. Women should, however, exercise the same degree of caution as they would anywhere – it's better not to walk or camp alone in isolated areas at night, for example.

Sexual harassment (at least in a mild form) is unfortunately still second nature to many Aussie males (who *hasn't* had someone try to 'sweet talk' them home from the pub?). Generally speaking, men in rural areas tend to be a bit more old fashioned – they're more likely to be an 'ocker' than a 'snag' (sensitive new-age guy)!

Call directory assistance ☎ 1223 for each state's sexual assault crisis phone line; most centres will accept reverse charges from women in crisis.

GAY & LESBIAN CYCLISTS

Australia is a popular gay and lesbian destination – and generally, it's a fairly gay-friendly place, although you're more likely to come across homophobic attitudes outside tourist areas. Homosexual acts are legal in all states.

Exclusively gay or gay-friendly tour operators, travel agents, resorts and accommodation exist throughout the country. Areas with a particular gay focus include Cairns and Noosa in Queensland; Sydney, the Blue Mountains and the south coast in NSW; and Melbourne, Daylesford and Hepburn Springs in Victoria. Gay & Lesbian Tourism Australia (GALTA; 🖳 www.galta.com.au) has information on gay-friendly operators.

Gay telephone counselling services are often a useful source of general information; see the ATC Web site 🖳 www.australia.com for a listing (go to Gay & Lesbian Travel under Activities & Adventures).

Major cities have gay newspapers, available from gay and lesbian venues. National gay lifestyle magazines include *OutRage*, *Campaign* and the art magazine *Blue*.

Gay and lesbian bike clubs include Bent Kranks (☎ 0407-358 180) in Melbourne (off-road); Sydney Spokes Mountain Bike Club (🖳 www.sydneyspokes.one.net.au); and Adelaide Spokes (🖳 www.merlin.net .au/~llew/spokes).

CYCLISTS WITH A DISABILITY

Disability awareness in Australia is reasonably high, and was heightened by the 2000 Paralympic Games in Sydney. Most tourist commissions are gathering information in their state about accessible tourist attractions and accommodation. Legislation requires that new accommodation must meet accessibility standards and tourist operators must not discriminate.

The best source of reliable information for travellers with a disability is Nican (☎ TTY 02-6285 3713 or ☎ TTY 1800-806

769, 🖳 www.nican.com.au), PO Box 407, Curtin, ACT 2605. It's a national free service on sport, recreation, tourism and the arts for people with disabilities. The Nican Web site links to a database of organisations catering for people with disabilities.

The recreational services section of the Vision Australia Foundation (☎ 03-9864 9237, 🖳 www.visionaustralia.org.au) can provide information about resources for cyclists who are vision-impaired.

The ATC (see the Tourist Offices section earlier in this chapter) publishes a fact sheet about travel in Australia for people with disabilities on their Web site (🖳 www.aus tralia.com), which contains travel tips and transport and contact addresses of organisations on a state-by-state basis.

It's worth checking Lonely Planet's Web site (🖳 www.lonelyplanet.com) for travellers' experiences on the Travellers with Disabilities section of the Thorn Tree. The US-based Web site 🖳 www.cando.com has information about hand cycles.

SENIOR CYCLISTS

Many organisations offer discounts to seniors, but often only those with government-pension or seniors cards, which are only available to residents (it's still worth asking).

Senior cyclists are often well represented in touring clubs; and veteran (racing) cycling clubs are based around Australia. The Australian Veterans Cycling Council (AVCC) Cycling Gazette is published on the web within the *International Cycling Gazette* (🖳 users.senet.com.au/~ricko4u). It lists contact details for state-based clubs. The Australian Retired Peoples Association (☎ 03-9650 6144, 🖳 home.vicnet.net.au/~ar pao50), a national membership-based organisation for over 50s, has reciprocal arrangements with similar organisations overseas.

TRAVEL WITH CHILDREN

Generally, travelling children are fairly well-catered-for in Australia.

Most motels and the better-equipped caravan parks supply cots and baby's baths, and many have playgrounds and swimming pools. Most Youth Hostel Association (YHA) and some backpacker hostels have family rooms. Cafes and restaurants often have high chairs and can provide small serves from the main menu.

Touring with Children

Children can travel by bicycle from the time they can support their head and a helmet, at around eight months. There are some small, lightweight, cute helmets around, such as the L'il Bell Shell. To carry an infant to toddler requires a child seat or trailer. Child seats are more common for everyday riding and are cheaper, easier to move as a unit with the bike and let you touch and talk to your child while moving. Disadvantages, especially over long distances, can include exposure to weather, the tendency of a sleeping child to loll, and losing luggage capacity at the rear. The best makes, such as the Rhode Gear Limo, include extra moulding to protect the child in case of a fall, have footrests and restraints, recline to let the child sleep and fit very securely and conveniently onto a rack on the bike.

With a capacity of up to 50kg (versus around 18kg for a child seat), trailers can accommodate two bigger children and luggage. They give better, though not always total, protection from sun and rain and let children sleep comfortably. Look for a trailer that is lightweight, foldable, conspicuous (brightly coloured, with flag) and that tracks and handles well. It's also handy to be able to swap the trailer between bikes so adults can alternate towing and riding beside the trailer. Child trailers tend to be preferred for serious touring, but may be illegal in some places, for example, Western Australia. Trailers or seats are treated as additional luggage items when flying.

Be sure that the bike to which you attach a child seat or trailer is sturdy and low-geared to withstand – and help *you* withstand – the extra weight and stresses. From the age of about four, children can move on to a 'trailer-bike' (effectively a child's bike, minus a front wheel, which hitches to an adult's bike) or to a tandem (initially as 'stoker' – the rider at the back – with 'kiddy cranks', or crank extensions) – this lets them help pedal. The tandem can be a long-term solution, keeping you and your child together and letting you compensate if the child tires. The British publication *Encycleopedia*, by Alan Davidson et al, is a good guide to quality trailers, trailer-bikes and tandems available from manufacturers around the world.

Be careful of children rushing into touring on a solo bike before they can sustain the effort and concentration required. Once they are ready and keen to ride solo, at about age 10 to 12, they will need a good quality touring bike, properly fitted (A$300, US$200, UK£130 up).

Bike touring with children requires a new attitude as well as new equipment. Be sensitive to their needs – especially when they're too young to communicate them fully. In a seat or trailer, they're not expending energy and need to be dressed accordingly. Keep them dry, at the right temperature and protected from the sun. Keep their energy and interest up. When you stop, a child travelling in a seat or trailer will be ready for action, so always reserve some energy for parenting. This means more stops, including at places like playgrounds. Older children will have their own interests and should be involved in planning a tour. Before setting off on a major journey, try some day trips to check your set-up and introduce your child to cycling.

Children need to be taken into account in deciding each day's route – traffic and distances need to be moderate and facilities and points of interest adequate. Given the extra weight of children and their daily needs, you may find it easier to leave behind the camping gear and opt for indoor accommodation or day trips from a base or series of bases. The very fit and adventurous may not need to compromise to ride with children, but those who do will still find it worthwhile.

As with other activities, children bring a new perspective and pleasure to cycle touring. They tend to love it.

Alethea Morison

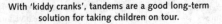

With 'kiddy cranks', tandems are a good long-term solution for taking children on tour.

PETER HINES

Child concessions (up to 50% of the adult rate) are common for accommodation, entry fees and transport. However, the definition of 'child' varies from under 12 to under 18 years.

For accommodation, concessions generally apply to children under 12 years sharing the room with adults. With the major airlines, infants travel free provided they don't occupy a seat – child fares apply up to 15 years old (but other discounts are usually more attractive). Bus and train companies have various arrangements for children.

Lonely Planet's *Travel with Children* contains plenty of useful information. As well, the various Travellers Medical & Vaccination Centres around Australia (at least one in every capital city) have a leaflet on the subject.

USEFUL ORGANISATIONS
National Parks Agencies

Australia's conservation areas are generally managed by the state and territory conservation departments.

The main addresses for information are:

New South Wales
National Parks & Wildlife Service (☎ 02-9585 6333 or ☎ 1300 36 1967, ▣ www.npws.nsw.gov .au) Level 1, 43 Bridge St, Hurstville, NSW 2220.

Northern Territory
Parks & Wildlife Commission of the Northern Territory (☎ 08-8999 5511, ▣ www.nt.gov .au/paw) 25 Chung Wah Terrace, Palmerston, NT 0830.

Queensland
Environmental Protection Agency (☎ 07-3227 8197, ▣ www.env.qld.gov.au) 160 Ann St, Brisbane, 4002.

South Australia
Parks & Wildlife South Australia (☎ 08-8204 1910, ▣ www.denr.sa.gov.au) The Environment Shop, 77 Grenfell St, Adelaide, 5000.

Tasmania
Tasmania Parks & Wildlife Service (☎ 03-6233 6191, ▣ www.parks.tas.gov.au) 134 Macquarie St, Hobart, Tasmania 7000.

Victoria
Department of Natural Resources & Environment (☎ 03-9637 8325, ▣ www.nre.vic.gov.au) 8 Nicholson St, East Melbourne, Victoria 3002. *Parks Victoria* (☎ 13 1963, ▣ www.parkweb .vic.gov.au) 35 Whitehorse Rd, Deepdene, Victoria 3103.

Western Australia
Department of Conservation & Land Management (☎ 08-9334 0333, ▣ www.calm.wa .gov.au) Technology Park, Western Precinct, 17 Dick Perry Ave, Kensington, WA 6151.

Kakadu and Uluru national parks in the NT and national parks in the Australian Capital Territory (ACT) are managed by the Commonwealth through Environment Australia's Biodiversity Group (☎ 02-6274 1221 or ☎ 1800-803 772, ▣ www.biodiversity.enviro nment.gov.au) John Gorton Building, King Edward Terrace, Parkes, Canberra 2601.

Nongovernment conservation organisations include:

Australian Conservation Foundation (☎ 03-9416 1166, ▣ www.acfonline.org.au) 340 Gore St, Fitzroy, Victoria 3065. *Offices also in Sydney, Canberra and Adelaide.*
The Wilderness Society (☎ 03-6234 9799, ▣ www.wilderness.org.au) 130 Davey St, Hobart, Tasmania 7000.

National Cycling Organisations

The Bicycle Federation of Australia (BFA; ☎ 02-6355 1570, ▣ www.bfa.asn.au/), GPO Box 3222, Canberra, ACT 2601, is a national federation of major bicycle-advocacy groups, dedicated to promoting cycling for transport and recreation. Most state advocacy organisations are represented by the BFA.

State bodies vary from large organisations to small, volunteer-run groups. The larger ones run popular tours and some provide useful touring information – check their Web sites. As well as nongovernment lobby groups, WA and SA have government cycling bodies within the state transport departments.

The main state bodies are:

Bicycle Institute of SA (☎ 08-8271 5824, ▣ www.bisa.asn.au/) GPO Box 792, Adelaide, SA 5001. Volunteer-run organisation. Concentrates on bicycle lobbying.
Bicycle New South Wales (☎ 02-9283 5200, ▣ www.bicyclensw.org.au) 209 Castlereagh St, Sydney 2001. Runs popular rides and a mail-order bookshop.
Bicycle Queensland (☎ 07-3844 1144) PO Box 8321, Woolloongabba, Qld 4102. This volunteer-run group organises popular mass day rides and lobbies governments.
Bicycle Tasmania (☎ 03-6226 7168, ▣ www.nets pace.net.au/~dmurphy/bt.htm) 102 Bathurst St, Hobart, 7000 (postal address only). Has a useful Web site and is run by volunteers.
Bicycle Victoria (☎ 03- 9328 3000, ▣ www .bv.com.au) 19 O'Connell St, North Melbourne. The largest nongovernment state organisation. Runs popular events such as the Great Victorian Bike Ride (see Organised Rides in the Getting Around chapter). Not a BFA member.

Tandeming in Australia

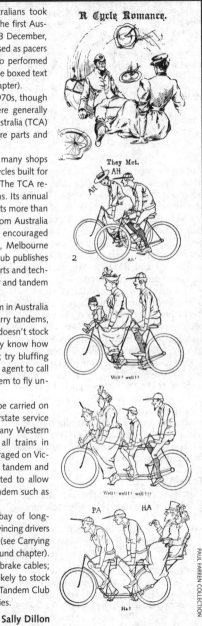

A Cycle Romance.

They Met.

Well ! well !!

Well ! well !! well !!!

Always eager to adopt new innovations, Australians took eagerly to tandeming in the late-19th century. The first Australian tandem race was held in Melbourne on 13 December, 1894, as part of the Austral Wheel Race. Often used as pacers in early time trials, Australian tandem teams also performed well in their own right on the racing circuit (see the boxed text 'Olympic Cycling' in the Facts about Australia chapter).

Tandem riding saw a resurgence in the late 1970s, though parts were difficult to source and tandems were generally bought overseas. The current Tandem Club of Australia (TCA) formed in 1980 to help members source obscure parts and share stockist information.

These days, the scene is alive and growing: many shops carry tandem spares and are willing to order bicycles built for two, while a few keep them on the shop floor. The TCA remains active, with more than 100 member teams. Its annual weekend rally, in late-October/November, attracts more than 50 tandems and their owners. Non-members from Australia or overseas are welcome to join club events and encouraged to contact the club for advice (PO Box 12259, Melbourne 8006, ⌨ home.vicnet.net.au/~tandem/). The club publishes a two-monthly newsletter with events, tour reports and technical tips. Newsletter back issues, a rides calendar and tandem stockists' details are published on the Web site.

As in most countries, transporting your tandem in Australia poses some difficulties. Australian airlines will carry tandems, though Qantas, which requires bikes be boxed, doesn't stock bike boxes big enough, and check-in staff rarely know how to deal with the situation. Bring your own box; try bluffing your way through; or, better still, get your travel agent to call the airline and ask that a note allowing the tandem to fly unboxed be entered in your passenger file.

Train travel is problematic; tandems cannot be carried on any NSW train services (including the XPT interstate service between Melbourne, Sydney and Brisbane) or any Western Australian services. They can be carried on all trains in Queensland and Victoria, though they're discouraged on Victoria's smaller sprinters. If you want to combine tandem and train travel, consider getting S&S couplings fitted to allow your bike to pack down, or look at a folding tandem such as Bike Friday's Tandem Two'sDay.

Many tandems will fit across the luggage bay of long-distance buses, though you may have trouble convincing drivers of this; the normal bike carriage conditions apply (see Carrying Your Bicycle in the Bus section of the Getting Around chapter).

Carry basic spares such as extra-long gear or brake cables; bike shops in country towns, especially, are unlikely to stock tandem-specific parts. Most shops listed on the Tandem Club of Australia Web site will mail emergency supplies.

Sally Dillon

PAUL FARREN COLLECTION

Bike South (☎ 08-8343 2911, 🖳 www.trans
port.sa.gov.au/bikesouth/index.html) Part of
the government department Transport SA.

Bikewest (☎ 9320 9301, 🖳 www.transport
.wa.gov.au/metro/bikewest) 441 Murray St,
Perth. A section of the state government's
transport department.

Bicycle Transportation Alliance (☎ 08-9420
7210, 🖳 sunsite.anu.edu.au/wa/bta/) 2 Delhi St,
West Perth. WA's community-run lobby group.

Pedal Power (☎ 02-6248 7995, 🖳 sunsite.anu.edu
.au/community/pedalpower/index.htm) GPO
Box 581, Canberra, ACT 2601. Volunteer-run
group. Organises Canberra's bike week, encourages commuting and runs rides.

Audax Australia (🖳 www.audax.org.au) runs
noncompetitive, long-distance rides, on- and
off-road. Visitors are welcomed. The Web
site lists state contacts and regional events.

Cycling Australia (🖳 www.cycling.org
.au), Dunc Gray Velodrome, Carysfield Rd,
Bass Hill NSW 2197, is the national body
for competitive cycling (road, track, mountain biking and BMX) in Australia; it has
separate bodies in each state.

Mountain Bike Australia (☎ 02-6249
0750, 🖳 members.optusnet.com.au/~mtba
/home.html) formed in 1999, is a separate
coalition of mountain-bike clubs around the
country. MTBA runs the MTBA Nationals
(which are separate from the CA Nationals).

OzHPV (🖳 sunsite.anu.edu.au/commu
nity/ozhpv/index.htm), PO Box 1053,
Auburn, NSW 2144 is the national body for
human-powered vehicles. It has affiliate
groups in some states.

The Tandem Club of Australia (🖳 home
.vicnet.net.au/~tandem/), PO Box 12259,
Melbourne 8006, has a rides program in each
state and an annual rally.

Touring Clubs

Most these clubs run regular weekend rides,
on which visitors are generally welcome.

Brisbane Bicycle Touring Association (🖳 www
.maxpages.com/bbta) PO Box 286, Ashgrove,
Qld 4060. Runs weekend rides; visitors are
welcome.

East Coast Touring Cycling Club (☎ 02-4964
1256, 🖳 users.hunterlink.net.au/~derk/) Organises at least three events every year.

Illawarra Touring Cycling Club (☎ 02-4229
6194, 🖳 www.illawarra.net.au/itcc/index.htm)
PO Box U30, University Post Office, Wollongong, NSW 2500.

Melbourne Bicycle Touring Club (🖳 home.vic
net.net.au/~mbtc/) Has been active for more
than 25 years – rides program on their Web
site.

Salamanca Cyclists Touring Club (☎ 03-6234
2730) Hobart's touring club.

Sunshine Coast Bicycle Touring Club (☎ 07-
5475 4249, 🖳 www.ozemail.com.au/~jcurrie
/index.html)

Team Chaos (🖳 www.zipworld.com.au/~braid
ing/team_chaos) Runs unsupported weekend
off-road bush rides, mostly in NSW. Numbers
are limited – contact through the Web site.

BUSINESS HOURS

Standard office hours are weekdays from
9am to 5pm. Shops usually open weekdays
from 9am to 5pm or 5.30pm and Saturdays
till either 12.30pm or 5pm. Sunday trading is
increasingly common, but currently limited
to major cities and parts of regional Victoria. City businesses tend to have longer
opening hours than in the country. Most
towns have one or two late-shopping nights,
usually Thursday and/or Friday (until 9pm).
Other hours include:

Banks Open weekdays from 9.30am to 4pm
(5pm Fridays). In country towns, some banks
only open a few days a week.

Bike Shops Open weekdays from 9am to 5.30pm
and Saturday morning until 12.30pm.

Convenience Stores Open seven days, usually
from 7am to 7pm.

Newsagents Open Monday to Friday from 7am to
6pm and Saturday until 12.30pm.

Post offices Open Monday to Friday from 9am to
5pm (In major cities Australia Post Shops also
open Saturday morning).

Supermarkets Open Monday to Friday 9am to
5.30pm and Saturday until 12.30pm or 5pm. In
cities and regional centres, seven-day trading
with longer hours – even 24-hour trading – is
becoming more the norm.

Tourist offices State tourist offices in capital
cities usually open 9am to 5pm, but close Saturday afternoon and Sunday.

Visitor centres Local or regional visitor centres
usually open 9am to 5pm daily (some close
weekends).

PUBLIC HOLIDAYS & SPECIAL EVENTS

The main school summer vacation is from
mid-December to late January. Other
shorter holiday periods vary slightly between states. They fall around April (generally coinciding with Easter), late June/July,
and late September/October.

Public Holidays

These also vary from state to state. The main national and state public holidays are:

New Year's Day 1 January

Australia Day 26 January – Commemorates the arrival of the First Fleet in 1788; this has been dubbed 'Invasion Day' by Aboriginal rights supporters

Eight Hours Day (Tas) 1st Monday in March

Labour Day (Vic, WA) 2nd Monday in March

Easter March/April – Good Friday to Easter Monday inclusive

Anzac Day 25 April – Commemorates the landing of Australian and New Zealand troops at Gallipoli in 1915

Labour Day (Queensland) 1st Monday in May

Foundation Day (WA) 1st Monday in June

Queen's Birthday (except WA) 2nd Monday in June

Queen's Birthday (WA) Last Monday in September

Labour Day (ACT, NSW, SA) 1st Monday in October

Christmas Day 25 December

Boxing Day 26 December

Proclamation Day (SA) Last Tuesday in December

Cycling Events

Australia has hundreds of cycling events, from club events and social rides to large public events and professional races. Here's a selection of the better known:

When	Where	Event
Jan	Adelaide	**Tour Down Under**, a six-day stage race (see the boxed text in the South Australia chapter).
Jan	Bright, Vic	**Audax Alpine Classic**, a very popular Audax event: 100km, 160km or 200km through the Victorian Alps; Australia Day long weekend.
Feb	Evandale, Tas	**Penny Farthing Championships** (see Tassie's West Coast ride)
Mar	Northern NSW	**Loop the Lake**, a one-day ride around Lake Macquarie attracting more than 1000 participants.
Mar	Northcliffe, WA	**Karri Cup,** WA's most lucrative mountain-bike race.
Mar/Apr	NSW	**The RTA Big Ride**, a nine-day noncompetitive supported tour that draws around 1500 participants.
Apr	Melbourne	**Melbourne Autumn Daytour (MAD Ride)**, Melbourne Bicycle Touring Club's noncompetitive road or mountain-bike ride through Melbourne's north-eastern ranges.
May	Brisbane	**Brissie to the Bay**, Queensland's largest recreational bike ride.
Oct	WA	**Perth-Albany-Perth**, Audax 90-hour, 1200km event.
Oct	Melbourne	**Around the Bay in a Day**, a one-day, noncompetitive 210km ride around Melbourne's Port Phillip Bay.
Oct	WA	**On Your Bike Tour**, WA's Cycle Touring Association's nine-day, noncompetitive, supported ride.
Oct	Canberra	**Tour de Capital**, Community race.
Oct	Victoria	**Melbourne to Warrnambool**, the world's longest running one-day handicap road race; open to licensed riders.
Oct/Nov	most states	**Fleche Opperman**, Audax 24-hour team event, at least 360km long.
Oct/Nov	varies	**TwoUp**, the Tandem Club of Australia's annual weekend rally.
Nov	NSW	**Sydney to the Gong**, hugely popular one-day ride from Sydney to Wollongong, with a 92km or 58km option.
Nov	Rutherglen, Vic	**Tour de Muscat**, supported weekend winery tour.
Nov	Geelong, Vic	**Geelong Otway Classic**, fund-raiser through the Otway Ranges.
Nov/Dec	Sydney	**Cycle Sydney**, a popular, one-day 50km ride through Sydney and suburbs on traffic-free roads.
Dec	Victoria	**Great Victorian Bike Ride**, a nine-day, noncompetitive supported ride drawing around 3000 participants.
Dec	Tasmania	**Annual Seven Hills Dash (ASH Dash)**, a hard, hilly, 200km Audax ride south of Hobart.

Special Events

Some of Australia's major festivals and events are (tourist offices have details):

Sydney to Hobart Yacht Race (Dec/Jan) Yachts leave Sydney Harbour on 26 December, arriving in Hobart from 29 December to 2 January.

Hobart Summer Festival (Jan) Month-long festival incorporating the Taste of Tasmania food festival at the docks.

Sydney Gay & Lesbian Mardi Gras (Feb) It's fun: it includes an extravagant procession and an incredible party along Oxford St.

Moomba (Mar) Melbourne festival featuring cultural and sporting events plus a huge street procession.

Port Fairy Folk Festival (Mar) Little Port Fairy, on Victoria's southern coast, hosts Australia's biggest folk-music festival.

Melbourne International Comedy Festival (Mar/Apr) No joke, it's one of the largest comedy festivals in the world.

Byron Bay Blues & Roots Festival (Easter) Artists from around the world perform at this NSW beach resort.

Bell's Beach Surf Classic (Easter) Bells Beach, Torquay, west of Melbourne, hosts the longest-running professional surfing event in the world.

Sydney City to Surf (August) Australia's biggest foot race is the 14km from Hyde Park to Bondi Beach.

AFL (Aussie Rules Football) Grand Final (Sep) The nation's biggest sporting event, held in Melbourne.

Melbourne Cup (Nov) Australia's premier horse race captures the country.

CYCLING ROUTES
Route Descriptions

This guide details bike tours in seven of Australia's eight states and territories, with the ACT rides included in the NSW chapter. While it doesn't promise comprehensive coverage, we're confident it describes the best cycling Australia has to offer.

In each state is a series of rides, each short enough for a visitor with limited time, which also link easily to one another. In addition, the Melbourne to the Gold Coast chapter describes the ride along the east coast between Cowes (near Melbourne) and Surfers Paradise (on the Gold Coast) in 31 days. Transport options are detailed for getting to and from each ride – including by bike.

The rides have been designed to make carrying camping gear and food optional, in all but a few instances. Every ride is divided into a set number of days, with a range of accommodation and food options described for each.

Ride Difficulty

Each ride is graded according to its difficulty in terms of distance, terrain, road surface and navigation. The grade appears in the table at the front of this book and in the introduction to the ride.

Grading is unavoidably subjective and is intended as a guide only; the degree of difficulty of a particular ride may vary according to the weather, the weight in your panniers or how hungry and tired you are. Many rides also involve easy and hard days, which are weighed up to create an overall grading.

Easy These rides involve no more than a few hours riding each day, over *mostly* flat terrain with good, sealed road surfaces and are navigationally straightforward. They are suitable for children over 10 years of age.

Moderate These rides present a moderate challenge to someone of average fitness: they are likely to include some hills, three to five hours riding each day and may involve some unsealed roads and/or more navigation.

Hard These are for fit riders who want a challenge: they involve long daily distances and/or challenging climbs, may negotiate rough and remote roads or present navigational challenges.

Times & Distances

Each ride is divided into stages and we've suggested a day be spent on each stage. In some cases the distance for a particular stage is relatively short, but other attractions in the region warrant spending time there – distance junkies may want to condense two stages into one day.

The route directions (cues) are given in kilometres from the start point of that stage.

A suggested riding time is given for each day, which should be used as a guide only. The times are, in most cases, based on an average speed of between 10km/h and 18km/h. They do not include time taken for rest stops, taking photographs or eating.

Mountain Biking in Australia

Mountain bikes began to infiltrate the Australian market in the early to mid-1980s, bridging the gap between BMX bikes and racers, suitable for both getting around and getting up mountains. The craze took off, with several clubs forming early on; one of the first was Melbourne's Fat Tyre Flyers in 1983.

The sport's popularity has grown immensely since the 1980s. Today, as in other parts of the world, it's mountain bikes that are crowding the bike-shop floor: in Australia (population 19 million), about half a million are sold every year. However, the number of 'serious' off-road riders remains relatively small. The proportion of semi-professional and professionals is increasing though, with several Australian riders in the international scene. While women are welcomed into – and enthusiastic about – the sport, it remains decidedly male-dominated.

There are more than 100 mountain-bike clubs around the country: some are race-oriented, others run social rides or tours (find club listings in the back of the *Australian Mountain Bike* magazine, available from newsagents). There are two separate national championships series: the MTBA (Mountain Bike Australia; a national body) nationals; and the Cycling Australia (a cycle-racing umbrella body) nationals. Confusingly, the International Cycling Union (UCI)-sanctioned Cycling Australia event is still referred to as the AMBA (the now-defunct Australian Mountain Bike Association) nationals.

As mountain biking increases in popularity, access is becoming an issue (in national parks it has been tightened already) and conflict with horse-riders and walkers occurs.

Bikes are allowed on most roads and vehicle tracks, including 'management-vehicles only' roads, but not on walking tracks or in wilderness areas. There are few purpose-built tracks in Australia, although enterprising operators have recently instituted downhilling on the summer slopes of winter ski resorts. The longevity of this activity remains to be seen, given concerns about environmental damage. Indeed, the other major access issue for mountain bikers is environmental sensitivity. Proactive clubs are working with authorities to develop a workable compromise. They're also educating riders about ways to minimise damage and avoid upsetting other users.

The Fat Tyre Flyers publish a basic list of off-road codes on the Web site ⌨ www.ftf.com.au:

SALLY DILLON

- Ride in control at all times.
- Respect the rights of others.
- Give walkers right of way and announce your presence.
- Always give horses right of way.
- Avoid skidding, which damages tracks and leads to erosion.
- Don't cut corners; stay on the track.
- Stay away from wet, muddy areas, which are prone to damage.
- Stay on roads and obey signs.

Despite the environmental concerns in heavy-use areas, the country has huge areas of prime mountain-bike country – many crisscrossed by fire trails – which are far less trafficked; the bush around central Victoria (featured in the Central Gold & Spa Country ride) is just one example.

Mountain bikes are also ideal for touring Australia; since so much of the best country is only accessible on dirt roads. Some rides in this book include short unsealed sections which, while quite rideable on touring bikes, are, of course, more comfortable on a mountain bike. There are also some specific mountain-bike rides featured, in areas where you can hire a decent mountain bike. And there are tips on where to get more information about areas to ride.

Cue Sheets & Elevation Charts

Elevation charts are given for days with significant changes in altitude. Information about terrain is also found in the ride description and cues. A ride with no elevation chart is not necessarily *flat*, but it won't have major climbing throughout the day.

See the Foreword for a description of how to use cue sheets.

ACTIVITIES

Need a break from the bike? Here's a list of some other activities around the country:

Bushwalking

Bushwalking is popular in Australia's national parks – but it's still easy enough to find solitude. As well as multi-day expeditions, there are plenty of marked day walks or short excursions. Especially in the more popular areas, there's often free walks information and maps at the park or from the local tourist body or national parks service.

The regional chapters of this book point you towards some bushwalking opportunities, while Lonely Planet's *Walking in Australia* details 72 of the best walks in the country.

Surfing & Swimming

Australia abounds in great beaches and surfing. Prime surfing spots include Margaret River, south-west WA; Bells Beach, Torquay and the Great Ocean Rd, Victoria; dozens of beaches on the NSW coast; and the Gold Coast in Queensland. You can hire boards and take lessons in some areas, but make sure you're aware of surf etiquette: increasing wave traffic and incidents of 'surf rage' have prompted surfing groups to publish surfing codes, often posted at beaches.

Scuba Diving

There's great scuba diving at a number of places around the coast, particularly along Queensland's Great Barrier Reef where there are also many dive schools. Dive courses are also available in other states.

Horse Riding

Opt for a different kind of saddle soreness: whether you're after a 30-minute stroll or an extended trail ride, any number of places around the country offer horse riding opportunities. many through natural areas.

Bird Watching

Birds Australia (formerly the Royal Australasian Ornithologists Union) runs bird observatories in NSW, Victoria, SA and WA. Its headquarters are at 415 Riversdale Rd, Hawthorn East, Victoria 3123 (☎ 03-9882 2622, ☐ www.birdsaustralia.com.au).

Other Activities

Windsurfing, paragliding, rafting, hot-air ballooning, bungee-jumping and hang-gliding are among the many other outdoor activities available. The places offering the most activities are usually also those with the most backpackers; places like Airlie Beach and Cairns in Queensland have a huge range.

ACCOMMODATION

Almost anywhere in Australia there's a caravan park or somewhere you can pitch a tent (except the middle of big cities). While cities and some country areas have plenty of budget hostel accommodation, away from backpacker areas the cheapest (and, occasionally, the only) bed will be the pub. Many country towns also have at least one motel.

Guesthouses and B&Bs are less common outside tourist areas; many also tend to aim towards the luxury 'treat yourself' end of the market, perfect for romantic getaways, but not so great for budget-minded singles.

For small groups, family motel rooms and caravan-park cabins are an economic option: many sleep up to six people.

A couple of free backpacker newspapers and booklets are available at hostels; they list hostels (although without details). State automobile clubs produce (large) directories listing caravan parks, hotels, motels, holiday flats and hostels in practically every Australian town. They're available for a nominal charge to members (or members of affiliated overseas clubs).

Camping & Caravan Parks

In caravan parks, unpowered tent sites generally cost around $10 to $15 for two people, more in the 'resort'-type places. Except during peak times, there's rarely any difficulty getting a site. A few caravan parks don't have tent sites, and in some areas, caravanners are evidently the more important customers.

Most caravan parks are well kept and good value – almost all have hot showers, flush toilets and laundry facilities. Some have barbecue shelters; a few have lock-up facilities for bikes.

Many have on-site vans that you can rent for the night (they generally cost $30 to $35). More widely available are (fully or partially) self-contained, on-site cabins, which generally start at around $45 for two people (bedding is only supplied in the more expensive units).

Camping in the bush, either in national parks and reserves or in the open, is for many people one of the highlights of a visit 'Down Under'. Many national parks have designated camping areas, with pit toilets, water and fireplaces. These often attract a small fee, payable to a patrolling ranger or through an honesty box.

Camping in undesignated areas should be done with sensitivity to the surrounding environment: don't leave rubbish; bury toilet waste – away from watercourses; and avoid using detergents and lighting fires. Ask permission if camping on private property. See the boxed text 'Bicycle Campers' Guide' for tips on safe bush camping.

Hostels

YHA hostels provide basic accommodation, usually in small dormitories or bunk rooms, although more and more are providing twin or double rooms. Australia has more than 130 YHA or associate hostels, with nightly charges of between $10 and $25 (most around $14–16) a night for members – most hostels also take nonmembers, who are charged an extra $3; this guide quotes non-member prices. You need to carry a sheet (or hire one – usually $3).

YHA advises joining in your home country. In Australia, you can join for $49 a year at any state office or youth hostel; non-member visitors can buy a Hostelling International card for $30. An introductory membership scheme is also available, where you pay no initial fee, but instead pay the additional $3 per night at any hostel; after 10 nights, you get full membership.

The annual *YHA Accommodation & Discounts Guide* is available from local and some overseas YHA offices.

Backpacker hostels are also plentiful within Australia, but are scarce outside cities and established backpacker areas such as Cairns and Byron Bay. Some are run-down hotels where the owners have tried to fill empty rooms; occasionally they're former motels, with TVs in every room; the best – at least in terms of facilities – are

---

Bicycle Campers' Guide

If you're bush camping, follow a few simple rules for your own safety, and to care for the environment:

- Tell someone of your itinerary and expected return time; *don't* forget to tell them when you return!
- If you do use a national-park bush hut, clean it, make sure the fire is out and replace firewood when leaving. Close the door securely. Carry out all rubbish.
- Camp at least 30m off tracks and 50m from waterways. To minimise impact, use an existing camp site if possible.
- Take a fuel stove for cooking. Carry out all rubbish.
- Wash at least 50m from streams and lakes and don't use soap. Scatter wash water. Boil water or use water-purification tablets before drinking.
- If there's a toilet where you're staying use it, but always take a trowel for burying faecal waste. Choose a spot at least 100m from water or campsites, dig a 15cm-deep hole and mix faeces and paper with soil when burying.
- Many Australian animals, such as possums, native bush rats, Tasmanian devils and bandicoots, will be happy to relieve you of your food supplies in the middle of the night. Clean up food scraps after eating and pack away your food and rubbish. Either suspend your food pannier on a cord out of reach of nearby branches or store it in a plastic container. For longer trips, pack food supplies in a pannier-sized plastic box, which doubles nicely as a workbench. Leaving your food in a pannier or tent won't keep bush rats from eating it – instead you may find yourself with a large hole to repair.
- Avoid camping under red gums, which are notorious for dropping branches without warning.

purpose-built as backpacker hostels. Prices are typically $15 to $22, although discounts can reduce this.

Some are promoted as 'party' places; avoid them if you want a quiet time. A few only admit overseas backpackers. If you're an Aussie and encounter this kind of reception, the best you can do is persuade the person at the desk that you're genuinely travelling the country, and are not a local there to play up.

You can join several backpacker organisations to receive discounts: VIP Backpacker Resorts (☎ 07-3395 6111), PO Box 600, Cannon Hill, Queensland 4170, has 134 hostel franchisees in Australia and more overseas. Nomads World (☎ 08-8363 7633 or ☎ 1800-819 883), 43 The Parade West, Kent Town, SA 5067, has around 40 franchisees in Australia and more internationally. Check their Web sites (🖳 www.backpackers.com.au and 🖳 www.nomadsworld.com) for hostel locations.

Membership of VIP costs $29, and Nomads $25 per year, giving a $1 discount on accommodation and, like YHA membership, discounts on transport, tours and activities. Join at participating hostels, backpacker travel agencies or through the organisations.

Most YHA and backpacker hostels have cooking and laundry facilities and a communal lounge area. Larger ones have excellent notice boards and travel offices. Only a few have 24-hour reception; especially in the country, the office is often closed for part of the day. Bicycle-storage facilities are variable – and often limited in city hostels; those recommended in this guide have adequate facilities.

Guesthouses & B&Bs

Options here include everything from restored miners' cottages, converted barns, rambling old guesthouses, up-market country homes and romantic escapes, to a simple bedroom in a family home. Tariffs cover a wide range, but are typically in the $50 to $100 (per double) bracket. Some serve breakfast; others simply leave provisions for you to make your own.

Hotels

Capital cities and big tourist destinations such as the Gold Coast have an abundance of up-market hotels, run by groups such as

the Sheraton or Hilton chains. Expect to pay around $220 for a double room. For the budget traveller, affordable hotel accommodation in Australia is usually in a pub.

Pubs

These are usually older places where accommodation is upstairs from the bar. Relatively few old city pubs still have rooms to rent, but many in the country do.

Pubs are invariably found in the centre of country towns. Many were built during boom economic times, so they're often among the largest and most extravagant buildings in town – they're typically double-storey, with huge balconies. However, the

Seasons to Stay

Seasonal prices for accommodation vary widely. Generally high season in beachside towns is from October through to Easter. In ski-resort areas (the NSW and Victorian High Country) high season is from the Queen's Birthday weekend – the second Monday in June – through August.

In addition to the normal high-season rates, prices in major holiday locations can be further inflated during school-holiday peak times (notably Christmas and Easter breaks, and sometimes during the two-week September break) and long weekends. It pays to avoid tourist areas during these times. For example, a beachside caravan park may charge $12 to $20 for a tent site most of the warmer months, but up to $30 between Christmas and mid-January. Week-long bookings are often required over this period.

Despite the prices, popular beachside towns fill up fast during summer holidays, so *always* check accommodation availability and prices before setting out.

If your heart's set on a summer cycling tour, ride before mid-December or in February and March. There will be less traffic on the roads, accommodation will be readily available, prices down and hosts much more relaxed.

Weekend accommodation is also frequently more expensive in popular areas. Places book up quickly, and a two-night stay is often the minimum for advance bookings. Mid-week deals can be great value.

We give high-season prices in this guide.

rooms themselves can be pretty old-fashioned and unexciting. Often their main occupants are itinerant workers. Never book a room above the bar if you're a light sleeper. On the plus side, country hotels are often the town's social focus so staying there is a good way to find out what makes the place tick. You can also usually get substantial meals for very reasonable prices.

Generally, pubs have twin rooms with shared facilities for around $25 to $35 (more with private bathroom). For secure bike storage, you'll often have to carry it up the back stairs, unless they can fit it in the cellar. Few have a separate reception area – ask in the bar if they have rooms available.

Motels, Serviced Apartments & Holiday Flats

Motel rooms are generally a bit newer than those at pubs and include bathrooms. Prices vary and at motels, unlike hotels, singles are rarely much cheaper than doubles. You'll sometimes find motel rooms for less than $40, but in most places they'll cost at least $50. They're a good option for small groups though – typically the rate is for doubles plus $10 or $15 per extra person. Most motels provide at least tea- and coffee-making facilities and a small fridge.

Holiday flats are found in holiday areas, and serviced apartments in big cities. A holiday flat is much like a motel unit but has a kitchen or cooking facilities; it usually has two or more bedrooms. In some, you have to provide your own bedding. Holiday flats are often rented on a weekly basis but it's still worth asking if daily rates are available. Paying for a week, even if you're only staying for a few days, can still be cheaper than paying the higher daily rate.

Serviced apartments are self-contained, with bathroom and kitchenette, and are cleaned daily. Often very central, they can be a great alternative to hotels, especially for families. They are sometimes available by the night, but more often by the week. Rates are around $70 to $100 per night or $350 to $600 per week.

Other Possibilities

Australia is a land of farms and some offer accommodation – some let you sit back and watch how the work's done, while others like to involve you in day-to-day activities.

Wwoof (Willing Workers on Organic Farms) has about 1300 participating farms in Australia, mostly on the east coast. You do a few hours' work each day on a farm in return for bed and board.

Join the organisation ($35/40 for singles/couples) to receive a book of participating places. Wwoof (☎ 03-5155 0218, 🖳 www .wwoof.com.au) is at Mt Murrindal Coop, Buchan, Victoria 3885.

FOOD

Culinary delights can be one of the real highlights of Australia. There was a time – around 25 years ago – when Australia's food (mighty steaks apart) had a reputation for being like England's, only worse. But miracles do happen and Australia's miracle was immigration. The Greeks, Yugoslavs, Italians, Lebanese and many others who flooded into Australia in the '50s and '60s brought their food with them. More recent arrivals include the Vietnamese, whose communities are thriving in several cities.

Local Food

In Australia today you can have excellent Greek moussaka (and a bottle of retsina to wash it down), delicious Italian saltimbocca and pasta, or good, heavy German dumplings; you can perfume the air with garlic after stumbling out of a French bistro, try a takeaway Middle Eastern felafel or indulge in sushi by the sea. The Chinese have been sweet-and-souring since the gold-rush days, while more recently, Indian, Thai and Malaysian restaurants have been all the rage. And for cheap eats, you can't beat some of the Vietnamese places.

Although there is no real Australian cuisine there is certainly some excellent Australian food to try. There's been a great rise in the popularity of local and 'bush' foods. Kangaroo and emu are often featured, as are regional delicacies such as marron (freshwater crayfish) in south-west WA; bush herbs such as roasted wattle seed (coffee flavoured) and native lemon myrtle are increasingly popular. Look out for kangaroo-tail samosas, emu pâté, gum-leaf smoked venison, salt-bush lamb, native aniseed frittata, Warrigal-greens salad or wattle-seed ice cream.

There are also cafes and restaurants in all the major cities serving food that can be termed 'modern Australian'. These dishes borrow heavily from a wide range of foreign cuisines, but have a definite local flavour. At these places seemingly anything goes, so you might find Asian-inspired curry-type dishes sharing a menu with European or Mediterranean-inspired dishes. It all adds up to exciting dining.

Some more traditional Aussie dishes are:

meat pies – vary from gourmet standard to an awful concoction of anonymous meat and gravy in a soggy pastry case (a 'pie 'n' sauce' is part of 'Sat'dy arvo at the footy'; see also the boxed text 'The Pie Floater' in the South Australia chapter).
lamingtons – squares of sponge cake covered in chocolate icing and coconut.
pavlovas – a nest of meringue, filled with cream and topped with fresh fruit; this typically comes out after the snags (sausages) and steaks at a barbie (barbecue).
Vegemite – a dark, salty yeast extract (similar to British Marmite), generally spread on toast or bread; newcomers beware, spread it thinly for your first try.

Vegetarians are well catered for in most major centres; in fact, while you won't always find inspired vegetarian cooking, there's few places in Australia where you won't find *something* vegetarian. There are few dedicated vegetarian restaurants outside capital cities and the more 'alternative' holiday spots, such as Byron Bay, Nimbin and Daylesford, but most modern cafes and restaurants have a few vegetarian dishes on the menu.

Where to Eat The best Australian eateries serve food as exciting and as innovative as you'll find anywhere, and it doesn't need to cost a fortune. Best value are the modern and casual cafes, where you can get an excellent feed for less than $20. A plate of pasta typically costs $12 to $18. Otherwise, most pubs have substantial, if basic, meals for under $10.

All over Australia you'll find BYO (Bring Your Own) restaurants which don't sell alcohol but allow you to bring it yourself – a much cheaper option than buying wine at restaurant prices. Most BYO restaurants have a small 'corkage' charge (typically $1 to $2 per person).

In some states (NSW, ACT, WA and Victoria), it is illegal to smoke in places that

Water & Food

Cycling in Australia can involve long distances with no services or even water en route. Be sure to carry at least two water bottles – perhaps more in remote areas – and enough food. See also the Health & Safety chapter.

serve food; otherwise, places often have a 'no smoking' area.

Most hotels (or pubs) serve two types of meal: bistro meals, which are usually in the $10 to $15 range and are served in the dining room or lounge bar; and bar (or counter) meals, which are eaten in the public bar and usually cost between $5 and $10.

While pub food is often fairly basic, it's generally pretty good value. The usual meal times are from noon to 2pm and 6pm to 8pm. Occasionally, you'll find fashionable hotels with fancier food (and restaurant prices).

Outdoor food stalls and markets can be excellent places to sample a variety of affordable cuisines. Produce markets are also great value for fresh groceries (see also Self-Catering). Food halls (generally found in shopping precincts and serving mostly Asian food and salads) are also quick and cheap.

Self-Catering

Good, fresh food is plentiful, economical and enormously varied in Australia – and most of it is locally produced. Particularly in the last 15 or so years, dozens of small enterprises have begun producing quality food products, from cheeses and breads to olives and pastas.

Large supermarkets stock a wide range of products, including fruit and vegetables; smaller towns often have just the basics, and fresh produce is delivered only once or twice a week. It's also common to find bulk food stores – where you can buy as much or as little pasta, muesli, rice, dried fruit and nuts (and often 'health foods' as well) as you like. Markets are great for cheap, fresh vegies.

In farming areas many producers will set up stalls by the road, where you can buy freshly-picked fruit and vegetables, and often jam and pickles. You usually pay via an honesty box, so carry some loose change.

Look for sweet bananas or macadamia nuts in Queensland, berries in Victoria, cherries in Tasmania and bush honey in WA.

DRINKS
Nonalcoholic Drinks

Australian tap water is, in all but a few instances, clean and safe. It mostly tastes good, too (although Adelaide is a notable exception). Though it's often safe, it's nevertheless recommended that water from streams be sterilised before drinking (see Water in the Health & Safety chapter).

Tea and coffee is widely available in Australia – and both are grown in northern Australia. Thanks to the influx of Italian migrants during the 1950s, Melbourne's coffee is excellent and many cafes pride themselves on serving a good brew. Other capital cities also serve very good coffee, though, interestingly, there's a bit of local variation: a macchiato in Sydney is different from one in Melbourne and different again in Fremantle. Increasingly, proprietors who care about good coffee are setting up in country areas as well. Having said that, there are plenty of places around the country where you can get something, but you might wish you'd brought your stove-top espresso maker.

In addition to the usual carbonated drinks and fruit juices, caffienated 'energy' drinks have infiltrated the drinks fridges (beware of using these in place of water and becoming dehydrated – see Sports Drinks in the Health & Safety chapter).

Sports Drinks Sports drinks such as PowerAde, Gatorade and Lucozade are widely available in corner stores and supermarkets (from the latter, also in powder form).

All's Well that Eats Well

It's eminently possible to eat well on the road without too much trouble or expense. (And why all that cycling if you can't indulge?) A far cry from the hardy overland cyclists of a century ago, whose evening 'tucker' (food) sometimes consisted of 'a tuck in the belt', gourmets today can pedal without fear.

Lunch? Here's mine.

Still dreaming about the morning's melt-in-the-mouth almond croissant from the Dunsborough bakery in south-west Western Australia, I break into a soft, crusty roll, cut a wedge from my mini wheel of Watsonia matured cheddar (made up the road in Capel), slice a sun-ripened tomato and add some fresh basil and rocket (available by the leaf at many grocers in the south-west). Admiring the view from the lawns of a Margaret River winery (having just tasted a delicious cabernet sauvignon), I tuck in, reflecting that life on the road ain't too bad.

Nicola Wells

Dear Mum, The tour is rather hard and filled with deprivation. Please send more money...

DON HATCHER

Alcoholic Drinks

Apart from beer, wine and spirits, so-called 'designer drinks' such as alcoholic lemonades and sodas or premixed drinks such as rum and coke or vodka and lemon soda are becoming very popular. Many places also sell Strongbow cider, which comes in sweet, dry and other variations.

Takeaway alcohol is sold at bottle shops ('bottlos'), some attached to a pub as a 'drive in' or even within smaller pubs. In many states, liquor is sold in outlets attached to supermarkets.

Beer The consistency of Australian beer will be fairly familiar to North Americans, though it generally has a higher alcohol content; it's also similar to what's known as lager in the UK. It may taste like lemonade to the European real-ale addict, but it packs quite a punch. It is invariably chilled before drinking.

Foster's is the best-known international brand, but there's a bewildering array of Australian beers. Among the most well known are XXXX (pronounced 'four-ex'), Tooheys, Foster's, Carlton and VB (Victoria Bitter).

However, the tastiest beers are usually produced by the smaller breweries. Cascade (Tasmania) and Coopers (SA) beers are sold widely; 'boutique' beers such as Mountain Goat (Melbourne) and Redback (Fremantle, WA) are definitely worth a try, though they're harder to find and more expensive than the big commercial beers. For the homesick European, there are a few pubs in the major cities that brew their own beer. Guinness is occasionally found on tap.

Standard beer normally contains around 5% alcohol, although the trend in recent years has been towards low-alcohol beers (between 2% and 3.5%). While Australians are generally considered to be heavy beer drinkers, per capita beer consumption has fallen by 20% in the past decade.

And a warning: driving – and cycling – under the influence of alcohol (0.05% is the legal limit) risks a fine and the loss of your drivers licence. 'Booze buses' (random breath-testing units) are used throughout Australia, especially in holiday periods.

Wine Wine is one of Australia's success stories – with a great climate for wine growing, the industry is rapidly gaining international recognition, and wine is being drunk in increasing quantities by Australians.

The best-known wine-growing regions are the Hunter Valley of NSW and the Barossa Valley of SA, but there are plenty of other fine areas. In Victoria the main region is the Rutherglen/Milawa area of the north-east, and there's also the Yarra Valley, the Mornington Peninsula, Geelong and central Victoria. SA also has the Coonawarra, McLaren Vale and the picturesque Clare Valley districts. In WA, increasingly sophisticated wines are being produced in the Margaret River area.

Each wine-growing area is generally renowned for a particular style of wine, although there's much more experimentation and blending of grapes these days. The Hunter Valley is famous for its whites (especially Chardonnay), the Barossa is even more famous for its shiraz, the Coonawarra produces excellent heavy reds, Margaret River is known for cabernets and the Rutherglen region is great for port and Muscat.

It takes a little while to become familiar with Australian wineries and their styles but it's an effort worth making. The most enjoyable way to do this is to visit the wineries and sample their products at the cellar door.

Health & Safety

Keeping healthy on your travels depends on your predeparture preparations, your daily health care and diet while on the road, and how you handle any medical problem that develops. Few touring cyclists experience anything more than a bit of soreness, fatigue and chafing, although there is potential for more serious problems. The sections that follow aren't intended to alarm, but they are worth skimming before you go.

Before You Go

HEALTH INSURANCE
Make sure that you have adequate health insurance. See Travel Insurance in the Visas & Documents section in the Facts for the Cyclist chapter.

MEDICAL COVER
Under reciprocal arrangements, residents of the UK, New Zealand, the Netherlands, Sweden and Italy are entitled to free or subsidised medical and hospital treatment under Medicare, Australia's compulsory national health-insurance scheme. To enrol, show your passport and health-care card or certificate from your own country; you are then given a Medicare card. Residents of Ireland can present their passport at a public hospital and be given free medical treatment.

Visits to private doctors are also claimable under Medicare. Clinics that advertise 'bulk billing' are the easiest to use as they charge Medicare direct. For more information, phone Medicare on ☎ 13 2011 or visit their Web site ☐ www.hic.gov.au.

IMMUNISATIONS
You don't need any vaccinations to visit Australia. However, it's always wise to keep up-to-date with routine vaccinations such as diphtheria, polio and tetanus – boosters are necessary every 10 years and are highly recommended.

FIRST AID
It's a good idea at any time to know the appropriate responses in the event of a major accident or illness, and it's especially important

First-Aid Kit

A possible kit could include:

First-Aid Supplies
- ☐ **sticking plasters (Band Aids)**
- ☐ **bandages (including elastic) & safety pins**
- ☐ **elastic support bandage** for knees, ankles etc
- ☐ **gauze swabs**
- ☐ **nonadhesive dressings**
- ☐ **small pair of scissors**
- ☐ **sterile alcohol wipes**
- ☐ **butterfly closure strips**
- ☐ **latex gloves**
- ☐ **syringes & needles** – for removing gravel from road-rash wounds
- ☐ **thermometer** (note that mercury thermometers are prohibited by airlines)
- ☐ **tweezers**

Medications
- ☐ **antidiarrhoea, antinausea drugs** and **oral rehydration salts**
- ☐ **antifungal cream** or **powder** – for fungal skin infections and thrush
- ☐ **antihistamines** – for allergies, eg, hay fever; to ease the itch from insect bites or stings; and to prevent motion sickness
- ☐ **antiseptic powder** or **solution** (eg, povidone-iodine) and **antiseptic wipes** for cuts and grazes
- ☐ **nappy rash cream**
- ☐ **calamine lotion, sting-relief spray** or **aloe vera** – to ease irritation from sunburn and insect bites or stings
- ☐ **cold** and **flu tablets, throat lozenges** and **nasal decongestant**
- ☐ **painkillers** (eg, aspirin or paracetamol/ acetaminophen in the USA) – for pain and fever
- ☐ **laxatives**

Miscellaneous
- ☐ **insect repellent, sunscreen, lip balm** and **eye drops**
- ☐ **water purification tablets** or **iodine**

Getting Fit for Touring

Ideally, a training program should be tailored to your objectives, specific needs, fitness level and health. However, if you have no idea how to prepare for your cycling holiday these guidelines will help you get the fitness you need to enjoy it more. Things to think about include:

Foundation You will need general kilometres in your legs before you start to expose them to any intensive cycling. Always start out with easy rides – even a few kilometres to the shops – and give yourself plenty of time to build towards your objective.

Tailoring Once you have the general condition to start preparing for your trip, work out how to tailor your training rides to the type of tour you are planning. Someone preparing for a three-week ride will require a different approach to someone building fitness for a one-day or weekend ride. Some aspects to think about are the ride length (distance and days), terrain, climate and weight to be carried in panniers. If your trip involves carrying 20kg in panniers, incorporate this weight into some training rides, especially some of the longer ones. If you are going to be touring in mountainous areas, choose a hilly training route.

Recovery You usually adapt to a training program during recovery time, so it's important to do the right things between rides. Recovery can take many forms, but the simple ones are best. These include getting quality sleep, eating an adequate diet to refuel the system, doing recovery rides between hard days (using low gears to avoid pushing yourself), stretching and enjoying a relaxing bath. Other forms include recovery massage, spas and yoga.

If you have no cycling background this program will help you get fit for your cycling holiday. If you are doing an easy ride (each ride in this book is rated; see Cycling Routes in the Facts for the Cyclist chapter), aim to at least complete Week 4; for moderate rides, complete Week 6; and complete the program if you are doing a hard ride. Experienced cycle tourists may start at Week 3, while those who regularly ride up to four days a week could start at Week 5.

Don't treat this as a punishing training schedule: try cycling to work or to the shops, join a local touring club or get a group of friends together to turn weekend rides into social events.

	Monday	Tuesday	Wednesday	Thursday	Friday	Saturday	Sunday
Week 1	10km*	–	10km*	–	10km*	–	10km*
Week 2	–	15km*	–	15km*	–	20km*	–
Week 3	20km*	–	20km†	25km*	–	25km*	20km†
Week 4	–	30km*	–	35km*	30km†	30km*	–
Week 5	30km*	–	40km†	–	35km*	–	40km†
Week 6	30km*	–	40km†	–	–	60km*	40km†
Week 7	30km*	–	40km†	–	30km†	70km*	30km*
Week 8	–	60km*	30km†	–	40km†	–	90km*

* steady pace (allows you to carry out a conversation without losing your breath) on flat or undulating terrain
† solid pace (allows you to talk in short sentences only) on undulating roads with some longer hills

The training program shown here is only a guide. Ultimately it is important to listen to your body and slow down if the ride is getting too hard. Take extra recovery days and cut back distances when you feel this way. Don't panic if you don't complete every ride, every week; the most important thing is to ride regularly and gradually increase the length of your rides as you get fitter.

For those with no exercise background, be sure to see your doctor and get a clearance to begin exercising at these rates. This is especially important for those over 35 years of age with no exercise history and those with a cardiac or respiratory condition of any nature.

Kevin Tabotta

if you are intending to ride off-road in a remote area. Consider learning basic first aid through a recognised course before you go, and carrying a first-aid manual and small medical kit.

Although detailed first-aid instruction is outside the scope of this guide, some basic points are listed in the section on Traumatic Injuries later in this chapter. Undoubtedly the best advice is to avoid an accident in the first place. The Safety on the Ride section at the end of this chapter contains tips for safe on-road and off-road riding, as well as information on how to summon help should a major accident or illness occur.

PHYSICAL FITNESS

Most of the rides in this book are designed for someone with a moderate degree of cycling fitness. As a general rule, however, the fitter you are, the more you'll enjoy riding. It pays to spend time preparing yourself physically before you set out, rather than let a sore backside and aching muscles draw your attention from some of the world's finest cycle-touring countryside.

Depending on your existing level of fitness, you should start training a couple of months before your trip. Try to ride at least three times a week, starting with easy rides (even 5km to work, if you're not already cycling regularly) and gradually building up to longer distances. Once you have a good base of regular riding behind you, include hills in your training and familiarise yourself with the gearing on your bike. Before you go you should have done at least one 60km to 70km ride with loaded panniers.

As you train, you'll discover how to adjust your bike to increase your comfort – as well as any mechanical problems.

Staying Healthy

The best way to have a lousy holiday (especially if you're relying on self-propulsion) is to become ill. Heed the following advice and the only thing you're likely to suffer from is that rewarding tiredness at the end of a full day.

Reduce the chances of falling ill by washing your hands frequently, particularly after working on your bike or going to the toilet and before handling or eating food.

HYDRATION

You may not notice how much water you're losing as you ride, because it evaporates in the breeze. However, don't underestimate the amount of fluid you need to replace – particularly in warmer weather. The magic figure is supposedly 1L per hour, though many cyclists have trouble consuming this much – remembering to drink enough can be harder than it sounds. Sipping little and often is the key; try to drink a mouthful every 10 minutes or so and don't wait until you get thirsty. Water 'backpacks' can be great for fluid regulation since virtually no physical or mental effort is required to drink. Keep drinking before and after the day's ride to replenish fluid.

Use the colour of your urine as a rough guide to whether you are drinking enough. Small amounts of dark urine suggest you need to increase your fluid intake. Passing reasonable quantities of light yellow urine indicates that you've got the balance about right. Other signs of dehydration include headache and fatigue. For more information on the effects of dehydration, see Dehydration & Heat Exhaustion later in this chapter.

Water

With few exceptions, tap water in Australia is safe to drink. Bore water (from underground sources) in some remote towns may be unfit for human consumption. Here, use the stored rainwater the locals drink.

Always beware of natural sources of water. A gurgling creek in the bush may look clear but the risk of infection from human or animal sources is real. For information on giardiasis, see Infectious Diseases later in this chapter.

The simplest way of purifying water is to boil it thoroughly. Vigorous boiling for five minutes should do the job. Simple filtering will not remove all dangerous organisms, so if you can't boil water treat it chemically. Chlorine tablets will kill many pathogens, but not *Giardia lamblia*. Iodine is very effective in purifying water and is available in tablet and liquid form, but follow the directions carefully and remember that too much iodine can be harmful. Flavoured powder will disguise the taste of treated water and is a good thing to carry if you are spending time away from town water supplies.

Sports Drinks

Commercial sports drinks such as Gatorade and PowerAde are an excellent way to satisfy your hydration needs, electrolyte replacement and energy demands in one. On endurance rides, especially, it can be difficult to keep eating solid fuels day in, day out, but sports drinks can supplement these energy demands and allow you to vary your solid fuel intake a little for variety. The bonus is that those all-important body salts lost through perspiration get restocked.

Make sure you drink plenty of water as well; if you have two water bottles on your bike (and you should), it's a good idea to fill one with sports drink and the other with plain water.

If using a powdered sports drink, don't mix it too strong (follow the instructions) because, in addition to being too sweet, too many carbohydrates can actually impair your body's ability to absorb the water and carbohydrates properly.

NUTRITION

One of the great things about bike touring is that it requires lots of energy, which means you can eat more. Depending on your activity levels, it's not hard to put away huge servings of food and be hungry a few hours after.

Because you're putting such demands on your body, it's important to eat well – not just lots. As usual, you should eat a balanced diet from a wide variety of foods.

Avoiding the Bonk

The bonk, in a cycling context, is not a pleasant experience; it's that light-headed, can't-put-power-to-the-pedals weak feeling that engulfs you (usually quite quickly) when your body runs out of fuel.

If you experience it the best move is to stop and refuel immediately. It can be quite serious and risky to your health if it's not addressed as soon as symptoms occur. It won't take long before you are ready to get going again (although most likely at a slower pace), but you'll also be more tired the next day so try to avoid it.

The best way to do this is to maintain your fuel intake while riding. Cycling for hours burns considerable body energy, and replacing it is something that needs to be tailored to each individual's tastes. The touring cyclist needs to target foods that have a high carbohydrate content. Foods that contain some fat are not a problem occasionally, as cycling at low intensity (when you're able to ride and talk without losing your breath) will usually trigger the body to draw on fat stores before stored carbohydrates.

Good cycle-touring foods include:

- bananas (in particular) and other fruits
- bread with jam or honey
- breakfast and muesli bars
- rice-based snacks
- muffins
- prepackaged high-carbohydrate sports bars (eg, PowerBar)
- sports drinks

During lunch stops (or for breakfast) you can try such things as spaghetti, cereal, creamed rice, pancakes, baked beans, sandwiches and rolls.

It's important not to get uptight about the food you eat. As a rule of thumb, base all your meals around carbohydrates (eg, pasta, rice, bread and potatoes) of some sort, but don't be afraid to also indulge in local culinary delights.

This is easy in Australia, with so much fresh food widely available (see Food in the Facts for the Cyclist chapter).

The main part of your diet should be carbohydrates rather than proteins or fats. While some protein (for tissue maintenance and repair) and fat (for vitamins, long-term energy and warmth) is essential, carbohydrates provide the most efficient fuel. They are easily digested into simple sugars, which are then used in energy production. Less-refined foods like pasta, rice, bread, fruits and vegetables are all high in carbohydrates.

Eating simple carbohydrates (sugars, such as lollies or sweets) gives you almost immediate energy – great for when you need a top-up (see the boxed text 'Avoiding the Bonk'); however, because they are quickly metabolised, you may get a sugar 'high' then a 'low'. For cycling it is far better to base your diet around complex carbohydrates, which take longer to process and provide 'slow-release' energy over a longer period.

The book *High-Performance Bicycling Nutrition*, by Richard Rafoth, is a useful reference for nutrition and health advice for all cyclists.

Day-to-Day Needs

Eat a substantial breakfast – wholegrain cereal or bread is ideal – and fruit or juice for vitamins. If you like cooked breakfasts, try to include carbohydrates (such as porridge, toast or potatoes) and avoid foods high in fat (such as greasy bacon and eggs), which take longer to digest.

Bread is the easiest food for lunch, topped with ingredients like cheese, peanut butter, salami and fresh salad vegetables. If you're in a town, salad rolls or focaccias make for a satisfying meal (chips or pizza, with their high fat content, will feel like a lump in your stomach if you continue straight away).

Keep topping up your energy during the ride. See the boxed text 'Avoiding the Bonk' for tips. Try to eat a high-carbohydrate meal in the evening. If you're eating out, Italian or Asian restaurants tend to offer more carbohydrate-based meals.

Rice, pasta and potatoes are good staples if you're self-catering. Team them with fresh vegetables and ingredients such as instant soup, canned beans, fish or bacon. Remember that even though you're limited in terms of what you can carry on a bike, it's possible – with some imagination and preparation – to eat delicious as well as nutritious camp meals.

AVOIDING CYCLING AILMENTS
Saddle Sores & Blisters

While you're more likely to get a sore bum if you're out of condition, riding long distances does take its toll on your behind. To minimise the impact, always wear clean, preferably padded, bike shorts (also known as 'knicks'). Brief, unfitted shorts can chafe, as can underwear (see Clothing under What to Bring in the Facts for the Cyclist chapter). Shower as soon as you stop and put on clean, preferably nonsynthetic clothes. Moisturising or baby nappy-rash creams also guard against chafing – apply liberally around the crotch area before riding. For information on correctly adjusting your bike seat, see the Your Bicycle chapter.

If you do suffer from chafing, wash and dry the area and carefully apply a barrier (moisturising) cream.

You probably won't get blisters unless you do a very long ride with no physical preparation. Wearing gloves and correctly fitted shoes will reduce the likelihood of blisters on your hands and feet. If you know you're susceptible to blisters in a particular spot, cover the area with medical adhesive tape before riding.

Knee Pain

Knee pain is common among cyclists who pedal in too high a gear. While it may *seem* that you'll go faster by turning the pedals slowly in a high gear, it's actually more efficient (and better for your knees) to 'spin' the pedals – that is, use a low enough gear so you can pedal quickly with little resistance. For touring, the ideal cadence (the number of pedal strokes per minute) ranges from 70 to 90. Try to maintain this cadence even when you're climbing.

It's a good idea to stretch before and after riding, and to go easy at the start of each day. This reduces the chance of injury and helps your muscles work more efficiently.

You can also get sore knees if your saddle is too low, or if your shoe cleats (for use with clipless pedals) are incorrectly positioned. Both are discussed in greater detail in the Your Bicycle chapter.

Stretching

Stretching is important when stepping up your exercise levels: it improves muscle flexibility, which allows freer movement in the joints; and prevents the rigidity developing in muscles that occurs through prolonged cycling activity.

Ideally, you should stretch for 10 minutes before and after riding and for longer periods (15 to 30 minutes) every second day. Stretching prepares muscles for the task ahead, and limits the stress on muscles and joints during exercise. It can reduce post-exercise stiffness (decreasing the recovery time between rides) and reduce the chance of injury during cycling.

You should follow a few basic guidelines:

- before stretching, warm up for five to 10 minutes by going for a gentle bike ride, jog or brisk walk
- ensure you follow correct technique for each stretch
- hold a stretch for 15 to 30 seconds
- stretch to the point of discomfort, not pain
- breathe freely (ie, don't hold your breath) and try to relax your body whenever you are stretching
- don't 'bounce' the stretch; gradually ease into a full stretch
- repeat each stretch three times (on both sides, when required)

Do not stretch when you have an injury to a muscle, ligament or tendon (allow it to heal fully), as it can lead to further injury and/or hinder recovery. Warming up the muscles increases blood flow to the area, making it easier to stretch and reducing the likelihood of injury.

The main muscle groups for the cyclist to stretch are: quadriceps, calves, hamstrings, lower back and neck. Use the following stretches as a starting point, adding extra stretches that are already part of your routine or if you feel 'tight' in other areas (eg, add shoulder rolls if your shoulders feel sore after a day's cycling).

Quadriceps

Facing a wall with your feet slightly apart, grip one foot with your hand and pull it towards the buttocks. Ensure the back and hips are square. To get a better stretch, push the hip forward. You should never feel pain at the knee joint. Hold the stretch, before lowering the leg and repeating the stretch with the other leg.

Calf

Stand facing a wall, placing one foot about 30cm in front of the other. Keep the heels flat on the ground and bend the front leg slowly toward the wall – the stretch should be in the upper-calf area of the back leg. Keep the back straight and bend your elbows to allow your body to move forward during the stretch. Hold the stretch; relax and repeat with the other leg.

Hamstrings

Sit with one leg extended and the other leg bent with the bottom of the foot against the inside of the extended leg. Slide your arms down the extended leg – bending from the waist – until you feel a pull in the hamstring area. Hold it for 15 seconds, before returning to the start position. Keep the toes pointed up; avoid hunching the back.

Lower-Back Roll

Lie on your back (on a towel or sleeping mat) and bring both knees up towards the shoulders until you feel a stretch in the lower back. Hold the stretch for 30 seconds; relax.

'Cat Stretch' Hunch

Another stretch for the lower back. Move to the ground on all fours (hands shoulder-width apart; legs slightly apart), lift the hips and lower back towards the sky until you feel a stretch. Hold it for 15 seconds; return to start position.

'Cat Stretch' Arch

One more stretch for the lower back. With hands and knees in the same position as for the Cat Stretch above, roll the hips and lower back toward the ground until you feel a stretch. Hold it for 15 seconds; return to start position.

Neck

Gently and smoothly stretch your neck each of the four ways: forward, back and side to side. Do each stretch separately. (Do not rotate the head in a full circle.) For the side stretches, use your hand to pull the head very gently in the direction of the stretch.

Numbness & Backache

Pain in the hands, neck and shoulders is a common complaint, particularly on longer riding days. It's generally caused by leaning too much on your hands. Apart from discomfort, you can temporarily damage the nerves and experience numbness or mild paralysis of the hands. Prevent it by wearing padded gloves, cycling with less weight on your hands and changing your hand position frequently (if you have flat handlebars, fit bar ends to provide more hand positions).

When seated your weight should be fairly evenly distributed through your hands and seat. If you're carrying too much weight on your hands there are two ways of adjusting your bike to rectify this: either by raising your handlebars or, if you are stretched out too much, fitting a smaller stem (talk to your local bike shop). For more guidance on adjusting your bicycle for greater comfort, see the Your Bicycle chapter.

Fungal Infections

Warm, sweaty bodies are ideal environments for fungal growth; physical activity, combined with inadequate washing of your body and/or clothes, can lead to fungal infections. The most common are athlete's foot (tinea) between the toes or fingers, and infections on the scalp, in the groin or on the body (ringworm). You can get ringworm (which is a fungal infection, not a worm) from infected animals or other people.

To prevent fungal infections, wash frequently and dry yourself carefully. Change out of sweaty bike clothes as soon as possible.

If you do get an infection, wash the infected area at least daily with a disinfectant or medicated soap and water, and rinse and dry well. Apply an antifungal cream or powder like tolnaftate. Expose the infected area to air or sunlight as much as possible; avoid artificial fibres; and wash all towels and underwear in hot water, change them often and let them dry in the sun.

Staying Warm

Except on extremely hot days, put on another layer of clothing when you stop cycling – even if it's just for a quick break. Staying warm when cycling is as important as keeping up your water and food intake. Particularly in wet or sweaty clothing, your body cools down quickly after you stop working.

Muscle strains occur more easily when your body is chilled and hypothermia can result from prolonged exposure (for prevention and treatment, see Hypothermia later in this chapter). Staying rugged up will help prevent picking up chest infections, colds and the flu.

It's not advisable to cycle at high altitude during winter; however, you *can* get caught suddenly in bad weather at any time of year, especially in the mountains. No matter when you go, always be prepared with warm clothing and a waterproof layer. Protect yourself from the wind on long downhill stretches – even stuffing a few sheets of newspaper under your shirt cuts the chill considerably.

Medical Problems & Treatment

ENVIRONMENTAL HAZARDS
Sun

You can get sunburnt quite quickly, even on cool or cloudy days, and especially when riding on shadeless roads.

Take sun protection seriously – unless you want to be fried and increase your chances of heatstroke and skin cancer:

- Cover up wherever possible: wear a long-sleeved top with a collar, and a peaked helmet cover – you may want to go the extra step and add a 'legionnaire's flap' to your helmet to protect the back of your neck and ears. Make sure your shirt is sunproof: very thin or loosely woven fabrics still let sun through. Some fabrics are designed to offer high sun protection.
- Use high-protection sunscreen (30+). Choose a water-resistant 'sports' sunscreen and reapply every few hours as you sweat it off. Don't forget to protect your neck, ears, hands, and feet if wearing sandals. Zinc cream is good for sensitive noses, lips and ears.
- Wear good sunglasses; they will also protect you from wind, dust and insects and are essential protection against sticks and flying objects if you're mountain biking.
- Sit in the shade during rest breaks.
- Wear a wide-brimmed hat when off the bike.

Mild sunburn can be treated with calamine lotion, aloe vera or sting-relief spray.

Heat

Treat heat with respect. Australia can get extremely hot, so don't set a demanding touring schedule as soon as you arrive; take things easy until you acclimatise.

Dehydration & Heat Exhaustion Dehydration is a potentially dangerous and easily preventable condition caused by excessive fluid loss. Sweating and inadequate fluid intake are common causes of dehydration in cyclists, but others include diarrhoea, vomiting and high fever – see Diarrhoea later in this chapter for details on appropriate treatment in these circumstances.

The first symptoms are weakness, thirst and passing small amounts of very concentrated urine. This may progress to drowsiness, dizziness or fainting when standing up and, finally, coma.

It's easy to forget how much fluid you are losing via perspiration while you are cycling, particularly if a strong breeze is drying your skin quickly. Make sure you drink sufficient liquids (see Hydration earlier in this chapter). Refrain from drinking too many caffeinated drinks such as coffee, tea and some soft drinks (which act as a diuretic, causing your body to lose water through urination) throughout the day; don't use them as a water replacement.

Dehydration and salt deficiency can cause heat exhaustion. Salt deficiency is characterised by fatigue, lethargy, headaches, giddiness and muscle cramps; salt tablets may help, but adding extra salt to your food is probably sufficient.

If one of your party suffers from heat exhaustion, lie the casualty down in a shady spot and encourage them to drink slowly but frequently. If possible, seek medical advice.

Heatstroke This serious and occasionally fatal condition can occur if the body's heat-regulating mechanism breaks down and the body temperature rises to dangerous levels. Continuous periods of exposure to high temperatures and insufficient fluids can leave you vulnerable to heatstroke.

The symptoms are feeling unwell, not sweating very much (or at all) and a high body temperature (39° to 41°C or 102° to 106°F). Where sweating has ceased, the skin becomes flushed and red. Severe, throbbing headaches and lack of coordination will also occur, and the sufferer may be confused or aggressive. Eventually the victim will become delirious or convulse.

Hospitalisation is essential; in the interim get the casualty out of the sun, remove their clothing, cover them with a wet sheet or towel and then fan continuously. Give them plenty of fluids (cool water), if conscious.

Cold

Hypothermia This occurs when the body loses heat faster than it can produce it and the body's core temperature falls. It is surprisingly easy to progress from very cold to dangerously cold because of a combination of wind, wet clothing, fatigue and hunger, even if the air temperature is above freezing.

Symptoms of hypothermia are exhaustion, numb skin (particularly toes and fingers), shivering, slurred speech, irrational or violent behaviour, lethargy, stumbling, dizzy spells, muscle cramps and powerful bursts of energy. Irrationality may take the form of sufferers claiming they are warm and trying to take off their clothes.

To prevent hypothermia, dress in layers (see Clothing under What to Bring in the Facts for the Cyclist chapter). A strong, waterproof outer layer is essential. Protect yourself against wind, particularly for long descents. Eat plenty of high-energy food when it's cold; it's important to keep drinking too – even though you may not feel like it.

To treat mild hypothermia, first get the person out of the wind and/or rain, remove wet clothing and replace it with dry, warm clothing. Give them hot liquids – not alcohol – and some high-kilojoule, easily digestible food. Do not rub victims: instead, allow them to slowly warm themselves. This should be enough to treat the early stages of hypothermia; however, medical treatment should still be sought, urgently if the hypothermia is severe. Early recognition and treatment of mild hypothermia is the only way to prevent severe hypothermia, which is a critical condition.

Asthma & Hay Fever

Australia has one of the world's highest incidences of asthma, the main culprits being air-borne allergens such as dust and pollen, which are also hazards for hay-fever sufferers. The main danger periods are May to late November in the south and April, May and October in the north.

Inhalers (puffers) are available without prescription at pharmacies.

INFECTIOUS DISEASES
Diarrhoea

Simple things like a change of water, food or climate can cause a mild bout of diarrhoea, but a few rushed toilet trips with no other symptoms are not indicative of a major problem. More serious diarrhoea is caused by infectious agents transmitted by faecal contamination of food or water, by using contaminated utensils, or directly from one person's hand to another. Paying particular attention to personal hygiene, drinking purified water and taking care of what you eat are important measures to take to avoid getting diarrhoea while touring.

Dehydration is the main danger with any diarrhoea, particularly in children or the elderly, as it can occur quickly. Under all circumstances, the most important thing is to replace fluids (at least equal to the volume being lost). Urine is the best guide to this – if you have small amounts of dark-coloured urine, you need to drink more. Weak black tea with a little sugar, soda water, or soft drinks allowed to go flat and diluted 50% with clean water are all good. With severe diarrhoea it's better to use a rehydrating solution to replace lost minerals and salts. Commercially available oral rehydration salts should be added to boiled or bottled water. In an emergency, make a solution of six teaspoons of sugar and a half teaspoon of salt in a litre of boiled or bottled water. Keep drinking small amounts often. Stick to a bland diet as you recover.

Gut-paralysing drugs such as diphenoxylate or loperamide can bring relief from the symptoms, although they don't cure the problem. Only use these drugs if you do not have access to toilets, that is, if you *must* travel. These drugs are not recommended for children under 12 years of age, or if you have a high fever or are severely dehydrated.

Seek medical advice if you pass blood or mucus, are feverish or suffer persistent or severe diarrhoea. Another cause of persistent diarrhoea in travellers is giardiasis.

Giardiasis

An intestinal disorder contracted by drinking water contaminated with the *Giardia lamblia* parasite, giardiasis' symptoms are stomach cramps, nausea, a bloated stomach, watery and foul-smelling diarrhoea, and frequent gas. It can appear several weeks after exposure. The symptoms may disappear for a few days and then return; this can go on for several weeks. Seek medical advice if you think you have giardiasis but, where this is not possible, tinidazole or metronidazole are the recommended drugs. Treatment is a 2g single dose of tinidazole or 250mg of metronidazole three times daily for five to 10 days.

Tetanus

This disease is caused by a germ that lives in soil and in the faeces of horses and other animals. It enters the body via breaks in the skin. The first symptom may be discomfort in swallowing or stiffening of the jaw and neck; this is followed by painful convulsions of the jaw and whole body. The disease can be fatal but can be prevented by vaccination.

INSECT-BORNE DISEASES
Ross River Fever

This viral disease, properly known as epidemic polyarthritis, is transmitted by some species of mosquito. The disease is more common in northern Australia; outbreaks are most likely in January and February. Cases have also been recorded in southwest Western Australia (WA) and in coastal New South Wales (NSW). Flu-like symptoms (muscle and joint pain, rashes, fever, headache and tiredness) are possible indicators, but blood tests are necessary for a positive diagnosis. Risk of infection for travellers is usually very low.

Unfortunately, there is no treatment for Ross River fever, although the symptoms can be relieved. The symptoms do not usually last for more than a few months, but some people still feel the effects, mainly chronic fatigue, for some years. Avoiding mosquito bites is the best preventive.

BITES & STINGS
Bees & Wasps

These are usually painful rather than dangerous. However, anyone allergic to these can suffer severe breathing difficulties and will need medical care. Calamine lotion or a commercial sting-relief spray will ease discomfort, and ice packs will reduce the pain and swelling. Antihistamines can also help.

Jellyfish

Avoid contact with these sea creatures, which have stinging tentacles – ask locals before swimming. Stings from most jellyfish are simply painful, but the box jellyfish, or 'stinger', found in northern Australia is potentially fatal – stay out of the water from October through April unless you're wearing protective clothing such as a 'stinger suit' (some people improvise by wearing pantihose over arms and legs).

Douse the stings with vinegar (carry some with you if you're heading to stinger territory for a swim) and don't try to remove the tentacles from the victim's skin. Be prepared to resuscitate, as the victim may stop breathing.

For minor stings calamine lotion, antihistamines and analgesics may relieve the pain.

Leeches

These are almost inseparable from rainforest; they attach themselves to your skin and suck your blood. Salt or a lit match will dislodge them. Do not pull them off, as the bite is more likely to become infected. Clean it and apply pressure if the bite is bleeding.

Snakes

Australia is home to many venomous snakes but few are aggressive – unless you interfere with or stand on one. Wear shoes, socks and long trousers when walking through undergrowth where snakes may be present; don't put your hands into holes and crevices; and take care collecting firewood as snakes like to hide among dry branches. If you see a snake, leave it alone. *Don't* try to catch it or kill it.

Snake bites, rarely fatal, do not cause instant death and antivenins are usually available. Immediately wrap the bitten limb tightly: begin at the bite area and move up to cover as much of the limb as possible, then down again if the bandage permits. Attach a splint to immobilise the limb. Keep the victim still and calm and seek medical assistance. It may help if you can describe the offending reptile, but ensuring the venom remains on the victim's skin or clothing (eg, by covering the bite site with a sticking plaster before bandaging) is more reliable. The old methods of tourniquets and sucking out the poison have now been comprehensively discredited.

Spiders & Scorpions

Most Australian spiders bite but very few are dangerous, although the funnel-web (widespread in NSW) is extremely poisonous, and a redback bite is potentially serious. If bitten by a funnel-web, treat as for a snake bite and seek urgent medical attention (capture a specimen for identification if possible). If bitten by a redback, apply ice to the area (it is not necessary to bandage as for snake bite) and seek medical attention immediately. For other spider bites (eg, white-tail or huntsman), ice the area and seek medical attention if symptoms persist or worsen.

Scorpion stings are notoriously painful but not very venomous compared with overseas species. Scorpions like sheltering in boots or clothing.

Ticks

Ticks can cause skin infections and more serious diseases, so always check all over your body if you have been walking or camping in a potentially tick-infested area. They are most active from spring to autumn, and usually lurk in overhanging vegetation.

To remove a tick, press down around its head with tweezers, grab the head and gently pull upwards. Avoid pulling the rear of the body as this may squeeze the tick's gut contents through the attached mouth parts into your skin, increasing the risk of infection. Smearing chemicals on, or burning, the tick is no longer recommended. After removing the tick, clean the wound and apply an antiseptic solution like povidone-iodine.

WOMEN'S HEALTH

Cycle touring is not hazardous to your health, but women's health issues are relevant wherever you go, and can be a bit more tricky to cope with when you are on the road.

If you experience low energy and/or abdominal or back pain during menstruation, it may be best to undertake less strenuous rides or schedule a rest day or two at this time.

Gynaecological Problems

If you have a vaginal discharge that is not normal for you with or without any other symptoms, you've probably got an infection.

• If you've had thrush (vaginal candidiasis) before and think you have it again, it's worth self-treating for this (see the following section).
• If not, get medical advice, as you will need a laboratory test and an appropriate course of treatment.
• It's best not to self-medicate with antibiotics because there are many causes of vaginal discharge, which can only be differentiated with a laboratory test.

Thrush (Vaginal Candidiasis) Symptoms of this common yeast infection are itching and discomfort in the genital area, often with thick white vaginal discharge (said to resemble cottage cheese). Many factors, including diet, pregnancy, medications and hot climatic conditions can trigger thrush.

You can help prevent it by wearing cotton underwear off the bike and loose-fitting bicycle shorts; maintaining good personal hygiene is particularly important when wearing cycling knicks. It's a good idea to wash regularly, but don't use soap, which can increase the chance of thrush occurring.

Bleeding Wounds

Most cuts will stop bleeding on their own, but if a blood vessel of any size has been cut it may bleed for some time. Wounds to the head, hands and at joint creases tend to be particularly bloody.

To stop bleeding from a wound:

• Wear gloves if you are dealing with a wound on another person.
• Lie the casualty down if possible.
• Raise the injured limb above the level of the casualty's heart.
• Use your fingers or the palm of your hand to apply direct pressure to the wound, preferably over a sterile dressing or clean pad.
• Apply steady pressure for at least five minutes before looking to see if the bleeding has stopped.
• Put a sterile dressing over the original pad (don't move this) and bandage it in place.
• Check the bandage regularly in case bleeding restarts.

Never use a tourniquet to stop bleeding as this may cause gangrene – the only situation in which this may be appropriate is if the limb has been amputated.

Washing gently with a solution of one teaspoon of salt dissolved in 1L warm water can relieve the itching. If you have thrush a single dose of an antifungal pessary (vaginal tablet), such as 500mg of clotrimazole is an effective treatment. Alternatively, you can use an antifungal cream inserted high in the vagina (on a tampon if you don't have an applicator). A vaginal acidifying gel may help prevent recurrences.

If you're stuck in a remote area without medication, you could use natural yoghurt (applied directly to the vulva or on a tampon and inserted in the vagina) to soothe and help restore the normal balance of organisms in the vagina.

It may also help to avoid eating yeast products like bread and beer, and eat yoghurt with acidophilus culture.

Urinary Tract Infection

Cystitis, or inflammation of the bladder, is a common condition in women. Symptoms include burning when urinating and having to urinate urgently and frequently. Blood can sometimes be passed in urine.

If you think you have cystitis:

• Drink plenty of fluids to help flush the infection out; citrus fruit juice or cranberry juice can help relieve symptoms.
• Take a nonprescription cystitis remedy to help relieve the discomfort. Alternatively, add a teaspoon of bicarbonate of soda to one glass of water when symptoms first appear.
• If there's no improvement after 24 hours despite these measures, seek medical advice because a course of antibiotics may be needed.

TRAUMATIC INJURIES

Although we give guidance on basic first-aid procedures here remember that, unless you're an experienced first aider and confident in what you're doing, it's possible to do more harm than good. Always seek medical help if it is available, but if you are far from any help, follow these guidelines.

Cuts & Other Wounds

Here's what to do if you suffer a fall while riding and end up with road-rash (grazes) and a few minor cuts. If you're riding in a hot, humid climate or intend continuing on your way, there's likely to be a high risk of infection, so the wound needs to be cleaned and dressed. Carry a few antiseptic wipes in your first-aid kit to use straight away, especially if no clean water is available. Small wounds can be cleaned with an antiseptic wipe (only wipe across the wound once with each). Deep or dirty wounds need to be cleaned thoroughly:

- Clean your hands before you start.
- Wear gloves if you are cleaning somebody else's wound.
- Use bottled or boiled water (allowed to cool) or an antiseptic solution like povidone-iodine.
- Use plenty of water – pour it on the wound from a container.
- Embedded dirt and other particles can be removed with tweezers or flushed out using a syringe to squirt water (you can get more pressure if you use a needle as well) – this is especially effective for removing gravel.
- Dry wounds heal best, so avoid using antiseptic creams that keep the wound moist; instead apply antiseptic powder or spray.
- Dry the wound with clean gauze before applying a dressing (use any clean material that's not fluffy; avoid cotton wool as it will stick).

Cuts and wounds make you vulnerable to tetanus infection – if you didn't have a tetanus injection before you went on tour, get one now.

A dressing will protect the wound from dirt, dust and flies. Alternatively, if the wound is small and you are confident you can keep it clean, leave it uncovered. Change the dressing regularly (once a day to start with), especially if the wound is oozing, and watch for signs of infection.

If you have any swelling around the wound, raising the affected limb can help the swelling settle and the wound to heal.

It's best to seek medical advice for any wound that fails to heal after a week or so.

Major Accident

Crashing or being hit by an inattentive driver in a motor vehicle is always possible when cycling. When a major accident does occur what you do is determined to some extent by the circumstances you are in and how readily available medical care is. However, remember that emergency services may be different from what you're used to at home. If you are outside a major town they may be much slower at responding to a call, so be prepared to do at least an initial assessment and to ensure the casualty comes to no further harm.

First of all, check for danger to yourself. If the casualty is on the road ensure oncoming traffic is stopped or diverted. A basic plan of action is:

- Keep calm and think through what you need to do and when.
- Get medical help urgently; send someone to phone ☎ 000.
- Carefully look over the casualty in the position in which you found them (unless this is hazardous for some reason, eg, on a cliff edge).
- Call to the casualty to see if there is a response.
- Check for pulse (at the wrist or on the side of the neck), breathing and major blood loss.
- If necessary (ie, no breathing or no pulse), and you know how, start resuscitation.
- Check the casualty for injuries, moving them as little as possible; ask them where they have pain if they are conscious.
- Don't move the casualty if a spinal injury is possible.
- Take immediate steps to control any obvious bleeding by applying direct pressure to the wound.
- Make the casualty as comfortable as possible and reassure them.
- Keep the casualty warm by insulating them from cold or wet ground (use whatever you have to hand, such as a sleeping bag).

Safety on the Ride

ROAD RULES

Generally cyclists must follow the same rules as motorists in Australia. An important road rule is 'give way to the right' – if an intersection is unmarked, you must give way to vehicles entering from the right. The speed limit in built-up areas is 50km/h or 60km/h; on the open highway it's usually 100km/h or 110km/h. Cyclists should follow these rules:

- Ride on the left side of the road and as far to the left as practicable.
- Riding two abreast is permitted; however, cyclists must ride no more than 1.5m apart.
- In Queensland, the Australian Capital Territory (ACT) and the Northern Territory (NT), cyclists can ride on footpaths. In other states, it's not allowed unless the cyclist is under 12 years of age. However, an adult can accompany children aged under 12 and children between 12 and 17 can join that adult. Tasmania was deciding the issue at the time of publication.
- Cyclists must ride in bicycle lanes when they are marked on the roads.
- On shared footways cyclists must ride in single file, keep to the left and give way to pedestrians.

Tips for Better Cycling

These tips on riding technique are designed to help you ride more safely, comfortably and efficiently:

- Ride in bike lanes if they exist.
- Ride about 1m from the edge of the kerb or from parked cars; riding too close to the road edge makes you less visible and more vulnerable to rough surfaces or car doors being opened without warning.
- Stay alert: especially on busy, narrow, winding and hilly roads it's essential to constantly scan ahead and anticipate the movements of other vehicles, cyclists, pedestrians or animals. Watch for potholes and other hazards as well.
- Keep your upper body relaxed, even when you are climbing.
- Ride a straight line and don't weave across the road when reaching for water bottles or climbing.
- To negotiate rough surfaces and bumps, take your weight off the saddle and let your legs absorb the shock, with the pedals level (in the three and nine o'clock positions).

At Night

- Only ride at night if your bike is equipped with a front and rear light; consider also using a reflective vest and/or reflective ankle bands.

Braking

- Apply front and rear brakes evenly.
- When your bike is fully loaded you'll find that you can apply the front brake quite hard and the extra weight will prevent you doing an 'endo' (flipping over the handlebars).
- In wet weather gently apply the brakes occasionally to dry the brake pads.

Cattle Grids

- These metal grates across the road are potential bike eaters. Ensure you have enough speed to carry you across; coast over them at 90 degrees, standing out of the saddle and balancing on the pedals.

Climbing

- Change down to your low gears to keep your legs 'spinning'.
- When climbing out of the saddle, keep the bike steady; try not to rock the handlebars from side to side.

Cornering

- Loaded bikes are prone to sliding on corners; approach corners slowly and don't lean into the corner as hard as you normally would.
- If traffic permits, take a straight path across corners; hit the corner wide, cut across the apex and ride out of it wide – but never cross the dividing line on the road.
- Apply the brakes before the corner, not while cornering (especially if it's wet).

Corrugations (Ruts)

- For short sections, stand up out of the seat and let the bike rock beneath you. On longer sections, look for the least corrugated area (often the edges or middle of the road), grin and bear it.

Descending

- Stay relaxed, don't cramp up: let your body go with the bike.
- A loaded bike is more likely to wobble and be harder to control at speed, so take it easy.
- Pump the brakes to shed speed rather than applying constant pressure; this avoids overheating the rims, which can cause your tyre to blow.

Tips for Better Cycling

Gravel Roads
- Avoid patches of deep gravel (often on the road's edge); if you can't, ride hard, as you do if driving a car through mud.
- Look ahead to plan your course; avoid sudden turning and take it slowly on descents.
- Brake in a straight line using your rear brake and place your weight over the front wheel if you need to use that brake.
- On loose gravel, loosen toe-clip straps or clipless pedals so you can put your foot down quickly.

Group Riding
- If you're riding in a group, keep your actions predictable and let others know, with a hand signal or shout, before you brake, turn, dodge potholes etc.
- Ride beside, in front or behind fellow cyclists. Don't overlap wheels; if either of you moves sideways suddenly it's likely both of you will fall.
- Ride in single file on busy, narrow or winding roads.

In Traffic
- Obey the rules of the road, and signal if you are turning.
- Look at the wheels to see if a car at a T-junction or joining the road is actually moving or not.
- Scan for trouble: look inside the back windows of parked cars for movement – that person inside may open the door on you.
- Look drivers in the eye; make sure they've seen you.
- Learn to bunny hop your bike (yes, it can be done with a loaded touring bike; just not as well) – it'll save you hitting potholes and other hazards.

In the Wet
- Be aware that you'll take longer to slow down with wet rims; exercise appropriate caution.
- When descending apply the brakes lightly to keep the rims free of grit/water etc and allow for quicker stopping.
- Don't climb out of the saddle (unless you want a change); shift down a gear or two and climb seated.

OH NO... I'M STUCK IN THE TRAM TRACKS!

MAYBE YOU COULD PICK UP SOME PASSENGERS?

DON HATCHER

On Bikepaths
- Use a bell or call out to warn of your approach.

Pick-a-Plank Bridges
- Timber bridges with planks running parallel to the road should be approached with caution.
- Unless you have wide tyres, look carefully at the gaps between the planks and decide whether you can safely ride across the bridge without your wheels falling into a gap; otherwise, walk. To ride, pick a line and stick to it by looking ahead rather than straight down.

Tram & Train Tracks
- Hit these as near to 90 degrees as possible to avoid getting your wheel stuck in the gap. In the wet, the metal rails are especially slippery and dangerous; take special care.

- In all states, hand signals are required if a cyclist is turning or diverging to the right. The ACT and NT, however, require you to also signal when stopping; WA requires signals for all turns; and NSW, for all turns and when stopping.
- Cyclists must not ride within 2m of a moving vehicle for a distance greater than 200m.
- Overtaking on the left is allowed unless the vehicle is turning left, or indicating to turn left.
- Cyclists are allowed to tow trailers only if the cyclist is aged over 16, the trailer passenger aged under 10, and the trailer no wider than 66cm.

Two-Lane Roundabouts

Two-lane roundabouts (traffic circles) can be extremely tricky. While motorists turning right are required to enter the roundabout and complete the turn from the right lane, cyclists can enter and turn from either lane (see Figures 1 and 2). But it's not as easy as it sounds. If riding in the left lane, you must give way to any vehicle which crosses your path to leave the roundabout (see Figure 2).

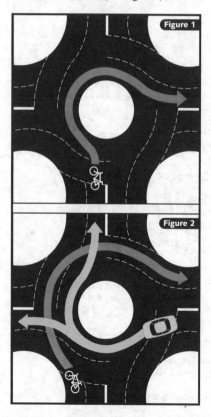

Figure 1

Figure 2

Mandatory Equipment

It is compulsory to wear an approved helmet in Australia, and a fine – of between $30 and $80 depending on the state – results if you are caught riding without one. To fit properly, the helmet should sit far enough forward that only 3–4cm of your forehead is exposed; it should be firm but not tight, with the strap fastened. If it has been in a crash, replace it.

Your bike must be fitted with an effective brake, plus a bell or warning device. For night riding, a red rear light, white front light and reflectors are also essential. Do not hesitate to use your bell or voice to make your presence felt.

Visible Clothing

Always wear brightly coloured clothing and, at night, garments with reflective strips.

RIDING OFF-ROAD

Although most rides are not far from civilisation, you should always remember one of the first rules about mountain-bike riding: never go alone. It's not uncommon for people to go missing in the Australian bush, either through injury or after losing their way. It's best, if possible, to go in a small group – four is usually considered the minimum number. This way, if someone has an accident or is taken ill, one person can stay with the casualty and the others can go for help.

Always tell someone where you are going and when you intend to be back – and make sure they know that you're back! Take warm clothing, matches and enough food and water in case of emergency. Carry enough tools so you can undertake any emergency repairs (see the Your Bicycle chapter for advice on a basic tool kit).

Carry a map and take note of your surroundings as you ride (terrain, landmarks, intersections and so on) so if you do get lost, you're more likely to find your way again. If you get really lost, stay calm and stop. Try to work out where you are or how to retrace your route. If you can't, or it's getting dark, find a nearby open area, put on warm clothes and find or make a shelter. Light a fire for warmth and help searchers by making as many obvious signs as you can (such as creating smoke, displaying brightly coloured items, or making symbols out of wood or rocks).

TOURING DANGERS & ANNOYANCES

Australia's overseas reputation as a wild and dangerous place is somewhat undeserved, though the large distances between towns, the sometimes harsh climate, and the country's larger than usual share of things that bite and sting do pose some challenges for travellers heading outside major cities. Most problems can be avoided by following some of the simple advice provided here. (For treatment of snake and spider bites, see Bites & Stings under Medical Problems & Treatment earlier in this chapter.)

Bushfires

Bushfires happen every year in Australia. Don't be the mug who starts one. In hot, dry, windy weather be extremely careful with any naked flame – cigarette butts thrown out of car windows have started many a fire.

Take local advice before setting out on a ride. On a day of total fire ban, don't go – delay your trip until the weather changes. Chances are that it will be so unpleasantly hot and windy you'll be better off anyway in an air-conditioned pub sipping a cool drink.

If you're in the bush and see smoke, even at a great distance, you should take it seriously. Go to the nearest open space, downhill if possible. A forested ridge is the most dangerous place to be. Bushfires move very quickly and change direction with the wind.

Having said all that, in the outdoors, more people die of cold than in bushfires! Even in summer, temperatures can drop below freezing at night in the mountains.

Bush Camping

Camping outside of commercial camping grounds requires some knowledge of bush safety and sound environmental practices. See the boxed text 'Bicycle Campers' Guide' in the Facts for the Cyclist chapter for a list of tips.

Crocodiles

Up north (north Queensland and the NT), saltwater crocodiles – 'salties' – are a real danger; they are known to sample humans. As well as living around the coast they are found in estuaries, creeks and rivers, sometimes a long way inland. Observe safety signs or ask locals whether waterholes are croc-free before plunging in.

> ### Warning
>
> On a total-fire-ban day (listen to the radio or watch the billboards on country roads), it is forbidden even to use a camping stove in the open. The locals will not be amused if they catch you breaking this particular law; they'll happily dob you in, and the penalties are severe.

Avoid collecting water from rivers or waterholes in crocodile areas; if you have to, go back to a different spot, at a different time each day.

Insects

For four to six months of the year you'll have to cope with those two banes of the Australian outdoors – the fly and the mosquito (mozzie).

In the cities the flies are not too bad; it's in the country that they start getting out of hand. The humble fly net – which fits over a hat or helmet and is rather like a string onion bag – is very effective. Repellents such as Aerogard and Rid may also help to deter the little bastards; citronella is a natural deterrent and is one of the ingredients in many barbeque candles.

Mozzies can be a problem, especially near wetlands in tropical areas – some species are carriers of Ross River Fever; see

Don't expect all of Australia's nasties to appear on your doorstep at once!

the Insect-Borne Diseases section earlier in this chapter. In areas where mosquitoes or sand flies are a problem, wear light-coloured clothing with long sleeves and legs at night and avoid wearing perfume.

Swimming

Many surf (ocean) beaches can be dangerous places to swim if you are not used to the conditions. Undertows (or 'rips') are the main problem, but a number of people are paralysed each year by diving into waves in shallow water and hitting a sand bar – check the depth first.

Many popular beaches are patrolled by surf lifesavers, and patrolled areas are marked by flags. If you swim between the flags assistance should arrive quickly if you get into trouble; raise your arm if you need help.

If you find yourself being carried out by a rip, the main thing to do is keep afloat; don't panic or try to swim against the rip. In most cases the current stops within a couple of hundred metres of the shore, and you can then swim parallel to the beach for a short way to get out of the rip, then make your way back.

EMERGENCY PROCEDURES

If you or one of your group has an accident (even a minor one), or falls ill during your travels, you'll need to decide on the best course of action, which isn't always easy. Obviously, you will need to consider your individual circumstances, including where you are and whether you have some means of direct communication with emergency services, such as a mobile phone (cell phone). Some basic guidelines follow.

Emergency Number

Call ☎ 000 to reach police, ambulance and fire services; the number can be dialled toll-free from any private or public phone without a phonecard or coins.

If there is an accident, give the dispatcher all the details, including where you are, how many people are injured, and the injuries.

- Use your first-aid knowledge and experience, as well as the information in this guide if necessary, to make a medical assessment of the situation.
- For groups of several people, the accepted procedure is to leave one person with the casualty, together with as much equipment, food and water as you can sensibly spare, and for the rest of the group to go for help.
- If there are only two of you, the situation is more tricky; you will have to make an individual judgement of the best course of action.
- If you leave someone, mark their position carefully on the map (take it with you); you should also make sure they can be easily found by marking the position with something conspicuous, such as bright clothing or a large stone cross on the ground. Leave the person with warm clothes, shelter, food, water, matches and a torch (flashlight).
- Try attracting attention by using a whistle or torch, lighting a smoky fire (use damp wood or green leaves) or waving bright clothing; shouting is tiring and not very effective.

The uncertainties associated with emergency rescue in remote wilderness areas should make it clear how important careful planning and safety precautions are, especially if you are travelling in a small group.

YOUR BICYCLE

Fundamental to any cycle tour you plan is the bicycle. In this chapter we look at choosing a bicycle and accessories, setting it up for your needs, learning basic maintenance, and loading and carrying your gear. In short, everything you need to gear up and get going.

CHOOSING & SETTING UP A BICYCLE

The ideal bike for cycle touring is (strangely enough) a touring bike. These bikes look similar to road bikes but generally have relaxed frame geometry for comfort and predictable steering; fittings (eyelets and brazed-on bosses) to mount panniers and mudguards; wider rims and tyres; strong wheels (at least 36 spokes) to carry the extra load; and gearing capable of riding up a wall (triple chainrings and a wide-range freewheel to match). If you want to buy a touring bike, most tend to be custom-built these days, but Cannondale (🖳 www.cannondale.com) and Trek (🖳 www.trekbikes.com) both offer a range of models.

Of course you can tour on any bike you choose, but few will match the advantages of the workhorse touring bike.

Mountain bikes are a slight compromise by comparison, but are very popular for touring. A mountain bike already has the gearing needed for touring and offers a more upright, comfortable position on the bike. And with a change of tyres (to those with semi-slick tread) you'll be able to reduce the rolling resistance and travel at higher speeds with less effort.

Hybrid, or cross, bikes are similar to mountain bikes (and therefore offer similar advantages and disadvantages), although they typically already come equipped with semi-slick tyres.

Racing bikes are less appropriate: their tighter frame geometry is less comfortable on rough roads and long rides. It is also difficult to fit wider tyres, mudguards, racks and panniers to a road bike. Perhaps more significantly, most racing bikes have a distinct lack of low gears.

Tyres Unless you know you'll be on good, sealed roads the whole time, it's probably safest to choose a tyre with some tread. If you have 700c or 27-inch wheels, opt for a tyre that's 28–35mm wide. If touring on a mountain bike, the first thing to do is get rid of the knobby tyres – too much rolling resistance. Instead, fit 1–1½ inch semi-slick tyres or, if riding unpaved roads or off-road occasionally, a combination pattern tyre (slick centre and knobs on the outside).

To protect your tubes, consider buying tyres reinforced with Kevlar, a tightly woven synthetic fibre very resistant to sharp objects. Although more expensive, Kevlar-belted tyres are worth it.

Pedals Cycling efficiency is vastly improved by using toe clips, and even more so with clipless pedals and cleated shoes. Mountain bike or touring shoes are best – the cleats are recessed and the soles are flexible enough to comfortably walk in.

Fold & Go Bikes

Another option is a folding bike. Manufacturers include: Brompton (🖳 www.phoenixcycles.com), Bike Friday (🖳 www.bikefriday.com), Slingshot (🖳 www.slingshotbikes.com), Birdie (🖳 www.whooper.demon.co.uk) and Moulton (🖳 www.alexmoulton.co.uk). All make high-quality touring bikes that fold up to allow hassle-free train, plane or bus transfers. The Moulton, Birdie, Brompton and Slingshot come with suspension and the Bike Friday's case doubles as a trailer for your luggage when touring.

Touring Bike

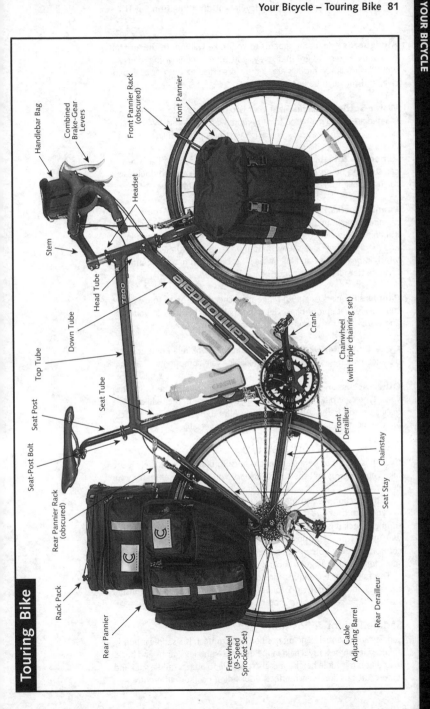

Handlebar Bag

Combined Brake-Gear Levers

Front Pannier Rack (obscured)

Front Pannier

Headset

Stem

Head Tube

Down Tube

Top Tube

Seat Post

Seat-Post Bolt

Seat Tube

Rear Pannier Rack (obscured)

Rack Pack

Rear Pannier

Freewheel (9-Speed Sprocket Set)

Cable Adjusting Barrel

Rear Derailleur

Seat Stay

Chainstay

Front Derailleur

Chainwheel (with triple chainring set)

Crank

Mudguards Adding mudguards to your bike will reduce the amount of muddy water and grit that sprays you when it rains or the roads are wet. Plastic clip-on models are slightly less effective but not as expensive, and they can be less hassle.

Water Bottles & Cages Fit at least two bottle cages to your bike – in isolated areas you may need to carry more water than this. Water 'backpacks', such as a Camelbak, make it easy to keep your fluids up.

Reflectors & Lights If riding at night, add reflectors and lights so you can see, and others can see you. A small headlight can also double as a torch (flashlight). Flashing tail-lights are cheap and effective.

Pannier Racks It's worth buying good pannier racks. The best are aluminium racks made by Blackburn. They're also the most expensive, but come with a lifetime guarantee. Front racks come in low-mounting and mountain bike styles. Low-mounting racks carry the weight lower, which improves the handling of the bike, but if you're touring off-road it is a better idea to carry your gear a bit higher.

Panniers Panniers (see p98) range from cheap-and-nasty to expensive top-quality waterproof bags. Get panniers that fit securely to your rack and watch that the pockets don't swing into your spokes.

Cycle Computer Directions for rides in this book rely upon accurate distance readings, so you'll need a reliable cycle computer.

Other Accessories A good pump is essential. Make sure it fits your valve type (see p86). Some clip on to your bicycle frame, while others fit 'inside' the frame. Also carry a lock. Although heavy, U- or D-locks are the most secure; cable locks can be more versatile.

Riding Position Set Up

Cycling is meant to be a pleasurable pursuit, but that isn't likely if the bike you're riding isn't the correct size for you and isn't set up for your needs.

In this section we assume your bike shop did a good job of providing you with the correct size bike (if you're borrowing a bike get a bike shop to check it is the correct size for you) and concentrate on setting you up in your ideal position and showing you how to tweak the comfort factor. If you are concerned that your bike frame is too big or small for your needs get a second opinion from another bike shop.

The following techniques for determining correct fit are based on averages and may not work for your body type. If you are an unusual size or shape get your bike shop to create your riding position.

Saddle Height & Position

Saddles are essential to riding position and comfort. If a saddle is poorly adjusted it can be a royal pain in the derriere – and legs, arms and back. In addition to saddle height, it is also possible to alter a saddle's tilt and its fore/aft position – each affects your riding position differently.

Saddle Tilt Saddles are designed to be level to the ground, taking most of the weight off your arms and back. However, since triathletes started dropping the nose of their saddles in the mid-1980s many other cyclists have followed suit without knowing why. For some body types, a slight tilt of the nose might be necessary. Be aware, however, that forward tilt will place extra strain on your arms and back. If it is tilted too far forward, chances are your saddle is too high.

Fore/Aft Position The default setting for fore/aft saddle position will allow you to run a plumb bob from the centre of your forward pedal axle to the protrusion of your knee (that bit of bone just under your knee cap).

Fore/Aft Position: To check it, sit on your bike with the pedals in the three and nine o'clock positions. Check the alignment with a plumb bob (a weight on the end of a piece of string).

Saddle Height The simplest method of roughly determining the correct saddle height is the straight leg method. Sit on your bike wearing your cycling shoes. Line one crank up with the seat-tube and place your heel on the pedal. Adjust the saddle height until your leg is almost straight, but not straining. When you've fixed the height of your saddle pedal the cranks backwards (do it next to a wall so you can balance yourself). If you are rocking from side to side, lower the saddle slightly. Otherwise keep raising the saddle (slightly) until on the verge of rocking.

The most accurate way of determining saddle height is the Hodges Method. Developed by US cycling coach Mark Hodges after studying the position of dozens of racing cyclists, the method is also applicable to touring cyclists.

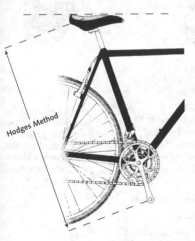

Hodges Method

Standing barefoot with your back against a wall and your feet 15cm apart, get a friend to measure from the greater trochanter (the bump of your hip) to the floor passing over your knee and ankle joints. Measure each leg (in mm) three times and average the figure. Multiply the average figure by 0.96.

Now add the thickness of your shoe sole and your cleats (if they aren't recessed). This total is the distance you need from the centre of your pedal axle to the top of your saddle. It is the optimum position for your body to pedal efficiently and should not be exceeded; however, people with small feet for their size should lower the saddle height slightly. The inverse applies for people with disproportionately large feet.

If you need to raise your saddle significantly do it over a few weeks so your muscles can adapt gradually. (Never raise your saddle above the maximum extension line marked on your seat post.)

Handlebars & Brake Levers

Racing cyclists lower their handlebars to cheat the wind and get a better aerodynamic position. While this might be tempting on windy days it doesn't make for comfortable touring. Ideally, the bars should be no higher than the saddle (even on mountain bikes) and certainly no lower than 75mm below it.

Pedals

For comfort and the best transference of power, the ball of your foot should be aligned over the centre of the pedal axle (see right).

If using clipless pedals consider the amount of lateral movement available. Our feet have a natural angle that they prefer when we walk, run or cycle. If they are unable to achieve this position the knee joint's alignment will be affected and serious injury may result. Most clipless pedal systems now have some rotational freedom (called 'float') built in to allow for this, but it is still important to adjust the cleats to each foot's natural angle.

Comfort Considerations

Now that you have your optimum position on the bike, there are several components that you can adjust to increase the comfort factor.

Handlebars come in a variety of types and sizes. People with small hands may find shallow drop bars more comfortable. Handlebars also come in a variety of widths, so if they're too wide or narrow change them.

With mountain bike handlebars you really only have one hand position, so add a pair of bar-ends. On drop bars the ends should be parallel to the ground. If they're pointed up it probably means you need a longer stem; pointed down probably means you need a shorter stem.

On mountain bikes the **brake levers** should be adjusted to ensure your wrist is straight – it's the position your hand naturally sits in. For drop bars the bottom of the lever should end on the same line as the end section.

Getting the right **saddle** for you is one of the key considerations for enjoyable cycling. Everybody's sit bones are shaped and spaced differently, meaning a saddle that suits your best friend might be agony for you. A good bike shop will allow you to keep changing a new (undamaged) saddle until you get one that's perfect. Women's saddles tend to have a shorter nose and a wider seat, and men's are long and narrow.

If you feel too stretched out or cramped when riding, chances are you need a different length **stem** – the problem isn't solved by moving your saddle forward/aft. Get a bike shop to assess this for you.

Pedal Alignment: The ball of your foot should be over the centre of the pedal axle for comfort and the best transfer of power.

Brake Levers: Adjust your drop bars so the end section is parallel to the ground and the brake lever ends on this same line.

🔧 Record Your Position

When you've created your ideal position, mark each part's position (scratch a line with a sharp tool like a scribe or use tape) and record it, so you can recreate it if hiring a bike or when reassembling your bike after travel. The inside back cover of this book has a place to record all this vital data.

MAINTAINING YOUR BICYCLE

If you're new to cycling or haven't previously maintained your bike, this section is for you. It won't teach you how to be a top-notch mechanic, but it will help you maintain your bike in good working order and show you how to fix the most common touring problems.

If you go mountain biking it is crucial you carry spares and a tool kit and know how to maintain your bike, because if anything goes wrong it's likely you'll be miles from anywhere when trouble strikes and face a long walk home.

If you want to know more about maintaining your bike there are dozens of books available (*Richard's Bicycle Book*, by Richard Ballantine, is a classic; if you want to know absolutely everything get *Barnett's Manual for Bicycle Maintenance* or *Sutherland's Handbook*) or inquire at your bike shop about courses in your area.

Predeparture & Daily Inspections

Before going on tour get your bike serviced by a bike shop or do it yourself. On tour, check over your bike every day or so (see the boxed text 'Pre-Departure & Post-Ride Checks' on p89).

Spares & Tool Kit

Touring cyclists need to be self-sufficient and should carry some spares and, at least, a basic tool kit. How many spares/tools you will need depends on the country you are touring in – in Britain, bike shops are common and the towns are not too spread out so you should get by with the following.

Multi-tools (see right) are very handy and a great way to save space and weight, and there are dozens of different ones on the market. Before you buy a multi-tool though, check each of the tools is usable – a chain breaker, for example, needs to have a good handle for leverage otherwise it is useless.

Adjustable spanners are often handy, but the trade-off is that they can easily burr bolts if not used correctly – be careful when using them.

The bare minimum:
- [ ] pump – ensure it has the correct valve fitting for your tyres
- [ ] water bottles (2)
- [ ] spare tubes (2)
- [ ] tyre levers (2)
- [ ] chain lube and a rag
- [ ] puncture repair kit (check the glue is OK)
- [ ] Allen keys to fit your bike
- [ ] small Phillips screwdriver
- [ ] small flat screwdriver
- [ ] spare brake pads
- [ ] spare screws and bolts (for pannier racks, seat post etc) and chain links (2)

For those who know what they're doing:
- [ ] spoke key
- [ ] spare spokes and nipples (8)
- [ ] tools to remove freewheel
- [ ] chain breaker
- [ ] pliers
- [ ] spare chain links (HyperGlide chain rivet if you have a Shimano chain)
- [ ] spare rear brake and rear gear cables

Always handy to take along:
- [ ] roll of electrical/gaffer tape
- [ ] nylon ties (10) – various lengths/sizes
- [ ] hand cleaner (store it in a film canister)

YOUR BICYCLE

Fixing a Flat

Flats happen. And if you're a believer in Murphy's Law then the likely scenario is that you'll suffer a flat just as you're rushing to the next town to catch a train or beat the setting sun.

Don't worry – this isn't a big drama. If you're prepared and know what you're doing you can be up and on your way in five minutes flat.

Being prepared means carrying a spare tube, a pump and at least two tyre levers. If you're not carrying a spare tube, of course, you can stop and fix the puncture then and there, but it's unlikely you'll catch that train and you could end up doing all this in the dark. There will be days when you have the time to fix a puncture on the side of the road, but not always. Carry at least two spare tubes.

1 Take the wheel off the bike. Remove the valve cap and unscrew the locknut (hex nut at base; see Valve Types) on Presta valves. Deflate the tyre completely, if it isn't already.

2 Make sure the tyre and tube are loose on the rim – moisture and the pressure of the inflated tube often makes the tyre and tube fuse with the rim.

3 If the tyre is really loose you should be able to remove it with your hands. Otherwise you'll need to lift one side of the tyre over the rim with the tyre levers. Pushing the tyre away from the lever as you insert it should ensure you don't pinch the tube and puncture it again.

4 When you have one side of the tyre off, you'll be able to remove the tube. Before inserting the replacement tube, carefully inspect the tyre (inside and out); you're looking for what caused the puncture. If you find anything embedded in the tyre, remove it. Also check that the rim tape is still in

Valve Types

The two most common valve types are Presta (sometimes called French) and Schraeder (American). To inflate a Presta valve, first unscrew the round nut at the top (and do it up again after you're done); depress it to deflate. To deflate Schraeder valves depress the pin (inside the top). Ensure your pump is set up for the valve type on your bike.

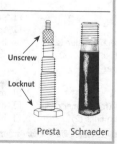

Unscrew

Locknut

Presta   Schraeder

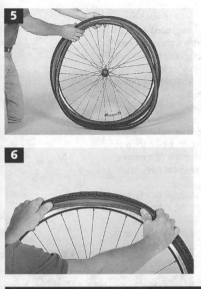

place and no spoke nipples (see p95) protrude through it.

5 Time to put the new tube in. Start by partially pumping up the tube (this helps prevent it twisting or being pinched) and insert the valve in the hole in the rim. Tuck the rest of the tube in under the tyre, making sure you don't twist it. Make sure the valve is straight – most Presta valves come with a locknut to help achieve this.

6 Work the tyre back onto the rim with your fingers. If this isn't possible, and again, according to Murphy's Law, it frequently isn't, you might need to use your tyre levers for the last 20–30cm. If you need to use the levers, make sure you don't pinch the new tube, otherwise it's back to Step 1. All you need to do now is pump up the tyre and put the wheel back on the bike. Don't forget to fix the pucture that night.

Fixing the Puncture

To fix the puncture you'll need a repair kit, which usually comes with glue, patches, sandpaper and, sometimes, chalk. (Always check the glue in your puncture repair kit hasn't dried up before heading off on tour.) The only other thing you'll need is clean hands.

1. The first step is to find the puncture. Inflate the tube and hold it up to your ear. If you can hear the puncture, mark it with the chalk; otherwise immerse it in water and watch for air bubbles. Once you find the puncture, mark it, cover it with your finger and continue looking – just in case there are more.

2. Dry the tube and lightly roughen the area around the hole with the sandpaper. Sand an area larger than the patch.

3. Follow the instructions for the glue you have. Generally you spread an even layer of glue over the area of the tube to be patched and allow it to dry until it is tacky.

4. Patches also come with their own instructions – some will be just a piece of rubber and others will come lined with foil (remove the foil on the underside but don't touch the exposed area). Press the patch firmly onto the area over the hole and hold it for 2–3 minutes. If you want, remove the excess glue from around the patch or dust it with chalk or simply let it dry.

5. Leave the glue to set for 10–20 minutes. Inflate the tube and check the patch has worked.

Chains

Chains are dirty, greasy and all too often the most neglected piece of equipment on a bike. There are about 120 or so links in a chain and each has a simple but precise arrangement of bushes, bearings and plates. Over time all chains stretch, but if dirt gets between the bushes and bearings this 'ageing' will happen prematurely and will likely damage the teeth of your chainrings, sprockets and derailleur guide pulleys.

To prevent this, chains should be cleaned and lubed frequently (see your bike shop for the best products to use).

No matter how well you look after a chain it should be replaced regularly – about every 5000–8000km. Seek the advice of a bike shop to ensure you are buying the correct type for your drivetrain (the moving parts that combine to drive the bicycle: chain, freewheel, derailleurs, chainwheel and bottom bracket).

If you do enough cycling you'll need to replace a chain (or fix a broken chain), so here's how to use that funky-looking tool, the chain breaker.

1 Remove the chain from the chainrings – it'll make the whole process easier. Place the chain in the chain breaker (on the outer slots; it braces the link plates as the rivet is driven out) and line the pin of the chain breaker up with the rivet.

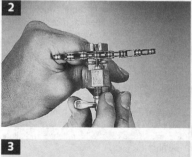

2 Wind the handle until the rivet is clear of the inner link but still held by the outer link plate.

3 Flex the chain to 'break' it. If it won't, you'll need to push the rivet out some more, but not completely – if you push it all the way out, you'll have to remove two links and replace them with two spare links. If you're removing links, you'll need to remove a male and female link (ie, two links).

4 Rejoining the chain is the reverse. If you turn the chain around when putting it on you will still have the rivet facing you. Otherwise it will be facing away from you and you'll need to change to the other side of the bike and work through the spokes.

Join the chain up by hand and place it in the breaker. Now drive the rivet in firmly, making sure it is properly lined up with the hole of the outer link plate. Stop when the rivet is almost in place.

5 Move the chain to the spreaders (inner slots) of the chain breaker. Finish by winding the rivet into position carefully (check that the head of the rivet is raised the same distance above the link plate as the rivets beside it). If you've managed to get it in perfectly and the link isn't 'stiff', well done!

Otherwise, move the chain to the spreaders on the chain breaker and gently work the chain laterally until the link is no longer stiff.

If this doesn't work (and with some chain breakers it won't), take the chain out of the tool and place a screwdriver or Allen key between the outer plates of the stiff link and carefully lever the plates both ways. If you're too forceful you'll really break the chain, but if you're subtle it will free the link up and you'll be on your way.

Chain Options

Check your chain; if you have a Shimano HyperGlide chain you'll need a special Hyper-Glide chain rivet to rejoin the chain. This will be supplied with your new chain, but carry a spare.

Another option is to fit a universal link to your chain. This link uses a special clip to join the chain – like the chains of old. You'll still need a chain breaker to fix a broken chain or take out spare links.

Pre-Departure & Post-Ride Checks

Each day before you get on your bike and each evening after you've stopped riding, give your bike a quick once-over. Following these checks will ensure you're properly maintaining your bike and will help identify any problems before they become disasters. Go to the nearest bike shop if you don't know how to fix any problem.

Pre-Departure Check List

☐ brakes – are they stopping you? If not, adjust them.
☐ chain – if it was squeaking yesterday, it needs lube.
☐ panniers – are they all secured and fastened?
☐ cycle computer – reset your trip distance at the start.
☐ gears – are they changing properly? If not, adjust them.
☐ tyres – check your tyre pressure is correct (see the tyre's side wall for the maximum psi); inflate, if necessary.

Post-Ride Check List

☐ pannier racks – check all bolts/screws are tightened; do a visual check of each rack (the welds, in particular) looking for small cracks.
☐ headset – when stationary, apply the front brake and rock the bike gently; if there is any movement or noise, chances are the headset is loose.
☐ wheels – visually check the tyres for sidewall cuts/wear and any embedded objects; check the wheels are still true and no spokes are broken.
☐ wrench test – wrench (pull) on the saddle (if it moves, tighten the seat-post bolt and/or the seat-clamp bolt, underneath); wrench laterally on a crank (if it moves, check the bottom bracket).

Brakes

Adjusting the brakes of your bike is not complicated and even though your bike shop will use several tools to do the job, all you really need is a pair of pliers, a spanner or Allen key, and (sometimes) a friend.

Check three things before you start: the wheels are true (not buckled), the braking surface of the rims is smooth (no dirt, dents or rough patches) and the cables are not frayed.

Begin by checking that the pads strike the rim correctly: flush on the braking surface of the rim (see right and p91) and parallel to the ground.

Calliper Brakes

It's likely that you'll be able to make any minor adjustments to calliper brakes by winding the cable adjusting barrel out. If it doesn't allow enough movement you'll need to adjust the cable anchor bolt:

1 Undo the cable anchor bolt – not completely, just so the cable is free to move – and turn the cable adjusting barrel all the way in.

2 Get your friend to hold the callipers in the desired position, about 2–3mm away from the rim. Using a pair of pliers, pull the cable through until it is taut.

3 Before you tighten the cable anchor bolt again, check to see if the brake lever is in its normal position (not slack as if somebody was applying it) – sometimes they jam open. Also, ensure the brake quick-release (use it when you're removing your wheel or in an emergency to open the callipers if your wheel is badly buckled) is closed.

4 Tighten the cable anchor bolt again. Make any fine-tuning to the brakes by winding the cable adjusting barrel out.

 Brake Cables

If your brakes are particularly hard to apply, you may need to replace the cables. Moisture can cause the cable and housing (outer casing) to bond or stick. If this happens it's often possible to prolong the life of a cable by removing it from the housing and applying a coating of grease (or chain lube) to it.

If you do need to replace the cable, take your bike to a bike shop and get the staff to fit and/or supply the new cable. Cables come in two sizes – rear (long) and front (short) – various thicknesses and with different types of nipples.

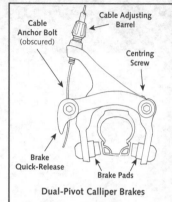

Cable Anchor Bolt (obscured)

Cable Adjusting Barrel

Centring Screw

Brake Quick-Release

Brake Pads

Dual-Pivot Calliper Brakes

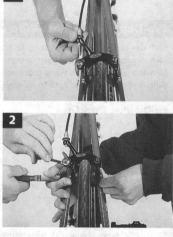

Cantilever Brakes

These days most touring bikes have cantilever rather than calliper brakes. The newest generation of cantilever brakes (V-brakes) are more powerful and better suited to stopping bikes with heavy loads.

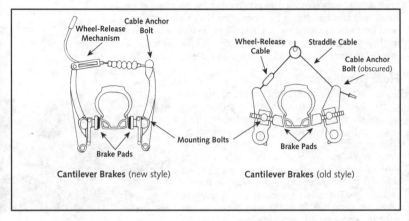

Cantilever Brakes (new style) **Cantilever Brakes** (old style)

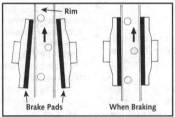

Cantilever Brake Toe-In: This is how the brake pads should strike the rim (from above) with correct toe-in.

On cantilever brakes ensure the leading edge of the brake pad hits the rim first (see left). This is called toe-in; it makes the brakes more efficient and pre-vents squealing. To adjust the toe-in on cantilever brakes, loosen the brake pad's mounting bolt (using a 10mm spanner and 5mm Allen key). Wiggle the brake pad into position and tighten the bolt again.

If you only need to make a minor adjustment to the distance of the pads from the rim, chances are you will be able to do it by winding the cable ad-justing barrel out (located near the brake lever on mountain bikes and hybrids). If this won't do you'll need to adjust the cable anchor bolt:

1 Undo the cable anchor bolt (not completely, just so the cable is free to move) and turn the cable adjusting barrel all the way in. Depending on the style of your brakes, you may need a 10mm spanner (older bikes) or a 5mm Allen key.

2 Hold the cantilevers in the desired position (get assistance from a friend if you need to), positioning the brake pads 2–3mm away from the rim. Using a pair of pliers, pull the cable through until it is taut.

3 Before you tighten the cable anchor bolt again, check to see if the brake lever is in its normal pos-ition (not slack as if somebody was applying it) – sometimes they jam open.

4 Tighten the cable anchor bolt again. Make any fine-tuning to the brakes by winding the cable ad-justing barrel out.

Gears

If the gears on your bike start playing up – the chain falls off the chain-rings, it shifts slowly or not at all – it's bound to cause frustration and could damage your bike. All it takes to prevent this is a couple of simple adjustments: the first, setting the limits of travel for both derailleurs, will keep the chain on your drivetrain, and the second will ensure smooth, quick shifts from your rear derailleur. Each will take just a couple of minutes and the only tool you need is a small Phillips or flat screwdriver.

Front Derailleur

If you can't get the chain to shift onto one chainring or the chain comes off when you're shifting, you need to make some minor adjustments to the limit screws on the front derailleur. Two screws control the limits of the front derailleur's left and right movement, which governs how far the chain can shift. When you shift gears the chain is physically pushed sideways by the plates (outer and inner) of the de-railleur cage. The screws are usually side by side (see photo No 1) on the top of the front derailleur. The left-hand screw (as you sit on the bike) adjusts the inside limit and the one on the right adjusts the outside limit.

Screws

Cage Plates

Front Derailleur: Before making any adjustments, remove any build-up of grit from the screws (especially underneath) by wiping them with a rag and applying a quick spray (or drop) of chain lube.

After you make each of the following adjustments, pedal the drive-train with your hand and change gears to ensure you've set the limit correctly. If you're satisfied, test it under strain by going for a short ride.

Outer Limits Change the gears to position the chain on the largest chainring and the smallest rear sprocket. Set the outer cage plate as close to the chain as you can without it touching. Adjust the right-hand limit screw to achieve this.

Inner Limits Position the chain on the smallest chainring and the largest rear sprocket. For chainwheels with three chainrings, position the inner cage plate between 1–2mm from the chain. If you have a chainwheel with two chainrings, position the inner cage plate as close to the chain as you can without it touching.

Rear Derailleur

If the limit screws aren't set correctly on the rear derailleur the conse-quences can be dire. If the chain slips off the largest sprocket it can jam between the sprocket and the spokes and could then snap the chain, break or damage spokes or even break the frame.

The limit screws are located at the back of the derailleur (see photo No 2). The top screw (marked 'H' on the derailleur) sets the derailleur's limit of travel on the smallest sprocket's (the highest gear) side of the free-wheel. The bottom screw ('L') adjusts the derailleur's travel towards the largest sprocket (lowest gear).

Outer Limits Position the chain on the smallest sprocket and largest chainring (see photo No 3). The derailleur's top guide pulley (the one

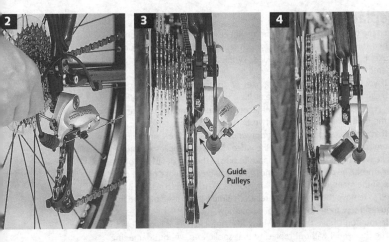

Guide
Pulleys

closest to the sprockets) should be in line with the smallest sprocket; adjust the top screw ('H') to ensure it is.

Inner Limits Position the chain on the largest rear sprocket and the smallest chainring (see photo No 4). This time the guide pulley needs to be lined up with the largest sprocket; do this by adjusting the bottom screw ('L'). Make sure the chain can't move any further towards the wheel than the largest sprocket.

Cable Adjusting Barrel

If your gears are bouncing up and down your freewheel in a constant click and chatter, you need to adjust the tension of the cable to the rear derailleur. This can be achieved in a variety of ways, depending on your gear system.

The main cable adjusting barrel is on your rear derailleur (see photo No 5). Secondary cable adjusting barrels can also be found near the gear levers (newer Shimano combined brake-gear STI levers) or on the downtube of your frame (older Shimano STI levers and Campagnolo Ergopower gear systems) of some bikes. Intended for racing cyclists, they allow for fine tuning of the gears' operation while on the move.

Raise the rear wheel off the ground – have a friend hold it up by the saddle, hang it from a tree or turn the bike upside down – so you can pedal the drivetrain with your hand.

To reset your derailleur, shift gears to position the chain on the second smallest sprocket and middle chainring (see photo No 6). As you turn the crank with your hand, tighten the cable by winding the rear derailleur's cable adjusting barrel anti-clockwise. Just before the chain starts to make a noise as if to shift onto the third sprocket, stop winding.

Now pedal the drivetrain and change the gears up and down the free-wheel. If things still aren't right you may find that you need to tweak the cable tension slightly: turn the cable adjusting barrel anti-clockwise if shifts to larger sprockets are slow, and clockwise if shifts to smaller sprockets hesitate.

Replacing a Spoke

Even the best purpose-made touring wheels occasionally break spokes. When this happens the wheel, which relies on the even pull of each spoke, is likely to become buckled. When it is not buckled, it is considered true.

If you've forgotten to pack spokes or you grabbed the wrong size, you can still get yourself out of a pickle if you have a spoke key. Wheels are very flexible and you can get it roughly true – enough to take you to the next bike shop – even if two or three spokes are broken.

If you break a spoke on the front wheel it is a relatively simple thing to replace the spoke and retrue the wheel. The same applies if a broken spoke is on the non-drive side (opposite side to the rear derailleur) of the rear wheel. The complication comes when you break a spoke on the drive side of the rear wheel (the most common case). In order to replace it you need to remove the freewheel, a relatively simple job in itself but one that requires a few more tools and the know-how.

If you don't have that know-how fear not, because it is possible to retrue the wheel without replacing that spoke *and* without damaging the wheel – see Truing a Wheel (below).

1 Remove the wheel from the bike. It's probably a good idea to remove the tyre and tube as well (though not essential), just to make sure the nipple is seated properly in the rim and not likely to cause a puncture.

2 Remove the broken spoke but leave the nipple in the rim (if it's not damaged; otherwise replace it). Now you need to thread the new spoke. Start by threading it through the vacant hole on the hub flange. Next lace the new spoke through the other spokes. Spokes are offset on the rim; every second one is on the same side and, generally, every fourth is laced through the other spokes the same way.

3 With the spoke key, tighten the nipple until the spoke is about as taut as the other spokes on this side of the rim. Spoke nipples have four flat sides – to adjust them you'll need the correct size spoke key. Spoke keys come in two types: those made to fit one spoke gauge or several. If you have the latter, trial each size on a nipple until you find the perfect fit.

Truing a Wheel

Truing a wheel is an art form and, like all art forms, it is not something mastered overnight. If you can, practise with an old wheel before leaving home. If that's not possible – and you're on the side of the road as you read this – following these guidelines will get you back in the saddle until you can get to the next bike shop.

1 Start by turning the bike upside-down, so the wheels can turn freely. Check the tension of all the spokes on the wheel: do this by

squeezing each pair of spokes on each side. Tighten those spokes that seem loose and loosen those that seem too tight. Note, though, the spokes on the drive side of the rear wheel (on the same side as the freewheel) are deliberately tighter than the non-drive side.

2 Rotate the wheel a couple of times to get an idea of the job at hand. If the wheel won't rotate, let the brakes off (see pp90–1).

3 Using the chalk from your puncture repair kit, mark all the 'bumps'. Keep the chalk in the same position (brace the chalk against the pannier rack or bike's frame) and let the bumps in the wheel 'hit' the chalk.

4 In order to get the bumps out you'll need a constant point of reference – to gauge if the bumps are being removed. Often, if it is not a severe buckle, you can use a brake pad. Position the brake pad about 2–3mm from the rim (on the side with the biggest buckle).

5 With your spoke key, loosen those spokes on the same side as the bump within the longest chalked area, and tighten those on the opposite side of the rim. The spokes at the start and the finish of the chalked area should only be tightened/loosened by a quarter-turn; apply a half-turn to those in between.

6 Rotate the wheel again; if you're doing it correctly the buckle should not be as great. Continue this process of tightening and loosening spokes until the bump is as near to gone as you can get it – as the bump is removed turn the nipples less (one-eighth of a turn on the ends and a quarter-turn in between). Experienced exponents can remove buckles entirely, but if you can get it almost out (1mm here or there) you've done well.

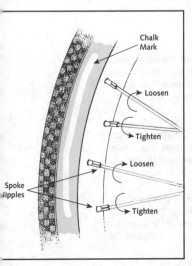

7 If the wheel has more than one bump, move onto the second-longest chalk mark next. As each bump is removed you might find it affects the previous bump slightly. In this case, remove the previous chalk mark and repeat Steps 4–6. Continue to do this until all the buckles are removed.

Don't forget to readjust the brakes.

If you've trued the wheel without replacing the broken spokes, have them replaced at the next bike shop.

YOUR BICYCLE

LOADING YOUR BICYCLE

If you've ever been to Asia and seen a bike loaded with boxes piled 2m high or carrying four, five or six people, plus a chicken or two, you'll realise that there are more ways to carry your gear than would otherwise seem. More realistic options for you come from a combination of front and rear panniers, a handlebar bag or trailer.

'Credit-card tourists', who are intent on travelling lighter, further and faster and who are happy to stay in hotels or hostels, can get by with a handlebar bag and/or rear panniers (see top right). The downside to this configuration is poor bike-handling; the steering feels particularly 'airy'. It's possible to adopt the 'lighter, further, faster' principle and still camp, but it means frugal packing.

If you want to be more self-sufficient or you're carrying 20kg or more, you'll probably find it easier (and your bike will handle better) with front and rear panniers. The tried-and-tested configuration that works best for a touring bike is to use four panniers: two low-mounting front panniers with two high-mounting rear panniers (see bottom right). The only other thing you might want to add is a small handlebar bag for this book, snacks, sunblock, money, camera etc.

Pannier configurations: the four-pannier system is the best way of carrying your gear and having a bike that handles well; packing light saves weight but the compromise can be poor bike handling

This combination, with a few light but bulky items on the rear rack (eg, tent, sleeping mat etc), allows you to carry a large load and still have predictable and manageable bike-handling.

If you're riding a mountain bike and riding off-road you'll probably want high-mounting front panniers to give you more clearance.

Packing Your Gear

It's frequently said that, in packing for a cycle tour, you should lay out everything you need to take and then leave half of it behind. The skill is in knowing which half to leave behind. Almost as much skill is needed in organising the gear in your panniers. Here are some tried and tested tips.

Compartmentalise Pack similar items into nylon drawstring bags (stuff sacks), to make them easier to find again (eg, underwear in one, cycling clothes in another, and even dinner food separated from breakfast food). Using different coloured stuff sacks makes choosing the right one easier.

Waterproof Even if your panniers are completely waterproof, and especially if they're not, it pays to put everything inside heavy-duty plastic bags. Check bags for holes during the trip; replace them or patch the holes with tape.

Reduce Flood Damage If your panniers are not waterproof and they pool water, you can reduce problems by putting things that are unaffected by water, say a pair of thongs, at the bottom of the bag. This keeps the other stuff above 'flood level'. Try using seam sealant on the bags' seams beforehand, too.

Load Consistently Put things in the same place each time you pack to avoid having to unpack every bag just to find one item.

Balance the Load Distribute weight evenly – generally around 60% in the rear and 40% in the front panniers – and keep it as low as possible by using low-mounting front panniers and packing heavy items first. Side-to-side balancing is just as critical.

Group Gear Pack things used at the same time in the same pannier. Night/camp things like your mat, sleeping bag and pyjamas, which you don't need during the day, could all be in the bag most difficult to access – likely to be on the same side as the side of the road you are riding on, since you will probably lean that side of the bike against a tree, pole or roadside barrier.

Put all clothing in one pannier, if possible, sorted into separate bags of cycling clothes, 'civilian' clothes, underwear, wet weather gear and dirty clothes. Keep a windproof jacket handy on top for descents.

In the Front Food and eating utensils are convenient to have in a front pannier along with a camping stove. Toiletry items, towel, first-aid kit, reading material, torch and sundry items can go in the other front bag.

In the Pockets or Bar Bag Easily accessible pockets on panniers or on your cycling shirt are useful for items likely to be needed frequently or urgently during the day, such as snacks, tool kit, sun hat or sunscreen. A handlebar bag is good for these items if your panniers don't have pockets, but remember that weight on the handlebars upsets a bike's handling.

Keep Space Spare Remember to leave some spare space for food and, if using a camping stove, for the fuel canister. Be mindful when

Another Option – Trailers

Luggage trailers are gaining in popularity and some innovative designs are now on the market. By spreading the load onto more wheels they relieve the bike and can improve rolling resistance. Their extra capacity is a boon for travelling on a tandem or with a young family. They can be combined with racks and panniers, but the hitch (point it connects with the bike) of some trailers may interfere with your panniers, so check first.

Two-wheeled trailers are free standing and can take very heavy loads, including babies and toddlers. Often brightly coloured, they give a strong signal to car drivers who tend to give you a wide berth. However, their relatively wide track can catch a lot of wind and makes them ungainly on rough, narrow roads or trails.

Single-wheeled trailers such as the BOB Yak share the load with the bike's rear wheel. They track well and can be used on very rough trails and may be the easiest option for full-suspension bikes. The load capacity of these units is somewhere between that of a bike with a rear rack only and a fully loaded (four panniers plus rack-top luggage) touring bike.

packing foods that are squashable or sensitive to heat and protect or insulate them – unless you're working on a gourmet pasta sauce recipe that includes socks.

Prevent 'Internal Bleeding' Act on the premise that anything that can spill will, and transfer it to a reliable container, preferably within a watertight bag. Take care, too, in packing hard or sharp objects (tools, utensils or anything with hooks) that could rub or puncture other items, including the panniers. Knives or tools with folding working parts are desirable.

Fragile Goods Valuables and delicate equipment such as cameras are best carried in a handlebar bag, which can be easily removed when you stop. Alternatively, carry these items in a 'bum bag', which will accompany you automatically.

Rack Top Strap your tent lengthways on top of the rear rack with elastic cord looped diagonally across from front to rear and back again, and round across to anchor the rear end. Be sure the cord is well-tensioned and secure – deny its kamikaze impulses to plunge into the back wheel, jamming the freewheel mechanism, or worse.

What to Look for in Panniers

Panniers remain the popular choice for touring luggage. They offer flexibility, in that one, two or four can be used depending on the load to be carried and they allow luggage to be arranged for easy access.

Many people initially buy just a rear rack and panniers, and it is wise to buy the best quality you can afford at this stage. These bags will accompany you on all of your tours as well as for day-to-day shopping and commuting trips for years to come.

The attachment system should be secure, but simple to operate. That big bump you hit at 50km/h can launch a poorly designed pannier and your precious luggage.

The stiffness of the pannier backing is another concern – if it can flex far enough to reach the spokes of the wheel the result can be catastrophic. Good rack design can also help avoid this.

The fabric of the panniers should be strong and abrasion- and water-resistant. You can now buy roll-top panniers, made from laminated fabrics, that are completely waterproof. Bear in mind that these bags are only waterproof until they develop even the smallest hole, so be prepared to check them and apply patches occasionally. Canvas bags shed water well, but should be used in conjunction with a liner bag to keep things dry. Cordura is a heavy nylon fabric with excellent abrasion resistance. The fabric itself is initially waterproof, but water tends to find the seams, so using a liner bag is a good idea once again.

Pockets and compartments can help to organise your load, but the multitude of seams increase the challenge of keeping the contents dry in the wet. A couple of exterior pockets are great for sunscreen, snacks and loose change that you need throughout the day. Carrying front panniers as well as rear ones allows more opportunities to divide and organise gear.

When fitting rear panniers check for heel strike. Long feet, long cranks and short chain-stays will all make it harder to get the bags and your body to fit.

Getting There & Away

AIR

Australia is a long way from just about everywhere, and getting there basically means flying. If you want to fly to Australia at a particularly popular time of year (the middle of summer – ie, over Christmas – is notoriously difficult) or on a particularly popular route (eg, Hong Kong or Singapore to Sydney or Melbourne) then you need to plan well ahead.

Airports & Airlines

Australia has a number of international gateways. Sydney and Melbourne are the two busiest. Perth gets many flights from Asia and Europe and has direct flights to New Zealand and Africa. The other main international airports are Adelaide, Brisbane, Cairns and Darwin. Hobart's 'International' airport only receives domestic flights. One place you can't fly to direct from overseas is Canberra, the national capital.

Sydney airport is notoriously busy – unless you're planning to visit only New South Wales, it's worth considering alternative entry and exit points such as Melbourne, Brisbane or Perth.

Australia's main international carrier is Qantas, part of the oneworld Alliance, which includes British Airways, American Airlines, Cathay Pacific and Finnair. Domestic airline Ansett also does some international flights; it's part of Star Alliance, which includes Air New Zealand, Lauda Air, Singapore Airlines, Thai and United Airlines.

Buying Tickets

The plane ticket will probably be the single most expensive item in your budget, and buying it can be an intimidating business. There is likely to be a multitude of airlines and travel agents hoping to separate you from your money, and it is always worth putting aside a few hours to research the current state of the market. Start early: some of the cheapest tickets have to be bought months in advance, and some popular flights sell out quickly. Talk to other recent travellers – they may be able to stop you making some of the same old mistakes.

> ### Warning
>
> The information in this chapter is particularly vulnerable to change: prices for international travel are volatile, routes are introduced and cancelled, schedules change, special deals come and go, and rules and visa requirements are amended.
>
> You should check directly with the airline or a travel agent to make sure you understand the conditions of your ticket. The details given in this chapter should be regarded as pointers and are not a substitute for your own careful, up-to-date research.

Look at ads in newspapers and magazines, consult reference books and watch for special offers. Then phone around travel agents for bargains. (Airlines can supply information on routes and timetables; however, except at times of inter-airline warfare, they do not supply the cheapest tickets.) Find out the fare, the route, the duration of the journey and any restrictions on the ticket. Then sit back and decide which is best for you.

Use the fares quoted in this book as a guide only. They are approximate and based on the rates advertised by travel agents at the time of going to press. Quoted air fares do not necessarily constitute a recommendation for the carrier.

If you are travelling from the UK or the USA, you will probably find the cheapest flights are being advertised by obscure bucket shops whose names haven't yet reached the telephone directory. Many such firms are honest and solvent, but there are a few rogues who will take your money and disappear, to reopen elsewhere a month or two later under a new name. If you feel suspicious about a firm, don't give them all the money at once – just leave a deposit of 20% or so and pay the balance when you get the ticket. If they insist on cash in advance, go somewhere else. And once you have the ticket, ring the airline to confirm you are actually booked on the flight.

Packing for Air Travel

We've all heard the horror stories about smashed/lost luggage when flying, but a more real threat to cycle tourists is arriving in a country for a two-week tour and finding their bike with broken wheels or in little bits spread out around the baggage carousel. Fixing a damaged bike could take days, and the delay and frustration could ruin your holiday.

How do you avoid this? Err on the side of caution and box your bike. Trust airline baggage handlers if you want (we're told some people actually do) and give your bike to them 'as is' – turn the handlebars 90°, remove the pedals, cover the chain with a rag or bag (to protect other people's baggage) and deflate your tyres (partially, not all the way) – but is it worth the risk? If you want to take that sort of a risk do it on your homeward flight, when you can get your favourite bike shop to fix any damage any time.

Some airlines sell bike boxes at the airport, but most bike shops give them away. Fitting your bike into a box requires a few simple steps and only takes about 15 minutes:

1 Loosen the stem bolt and turn the handlebars 90°; loosen the clamp bolt(s) and twist the handlebars as pictured.

2 Remove the pedals (use a 15mm spanner, turning each the opposite way to how you pedal), wheels and seat post and saddle (don't forget to mark its height before removing it).

3 Undo the rear derailleur bolt and tape it to the inside of the chainstay. There's no need to undo the derailleur cable. You can remove the chain (it will make reassembly easier) but it isn't necessary.

4 Cut up some spare cardboard and tape it beneath the chainwheel to prevent the teeth from penetrating the floor of the box and being damaged.

5 Remove the quick-release skewers from the wheels and wrap a rag (or two) around the cluster so it won't get damaged or damage anything else.

If you run your tyres at very high pressure (above 100psi), you should partially deflate them – on most bikes this won't be necessary.

6 Place the frame in the box, so it rests on the chainwheel and forks – you might want to place another couple of layers of cardboard underneath the forks.

Most boxes will be too short to allow the front pannier racks to remain on the bike; if so, remove them. The rear rack should fit while still on the bike, but may require the seat stay bolts to be undone and pushed forward.

Packing for Air Travel

Side View

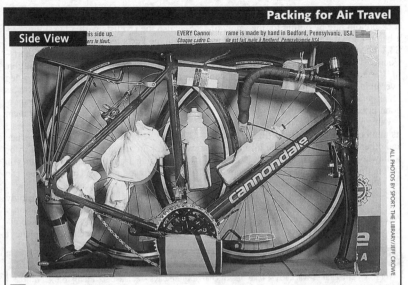

EVERY Cannondale frame is made by hand in Bedford, Pennsylvania, USA.
Chaque cadre Cannondale est fait main à Bedford, Pennsylvanie USA

This side up.
Vers le Haut.

ALL PHOTOS BY SPORT: THE LIBRARY/JEFF CROWE

7 Place the wheels beside the frame, on the side opposite the chainwheel. Keep the wheels and frame separate by inserting a piece of cardboard between them and tying the wheels to the frame (to stop them moving around and scratching the frame).

8 Slot the saddle and seatpost, your helmet, tools and any other bits and pieces (eg, tent, sleeping bag) into the vacant areas. Wrap the skewers, chain and other loose bike bits in

newspaper and place them in the box. Add cardboard or newspaper packing to any areas where metal is resting on metal.

9 Seal the box with tape and write your name, address and flight details on several sides.

Now all you need to do is strap your panniers together and either take them with you as carry-on luggage or check them in.

Top View

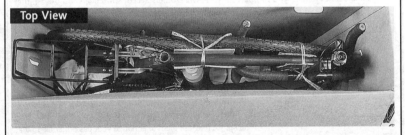

Bike Bags

If you're planning on travelling between regions via train, plane or bus then consider taking a bike bag. The simplest form of zippered bike bag has no padding built into it, is made of Cordura or nylon, and can be rolled up and put on your rear pannier rack and unfurled when you need to travel again.

Some of the smaller ones require you to remove both wheels, the front pannier racks, pedals and seatpost to fit inside the bag. However, these make for (relatively) easy and inconspicuous train, plane or bus transfers so the extra effort is worthwhile.

You may decide to pay more than the rock-bottom fare by opting for the safety of a better-known travel agent. Firms such as STA Travel, which has offices worldwide; Council Travel in the USA; or Travel CUTS in Canada are not going to disappear overnight, leaving you clutching a receipt for a nonexistent ticket, and they do offer good prices to most destinations.

Once you have your ticket, write down its number, together with the flight number and other details, and keep the information somewhere separate. If the ticket is lost or stolen, this will help you get a replacement. It's sensible to buy travel insurance as early as possible. If you buy it the week before you fly, you may find, for example, that you're not covered for delays to your flight caused by industrial action.

Cyclists with Special Needs

See also the Cyclists with a Disability section in the Facts for the Cyclist chapter.

If you have special needs of any sort – you're vegetarian, taking young children, terrified of flying or have broken a leg (Heaven forbid!) – let the airline know as soon as possible so they can make arrangements accordingly. You should remind them when you reconfirm your booking (at least 72 hours before departure) and again when you check in at the airport. It may also be worth ringing around the airlines before you make your booking to find out how they can handle your particular needs.

Airports and airlines can be surprisingly helpful, but they do need advance warning. Most international airports will provide escorts from the check-in desk to the plane if

Cycle-Friendly Airlines

Not too many airlines will carry a bike free of charge these days – at least according to their official policy. Most airlines regard the bike as part of your checked luggage. Carriers working the routes to Australia from Europe, Asia and the Pacific usually allow 20kg of checked luggage (excluding carry-on), so the weight of your bike and bags shouldn't exceed this. If you're over the limit, technically you're liable for excess-baggage charges.

Carriers flying routes to Australia from or through North America use a different system. Passengers are generally allowed two pieces of luggage, each of which must not exceed 32kg. Excess baggage fees are charged for additional pieces, rather than for excess weight. On some airlines a bike may be counted as one of your two pieces; others charge a set fee for carrying a bike, which may then be carried in addition to your two other pieces. Check whether these fees are paid for the whole journey, each way or per leg.

Some airlines require you to box your bike, while others accept soft covers, or just ask that you turn the handlebars, remove the pedals and cover the chain. Check this policy before getting to the airport; only a few airlines sell sturdy boxes at the check-in counter.

When we looked into the policies of different carriers, we found that not only does the story sometimes change depending on who you talk to – and how familiar they are with the company's policy – but the official line is not necessarily adhered to at the check-in counter. If a company representative or agent reassures you that your bike travels for free, ask them to annotate your passenger file to that effect. If your flight is not too crowded, the check-in staff are often lenient with the excess charges, particularly with items such as bikes. The times when you are most likely to incur excess baggage charges are on full flights and, of course, if you inconvenience the check-in staff. If you suspect you may be over the limit, increase your chances of avoiding charges by checking in early and being well organised, friendly and polite – a smile and a 'Thankyou' can go a long way!

DON HATCHER

needed, and there should be ramps, lifts, accessible toilets and reachable phones. Aircraft toilets, on the other hand, may present a problem; travellers should discuss this with the airline at an early stage and, if necessary, with their doctor.

Hearing-impaired travellers can ask for airport and in-flight announcements to be written down for them.

Children under two travel for 10% of the standard fare (or free, on some airlines), as long as they don't occupy a seat. They don't get a baggage allowance either. Children aged between two and 12 can usually occupy a seat for half to two-thirds of the full fare and do get a baggage allowance.

Departure Tax

Departure tax (equivalent to A$30) is prepaid (and noted) with your ticket purchase. Children under 12 are exempt.

Round-the-World Tickets

Round-the-world (RTW) tickets are often real bargains. They are usually put together by a combination of two airlines and permit you to fly anywhere you want on their route systems so long as you do not backtrack. There may be restrictions on how many stops you are permitted and usually the tickets are valid for 90 days up to a year. The cost of a South Pacific RTW ticket including Australia typically starts around US$2100.

An alternative type of RTW ticket is one put together by a travel agent using a combination of discounted tickets. A good UK agent like Trailfinders can put together interesting London-to-London RTW combinations that include Australia for £800 to £1200. The cheapest times to depart the UK are February to early April and October–November.

Also worth investigating is the Global Explorer – a RTW ticket put together by Qantas, British Airways, American Airlines and several others. The number of stops on this one is normally limited to 15.

The UK

Trailfinders in west London produces a lavishly illustrated brochure which includes air fare details. Look in the Sunday papers and *Exchange & Mart* for ads. Also look out for the free magazines widely available in London – start by looking outside the main train and underground stations. STA Travel also has branches in the UK.

Most British travel agents are registered with the Association of British Travel Agents (ABTA). If you bought your ticket from an ABTA-registered agent which then goes out of business, ABTA will guarantee a refund or an alternative. Unregistered 'bucket shops' are riskier but also sometimes cheaper.

Trailfinders (☎ 020-7938 3939) at 194 Kensington High St, London W8 6BD, and STA Travel (☎ 020-7581 4132) at 86 Old Brompton Rd, London SW7 3LQ, and 117 Euston Rd, London NW1 2SX (☎ 020-7465 0484), are good, reliable agents for cheap tickets.

Standard direct fares from London to Sydney or Perth are around £376/688 one way/return during the low season, plus tax (£30/45). High-season fares are typically around £399/740 plus tax.

From Australia the cheaper fares are around A$949/1515 to London and other European capitals in the low season, and $A1049/1739 in the high season.

Continental Europe

Frankfurt is the major arrival and departure point for Australian flights, with connections to other European centres.

There are many bucket shops on mainland Europe where you can buy discounted air tickets. The international student and discount travel agencies STA and Council Travel also have a number of offices in various European countries. In Amsterdam, make sure your travel agent has an 'SGR' certificate or you may never see your money again.

Standard Frankfurt–Sydney fares are around DM1800/2000 return plus tax (around DM100) in low/high season – though you can find cheaper fares, depending on the airline. Expect to pay around DM1500/1300 one way, plus tax (around DM60).

The USA & Canada

A variety of connections cross the Pacific from Los Angeles or San Francisco to Australia, including direct flights, flights via New Zealand, island-hopping routes and more circuitous Pacific-rim routes via nations in Asia. Qantas, Air New Zealand and

United Airlines fly USA–Australia. An interesting option from the east coast is the Japan Airlines flight via Japan.

The *New York Times*, the *LA Times*, the *Chicago Tribune*, the *San Francisco Examiner*, the Toronto *Globe & Mail* and the *Vancouver Sun* produce weekly travel sections in which you'll find any number of travel agents' ads. *Travel Unlimited* magazine publishes details of the cheapest air fares and courier possibilities for destinations all over the world from the USA. Council Travel and STA Travel have offices in major cities nationwide. Travel CUTS has offices in major Canadian cities. Qantas, Air New Zealand, Japan Airlines and Canadian Airlines International all fly from Canada to Australia.

You can typically get a one-way/return ticket from the west coast for US$849/999 in the low season, US$874/1028 in the high season (Australian summer – over Christmas), both excluding tax; or from the east coast for US$1064/1199 in the low season, or US$1140/1450 in the high season, plus tax.

Airfares out of Vancouver will be similar to those from the US west coast. From Toronto, fares go from around C$1480/1820 during the low season and C$1800/2135 in the high season.

Return fares from Australia include: San Francisco for A$1589/A$1895 low season/high season; New York for A$1845/2205; and Vancouver for A$1639/2049.

If Pacific-island hopping is your aim, check out the airlines of Pacific island nations, some of which have good deals on indirect routings. Qantas can give you Fiji or Tahiti along the way, while Air New Zealand can offer both these stopovers and the Cook Islands as well.

New Zealand

Air New Zealand, Ansett and Qantas operate a network of trans-Tasman flights linking Auckland, Wellington and Christchurch in New Zealand (NZ) with most major Australian gateway cities. STA Travel and Flight Centres International are popular travel agents in NZ.

For a full-economy 21-day advance purchase Auckland–Sydney fare, you're looking at around NZ$450/600 one way/return (must return in 30 days) in the low season and NZ$450/700 in the high season – it costs a little more to Melbourne. There is a lot of competition on these routes, so there is bound to be some good discounting going on.

Depending on which airline you choose, cheap fares to NZ from Europe are via the USA or Asia. A straightforward London–Auckland return bucket-shop ticket costs around £695 in the low season, or £998 in high season. With a RTW ticket (from around £800), you can make Australia a stop before continuing on to NZ.

Asia

Ticket discounting is widespread in Asia, particularly in Singapore, Hong Kong, Bangkok and Penang. A lot of fly-by-nights occupy the Asian ticketing scene so a little care is required. STA Travel, which is reliable, has branches in Hong Kong, Tokyo, Singapore, Bangkok and Kuala Lumpur.

Asian routes have been particularly caught up in the capacity shortages on flights to Australia. Flights between Hong Kong and Australia are notoriously heavily booked while flights to or from Bangkok and Singapore are often part of the longer Europe-Australia route so they are also sometimes full. Plan ahead. For more information on South-East Asian travel, and travel on to Australia, see Lonely Planet's *South-East Asia on a shoestring*.

Low-season return fares from Japan are typically between ¥60,000 and ¥73,000; in the high season, expect to pay around ¥102,000 to ¥130,000.

South Africa

A number of direct flights leave each week between Africa and Australia, but they only travel between Perth and Harare or Johannesburg. Fares vary, but from Perth to Johannesburg expect to pay up to A$1650 return in the low season (excluding tax) with Qantas or Malaysian Airlines. Air Mauritius offers the cheapest flights (A$747/1156 one way/return), which include at least a day stopover in Mauritius.

Other airlines that connect southern Africa and Australia include Singapore Airlines, South African Airways and Air Zimbabwe.

From East Africa the options are to fly via Mauritius or Zimbabwe, or via the Indian subcontinent and on to South-East Asia, then connect to Australia.

ORGANISED TOURS

Several companies around the world (mostly US-based) run organised tours to Australia – some of them combining cycling with other adventure activities such as canoeing, bushwalking and diving. The Internet is a good place to look for tour companies – sites such as Cybercyclery (💻 www.cycling.org) have hundreds of touring links. See Organised Rides in the Getting Around chapter for listings of Australian-based tour operators.

Texas-based Travel Innovations (☎ 512-443 5393, 💻 www.io.com/~jmc12), 2711 Market Garden, Austin, TX 78745, offers five-day mountain-biking (camping) trips for US$650, including food; and six-day on-road tours (with indoor accommodation) for around US$1200.

Multi-activity trips, combining mountain biking, canoeing, kayaking, diving and walking (at a moderately easy level) in Queensland are offered by Outer Edge Expeditions (☎ 800-322 5235, 💻 www.outer-edge.com), 4830 Mason Rd, Howell, MI 48843-9697; and The World Outside (☎ 800-480 8483, 💻 www.theworldoutside.com), 2840 Wilderness Place, #F, Boulder, CO 80301. You'll pay around US$1675/1398 for 14/11 days.

In the UK, the Cyclists' Touring Club (CTC; ☎ 1483-417 217, 💻 www.ctc.org.uk), Cotterell House, 69 Meadow, Godalming, Surrey GU7 3HS, coordinates a large number of independently organised, well-priced tours to around-the-world destinations (including Australia), led by experienced volunteer members.

Getting Around

AIR
Domestic Air Services
Although Australia's airline industry is deregulated, there are only two main domestic carriers: Qantas (☎ 13 1313, ⊑ www.qantas.com.au) and Ansett (☎ 13 1300, ⊑ www.ansett.com.au). From time to time, new airlines appear to compete on the popular routes, bringing prices down. Currently, two budget airlines, Impulse (☎ 13 1381, ⊑ www.impulseairlines.com.au) and Virgin Blue (☎ 13 6789, ⊑ www.virginblue.com.au) have begun flying the main east coast routes, but it remains to be seen whether they will become major players.

A number of smaller companies fly between regional centres and link with capital cities. These are affiliated (and booked) with either Qantas or Ansett.

The full-economy fare for Qantas and Ansett flights between Brisbane and Melbourne is $513; from Sydney to Melbourne it's $375; Cairns to Sydney is $667; Sydney to Perth is $806; Adelaide to Perth is $648; and Melbourne to Hobart is $289. Three-week advance fares are readily available and usually much cheaper, for example Melbourne to Sydney costs $289 return.

However, you can almost always buy tickets for well below full fare. Increased competition has encouraged the major airlines to slash instant-purchase fares for popular east-coast routes (Sydney to Melbourne fares, for example, are available from $143 return). At short notice it's sometimes cheaper to buy a return ticket on special than a one-way regular economy fare. Other special deals (often with conditions attached)

Warning
As this book was researched before the introduction of the GST (Goods and Services Tax; introduced in July 2000), prices listed may not include the 10% increase imposed on goods and services, including domestic transport, accommodation and prepared food. See Taxes & Refunds in the Facts for the Cyclist chapter for more information on how the GST may affect your budget.

and advance purchase fares are available through travel agents or exclusively through the airlines' Web sites. It's worth checking prices with agents as well as through the airlines direct to find the best fare.

Impulse Airlines one-way fares include: Sydney to Melbourne $167, Sydney to Brisbane $179, Melbourne to Brisbane $300.

Air Passes
Both Qantas and Ansett offer air passes, which offer substantial savings on full-economy fares if you're planning to take several flights within Australia. However, with heavy discounting of many point-to-point fares, the difference may not be all that much.

Essentially, an air pass is at least three or four pre-booked flights, so it's only useful if you know in advance where and when you want to fly.

Qantas' Boomerang Pass can only be purchased overseas. The Qantas Backpacker Pass is sold in Australia. Check the Ansett and Qantas Web sites for international telephone numbers, or to email an inquiry.

Carrying Your Bicycle
Both Ansett and Qantas allow one piece of checked luggage (with maximum weights of 20kg and 32kg, respectively). Unless your total luggage falls within that limit, your bike may be charged an additional $10 – at the airline's discretion.

Ansett will take bikes unboxed, but they must be partially disassembled: handlebars turned; pedals removed; front wheel removed and attached to the rear; and chain covered. Qantas requires the bike to be boxed ('bike packs' cost $15 at the airport, or bring your own); see the boxed text 'Packing for Air Travel' in the Getting There & Away chapter.

Impulse carries bikes intact, requiring only that the tyres are slightly deflated. However, there's no guarantee that bikes will travel on the same service, particularly if there are several. Total luggage allowance is 20kg; excess baggage is charged at $1/kg at the discretion of the check-in staff.

Virgin Blue carries bikes as freight – they must be boxed securely and checked in at the airport's cargo section (follow the signs at the terminal) at least one hour before departure. If your bike and luggage falls within the 20kg limit, there's no charge – otherwise excess-baggage charges apply (around $5/kg).

Domestic Tax

Flights through Sydney may be subject to a small additional charge as a result of the Federal Government's airport-noise levy on airlines using the airport ($3.40). Other airports charge 'improvements' taxes from time to time (eg, Cairns airport charges $9.25).

BUS

Bus travel is generally the cheapest way to get from A to B. Buses go to areas that trains don't and, although the usual policy on carrying bikes is 'at the driver's discretion', outside of peak periods it's generally not too hard to get your bike around.

Greyhound Pioneer (☎ 13 2030, ☐ www.greyhound.com.au), with services throughout mainland Australia, and McCafferty's (☎ 13 1499, ☐ www.mccaffertys.com.au), which operates in all mainland states except Western Australia (WA), are the main national carriers. Tasmanian Redline Coaches (☎ 03-6336 1444 from interstate or ☎ 1300-360 000 in Tasmania) and TWT Tassielink (☎ 1300-300 520, ☐ www.tigerline.com.au) are the main operators in Tasmania.

Other bus companies cover specific areas. Some, such as V/Line in Victoria and Westrail in WA, are run by the state's rail operator; others are privately owned. Details of

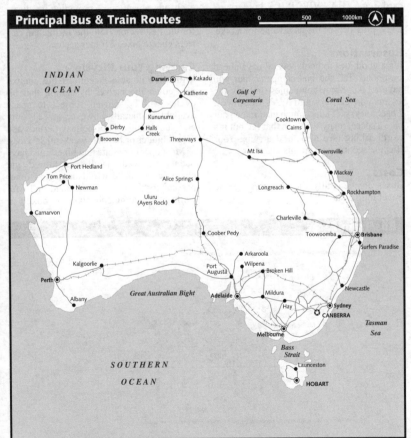

Principal Bus & Train Routes

relevant operators are given in the rides chapters of this book.

Bus Passes

Bus passes allow more flexibility and can be cheaper than a series of express (or point-to-point) tickets. It's worth checking prices if you're planning on doing several bus journeys.

Greyhound's kilometre passes are valid for one year and don't have a set itinerary. The minimum is a 2000km pass ($233) which enables you to travel 2000km anywhere (eg, Brisbane to Cairns); they go up in increments of 1000km. It costs either $22 or 10% of the pass price (whichever is more) to carry a bike. McCafferty's also offers kilometre passes to concession- or discount-card (eg, YHA, VIP, ISIC) holders. A 2000km pass costs $205, 5000km costs $427, plus 10% of the pass value for a bike.

Reservations

It's a good idea to book several days ahead by phone. Tell the bus company that you have a bike. Some companies (notably the Tasmanian carriers and WA's Southwest Coachlines) will fairly much guarantee your bike a space; many won't go that far, but it's worth asking (see also the Carrying Your Bicycle section later in this chapter).

Costs

Buses are generally the cheapest way to travel long distances.

For examples of Greyhound adult fares see the table 'Bus/Train Fares'; McCafferty's fares for the same journeys are slightly cheaper.

Both Greyhound and McCafferty's offer 10% discounts on express tickets and passes for YHA, VIP, ISIC and seniors or pension cards (20% for Australian seniors and students, and children). Discounts of up to 35% are also available (limited seats) on advance-purchase fares.

On Greyhound express tickets, bikes are charged $22 per sector (a sector can be any length – Melbourne to Sydney or Melbourne to Cairns – as long as it's all in one stint). If you book several sectors at the same time with McCafferty's they charge bikes $27 for the first sector and $11 for each subsequent one – providing it's disassembled. Fully assembled bikes cost $49 for the first sector. Both the Tasmanian carriers charge bikes $10 per sector.

Carrying Your Bicycle

With a few notable exceptions, bus companies cover themselves by stating that bicycles will be carried subject to space available. Generally, however, space is only an issue during school-holiday periods and on commuter or popular weekend services.

Most operators state that bikes must have pedals removed, handlebars turned and chains covered, to avoid damaging other passengers' luggage. Greyhound and McCafferty's recommend bikes be boxed or

Bus/Train Fares

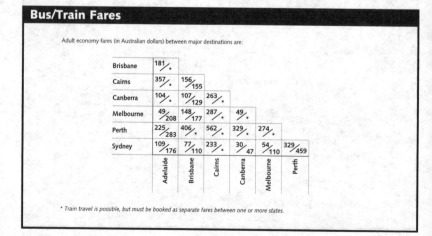

Adult economy fares (in Australian dollars) between major destinations are:

	Adelaide	Brisbane	Cairns	Canberra	Melbourne	Perth
Brisbane	181/*					
Cairns	357/*	156/155				
Canberra	104/*	107/129	263/*			
Melbourne	49/208	148/177	287/*	49/*		
Perth	225/283	406/*	562/*	329/*	274/*	
Sydney	109/176	77/110	233/*	30/47	54/110	329/459

* Train travel is possible, but must be booked as separate fares between one or more states.

wrapped. Some drivers may take your bike fully assembled (McCafferty's charges substantially more to do so; $49 for the first sector) but make sure you have the requisite tools to dismantle it quickly if required. See the Costs section earlier for bike fares.

The two main Tasmanian operators carry bikes intact (on smaller coaches, wheels may need to be removed), and virtually guarantee your bike's passage – providing you're at the depot an hour (Tasmanian Redline) or 30 minutes (TWT Tassielink) before departure.

TRAIN

Train services fall into three categories: state-specific country trains; interstate services; and metropolitan commuter trains (the latter are covered under Local Transport at the end of this chapter). State rail bodies also run buses to supplement the train network.

State Services Unfortunately, while train travel would seem to be a perfect partner to cycling, most government-run state rail systems in Australia pull in way under potential. Gone are the days when bikes could be wheeled straight into the guard's van: nowadays, most state rail services have limited luggage space and, despite the odd sympathetic staffer, the regulations in some states are about as bike-friendly as a head wind on a busy highway.

You'll find these regulations outlined under the Carrying Your Bicycle section later in this chapter; further details of relevant services are in the regional chapters.

Interstate Services Countrylink (☎ 13 2232, 🖳 www.countrylink.nsw.gov.au), run by the State Rail Authority in NSW, operates the XPT interstate services on the east coast between Melbourne, Sydney and Brisbane. However provision for bikes is limited (see Carrying Your Bicycle).

Private operator Great Southern Railway (☎ 13 2147, 🖳 www.gsr.com.au) runs three major interstate services: the *Overlander*, between Melbourne and Adelaide; the *Indian Pacific*, between Sydney and Perth via Adelaide; and the *Ghan*, between Adelaide and Alice Springs. Aimed at the tourist market, these services are more customer-focussed and have plenty of luggage space.

Classes

Most state rail services have either all economy, or economy and first-class carriages. First-class sleepers are also available on Countrylink's XPT overnight services.

Classes available on Great Southern Railway services and most long-distance services in Queensland are: economy ('coach class'); economy sleeper ('holiday class'); and 1st-class sleeper – which may include meals.

Reservations

It's generally a good idea to book state rail travel in advance, especially if you're travelling during school holidays, although reservations are not taken on all services.

It's mandatory to make advance bookings for bikes on Countrylink (regional NSW and east-coast interstate services) and Westrail (WA) trains, but bookings are not required on QR (Queensland) or V/Line (Victoria) services.

It's advisable to book on Great Southern Railways services well in advance (nine months during wild flower season, from August to October). However, outside peak season, you may still get a seat a couple of days ahead.

Costs

For adult economy fares see the table 'Bus/Train Fares' earlier. Sleeper fares generally cost about double an economy fare, eg, Countrylink adult fares from Sydney to either Melbourne or Brisbane are $110, while a 1st-class sleeper costs $231. Bikes cost $11.

On Great Southern Railway services, bikes are charged $30/40 boxed/unboxed per sector. Regional chapters have details of relevant state services. See also Carrying Your Bicycle.

Carrying Your Bicycle

Make sure you're familiar with the rules for carrying bikes on the train service that you're using. It's a good idea to arrive early at the station and, if you can, load your bike yourself – train staff are not generally known for careful handling.

Various rail services' requirements for carrying bikes are:

NSW The State Rail Authority's Countrylink (☎ 13 2232) operates regional state services and the interstate XPT. Each service has space for only three bikes or surfboards, and will *only* take boxed bikes (boxes are provided or bring your own – don't even try travelling without one). Bikes are charged $11 and must be booked in advance.

Queensland QR (☎ 13 2232 in Qld or ☎ 1800-806 468 from interstate, 🖳 qroti.bit.net.au/traveltrain/) has space for bikes on *most* services. Front wheels and pedals must be removed and handlebars turned; and they're loaded by rail staff. Bikes are charged 20% of the adult fare.

Victoria V/Line (☎ 13 6196, 🖳 www.vline.vic.gov.au) services take bikes intact. Older 'locomotive' trains take up to six bikes in luggage vans; the newer 'sprinters' take two per carriage. Except for peak services, there's generally space, although V/Line advises booking ahead on ☎ 9619 2338. Bikes are charged $3 one way.

WA Westrail (☎ 13 1053 in WA or ☎ 1800-099 150 from interstate) train services have little or no capacity for carrying bikes: they are banned from all services except the Australind between Bunbury and Perth (on which they are merely discouraged) – it has room for two only. Bikes (carried intact) are charged $8 one way.

Australia-wide – Great Southern Railway services have plenty of space for bicycles and will take them unboxed ($40 per sector) or boxed ($30).

See the boxed text 'Tandeming in Australia' in the Facts for the Cyclist chapter for details of transporting tandems on trains.

CAR

Driving is generally easy in Australia: although distances are great, the roads are well signposted and in good condition in the main areas – although dirt roads are common once you get into quieter rural and the remote countryside of the 'Outback'. Petrol (gasoline) is reasonably expensive at about 95 cents a litre (US$3.60 a gallon).

Australians drive on the left side of the road. The general speed limit in built up areas is 50km/h or 60km/h and on the open highway it's usually 100km/h or 110km/h. Serious campaigns against speeding and drink-driving have made Australians less likely to indulge in such behaviour (you'll risk a fine and possible loss of licence if you do), although they're far from eliminated.

Beware of theft from cars, particularly in isolated parking areas such as those in national parks. Don't leave valuables in the car and be careful about leaving your bike inside while you go off walking.

Car Rental

The many rental companies in Australia range from the major ones such as Budget, Hertz, Avis and Thrifty, with offices in most major towns, to smaller, local operators and the 'rent-a-wreck' companies that rent out older, cheaper cars. One day's hire of a small car from a major company costs around $51/day, plus $19.80 insurance to reduce the excess liability from $2200 to $275, and covers windscreen and tyre damage.

Be aware that if you are travelling on dirt roads you will probably not be covered by insurance – and you should know exactly what your liability is in the event of a crash.

To hire a car, visitors from non-English speaking countries require an international drivers licence. The same is preferred even if you're from an English-speaking country, but a normal licence (at least 12 months old) is accepted. Some rental companies have minimum-age restrictions. Credit cards are useful – without one, you may need to leave a large cash bond with the hire company.

Be aware that hire companies may restrict the attachment of bike carriers to the car (read any fine print carefully!).

BOAT

The main boat travel in Australia is between Victoria and Tasmania. See the Gateway Cities section in the Tasmania chapter for details of the *Devil Cat* and the *Spirit of Tasmania* services.

Regional chapters also have details of relevant short ferry trips. Bikes are usually carried free of charge or for a small fee.

LOCAL TRANSPORT

The metropolitan train services in many of Australia's capital cities are handy for getting quickly through suburban sprawl to better cycling country. Bikes are not carried on metropolitan buses or trams.

Services in Melbourne, Perth, Brisbane and Sydney carry bikes either for free or for a concession fare. The main restrictions are during commuter peak periods. More information about local transport is in the regional chapters.

ORGANISED RIDES

A number of guided cycling tours are available around Australia. They are generally small-group, set-itinerary affairs, though some offer customised tours. Most include indoor accommodation, vehicle support, bike hire (optional) and some or all meals. There are also some excellent tours run by the bicycle advocacy organisations. These are typically much larger, involve camping and represent excellent value – they're also suitable for families.

A list of tour operators follows – it's also worth surfing the net for others (try 🖳 www .jub.com.au/cycling/ for starters):

Boomerang Bicycle Tours (☎ 02-9890 1996, 🖳 www.ozemail.com.au/~ozbike/) PO Box 6543, Parramatta, NSW 2150. Runs discovery and post-Olympic day tours of Sydney and supported tours of up to seven days in NSW and Victoria (daily distances tailored – 15km to 140km), from $125 to $225 per day, including meals, guides and indoor accommodation.

Terry's Cycling Adventures (☎ 0412-603 831, Ⓔ terrycycling@shoal.net.au) PO Box 258, Nowra, NSW 2541. Runs fully supported, guided tours between major cities in south-eastern Australia. The cost of the two- to 15-day tours (averaging 85km/day or more) cost around $100 per day, including meals and indoor accommodation.

Remote Outback Cycle Tours (☎ 08-9244 4614, 🖳 www.cycletours.com.au) PO Box 1179, West Leederville, WA 6901. Runs outback tours combining cycling with four-wheel driving. Four- to 15-day tours are priced from $450 to $1390.

Tasmanian Expeditions (☎ 1800-030 230, 🖳 www.tasmanianexpeditions.com.au). Runs all-inclusive four- to six-day tours from $545 to $1485 with camping, hostel and B&B accommodation options (20km to 60km/day). Walking and rafting options are also available.

Silver City Bush Treadlers (☎/fax 08-8088 3764) 231 Argent St, Broken Hill, NSW 2880. Runs a two-week supported outback mountain-bike tour around July each year. It costs around $700 including meals (fundraising for the Royal Flying Doctor Service), with accommodation from camping to pubs (BYO bike and tent).

Bicycle Victoria (☎ 03-9328 3000, 🖳 www .bv.com.au) GPO Box 1961R, Melbourne, Victoria 3001. Famous for its Great Victorian Bike Ride, a nine-day supported ride held annually in early December, with around 3000 participants. This ride costs around $500, including meals (BYO bike and tent). Other events are held during the year. Similar rides are also organised by Bicycle NSW (☎ 02-9283 5200, 🖳 www.bic yclensw.org.au), PO Box 272, Sydney 2000; some other state groups organise smaller-scale events.

New South Wales

Bigger than France and the UK combined – indeed, bigger than Texas – Australia's most populous state provides cyclists with a rich choice of destinations and a fascinating range of terrain. The state capital, Sydney, is internationally renowned for its vibrancy and beautiful setting on Port Jackson. The 2000km-long coastline includes sparkling beaches and lively towns. West, the Great Dividing Range separates the populated coastal fringe from the scattered towns and villages of the New South Wales (NSW) interior. The range includes World Heritage rainforests, elevated farmlands and, in the Snowy Mountains, alpine wilderness and peaks rising above 2000m. Just north of the 'Snowies' is the Australian Capital Territory (ACT) and the national capital, Canberra. West of the divide are farmlands of one type or another, national parks showcasing Aboriginal endurance and culture, and almost unimaginable light and space.

HISTORY

Aboriginal people inhabited the area now known as NSW for at least 50,000 years before the arrival of Europeans. It's thought they comprised about 60 language groups, and estimates of their numbers vary anywhere from 300,000 to one million.

Earlier explorers had long since charted the west and north coasts of Australia (then known as New Holland) when, in 1770, English navigator James Cook landed on the east coast, just south of present-day central Sydney at Botany Bay. Eighteen years later, Arthur Phillip and the First Fleet landed at Port Jackson, just north, to establish the British penal colony of NSW.

It's believed there were about 3000 Aboriginal people in the Sydney region at this time. They belonged to three main language groups – the Ku-ring-gai, the Dharawal and the Dharug – encompassing several dialects and subgroups. Sydney Cove itself, where Phillip's fleet landed, was the estate of the Eora people.

Early attempts at farming were unsuccessful, and the colony remained dependent on infrequent supply fleets from Britain. NSW was a harsh place. Colonists, many of whom were convicts displaced from their homeland,

in turn set about dispossessing Aboriginal people. The colonial 'fathers' of the time – officers of the NSW Corps – were more interested in lining their own pockets than good governance, and the era was characterised by harsh discipline and punctuated with various uprisings. It wasn't until Lachlan Macquarie began his term as governor in 1810 that things improved. It was during his tenure that colonists pushed westwards over the Blue Mountains to the broad-acre pasture and crop lands that would support the maturing colony – and make some of its settlers very rich.

Transportation of convicts to NSW ceased by 1850. Meanwhile, new colonies in present-day Victoria and South Australia were carving off areas of NSW, whose boundaries once covered more than half the continent (the state's present-day size accounts for little more than 10% of the total area of Australia).

The gold rushes of the 1850s and later 19th century secured NSW's future. They attracted new migrants, many of whom remained to build the population and labour base. With Federation, on 1 January 1901, when the various Australian colonies joined as a nation, the colony of NSW became a state.

The 20th century saw NSW maintain its position as the dominant Australian state in terms of population and economic activity. An extended period of economic growth began during WWII, while austere periods in both the 1970s and early 1990s were followed by booms, the late '90s version stimulated in no small part by preparations for the Sydney 2000 Olympic Games.

NATURAL HISTORY

The Great Dividing Range runs most of the length of Australia's east coast and incorporates many of the state's natural highlights, including the popular resort area of the Blue Mountains, west of Sydney. The Snowy Mountains in the south include the continent's highest peak, Mt Kosciuszko (2228m).

The eastern side of the range forms a generally steep escarpment, usually heavily forested. Most of the ancient range's peaks have been worn down to plateaus. The western side is less steep and dwindles into a series of foothills and valleys, which provide fertile farmland. From here west, the state is almost entirely flat.

NSW's native vegetation is enormously diverse, including dry plains, coastal heath and temperate and subtropical rainforests. Eucalypt forest is especially common, towering above banksias, grevilleas, bottlebrushes and boronias.

Despite extensive clearing for agriculture, vast areas of vegetation remain little changed. Wollemi National Park, less than 100km north-west of Sydney, contains the state's largest officially recognised wilderness area – 3610 sq km. It's so wild, in fact, that in 1994 an unknown tree, the Wollemi pine, was discovered (see the boxed text 'The Tree That Time Forgot' later in this chapter).

Aborigines' land-management practices prior to European settlement – especially undergrowth burning to encourage feed for mammals – gave early Sydney a park-like appearance. The dense scrub that's common today was largely absent; it was possible to gallop a horse through the bush.

If you want to see a kangaroo or wallaby you won't be disappointed – at some picnic and camping grounds you literally have to shoo them off (don't get aggressive about it – they're powerful animals!). Cheeky and nocturnal, brush-tailed possums are the great urban survivors; they're are a common sight, even in cities. Koalas, echidnas and platypuses are less so, but an encounter with any one is not out of the question.

The NSW bush is home to some of the world's most raucous bird species, such as kookaburras and various species of parrot, as well as several species of venomous snake. In spite of popular perceptions, they're rarely aggressive – if you do see a snake, simply stand back and enjoy the sight of a magnificent predator; 99% of the time the snake will leave you well alone.

CLIMATE

As a general rule, NSW is hotter the further north you go and drier the further west. The coastal strip, especially in central and southern parts, is generally temperate, although temperatures can get uncomfortably hot in midsummer, especially in the north. On the Great Dividing Range, expect milder summer temperatures and cool to cold winters. The Snowy Mountains are generally snow-covered for only a few months of the year. West of the divide, summer days can be dangerously hot and cycling is probably best avoided, especially in the far west.

Rainfall also varies according to region, with annual averages generally highest along the coast and lowest in the far west. Late summer to early winter is the wettest period on the coastal fringe.

Prevailing winds are from the east in summer and west in winter, although the eastward march of cold fronts can produce cooler southerlies and south-westerlies at any time. Close to the coast, summer north-easterlies often provide relief on warm days.

INFORMATION
Maps
NSW is covered by Auslig's 1:250,000-scale Natmap series; these have sufficient contour detail for touring and are the most practical scale. The only drawback is many maps haven't been revised for some years. Auslig's 1:100,000 Natmap series, with more contour detail, are available for the eastern two-thirds of the state. They're available at map retailers or by credit card from Auslig (☎ 6201 4300 or ☎ 1800-800 173, ℮ mapsales@auslig.gov.au). In Sydney, Mapworld (☎ 9966 5770), the corner of Willoughby Rd and Albany St, Crows Nest, is the best map shop.

Best for mountain-bike rides are the topographic maps (1:50,000; $7.50 each) produced by the Land and Property Information office (LPI). Both offices, in central Sydney (☎ 9228 6315), 23–33 Bridge St, and Bathurst (☎ 6332 8200), take credit card orders; the Sydney office sells maps over the counter. The maps are also available from map retailers.

The NSW motoring organisation NRMA (☎ 13 2132) publishes a fine series of road-touring maps that cover the state in varying scales (but have no contour detail). Regularly updated and with a town index, they're free to NRMA members, $5 to nonmembers.

Sydney-based Cartoscope (☎ 9929 7431, 🖳 www.cartoscope.com.au) produces a series of free tourist maps available in visitor centres. They cover the NSW east coast only, but include useful town maps of many smaller centres described in this book. Unlike some Auslig maps, they're generally up-to-date – a good (cheap!) resource.

Books
Lonely Planet's *New South Wales* is a useful supplement to this guide.

Fewer NSW-specific cycling books exist. Amanda Lulham's *Discovering NSW & Canberra's Bike & Walking Paths* has good general coverage of the bikepaths in and around Sydney, Canberra and 11 regional centres. Sven Klinge's *Cycling the Bush:*

100 Rides in NSW is a useful mountain-bike resource.

For excellent reading, *1788* is a collection of the writings of First Fleet officer Watkin Tench, a keen observer of the colony's earliest days; Eric Rolls' *A Million Wild Acres* is a remarkable examination of NSW's natural history.

Information Sources
The state cycling advocacy body, Bicycle NSW (☎ 9283 5200, ℮ info@bicyclensw.org.au), Level 2, 209 Castlereagh St, Sydney 2000, can provide information on cycling routes throughout the state and direct you towards touring clubs. Find listings of touring clubs and organised rides in the bimonthly *Australian Cyclist* magazine.

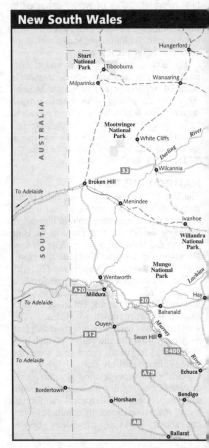

New South Wales

For budget travellers, the YHA Membership and Travel Centre (☎ 9261 1111, 🖳 www.yha.org.au), 422 Kent St, Sydney, is a good starting point.

GATEWAY CITIES
Sydney

The state capital is the best place to begin your NSW travels. Australia's oldest and largest settlement is a vibrant city built around one of the world's most spectacular harbours – more correctly called Port Jackson. The harbour, its opera house and bridge are known worldwide; so too is the fact that Sydney hosted the 2000 Olympic Games. Sydney's lesser-known attractions include lively nightlife and great food; beautiful beaches north, south and east of the city; and superb national parks within the city and on its fringe.

Outwardly, Sydney is a welcoming place, with strong gay and lesbian and many ethnic communities lending the city a diverse and tolerant air. This isn't an illusion; it *is* an easygoing place. The worst visiting cyclists will have to contend with is the ratbag drivers – and they're definitely *not* an illusion.

Information Your best bet is the Sydney visitor centre (☎ 9255 1788 or ☎ 1800-067 676), 106 George St, The Rocks. Another visitor centre (☎ 9286 0111) is at Darling Harbour, next to the IMAX Cinema; the National Parks Information Centre is at Cadman's Cottage (☎ 9247 5033) in The Rocks. Printed information sources include *TNT*, a

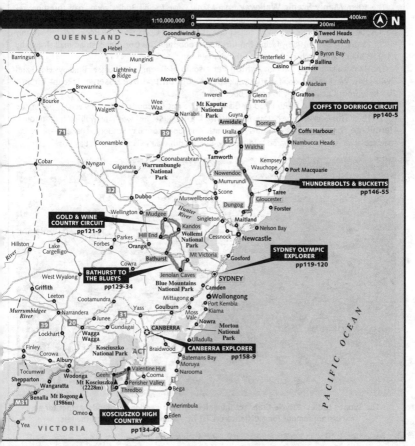

backpackers magazine, free from hostels and tourist offices. *OVG* (Overseas Visitors Guide) is a free monthly publication available from the airport that combines maps and places of interest with what's-on listings.

Lonely Planet's *Sydney City Map* ($7.95) covers the city centre, the Blue Mountains and the Olympic site at Homebush Bay.

Sydney's bike-touring specialist is Inner City Cycles (☎ 9660 6605), 31 Glebe Point Rd, Glebe. Other good central bikeshops are Clarence Street Cyclery (☎ 9299 4962), 104 Clarence St, right in the city and with the largest range of any bike shop in Australia; and Woolys Wheels (☎ 9331 2671), 82 Oxford St, Paddington.

Harbourside Rides & Walks

Even if you decide to do most of your Sydney sightseeing by train, bus or on foot, a ride across the **Harbour Bridge Cycleway** is essential. Enter from Watson Rd, near the Sydney Observatory; it's 1.4km – about 500m of which is over the water – to Milsons Point. Views west are wonderful. Elsewhere on the harbour foreshores, riding is a mixed experience. It's very up-and-down and many of the roads closest to the water are crowded. A detailed road-map is essential if you're keen to ride (a street directory such as Gregory's – $29.95 – is best), but you'll have a more peaceful experience and enjoy better views if you go on foot.

The 10km **Manly Scenic Walkway** from Manly Cove to Spit Bridge winds past foreshore reserves, quiet harbour beaches and through pretty Dobroyd Head Scenic Area, part of Sydney Harbour National Park. A map is handy; collect one at Cadman's Cottage in The Rocks or at the Manly visitor centre (☎ 9977 1088), facing the surf beach opposite The Corso pedestrian mall. Travel by ferry to Manly and catch a bus back to the city centre.

The 4km walking track through **Ashton Park**, south of Taronga Zoo, passes Bradleys Head and Taylors Bay. West of the zoo, a shorter walk goes through **Sirius Cove Reserve.** Take the Taronga Zoo ferry from Circular Quay to access both walks.

The 2.6km walk from South Head to Clarke Reserve has harbour and ocean views; it passes the high cliffs at **The Gap** and the historic **Macquarie Lighthouse**. Just west, the walking track through **Hermitage Foreshore Reserve** runs from plush Kincoppal-Rose Bay School to Nielsen Park, giving spectacular views down the harbour to the city. Reach both walks via a Watsons Bay bus.

The Sydney Ladies' Bicycle Club, accompanied by their gentlemen friends, gather for an excursion; famous long-distance cyclist Mrs Maddock is fifth from the left.

Things to See & Do For a comprehensive list of activities, find a copy of Lonely Planet's *Sydney*. Weekly entertainment listings are in the *Metro* lift-out in Friday's *Sydney Morning Herald* and in free music and entertainment newspapers such as *Drum Media*, *Revolver*, *3D World*, *Sydney City Hub*. *Capital Q Weekly* and *Sydney Star Observer* cover the gay and lesbian scene.

Across Sydney Cove from The Rocks sits the world-famous **Sydney Opera House**. Attend a performance here (box office ☎ 9250 7777) or at least take a tour (☎ 9250 7250).

Between The Rocks and the Opera House is Circular Quay, home of Sydney Ferries and one of the city's focal points – there's almost always something happening here.

East of the central business district lies Macquarie St, with Sydney's greatest concentration of early public buildings. Two of the best known are on Queens Square, at the northern end of Hyde Park: **St James Church** (built 1819–24) and the Georgian-style **Hyde Park Barracks** (1819).

The **Australian Museum** (☎ 9320 6000), corner College and William Sts, is worth visiting for its natural history, wildlife and Aboriginal history displays. The **Art Gallery of NSW** (☎ 9225 1744), in the Domain, has permanent displays of Australian, Aboriginal, European and Asian art, and fine temporary exhibits. The **Powerhouse Museum** (☎ 9217 0111), behind Darling Harbour at 500 Harris St, Ultimo, has good exhibits on decorative arts, social history, science and technology; while the **Museum of Sydney** (☎ 9251 5988), corner Bridge and Phillip Sts, shows early Sydney history. The **Museum of Contemporary Art** (☎ 9241 5892 or ☎ 9252 4033), Circular Quay West, features eclectic modern art.

Worthwhile attractions at Darling Harbour are the stunning **Sydney Aquarium** (☎ 9262 2300), near the eastern end of Pyrmont Bridge; the **National Maritime Museum** (☎ 9552 7777), at the bridge's western end; and the exquisite **Chinese Garden** (☎ 9281 6863), near the Sydney Entertainment Centre.

First-time visitors will certainly want to see and experience the harbour. The **Manly ferry** does nicely – you'll see all the famous sites such as the harbour bridge and opera house. **Sydney Harbour National Park** protects pockets of bushland around the harbour and includes several small islands,

all accessible by ferry or water taxi. A picnic on **Clarke Island**, off Darling Point, or **Shark Island**, off Rose Bay, is a treat. For information and permits (which you'll need), go to the National Parks Information Centre at **Cadman's Cottage** (☎ 9247 5033) – Sydney's oldest house – in The Rocks. There, you can also check times for tours to **Fort Denison**, a small fortified island off Mrs Macquarie's Point with great city views.

The Rocks itself is well worth a wander. The site of Sydney's first European settlement, if you ignore the kitsch you can get a real sense of early Sydney. The **Sydney Harbour Bridge** spears north across Port Jackson near The Rocks. You can climb inside the bridge's south-eastern stone pylon, which houses the Harbour Bridge Museum (☎ 9247 3408); scale the bridge itself with Bridge-climb (☎ 9252 0077); or take a spin across the Harbour Bridge Cycleway (see the boxed text 'Harbourside Rides & Walks' opposite).

Places to Stay There are no camping grounds close to central Sydney. *Sheralee Tourist Caravan Park* (☎ *9567 7161; 88 Bryant St, Rockdale*) is 13km south-west, close to the East Coast Explorer route entering Sydney; sites cost $25 for one or two people. *Lakeside Caravan Park* (☎ *9913 7845; Lake Park Rd, Narrabeen*) is 26km north, close to the East Coast Explorer route exiting Sydney. Sites are $25 but week-long bookings are required during school holidays.

Of the many central hostels, few have space for bikes. The biggest is the modern *Sydney Central YHA* (☎ *9281 9111, 11 Rawson Place*) where dorm beds cost $27.50, and twin rooms $40 per person. Bikes are stored indoors, but bring a lock.

Glebe Point YHA (☎ *9692 8418; 262–264 Glebe Point Rd, Glebe*) is in a quiet and leafy inner-city suburb; dorm beds cost $26, twin rooms $31 per person. Book your bike ahead.

Further out (but still handy to the city), the lovely *Billabong Gardens* (☎ *9550 3236; 5–11 Egan St, Newtown*) has great facilities in a great suburb – arguably Sydney's best budget restaurant zone. Beds in standard dorms cost $20; doubles cost $66. Bike parking is secure but limited.

Mid-range hotel and motel accommodation is plentiful but, again, cycle parking is scarce. An exception is the *George Hotel* (☎ *9211 1800, 700A George St*), not far from Central Station. Singles cost $50. Nearby, the big *CB Private Hotel* (☎ 9211 5115, 417 Pitt St) stores bikes in their basement (at owners' risk). Singles/doubles cost $45/65, with shared bathrooms.

In Glebe, there's a couple of good options if you're cycling with a mate. The *Rooftop Motel* (☎ 9660 7777 or ☎ 1800-227 436, 146–48 Glebe Point Rd) has fairly basic rooms for $99. Just up the road at the *Haven Inn* (☎ 9660 6655, 196 Glebe Point Rd), a room costs $140, with secure bike parking.

In Newtown, the neat *Australian Sunrise Lodge* (☎ 9557 4400, 485 King St) has no objections to cycles in rooms. Their budget singles cost $69.

If you're up for a splurge, try one of the hotels near Circular Quay, with harbour views. The *Old Sydney Parkroyal* (☎ 9252 0524 or ☎ 1800-221 493, 55 George St), the *Regent* (☎ 9238 0000 or ☎ 1800-222 200, 199 George St) and *Hotel-Intercontinental* (☎ 9230 0200 or ☎ 1800-221 828, 117 Macquarie St) are all a stroll from Circular Quay. Expect standard rates to be $350 at the least.

Places to Eat If you plan to do some serious eating, pick up Lonely Planet's *Out to Eat – Sydney*; the *Good Living* lift-out in Tuesday's *Sydney Morning Herald* reviews the latest and grooviest places.

Southern Central Sydney Near the George St cinema strip, *Banana Leaf Curry House* (☎ 9283 7833, 605–609 George St) has a big range of Asian food. Near the Queen Victoria Building, *Lola's Bistro* (☎ 9267 1116, 236 Clarence St) is in Hotel Sweeney's. Both places will *really* fill you up for under $15.

Chinatown Just wander in to this area, just north of Central Station, and see where your nose leads you. Ever-reliable *BBQ King* (☎ 9267 2433, 18–20 Goulburn St) has a huge choice of mains from $11. For yum cha lunch and seafood dinners, head to *Kam Fook Sharks Fin Seafood* (☎ 9211 8988; Market City, 9 Hay St, Haymarket).

Liverpool St South of Town Hall Station near George St, Sydney's Little Spain is the place to come for sangria and smoky rooms. Try *Capitan Torres* (☎ 9264 5574, No 73) for a $15 vegetarian paella, or *Miró* (☎ 9267 3126, No 76) for tapas and joyful atmosphere.

Newtown Lined with restaurants and cafes, King St is the main drag in this Inner West suburb. *Cinque* (☎ 9519 3077, No 261A) is in the Dendy cinema, serving generous portions for around $15. *Efes Turkish Pizza* (☎ 9516 4276, No 124) will fill your belly for under $10. King St is also Sydney's Thai cuisine central; visit *Simply Thai* (☎ 9565 5111, No 186) for the laksa.

Glebe Welcome to cafe heaven, south-east of the city. Give *digi.kaf* (☎ 9660 3509, 174 St Johns Rd) a go for lunch (dinner only on Friday) or Web surfing. For a large coffee fix and yummy cake, stop in at the *Blackwattle Canteen* (☎ 9552 1792, 456 Glebe Point Rd). It's hard to go past *Iku* (☎ 9692 8720, 25A Glebe Point Rd) and the legendary $6.20 macro burger.

Getting There & Away If you're flying into NSW from abroad you will most likely arrive in Sydney.

Air Sydney Airport, about 8km south of the city, is Australia's busiest international air gateway. Regular services fly to Sydney and Canberra from all state capitals and many NSW regional centres.

Cityrail (☎ 13 1500) trains run regularly from stations at the international and domestic terminals to Sydney's Central Station ($10, 10 minutes). Bikes travel free outside peak period (see the boxed text below).

The ride from the airport will be uncomfortable for anyone lacking experience in

---

Bikes on Buses & Trains

If you're travelling on New South Wales' Countrylink's regional train services, you'll need to box your bike. Bikes cost $11 on any service; only three bikes are allowed per service (request a box when you book).

Bikes travel free on Sydney's Cityrail services outside peak periods (6am–9am and 3.30pm–7.30pm weekdays); otherwise, you must pay a child's fare (half fare) for them. They can travel in any carriage, unboxed.

Standard charges and packing conditions also apply to transporting bikes on buses; see Carrying Your Bicycle in the Bus section of the Getting Around chapter.

heavy traffic. Go via O'Riordan, Bourke, Elizabeth, Redfern and Chalmers Sts.

A taxi to central Sydney costs \$20 to \$25.

Bus Countrylink (☎ 13 2232) runs the most comprehensive bus network in NSW and sometimes has discounts of up to 40% on economy fares. Major bus companies also serve many towns on their express runs from Sydney to other capitals; see the Bus section in the Getting Around chapter for more information. Sydney Coach Terminal (☎ 9281 9366) is on Eddy Ave outside Central Station; Greyhound and McCafferty's have offices in the same street.

Train NSW's Countrylink rail network is the most comprehensive in Australia. However, it's also one of the most bicycle unfriendly, with only two bikes allowed per service, and bookings required.

All of the interstate and principal regional services operate from Central Station; a Countrylink Travel Centre is on the main concourse. Call ☎ 13 2232 for recorded arrival/departure information. See the Getting Around chapter for more information.

Cityrail (☎ 13 1500), the Sydney metropolitan service, is more bike-friendly and the network is big enough to get you into some great cycling country – as far as Newcastle in the north, Katoomba in the west, through Wollongong to Bomaderry south, or Goulburn in the south-west.

Bicycle See Days 17 (p416) and 18 (p418) of the East Coast Explorer ride (in the Melbourne to the Gold Coast chapter) for details of cycling into Sydney from the south and north, respectively.

Sydney Olympic Explorer

Duration	2–3 hours
Distance	30km
Difficulty	easy–moderate
Start/End	Centennial Park, Woollahra

In part, the route follows the 2000 Olympic road-cycling course, and also takes in Bondi Beach and parts of Sydney's plush eastern suburbs. Wonderful views of the city and the harbour are a feature.

Olympic Wannabe?

Test yourself against the winners of the 2000 Olympics mens and womens road cycling. Jan Ullrich (Germany) completed 14 laps of the course (239.4km) in five hours, 29 minutes and eight seconds; while Leontien Zijlaard-van Moorsel (Netherlands) rode seven laps (119.7km) in three hours, six minutes and 31 seconds.

PLANNING
The ride can be tackled year-round. Expect crowded roads if riding on a sunny weekend in midsummer. Navigating by street signs is easy.

GETTING TO/FROM THE RIDE
Centennial Park is about 2km from Central Station and about 3.5km from Circular Quay.

THE RIDE
The **Centennial Park** gate at Oxford St, Woollahra, is only 2km to 3km east of central Sydney, a key reason why the park's shady roads were lined with spectators during the 2000 Olympic road-cycling races. The course followed a serpentine path through the park before returning to the start and finish line about 1km away, near the **Sydney Cricket Ground**.

We'd suggest you spend as much time as possible exploring the park's roads; it's arguably the most pleasant – and certainly one of the most popular – places in Sydney to ride a bicycle. When you do leave, exit onto Darley Rd, Randwick.

At the bottom of Bronte Rd, leave the Olympics course and go right into **Bronte Park** through the gates near the bus stop. Follow the path that loops behind the surf club, near the playground equipment – that way you can ride up the short rise to Bronte Marine Drive. A stop for coffee somewhere along Campbell Parade – the road that curves past famous **Bondi Beach** – is a must. Cycle along the promenade on a sunny day and you'll see why Bondi is known as the most cosmopolitan of Sydney beaches. Another must-stop spot is the **Dudley Page Reserve** at Dover Heights, renowned as the best (public) place in eastern Sydney for city and harbour views. Further along Old South Head Rd the route passes **Macquarie Lighthouse**, built in 1833

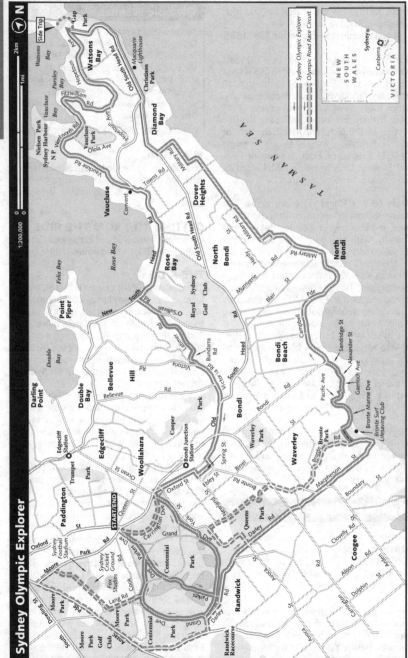

Sydney Olympic Explorer

to the design of an earlier light raised by convict architect Francis Greenway.

It's worth the side trip to pretty and popular **Watsons Bay** (the 'Watto Bay' *pub* is a fine place for liquid refreshments) before looping back into Vaucluse. **Vaucluse House** (☎ 9388 7922) was the grand residence of early patriot WC Wentworth and is a pleasant sojourn, both for its historical interest and lovely grounds. Continue past **Neilsen Park** (20.3km) – a *very* popular harbour beach and reserve that's part of Sydney Harbour National Park – to **Kincoppal-Rose Bay Convent**, surely the school with Sydney's best view.

There are more nice views from the route on the way up Bellevue Hill, after which the roads are much busier, and it's probably best not to dither en route back to Centennial Park.

Gold & Wine Country Circuit

Duration	4 days
Distance	307.5km
Difficulty	moderate–hard
Start/End	Bathurst

Beginning and ending at historic Bathurst, the tour passes through former gold-mining towns en route to Mudgee, today the thriving service centre for nearby wineries. At its eastern extremity, the tour route runs within sight of the extraordinarily rough terrain of Wollemi National Park, one of NSW's largest wilderness areas.

HISTORY

The central west region was originally occupied by the Wiradjuri people, NSW's largest Aboriginal group. The explorers Blaxland, Lawson and Wentworth breached the Blue Mountains in 1813 and Bathurst, the first town established west of the Great Dividing Range, was founded on the orders of Governor Macquarie in 1815. The Wiradjuri fought for their lands and were slaughtered in large numbers after martial law was declared in 1824. The region remained isolated and settler numbers small until the 1850s, when the first of a series of gold rushes brought people flooding across the mountains.

PLANNING
When to Ride

Spring and autumn are best. The central west can be very hot in midsummer and cool to cold in midwinter.

Maps

The NRMA's NSW Touring map No 5 *Central West, New England, North West* (1:550,000) has the most up-to-date information. For contour detail, use Auslig's Natmap maps *Bathurst* and *Dubbo* (1:250,000).

GETTING TO/FROM THE RIDE

Bathurst is also the start of the Bathurst to the Blueys ride, later in this chapter.

Bathurst

Inland and 210km west, Bathurst is linked to Sydney by the Great Western Hwy, which crosses the Blue Mountains.

Bus Greyhound Pioneer (☎ 13 2030) runs one service daily between Sydney and Bathurst ($28.60, 4½ hours).

Train Countrylink (☎ 13 2232) runs services between Sydney and Bathurst ($37.40, three to four hours, two daily).

Bicycle Cyclists coming from Sydney would be advised to catch a train at least as far as Katoomba (101km east of Bathurst) to avoid both traffic and long climbs up the eastern flank of the Blue Mountains.

THE RIDE
Bathurst

In rolling countryside at about 670m elevation, Bathurst has long been a thriving centre for the rich surrounding rural lands. Nowadays education is its main industry – it's home to the Charles Sturt University and six high schools.

Information The Bathurst visitor centre (☎ 6332 1444 or ☎ 1800-681 000, @ visitors@bathurst.nsw.gov.au), 28 William St, provides excellent information sheets for local attractions and has a restored Cobb & Co coach on display. Banks (with ATMs) are on William and Howick Sts. Winning Edge Cycles (☎ 6332 4025), 88 Durham St, does repairs and has a good range of spares. The main post office is on Howick St.

Things to See & Do Bathurst is packed with historical points of interest; walk up **William St**, with its historical markers at cross-street corners, to get a taste. The striking **Bathurst Court House** (1880) on Russell St is regarded as one of Australia's most significant Victorian-era public buildings. The east wing houses the **Historical Society Museum** (☎ 6332 4755).

The Bathurst Regional Art Gallery (☎ 6331 6066), 70–78 Keppel St, concentrates on Australian artists since the mid-1900s. The Slattery Museum (☎ 6331 4177) in St Stanislaus College, Bentinck St, is dedicated to Father Slattery, who took Australia's first X-ray at this site in 1896. Ben Chifley's House (☎ 6332 1444), 10 Busby St, is the former home of post-WWII prime minister Ben Chifley (1885–1951). Old Government Cottage (☎ 6332 4755), 1 George St, was built between 1817 and 1820 and is the oldest brick building west of the Macquarie River. There's also a fine colonial-era collection at Miss Traill's House (☎ 6332 4232), corner Russell and Peel Sts.

Places to Stay & Eat The only camping ground close to the centre of town, *Bathurst Holiday Park (☎ 6331 8286; Sydney Rd, Kelso)* charges $15 for two people.

The *Bathurst Explorers Motel (☎ 6331 2966, 357 Stewart St)* has single/double rooms for $59/69. The *Knickerbocker Hotel Motel (☎ 6332 4500, cnr William & Russell Sts)* is centrally located and does B&B at $50/77. For luxury, try *Strathmore Victorian Manor (☎ 6332 3252, 202 Russell St)*, where B&B is $82.50/110.

William St is home to a *Coles (No 41)* and *Woolworths* supermarket, plus two *bakeries*.

The *Acropole Restaurant (cnr William & Howick Sts)* does big breakfasts from $7 and has a good selection of pastas. *Hipster Cafe (☎ 6332 1499, 138 William St)* opens late and also serves filling pastas. *Crowded House Cafe Restaurant (☎ 6334 2300, 1 Ribbon Gang Lane)* has pricier meals in a lovely 1840s school house. *G&T Bar & Grill (☎ 6331 1264, 73 William St)* does a good vegetable and lentil curry for $13.90. Both the *Edinboro (☎ 6331 5020, 134 William St)* and *Knickerbocker* hotels have bistros; the 'Eddy's' burgers and veggie burgers are a bargain.

Day 1: Bathurst to Hill End

5½–7 hours, 81.4km

Given the distance spent on dirt (32km, all of it in the day's second half), this is a longish day. Happily, the dirt road is well maintained (it's an official NSW Tourist Drive route). Wonderful rural and bushland scenery, some interesting towns and – if the route's tackled midweek – an absence of traffic more than make up for dusty tyres. Of several climbs, a couple have some sting. A highlight is the rollicking downhill to the Turon River and Sofala.

The small community of Wattle Flat is reached at 36km, where the 5km **Buurree Walking Trail** winds past evidence of 19th-century gold mining and includes some fantastic views.

Sofala (44.7km) is a fascinating and quirky little town, a remnant of the earliest gold rush days (the 1850s) where many timber buildings have been preserved. It's nice to stop for a cool drink at the 1862 *Royal Hotel*; if you're short of time, at least have a quiet spin around Sofala's narrow streets.

The dirt road begins almost immediately after Sofala and involves several climbs. It's quite a relief to reach the privately owned **History Hill** complex (☎ 6337 8222; 79.9km), just before Hill End. The exhibits at the museum and underground tourist mine provide a good insight into the extraction of gold during the 19th century.

Hill End

A gold-rush boomtown in the 1870s, Hill End was declared a historic site in 1967 and has an authentic charm that's irresistible.

Information The visitor centre (☎ 6337 8206, e hill.end@npws.nsw.gov.au), operated by the National Parks & Wildlife Service (NPWS), is outside the town centre in the restored hospital (built in the 1870s and closed in 1929). Its museum and theatrette provide background on the town and gold rushes (which is essential before you continue explorations). It takes bookings for the NPWS camping grounds. All businesses in town have Eftpos facilities. The post office is on Tambaroora St (open weekday afternoons).

Things to See & Do The key to Hill End's revival is a remarkable set of **photographs** taken in 1872 by Beaufoy Merlin. Although

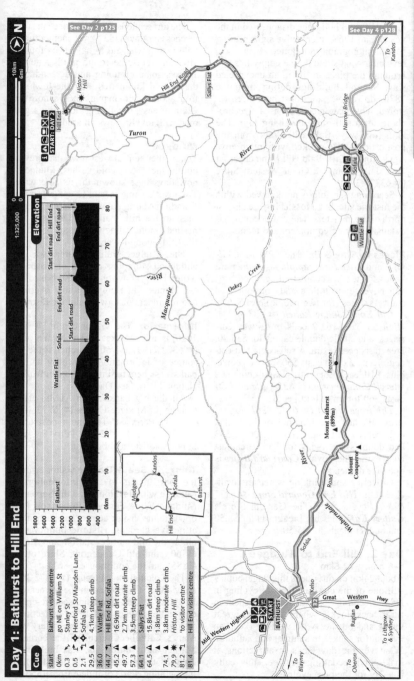

NEW SOUTH WALES

Day 1: Bathurst to Hill End

Cue

start		Bathurst visitor centre
0km		go NE on William St
0.3		Stanley St
0.5		Hereford St/Marsden Lane
2.1		Sofala Rd
29.5	◄	4.1km steep climb
36.0		Wattle Flat
44.7		Hill End Rd, Sofala
45.2	◄	16.9km dirt road
49.7	◄	2.7km moderate climb
57.3	◄	3.5km steep climb
64.1		Sallys Flat
64.5	◄	15.8km dirt road
74.1	◄	1.8km steep climb
79.9	✳	3.8km moderate climb
		History Hill
81.2		'to visitor centre'
81.4		Hill End visitor centre

Elevation

1:325,000

Turon River

History Hill

START: DAY 2
Hill End

See Day 2 p125

See Day 4 p128

To Kandos

Sallys Flat

Narrow Bridge

Sofala

Wattle Flat

Oakey Creek

Macquarie River

Start dirt road

End dirt road

Peronne

Mount Bathurst (899m)

Mount Conqueror

Withinmale

Sofala Road

Kelso

Great Western Hwy

Mid Western Highway

START
BATHURST

To Blayney

To Oberon

To Raglan

To Lithgow & Sydney

Kandos
Mudgee
Sofala
Hill End
Bathurst

many Hill End buildings disappeared in the years up to 1967, interpretive signs bearing Merlin photographs are dotted about town, revealing what stood on the empty lots and bringing the place to life in an unexpected way. Several buildings dating from the 1870s do remain, and most have been restored. The visitor centre has a free brochure for a self-guided **walking tour**. The 2km (one-way) **Bald Hill Walk** from the post office is also marked with interpretive signs. Tours of the **Bald Hill Mine** depart at 1pm daily from the Great Western Store (☎ 6337 8377).

Searching for gold is not allowed within the historic site, but a **fossicking** area is just north of the cemetery. The visitor centre has details for hiring equipment and tours.

Places to Stay & Eat The NPWS-run *Village* and *Glendora camping grounds* are handy to the town centre (Village is closest) and have septic toilets and coin-operated showers. Sites (for two people) cost $10.

Hill End Holiday Ranch (☎ 6337 8224, High St) has $16.50 beds in railway carriages, and single/double cabins for $30/40; breakfasts costs extra. A self-contained cottage sleeps six and costs $60 for two people, plus $10 each for extras. Self-contained *'Beryl' Cottage (☎ 6337 8258, Fletcher St)* costs $60 for up to four people.

The Royal Hotel (☎ 6337 8261, Beyers Ave) – the last remaining pub of the 28 that once served Hill End – has singles for $33 and doubles and twins for $55. Breakfast costs extra. The Royal's *Courtyard Bistro* is open for dinner.

Groceries and drinking water are available at the *Hill End General Store (☎ 6337 8237, Beyers Ave)*. The General Store's *Gallery Cafe* does big breakfasts for $8.50 and budget meals for $5.50.

Day 2: Hill End to Mudgee
5–6 hours, 72.6km

About 24km on dirt opens this stage, but it's still one of the classiest days of cycling in NSW's central west. Most of it is spent in rural backblocks, where there are great views and brushes with wildlife (keep an eye out for snakes in summer and autumn). Whatever the day lacks in attractions, it makes up in pedalling pleasure – this really is a day for the pure cyclists.

The dirt sections are passed once the route reaches **Hargraves** (33.5km); another former gold-rush town, said to have been founded after an Aborigine found a 48kg nugget. There's some climbing and descending in the several kilometres after the town, but from about the 46km mark there's more than 22km of easy, undulating riding on a good road with lovely views all around.

Mudgee
Yet another central west town that grew up during the 1850s gold rushes, Mudgee is nowadays best known for its fine wines. The town's name is said to come from the Wiradjuri Aboriginal word *moothi*, meaning 'nest in the hills', and Mudgee is indeed nestled among attractive ranges in the fertile Cudgegong River valley.

The Mudgee-Gulgong area was the childhood stomping ground of Australian writer Henry Lawson (see the boxed text 'At Home with Henry Lawson' overleaf), and reminders of Lawson dot the district.

Information The visitor centre (☎ 6372 1020) is at 84 Market St. The NPWS office (☎ 6372 7199) at 1/60 Church St is the best source of information on nearby national parks – ask here for information on Wollemi National Park (see Day 3).

All the big banks (with ATMs) are on Church St. Mudgee Cycles (☎ 6372 4600) is at 39 Perry St. The main post office (1862), corner Market and Perry Sts, is an important historical building.

Things to See & Do The visitor centre is the best place to get information on **Mudgee wineries**, tours and the September **Mudgee Wine Festival. Robertson Park**, opposite the visitor centre, has particularly attractive gardens. **Historic buildings** include the old police station and stables (1860), the old Cudgegong Shire offices (1885) and the courthouse (1861).

The **Colonial Inn Museum** (☎ 6372 3078) on Market St is housed in the former West End Hotel (1856). It contains some re-created colonial-era rooms and a fine collection of historic photographs. The presbytery at **St Mary's Catholic Church**, on the corner of Market and Church Sts, was built in the early 1850s and is Mudgee's oldest remaining building. Parts of it date from 1857, but

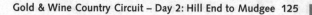

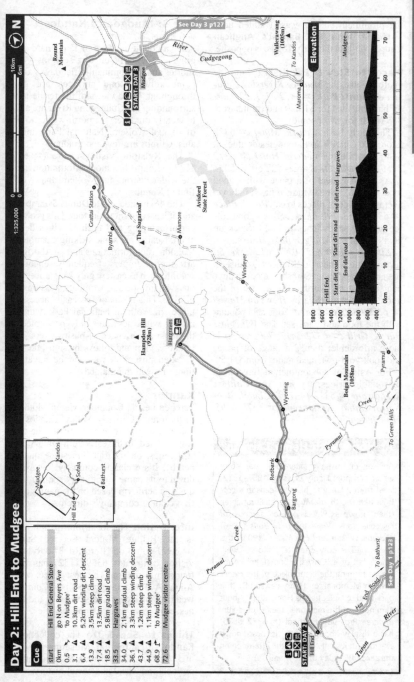

Day 2: Hill End to Mudgee

Cue

start		Hill End General Store
0km	↖	go N on Beyers Ave
0.5	↘	'to Mudgee'
3.1	◣	10.3km dirt road
6.4	◣	5.2km winding dirt descent
13.9	◣	3.5km steep climb
17.4	◣	13.5km dirt road
18.5	◣	5.8km gradual climb
33.5		Hargraves
34.0	◣	2.1km gradual climb
36.1	◣	3.3km steep winding descent
43.7	◣	1.2km steep climb
44.9	◣	1.1km steep winding descent
68.9	↳	'to Mudgee'
72.6		Mudgee visitor centre

Elevation

Hill End
Start dirt road
End dirt road
Start dirt road
End dirt road
Hargraves
Mudgee

the prominent steeple wasn't added until 1911. **St John the Baptist's Anglican Church**, built in the early 1860s, is opposite.

Places to Stay & Eat Right behind the visitor centre, the *Mudgee Riverside Caravan & Tourist Park* (☎ 6372 2531, 22 Short St) has tent sites for $13.20 and cabins from $55 (both for two people).

The fairly basic *Central Motel* (☎ 6372 2268, 120 Church St) has singles/doubles at $44/55, while the *Federal Hotel* (☎ 6372 2150, 34 Inglis St) charges $27.50/49.50.

As you'd expect of a place with a good local drop of wine, Mudgee has an above-average choice of places to eat. *Rose's Place* (☎ 6372 4353, 79B Market St) has good coffee and big sandwiches from $4. Stock up next door at the *Mudgee Bake House*.

Eltons Cafe (☎ 6372 0772, 81 Market St) serves some wonderful 'Modern Oz' dishes. It's not cheap (about $40 should cover three courses) but it's worth it for a taste of the home-made chips. Nearby *Troy's on Market* (☎ 6372 0880, 67 Market St) is also popular with the food and wine set. The *Wineglass Bar & Grill* (☎ 6372 3417, 7 Perry St) is more affordable; there's a range of pastas and cook-your-own meat mains from $11.50.

For Asian or subcontinental flavours at reasonable prices, try *Kai Sun Chinese Restaurant* (☎ 6372 1487, 42 Church St) or *Natraj Indian Restaurant* (☎ 6372 6895, 113 Church St).

At Home with Henry Lawson

An icon of Australian literature, short-story writer and poet Henry Lawson (1867–1922) lived from infancy to his mid-teens in a cottage 8km north of Mudgee, at Eurunderee (then known as Pipeclay). Most famous for his collections *While the Billy Boils* (1896) and *Joe Wilson and His Mates* (1901), this poet's pad is now open to visitors – well, what's left of it. Only the brick fireplace remains; forming the centrepiece of the Henry Lawson Memorial, on Henry Lawson Dr (the back road to Gulgong, via Home Rule). About 1km north of the memorial, the restored Eurunderee Provisional School (☎ 6372 5875) has a display about Lawson, its best-known ex-student; it's only open in the afternoon on the second Sunday of the month.

Day 3: Mudgee to Kandos
4–5 hours, 60.1km
After a couple of days of fairly hard slogging – especially on dirt sections – this shorter and predominantly flat day is a welcome relief. Road surfaces are good throughout. Wide views of the fertile lands surrounding the Cudgegong River are a feature early on; later, the north-western flank of rugged Wollemi National Park dominates. Climbs are few and gradual.

The Rylstone visitor centre (☎ 6379 1132; 52.6km) has more information about the wider district and Wollemi than you'll find at Kandos.

The 46km side trip to **Dunns Swamp** will add at least a night to the tour. This is a wonderful camping and bush-activities destination. Nearby are some striking examples of 'pagoda' rock formations and an Aboriginal art site. Campers frequently encounter wildlife such as eastern grey kangaroos, various wallaby species, wombats, possums and birdlife. This is one of few easily accessible places in Wollemi National Park, which is mostly wilderness and only penetrated by the most experienced of bushwalkers. Turn left at 53.9km and follow the signs; the road is sealed most of the way, and the gravel sections are well maintained.

Kandos
Perched beside Coomber Melon Mountain in the pretty Capertee Valley, Kandos is a name synonymous with cement. The town was founded (in the early 20th century), and still relies, on the rich limestone quarries nearby. It's a classic company town, right down to its name – originally spelled 'Candos', an acronym based on the names of the first cement company's directors.

Information The local information outlet is the Bridge Motors Service Station (☎ 6379 4004) on Ilford Rd. The Rylstone visitor centre (☎ 6379 1132) has more tourist information. The post office, corner Angus Ave and Jacques St, is a Commonwealth bank agent and several of the businesses in town have Eftpos facilities.

Things to See & Do The collection at **Kandos Bicentennial Museum** (☎ 6379 4057/4595), 22 Buchanan St, concentrates on local industrial and social history.

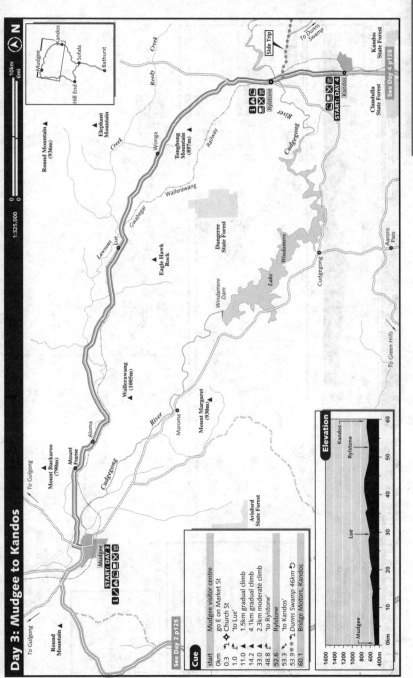

Day 3: Mudgee to Kandos

NEW SOUTH WALES

Cue

start		Mudgee visitor centre
0km		go E on Market St
0.3		Church St
1.0		'to Lue'
11.0		1.5km gradual climb
14.2		4.1km gradual climb
33.0		2.3km moderate climb
48.8		'to Rylstone'
52.6		Rylstone
53.3		'to Kandos'
53.9		Dunns Swamp 46km ↺
60.1		Bridge Motors, Kandos

Elevation

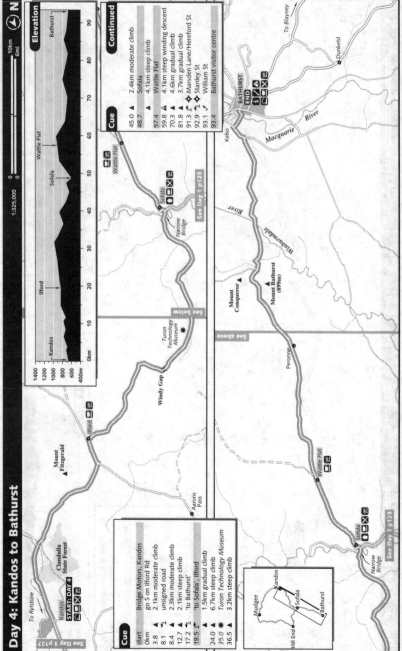

Day 4: Kandos to Bathurst

NEW SOUTH WALES

Elevation

1:325,000

0   10km
0   6mi

Cue

start		Bridge Motors, Kandos
0km	◀	go S on Ilford Rd
3.8	◀	2.1km moderate climb
8.1	◀	unsigned road
8.4	◀	2.3km moderate climb
12.7	◀	2.1km steep climb
17.2	◀	'to Bathurst'
19.5	◀	'to Sofala', Ilford
24.0	◀	1.5km gradual climb
35.0	✳	6.7km steep climb
36.5	◀	*Turon Technology Museum*
		3.2km steep climb

Cue Continued

45.0	◀	2.4km moderate climb
48.7		Sofala
57.4	◀	4.1km steep climb
59.8	◣	Wattle Flat
70.3	◀	4.1km steep winding descent
81.8	◀	4.6km gradual climb
91.3	◇	3.7km gradual climb
92.9	◇	Marsden Lane/Hereford St
93.1	◢	Stanley St
93.4		William St
		Bathurst visitor centre

Sydney Harbour Bridge and the Opera House – see the icons then escape the city to explore NSW by bike.

Keep an eye out for king parrots in the Blue Mountains, near Sydney.

Enjoy Sydney from a ferry deck.

Relax in charming old gold-rush boom towns such as Hill End, on the Gold & Wine Country Circuit.

Go bush on a High Country mountain-bike ride (Valentine Fire Trail).

Relax in the fabulous rainforest of Dorrigo National Park, NSW.

Welcoming Walcha sculptures.

Canberra's Parliament House... inside and out – see it all on the Canberra Explorer ride.

From Kandos, it's about 25km to the western fringe of **Wollemi National Park**, a place so rugged that rare organisms are still discovered within its boundaries (see the boxed text 'The Tree That Time Forgot'). There's good fishing at **Windamere Dam**, on the Cudgegong River about 20km northwest of Kandos.

Places to Stay & Eat The nearest camping ground is about 7km north in Rylstone, at the small *Apex Caravan Park* (☎ 6379 1165, Carwell St); sites are \$8.80 per tent.

The *Kandos Hotel* (☎ 6379 4030, 2 Angus Ave) has singles for \$22 and doubles for \$33, including a light breakfast. The pub also serves dinner (except Sunday). The *Railway Hotel* (☎ 6379 4403, Ilford Rd) has singles/doubles for \$20/38, including light breakfast. Typical pub fare is on offer here for dinner (\$11 steaks, \$8 fish and chips), but it's roast only on Sunday. The *Fairway Motel* (☎ 6379 4406, cnr Ilford Rd & Henbury Ave) charges \$62/71.50.

You'll find good sandwiches at *Goldie's* (22 Angus Ave) and assorted takeaways at *Bowers Burgers* (☎ 6379 4180, 37 Angus Ave). Another alternative is *Kandos Chinese Restaurant* (☎ 6379 4308, 19 Angus Ave).

The Tree That Time Forgot

In August 1994, ranger David Noble and two friends were exploring a deep, damp and very sheltered gorge in Wollemi National Park when Noble made the discovery of a lifetime – a tree with palm-frond-like leaves and bubbly looking bark, quite unlike anything he'd seen before.

Four months later, the discovery was announced: the tree, named *Wollemia nobilis* – the Wollemi pine – had previously been known only from 100-million-year-old fossils. It was placed in a genus all its own, and became the third living genus of the conifer family, Araucariaceae.

Another stand of Wollemi pines was found near the first, in May 1995, bringing to 38 the number of adult specimens in existence. The pine is so rare that its sites in the wild are unlikely ever to be officially made public. You can see the Wollemi pine (in a cage!) at the Royal Botanic Gardens, in Sydney, and the Mt Annan and Mt Tomah Botanic Gardens.

Day 4: Kandos to Bathurst
6½–8 hours, 93.4km

A long day rounds out this ride, and it's solid as well. The first 19.5km of the day are likely to be the worst for traffic, and it's wise to get an early start. Once past Ilford, the route – much of which has only recently been sealed – is an absolute joy for cycle touring, combining good road surfaces, manageable climbs, lively descents and wide, wide views.

Midway between two of the day's longest climbs, the **Turon Technology Museum** (☎ 6358 8434) is worth a visit if you're there on the first weekend of the month. Exhibits trace the development of the internal combustion engine since the 1850s, and include working steam engines.

From Sofala (48.7km), the route retraces its Day 1 path (see p122), the first part of which is a 4km uphill grind.

Bathurst to the Blueys

Duration	2 days
Distance	132.9km
Difficulty	hard
Start	Bathurst
End	Mt Victoria

First passing the forests and farmlands that dot the Oberon plateau, the route features a visit to spectacular Jenolan Caves and wonderful views from the west towards the upper Blue Mountains. While sections of the route are flat or gently undulating, the formidable climbs and descents near Jenolan Caves are best attempted only by fit and experienced riders.

HISTORY

The route covers a region that extends from traditional Wiradjuri Aboriginal lands to the western lands of the Dharug people. Because of its proximity to the Sydney to Bathurst road, Europeans were exploring the land here soon after the Blue Mountains were breached in 1813; the Oberon area was being settled as early as the 1820s. The Jenolan Caves' extraordinary, open-ended Grand Arch was discovered in the late 1830s by bushranger James McKeown and first came to public attention when McKeown was tracked down. The cave system was explored further over subsequent decades and the area was declared a reserve in 1866. A cave was opened to tourists as early as 1867.

Jenolan Caves was a popular cycling destination from Sydney in the late-19th century. Some rode the full 180km as a challenge; others took the train to Mt Victoria and rode the final 65km.

NATURAL HISTORY

The cold and windy Oberon Plateau, rising to more than 1300m, is at the western edge of the Blue Mountains (the 'mountains' are in fact an elevated plateau that slopes gradually west to east, and the Oberon Plateau is among its highest points). Streams flowing eastward across the Blue Mountains for aeons have created the spectacular cliff lines and steep-sided valleys for which the region is renowned. The Jenolan Caves, further west, have been eroded from limestone sediments, the oldest of which were laid down about 400 million years ago.

PLANNING
When to Ride

Weekdays in spring and autumn are best.

Maps

Use NRMA's NSW Touring map No 5 *Central West, New England, North West* (1:550,000). For contour detail, use Auslig's Natmap maps *Bathurst* and *Sydney* (1:250,000).

GETTING TO/FROM THE RIDE

The Gold & Wine Country Circuit, detailed earlier in this chapter, links directly: it starts and ends at Bathurst.

Bathurst

See the Gold & Wine Country Circuit (p121) for details on getting to/from Bathurst.

Mt Victoria

Train Cityrail (☎ 13 1500) runs regular services to Sydney ($12.60, 2½ hours). Bikes cost $6.30 during peak times (6am–9am and 3.30pm–7.30pm weekdays); otherwise they travel free.

Bicycle It's a 77km ride, on the Great Western Hwy, to Penrith, on Sydney's western fringe. The route passes iconic Blue Mountain features such as the Three Sisters and the Jamison Valley; though it's mostly downhill, there's plenty of traffic. For a further 32km, from Penrith to Parramatta, there's a wide cycling lane beside the noisy and fast M4 motorway – a great way to experience Sydney's amazing urban sprawl. Trains go to the city from both Penrith and Parramatta stations.

THE RIDE
Bathurst

See Bathurst (p121–22) in the Gold & Wine Country Circuit for information about accommodation and other services.

Day 1: Bathurst to Jenolan Caves

5½–7 hours, 76.2km

Big landscapes, big climbs and roaring descents are the hallmark of this tiring but satisfying day. The Bathurst to Oberon road is sublime on a cool weekday, with light traffic allowing plenty of space to take in views. The rise from O'Connell (about 700m elevation) to Oberon (nearly 1100m) occurs in a number of stages over 24km; the later rise to the route's high point (above 1300m) is unbroken over 7km, all on dirt road. A brake check before setting out is essential.

It's delightfully easy going to the village of O'Connell (22km). Here, National Trust-registered buildings date back to the 1830s. Pity it's a bit early in the day for a beer at the historic O'Connell pub, an oasis for thirsty locals.

Oberon (46.6km) is the last place to buy food if you're camping or staying in self-catering accommodation at Jenolan Caves. There's a NPWS office (☎ 6336 1972) at 38 Ross St for last-minute information on national parks in the region – ask here if you plan to visit Kanangra-Boyd National Park from Jenolan.

There's a nice view of Lake Oberon from the route out of Oberon; the terrain here is also noticeably lumpier – big, smooth-sided hills on which the road seems but a scratch.

Thankfully, the dirt climb (from 60.6km) rises moderately for most of the way, just occasionally steepening. In contrast, the descent to Jenolan Caves is unrelentingly steep, the road narrow and twisting with severe hairpins. Stop frequently to ensure rims and brakes don't overheat.

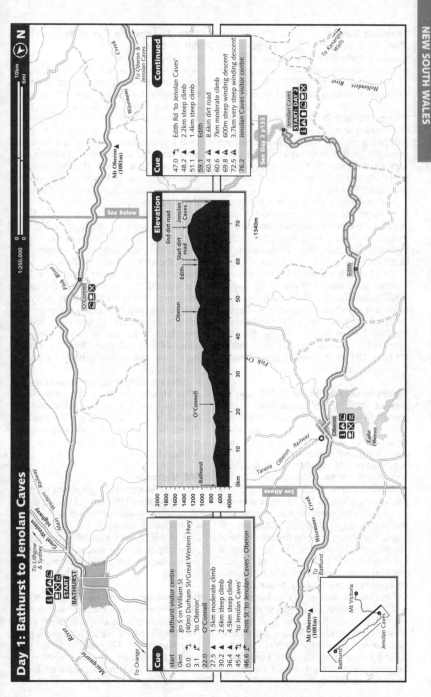

NEW SOUTH WALES

Day 1: Bathurst to Jenolan Caves

Cue

start	Bathurst visitor centre
0km	go S on William St
0.0	(40m) Durham St/Great Western Hwy 'to Oberon'
3.1	'to Oberon'
22.0	O'Connell
27.5	1.5km moderate climb
30.2	2.6km steep climb
36.4	4.5km steep climb
45.4	'to Jenolan Caves'
46.6	Ross St to Jenolan Caves', Oberon

Cue Continued

47.0	Edith Rd 'to Jenolan Caves'
48.2	2.2km steep climb
51.1	1.4km steep climb
59.1	Edith
60.4	8.6km dirt road
60.6	7km moderate climb
69.8	600m steep winding descent
72.5	3.7km very steep winding descent
76.2	Jenolan Caves visitor centre

See Day 2 p133

Elevation

2000
1800
1600
1400
1200
1000
800
600
400m

0km 10 20 30 40 50 60 70

+1340m

Bathurst
O'Connell
Oberon
Edith
Start dirt road
End dirt road
Jenolan Caves

See Above
See Below

Mt Oberon ▲ (1081m)

O'Connell

Fish River

Fish Creek

Tarana Oberon Railway

Oberon

Lake Oberon

Wisemans Creek

Edith

Hollanders River

To Kanangra Walls

Jenolan Caves
START: DAY 2

To Oberon & Jenolan Caves

Creek

Wisemans

To Lithgow & Sydney

Main Western Highway

Great Western Hwy

Western Railway

Macquarie River

To Orange

BATHURST
START

To Bathurst

Mt Victoria

Bathurst
Mt Oberon ▲ (1081m)
Jenolan Caves

1:250,000
0
0   10km
0   6mi
N

NEW SOUTH WALES

Jenolan Caves

Deep in a beautiful, steep-sided valley, these are Australia's best-known, most accessible and popular limestone caves. The visitor centre (☎ 6359 3311, @ jencaves @jenolan.org.au) is opposite Caves House.

Things to See & Do Of the 22 known major **caves** in the Jenolan system (which is still being explored), nine 'dark' caves are open for guided tours. If enclosed caves aren't your thing, the Grand Arch offers a taste: it's nearly 130m long and soars to more than 20m high.

Bushwalking in the area is a big attraction. Plants and animals are protected in the Jenolan Reserve and visitors regularly encounter wallabies, kangaroos and birdlife, including lyrebirds. The visitor centre has details of walks nearby the caves.

It's a long ride – about 70km return – from Jenolan to **Kanangra Walls** in **Kanangra-Boyd National Park**, but the walls are one of NSW's most extraordinary natural features. To reach the walls, retrace the last 4km of the Day 1 route (yes, *up* the big hill) and turn left. The Oberon NPW+S office (☎ 6336 1972), 38 Ross St, is the best information source.

Places to Stay & Eat The NPWS *camping ground (☎ 6359 3311 for bookings)*, about 3km north of the caves, has sites for $11, and toilets and showers. Cabins sleeping six to eight people cost $121.50 per night; the Bellbird Cottage, which sleeps eight, costs $143. You must be self-sufficient if you're staying here; pay fees at the visitor centre.

Jenolan Caves House (☎ 6359 3322) is the booking point for the other accommodation listed; it's considerably more expensive on Saturdays, long weekends and school holidays. The cheapest rooms in Jenolan Caves House are $110 off-peak (for two people), but dorm beds in the Vernon Wing are $22. Meals are extra (breakfast is $16, two-/three-course dinners are $36/44). *Trails Bistro* in Caves House is the best bet for lunch.

The best option for groups is a room in either of the 'bushwalking lodges': the *Gate House* charges $71.50/88 for four-/eight-bed rooms; *Binoomea Cottage* charges $82.50 for 4-bed rooms. Both have shared kitchens, but you must bring food: there's no store near the caves.

Day 2: Jenolan Caves to Mt Victoria

4½–6 hours, 56.7km

With fair weather and light traffic, this is definitely a ride to remember, spent on roads that cross dramatic country and allow expansive views. It's also a fitness challenge to rival Day 1.

The best news comes first: the sealed road leaving Jenolan climbs at a far tamer pitch than that which led in. It's still a long haul out – about 13km of climbing – and following is an undulating ridge-top run providing 360-degree views of the Great Dividing Range.

Shortly after the turn to Coxs River (34.1km) comes a stretch of sealed road that's so bad it would better as dirt – a real skull-rattler. After a series of sweeping descents, the route crosses **Coxs River** (44.1km), one of the major feeder streams for Lake Burragorang – Sydney's main water supply reservoir. Deep in the Kanimbla Valley and shaded by casuarina trees, the river presents a believable picture of a pristine mountain stream, but in fact at this point about 75% of its natural flow has already been taken for power stations upstream, near Lithgow.

After rejoining the Great Western Hwy at Little Hartley (50.7km), the route climbs Victoria Pass on a road surveyed and first opened in the early 1830s. The road replaced the much steeper and rougher earlier routes pioneered by William Cox and William Lawson.

Mt Victoria

The Blue Mountains' highest and westernmost township, Mt Victoria (known as 'Mt Vic') is a compact and friendly eyrie that's a popular destination for bushwalkers, rock climbers and sundry city escapees. Its proximity to Sydney means it can be busy on weekends, but it is invariably quiet midweek.

Information There's no visitor centre in Mt Vic itself; information on the Blue Mountains region is available on (☎ 1800-041 227). The NPWS Blue Mountains Heritage Centre (☎ 4787 8877) is the best source for national park and bushwalking information; it's 8km south-east at Govetts Leap, near Blackheath.

Day 2: Jenolan Caves to Mt Victoria

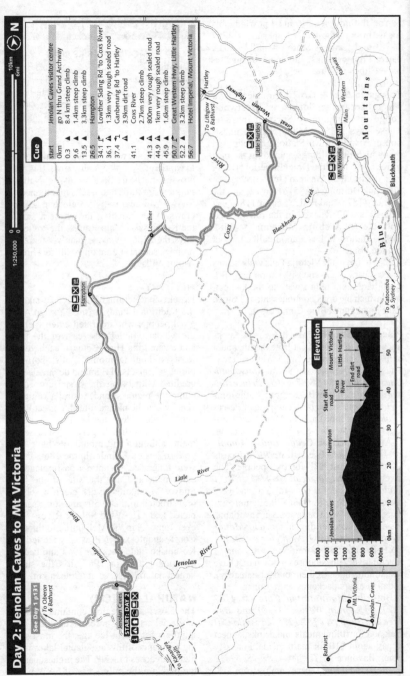

Cue

start	Jenolan Caves visitor centre
0km	go N thru Grand Archway
0.3	8.4 km steep climb ▲
9.6	1.4km steep climb ▲
13.5	3.3km steep climb ▲
26.5	Hampton
34.1	Lowther Siding Rd 'to Coxs River' ↰
36.1	1.3km very rough sealed road
37.4	Ganbenang Rd 'to Hartley' ↰
	3.9km dirt road ▲
41.1	Coxs River
41.3	2.7km steep climb ▲
44.9	800m very rough sealed road
45.9	1km very rough sealed road
	1.6km steep climb ▲
50.7	Great Western Hwy, Little Hartley ↰
52.2	3.2km steep climb ▲
56.7	Hotel Imperial, Mount Victoria

Elevation

Jenolan Caves • Hampton • Start dirt road • Coxs River • Little Hartley • Mount Victoria • End dirt road

START–DAY 2
Jenolan Caves

To Oberon & Bathurst
See Day 1 p131

To Kanangra Walls

Jenolan River
Little River
Jenolan River

Lowther
Hampton

Coxs River
Blackheath Creek

To Lithgow & Bathurst
Hartley
Little Hartley
Mt Victoria
END

Great Western Highway
Main Western Railway

Blue Mountains
Blackheath

To Katoomba & Sydney

N

10km
6mi

1:250,000

Bathurst
Mt Victoria
Jenolan Caves

You'll find friendly and knowledgable locals in both the Hotel Imperial (☎ 4787 1878) and General Store (☎ 4787 1231). There are no banks, but most businesses have Eftpos facilities.

Things to See & Do The grandest of Mt Vic's heritage buildings is **Westwood Lodge** in Montgomery St, built in 1876. These days it's the Manor House guest-house. A walk down Station St leads past many **historic buildings**, including the post office (1897) and the Hotel Imperial (1878), both on the Great Western Hwy corners; the old Bank Building (1885) at No 22; and the Library (1875) and Police Station (1887), at Nos 30 and 32. Tucked in the railway station, the **Mt Victoria Museum** (☎ 4787 1190), Station St, has a good collection but limited hours.

East of town, the **Victoria Falls walk** begins at a car park at the end of Victoria Falls Rd. It's a hard, 6km return walk to the lookout, from which the track continues into the **Grose Valley** and famed **Blue Gum Forest**.

Places to Stay & Eat The nearest camping ground to Mt Vic is at Blackheath, about 6km south-east on the Great Western Hwy. Sites for two people cost $21 at ***Blackheath Caravan Park*** *(☎ 4787 8101, Prince Edward St)*; cabins with/without bathrooms $69/50. There's also bush camping at ***Perrys Lookdown***; phone the Blue Mountains Heritage Centre (☎ 4787 8877) for information.

A dorm bed at ***Cedar Lodge Cabins*** *(☎ 4787 1256, 42 Great Western Hwy)* costs $35; cabins cost $71 for two people. The lovely old ***Hotel Imperial*** *(☎ 4787 1878, 1 Station St)* has dorm beds for $26 and very basic singles/doubles from $40/59; more expensive rooms with bathrooms are available. It's a good place for dinner, too. ***The Manor House*** *(☎ 4787 1369, Montgomery St)* has B&B from $105/145 midweek; it's one of several lovely guesthouses in town that have restaurants (none of them budget-category), and also offers packages with dinner.

Both the ***Mountaintop Cafe*** *(☎ 4787 1221, 115 Great Western Hwy)* and ***Bay Tree Tea Shop*** *(☎ 4787 1275, 26 Station St)* are good for filling meals and drinks; expect to pay about $10 for main meals. For tasty Asian flavours, ***K. Ti's*** *(☎ 4787 1898, 112 Great Western Hwy)* serves mains from $18.

Kosciuszko High Country

MOUNTAIN-BIKE RIDE

Duration	3 days
Distance	128.4km
Difficulty	moderate–hard
Start	Perisher Valley
End	Thredbo

Blocked by snow during winter and subject to capricious weather at any time, this route crosses the heart of Kosciuszko National Park on fire trails and tracks maintained for Snowy Mountains hydro-electric scheme crews. After reaching the western side of the Kosciuszko Main Range, the route follows the Alpine Way, arguably Australia's premier scenic mountain road, to Thredbo Alpine Village.

HISTORY

Kosciuszko National Park (KNP) takes in the traditional lands of the Ngarigo Aboriginal people, who migrated extensively on the Monaro Tablelands (east of the park) and entered the High Country each year to feast on bogong moths. Polish-born explorer/scientist Paul Edmund de Strzelecki is credited with being the first European to climb the region's (and Australia's) highest peak, which he named after the great Polish patriot Tadeusz Kosciuszko. The Kosciuszko High Country has largely resisted settlement, although the mountains have seen gold rushes (at Kiandra in the 1860s); they were long used as summer pasturelands by cattlemen; and are the site of the huge Snowy Mountains hydro-electric scheme (constructed in the 1950s and '60s; see the boxed text 'The Wild Snowy River – Forever Tamed?' in the Melbourne to the Gold Coast chapter). KNP was gazetted (as Kosciusko State Park) in 1944 and became a national park in 1967. It's the state's largest natural reserve at 6900 sq km.

NATURAL HISTORY

The Kosciuszko region contains evidence of glacial activity – rare in Australia – during the most recent Ice age; the most striking remnants of this are glacial lakes in the highest reaches of KNP. The highest parts in the park are the only areas of NSW which are consistently snow-covered in winter and harbour many plants and animals found nowhere else in Australia. High-country wildlife includes the rare mountain pygmy possum and the striking, black-and-yellow corroboree frog; at lower reaches wombats, wallabies, grey kangaroos and emus are commonly seen. The park includes six designated wilderness areas (about 3000 sq km of its total area).

PLANNING
Cyclists are free to use roads and management vehicle tracks in KNP (unless signs indicate these are closed) but not walking tracks. Park authorities ask that cyclists travel in small groups (four to eight people), respect other park users (particularly walkers) and try to minimise their impact by avoiding skidding and wet and muddy areas. Camping is permitted throughout the park, except in the catchment areas of the glacial lakes, in the ski resorts and at Yarrangobilly Caves. Designated picnic/camping areas usually have basic facilities such as pit toilets and fireplaces. If you're bush camping, especially in the higher reaches of the park, observe the tips in the boxed text 'Bicycle Campers' Guide' in the Facts for the Cyclist chapter.

When to Ride
Late spring and early autumn are best. Midsummer temperatures are comfortable, but the flies can be intense and quite unpleasant. The higher reaches of the off-road route are often impassable due to snow from late May until September/October.

Check the Skitube operating times when planning your ride (see the Getting to/from the Ride section for details).

Maps & Books
The LIC maps *Thredbo*, *Mt Kosciusko* and *Khancoban* (all 1:50,000; $7.50 each) cover the route. While it's advisable to have all three, take the *Mt Kosciusko* sheet at the minimum, as it covers all the dirt terrain except a shortish stretch of the Valentine Fire Trail.

Gavin Scott's *Mountain Bike Trails of the Snowys* contains some good general information about riding in the mountains and is handy for planning further explorations; it's generally only available in the region.

What to Bring
This is a mountain-bike-only tour (although all of the Day 3 route could easily be completed on a touring bike). Several businesses in Jindabyne hire mountain bikes; at Paddy Pallin (☎ 6456 2922, e paddys@jindabyne .snowy.net.au), near the Alpine Way turnoff, a mountain bike for three/four days will cost $82/91 (panniers $23/26). It's advisable to book ahead if you're going to ride during school holidays; the shop is open daily.

You must be self-sufficient for this ride and carry all food and cooking and sleeping gear. Some parts of the park are fuel-stove only – check before your departure.

Take a tent: high-country huts such as Valentine are to be used for emergency shelter only. Always come equipped for four-season travel; warm, windproof and waterproof clothing is essential. Pack sunscreen and insect repellent.

GETTING TO/FROM THE RIDE
The Kosciuszko region lies about midway between Sydney and Melbourne and 180km south of Canberra. The main villages, Thredbo and Jindabyne, are 33km apart on the Alpine Way. The Bullocks Flat skitube terminal on the Alpine Way is 18km west of Jindabyne (with some decent climbs on the way) and 15km east of Thredbo.

Perisher Valley is all but deserted from October through May; Jindabyne is the region's year-round tourist capital and a good base. It's reached on Day 9 of the East Coast Explorer ride (see the Melbourne to the Gold Coast Chapter).

Perisher Valley
At around 1730m, Perisher is most easily accessed via the skitube which climbs onto the range from the Bullocks Flat terminal.

Bus & Skitube Greyhound Pioneer (☎ 13 2030) runs services from Canberra, stopping at Jindabyne, Bullocks Flat and Thredbo ($49, three hours, four per week), and from Albury ($65, Sunday and Tuesday).

Trains from the Bullocks Flat terminal (☎ 6456 2010) to Perisher Valley ($15, 20 minutes) run every two hours, Thursday to Sunday between mid-October and mid-December; Tuesday to Sunday from late January until Easter; and daily during summer school holidays.

Thredbo

It's a mostly downhill, and very pleasant, ride from Thredbo to Jindabyne on the Alpine Way. Snowy Mountains Taxi Services (☎ 6457 2444) will take you there for around $80 (mention bikes when you phone).

Bus Greyhound Pioneer (☎ 13 2030) runs from Thredbo and Jindabyne to Canberra ($49, three hours, Sunday and Tuesday).

THE RIDE
Day 1: Perisher Valley to Valentine Hut
3–4½ hours, 28.9km

While it sounds like a short day, it isn't over quickly – the long climb to Schlink Pass and rough terrain over the last 5km to Valentine Hut take their toll. To ensure you reach Valentine with plenty of daylight available, be at Bullocks Flat **Skitube** terminal (☎ 6456 2010) in time for the 11am train.

Leave the Skitube terminal at Perisher Valley and go east on Summit Rd to Smiggin Holes. Turn left into Smiggin village (2km) and climb away from it on the Link Rd; a right at the orange snow gates (7.2km) and a left at 9.7km leads to Guthega Power Station. Cross the bridge over the Snowy River (10.1km) and roll left of the power station. The trailhead to Schlink Pass and Valentine starts at 10.2km (go through the gate); the first 2.5km of the track is steepest, rising more than 200 vertical metres through three stony, hairpin corners. Take the right fork at 12.6km and keep following the track, which rolls upwards from here at a comfortable gradient. **Whites River Hut**, a short detour left at 18.5km, is a nice place for a break.

Schlink Pass (20km) is the tour's high point – 1810m. It was named for Dr Herbert Schlink, a pioneering ski-tourer who was among the first party to ski from the Hotel Kosciusko (east of Smiggin Holes) to Kiandra, about 60km north, in 1927. Go right into the Valentine Fire Trail at 23.8km; there's an Australian Alps Walking Track marker near the turn. The last few kilometres are rough, including a couple of wobbly creek crossings and a nasty 1.5km ascent at 24.5km.

Valentine Hut & Surrounds

Set at about 1680m elevation in a pretty snowgum grove above the Valentine River, Valentine Hut is a popular stopping point for walkers and skiers making extended journeys in KNP through the 66,300-hectare **Jagungal Wilderness**. There are several deepish holes in the Valentine River where you can take a cooling dip, but remember not to use soap in or anywhere near the river. Pretty **Valentine Falls** are downstream of the hut – it's not an easy walk. A further 6km to 7km of hard riding along the fire trail is **Grey Mare Hut**, with wonderful views of **Mt Jagungal** (2061m).

Day 2: Valentine Hut to Geehi
4–5 hours, 51.7km

All of the hard work on Day 1 is rewarded today, after a tricky 5km on Valentine Fire Trail.

From the right turn onto the Geehi Fire Trail (5km; 1730m), there's 14km of virtually uninterrupted downhill on a brilliantly smooth track. The track shadows the Geehi River much of the way, and the rushing water is a pleasant background sound. After crossing the concrete bridge over the Geehi (19.1km; 1110m), a couple of short, intense climbs give nice views of **Geehi Reservoir**. Ride around the locked gate at 22.7km and continue; the route is now on the Olsens Lookout/Geehi Reservoir Rd and you can expect a few cars. Despite some side tracks off the route over the next several kilometres, the major road is always obvious.

From about 32km onwards views of the western faces of the Kosciuszko Main Range – including well-known features such as **The Sentinel** and **Watsons Crags** – sharpen with each pedal stroke. **Olsens Lookout**, reached via a left turn at 38.4km, has the best views, enhanced by interpretive signs – it's well worth the 1.6km return side trip. From 40.7km (elevation 1050m), the day is practically over. A rollicking 7.3km downhill leads back to the sealed **Alpine Way** (go left here), after which there's a short climb before another speedy descent to the Geehi camping area.

Geehi & the Swampy Plain River

Geehi is a large, open area, the primary features of which are a number of old huts, a disused airstrip (a hydro-electric scheme construction camp was established here in 1958) and spectacular views east, to the Kosciuszko Main Range. It's a popular camping area and facilities are good. There

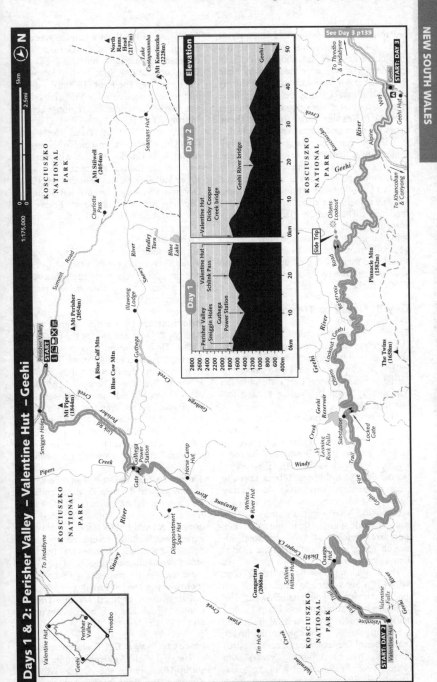

Days 1 & 2: Perisher Valley – Valentine Hut – Geehi

are toilets, picnic tables and interpretive signs near the Alpine Way and another toilet block near **Geehi Hut**, about 1km west of the road. Camping near the **Swampy Plain River**, a major tributary of the Murray River, is pleasant at any point along here; there are quieter sites about 1km further west near **Keebles Hut** – to reach them, cross the river and ride across **Bears Flat**.

Wildlife, especially kangaroos and wallabies, are a feature of any stay at Geehi. They graze out in the open, sometimes in great numbers, around the airstrip and on Bears Flat, often wandering close to camp sites en route to the river for a drink (*don't feed them*). The Swampy Plain River is popular for trout fishing, and it's worth packing some kit if you have room. Conditions can get quite humid at Geehi in midsummer, something that doesn't go unnoticed when you've spent the previous night more than 1200m higher.

Day 3: Geehi to Thredbo
4–5 hours, 47.8km

There's nothing too complicated about the Day 3 route: it serves up a supreme fitness challenge and just happens to include Australia's best alpine views. There's no navigating to worry about: turn right onto the Alpine Way when leaving Geehi, and follow it to Thredbo.

The first physical challenge comes practically before there's been time for a warm-up. From 3.1km, a climb of nearly 7km through magnificent eucalypt forest takes the route towards 800m elevation before a superb, swooping downhill brings it back down to cleared country surrounding the **Murray River** – which forms the border between Victoria and NSW – in the vicinity of Tom Groggin cattle station. Beginning at 22.1km, there are stretches of good dirt road, although a program to seal the entire road is nearing completion.

The Tom Groggin picnic area (at 22.3km; 540m) is a good place to stop, stretch and snack – a long time going uphill awaits. The route steepens at around the 24km (600m) mark, and climbs 450m vertical in a little over 5km; the 1km downhill to the lovely **Leatherbarrel Creek** picnic and camping area provides a nice break but robs you of 60m vertical. From Leatherbarrel, it's 11km to the top of the climb and most the remaining

570m feels like it's at a gentler grade (although much of it isn't!). The outlook is pleasant throughout, but the view from **Pilot Lookout** (36.5km; 1430m) is special. It's named for **The Pilot** (1830m), a distant and solitary peak near the Victorian border, and marks the wilderness region where the Murray River rises.

The road crests at **Dead Horse Gap** (41.5km; 1582m), after which it's almost all downhill to Thredbo village, with beautiful views of the Ramshead Range and Thredbo River Valley. Take the first turn left (Banjo Dr) into Thredbo, then turn left again into Diggings Terrace. Continue into Friday Dr to reach the Alpine Hotel and Valley Terminal.

Thredbo
Stylish and in a breathtaking position, Thredbo lays claim to the title of Australia's premier alpine resort. Its ease of access to the Kosciuszko High Country and range of facilities make it hard to dispute.

Information The visitor centre (☎ 6459 4100 or ☎ 1800-020 589) at the bus stop on Friday Dr is good for general orientation, transport and accommodation. The Sports Centre, across the river in Valley Terminal, is best for activities. There are ATMs dotted about Thredbo and most businesses have Eftpos and accept credit cards. Raw NRG Mountain Bike Centre (☎ 6457 6282) in Valley Terminal carries spares and does repairs; it's open daily. The post office is in the supermarket under Mowamba Apartments.

Things to See & Do It would be easy to occupy several days walking and mountain biking around the village. Go to Raw NRG if you want to cycle Thredbo's famed **Cannonball downhill MTB run** (it's a blast, but expensive). Walking is a cheaper option; the Sports Centre has a free map of the many **walks** in and around Thredbo. In the village there are tennis courts, a golf course, a 'bobsled' run and, at Friday Flat, the Australian Institute of Sport/Thredbo Training Centre, which has a 50m pool, gym and climbing wall.

Places to Stay & Eat There's no camping in Thredbo itself; *Ngarigo* camping area is about 10km down the Alpine Way and *Thredbo Diggings* a few kilometres further.

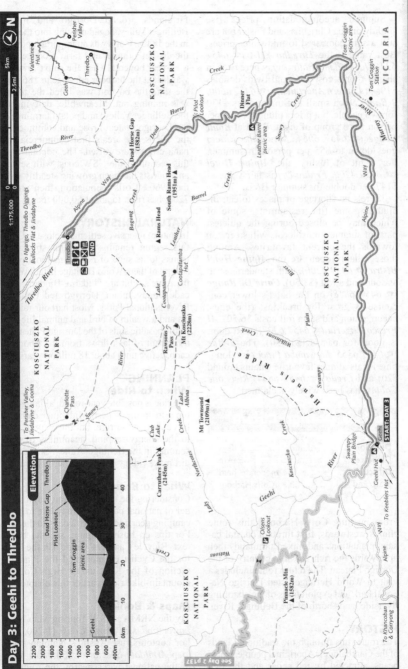

NEW SOUTH WALES

Day 3: Geehi to Thredbo

Summer accommodation prices rise slightly during Christmas and Easter but are still a snip compared to midwinter prices. Best value is the *Thredbo YHA* (☎ *6457 6376, Jack Adams Pathway)*, where beds in shared rooms cost $16, and twins/doubles $19. At *Lantern Apartments* (☎ *6457 6600, 2 Banjo Dr)* a small apartment costs $130 for two people, but prices plunge to $25 per person for a group of eight. B&B at *Boali Lodge* (☎ *6457 6064, Mowamba Place)* goes down to $55 per person in summer. For a bit of luxury, the *Alpine Hotel* (☎ *6459 4200, Friday Dr)* is fair value at $147 per double for summer B&B.

There's no shortage of places to eat, including some fine restaurants, some of which may be closed during the quietest parts of summer; most locals will steer you towards the current favourites. Among those reliably open are the *Alpine Hotel Bistro* (☎ *6459 4200)*, with standards such as soup and a roll ($3.50). *Carte De Range* (☎ *6457 6818)* on the hotel's lower concourse is great for breakfast (the eggs, bacon, onion and salsa roll costs $6.50). *Al Fresco Pizzeria* (☎ *6457 6327)*, next door, is good for pastas ($10.50). The *T-Bar* (☎ *6457 6355, Mowamba Place)* is a longtime locals' dinner favourite (mains around $20) and *Credo* (☎ *6457 6844, Riverside Cabins)* has been widely acclaimed.

Coffs & Dorrigo Circuit

Duration	2 days
Distance	136.6km
Difficulty	moderate–hard
Start/End	Coffs Harbour

From bustling Coffs Harbour, this route climbs westwards, first through coastal banana plantations and mixed farmlands then up towards the rich volcanic country of the Dorrigo Plateau. The return route includes a visit to World Heritage-listed Dorrigo National Park and explorations of the charming riverside lands north of the Bellinger River.

HISTORY

The route runs through the traditional lands of the Gumbainggir Aboriginal people. Europeans, attracted by red cedar and the rich farmlands around Dorrigo and in the Bellinger Valley, began moving into the area in the 1840s. Coffs was an important port for the district's timber and farm produce until a 13-year boycott, when the ship *Carrywell* was lost at the harbour entrance in 1865. By the time the boycott was lifted the timber was running out. Meanwhile, dairying (in the Bellinger Valley) and potato farming (on the Dorrigo Plateau) rose and continued. In the 1920s, the area's first commercial banana crops were raised. The popularity of this section of the NSW coast with settlers and tourists has been growing steadily since the 1960s. Coffs' population, then around 7200, has risen to about 50,000 today.

NATURAL HISTORY

In spite of intensive settlement close to Coffs, this region remains a natural stronghold thanks to its suite of nearby national parks, several of them World Heritage listed. Within the route's orbit are Ulidarra, Bindarri, Cascade, Junuy Julum, Dorrigo and Bellinger River National Parks. Most harbour rainforest and a wealth of bird and animal life. The fertile basaltic soils of the Dorrigo Plateau are a remnant of lava flows from the Ebor volcano, active until about 18 million years ago.

PLANNING
When to Ride

The ride is possible year-round, although autumn to spring is best. Midwinter days can be cool up at Dorrigo, but this is preferable to the energy-sapping steaminess of midsummer in the Bellinger Valley. Sections of dirt make riding in dry weather preferable.

What to Bring

Considering the ride's proximity to a number of national parks, you may like to bring camping gear and add extra days to the tour. For tips on bush camping, see the boxed text 'Bicycle Campers' Guide' (in the Facts for the Cyclist chapter) and the Planning section of the Kosciuszko High Country mountain-bike ride (earlier this chapter).

Maps & Books

Try the NRMA's NSW Touring Map No 1, *Lower and Mid North Coast* (1:200,000). For contours, use Auslig's Natmap series map *Armidale Special* (1:250,000). Maps of the national parks nearby the route are available from the Dorrigo NPWS office/ Rainforest Centre (☎ 6657 2309), PO Box 170, Dorrigo 2453.

GETTING TO/FROM THE RIDE

On the coast between Sydney and Brisbane, Coffs Harbour is around 555km north-east of Sydney, by most direct route. Coffs is reached on Day 25 of the East Coast Explorer ride (see the Melbourne to the Gold Coast chapter).

Train Countrylink (☎ 13 2232) runs three daily services between Sydney and Coffs ($79.20, nine hours).

Bus Greyhound Pioneer (☎ 13 2030) runs three daily services between Sydney and Coffs ($64.90, eight to 10 hours). McCafferty's Coaches (☎ 13 1499) have five daily services between Sydney and Coffs ($62).

THE RIDE
Coffs Harbour

The biggest town between Newcastle and the Gold Coast, adrenalin junkies love Coffs Harbour for its huge variety of adventure sports. Everything from **whale-watching** to **indoor rock climbing** is available and it's one of the cheapest places on the coast to get **dive** certified.

Information The visitor centre (☎ 6652 1522 or ☎ 1300-369 070) is on the corner of Grafton and McLean Sts, in Urara Park. The main post office is on the ground floor of the Palms Centre shopping complex in the mall. There's another at the jetty, opposite the Pier Hotel.

There are at least three bike shops: try Bob Wallis Bicycle Centre (☎ 6652 5102), corner of Orlando and Collingwood Sts.

Things to See & Do Enjoy the views from **Beacon Hill Lookout**, at the top of Edinburgh St, and **Corambirra Point**, south of the harbour.

The excellent **Coffs Creek Walk** is an easy 3.5km; start opposite the council chambers on Coff St. It passes the very worthwhile **North Coast Botanic Gardens**, at the end of Hardacre St. The **Historical Museum**, 191 High St, covers the area's Aboriginal and European past (open 1.30pm to 4pm Tuesday to Thursday and Sunday).

The kitsch-plus **Big Banana** is hard to miss, on the highway north of town. Entry is free, but the guided Plantation Tour (☎ 6652 4355) costs $10.

The main town beach, **Park Beach**, is patrolled from October to April and in school holidays – watch for rips. Ride north on the highway to **Diggers Beach**, turn off near the Big Banana; **Moonee Beach**, about 14km out of town; and **Emerald Beach**, 6km farther on.

Check out the **activities** on offer at the Marina Booking Centre (☎ 6651 4612), although often the hostels have better deals. Gambaarri Tours (☎ 6655 4195) has excellent half-day trips to a number of **Aboriginal sites** on the coast ($50).

Places to Stay Except in hostels and hotels, expect these prices to rise by about 50% in school holidays and by as much as 100% at Christmas/New Year.

The *Park Beach Caravan Park (☎ 6648 4888, Ocean Parade)* has tent sites from $17.60 for two people. Cabins cost from $75.50. Plenty of other places are along the highway north and south of town.

Choose from four good hostels. *Coffs Harbour YHA (☎ 6652 6462, 110 Albany St)*, not far from the city centre, has dorm beds for $20 and doubles for $44. *Barracuda Backpackers (☎ 6651 3514, 19 Arthur St)* is a long way from anywhere, out near the Park Beach Plaza, but gets rave reviews for its facilities; dorm beds cost $20, doubles $46.

Hotel accommodation is good value in summer, as prices tend to stay the same year-round. *Fitzroy Hotel (☎ 6652 3007, 2 Moonee St)*, on the corner of Grafton St, charges $22/33 for singles/doubles. Near the harbour, the *Pier Hotel (☎ 6652 2110, cnr High & Camperdown Sts)* has large clean rooms for $20 per person.

Low-season motel prices can also be reasonable. Grafton has a string of options; *Toreador (☎ 6652 3887, 31 Grafton St)* charges from $58 a double. A bunch of motels around Park Beach have similar rates, including the *Ocean Parade Motel (☎ 6652 6733, 41 Ocean Parade)*, which has $55 doubles.

Places to Eat Supermarkets are dotted all over town, including a *Woolworths (cnr Pacific Hwy & Park Beach Rd)*. The mall is full of *cafes* and *takeaway joints* and all the pubs in the area have counter meals.

Cheap eats can be found at the *Ex-Services Club* (☎ 6652 3888, cnr Grafton & Vernon Sts) and the *Catholic Club* (☎ 6652 1477, 61A West High St), about 1km inland from Grafton St.

For choice, you can't beat the cluster of restaurants at the jetty end of High St. *Foreshores Cafe* (☎ 6652 3127, No 394) offers good-value breakfast (open from 7.30am daily). The lively *Tahruah Thai Kitchen* (☎ 6651 5992, No 360) has a great selection of stir-fries from $10.

Head to the harbour for seafood. *Coffs Harbour Fishermen's Co-op* has a sushi/sashimi bar as well as uncooked seafood and takeaway. The nearby *Yacht Club* serves lunches from $7 in the bar. *Tide & Pilot Brasserie* (☎ 6651 6888, Marina Dr) offers fantastic views up the coast; mains cost $12 to $20.

Day 1: Coffs Harbour to Dorrigo
4½–6 hours, 73km
This is a day for climbers, with the route rising from just above sea level to more than 700m elevation. Happily, the ascents (with a few exceptions) tend to be steady rather than real grinds. Still, the day won't be over quickly, and an early start and leisurely pace

is recommended. About 20km of the day is spent on well-maintained dirt roads. These are best tackled when dry, and it's advisable to check conditions before setting out.

Banana plantations and rolling farmlands line the roadside between Coffs and Coramba (15.8km), but these give way to timbered escarpment as the route climbs Eastern Dorrigo Way – rainforest at first, then the tall timber of Orara West State Forest, and some striking pockets of rainforest towards the climb's top. Following are a series of breathtakingly beautiful farming valleys spaced between wild climbs through wild, whispering forest. Around 50.6km, the route runs briefly beside the border of **Dorrigo National Park** near Coopernook Creek; on the climb away from the creek is the **Jack Feeney Memorial Tallowood** (52.8km), a massive forest eucalypt.

From about 66km, wide views of the rolling, green Dorrigo Plateau signal the day's last few kilometres. At 71km, Dangar Falls on Dorrigo's outskirts are worth a stop. They're not big falls by New England standards, but very pretty and accessible thanks to an excellent lookout.

Dorrigo
Perched on the edge of the New England escarpment, Dorrigo is the main service centre

The Main Street Digger

Australia's many WWI memorials come in a variety of forms: while statues of solitary Australian soldiers ('diggers') aren't the most common, they do catch the eye.

Though many are not actually cenotaphs (literally, empty tombs), the memorials are a kind of distant grave-marker. The nearly 60,000 Australians who died in WWI truly never came home: all are interred in Europe, the Middle East and the Dardenelles.

The memorials also honour what was an all-volunteer force. From a total population of about four million, Australia raised more than 300,000 battlefield soldiers for WWI service, and none were conscripts.

It's thought that Australia has more WWI memorials in proportion to lost soldiers than any other country: about 2000, or one for every 30 men killed during the war.

IAN CONNELLAN

Day 1: Coffs Harbour to Dorrigo

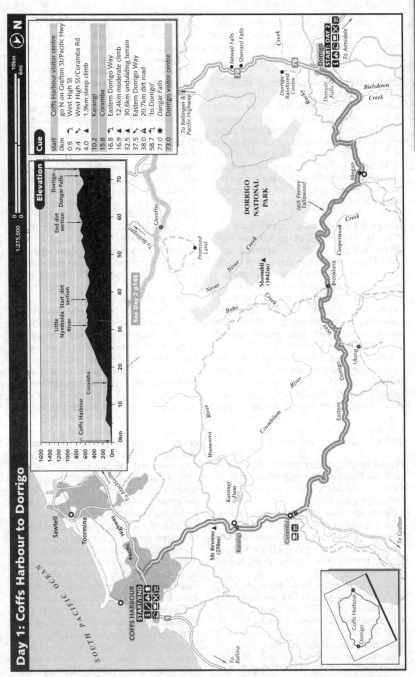

Cue

start		Coffs Harbour visitor centre
0km		go N on Grafton St/Pacific Hwy
0.5	↰	West High St
2.4	↖	West High St/Coramba Rd
4.0	◢	1.9km steep climb
10.2	◢	Karangi
15.8		Coramba
16.8	↰	Eastern Dorrigo Way
16.9	◢	12.4km moderate climb
32.5	◢	30.6km undulating terrain
37.5	◢	Eastern Dorrigo Way
38.0	◢	20.7km dirt road
58.7	↰	'to Dorrigo'
71.0	✳	Dangar Falls
73.0		Dorrigo visitor centre

Elevation

of a rich agricultural district and the magnificent rainforests in several nearby national parks. It's increasingly geared for tourists, but remains an easygoing, charming place.

Information The visitor centre (☎ 6657 2486), 36 Hickory St, is staffed by helpful volunteers. The Dorrigo Rainforest Centre (☎ 6657 2309), Dome Rd, is the best source of information for regional national parks and World Heritage areas; it's 3.6km south of town (see Day 2). The post office, 45 Hickory St, is a Commonwealth Bank agent; the National Australia Bank is on the corner of Hickory and Cudgery Sts; and many businesses have Eftpos facilities.

Things to See & Do Inscribed on the World Heritage List, **Dorrigo National Park** (☎ 6657 2309) conserves some of Australia's most accessible rainforests. More than 100 bird species have been recorded here, including fascinating ground-dwellers such as the lyrebird, logrunner and brush turkey. Starting at the Rainforest Centre, the 5.8km **Wonga Walk** leads through subtropical rainforest and past pretty Crystal Shower Falls and Tristania Falls.

Just west of town on Tallowood St, the privately-owned **Dorrigo Steam Railway and Museum** claims to have the southern hemisphere's largest collection of railway rolling stock: about 280 carriages and wagons. You can see much of this steel-wheeled bounty from the street but no one's quiet sure when, if ever, the museum will be open.

Places to Stay & Eat About 1.5km east of town, the *Dorrigo Mountain Resort (☎ 6657 2564, 1 Bellingen Rd)* has tent sites for $15 for two people.

Splendidly situated about 5km from town (turn left and continue 2km past the rainforest centre), *Gracemere Grange (☎ 6657 2630, 325 Dome Rd)* has B&B for $20 per person. The $7.50 two-course dinner is well recommended.

In town, *Dorrigo Hotel Motel (☎ 6657 2016, cnr Cudgery & Hickory Sts)* has singles and doubles from $39 and counter meals. The *Commercial Hotel Motel (☎ 6657 2016, 15 Cudgery St)* has rooms in the same price range and good-value food.

Stock up on rolls and cakes at the *Dorrigo Bakery (Hickory St)*. The *Waterfall Way*

Cafe (Cudgery St) does big breakfasts for $7.50, serves great coffee and has lunchtime treats such as tofu rice balls. You'll also get a big breakfast ($6.50) at *Nick's Cafe (☎ 6657 2046, 26 Hickory St)*, as well as $3 burgers. *Misty's Restaurant (☎ 6657 2855, 33 Hickory St)* serves renowned food (dinner Thursday to Sunday) and also offers accommodation for $65 per double in a cottage.

Day 2: Dorrigo to Coffs Harbour
4–5½ hours, 63.6km

Spectacular views and charming rural lands are constant and pleasant distractions during this mid-length day. The hard climbing from Day 1 is rewarded with an exhilarating descent early but undulating back roads in the Bellinger Valley and a further 16.2km of dirt roads make it a solid ride.

The **Dorrigo Rainforest Centre** (☎ 6657 2309), a side trip at 2km, is an essential stop, if only to take a short stroll on the 'skywalk', which provides a bird's-eye perspective of the rainforest canopy and big views southeast, across the Bellinger Valley to the ocean.

Rest tired brake hands during the 10.1km Waterfall Way descent at both **Sherrard Falls** (7.4km) and **Newell Falls** (8.5km), the features from which the road takes its name. The few narrow sections on the descent are relieved by wide verges in the trickier sections.

It's hard to pick the prettiest spot in the Bellinger Valley, but the stretch on Gordonville Rd (22.1km) is in the running. Take care on the cattle grids and pick-a-plank bridges. To see another contender, take the side trip (at 28.2km) north from Gleniffer to **Promised Land**. The peaceful hills have lured several notable Australians; Booker Prize-winning novelist Peter Carey lived here in the 1980s and David Helfgott (subject of the acclaimed movie *Shine*) has a house here. The side trip south (also at 28.2km) leads to **Bellingen**, the bright, friendly, somewhat bohemian centre of the Bellinger Valley.

From Gleniffer to the 37km mark is the day's hardest riding. The dirt road can be rough after heavy rain and it includes the day's longest climbs. Take care on descents.

The back way into Coffs Harbour (from 50.5km) avoids the busy Pacific Hwy. A recent upgrade will make the highway more pleasant for cyclists; taking it will shave about 3.5km off the route. Walk through the pedestrian mall, just before the final turn.

NEW SOUTH WALES

Day 2: Dorrigo to Coffs Harbour

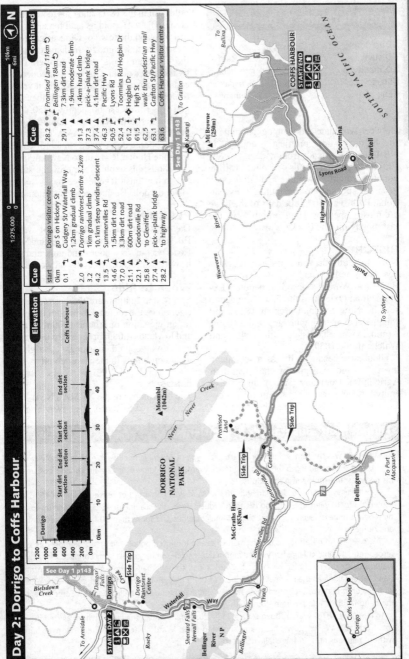

Elevation

Cue

start	Dorrigo visitor centre
0km	go S on Hickory St
0.1	Cudgery St/Waterfall Way
	1.2km gradual climb
2.0	*Dorrigo rainforest centre 3.2km*
3.2	1km gradual climb
4.2	10.1km steep winding descent
13.5	Summervilles Rd
14.6	1.5km dirt road
17.0	3.3km dirt road
21.1	600m dirt road
22.1	Gordonville Rd
25.8	'to Gleniffer'
27.4	pick-a-plank bridge
28.2	'to highway'

Cue — Continued

28.2	*Promised Land 11km*
	Bellingen 18km
29.1	7.3km dirt road
	1.9km moderate climb
31.3	1.4km hard climb
37.3	pick-a-plank bridge
37.4	4.1km dirt road
46.3	Pacific Hwy
50.5	Lyons Rd
52.4	Toormina Rd/Hogbin Dr
61.2	Hogbin Dr
61.5	High St
	walk thru pedestrian mall
62.5	Grafton St/Pacific Hwy
63.1	Coffs Harbour visitor centre
63.6	

See Day 1 p143

NEW SOUTH WALES

Thunderbolts & Bucketts

Duration	.4 days
Distance	.281.4km
Difficulty	moderate–hard
Start	Armidale
End	Dungog

Between Armidale and Dungog lies some of the highest – and prettiest – country in NSW. The route leads from wide, high New England grazing lands, through rolling country around Nowendoc and Gloucester, near the spectacular Barrington Tops National Park. The first three days of the route are mostly spent on Thunderbolts Way, the last mostly on The Bucketts Way.

HISTORY

North to south, the route passes through or near lands of the Nganyaywana, Dainggatti, Biripi and Worimi Aboriginal peoples. Explorer John Oxley was the first European to see the New England area in 1817, and squatters began taking up land in the 1830s. Armidale was established in the 1840s, and Walcha in the 1850s.

Gloucester began its life as a 'company town' on land managed by the Australian Agricultural Company (AAC), an English entity formed in the 1820s. A settlement grew around the AAC's buildings, but it took a gold rush in the 1870s and '80s to kick things along. The AAC sold its land for subdivision in 1903, and the town of Gloucester grew.

Settlers first came to the Dungog area in the 1820s and '30s – many of them drawn by the area's cedar. One account concerns a cedar tree nearly 9m wide which, it was estimated, would yield 9km of timber. Dungog was firmly established by 1850.

Thunderbolts Way was named for the bushranger Fred Ward – AKA Thunderbolt – who operated in a wide stretch of country from the Hunter River up to New England in the 1860s; his exploits are now the stuff of Australian bush legend (see the boxed text 'Thunderbolt: Bushranger & Gentleman?').

PLANNING

Day 4 is optional. At the time of writing, Bucketts Way between Gloucester and Stroud Road was in very poor condition, and quite heavily trafficked, especially on weekends.

When to Ride

Spring and autumn are the best seasons to ride. Since the route takes in both tablelands (at an elevation of around 1000m or more) and lowlands (300m or lower), winter riding will involve cold mornings up high, but ideal conditions in the lower country.

Maps

The best maps are the NRMA's NSW Touring Maps No 5 *Central West, New England,*

Thunderbolt: Bushranger & Gentleman?

'Bushranger' was the term coined for a particular type of Australian baddie: a robber, usually armed, who based his operations in the bush. Frederick Ward, better known as Captain Thunderbolt, made his name as a bushranger in the 1860s.

Born near Windsor outside Sydney in 1836, Ward was convicted of horse stealing in 1856 and sentenced to 10 years at Cockatoo Island in Sydney Harbour. Escaping in 1863, he made up for lost time over the next seven years, robbing 25 mail coaches and more than 30 hotels, stores, stations and homes.

Ward relied on his ability as a horseman to evade mounted police – firing at them only as a last resort – and his time at large has yielded innumerable stories of his gentlemanly conduct. Once, while waiting to steal a racehorse he fancied, Ward is said to have bailed up a group of German musicians. After taking all their money (£16), he had them play by the roadside and, apparently pleased with the entertainment, returned some money and asked for a forwarding address. Some time later, the band received a letter from Ward with £16 tucked inside.

In late May 1870, Ward robbed several individuals near Uralla, the last of whom alerted the police. Constable Walker gave chase, and shot and killed Ward at Kentucky Creek. He was buried, without religious rites, in the Uralla cemetery.

North West (1:550,000) and No 1 *Lower and Mid North Coast* (1:200,000). For contour detail, use Auslig's Natmap sheets *Armidale Special, Hastings* and *Newcastle* (1:250,000; $7.70 each).

GETTING TO/FROM THE RIDE

Armidale is about 200km inland from Coffs Harbour: the start/end of the Coffs to Dorrigo Circuit (earlier in this chapter) and the Day 25 destination on the East Coast Explorer (in the Melbourne to the Gold Coast chapter).

Armidale

Bus Greyhound Pioneer (☎ 13 2030) runs one service daily from Sydney to Armidale. ($60.50, eight hours). McCafferty's Coaches (☎ 13 1499) has one daily service between Sydney and Armidale ($57). Keans Coaches (☎ 6543 1322) runs between Coffs Harbour and Armidale ($26.50, 3½ hours, three per week).

Train Countrylink (☎ 13 2232) runs one daily service from Sydney to Armidale ($79.20, eight hours).

Dungog

Dungog is about 65km from Bulahdelah, which is reached on Day 21 of the East Coast Explorer (in the Melbourne to the Gold Coast chapter). Countrylink (☎ 13 2232) runs three daily trains from Dungog to Sydney ($37.40, 3½ hours).

Gloucester

Countrylink (☎ 13 2232) runs a daily train from Gloucester to Sydney ($41.80, four hours).

THE RIDE
Armidale

Roughly equal distances from both Sydney and Brisbane, graceful Armidale is a major centre of the NSW northern tablelands. It's renowned for cool summers, the autumn colours of its introduced trees and cold winters. The region's long-established grazing industry accounts for many of the city's fine heritage buildings; a thriving student population at the University of New England (UNE) gives it a lively feel.

Information The visitor centre (☎ 6772 8527 or ☎ 1800-627 736) is on the corner of Dumaresq and Marsh Sts, near Curtis Park. The NPWS visitor centre (☎ 6773 7211) is at 85 Faulkner St. Banks (with ATMs) are all on Beardy St, part of which is a pedestrian mall. The main post office is on the corner of Beardy and Faulkner Sts. Armidale Bicycle Centre (☎ 6772 3718), 244 Beardy St, has a great range of gear and spares and does quality repairs.

Things to See & Do Armidale is home to some fine museums. The **Folk Museum** (☎ 6770 3536), corner Faulkner and Rusden Sts, has a good collection of local artefacts. The **New England Regional Art Gallery** (Neram; ☎ 6772 5255), Kentucky St, has a collection that's strong on Australian artists of the late 19th and early 20th centuries. Nearby on Kentucky St, the **Aboriginal Cultural Centre and Keeping Place** (☎ 6771 1249) has exhibitions but is primarily dedicated to preserving Aboriginal and Torres Strait Island art and culture. The **Bicentennial Railway Museum** (☎ 6770 3536) in Brown St has rolling stock and other railway memorabilia.

A good place to get oriented is the **Apex Memorial Lookout** in Drummond Park, on the corner of Jessie and Donnelly Sts. Tours of Armidale's many **heritage buildings** are popular; pick up the *Armidale Heritage Walk* guide at the visitor centre.

The bikepath that winds through central Armidale's park belt (join it near the visitor centre) leads west to **UNE**, the first Australian university outside of a capital city. There are some lovely old buildings and several museums on campus, including the **Museum of Antiquities** (☎ 6773 2555), in the Arts building, and the **Zoology Museum** (☎ 6773 2865), in the Zoology Building.

Further afield, **Dumaresq Dam** (8km north-west of town), **Dangars Falls** (22km south) and **Wollomombi Falls** (40km east) are popular attractions. Ask at the visitor centre for details.

Places to Stay About 2km east of the city centre, *Pembroke Tourist and Leisure Park* (☎ 6772 6470, 39 Grafton Rd) offers tent sites for $16.50, on-site vans for $38 and cabins for $56 (all for two people). The park includes a *YHA hostel*: a comfortable and well-equipped bunkhouse with beds for $16. At *Highlander Van Village* (☎ 6772 4768,

76 Glen Innes Rd), 2km north of the city, sites are $12, on-site vans $35, and cabins $58 (all for two people).

There are more than 20 motels around town, most are lower off-peak. The *Estelle Kramer Motor Inn (☎ 6772 5200, 113 Barney St)* is the best value close to the city; it has rooms for $50/60. The *Hideaway Motor Inn (☎ 6772 5177, 70 Glen Innes Rd)* is about 2km north of the centre, with doubles at $60.

There are some lovely B&Bs in town, most charging more than $50 for a single. An exception is *Smith House (☎ 6772 0652, 88 Barney St)*, where singles cost $28 (doubles $42). The visitor centre has details of other B&Bs.

Places to Eat As you'd expect, there's a wide choice; at the cheap and cheerful end of the scale are the usual suspects – most of the pubs and clubs about town serve bargain bistro or counter meals.

Stock up on rolls and pastries at *Brumby's Breads (cnr Beardy & Dangar Sts)*. For coffee, try *Caffiends (☎ 6772 0277, 182 Beardy St)* or, further afield, *NERAM Cafe (☎ 6772 5255, Kentucky St)*, which is great for lunch.

Dalmatia Pizza (☎ 6772 2300, 2/110 Marsh St) is a vegetarian haven, with pastas from $9 and yummy salads from $10. Try the home-made lemonade. A little more expensive, *Jitterbug Mood (☎ 6772 3022, 15*

Rusden St) has a fantastic wine list; expect to pay $18 to $25 for a main. In the mall, *Jean Pierre's Cafe Restaurant (☎ 6772 2201, Beardy St)* is the place to head for pasta; there's a wide range and plentiful servings for the price (small $10, large $12). *The Only Place (☎ 6772 2086, cnr Beardy & Jesse Sts)* is good for carnivores with steaks from $14.

Day 1: Armidale to Walcha
3½–5 hours, 65.9km

This is the first of a couple of glorious days on the high New England tablelands, gently undulating between 1000m and 1100m almost all the way to Walcha. The first part of the route follows the New England Hwy to Uralla (23.5km), final resting place of Thunderbolt (see the boxed text 'Thunderbolt: Bushranger & Gentleman?') earlier.

Between Armidale and Uralla, it's hard farming country. However, amid the stark bleached trunks of trees killed by New England dieback disease is evidence of tree plantings by local Landcare groups (see the boxed text 'Landcare' earlier in this chapter).

A statue of **Thunderbolt** atop his mount marks the turn into Salisbury St (23.9km) in Uralla. Thunderbolt's grave is a bit further south, in the old cemetery at the corner of John and Roman Sts. **McCrossins Mill Museum** (☎ 6778 3022), Salisbury St, has displays about Thunderbolt and is worth a visit.

Landcare

Neat rows of newly planted trees in a paddock beside the New England Hwy are a perfect example of the work of Landcare – a nationwide, community-based program of protecting Australia's natural resources. There's nothing sexy about the trees. They're small and protected by old milk cartons; it looks like a mob of farmers planted them in between more pressing jobs. But there's a lot of them, and they're growing.

Since the arrival of Europeans, the Australian landscape has been greatly altered and is, by universal agreement, in a parlous state. Erosion, soil salinity, degraded water resources and pest plants and animals are the bane of modern farmers. Many native animals have been driven to extinction while populations of others – kangaroos, for example – have exploded to pest proportions, and require culling.

Landcare is very much a grass-roots movement, and local groups – about 4250 across Australia; 1400 in NSW – are at its core. Groups operate autonomously, identifying local issues and supplying the volunteer workforce to deal with them; the Federal Government helps with project funds. There are urban as well as rural Landcare groups; particularly outside the cities, they're even providing a new social network in many communities – one in three Australian farmers is said to belong to a Landcare group.

Landcare isn't conservation of the marches-and-banners kind, but many Australians believe its grass-roots support gives it the best chance of effecting long-term results.

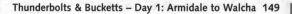

NEW SOUTH WALES

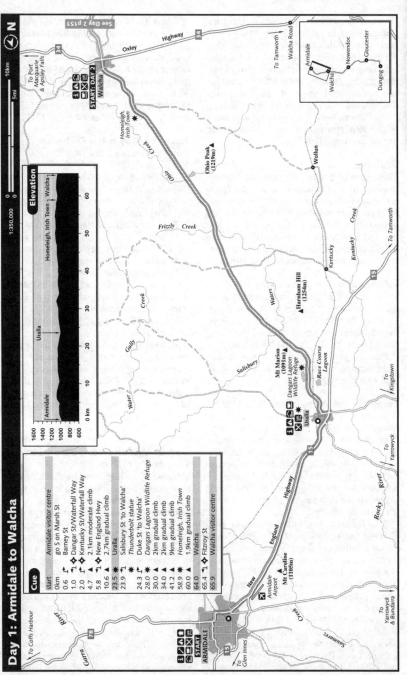

Day 1: Armidale to Walcha

1:350,000

Elevation

Homeleigh, Irish Town — Walcha

Armidale — Uralla — Walcha

| 1600 | 1400 | 1200 | 1000 | 800 | 600 |

0 km   10   20   30   40   50   60

Cue

start	0km	Armidale visitor centre
0.6		go S on Marsh St
1.0		Barney St
2.0		Dangar St/Waterfall Way
4.7		Kentucky St/Waterfall Way
5.8		2.1km moderate climb
10.6		New England Hwy
23.5		2.7km gradual climb
23.9		Uralla
		Salisbury St 'to Walcha'
24.3		Thunderbolt statue
28.0		Duke St 'to Walcha'
30.0		Dangars Lagoon Wildlife Refuge
34.0		2km gradual climb
41.2		2km gradual climb
58.9		9km gradual climb
60.0		Homeleigh, Irish Town
64.0		Walcha
65.4		1.9km gradual climb
65.9		Fitzroy St
		Walcha visitor centre

A conveniently located hide at **Dangars Lagoon Wildlife Refuge** (28km) allows fantastic views of the abundant birdlife that paddle the waters. Soon afterwards (32km), a hill crest opens up panoramic views of New England grazing country. There's far less traffic, and a delightful sense of solitude grows throughout the rolling country that follows.

At 58.9km, the old settler's hut at **Homeleigh, Irish Town** serves as a reminder of life on the Australian frontier.

Walcha

The centre of a wool-growing and timber-industry district, small, neat Walcha (pronounced 'Wolka') has a population of about 1800 people and is close to the eastern slopes of the Great Dividing Range. Strong Aboriginal and artistic communities give it an unusual feel: the signposts at the four main town entry points are sculptures by local artists.

Information The visitor centre (☎ 6777 1075, e walchatc@northnet.com.au) is in the old school, 106 Fitzroy St. The State Forests office (☎ 6777 2511), 19E Hill St, is the best source of information on the many forests between Walcha and Nowendoc.

Banks are on Derby St; the New England Credit Union has an ATM. The post office is at 44N Derby St.

Things to See & Do It's worth making an appointment to see the **Pioneer Cottage and Museum** (☎ 6777 1265), opposite Quota Park on Derby St, which otherwise opens Saturday only. The large collection includes an 1858 slab house, complete with period furnishings, a shearing shed, Aboriginal artefacts and the Tiger Moth biplane that's said to be the first aircraft used in Australia for aerial fertilising.

The **Amaroo Aboriginal Museum and Cultural Centre** (☎ 6777 1391), 38N Derby St, has a collection of artefacts as well as artwork, screen printing and contemporary clothing created by local Aboriginal people. It's a great place for whitefellas to meet Aboriginal people and learn about their culture.

More local art is on display at the **Old School Gallery** (☎ 6777 1111), in the same building as the visitor centre; it's open weekdays. You'll find sculptures around town at Captain Cook Park, near the Apsley River, and in McHattan Park, west on Fitzroy St.

About 20km east of Walcha, magnificent **Apsley Falls**, in **Oxley Wild Rivers National Park**, are worth the ride. An observation deck provides great views of the falls, which drop more than 300m. Much of the national park, World Heritage-listed for its rainforest, is part of the rugged **Macleay Gorges Wilderness**. For more information call the Armidale NPWS office (☎ 6773 7211).

Places to Stay & Eat Pitch a tent at quiet *Walcha Caravan Park (☎ 6777 2501, 113 Middle St)* for $10.

The *Commercial Hotel (☎ 6777 2551, Commercial Lane)* has singles/doubles for $30/55; the pub serves good-value meals, including breakfast.

The *New England Hotel Motel (☎ 6777 2532, 51E Fitzroy St)* has tidy motel rooms for $40/50 and cheaper rooms in the pub; there's also a Chinese restaurant there.

The *Walcha Motel (☎ 6777 2599, 31W Fitzroy St)* has rooms for $60/70; its *Embers* restaurant is licensed and cosy, with mains from $16. *Fenwicke House (☎ 6777 2713, 23E Fitzroy St)* charges $40/30 per person for B&B/room only.

McKays Bakery (Derby St) – 'the lamington capital of the world' – opens at 6.30am (except Sunday). The friendly *Apsley Take-Aways (☎ 6777 1000, 11 Fitzroy St)* does a wide variety of Aussie classics (including a $4.20 steak sandwich) until 8pm and has tables. The *Ex-Services Club (☎ 6777 2231, Fitzroy St)* serves classic pub meals.

Day 2: Walcha to Nowendoc

4½–6 hours, 72.7km

More wide, rolling New England country, light traffic, a good road and several flying descents – the longest about 8km – make this day a pleasure from start to finish.

Before leaving the Walcha limits, stop for a moment at the **Oxley cairn** (1km). Explorer John Oxley camped about 1.6km south-east of here en route to Port Macquarie in 1818, after leading the first party of Europeans across the Liverpool Plains. Just 1km farther on, **Langford homestead** marks the site of the original Wolka run, established in 1832, the first landholding in the New England. Langford is a striking presence: a two-storey, red-brick Italianate mansion, sporting a central tower and decorative cast-iron; nearby is the property's lake, complete with jetty.

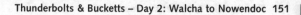

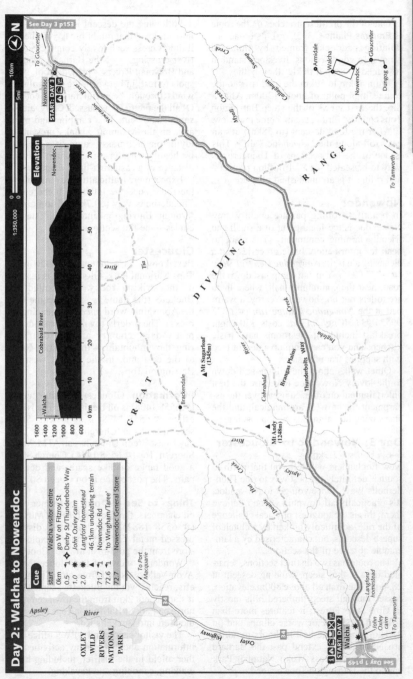

Day 2: Walcha to Nowendoc

Cue

start		Walcha visitor centre
0km		go W on Fitzroy St
0.5	◇	Derby St/Thunderbolts Way
1.0	✷	John Oxley cairn
2.0	▲	Langford homestead
		46.1km undulating terrain
71.7	⌐	Nowendoc Rd
72.6	⌐	'to Wingham/Taree'
72.7		Nowendoc General Store

Elevation

See Day 3 p153

One of the prettiest stretches on the route is **Brangas Plains** (33–38km), its broad undulating paddocks framed by timbered ranges. In good seasons, livestock stand in lush feed so deep it tickles their bellies.

From 40km to 50km the road rises to the route's high point of about 1300m. After a dip, the first views of the steep Barrington Tops country, further south, come into view.

After the long descent (to 58km), it's an easy roll along the Nowendoc Valley. This is one of the last sections of Thunderbolts Way to be sealed – a $7.1 million project – and riding it is an unabashed pleasure.

Nowendoc

In beautiful, rolling pasture country, tiny Nowendoc is the focal point of a small and friendly farming community. The place to head for information, basic groceries and a cleansing ale is the *Nowendoc General Store* (☎ 6777 0955). You can camp just down the road, near the community hall, where there are toilets but no showers. Nearby, a warm bed at the *Nowendoc Village Inn* (☎ 6777 0952/0934, Wingham Rd) costs $30 (light breakfast included); the rooms have basic kitchens and you can whip up a decent feed with supplies from the store.

Quiet walks about the village and down to the lovely Nowendoc River are the best entertainment on offer. Sunsets over the escarpment to the west are magical, and the star gazing hereabouts is as good as it gets.

Day 3: Nowendoc to Gloucester
5–6½ hours, 77.9km

New Englanders will tell you that north to south is definitely the best way to ride Thunderbolts Way: 'Once you get to Nowendoc, it's practically all downhill'. Don't believe them; this is the toughest physical challenge of the ride, admittedly broken by a clutch of superb descents, but characterised by a lamentable absence of flat sections.

The route has two distinct sections, separated by a 6.4km steep, winding descent at 28.4km. The first, all above 800m elevation, passes through steep timbered hills mostly in Giro State Forest; it features more than 13km of moderate or worse climbs and (at 21.1km) one of the best **lookouts** in northern NSW. Views extend past the Barnard River Valley, across Woko National Park and to the Barrington Tops beyond.

Following the descent is about 30km of up-and-down that might break your heart if it didn't cross such lovely country. Several river crossings – of the Barnard, Manning and Bowman Rivers – provide cool, shady spots to rest; in between, the road rolls and winds through beautiful farming country. Of all the pretty spots passed, **Gloryvale Reserve** stands out. This camping and picnic area on the Manning's banks presents an idyllic picture: grassy camp sites sheltered by healthy eucalypt trees within crawling distance of a casuarina-lined river.

Expect more traffic after the remainder of the route once the left turn at the end of Thunderbolts Way (69.7km). The final run through Barrington into Gloucester includes some flat sections – bliss!

Gloucester

Best known as a gateway to Barrington Tops National Park, Gloucester is just east of the striking rocky hills called The Bucketts (the name is said to come from the Aboriginal word *buccans*, meaning big rocks). The orderly town is surrounded by pretty dairy country and the district is ringed by mountains – the Mograni Range to the east and, in the distant west, the Barrington Tops.

Information Gloucester visitor centre (☎ 6558 1408) is on Denison St. The NPWS office (☎ 6558 1478) is at 34 King St. Of several banks on Church St, only the Holiday Coast Credit Union has an ATM. Valley Sport 'n' Toy (☎ 6558 1444), Church St, has a good range of bike spares and does repairs. The post office is on Queen St.

Things to See & Do In the former council chambers, the **Gloucester Folk Museum** (☎ 6558 1882), 12 Church St, displays pressed-metal ceilings and an explosives store from the gold-rush town of Copeland.

Wonderful views of the Gloucester and Avon Valleys extend from atop **The Bucketts**, reached via the **Bucketts Scenic Walk**. It starts about 2km from the town centre; go north on Park St/Barrington Tops Forest Rd, then left into Bucketts Rd.

The visitor centre and NPWS office have information about the many activities further afield in the district, including **bushwalking**, **canoeing** and **kayaking**.

Day 3: Nowendoc to Gloucester

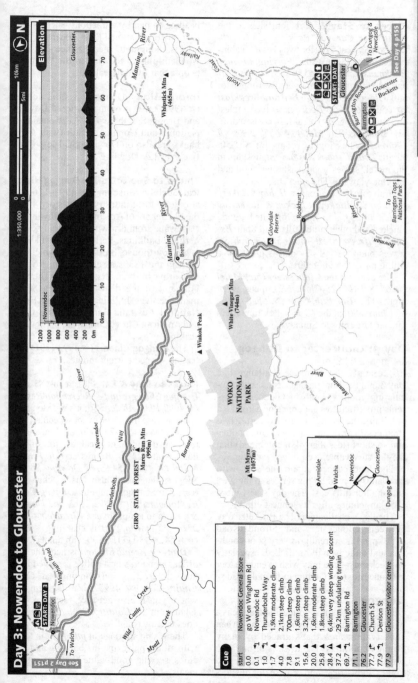

Elevation

Cue		
start		Nowendoc General Store
0.0		go W on Wingham Rd
0.1		Nowendoc Rd
1.0		Thunderbolts Way
1.7		1.9km moderate climb
4.0		2.1km steep climb
7.8		700m steep climb
9.1		1.6km steep climb
15.6		3.2km steep climb
20.0		1.6km moderate climb
25.8		1.8km steep climb
28.4		6.4km very steep winding descent
37.2		29.2km undulating terrain
69.7		Barrington Rd
71.1		Barrington
76.2		Gloucester
77.7		Church St
77.9		Denison St
77.9		Gloucester visitor centre

NEW SOUTH WALES

Places to Stay & Eat Tent sites at the *Gloucester Caravan Park* (☎ 6558 1720, *Denison St)* cost $16 (for two people); cabins range from $38 to $62. *Barrington Tops Backpackers HQ* (☎ 6558 9131, *Church St)* has $15 dorm beds and family rooms for $40. *Gloucester Cottage Bed and Breakfast* (☎ 6558 2658, 61 *Denison St)* has singles/ doubles at $65/76 (breakfast costs extra). The *Bucketts Way Motel* (☎ 6558 2588, 19 *Church St)* has lovely rooms for $71.50/ 82.50; *Thunderbolts Restaurant*, upstairs in the motel, serves good Australian food and has fine views of The Bucketts.

Grab rolls for the road at *Hebby's Bakery* (*Church St)*. *Blakeys Chicken & Takeaway* (☎ 6558 1253, 35 *Church St)* sells burgers, chicken and other quick fills until 8pm. *Escape Cafe* (☎ 6558 1407, 57 *Church St)* serves breakfast all day and is great for a filling pasta ($5.90–8.90).

The bistro at the *Gloucester Hotel Motel* (☎ 6558 1816, 28 *Church St)* opens every night. The *Top Pub Cafe* (☎ 6558 2491, 82 *Church St)*, at the Avon Valley Inn, offers fancier fare (closed Sunday).

Day 4: Gloucester to Dungog

4–5 hours, 64.9km

It's certainly not a fitness challenge like Day 3, but the final day has its hazards. Undulating country south of Gloucester presents no difficulties and, once on Stroud Rd (44.4km), the riding is very peaceful. Two stretches of dirt road are well maintained and so short (less than 4km combined) that they're survivable even in wet weather.

The landscape is again the star, with farmlands framed by big ranges to the west and smaller hills east. The day's best view, at 56km, comes after its longest climb.

The day's challenge is The Bucketts Way between Gloucester and Stroud Road (41.3km). It's currently in very poor condition and quite heavily trafficked, especially on weekends – you may wish to end the tour at Gloucester (see Getting to/from the Ride).

Dungog

Quiet Dungog's most noticeable feature is a wide main street (Dowling St), an urban conservation area that's graced by many original buildings. The town is primarily a service centre for the local dairying and timber industries, and a base for visitors heading to nearby attractions, such as Barrington Tops National Park. The name Dungog is thought to mean 'place of thinly wooded hills' to the clan of the Wonnarua people that lived hereabouts.

Information Dungog visitor centre (☎ 4992 2212) is on the corner of Dowling and Brown Sts; there's an ATM outside it. National and Commonwealth (with ATM) banks are also on Dowling St. The post office is at 129 Dowling St.

Things to See & Do The Dungog Historical Society Museum (☎ 4992 1760) is strong on local industry and history. It's in the old School of Arts building, Dowling St.

A walk around town will reveal several heritage buildings. Perhaps the best known is the courthouse, on Brown St, which was built in the 1830s as barracks for troopers who drove bushrangers, including Thunderbolt, out of the district. Dowling St has many heritage buildings; the Bank Hotel, National Australia Bank (formerly CBC) and Anglican Christ Church are particularly striking.

The Dungog Cinema (☎ 4992 1191) runs bargain-priced current movies.

Places to Stay & Eat Sites are just $5 at the *Dungog Showground & Recreation Reserve* (☎ 4992 1033, *Abelard St)*; it's wise to phone ahead in case there's an event scheduled. The *Royal Hotel* (☎ 4992 3070, 80 *Dowling St)* offers bed and light breakfast for singles/ doubles at $22/38. Rooms at *Tall Timbers Motel* (☎ 4992 1547, 167 *Dowling St)* cost $55/77; the motel also has a 'char-grill' restaurant. Groups could try *Dungog Country Apartments* (☎ 4992 2112, 262 *Dowling St)*. For a touch of luxury, *Kirralee* (☎ 4992 2210, 72 *Dowling St)* is charming – B&B costs $120/130 ($150/190 with dinner).

Dungog Bread Kitchen is near the post office. Dungog's best coffee is served in its most interesting surroundings at *Crazy Chairs Cafe* (☎ 4992 3272, *Dowling St)*, where you'll also get nice focaccias with salad from $6. *Country Grub* (*Dowling St)* does takeaways.

There's no shortage of *pub food* in town, with all the pubs, and the bowling and RSL clubs, serving good-value bistro or counter meals.

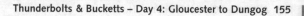

Day 4: Gloucester to Dungog

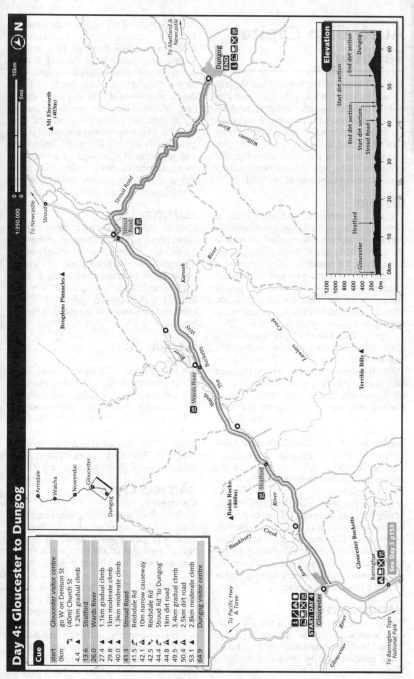

Cue	
start	Gloucester visitor centre
0km	go W on Denison St (40m) Church St
4.4	1.2km gradual climb
13.6	Stratford
26.0	Wards River
27.4	1.1km gradual climb
29.8	1km moderate climb
40.0	1.3km moderate climb
41.3	Stroud Road
41.5	Reidsdale Rd
42.1	10m narrow causeway
42.5	Reidsdale Rd
44.4	Stroud Rd 'to Dungog'
44.8	1km dirt road
49.5	3.4km gradual climb
50.4	2.5km dirt road
53.1	2.8km moderate climb
64.9	Dungog visitor centre

Elevation

Start dirt section
End dirt section
Dungog
End dirt section
Start dirt section
Stroud Road
Stratford
Gloucester

1200
1000
800
600
400
200
0m

0km   10   20   30   40   50   60

Australian Capital Territory

The ACT is one of the best – if not *the* best – place in Australia for cycling. Its only city and the national capital, Canberra, has Australia's best bikepath network. Except for the main arteries, many roads leading from Canberra into the surrounding countryside are quiet and the scenery is stunning. For mountain bikers, nearby forests and reserves have extensive networks of fire roads.

HISTORY

The ACT encompasses traditional lands of both the Ngunawal and Ngarigo Aboriginal peoples. Europeans first reached the area in the early 1820s and took up grazing lands there before the decade was out. There was a small community in the area of modern-day Canberra by the 1840s – when the longest surviving of the district's churches, the Church of St John the Baptist, was built – and the region was widely settled by the 1870s.

The ACT and Canberra were created as a compromise between colonial rivals NSW and Victoria, in the wake of Federation, in 1901. With neither Sydney nor Melbourne keen to see the other named national capital, it was decided to find another site. A Federal parliamentary committee inspected many towns and regions before the 2330 sq km patch was finally selected in 1908, and handed over to the Commonwealth Government in 1911. A competition to design a city for 25,000 people was launched the same year and won by the American Walter Burley Griffin.

Federal Parliament didn't sit in Canberra until 1927, and the main offices of Federal departments were slowly moved to the city over coming decades. The latter part of the 20th century saw the arrival of other institutions, including the High Court of Australia, and the various galleries and attractions that continue to grow in number.

NATURAL HISTORY

While pockets of eucalyptus woodland remain around Canberra – particularly near Black Mountain, Mt Ainslie and Mt Majura – the relatively early establishment of a European farming community resulted in much clearing of native plant communities. The best examples of native vegetation are found in Namadgi National Park and the Tidbinbilla Nature Reserve, which combined occupy most of south-western ACT. Nearer Canberra are large tracts of introduced pine forest. In the city itself there's been considerable alteration to the natural order. Both the Molonglo River and Ginninderra Creek have been dammed (to create lakes Burley Griffin and Ginninderra) and widespread plantings of introduced, mostly deciduous, trees in older parts of the city give it an appearance that's both very pretty in autumn and pretty un-Australian.

CLIMATE

Built on undulating terrain at about 550m to 700m above sea level, Canberra enjoys low humidity, a moderate rainfall (evenly spread throughout the year) and plenty of sunshine (an average of more than seven hours a day). Mean temperatures are approximately 0° to 11°C in midwinter and 13° to 28°C in midsummer. Snowfalls are rare but not unheard of.

INFORMATION
Maps

For cyclists, the ACT Government's *Canberra Cycleways* map ($5.95) is essential. It's waterproof and durable, and indicates the suitability of roads as well as major and minor bikepaths. It's available from the Canberra visitors centre (☎ 6205 0044). The NRMA NSW Touring Map 2, *Canberra and South East New South Wales*, includes a useful *Canberra & Suburbs* map (1:60,000).

GATEWAY CITIES
Canberra

In its growing-up years, Canberra was home to little more than federal public servants and their various service providers. Not so now. About 300,000 people live in the city and it continues to grow.

Information The Canberra visitors centre (☎ 6205 0044 or ☎ 1800-026 166) is about 2km north of Civic (the city centre), in Dickson, at 330 Northbourne Ave, the main north-bound artery. It has a tremendous range of maps and information. The big banks are all represented in Civic and most shopping centres dotted about Canberra have ATMs. Of the several bike shops around the city, Canberra Bicycle Centre (☎ 6248 8861) in Woolley St, Dickson, is close to the visitor centre. The main post office is at 53–73 Alinga St, in Civic.

Things to See & Do While Canberra is short on history, it contains a number of splendid museums and other attractions, and one can spend several very full days here. Several of the main attractions are detailed in the Canberra Explorer ride.

Just north of Lake Burley Griffin, the **National Film and Sound Archive** (☎ 6209 3111), in McCoy Circuit, Acton, has Australia's finest collection of old films (dating back to the 1890s) and sound recordings. On the nearby eastern slopes of Black Mountain, the **National Botanic Gardens** has outstanding displays of Australian native plants; guided walks leave the Gardens' visitor centre (☎ 6250 9540) daily. The **Australian Institute of Sport** (☎ 6214 1010), Leverrier Crescent, Bruce, offers tours (guided by elite athletes) and various exhibits. North again, the **National Dinosaur Museum** (☎ 1800-356 000) has all manner of displays, including original dinosaur fossils. **Blundells' Cottage** (☎ 6273 2667; c. 1860), Wendouree Dr, Parkes, was once the home of tenant farmers; now it's an interesting museum revealing much of pioneer life in the region.

It's possible to cycle to the lookouts atop **Black Mountain**, north of the lake, and **Red Hill**, south. The former features the none-too-attractive **Telstra Tower** (☎ 6248 1911), which has public viewing areas and a restaurant. Night views from Red Hill are striking.

Further from the city centre, attractions include the Australian National University's **Mt Stromlo Observatory** (☎ 6288 1111) at Weston Creek; the **Tidbinbilla Deep Space Tracking Station** (☎ 6201 7838), Paddys River Rd, Tidbinbilla; and **Tidbinbilla Nature Reserve** (☎ 6237 5120), the site of some lovely bushland walks and many Australian native animals.

Places to Stay Canberra caters for visitors on any budget. Call ☎ 1800-100 660 to book accommodation through the visitor centre.

Canberra Motor Village (☎ 6247 5466; *Kunzea St, O'Connor)* is closest to the city centre and in a nice bush setting. For two, tent sites/cabins cost $11/65. Its motel section has

rooms from $72. *Canberra Carotel Caravan Park* (☎ 6241 1377, Federal Hwy), a bit further north in Watson, is a little cheaper.

The lovely *Canberra YHA* (☎ 6248 9155, e canberra@yhansw.org.au; 191 Dryandra St, O'Connor) is in a bush setting; dorm beds cost $20, doubles $48.

Australian Capital Motor Inn (☎ 6257 8133; 193 Mouat St, Lyneham) has doubles/singles at $65/72: it's about 4km north of Civic. The *Canberra City Motor Inn* (☎ 6295 2056; cnr Canberra Ave & Burke Crescent, Manuka) is on the south side, close to Parliament House; rooms cost $79/89.

There's a lot of B&B accommodation in Canberra but not much of it is cost-effective for singles. *White Gum Place* (☎ 6248 9368; 23 Padbury Place, Downer)* charges $60/85; *Passmore Cottage B&B* (☎ 6247 4528; 3 Lilley St, O'Connor)* charges $75/95.

Several good hotels are close to Civic. Singles and doubles start at $153 (including breakfast) at *Rydges Canberra* (☎ 6247 6244, London Circuit)*, a well-known landmark that's close to the start/end of the Canberra Explorer ride.

Places to Eat Canberra is full of reasonably priced eateries and very good restaurants. If you're staying on the north side, head to Civic, where East Row and Garema Place are the happiest hunting grounds for tucker. For fine food, try *The Chairman & Yip* (☎ 6248 7109, 108 Bunda St) or *The Republic* (☎ 6247 1717, 20 Allara St)*.

If you're in Dickson to visit the Bicycle Museum (see the Canberra Explorer ride), stay for dinner at one of several Asian restaurants in Woolley St; *Madam Yip* (☎ 6247 1741, No 4/54) is sensational.

On the south side, Manuka and Kingston are the best places to troll. In Manuka, both *Ottoman Cuisine* (☎ 6239 6754, cnr Flinders Way & Franklin St) and *A Foreign Affair* (☎ 6239 5060, 8 Franklin St) are innovative and popular. *Juniperberry* (☎ 6295 8317, cnr Monaro Crescent & La Perouse St)*, at the Red Hill shops, serves arguably Canberra's best food.

Getting There & Away By the most direct routes, Canberra is about 280km southwest of central Sydney; 145km west of Batemans Bay, which is reached on Day 13 of the East Cost Explorer ride (see the

Melbourne to the Gold Coast chapter); and about 180km north of Jindabyne, reached on Day 9 of the East Coast Explorer ride, and close to the Kosciuszko High Country mountain-bike ride.

Air Canberra receives no international flights, but regular services fly from all Australian capitals. See the Getting There & Away and Getting Around chapters for more information about air travel to and within Australia.

The airport is 7km south-east of the city. Go west on Pialligo Ave, Morshead Dr and Parkes Way for the quickest and easiest ride to Civic.

Bus Greyhound Pioneer (☎ 13 2030) runs between Sydney and Canberra ($31.60, 4½ hours, several daily), as does McCafferty's Coaches (☎ 13 1499; $30, four daily).

Train Countrylink (☎ 13 2232) runs services between Sydney and Canberra ($47.30, four hours, three daily).

Canberra Explorer

Duration ....2½–3 hours
Distance 35.7km
Difficulty..............................easy–moderate
Start/End ....Acton Ferry Wharf

The bikepath that circles Lake Burley Griffin offers arguably Australia's most pleasant traffic-free riding, and can be enjoyed year-round. The route mainly follows this path, which passes most of the capital's museums and key buildings of state. Added to it are out-and-back detours to Mt Ainslie (for fine views of Canberra) and to Parliament House.

THE RIDE
Handy to Civic, the old Acton ferry wharf is a convenient spot to join the Lake Burley Griffin bikepath; a *Canberra Cycleways* map shows other access points. The ride is predominantly flat, with the climb to Mt Ainslie the only genuine ascent of the day.

Inside 1km the route passes the **Captain Cook Memorial Water Jet**, which shoots water more than 100m above the lake (and all over lakeside viewers, if there's a

southerly blowing) from 10am to noon and 2pm to 4pm daily.

You may choose to skip the climb to Mt Ainslie lookout (7.9km), but at least go to the **Australian War Memorial** (☎ 6243 4211; a side trip at 3.8km), where the extensive and sobering collection casts light on the conflicts in which Australians have fought; the Roll of Honour lists the 102,000 Australians who have died at war.

The round-the-lake route continues eastwards, passing the **National Carillon**, which has recitals on Wednesdays (from 12.45pm) and weekends (from 2.45pm).

After crossing the Kings Ave bridge and looping back to the lake, the route passes the **National Gallery of Australia** (☎ 6240 6411), which has a fine permanent collection and visiting exhibitions; and the **High Court** (☎ 6270 6811), Australia's highest court of appeal. Visitors are welcome to sit in on cases but most are fairly dry.

Another 3km deviation from the lake at 16.4km passes: the **National Library** (☎ 6262 1111), which has regular exhibitions, usually on a literary or historical theme; the **National Science and Technology Centre/Questacon** (☎ 1800-020 603), a 'hands-on' science museum; **Old Parliament House** (☎ 6270 8222), the seat of Federal Parliament from 1927 to 1988 and now home of the **National Portrait Gallery** and various exhibitions; and finally **Parliament House** (☎ 6277 5399), on Capital Hill, the federal law-makers' permanent home, opened in 1988.

From about 26km, the bikepath rolls past the extensive grounds of **Government House Yarralumla**, home of the Governor-General (not open to the public), en route to **Scrivener Dam**, at 28.4km, which holds back the waters of Lake Burley Griffin. On the western side of the dam, the **National Aquarium** (☎ 6287 1211) has a collection of both aquatic and terrestrial native animals. The complex housing the **National Museum** collection and the **Australian Institute of Aboriginal and Torres Strait Islander Studies** (AIATSIS) is further east at 34.5km.

From the Acton ferry wharf, it's 5.5km north via quiet suburban bikepaths to the **Canberra Bicycle Museum** (☎ 6248 0999), 2 Badham St, Dickson. More than 50 different bikes and many other cycling artefacts are on display (open 24 hours daily), with refreshments and food close at hand.

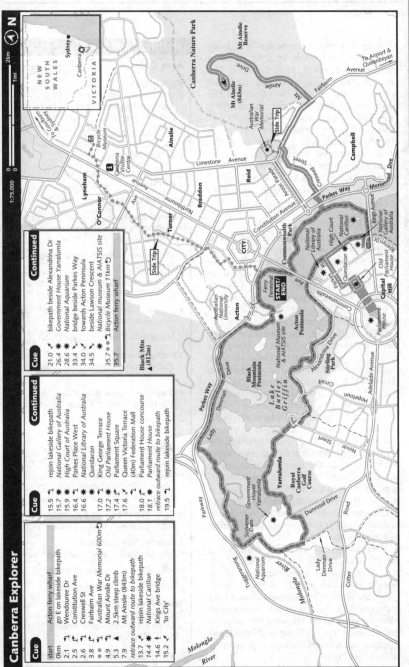

Canberra Explorer

Cue		
start		Acton ferry wharf
0km	↱	go E on lakeside bikepath
2.1	↱	Wendouree Dr
2.5	↱	Constitution Ave
2.6	↱	Creswell St
3.8	↱	Fairbairn Ave
● ●	●	Australian War Memorial 600m ↵
4.9	↱	Mount Ainslie Dr
5.3	◄	2.5km steep climb
7.9	▲	Mt Ainslie (843m)
		retrace outward route to bikepath
13.7	↱	rejoin lakeside bikepath
14.4	✸	National Carillon
14.6	↱	Kings Ave bridge
15.2	↱	'to City'

Cue		Continued
15.5	↱	rejoin lakeside bikepath
15.7	✸	National Gallery of Australia
15.9	✸	High Court of Australia
16.4	↱	Parkes Place West
16.6	✸	National Library of Australia
		Questacon
17.0	↱	King George Terrace
17.2	↱	Old Parliament House
17.4	↱	Parliament Square
17.6	↱	Queen Victoria Terrace
		(40m) Federation Mall
18.0	↱	Parliament House concourse
18.1	↱	Parliament House
		retrace outward route to bikepath
19.5	↱	rejoin lakeside bikepath

Cue		
21.0	↱	bikepath beside Alexandrina Dr
26.4	✸	Government House Yarralumla
28.6	✸	National Aquarium
33.4	↱	bridge beside Parkes Way
34.0	↱	towards Acton Peninsula
34.5		beside Lawson Crescent
	✸	National museum & AIATSIS site
35.7	● ● ↱	Bicycle Museum 11km ↵
35.7		Acton ferry wharf

Victoria

Victoria is a cyclist's paradise. In a small area, readily accessible by train, it has a tremendous diversity of landscapes. The coast is one of the most spectacular in the world, and the country rises from the flat plains around Rutherglen to the challenging High Plains, which rise to over 1800m.

Explore many small towns and sites steeped in gold-mining history along the quiet, sealed back roads that form an extensive network throughout the state. With the exception of snow in the High Country in winter, the temperate climate enables cycling all year.

HISTORY

Estimates of the numbers of Aborigines in Victoria at the time of European colonisation vary between 15,000 and 100,000 – although some may have already died from European disease spread from NSW before European settlement south of the Murray.

In 1803, a small party of convicts, soldiers and settlers arrived at Sorrento (on Port Phillip Bay) but abandoned the settlement within a year. Explorers Hume and Hovell made the first overland journey south from Sydney, in 1824, to Port Phillip Bay. In 1835, Tasmanian businessman John Batman 'purchased' 240,000 hectares of land from the chiefs of a number of tribes in the region (for an assortment of goods, including blankets, tomahawks, clothing and 50 pounds of flour) and established the settlement of Melbourne on the Yarra River. However, the chiefs were engaging in the practice of 'tanderrum' (where strangers are granted the right to travel through the country), not selling the land, and the agreement was not recognised by colonial authorities, as it contravened the doctrine of terra nullius.

Melbourne, on Port Phillip Bay, was a natural drawcard for free settlers, and, by the 1860s, squatters had settled much of the state's extensive lightly wooded areas (often the result of Aboriginal firestick land management), which were pronounced ideal for grazing. By this time, the colonisers' violence, land clearing and introduced diseases had reduced the Koorie population to less than 2000.

In Brief

Area Code: ☎ 03

Highlights
- wild flowers and Aboriginal culture in the **Grampians**
- the spectacular coast scenery of the **Great Ocean Road**
- wineries and gourmet food in the **north-east**
- the **High Plains'** sweeping vistas

Special Events
- **Melbourne International Food & Wine Festival** (Mar)
- **Melbourne International Comedy Festival** (Apr)
- **Melbourne Festival** arts and cultural events (Oct/Nov)
- Australian Rules Football **Grand Final** (Sept) Melbourne
- **Melbourne Cup** horse race (Nov)

Cycling Events
- **Audax Alpine Classic** 100–200km ride (Jan) Bright
- **Great Melbourne Bike Ride** one-day ride (Mar); contact Bicycle Victoria
- **MAD Ride** day ride (Apr) Melbourne; contact Melbourne Bicycle Touring Club
- **Melbourne to Warrnambool** world's longest-running handicap road race (Oct)
- **Tour de Muscat** supported weekend winery tour (Nov) Rutherglen; contact Rutherglen visitor centre
- **Great Victorian Bike Ride** nine-day mass ride (Dec); contact Bicycle Victoria

Gourmet Specialities
- coffee in Melbourne – Australia's best
- bullboars (spicy sausages), central Victoria
- Rutherglen's ports and muscats

State Tourist Information
Tourism Victoria (☎ 13 2842, 🖥 www.visitvictoria.com) Melbourne Town Hall, cnr Little Collins & Swanston Sts

Explore Australia's most bike-friendly city, Melbourne (top left), then cycle Victoria's scenic countryside: (clockwise from top right) bikepaths meander along Melbourne's Yarra River; Loch Ard Gorge, one of the Twelve Apostles, and the Bay of Martyrs on the Great Ocean Road; and Mt Difficult Range, Grampians.

The pretty town of Bright is a cyclist's mecca; visit in autumn for the spectacular colours.

Relax in charming Daylesford, close to Melbourne.

Bendigo's vibrant Chinese and gold-rush heritage.

Beechworth: historic buildings and famous bakery.

A day's reward – sit back to watch the late sun turn snow gums gold in Alpine National Park.

The discovery of gold in 1851 changed the fortunes of Melbourne and the new colony of Victoria. Hundreds of thousands of miners flocked to the goldfields of Ballarat, Bendigo and further afield. Magnificent homes and public buildings were built and, especially during the 1880s, the building industry boomed. By the 1870s much of the surface gold had run out, although the more lucrative reef mining continued until the 1890s. Now a rich city, Melbourne became Australia's premier bicycling city

Cycling in the City

Melbourne is *the* premier cycling city in Australia. It has almost 1000km of bikepaths and, particularly in the inner city, an excellent network of roads with designated bike lanes. The main road through the city, Swanston St, is largely dedicated to cyclists, pedestrians and trams. Melbourne is relatively flat and, fortuitously, the wide roads enable bikes and cars to travel together. More and more Melburnians are commuting by bicycle.

Bikepaths following rivers, the bay and disused rail lines provide scenic, quiet recreational cycling (although they can be congested at weekends). A series of maps highlighting specific trails can be obtained free from Bicycle Victoria or the Visitor Information Centre. Tourism Victoria's free cycling brochure in the Stepping Out series includes two city rides. Inner-city rides include the Capital City Trail and the Outer Circle Loop through the leafy suburbs of Kew and Camberwell. Cycling further afield along river corridors, it is possible to forget you are in a major city. The Main Yarra Trail follows the Yarra River to Westerfolds Park (about 35km); the Maribyrnong River Trail goes to Brimbank Park (about 28km). Alternatively, cycle the Bayside Bikepath along Port Phillip Bay.

Access to the hills east of Melbourne is easy, using the suburban rail network. Hurstbridge train station is the start of rides to Kinglake, Yarra Glen and Whittlesea; Lilydale and Belgrave stations give access to the Dandenong Ranges, which have some exciting mountain-bike tracks. The popular Warburton Rail Trail starts at Lilydale and follows the Yarra Valley to the foothills of the Yarra Ranges.

NATIONAL LIBRARY OF AUSTRALIA

Melbourne has always been a cycling hub – members of the Melbourne Cycling Club gather, in club uniform, outside Government House beside the Botanic Gardens, before an outing.

VICTORIA

VICTORIA

(see the History of Cycling section in the Facts about Australia chapter).

In the 1890s the property market collapsed and left Melbourne in a depression, from which it did not recover until the 1920s, with the establishment of coal, dairy and manufacturing industries. The latter suffered greatly during the Great Depression when more than one-third of Victoria's workforce became unemployed.

Following WWII there was a massive immigration scheme, primarily from southern Europe, designed to boost Melbourne's industrial base.

As it had a century earlier, Victoria boomed during the 1980s – and crashed the following decade.

NATURAL HISTORY

Victoria has vastly contrasting geographical regions. The Great Dividing Range runs parallel to the coast, heading east from the Grampians. It includes the peaks and plateaus of the Victorian Alps, which are known as the High Country. The volcanic plains of the Western District provide some of the country's best grazing. The hottest and driest areas are the northern Wimmera and Mallee regions, which make up the Victorian section of the Murray-Darling Basin. Coal is mined for electricity at Gippsland (in the south-east), which also has fertile dairy country and vast forests. The coast varies from seemingly endless sandy beaches to imposing rocky headlands.

Approximately 65% of the state has been cleared but the diversity of Victoria's vegetation is still apparent. Eucalypts – including the hardy scrub of the Mallee, towering mountain ash and the High Country's twisted snow gums – and acacias (wattles) are the most common trees. Wild flowers abound, especially in the Grampians and coastal regions.

Native fauna is concentrated in protected areas, although the ubiquitous possum and many honeyeaters are common in urban areas. On the road, kangaroos, wallabies, emus, wombats, koalas, cockatoos, galahs and rosellas are often seen.

CLIMATE

Victoria has a temperate climate and three climatic regions. The southern and coastal areas are subject to changeable weather patterns associated with frequent cold fronts and south-westerly winds.

The alpine areas have the most extreme and unpredictable conditions. The higher mountains, snow-covered in winter, can receive falls even in summer. The weather is generally more stable north of the Great Dividing Range.

The Mallee region of the north-west is hot and dry.

In summer the average daily maximum temperatures are around 25°C along the coast, around 20°C in alpine areas, and up to 35°C in the north-west. In winter the average maximums are around 13°C along the coast, between 3° and 10°C in the alpine areas and 17°C in the north-west.

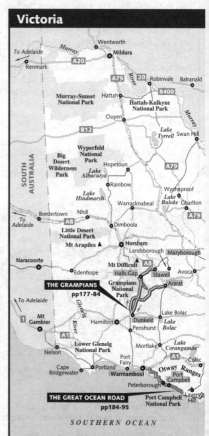

Rainfall is spread fairly evenly throughout the year, with the wettest areas being the Otway Ranges and the High Country, and the driest being the north-west corner.

INFORMATION
Maps

The best maps for cycle touring are the Royal Automobile Club of Victoria (RACV) regional maps (1:350,000). Available from RACV (☎ 13 1955), 360 Bourke St, Melbourne, they cost $3.95 (free to RACV and reciprocal Australian automobile association members).

The VicRoads Web site (🖳 www.vicroads.vic.gov.au) has a detailed map of cycling routes in Melbourne; look under Traffic Management.

Books

Lonely Planet's *Victoria* and *Melbourne city guide* are good companions to *Cycling Australia*.

Bike Paths Victoria has a good selection of car-free city and suburban rides, and *Railtrails of Victoria* details car-free country rides. For mountain biking around Melbourne, Keiran Ryan's *Off Road Cycling Adventures* offers more than 35 rides.

Many regional guides to Victorian natural history exist. The pocket-book *Trees of Victoria and Adjoining Areas*, by Leon Costermans, gives an excellent overview. Nelly Zola & Beth Gott's interesting *Koorie Plants: Koorie People* focuses on the traditional use of plants by Indigenous people. A fascinating insight into Koorie culture at the

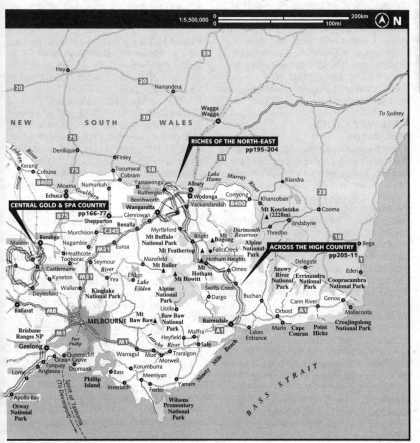

time of colonisation is *Buckley's Hope*, by William Buckley, the escaped convict who lived with Aboriginal people for 32 years.

Information Sources

Information Victoria (☎ 1300-366 356), 356 Collins St, Melbourne, has an extensive range of maps and books about Victoria.

The Department of Natural Resources and Environment (DNRE) information centre (☎ 9637 8325, @ infocentre@nre.vic .gov.au), 8 Nicholson St, East Melbourne, has many books on natural history, history and Aboriginal culture. Information on national and state parks and recreation is available from Parks Victoria (☎ 13 1963, 🖳 www.parkweb.vic.gov.au).

Bicycle Victoria (☎ 9328 3000, 🖳 www .bv.com.au), 19 O'Connell St, North Melbourne, runs public rides, notably the Great Victorian Bike Ride (see the Getting Around chapter). It also sells books and maps.

Victoria's cycling clubs are mostly based in Melbourne. The Melbourne Bicycle Touring Club (🖳 home.vicnet.net.au/~mbtc/) runs rides every weekend. It welcomes visitors; its program is on the Web site.

GATEWAY CITIES
Melbourne

Marvellous Melbourne has been voted Australia's most livable city in spite of the derision it cops for its changeable weather and less-than-inviting Yarra River.

It is Australia's cafe-society capital and has enough restaurants to eat at a different one every day for more than a year. It still has trams, remains in the grip of football fever for much of the year, and boasts lovely gardens and beautiful 19th-century buildings. But, best of all, Melbourne is the cycling capital of Australia (see the boxed text 'Cycling in the City' earlier in this chapter).

Information The Victoria Visitor Information Centre (☎ 13 2842, 🖳 www.visitvictoria.com) is in the Melbourne Town Hall, corner Little Collins and Swanston Sts. All major banks are represented in the city centre; most have currency exchange and ATMs.

Christie Cycles (☎ 9818 4011, @ chriscyc @ozemail.com.au), 80 Burwood Rd, Hawthorn, specialises in touring bikes and equipment and tandems. Bike hire costs $20/75 per day/week, including panniers.

In the city centre, Fitzroy Cycles (☎ 9639 3511), 224 Swanston St, hires mountain bikes for $35 per day, with cheaper rates for longer-term hire.

Things to See & Do The **Royal Botanic Gardens** in the Domain are world famous and the **Fitzroy Gardens** near historic East Melbourne include the Melbourne icons **Captain Cook's Cottage** and the **Fairy Tree**.

The **Queen Victoria Market**, on the corner of Victoria and Peel Sts, sells all manner of foodstuffs and mixed goods.

At night, explore the **Old Melbourne Gaol** (☎ 9663 7228) by candlelight or climb the **Rialto Tower** (☎ 9629 8222) for 360-degree views of the city.

Melbourne is a city of **festivals**, and there is always something on, either sporting or cultural.

Places to Stay The closest caravan park to the city, *Melbourne Holiday Park* (☎ 9354 3533; @ holidaypark@big4melb.com; 265 Elizabeth St, Coburg) is 10km north and a bit isolated. Camp sites cost $22; and cabins, $59 a double ($75 with en suite).

Toad Hall (☎ 9600 9010, 441 Elizabeth St) has dorm beds for $25 and rooms for $60. *Queensbury Hill YHA Hostel* (☎ 9329 8599; 78 Howard St, North Melbourne) has dorm beds ($21) and rooms ($55/62 per single/double). The *Nunnery* (☎ 9419 8637 or ☎ 1800-032 635; @ nunnery@bakpak .com; 116 Nicholson St, Fitzroy) is opposite gardens and close to the dining strips of Lygon and Brunswick Sts. Dorms ($22 per person) and rooms ($50/70) include a light breakfast.

Popular with cyclists, *Olembia Guesthouse* (☎ 9537 1412; 96 Barkly St, St Kilda) has dorm beds for $21 and rooms for $44/64. Booking is essential.

The great-value *Hotel Y* (☎ 9329 5188, 489 Elizabeth St) has rooms from $79.

Batman's Hill (☎ 9614 6344 or ☎ 1800-335 308, 66–70 Spencer St) has rooms from $125 to $165, including breakfast.

Overlooking parkland, the self-contained units at *Oxley Lodge* (☎ 9388 0055; 793 Park St, Brunswick) cost from $92.

The Victorian *Magnolia Court Boutique Hotel* (☎ 9419 4222; 101 Powlett St, East Melbourne) is charming, with rooms from $130 and suites from $203.

Places to Eat Melbourne is a foodie's paradise; many claim it to be Australia's top dining destination. Lonely Planet's *Out to Eat – Melbourne* helps narrow the choices, with more than 400 hand-picked places to eat detailed and updated annually. Here's a guide to some of the best areas to visit for a great feed.

Self-Catering The *Queen Victoria Market* (☎ 9320 5822, cnr Victoria & Elizabeth Sts) is great for fresh fruit and vegetables and delicatessen items. It's open Tuesday and Thursday from 6am to 2pm, Friday (6am–6pm), Saturday (6am–3pm) and Sunday (9am–4pm), when many of the produce stalls are closed and clothes, bric-a-brac etc take over.

Southgate Over the Yarra from the city, eateries here range from a food hall to five-star restaurants. Try the popular *Blue Train Cafe* (☎ 9696 0111; Mid Level, Southgate).

Brunswick St, Fitzroy This cool cafe strip on the northern edge of the city centre opens from early till late: *Babka Bakery Cafe* (☎ 9416 0091, 358 Brunswick St) is great for breakfast; try *Retro Cafe* (☎ 419 9103, 413 Brunswick St) for more substantial meals.

Central Melbourne Little Bourke St is Melbourne's Chinatown. The noisy, well-established *Kun Ming Cafe* (☎ 9663 1851, 212 Little Bourke St) has a huge, modestly priced menu. Just north of the city is *Maria's Trattoria* (☎ 9329 9016; 122–124 Peel St, North Melbourne), with its excellent, enormous pasta dishes (closed weekends).

Lygon St, Carlton Melbourne's 'Little Italy' has great pasta and gelati. For the best espresso and pastries, nothing beats *Brunetti* (☎ 9347 2801, 198 Faraday St), around the corner from the main restaurant strip.

Richmond The Bridge Rd shopping strip has some good day-time cafes. Victoria St is the place for Vietnamese food, especially at *Thy Thy 1* (☎ 9429 1104; Level 1, 142 Victoria St), where a feed costs around $10.

Acland St, St Kilda European cake shops helped make this restaurant strip famous. For great Malaysian food try *Chinta Ria Soul* (☎ 9525 4664, 94 Acland St). *Cafe di Stasio* (☎ 9525 3999, 31A Fitzroy St) is worth the cost of its fine Italian food.

Getting There & Away As Australia's second-largest city, Melbourne has plenty of transport options.

Air Melbourne airport is approximately 22km north of the city. International and domestic terminals are in the same building,

---

Cycling to/from the Airport

The 25km, relatively flat ride linking the city with Tullamarine airport is actually quite pleasant, with much of it meandering along the Moonee Ponds Creek Bikepath. Although not well signposted, if you stick to the main bikepath and keep the creek in sight you're unlikely to go wrong. However, look out for the many very sharp turns.

Airport–City Leaving the airport, follow Centre Rd and turn left into Melrose Dr; follow that for about 5.2km before turning sharp left (at a roundabout) into Mascoma St, which continues straight at the next roundabout as Boeing Dr. Continue through Boeing Reserve car park, past the big rock and the rotunda and turn right onto Moonee Ponds Creek Bikepath. Follow it towards the city. There is a small deviation at 14.6km into Primrose St and left into Vanberg St before joining the path again.

The choice at the end of Tullamarine Fwy will depend on your destination. Access to North Melbourne and the city is easiest along the bike lane on Flemington Rd. The bikepath continues along under the new City Link freeway to Southgate, which links, via St Kilda Rd, to St Kilda.

City–Airport Head north-east along Victoria St then Elizabeth St to reach the bikepath that parallels Flemington Rd; the left turn ('to Moonee Ponds') onto the bikepath to the airport comes just after passing under one (railway) bridge and crossing another (over the creek). Turn (left) off it at the big rock and rotunda after passing a baseball diamond and before another railway bridge. Then follow the Airport–City directions (above) in reverse.

VICTORIA

and the airport receives regular flights from other state capitals and Victorian and Tasmanian regional centres.

The pleasant ride to the city is mainly along bikepaths (see the boxed text 'Cycling to/from the Airport' on the previous page). Taxis to the city cost around $45; taxi vans take up to four boxed bikes. Skybus (☎ 9335 3066) runs a half-hourly service to the city ($11; bikes carried free, space permitting).

Bus McCafferty's (☎ 13 1499, 🖳 www.mcc affertys.co m.au) runs coaches between Melbourne's Spencer St Coach Terminal (next to Spencer St train station) and Adelaide or Sydney via Canberra. Greyhound Pioneer (☎ 13 2030, 🖳 www.greyhound .com.au) runs between Melbourne's Transit Centre, 58 Franklin St, and Adelaide, Brisbane, Sydney and Canberra. See the Getting Around chapter for fare details.

Train Interstate and V/Line trains arrive at Spencer St Station at the city's west end (see the Getting Around chapter for details of interstate services).

V/Line (☎ 13 6196, 🖳 www.vline.vic .gov.au) operates Victorian country train services, which service many of the state's regional centres. It's one of the better state rail systems for bikes, which are carried (intact) anywhere for $3. V/Line buses (which have replaced some rail services) are required to accept bikes; however, in practice, it's often at the discretion of the driver – try to travel at off-peak times.

Sea The overnight *Spirit of Tasmania* ferry (☎ 1800-030 344) crosses Bass Strait between Port Melbourne and Devonport three times weekly each way. A bikepath runs between the ferry terminal at Station Pier, Waterfront Place, and the city.

Getting Around Metropolitan Melbourne has a good public transport network of trains, trams and buses. Contact the Met Information Centre (☎ 13 1638, 🖳 www.victrip.vic .gov.au) or the city Met Shop, 103 Elizabeth St, for information about routes, timetables and fares. Bikes may be carried on trains for free, except during peak periods (7am–9am and 4pm–6pm), when a concession fare is charged. They cannot be carried on buses or trams.

Central Gold & Spa Country

Duration	5 days
Distance	307.1km
Difficulty	easy–moderate
Start/End	Bendigo

Undulating through pleasantly varied countryside, this ride explores one of Australia's richest goldfields. The enormous prosperity brought to central Victoria during the late 19th century is evident in the impressive Victorian architecture of the towns visited. Though some of these are now little more than quiet villages (a fraction the size of their mining heyday), each has plenty of character and historical lore.

The route visits the Daylesford-Hepburn area, where other mineral riches bubble from underground springs. Marketed as Victoria's spa centre, the region has become a massage and alternative therapy hub – and foodies will have a field day.

HISTORY
The first significant gold discovery in Australia was at Clunes in 1850. Once it was announced in 1851, the rush was on. Not long afterwards, more lucrative sites were discovered at Ballarat to the south, at Mt Alexander near Castlemaine and at Ravenswood near Bendigo.

Thousands of hopeful miners arrived from all around the world. Nowadays, Bendigo is proud of its Chinese heritage, but that wasn't always the case. Among predominantly western immigrants, it was Chinese prospectors who bore the brunt of racial tension, despite their large numbers.

By the 1860s, central Victoria's abundant surface gold was running out. Large and powerful mining companies with heavy machinery moved in to replace independent diggers. The reef-mining boom from the 1860s to the '80s produced enormous wealth, and it was during this period that many of the towns' impressive buildings were built.

By the end of the century even reef mining was ceasing to be profitable. Other industries took over in towns like Maryborough and Bendigo, which have grown into important regional centres; places like Clunes and

Maldon are now quiet villages with incongruously large buildings.

A more recent boom in central Victoria has been in wine production. Although the region's wine won European praise as early as 1873, it's in the last quarter of the 20th century that the industry has really taken off and wineries popping up everywhere.

NATURAL HISTORY

Central Victoria was once largely covered in relatively open box-ironbark forest (box and ironbark being the dominant eucalypt species). The relatively poor soil supports a variety of other plants including wattles, orchids and other wild flowers.

Eastern grey kangaroos and wallabies are common, as are possums. Koalas can be seen in the Leanganook Sanctuary (see Day 1). Other fauna includes snakes, echidnas and birds, such as eagles, kookaburras, cockatoos and galahs.

Mining, along with clearing for sheep and cattle grazing, has disturbed or removed much of the original forest. Introduced rabbits and salinity because of irrigation have further contributed to land degradation in some areas.

Classic Victorian Weekender

The gold country around Bendigo – with plenty of cosy B&Bs, antique-shop and cafe-filled towns, quiet country roads and proximity to Melbourne – is the perfect area for a weekend getaway. The Central Gold & Wine Country ride can be easily adapted to create a 127km, two-day ride to Castlemaine with plenty of time to indulge in cafe grazing and gallery hopping.

Catch the V/Line train to Bendigo and follow Day 1 (p168–70) of the ride to Castlemaine (58.2km), where many high-quality B&Bs beckon. Book early to secure accommodation on weekends. On the second day, return to Bendigo via charming Maldon. Follow the signs west to Maldon (18km): take the Midland Hwy then the Pyrenees Hwy to the Castlemaine–Maldon Rd (see p169 map). After lunch and some exploration of this historic town (p175–77) follow the Day 5 route (p177), for the 51km to Bendigo, from where trains return to Melbourne.

PLANNING

The Central Gold Country can still be enjoyed over a weekend; see the boxed text 'Classic Victorian Weekender'.

When to Ride

Autumn (March to May), with the best chance of still, clear days, and spring (September to November), the height of the wattle bloom, are the best seasons.

Accommodation is scarce at Easter and during festivals and, especially in Daylesford and Maldon, it's pricier and heavily booked on weekends.

Maps

The accurate VicRoads Nos 05 *Bendigo* and 10 *Melbourne* sheets (1:250,000; $7.95 each) are available from map shops or Information Victoria. The RACV has the convenient *Goldfields Regional Map* (1:350,000). For topographic information, you'll need Auslig *Bendigo*, *Melbourne*, *Ballarat* and *St Arnaud* (1:250,000) maps.

GETTING TO/FROM THE RIDE

Train V/Line (☎ 13 6196) runs regular services between Melbourne's Spencer St Station and Bendigo ($20.80 plus $3 per bike, two hours). Space for bikes is limited to two per carriage on some services.

Bicycle This ride connects to The Grampians rides from Maryborough, though the route is fairly exposed and not that interesting. Take the Pyrenees Hwy to Avoca, then head north-west on the Sunraysia Hwy for 13km; continue on the C221 past the wineries to Landsborough, then go east to Stawell (121km). Alternatively, after cycling The Grampians ride, take the Pyrenees Hwy from Ararat to Maryborough via Avoca (92km).

THE RIDE
Bendigo

This lively and attractive provincial centre was once one of Australia's richest gold-mining towns.

It's a sizeable place, with plenty of eateries and things to see, and the surrounding bush is great for mountain biking.

Information In the old post office is now the Bendigo visitor centre (☎ 5444 4445 or

VICTORIA

☎ 1800-813 153, e tourism@bendigo.vic .gov.au), at 51 Pall Mall.

On Mitchell St are several banks with ATMs and Moroni's Bike Shop (☎ 5443 9644) is at No 104, near the train station. Ask about mountain biking – the staff have good local knowledge and can put you in touch with other riders.

Things to See & Do Bendigo's impressive buildings include the sumptuous **Shamrock Hotel** (☎ 5443 0333), **law courts** and former **post office**, all on Pall Mall. The massive, Gothic-style **Sacred Heart Cathedral**, on the corner of High and Short Sts, is another landmark. View St, uphill from the Pall Mall's **Alexandra Fountain**, is worth a wander. Its interesting buildings include the **Capitol Theatre** at No 50, **Dudley House** next door and the **Rifle Brigade Hotel** across the road.

The **Art Gallery** (☎ 5443 8566) is the largest and one of the state's best provincial galleries.

The excellent **Golden Dragon Museum** (☎ 5441 5044), 9 Bridge St, houses Sun Loong, the world's longest Chinese processional dragon and the centrepiece of Bendigo's annual Easter Fair parade. The classical **Chinese gardens** are adjacent.

The 412m-deep **Central Deborah Gold Mine** (☎ 5443 8322), 76 Violet St, yielded 1000kg of gold before closing in 1954. Mining has since recommenced and an interesting tour goes 61m underground. A vintage 'Talking' Tram (☎ 5443 8322), with a running commentary, runs from the mine through the city to the **Tramways Museum** (☎ 5443 8322) and **Chinese Joss House** (☎ 5442 1685).

Bendigo's major festival is the carnival-style annual **Easter Fair**. The **Bendigo Madison**, a track-cycling event, is held annually on the Labor Day weekend in March.

Places to Stay Nearly 3km south-west of the city centre, *Central City Caravan Park (☎ 5443 6937; 362 High St, Golden Square)* has $14 tent sites for one or two people; small, bland backpacker cabins for $15 per person; on-site vans for $29/35 per single/ double; and cabins from $52.

Dorm beds cost $19 at the YHA-affiliated *Buzza's Bendigo Backpacker (☎ 5443 7680, 33 Creek St South)*.

The four-star *Barclay 'On View' Motor Inn (☎ 5443 9388, 181 View St)* has rooms

from $83/95. The older, but good-value *City Centre Motel (☎ 5443 2077, 26 Forest St)* has midweek rates at $49/58 (weekends $57).

Federation-style, self-contained suites at *Gardena B&B (☎ 5443 0551, 176 Williamson St)*, with pool, cost $77/110 (with continental breakfast).

Places to Eat The *Coles* supermarket *(Lyttleton Terrace & Myers St)* opens 24 hours; *Bendigo Wholefoods (☎ 5443 9492, 314 Lyttleton Terrace)* is opposite.

Cafe la Vache (☎ 5441 1855, 47 Bull St) serves breakfast, including pancakes ($4.50) and baked goodies.

A long-time local favourite, *Clogs (☎ 5443 0077, 106 Pall Mall)*, has pizzas from $7; pastas cost $9.50 to $11. It's licensed and open late. Good takeaway from the *Turkish Kitchen (Shop 4, 289 Lyttleton Terrace)* includes $3 felafels and $4.50 kebabs.

The bistro in the *Rifle Brigade Hotel (☎ 5443 4092, View St)* has mains from $10.50 to $17.50 (cheaper on Sunday and Monday) and house-brewed beer. Along with Irish stew, the theme pub *Darby O'Gills (☎ 5443 4916, cnr Bull & Hargreaves Sts)* has international dishes from $9.90.

The lovely *Whirrakee Restaurant & Wine Bar (☎ 5441 5557, 17 View Point)* has modern Australian mains (including vegetarian and kangaroo) from $14 to $21, plus an excellent range of local wines.

Day 1: Bendigo to Castlemaine
3–4½ hours, 58.2km

Heading out along the railway line, Bendigo (and all services) are quickly left behind for a quiet day's ride undulating through box-ironbark forest and open farmland. The most significant climb is a steep grunt over the shoulder of Mt Alexander (43km).

A **red gum** (20.8km), thought to be more than 700 years old, is the tree the rescue party of ill-fated explorers Burke and Wills camped under in 1862.

The Leanganook **Koala Sanctuary** is a 2km detour up Mt Alexander (at 44.1km). It's not touristy – the basic picnic area has toilets and water – and koalas are often seen from the walking trails through the sanctuary.

Across the Calder Hwy, the former **Faraday School** (47.9km) was the scene of an infamous kidnapping in 1972. Teacher Mary Gibbs and her six pupils later escaped,

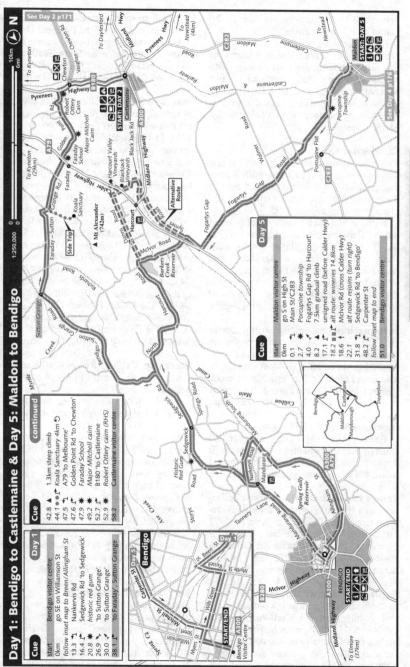

Day 1: Bendigo to Castlemaine & Day 5: Maldon to Bendigo

VICTORIA

N 1:250,000 0 10km / 6mi

See Day 2 p171

Day 1

Cue

start		Bendigo visitor centre
0km	↰	go SE on Williamson St
		follow inset map to Breen/Allingham St
13.3	↰	Nankervis Rd
16.4	↱	Sedgewick Rd 'to Sedgewick'
20.8	☀	historic red gum
26.9	↱	'to Sutton Grange'
30.0	↰	'to Sutton Grange'
38.1	↱	'to Faraday , Sutton Grange

Cue continued

42.8	▲	1.3km steep climb
44.1	•↰ ↻	Koala Sanctuary 4km
47.5	↰	A79 to Melbourne'
47.6	↱	Golden Point Rd 'to Chewton'
47.9	☀	Faraday School
49.2	☀	Major Mitchell cairn
52.7	↱	B180 'to Castlemaine
52.9	☀	Robert Ottery cairn (RHS)
58.2		Castlemaine visitor centre

Day 5

Cue

start		Maldon visitor centre
0km		go S on High St
0.1	↰	Main St/C283
2.7	☀	Porcupine township
4.0	↱	Fogartys Gap Rd 'to Harcourt'
8.2	▲	7.5km gradual climb
17.1	↱	unsigned road (before Calder Hwy)
18.2	▪▪▪	*alt route: wineries 14.8km*
18.6	↰	McIvor Rd (cross Calder Hwy)
22.1		*alt route rejoins (turn right)*
31.8	↱	Sedgewick Rd 'to Bendigo'
48.2	↰	Carpenter St
		follow inset map to end
51.0		Bendigo visitor centre

To Kyneton

Chewton

Pyrenees Highway

START: DAY 2 Castlemaine A300

To Kyneton (29km)

A79

Golden Grange Rd

Robert Ottery Cairn

Major Mitchell Cairn

Faraday School

Faraday

Calder Highway

Koala Sanctuary

Side Trip

▲ Mt Alexander (742m)

Faraday – Sutton Grange Rd

Sutton Grange

Harcourt Valley Vineyards

Blackjack Vineyards

Black Jack Rd

Harcourt

Midland Highway

Syms Rd

Alternative Route

Fogartys Gap

McIvor Road

Barkers Creek Reservoir

Sutton Grange Road

Myrtle Creek

Bendigo Sutton Road

Richards Road

Danns Road

North Harcourt Road

Sedgewick Road

Springs Road

Mandurang South Rd

Historic Red Gum

Sedgewick

Mandurang

Spring Gully Reservoir

Nankervis Road

Tannery Lane

Storys Road

Axe Creek

Spires Ck

Mandurang Road

Allingham

McIvor Highway A300

BENDIGO START/END

B280 Midland Highway

To Elmore (37km)

Bendigo Day 1

Breen St

Russell St

Myrtle St

Carpenter St Day 5

Mitchell St

Wills Street

Williamson Street

Myers Street

START/END A300

Bendigo Visitor Centre

Midland Hwy

Pyrenees Hwy

To Daylesford

Vaughan - Chewton Rd

Midland Hwy

Railway

Castlemaine & Maldon

Road

Walmer

Road

Fogartys Gap

Porcupine Flat

Porcupine Township

C283

To Newstead (4km)

C282

Maldon

START: DAY 5

See Day 4 p176

To Newstead

To Daylesford

Bendigo · Castlemaine · Maldon · Maryborough

Colban

Main

Canal

unharmed, by kicking out the door of the van in which they were held.

From here it's a delightful ride along the creek. Towards Castlemaine is evidence of the area's gold-mining past, along with **monuments** to 1830s explorer Major Mitchell (49.2km) and to Robert Ottery (52.9km), who found the first gold in the area after walking barefoot from Williamstown (a Melbourne suburb).

Castlemaine

The area around Chewton and Castlemaine was one of the world's richest shallow alluvial goldfields. Thousands flocked here in the early 1850s and Castlemaine was declared a municipality in 1855.

Without the rich quartz reefs found around Bendigo and Ballarat, Castlemaine didn't last as a major player, but the town today has other riches: a significant arts community, several galleries and a leading arts festival, as well as some delightful gardens. Less widely known is the wealth of mountain-biking opportunities in the region.

Information Castlemaine visitor centre (☎ 5470 6200, 🖥 www.mountalexander.vic .gov.au/tourism) is in the magnificent Castlemaine Market building on Mostyn St (entry also from Forest St). Free brochures include *Things to See & Do* and *Food & Wine*; town maps cost $1. The Mount Alexander Shire Council provides a free accommodation booking service (☎ 1800-171 888).

Banks (with ATMs) are on Barker and Mostyn Sts. Castlemaine Cycles (☎ 5470 5868), 28 Hargraves St, has mountain-biking maps, and can arrange a personal guide.

Things to See & Do The extensive collections of a Hungarian silversmith and his creative family are displayed at **Buda** (☎ 5472 1032), their historic home and garden at 42 Hunter St. The **Castlemaine Art Gallery & Historical Museum** (☎ 5472 2292), in Lyttleton St, includes contemporary and colonial Australian art. On Downes Rd, the **Castlemaine Botanic Gardens**, established in 1860, are among Victoria's oldest.

The imposing old **Castlemaine Gaol** (☎ 5470 5311), on Bowden St, provides excellent views of the town. Guided tours run on weekends – and you can even spend a night here. On the way into town, pat dingos

at the **Dingo Farm Australia** (☎ 5470 5711), on Dingo Park Rd, off the Pyrenees Hwy.

Every odd-numbered year, Castlemaine hosts the **Castlemaine State Festival** in April – one of Victoria's leading arts events – and the **Garden Festival** in November.

Places to Stay Book ahead well in advance at festival times. The prettiest camping is at the *Botanic Gardens Caravan Park* (☎ 5472 1125, 18 Walker St). Tent sites cost $9.50/11 for one/two people; on-site vans cost $27.50, and en suite cabins from $44. *Carracourt Caravan Park* (☎ 5472 2160, 101 Barker St) has double cabins for $50.

National Trust-classified *Campbell St Motor Lodge* (☎ 5472 3477, 33 Campbell St) has pleasant, older rooms for $58/76 a single/double. *Castlemaine Colonial Motel* (☎ 5472 4000, 252 Barker St) is a standard motor inn with rooms for $79/89.

The Edwardian *Green Gables* (☎ 5472 2482, 94 Hargraves St) is at the cheaper end of the town's many B&Bs, with rooms from $60/90. The *Midland Private Hotel* (☎ 5472 1085, 2–4 Templeton St) has a magnificent Art Deco foyer and Victorian club-style lounge. B&B costs $66/100; book ahead.

Places to Eat The *Rainbow IGA* supermarket is at the corner of Mostyn and Hargraves Sts.

Good cafes in Castlemaine include the rustic, yet stylish, *Tog's Cafe & Gallery* (☎ 5470 5090, 58 Lyttleton St), with good coffee and cakes; hearty evening meals (Friday and Saturday) cost from $13.50 to $17.50. Bright and airy *Saff's Cafe* serves evening meals Thursday to Saturday (laksa costs $12.50) and breakfast.

Capones Pizzeria (☎ 5470 5705, 50 Hargraves St), open every night, is not quite genuine 1920s Chicago: it's nonsmoking. The *Globe Bistro* (☎ 5470 5055, 81 Forest St) has pasta and pizza for around $12.50 every night; more upmarket fare is available in the adjoining *Globe Restaurant*.

Day 2: Castlemaine to Daylesford

2½–3½ hours, 48km

From mining to mineral springs, the ride undulates along mostly quiet roads (other than a 2.2km stretch from Guildford), becoming busier and more hilly in the final 15km.

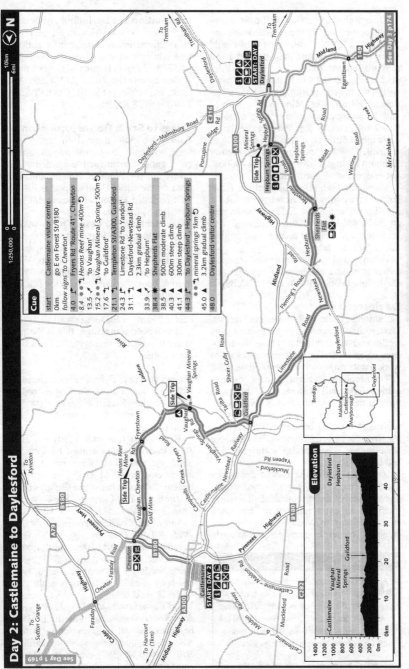

Day 2: Castlemaine to Daylesford

1:250,000

VICTORIA

See Day 3 p174

See Day 1 p169

START: DAY 3
Daylesford

Hepburn Springs

Shepherds Flat

Guildford

Vaughan Mineral Springs

START: DAY 2
Castlemaine

Chewton

Cue

start		Castlemaine visitor centre
0km		go E on Forest St/B180
		follow signs 'to Chewton'
4.0		Fryers Rd 'Route 41', Chewton
8.4		↰ Herons Reef mine 400m
13.5		↱ 'to Vaughan'
15.2		↰ Vaughan Mineral Springs 500m
17.6		↱ 'to Guildford'
21.1		↰ Templeton St/A300, Guildford
24.3		↱ Limestone Rd 'to Yandoit'
31.1		↰ Daylesford–Newstead Rd
33.9		◀ 2.3km gradual climb
		↱ 'to Hepburn'
38.4	✳	Shepherds Flat
38.5	◀	500m moderate climb
40.3	◀	600m steep climb
41.1	◀	300m steep climb
		↱ 'to Daylesford', Hepburn Springs
44.3		↰ mineral springs 1km
45.0	◀	3.2km gradual climb
48.0		Daylesford visitor centre

Elevation

Castlemaine
Vaughan Mineral Springs
Guildford
Hepburn
Daylesford

1400
1200
1000
800
600
400
200
0m

0km   10   20   30   40

Bendigo
Maldon
Castlemaine
Maryborough
Daylesford

Side Trip
Side Trip
Side Trip

Though the rush ended well over a century ago, the road between Castlemaine and Vaughan is littered with signs of the gold frenzy: from an **abandoned poppet head** (5.6km), **engine house** (10.2km) and degraded digging sites, to Irishtown – a name without a town – marking a one-time settlement. **Heron's Reef Mine** (8.4km; ☎ 5473 4387) is an open-air gold-mining museum with tours ($10, by appointment only).

Vaughan Springs, a side trip at 15.2km, is smaller and less touristy than the prettier **Hepburn Springs**, also a side trip at 44.3km, but both are well worth visiting.

Shepherds Flat, set among rolling farmland, has a *cafe* with **cricket memorabilia** (38.4km). The fragrant fields of **Lavendula** (☎ 5476 4393) are 500m on, along with lavender products and a *cafe* – all behind the $2.50 entry fee.

Urban sprawl – albeit attractive – connects the twin towns of Hepburn Springs and Daylesford (along with dozens of B&Bs).

Daylesford

Set among scenic hills, lakes and forests, Daylesford's prosperous past is evident in its well-preserved architecture, as is the influence of Swiss-Italian settlers who came to work tunnel mines in the surrounding hills.

The Hepburn mineral springs, discovered (before gold) in 1836, made the area a popular health resort by the 1870s. Daylesford and Hepburn Springs are enjoying a revival as the 'spa centre of Victoria', attracting – as before – droves of fashionable Melburnians. There's also a thriving gay and lesbian scene.

Weekends see the area inundated with visitors; accommodation is pricier and single-night bookings are discouraged. It's worth spending an extra night here, but book ahead. Monday to Wednesday is quieter – indeed, too quiet for many eateries to open.

Information The Daylesford visitor centre (☎ 5348 1339) is on Vincent St, next to the post office; limited tourist information is also available from the Hepburn post office (☎ 5348 1339) on Hepburn-Daylesford Rd.

Commonwealth (with ATM) and ANZ banks are on Vincent St. KC Cycles (☎ 5348 1010) is at 28 Raglan St.

Things to See & Do The popular **Convent Gallery** is a multi-storey 19th-century convent, brilliantly converted into an art and craft gallery in attractive gardens. Also lovely are the **Wombat Hill Botanic Gardens** on the hill in Central Springs Rd. The well-regarded **Historical Society Museum** is at 100 Vincent St.

The **Hepburn Spa Resort** (☎ 5348 2034), in the **Mineral Springs Reserve**, features such services as a relaxation pool, spas with essential oils, massage and saunas. Weekends are busy – and prices higher – you'll need to book. Perhaps as relaxing is a walk through the lovely reserve. Take a bottle to collect your own mineral water. The visitor centre has maps for longer **walks**.

If you need a **massage**, this is the place to get it – ask the visitor centre for a list of practitioners.

Places to Stay It's best to book ahead, but if you're caught short, the Daylesford Accommodation Booking Service (☎ 5348 1448), on Vincent St, is open until at least 7pm most nights.

The closest tent sites ($10) are at the *Daylesford Victoria Caravan Park (☎ 5348 3821, Ballan Rd)*, 1.5km south. Six-berth cabins cost from $44 to $83; most require bedding. More secluded and slightly cheaper is *Jubilee Lake Caravan Park (☎ 5348 2186, Lake Rd)*, 3.5km from town.

Sprawling *Continental House (☎ 5348 2005, 9 Lone Pine Ave)* is an alternative, vegetarian guesthouse 500m uphill from the spa centre. Beds cost from $15 to $20. Bring bedding – but no meat, fish or eggs – and book ahead. The Saturday night vegan buffet is good value.

Val Ragatz (☎ 5348 3315, 39 Vincent St) does $20, no-nonsense, no-frills B&B, the best value you'll find, and close to town. Also good value is the accommodating *35 Hill St (☎ 5348 3878)*, with spa. B&B in comfortable singles/doubles costs $50/70.

Traditional pub rooms at *Walshs Daylesford Hotel* (☎ *5348 2335, Burke Square*) cost $55 ($11 more on Saturday), including breakfast.

Places to Eat The *IGA* supermarket has entrances on Vincent and Albert Sts.

Daylesford has the highest concentration of good bakeries for kilometres: the *Farmhouse Bakery* (*57D Vincent St*) specialises in Italian-style breads; a few doors along, *Himalaya Bakery* bakes healthy, organic breads; buy muffins (from 7am) around the corner at *Not Just Muffins* (*Albert St*).

Champion Restaurant & Takeaway (*72 Vincent St*) does a burger with the lot for $3.80. *Valentino's Pizza Restaurant* (☎ *5348 1771, 28 Vincent St*) is the best value for a carbo fix: pasta costs $8 to $12.50.

The stylishly earthy *Harvest Cafe* (☎ *5348 3994, Albert St*) has evening mains (Thursday through Sunday) featuring vegetarian and seafood dishes. *Frangos & Frangos* (☎ *5348 2363, 82 Vincent St*) opens from breakfast till late; it's fashionable, with great coffee and evening mains from $18.50 to $25.90. Try bullboars ($18.90), a central-Victorian spiced sausage. The *Food Gallery* (☎ *5348 1677, Vincent St*) serves breakfast from 8am.

Day 3: Daylesford to Maryborough

3½–5 hours, 74.7km

Make sure you carry enough water for today, or buy or boil tap water in Clunes (see the 'Warning' boxed text earlier). After the scenic first 11km (and the day's main climb) on the Midland Hwy, it's an easy, quiet ride to Clunes. Though the highway carries trucks, it has a good shoulder. Traffic increases a little on the Maryborough Rd from Clunes, which undulates gently through attractive box-ironbark forest.

Mullock heaps, by-products of deep-lead mines, litter the paddocks between Blampied and Clunes. Many such mines operated in the area after surface gold ran out, some well into the 20th century. Along with gold, these mines turned up fossils – look out for two **information boards** (from 25.1km).

The population of **Clunes** (39.4km) skyrocketed to 30,000 with the first discovery of gold. Today, it's a cute little town (population 850) with big buildings, many of which have changed little since its heyday.

On the corner of Fraser St is a *bakery*, or try the quaint *FJ Cafe* (*51 Fraser St*) – spot the Malvern Star bike among all those Holden cars… **Clunes visitor centre** (☎ 5345 3896), 70 Bailey St, is also a bottle museum and is in a grand old red-brick school building as you leave town.

Talbot (57.8km) is another old gold town, again with some magnificent architecture – don't miss the bluestone *Bull & Mouth* (☎ *5463 2325, Ballaarat St*), now a well regarded restaurant and bar, with B&B. Things are pretty quiet in Talbot – oh, except for the annual yabby festival.

Maryborough

Maryborough was the name of a police camp established at the diggings after gold was discovered in 1854. At the height of the rush, the population was more than 40,000 – more than five times its current level.

Despite the beautiful Victorian architecture, Maryborough is less of a tourist town than a pleasant, bustling rural centre: you'll find few wine-quaffing trendy suburbanites here – more likely the local boys cruising in hotted-up cars. Its strong manufacturing base, including apiary, food processing and printing, had already developed by the time gold ran out around 1918.

Information The visitor centre (☎ 5460 4511 or ☎ 1800-356 511, 🖳 www.cgoldshire .vic.gov.au) is at the Maryborough Railway Station Complex (see Things to See & Do), off Tuaggra St. It's likely to move to the corner of Alma and Nolan Sts in 2001.

The DNRE and Parks Victoria (☎ 13 1963) are at 126 High St. The major banks (with ATMs) are in High St, as is Maryborough Cycles (☎ 5461 4150), at No 114.

Things to See & Do The architectural jewel in Maryborough's crown is the inordinately large **Maryborough Railway Station**, once described by Mark Twain as 'a train station with town attached'. Built in 1862, it now houses a mammoth antique emporium and delightful cafe.

Some fine **wineries** are close to Maryborough; most around Avoca (28km west) and the Pyrenees Ranges. To see them properly, stop overnight at Avoca.

Maryborough's annual events include the **RACV Energy Breakthrough** in November,

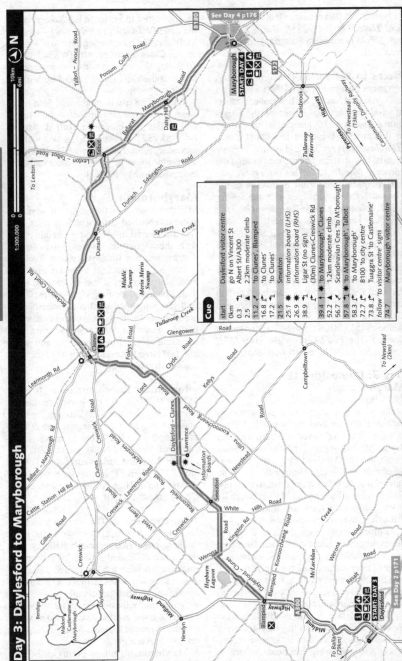

Day 3: Daylesford to Maryborough

VICTORIA

1:1,300,000

Cue		
start	0km	Daylesford visitor centre
		go N on Vincent St
	0.3	Albert St/A300
	2.5	2.2km moderate climb
	11.2	'to Clunes', Blampied
	16.8	'to Clunes'
	17.2	'to Clunes'
	21.5	Smeaton
	25.1	information board (LHS)
	26.9	information board (RHS)
	38.9	Ligar St (no sign)
		(30m) Clunes-Creswick Rd
	39.4	1.2km moderate climb
	52.2	to Maryborough, Clunes
	56.7	Scandinavian Cres 'to M'borough'
	57.8	'to Maryborough', Talbot
	58.3	'to Maryborough'
	72.7	B100 'to city centre'
	73.8	Tuagrra St 'to Castlemaine'
		follow 'to visitor centre' signs
	74.7	Maryborough visitor centre

See Day 4 p176

See Day 2 p171

which includes a Human Powered Vehicle Grand Prix; regular **Audax rides**; the **Australasian Goldpanning Championships**, held around the last weekend in October; and the New Year's Day **Highland Gathering**.

Places to Stay & Eat The well-equipped and bike-friendly *Maryborough Caravan Park (☎ 5460 4848, 7 Holyrood St)* has $11 tent sites and cabins from $49.

Although hotels offer the cheapest accommodation, there's little else to recommend them. The *Albion (☎ 5461 1035, 57 High St)* is perhaps less noisy than the others, with motor inn-style units for $35/60 a single/double, including breakfast.

The friendly *Wattle Grove Motel (☎ 5461 1877, 65 Derby Rd)* has pleasant enough units from $49/55. *Maryborough Guesthouse B&B (☎ 5460 5808, 44 Goldsmith St)* is good value, with en suite rooms from $95 weeknights (from $110 weekends). Guests can book bus or bus-and-bike winery tours ($50, including lunch).

Safeway supermarket is opposite the *Parkview Bakery & Cafe (☎ 5461 4655, 21 Tuaggra St)*, which serves breakfast from 5am.

Golden Wattle Pizza (96 High St) serves small/large pizzas from $5.50/10. Open until 6pm, *Station Cafe*, at the train station, has $6 generous pasta servings, plus cakes and snacks. For a carbo fix, order pancakes and pasta from $7, plus steak, seafood and espresso at the *Mandeville Coffee Palace (☎ 5460 4992, cnr Napier & Nolan Sts)*.

Standard bistro meals at the *Albion* are $9.50 to 12.50. The popular *Bunkers Restaurant (☎ 5460 4900, Park Rd)* at the golf club serves $10 mains Thursday to Sunday – no bike knicks please.

Day 4: Maryborough to Maldon
3½–5 hours, 75.2km
This ride through classic gold country is again quiet and relatively easy, rolling gently through farmland, old mining towns (with few services past Dunolly) and a lovely section of box-ironbark forest between Dunolly and Laanecoorie. A 3.6km dirt section (59km) can be avoided by taking the busier Bridgewater–Maldon Rd at 46.3km.

Timor (8.1km) is now little more than a locality. The (now-closed) general store is full of character and the lovely old school

(300m side trip at 8km) is a fine example, typical of the era.

Dunolly (22.4km) and the rich alluvial goldfields to its north were known as the 'Golden Triangle', yielding more gold nuggets than any other area in the country, including the world's largest, the 65kg Welcome Stranger, found in 1869 – a replica is at Dunolly's **Goldfields Historical Museum**.

For a small town, Dunolly's not bad on food. Broadway has a *bakery*; the *Welcome Stranger Cafe*, which serves huge ice-creams; and the groovy *Broadway Cockatoo Cafe (116 Broadway)*, which does coffee, cake and pizza.

Tarnagulla (2km off the route, at 35.6km) is worth a visit for its gold-rush architecture, which includes an inordinate number of **churches** and the **Victoria Theatre**, a former dance hall and vaudeville theatre. The sleepy, pretty village has a *store* and a *pub*.

Maldon
Declared by the National Trust as Australia's first 'Notable Town' in 1965, this village makes the most of its old-world charm – much of its historic architecture remains intact – while minimising tackiness. Though quieter during the week, it's a popular weekend tourist spot.

Information Maldon visitor centre (☎ 5475 2569) is in the Shire Gardens, on High St. Bendigo Bank is next door; the Commonwealth, in the post office a block north on High St, accepts some cards. Eftpos is available from the milk bar and Maldon Pharmacy, both on Main St.

Things to See & Do Main St is littered with **'olde worlde' shops** in which to browse; take a more scholarly look at the town's architecture on a **town walk**, described in the visitor centre's free *Town Walk* brochure. There's a collection of relics at the **historical museum** (☎ 5475 1633) in the Shire Gardens, on High St.

Weekend tours visit **Carman's Tunnel** (☎ 5475 2667), dug through solid rock in the 1880s in search of gold. It's 2.7km south of town. The Victorian Goldfields Railway (☎ 5475 2966) runs **steam-train rides** on Wednesday and Sunday. Climb **Mt Tarrengower** (180m in 1.6km) for 360-degree views.

VICTORIA

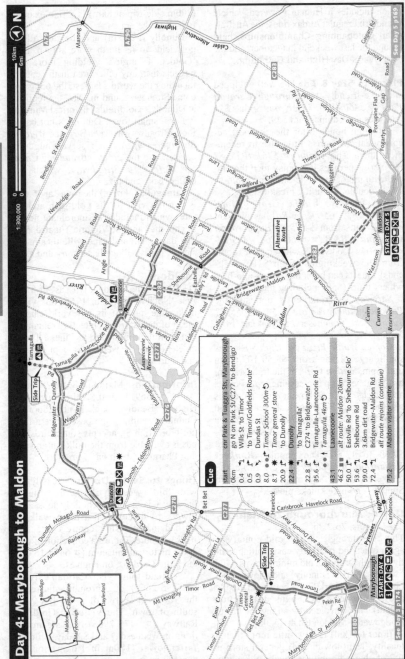

Day 4: Maryborough to Maldon

Cue	
start	cnr Park & Tuaggra Sts, Maryborough
0km	go N on Park St/C277 'to Bendigo'
0.4	Wills St 'to Timor'
0.5	'to Timor/Goldfields Route'
0.9	Dundas St
8.0	Timor School 300m ↰
8.1	Timor general store
20.9	'to Dunolly'
22.4	Dunolly
	'to Tarnagulla'
22.8	C274 'to Bridgewater'
35.6	Tarnagulla–Laanecoorie Rd
	Tarnagulla 4km ↰
43.1	Laanecoorie
46.3	alt route: Maldon 20km
50.0	Eastville Rd 'to Shelbourne Silo'
53.6	Shelbourne Rd
59.0	3.6km dirt road
72.4	Bridgewater–Maldon Rd
	alt route rejoins (continue)
75.2	Maldon visitor centre

The well-regarded **Maldon Folk Festival** is more than 25-years-old. It's on the first weekend in November. The **Maldon Easter Fair**, which began in 1877, includes an **Audax ride**.

Places to Stay & Eat Book accommodation early for long weekends, festivals and Christmas.

Tent sites at the secluded *Maldon Camping & Caravan Park* (☎ 5475 2344, Hospital St) cost $6.50 per person. On-site vans/cabins cost $33/50 to $60 (bedding required).

Derby Hill Accommodation Centre (☎ 5475 2033, Phoenix St) is a youth camp that opens as a motel on weekends. Beds cost $33 in dorms with two to 16 beds (cooking and bike-storage facilities are limited).

Maldon has dozens of B&Bs. For value, try the Victorian cottage, *Palm House* (☎ 5475 2532, e palmhous@netcon.net.au, 2 High St). Weekend prices are $45/80 per single/double (less midweek). *McArthur's* (☎ 5475 2519, 43 Main St) claims it is Victoria's oldest eating house still in operation. Two doubles are available behind the restaurant; B&B costs from $70/90 a single/double; book ahead. Popular for Devonshire teas, it also serves evening meals ($12–14) from Wednesday to Sunday.

Refurbished rooms at the atmospheric *Grand Hotel* (☎ 5475 1002, 26 Main St) start at $80, including continental breakfast (bikes outside). The pleasant dining room (plus nonsmoking area) serves good-value meals (mains $8 to $13.90).

The tiny *Maldon Historic Bakery* (☎ 5475 2713, 51 Main St) is crammed with goodies. *Cafe Maldon* (☎ 5475 2022, 51 Main St) has huge muffins, and lunch from $3.50. *Maldon Takeaway* (☎ 5475 2116, 10 Main St) sells pizza and more from 8am to 8pm.

Don't leave without trying out the old-fashioned Maldon Ice Block – 80 cents from the *Maldon Milkbar (21 Main St)*; the *Supermarket* is a few doors down.

Day 5: Maldon to Bendigo

2½–3½ hours, 51km
See the Day 1 map (p169) for the Day 5 route. A gradual climb through Fogarty's Gap is followed by some rolls through pretty Harcourt and a more relaxed climb back than on Day 1, over Mt Alexander's other shoulder (22.9km), before an easy run to Bendigo.

The country is attractive and lightly wooded, with no services and few cars until Bendigo.

The simulated village **Porcupine Township** (2.7km; ☎ 5475 1000) recreates life in the 1850s.

Enjoy more of the fruit-growing Harcourt Valley on an undulating alternative route via two wineries: **Blackjack Vineyards** (☎ 5474 2355) and **Harcourt Valley Vineyards** (☎ 5474 2223), where the Bendigo Wine Festival is held each Easter. Take Symes Rd to the Midland Hwy, go left and then right into Coolstore Rd (unsigned). After 1.5km, turn left into Black Rd (unsigned). Go right on the Calder Hwy for the wineries. Otherwise, continue on Blackjack and Danns Rds to McIvor Rd.

The ride retraces part of Day 1 (at 31.8km) through the Sedgwick district.

The Grampians

Duration	3 days
Distance	207.9km
Difficulty	easy–moderate
Start	Stawell
End	Ararat

The Grampians' 167,000-hectare national park, surrounded by rich agricultural land, has been one of the most popular tourist destinations in Victoria since the start of the 20th century. This three-day ride has stunning views, spectacular waterfalls and rock formations, Aboriginal rock art and, in spring, the most magnificent wild flower display. The tour focuses on sealed roads but you have plenty of opportunities for dirt-road riding and bushwalking throughout the park. The national park has a large number of basic camping grounds in idyllic locations.

HISTORY

Gariwerd, as the Grampians were originally known, is an area of immense cultural significance to Koorie people. In 1836 Major Thomas Mitchell named Gariwerd 'the Grampians' after the Scottish ranges and promoted European settlement of the rich grazing land. Within 10 years the Aboriginal

VICTORIA

population had dwindled, and by 1857, there were only 900 of the original 23,000 Indigenous inhabitants left.

While the mountains themselves were unsuited to agriculture or grazing, timber was extracted and water dammed to supply the growing towns. In 1984, after a lengthy campaign, the Grampians became a national park.

In recognition of the traditional custodians of the area the name reverted to Gariwerd in 1991, but the Kennett government revoked this change in 1994.

NATURAL HISTORY

The Grampians, at the western end of the Great Dividing Range, comprise a long spine that stands out dramatically from the surrounding flat landscape. They extend for 80km north-south and 50km east-west. Mt William (1167m) is the highest summit.

The ranges consist of layers of sandstone and shale laid down more than 500 million years ago. Hard, erosion-resistant sandstones form the ridges of the Serra and Mt William Ranges. The characteristic gentle western slope and steep eastern escarpment is known as a 'cuesta'. River valleys have formed in the more easily eroded shales. Erosion of the sandstones revealed granite, which was easily worn – its erosion resulting in the rounded hills and flat land of areas such as the Victoria Valley.

During high sea levels in the late Tertiary period, the Grampians were isolated from the rest of Victoria, which resulted in the evolution of unique plant species, notably the Grampians thryptomene (tiny white flowers). The area is famous for its spring wild flowers. The communities range from heathlands on the exposed Major Mitchell Plateau, dry sclerophyll forests of the lower slopes and rainforest in the gullies.

Honeyeaters abound in spring and noisy gang gang cockatoos frequent the drier bushland. Kangaroos and crimson rosellas are tame around Halls Gap.

PLANNING
When to Ride

The best months are September to November, for the profusion of wild flowers; and April to May, when the mornings are cool and the days warm. Summer is hot; winter can be cold and wet, with snow on the Major Mitchell Plateau.

The Grampians are busy during school holidays, especially at Easter, when accommodation can be scarce.

Maps

RACV's *The Grampians Holiday Map* provides excellent detail of road conditions around the Grampians together with town maps. Detailed walking maps are available from the national park office at Halls Gap, or the Stawell visitor centre.

What to Bring

You need to be self-sufficient to camp in the national park.

GETTING TO/FROM THE RIDE

For a circuit of western Victoria, bracket The Grampians ride with the Central Gold & Spa Country and The Great Ocean Road rides, both detailed in this chapter. From Maryborough (Day 4 of Central Gold & Spa Country) it's 121km on quiet roads to Stawell via Avoca and Landsborough. Link to The Great Ocean Road ride from Dunkeld (Day 2).

Stawell

V/Line (☎ 13 6196) runs trains to Ballarat, which connect with buses to Stawell ($31.60 plus $3 per bike, 3½ hours, two a day).

Dunkeld

Cycle to The Great Ocean Road ride from Dunkeld (Day 2). Take the C178 through Penshurst to Port Fairy, then head east on the Princes Hwy to Warrnambool (121km).

Ararat

The V/Line bus to Ballarat connects with a train to Melbourne ($26.90 plus $3 per bike, three hours, two a day).

THE RIDE
Stawell

Stawell is the closest major town to the Grampians' tourist hub, Halls Gap. Its prosperity, associated with gold, resulted in fine stone buildings, many of Grampians sandstone. The town is most famous for the **Stawell Gift** running race held every Easter at Centennial Park (which also has a **museum**). Accommodation at Easter can be scarce.

Information The visitor centre (☎ 1800-246 880) is on the Western Hwy.

Town facilities are 1.5km north of the highway, most centred around the Gold Reef Mall. Stawell is the only town with comprehensive banking facilities; Commonwealth, Bendigo and ANZ banks, all with ATMs, are in the mall. Boag's Cycles and Sports (☎ 5358 1308), in the mall, sells basic bicycle parts and does repairs; it is the only repair shop until Ararat.

Places to Stay The *Stawell Grampians Gate Caravan Park* (☎ 5358 2376, Burgh St) has camp sites from $11 for two people and double cabins from $36/45 without/ with en suite.

Town Hall Hotel (☎ 5358 1059, Main St) has pleasant rooms from $18.

The *Diamond House Motor Inn* (☎ 5358 3366, cnr Prince & Seaby Sts), has unusual brickwork and well-appointed single/double rooms from $60/72.

Places to Eat The *Safeway* supermarket *(Church St)* opens 24 hours. The popular *Chris n' Di's Bakery* (☎ 5358 4566, 76 Main St) opens from 7am.

The *Gold Reef Chinese Restaurant* (☎ 5358 1005, 98 Gold Reef Mall) has meals for around $7, with vegetarian options (closed Monday).

All the hotels have counter meals, but recommended is the bistro in the *Town Hall Hotel* (☎ 5358 1059, 62–68 Main St).

Of the few restaurants in Stawell, the best is in the *Diamond House Motel* (see Places to Stay) which has two- to four-course set menus from $21 to $29 (not suited to vegetarians).

Day 1: Stawell to Halls Gap
3–6 hours, 53km

It is a short ride from Stawell to Halls Gap through open farmland, with expansive views of the Mt William Range. Organise accommodation in Halls Gap before setting off on the second part of the ride, a circuit through the Wonderland Range.

A side trip to **Bunjil's Cave** (at 5.7km) visits one of the state's most important Aboriginal art sites, which contains a rare depiction of Bunjil, the creator spirit of the region. It is 3km along a corrugated road; unfortunately, it's had to be protected inside a wire cage.

Pomonal (21.4km), named after Pomona, the goddess of gardens and fruit, has the *Blue Wren Tea Rooms*, which serves wonderful Devonshire teas.

The **Wonderland Range** features exposed rock formations, such as the **Elephants Hide** (36km), which are good examples of the cuesta landform. A side trip (at 35.7km) leads to the **Wonderland Turntable**. Here, erosion of the sandstone has created deep canyons and formations, such as **The Nerve Test** and **Devils Peak**, which can be reached along walking tracks.

Dry sclerophyll forest, in which flowers abound in spring, is prominent after the Sundial Turntable turn-off (40.9km). Several walks leave **Sundial Turntable**; the circuit to **Lakeview Lookout** and **Devils Gap** boasts stunning views down the Serra Range and across to the Mt William Range.

From the Sundial Turntable the road descends past the **Silverband Falls** (44.3km) and emerges at Lake Bellfield. Towards Halls Gap is the **Brambuk Aboriginal Cultural Centre** (51.4km; ☎ 5356 4452), owned and operated by five Aboriginal communities. The award-winning building incorporates elements of cultural significance to all the communities and bush-food ingredients are used in the *cafe*. The adjacent **national park visitor centre** (☎ 5356 4381) has excellent natural-history interpretive displays and recreational information.

Halls Gap

In a narrow valley, Halls Gap is the only town in the Grampians. It is named after Charles Hall, a squatter who explored tracks through the gap where Fyans Creek emerges from the Mt William Range. With the advent of tourism in the early 20th century, the settlement grew as a service town.

Information The visitor centre (☎ 5356 4616) is on Dunkeld Rd. The national park visitor centre (see Day 1 ride) can provide information and maps for walks and mountain biking (which is permitted only on certain roads).

A Commonwealth Bank ATM is in the Mobil Service Station on Dunkeld Rd.

Action Adventures (☎ 5356 4540) hires mountain bikes for $15/25 per half/full day ($100 deposit). The Grampians Adventure Services (☎ 5356 4556), Shop 4, Stony Creek Shops, hires mountain bikes for $8/20 per hour/half day.

VICTORIA

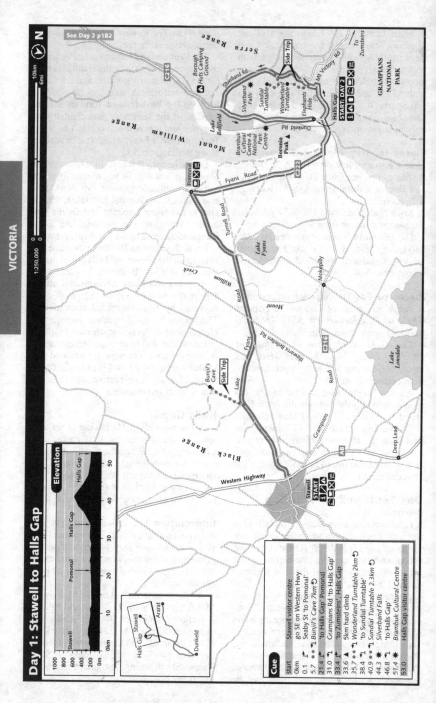

Day 1: Stawell to Halls Gap

Elevation

	Stawell	Pomonal	Halls Gap	Halls Gap
1000
800
600
400
200
0m

0km   10   20   30   40   50

Cue

start		Stawell visitor centre
0km		go SE on Western Hwy
0.1	↱	Seaby St 'to Pomonal'
5.7	↳	Bunjil's Cave 7km ⟲
21.4		'to Halls Gap' Pomonal
31.0	↱	Grampians Rd 'to Halls Gap'
33.4	↱	'to Zumsteins', Halls Gap
33.6	◄	5km hard climb
35.7	⟲	Wonderland Turntable 2km ⟲
38.4		'to Sundial Turntable'
40.9	⟲	Sundial Turntable 2.3km ⟲
44.3	✱	Silverband Falls
46.8	↱	'to Halls Gap'
51.4	✱	Brambuk Cultural Centre
53.0		Halls Gap visitor centre

Things to See & Do Halls Gap is the base for activities in the Grampians National Park. Action Adventures (☎ 5356 4540) runs **rock climbing**, **abseiling** and **canoeing** excursions.

Places to Stay Accommodation is spread about 5km around Halls Gap and can be scarce at Easter. September to Easter is the peak season.

The *Halls Gap Caravan Park* (☎ 5356 4251, Dunkeld Rd), close to town, has camp sites from $18, on-site vans from $45, cabin vans from $62 and self-contained double units from $74.

The eco-designed *Halls Gap YHA* (☎ 5356 4544, cnr Buckler St & Dunkeld Rd) has dorm beds for $23 and singles/doubles for $43/55. Opposite the national park office, the *Brambuk Backpackers* (☎ 5356 4250, Dunkeld Rd) has excellent facilities and views of the Mt William range. Dorm beds cost $20 and private rooms, $35/45 (including linen and a light breakfast).

Mountain Grand Guest House (☎ 5356 4232, Dunkeld Rd), open since the 1940s, has recently been renovated. Midweek B&B costs $108 a double; on weekends a weekend special ($218 a double) includes breakfast, a picnic hamper, lunch, Devonshire tea and dinner.

The cheaper rooms (from $75/85) at the quiet *Kookaburra Lodge* (☎ 5356 4395, 14 Heath St) have stunning views.

Places to Eat The *bakery* (Shop 3, Stony Creek Shops) opens from 8am; the licensed *supermarket* (Dunkeld Rd) opens from 7am to 10pm.

The *Halls Gap Tavern* (☎ 5356 4416, Dunkeld Rd) is open for breakfast, lunch and dinner. The $10 early-bird dinner special offers a set three-course meal between 5pm and 7pm; happy hour is 5pm to 6pm. The *Halls Gap Hotel* (☎ 5356 4566, Stawell Rd) has good pub meals and splendid views of the Mt Difficult Range.

A good range of pasta dishes is available at the BYO *Cafe Rosea* (Shop 7, Stony Creek Shops), open from 11am to late. The restaurant at the *Mountain Grand Guest House* has mains (some vegetarian) from $15 to $18.

Day 2: Halls Gap to Dunkeld
3½–6½ hours, 64.7km

The Grampians Tourist Rd follows Fyans Creek to the Great Dividing Range and then descends along the Wannon River valley. At all times it allows spectacular views of the Serra Range and the Mt William Range. The road has some steep stretches crossing the foothills of Mt Abrupt. *Camping grounds* along the route are in quiet, beautiful bush settings.

The *cafe* at the Brambuk Aboriginal Cultural Centre (2.5km; see Day 1) is the last shop.

The side trip to **Mt William** (12.4km) is a steep 10km climb, rewarded by stunning views across the Major Mitchell Plateau and an exhilarating descent.

Dunkeld

This tiny town at the southern end of the Grampians has spectacular views of Mt Sturgeon and Mt Abrupt, particularly at sunrise. A **museum** in Templeton St provides a self-guided tour of Dunkeld's historic buildings. It can be visited at any time by asking at the general store.

Information The visitor centre (☎ 5577 2558) is on Parker St. The post office, a Commonwealth Bank agent, is on Wills St.

Places to Stay & Eat Tent sites with views at the basic *Dunkeld Caravan Park* (☎ 5577 2578, Parker St) cost $7. Comfortable cabins at the *Southern Gate Caravan Park* (☎ 5577 2210, Parker St) cost from $44/55 a single/double; camp sites cost $12; and on-site vans, $25.

Dunkeld Lodge (☎ 5577 2584, Wills St) has cosy backpacker accommodation for $20, including breakfast, and dinner for $6.

Magnificent views of Mt Sturgeon are assured from the *Royal Mail Hotel* (☎ 5577 2241, Parker St). Rooms start from $83/99 midweek ($116/143 weekends). The hotel also runs the historic self-contained one- and two-bedroom ($176) *Mt Sturgeon Cottages* and backpacker accommodation ($25), on the adjacent Mt Sturgeon Homestead. Booking is essential.

The *Grampians View B&B* (☎ 5577 2450, McArthur St) has rooms for $60.

The *general store* and *take away* close early; but the *service station (cnr Western*

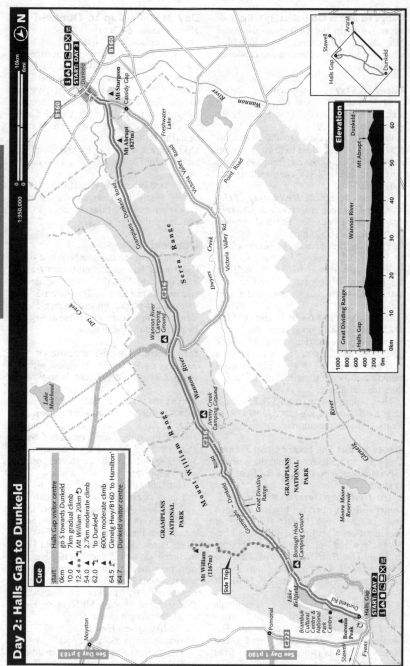

Day 2: Halls Gap to Dunkeld

VICTORIA

Cue

start		Halls Gap visitor centre
0km		go S towards Dunkeld
10.0	◀	7km gradual climb
12.4	●●◀	Mt William 20km ↻
54.0	◀	2.7km moderate climb
62.0	◀	'to Dunkeld'
64.5	◀	600m moderate climb
	◀	Glenelg Hwy/B160 'to Hamilton'
64.7		Dunkeld visitor centre

Elevation

See Day 3 p183

See Day 1 p180

Day 3: Dunkeld to Ararat

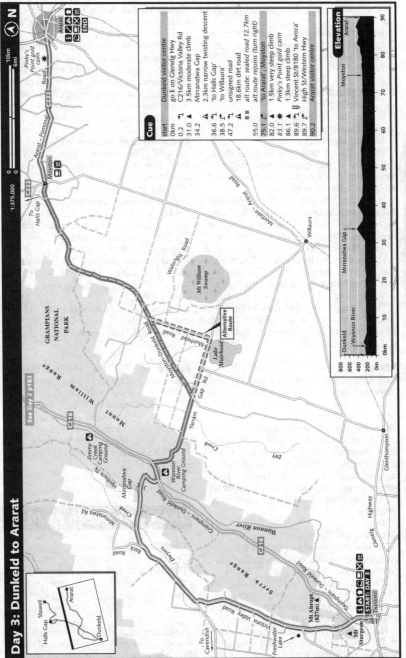

Cue

start		Dunkeld visitor centre
0km	⌐	go E on Glenelg Hwy
0.2	⌐◀	C216/Victoria Valley Rd
31.0	◀	3.5km moderate climb
34.2		Miranatwa Gap
	◀◀	2.3km narrow twisting descent
36.6	⌐◀	'to Halls Gap'
38.5	⌐◀	'to Willaura'
47.2	⌐◀	unsigned road
		18.6km dirt road
		alt route: sealed road 12.7km
		alt route rejoins (turn right)
55.0	⌐◀	'to Ararat', Moyston
75.1	⌐◀	1.5km very steep climb
82.0	✳	Pinky's Point gold cairn
83.1	◀	1.3km steep climb
86.1	⌐◀	Vincent St/B180 'to Avoca'
89.6	⌐◀	High St/Western Hwy
89.7	⌐◀	
90.2		Ararat visitor centre

Elevation

VICTORIA

Hwy & Templeton St) sells limited supplies until 8pm.

The hotel's *bistro* has substantial meals from $9 to $12.50; its *restaurant* features local produce – excellent mains cost $17.50 to $19.50.

Day 3: Dunkeld to Ararat
5–9 hours, 90.2km

This long, easy ride has more views of the ranges. A small *store* at Moyston (74.6km) is the only shop on the route.

The flat, rural landscape of the **Victoria Valley** has views of sheep and red gums bounded by the Serra Range in the east and the Victoria Range in the west.

In the Serra Range, near the **Henham Track**, a southern Grampians resort was proposed in the 1940s, but never built. The lookout at **Mirrinatwa Gap** (33.7km) provides expansive views.

The roughest sections of the 18.6km section of unsealed road before Moyston can be avoided by taking the slightly longer alternative route.

The strangely named **Pinky's Point** cairn (84km) marks the place where Joseph Pollard 'and his mates' found the first gold in the district in 1854.

Ararat

This agricultural town lies between the Grampians and the Pyrenees Ranges. The squatter Horatio Wills camped on the Black Range, and named the peak Mt Ararat, because 'like the Ark, we have rested here'.

With the discovery of gold in 1854 the town prospered and, as the centre of a rich pastoral region, continued to prosper after the gold declined. The town is still a rural service centre, although it now depends on the tourism boom. Cyclists are made very welcome.

Information The visitor centre (☎ 5355 0270) is at the station on High St. It has an excellent panorama of the region's attractions.

The main shopping street is Barkly St, which has five hotels in the short stretch between Vincent St and Ingor St. Ararat has most main banks, all with ATMs.

The friendly staff at Lardner Bros Sports (☎ 5253 1074), 2 Ingor St, offer a range of parts and full repair service.

Things to See & Do Tours of the austere **J-Ward Museum** (☎ 5352 3621) on Girdlestone St, the Institution for the Criminally Insane from 1887 to 1991, are fascinating. A **museum** in Queen St has a huge collection of artefacts and photographs. **Green Lake**, east of town, has excellent bird watching, particularly in summer when it is often the only water around. A short bikepath links the lake to town.

Places to Stay The *Acacia Caravan Park* (☎ 5352 2994, Acacia Ave) has camp sites from $16 and cabins and self-contained units from $55 a double.

Backpacker accommodation is available in the *Grampians Hotel* (☎ 5352 2393, 157 Barkly St). Rooms cost $15/30 a single/double, with use of a lounge and kitchen. The hotel even boasts a friendly ghost.

Ararat Hotel (☎ 5352 2477, 130 Barkly St) has pleasant rooms for $25/35. Closer to town, the *Ararat Central Motel* (☎ 5352 4444, 249 Barkly St) has standard rooms from $54/65.

Statesman Flag Motor Inn (☎ 5352 4111 or ☎ 1800-803 322, Western Hwy) has standard rooms ($77/88) with a delightful courtyard view.

Places to Eat The licensed *Safeway* supermarket *(Ingor St)* opens 24 hours.

The cosy *Vines Cafe & Bar* (☎ 5352 1744) serves mains ($17–$21) that include vegetarian choices, and coffee, cakes and lunches (open Thursday to Sunday).

The *Man Hing Chinese Restaurant* (☎ 5352 3311, 190 Barkly St) has takeaway and eat-in meals.

Ararat Hotel (☎ 5352 2477, 130 Barkly St) offers bistro meals for around $12.50.

The Great Ocean Road

Duration	5 days
Distance	281.4km
Difficulty	moderate
Start	Warrnambool
End	Geelong

The Great Ocean Road is Australia's – and one of the world's – great coastal routes. The landscape ranges from stunning coastal cliffs to beautiful beaches where steep green hills meet the azure sea. Add to this challenging climbs and exhilarating descents through the Otway Ranges, and you have a real coastal adventure.

This ride allows ample time to explore the many attractions. Camping enthusiasts can enjoy some beautiful isolated sites in the Otway Ranges.

HISTORY

The Great Ocean Road is only a relatively recent development; until the 1930s no road linked coastal settlements.

In 1859, during construction of the telegraph line between Victoria and Tasmania, a track was cut along the coast. As the area's population grew, so did the demand for a road linking settlements. Construction began in August 1918 and the lack of finance for the project was overcome by employing returning WWI servicemen and, during the Depression, unemployed men (called 'susso workers', because they worked for sustenance).

In 1932 the road was completed from Eastern View to Apollo Bay. It was called the Great Ocean Road and tolls applied. The

The Shipwreck Coast

The coast from Port Fairy to Apollo Bay is aptly called the Shipwreck Coast. In sailing's 'golden age', ships travelling to/from Australia's east coast had to cross Bass Strait's treacherous waters largely without detailed charts or navigational aids. Fierce winds often drove them off course, onto limestone reefs close to shore. More than 160 ships have been wrecked, giving names to such localities as Childers Cove (after the barque *Children*), Halladale Cove (after the *Falls of Halladale*) and Loch Ard Gorge (after the clipper *Loch Ard*).

Not all the wrecks occurred in bad weather. Legend has it that Captain James 'Bully' Forbes was below 'entertaining' when *The Schomberg* ran aground in sand close to Peterborough. All were rescued by a passing steamer but, ironically, the ship was destroyed days later in a storm.

Wrecks also occurred on the less-treacherous, eastern side of Cape Otway. Three men, including Captain Gortley and seaman Godfrey, drowned near Wye River. Later, the Great Ocean Road was built directly over their graves; a headstone, erected nearby, incorrectly identifies them as: 'Erected...in memory of Captain Devel, Parke and Godfrey'! (See Day 4.)

LIBRARY OF VICTORIA

Only two people survived the wreck of the *Loch Ard* in 1878; crewman Tom Pearce climbed the cliff from what's now known as Loch Ard Gorge to get help for passenger Eva Carmichael.

later extension of the road across the Otways to Port Campbell was called merely the 'Ocean Rd'.

NATURAL HISTORY

The broad plateau of the Port Campbell coast comprises limestone laid down about 50 million years ago. Most of the land has been cleared and remnant coastal heath is adapted to dryness and sea spray. There is little wildlife, although shearwaters and other ocean birds nest on the stacks and promontories.

In marked contrast is the steep Otway coast, which consists of folded and faulted sandstones and mudstones. The Otways' western side is exposed to storm waves and, near Moonlight Head, 90m-high slopes plunge into the ocean. On the more-protected eastern coast an extensive shore platform abuts the ranges.

The Otway Ranges' high rainfall has led to deeply cut valleys, deep soils, and dense forest. Wetter areas have ferns, myrtle beech and mosses, while eucalypt forests dominate higher land. Ironbark forests and heathlands occur in the rain shadow of the Otways between Anglesea and Geelong.

The ranges are home to a variety of animal and bird life. Cockatoos shriek high above the canopy and koalas are common in the manna gums near Cape Otway.

PLANNING
When to Ride

The Great Ocean Road is a popular tourist route, particularly during the January school holidays, when the road is very busy and accommodation is often scarce. Most weekends (particularly at Easter) are also busy between Lorne and Torquay. Late spring, summer and autumn are the best seasons; winter is cold and wet.

Maps & Books

The RACV *West Melbourne & Great Ocean Road* regional map covers the ride. Vicmap's *The Otways & the Shipwreck Coast Map* (1:50,000; $8.95) provides detailed topographic information.

The beautifully photographed *Great Ocean Road: A Traveller's Guide*, by Rodney Hyett, has an interesting account of a coastal walk from the Bellarine Peninsula to Warrnambool in 1879.

GETTING TO/FROM THE RIDE

Precede The Great Ocean Road ride with The Grampians ride, described earlier in this chapter – from Dunkeld, head south on the C178 through Penshurst to Port Fairy and then follow the Princes Hwy to Warrnambool (121km).

Warrnambool

Warrnambool train station is on Merri St, near Lake Pertobe. West Coast Rail (☎ 5226 6500) operates daily services between Melbourne and Warrnambool ($34.20 plus $3 per bike; three hours; three services daily on weekdays, two on weekends).

Geelong

Frequent V/Line (☎ 13 6196) services go between Geelong and Melbourne's Spencer St Station ($8.60 plus $3 per bike, one hour).

THE RIDE
Warrnambool

On the protected Lady Bay, Warrnambool is the largest city in Victoria's south-west. First established as a whaling station, the town was settled following the growth of harbour facilities. The main town is on a cliff overlooking Lake Pertobe, its skyline dominated by the Norfolk pines that line the streets. A manufacturing industry is still maintained, notably with the staff-owned clothing company Fletcher Jones.

Information The visitor centre (☎ 5564 7837), 600 Raglan Parade, has an excellent visitors guide, a map of local cycling routes (50 cents) and information about Port Campbell National Park – worth collecting as the Port Campbell visitor centre closes on weekends. Parks Victoria (☎ 5561 9900) is at 78 Henna St.

The major banks (with ATMs) are in Liebig and Koroit Sts.

Despite its road-racing heritage, Warrnambool has no major bike shops. The Warrnambool Shooters & Anglers Centre (☎ 5562 3502), 101 Liebig St, has some bicycle tools and basic spares.

Things to See & Do Warrnambool is an attractive town with many historic buildings and public gardens. The **Flagstaff Hill Maritime Museum** (☎ 5564 7841), on the corner of Merri and Banyan Sts, re-creates a

19th-century port, with many buildings using materials salvaged from wrecks; the **historical films** are a highlight.

Between June and September **Southern Right Whales** (so named because whalers felt they had the 'right' amount of blubber) return to the southern waters to calve. Look for them from a viewing platform at **Logan's Beach**.

Several beaches and lagoons are safe for **swimming** and **fishing**.

The town is also the finish of the 260km **Melbourne to Warrnambool** road race, held every October.

Places to Stay Close to town, the *Warrnambool Surfside Holiday Park* (☎ 5561 2611, Pertobe Rd) has beach access. Protected camp sites cost from $14/27 a single/double and cabins from $92.

The *Warrnambool Beach Backpackers* (☎ 5562 4874, ℮ johnpearson@hotmail .com, 17 Stanley St), near the beach and Lake Pertobe, has Internet access, a bar and a large lounge. Dorm beds cost $18 and doubles, $44, including linen.

Western Private Hotel & Motel (☎ 5562 2011, cnr Kepler & Timor Sts) has backpacker accommodation in single rooms for $16.50; breakfast costs $3.50. Motel units cost from $49/59, including a light breakfast.

Redwood Manor Motel (☎ 5562 3939, 251 Koroit St) has self-contained, quiet and comfortable motel units from $80/100.

The beautiful Victorian *Walsingham B&B* (☎ 5561 7978, 12 Henna St) charges from $108 per double, including breakfast.

Places to Eat The 24-hour *Coles* supermarket *(Lava St)* is close to the centre. In addition to great coffee from 7am, *Puds Pantry & Deli* (☎ 5562 5119, 60 Kepler St) sells delicious breads (closed Sunday).

Restaurants and cafes in Warrnambool are clustered around the southern end of Liebig St. *Fishtales Cafe* (☎ 5561 2957, 63 Liebig St) has a 'monster' breakfast for $8 and an innovative menu that caters to cyclists, vegetarian or carnivore.

Balenàs (☎ 5562 0900, 158 Timor St) is a modern Australian restaurant with mains from $18 to $25. Busy *Bojangles* (☎ 5562 8751, 61 Liebig St) serves pasta and fabulous wood-fired pizzas.

Day 1: Warrnambool to Port Campbell
4–6 hours, 69.1km

The ride along the coast is easy, particularly if the wind is south-westerly. Allansford and Peterborough have shops, but take food and water for the wonderful picnic spots along the way.

Join the **Great Ocean Road** after the small dairying community of Allansford (14.5km). The uninspiring **Cheese World** building (17.1km) has a **dairy museum** and a *coffee shop* that serves great ice creams and milk shakes.

The first opportunity to view the coast is on the side trip to spectacular **Childers Cove** (29.1km), where the barque *Children* was wrecked in 1839. **Walking tracks** explore the promontories and rock stacks of the **Bay of Islands** (49.9km). The wide **Crofts Bay**, just after, has beach access. Archaeological sites are found at the **Bay of Martyrs** (53.4km), where Koorie men were killed by driving them off the cliff.

The *general store* at **Peterborough** (55.5km) is off the main road. The *Schomberg Hotel* has good counter meals and accommodation; a *caravan park* is next door.

Numerous sights in the final 12km show the extent of erosion along the coast, including **The Grotto** (59km); **London Bridge** (60.7km), which did fall down in 1990; and **The Arch** (61.5km).

Evidence of a previous shoreline exists at **Two Mile Bay** (65.1km), where a broad shore platform protects the receding coastline.

Port Campbell
Nestled along Campbells Creek below steep cliffs is Port Campbell. Whalers used the bay during the early 19th century as it was the only sheltered section of coast between Warrnambool and Apollo Bay. The town was settled in the 1870s as a fishing village and, with transport connections to Timboon and the new Ocean Rd, the town became a holiday destination. Quiet in winter, the town's population swells during summer.

Information The visitor centre (☎ 5598 6088) and the national parks office (☎ 5598 6382) share a building in Morris St.

The general store in Lord St sells basic bike parts and houses the post office, which is a Commonwealth Bank agency.

VICTORIA

VICTORIA

Day 1: Warrnambool to Port Campbell

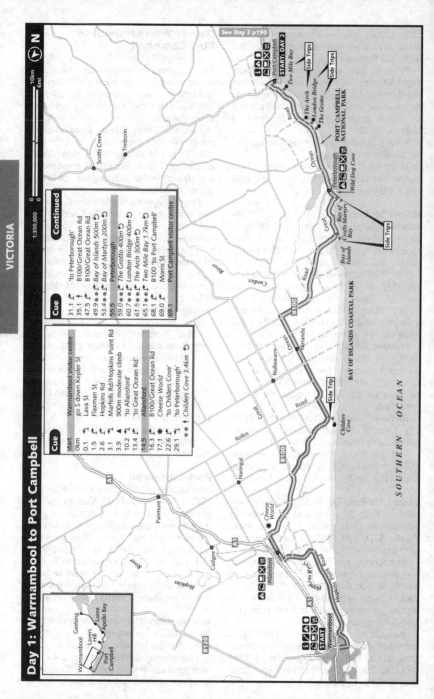

1:350,000

See Day 2 p190

Cue

start		Warrnambool visitor centre
0km		go S down Kepler St
0.1		Lava St
1.5		Flaxman St
2.6		Hopkins Rd
3.1		Marfells Rd/Hopkins Point Rd
3.9		900m moderate climb
10.2		'to Allansford'
13.4		'to Great Ocean Rd'
14.5		Allansford
16.3		B100/Great Ocean Rd
17.1		Cheese World
22.6		'to Childers Cove'
29.1		'to Peterborough'
		Childers Cove 3.4km

Cue — Continued

31.1		'to Peterborough'
35.1		B100/Great Ocean Rd
47.5		B100/Great Ocean Rd
49.9		Bay of Islands 500m
53.4		Bay of Martyrs 200m
55.5		Peterborough
59.0		The Grotto 400m
60.7		London Bridge 400m
61.5		The Arch 300m
65.1		Two Mile Bay 1.7km
68.1		B100 'to Port Campbell'
69.0		Morris St
69.1		Port Campbell visitor centre

Port Campbell — START: DAY 2

Two Mile Bay

Side Trips

The Arch
London Bridge
The Grotto

PORT CAMPBELL NATIONAL PARK

Ocean Road

Peterborough
Wild Dog Cove

Side Trips

Bay of
Crofts Martyrs
Bay

Bay of
Islands

Side Trips

Great Road

Curdies River

Nirranda

Nullawarre

Ocean Road

BAY OF ISLANDS COASTAL PARK

B100

Side Trip

Childers
Cove

Great Road

Rollos

Naringal

B100

SOUTHERN OCEAN

Scotts Creek

Timboon

Panmure

Cudgee

Hopkins River

Cheese
World

Allansford

Hopkins Point Road

Warrnambool — START

B120

B100

Hopkins River

(inset map)

Geelong
Warrnambool
Lavers Hill
Lorne
Apollo Bay
Port Campbell

Things to See & Do Port Campbell bay has a safe **swimming** beach near a shady picnic area. The **Shipwreck Museum** (☎ 5598 6463), 26 Lord St, has lots of memorabilia from ships wrecked near the Port Campbell coast. The **Old Hall Gallery**, in Lord St, has an eclectic collection that includes the last manual telephone exchange from Timboon.

Places to Stay The *Port Campbell Caravan Park* (☎ 5598 6492 or ☎ 5598 6369, *Tregear St)*, on Campbells Creek, has a shelter shed, barbecues, protected camp sites ($15) and en suite cabins from $95 a double.

Booking is essential for the popular *Port Campbell Youth Hostel* (☎ 5598 6305, @ portcampbellyha@ansonic.com.au, 18 Tregear St), which has a huge communal area. Dorm beds cost $16; doubles, $38; and cabins, from $56. Dorm beds in the YHA's adjacent *Mathieson House* cost $20.

The *Port O' Call Accommodation House* (☎ 5598 6206, 37 Lord St) has a pleasant garden and standard doubles from $85 and rooms with cooking facilities from $100.

Places to Eat Groceries are available from the *general store (Lord St)*.

The *Cray Pot Bistro* (☎ 5598 6320), in the Port Campbell Hotel, serves excellent pub meals, including crayfish from $26. The seafood platter ($38 for two) at *Napiers Restaurant* (☎ 5598 6231, Lord St) is also recommended.

Emma's Cottage (☎ 5598 6458, 25 Lord St) is a nonsmoking cafe and restaurant that serves scrumptious sundaes (closed Monday–Wednesday).

The *Koo-AAh Restaurant* (☎ 5598 6408, 26 Lord St) has delicious vegetarian curries (open daily from 6am and Wednesday to Saturday evening).

Day 2: Port Campbell to Lavers Hill

3–5 hours, 49.7km
After following the cliffs along Port Campbell National Park for the first half of Day 2, the route climbs into the Otway Ranges. The short distance allows ample time to explore the coast as well as grind the long climb to Lavers Hill! Princetown has a small *general store*, and Lavers Hill an even smaller one. Carry supplies from Port Campbell for camping in the Otway National Park.

It's easy to spend a couple of hours exploring the trails around **Loch Ard Gorge** (8.4km) where the *Loch Ard* was wrecked in 1878 (see the boxed text 'The Shipwreck Coast' earlier in this chapter).

The **Twelve Apostles** (12.1km), the Great Ocean Road's most-photographed icon, are best seen in the early morning light. **Gibson Steps** (13km) allows access to the beach and a different view of a couple of the Apostles.

Glenample Homestead (13.4km), where the survivors of the *Loch Ard* wreck were brought, has been restored with a picnic area and excellent **museum**.

The short detour to **Princetown** (18.4km) reaches the *Talk-o-the-Town Tavern* where, over coffee, the extensive Gellibrand River wetlands can be viewed.

The quiet, unsealed Old Ocean Rd is an alternative flat route that follows the Gellibrand River for 11km.

Moonlight Head, a 8km return short side trip on an unsealed road at 34.3km, is finally reached by a short walk to the headland, which affords spectacular views to 100m-high cliffs.

The Otways rainforest's jewel is **Melba Gully State Park**. A side trip at 47.2km drops to a delightful **walk** through dense rainforest, featuring a 300-year-old messmate tree.

Lavers Hill

High in the Otway Ranges, Lavers Hill is at the junction of roads to Colac, Apollo Bay and Port Campbell. Although once a busy timber town, it is now very quiet with few facilities. From the junction are commanding views of the Southern Ocean towards Johanna. The Gardenside Manor Tearooms runs the post office, which has Eftpos and sells basic groceries.

Places to Stay & Eat Camp sites at the *Lavers Hill Roadhouse Caravan Park & Tavern* (☎ 5237 3251, Great Ocean Rd) cost $12; the bunkhouse cost $40 a double; and on-site vans, from $30. It has a cafe, takeaway and highly recommended pub meals.

Otway Junction Motor Inn (☎ 5237 3295) has singles/doubles with wonderful views from $75/85; the *restaurant* serves mains (some vegetarian) from $15 to $22.

Buy light lunches, notably the Aussie Billabong damper, and Devonshire teas from the *Blackwood Tearooms* at the road junction.

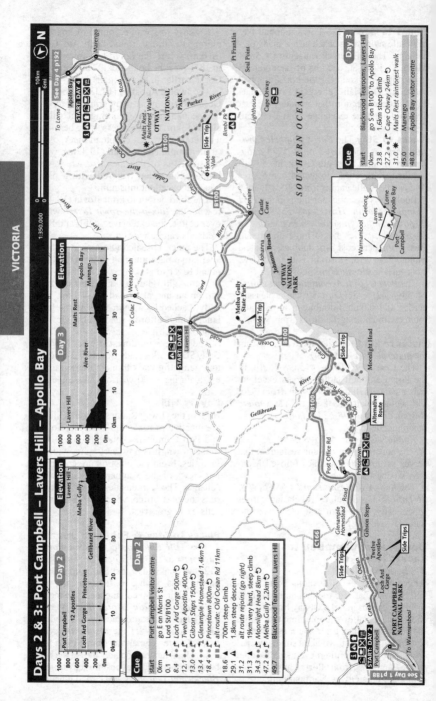

Days 2 & 3: Port Campbell – Lavers Hill – Apollo Bay

VICTORIA

1:350,000

Day 3 Elevation

Lavers Hill | Maits Rest | Apollo Bay
Marengo

Day 2 Elevation

Port Campbell | 12 Apostles | Princetown | Melba Gully
Loch Ard Gorge | Gellibrand River

Cue — Day 3

start	Blackwood Tearooms, Lavers Hill
0km	go S on B100 'to Apollo Bay'
23.8	1.6km steep climb
27.2	Cape Otway 24km
31.0	Maits Rest rainforest walk
45.0	Marengo
48.0	Apollo Bay visitor centre

Cue — Day 2

start	Port Campbell visitor centre
0km	go E on Morris St
0.1	Lord St/B100
8.4	Loch Ard Gorge 500m
12.1	Twelve Apostles 400m
13.0	Gibson Steps 150m
13.4	Glenample Homestead 1.4km
18.4	Princetown 800m
	alt route: Old Ocean Rd 11km
18.6	700m steep climb
29.1	1.8km steep descent
31.2	alt route rejoins (go right)
31.3	19km very hard, steep climb
34.3	Moonlight Head 8km
47.2	Melba Gully 2.2km
49.7	Blackwood Tearooms, Lavers Hill

SOUTHERN OCEAN

SEE Day 4 p192
START: DAY 4
Apollo Bay
Marengo
To Lorne
Maits Rest Rainforest Walk
OTWAY NATIONAL PARK
Parker River
Pt Franklin
Seal Point
Bimbi Pk
Lighthouse
Cape Otway
Hordern Vale
Calder River
Aire River
Ocean Road
Great Ocean Road
Glenaire
Castle Cove
Johanna
Johanna Beach
Ford River
Weeapionah
To Colac
Lavers Hill
START: DAY 3
Melba Gully State Park
Side Trip
OTWAY NATIONAL PARK
Ocean Road
Great Ocean Road
Old Ocean Road
Alternative Route
Moonlight Head
Side Trip
B100
Gellibrand River
Princetown
Post Office Rd
Glenample Homestead
Gibson Steps
Twelve Apostles
Side Trips
Loch Ard Gorge
Great Ocean Road
PORT CAMPBELL NATIONAL PARK
START: DAY 2
Port Campbell
To Warrnambool
See Day 1 p188

Warrnambool
Port Campbell
Lavers Hill
Apollo Bay
Lorne
Geelong

N
10km
6mi
0

Day 3: Lavers Hill to Apollo Bay
3–6 hours, 48km

Although short, Day 3 is tough. As there are no shops en route carry food and water.

After a long descent from Lavers Hill, past the **Johanna Beach** turn-off (9.1km) and its spectacular views, the route reaches the pancake-flat floodplain of the Aire and Calder Rivers. A long and, at times, steep climb leads through the spectacular tall timbers of the Otway National Park and past the turn-off to **Cape Otway** (27.2km; see Side Trip) to the **Maits Rest Rainforest Walk** (31km), a signposted boardwalk through spectacular remnant rainforest.

The ride finishes with another long descent (and more spectacular views) to the coast.

Side Trip: Cape Otway Lighthouse
24km return

The road to **Cape Otway** winds through the tall eucalypts of Otway National Park and emerges into farming country before reaching **Cape Otway lighthouse**. Built in 1848, this is Australia's second-oldest lighthouse. Self-guided tours cost $6.60. A *kiosk* is at the lighthouse and accommodation is available at *Cape Otway Lightstation* (☎ 5237 9240). Backpacker accommodation, camping and cabins are available at *Bimbi Park* (☎ 5237 9246), although the grunting of koalas during the night may be disturbing.

Apollo Bay
At the base of the Otway Ranges with a backdrop of steep, cleared hills, the crayfish port and holiday town of Apollo Bay is reminiscent of seaside villages of Scotland and Wales. The number of B&Bs, motels and restaurants is growing in response to an increase in weekend visitors from Melbourne.

Information The visitor centre (☎ 5237 6529) is on the foreshore, and has an excellent natural-history display.

The Commonwealth Bank and Bank of Melbourne are on the Great Ocean Rd and have ATMs. Basic bike parts are sold at Fishing Tackle & Bait (☎ 5237 6434), 39 Great Ocean Rd. Otway Expeditions (☎ 5237 6341), 7 Noel St, hires mountain bikes for $20/30 per half/full day.

Things to See & Do The **beach** here is a wonderful place to relax, swim and walk, as

is the **pier**, where you can watch the crayfish boats.

Mountain biking is becoming popular in the hinterland. For downhill thrills Otway Expeditions (☎ 5237 6341), 7 Noel St, run tours, providing transport to the top of the ranges and guiding cyclists down the steep tracks to Apollo Bay. They also run guided night rides.

Places to Stay The *Pisces Caravan Park* (☎ 5237 6749, Great Ocean Rd), 1.8km north of town, has tent sites overlooking the bay for $23 a double, including use of the camp kitchen. Cabins for two cost $52/63 without/with en suite.

Closer to town, the *Kooriengal Holiday Park* (☎ 5237 7111, 27 Cawood St) has uninspiring tent sites for $25 and en suite cabins for $75.

The friendly *YHA Surfside Backpackers* (☎ 5237 7263 or ☎ 1800-357 263, @ apoll obay@yhavic.org.au, cnr Great Ocean Rd & Gambier St) is a delight, with fabulous ocean views from the sitting room. Dorm beds cost $18; doubles from $40; and self-contained family rooms from $75.

The attractive *Beachfront Motel* (☎ 5237 6437, 163 Great Ocean Rd) has motel units for $89 a double and cottages with cooking facilities for $110.

Greenacres Country House by the Sea (☎ 5237 6309, cnr Great Ocean Rd & Nelson St) operates as both a guest house and a motel with rooms from $110 to $220 a double, including a light breakfast.

Places to Eat The *bakery (119 Great Ocean Rd)* opens from 7am. The *IGA* supermarket *(77 Great Ocean Rd)* is licensed.

The shark attack burgers are a knockout at *Cafe Nautigals* (☎ 5237 6610, 58 Great Ocean Rd), open from 8.30am.

Apollo Bay is famous for seafood and the best can be found at *Waynes Craypot Bistro* (☎ 5357 6240), in the Apollo Bay Hotel. The crayfish price depends on the season and starts at about $20. The range of good pub meals includes vegetarian pasta.

Delicious Asian-style dishes feature at the small, nonsmoking *Buffs Bistro & Bar* (☎ 5237 6403, 51 Great Ocean Rd), open from 9.30am. The *Seagrape Wine Bar & Grill* (☎ 5237 6610, 141 Great Ocean Rd) has a Mediterranean feel and is good value.

Day 4: Apollo Bay to Lorne
3–5 hours, 44.5km

This is the most spectacular section of the Great Ocean Road, where the route is carved into the cliffs as they plunge into the sea. The narrow, sometimes busy, road winds around the coastline passing small towns such as Skenes Creek, Kennett River and Wye River, whose populations explode with tourists in summer. Allow plenty of time to enjoy the views or swim at the beautiful beaches.

The short, steep climb up to **Cape Patton Lookout** (17km) is rewarded by expansive coast views.

From **Kennett River** (22.6km) the hills are covered by the eucalypts of Angahook-Lorne State Forest. Soon after is WB Godrey's gravesite (see the boxed text 'The Shipwreck Coast' earlier in this chapter) and the **Mt Defiance Lookout** (34.5km), where views extend to the Aireys Inlet lighthouse.

At **Cumberland River** (37km), a steep gorge has been cut through the sandstone. The beautiful *camping ground* here has a sheltered barbecue area and some lovely walks into the forest.

Lorne

Approaching Lorne from the south, with tall eucalypts framing Loutit Bay, it is easy to understand why it has always been the most popular holiday destination on this coast. The regular population of about 1000 swells at weekends and during holidays. Most of the action is along Mountjoy Parade, where cafe tables and chairs spill over the footpath.

Information The visitor centre (☎ 5289 1152), 144 Mountjoy Parade, has information about accommodation in Lorne (which can be scarce in summer), maps of Angahook-Lorne State Park and the *Cycling the Surf Coast Shire* brochure. The Bank of Melbourne and Commonwealth Bank on Mountjoy Parade have ATMs.

Things to See & Do Lorne is an excellent base to explore the **Angahook-Lorne State Park** – several walks start near town – but be prepared to do some climbing.

Great Ocean Road Adventure Tours, (GORATS; ☎ 5289 6841) is a **mountain-bike** hire company that specialises in downhill tours and supplies transport to the top of the range.

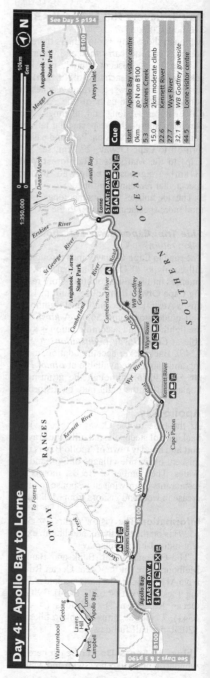

Cue		
start		Apollo Bay visitor centre
0km		go N on B100
5.3		Skenes Creek
15.0	▲	2km moderate climb
22.6		Kennett River
27.7		Wye River
32.1	✱	WB Godfrey gravesite
44.5		Lorne visitor centre

Lorne is also a good place to **relax** and shop, eat in the cafes or just laze on the beach. A book exchange is tucked behind 146 Mountjoy Parade.

Lorne is renowned for its riotous New Year's Eve activities and in early January is filled with swimmers attempting the **Pier to Pub** race across Loutit Bay.

Places to Stay The *Erskine River Caravan Park* (☎ 5289 1382), near the beach, has camp sites overlooking the river for $20 and standard cabins for $60 a double (from $80 with en suite).

The YHA-associate *Great Ocean Road Backpackers* (☎ 5289 1809, 10 Erskine Ave) has a stunning setting. Perched on the hillside among tall trees frequented by crimson rosellas and king parrots, it has dorm beds ($21) and doubles/twins ($25).

For great views over Loutit Bay the *Sandridge Motel* (☎ 5289 2180, cnr Mountjoy Parade & William St) has units from $75 a double.

The *Anchorage Motel* (☎ 5289 1891, 32 Mountjoy Parade) is one of the cheaper motels, with clean, basic doubles from $70 to $155.

Erskine House (☎ 5289 1209, Mountjoy Parade) has been a guest house since the 19th century. B&B costs from $160/195 per double without/with en suite.

Places to Eat Lorne has no shortage of places to eat; most cafes open for breakfast and restaurants stay open late.

The *Ridgeways* supermarket (1 Great Ocean Rd) opens from 8am to 7pm.

The *Loutit Bay Bakery* (46B Mountjoy Parade) has a fabulous range of breads and pies for a perfect picnic. *Lorne Ovenhouse (46A Mountjoy Parade)* has excellent wood-fired pizzas and calzone.

Marks Restaurant (☎ 5289 2787, 124 Mountjoy Parade), which overlooks Loutit Bay, is good value and serves vegetarian options ($10 to $12).

Pub meals are available at the *Lorne Hotel* (☎ 5289 1409), which has weekend bands.

Day 5: Lorne to Geelong
5–7 hours, 70.1km

More traffic uses the road from Lorne, but the route mostly has a good shoulder. Between Lorne and Anglesea the road hugs the coast,

with a climb over Big Hill. The **Memorial Arch**, spanning the road at 12.5km, commemorates the completion of the Great Ocean Road and, for some, is its official starting point. Much of the heathland extending to the coast near Aireys Inlet has been developed, with some architectural nightmares.

The side trip at 36km to **Point Addis** winds through box-ironbark forest before dropping to a car park where a track leads to the expansive swimming beach, backed by huge cliffs. From here a 1km interpretive trail leads through the Ironbark Basin, explaining the traditional lifestyle of local Koorie people.

Bells Beach (40.1km), home of Australia's largest surfing competition, provides a final view of the spectacular south-west coastline.

Torquay (46.5km) is quiet during the week but hectic at weekends. The Esplanade follows the city beach, which is lined with huge Norfolk pines. The *cafes* and shops are set back from the beach; on the highway is a fascinating **surf museum**.

The *caravan parks* (go straight at 67.5km) in Geelong are just off the route near the Barwon River, south of the city.

Geelong

Geelong, on Corio Bay, is Victoria's largest provincial city. The city prospered from wool and giant wool stores, many now converted to offices, still line Eastern Beach. After WWI, automotive, aluminium and chemical industries established a strong industrial base. The town suffered a major financial collapse in the late 1980s but is slowly recovering. Recent waterfront development is designed to boost tourism, although traders behind this facade feel neglected. Geelong was the first Victorian town to produce a bike plan (in 1978) and has a strong emphasis on ensuring cycling is feasible and safe.

Information Geelong's visitor centre (☎ 5222 2900), corner Moorabool and Brougham Sts, is in the National Wool Museum. It has a comprehensive range of maps and brochures – notably, cycling guides.

DeGrandi Cycle & Sport (☎ 5221 5099), 419 Moorabool St, has a large range.

Things to See & Do Experience the importance of wool to Geelong's development by visiting the **National Wool Museum** in

VICTORIA

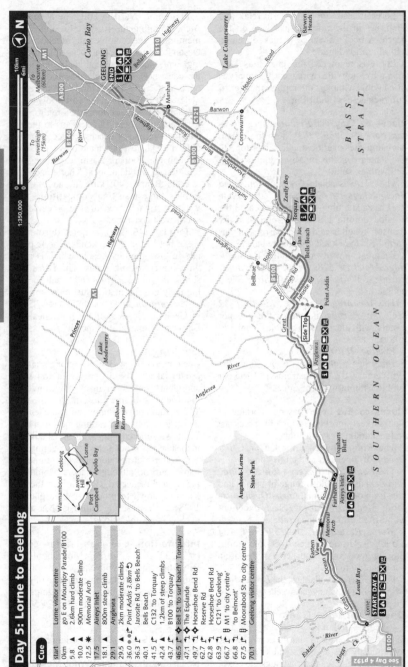

Day 5: Lorne to Geelong

Cue

start		Lorne visitor centre
0km		go E on Mountjoy Parade/B100
5.8	◄	2.6km hard climb
10.0	◄	900m moderate climb
12.5	✳	Memorial Arch
17.5	◄	Aireys Inlet
18.1	◄	800m steep climb
29.1		Anglesea
29.5	◄	2km moderate climbs
36.0	●↻	Point Addis 3.8km ↻
36.3	↲	Jarosite Rd 'to Bells Beach'
40.1		Bells Beach
41.5	↲	C132 'to Torquay'
42.4	↲	1.2km of steep climbs
43.7	↲	B100 'to Torquay'
46.5	↲	Bell St to surf beach', Torquay
47.1	◆	The Esplande
49.7	◆	Horseshoe Bend Rd
62.7	↲	Reserve Rd
62.8	↲	Horseshoe Bend Rd
63.9	↲	C121 'to Geelong'
66.7	↲	M1 'to city centre'
66.8	↲	'to Belmont'
67.5	↲	Mooraboo St 'to city centre'
70.1		Geelong visitor centre

the restored Dennys Lascelles Wool Store. Covering three storeys, permanent and temporary exhibitions range from the sheep's back to contemporary fashion.

The **Geelong Art Gallery**, in Little Malop St, has an excellent collection of Australian impressionist art.

Redevelopment of **Eastern Beach**, with walks, restaurants and parklands, has made it a delightful place to view Corio Bay. The **Industrial Heritage Track** along the Barwon River is a recommended ride. Brochures are available from the visitor centre.

In November the Geelong Touring Club runs the 160km **Geelong Otway Classic**, a fund-raising circuit ride through the Otway Ranges to Lorne.

Places to Stay Geelong's caravan parks are on the Barwon River in Belmont. The *City Southside Caravan Park (☎ 5243 3788, 87 Barrabool Rd)* has pleasant camp sites from $15 and cabins from $60 a double.

The Nomads National Hotel (☎ 5229 1211, 191 Moorabool St) has dorm beds from $19 and doubles for $22. It has a large kitchen and sells cheap meals.

The Kangaroo Motel (☎ 5221 4022, 16 The Esplanade South) has singles/doubles from $65/75 and is on Corio Bay.

The elegant Victorian *Pevensey House (☎ 5224 2810, 17 Pevensey Crescent)*, near Eastern Beach, offers rooms for $132/154, including silver-service breakfast.

Places to Eat Market Square Shopping Centre has a *Safeway* supermarket *(Malop St)*. The two 24-hour *Coles* stores are in Belmont Shopping Village *(65 High St)* and Bay City Plaza *(77 Malop St)*.

Near the caravan parks are some good restaurants. The Turkish-Italian *Magic Woodoven (☎ 5241 1278; 81 High St, Belmont)* serves fabulous bread, kebabs, and large pizzas for around $10. The *Mandarin Court Chinese Restaurant (☎ 5241 9888; 105 High St, Belmont)* has a large menu with mains for around $10.

Lamby's (☎ 5223 2392), in the National Wool Museum, has a lovely atmosphere and mains from $18 to $20.

On Cunningham Pier, with views across the bay, *Buccaneers (☎ 5222 6444)* serves enormous plates of fish and chips for $7.50.

Interesting eateries around the central Little Malop St include *Wholefoods Cafe & Gallery (☎ 5229 3909, 10 James St)*, which serves gourmet vegetarian lunches (closed weekends); and the popular, lively *Cats Cafe & Bar (☎ 5229 3077, 90 Little Malop St)*, which has a good range of vegetarian dishes.

Riches of the North-East

Duration...4 days
Distance...221.1km
Difficulty......................................moderate
Start..Wangaratta
End..Bright

Flat riding along the floodplains of the Murray and Ovens Rivers is combined with some steep climbs to the historic gold towns of Beechworth and Yackandandah in the foothills of Victoria's High Plains. This is a ride designed to enable you to relax and enjoy some of the best wine and food Victoria has to offer. The riding distances are short to allow time to explore historic towns and visit wineries and gourmet retreats. Off the usual backpacker route, hostel accommodation is scarce.

HISTORY
Aboriginal groups settled in the lowland areas and much of the hill country is sacred to them. Europeans, following the explorers Hume and Hovell, settled in the 1840s, but it was the discovery of gold in the 1850s that had the most dramatic effect on development. Beechworth, where 85 tonnes of gold was extracted, was one of the region's richest goldfields and miners flocked to the area.

Small mining settlements spread but, with the decline of gold, the area reverted to grazing and, on the lower slopes, forestry. Wine making, first established in the 19th century, was restabilised in the 1960s and the north-east was placed firmly on the map as a premier tourist attraction.

NATURAL HISTORY
The foothills of the High Country in the north-east are largely composed of folded and faulted sedimentary rocks and exposed granite intrusions injected with gold seams. With erosion, vast amounts of alluvial gold

were deposited in and around the Ovens, Goulburn, Kiewa and Murray Rivers.

Most of the land has been cleared for grazing or mined for gold. River red gums are prominent in the river valleys and adjacent floodplains. On drier land, the box-ironbark woodlands of the Chiltern National Park boast a show of spring wild flowers, especially orchids, and are frequented by honey-eaters, parrots and cockatoos.

The granite country of Beechworth features red gum, the endemic black cypress pine and, in spring, magnificent wattles.

PLANNING
When to Ride

The ride can be done at any time of the year. Holiday periods, especially Christmas and Easter, can be busy (but quieter than coastal areas). Summer can be hot. Wine and food festivals are held all year, particularly in early autumn and spring.

Maps & Books

The RACV regional maps *North Eastern Victoria* and *Goulburn Murray Waters* cover the ride.

The excellent *North-East Victoria: An Explorer's Guide*, by Chris Mclaughin, covers the north-east and the High Country.

The Wangaratta Bicycle User Group's *Unlimited Cycling: Wangaratta Recreation Rides* outlines 22 rides.

GETTING TO/FROM THE RIDE

Bright is also the start of the Across the High Country ride (described later in this chapter).

To link with the Central Gold & Spa Country ride (earlier in this chapter) spend two days riding from Bendigo to Wangaratta via Rushworth and Murchison. Alternatively, ride from Bendigo to Seymour to catch the Wangaratta train – it's a lovely day ride via Sutton Grange, Heathcote and Tooborac.

Wangaratta

The train station is about 800m west of the town centre. V/Line (☎ 13 6196) operates from Melbourne to Wangaratta ($29.30 plus $3 per bike, 2¾ hours, three times daily, twice on weekends).

Bright

Train V/Line (☎ 13 6196) runs buses between Wangaratta and Bright ($9.60 plus $3 per bike, 1½ hours, two daily on weekdays, one on weekends), which connect with trains to Melbourne and Sydney.

Bicycle It's 74km from Bright to Wangaratta; the road has a shoulder and is not very busy. The Alpine Rail Trail covers about half the route.

THE RIDE
Wangaratta

At the confluence of the Ovens and King Rivers, this town grew during the gold rush as a stopover point for travellers from NSW, southern Victoria and the High Country. On such a major transport route the area was alive with bushrangers out to exploit the unwary traveller. Still an important junction, Wangaratta is now mainly a rural and commercial town.

It has a strong racing fraternity and is the home-town of several prominent cyclists: Dean Woods, a three-time Olympian (winner of gold, silver and bronze medals); Damian McDonald, who competed in the road race at the Atlanta Olympics, and veteran legend Barry Burns.

Dan 'Mad Dog' Morgan

Dan 'Mad Dog' Morgan was a bushranger who is perhaps more famous in death than in life. His hairy body was more ape-like than human and he was prone to violent psychopathic rages. On the run after stealing horses, he rested too long at Peechalba Station, 35km north of Wangaratta. The police were alerted and in the ensuing 'roundup' he was fatally wounded.

His body was returned to Wangaratta and, by popular demand, put on display with matchsticks holding his eyes open to enable photos to be taken! While on display his beard was skinned from his face and taken to Benalla; legend has it that his scrotum was removed and sewn into money pouches. Later, his head was removed and sent to Melbourne for examination by phrenologists to see if there was any connection between his brain and crimes. Finally, after public outcry at his defilement, the headless, beardless and ball-less body was removed and buried next to the Wangaratta Cemetery, south of the present-day visitor centre, where the grave can still be found.

Information
The visitor centre (☎ 5721 5711), on the corner of Tone Rd and Handley St, is on the Melbourne side of town on the Hume Hwy.

The Commonwealth Bank and Bank of Melbourne are in Murphy St and the ANZ is in Reid St; all have ATMs. Wangaratta City Cycles (☎ 5721 4744), 90 Murphy St, has a repair service.

Things to See & Do
The main tourist attraction is **Airworld**, an aviation museum at the Wangaratta airport, signposted 4km east of the freeway. It has a collection of 40 vintage aircraft and aviation memorabilia. Visit 'Mad Dog' Morgan's grave (see the boxed text).

The town is also famous for its **Festival of Jazz**, held in early November.

Places to Stay
The *Painters Island Caravan Park (☎ 5721 3380, Pinkerton Crescent)* has riverside camping ($14), on-site vans ($28) and en suite cabins from $55 a double.

Charming *Millers Cottage Motel (☎ 5721 5755, cnr Great Alpine Rd & Old Hume Hwy)* has singles/doubles from $42/50.

Close to the station, the *Wangaratta Motor Inn (☎ 5721 5488 or ☎ 1800-811 049, 6 Roy St)* has rooms from $55/67.

Places to Eat
The *Coles* supermarket *(Ryley St)* is open 24 hours. *Montys Bakery (58 Reid St)* opens early.

Scribblers Cafe (66 Reid St) displays works by local artists (open from 8.30am).

Vespas (cnr Ovens & Reid Sts) serves modern Mediterranean-style food in a pleasant outdoor eating area.

The popular *Cafe Martini (87 Murphy St)* is good for Italian bistro food and has excellent wood-fired pizzas.

Day 1: Wangaratta to Beechworth
2½–5 hours, 47.6km
Along quiet roads via Milawa, views of Mt Buffalo dominate the horizon. Be sure to carry adequate water after Everton.

Red gums on the Ovens River floodplain provide shade on the flat road to Milawa (17.1km), which has a *caravan park* and *motel*. The town is synonymous with gourmet food; sample unusual cheeses at the Milawa Cheese Company (15.3km), which

also sells coffee and light lunches. **Milawa Mustards**, in town on Factory Rd, has samples of mustard flavoured with local herbs. Detour to **Brown Brothers Winery**, which has tastings in the cool cellars. Lunch at *The Brown Brothers Epicurean Centre* includes a glass of wine to complement the meal.

Alternatively, bread, cheese, mustard and wine can be enjoyed at the beautiful picnic ground beside the Ovens River at 26.8km.

Everton (28.4km) has a *general store*, *camping ground* and *pub*.

Beechworth
Beechworth was the administrative centre of the north-east's lucrative gold mining areas. National-Trust preservation since the 1960s has resulted in a town little changed from the 19th century, bringing new prosperity as a tourist town with an emphasis on antiques, craft, cafes and restaurants.

Information
The visitor centre (☎ 5728 3233, 🖳 www.beechworth-index.com.au), on Ford St, has touring guides to Chiltern, Rutherglen and Yackandandah. The DNRE (☎ 5728 1501), on Albert Rd, has maps of the state forest.

A Commonwealth Bank (with ATM) is in Ford St. Beechworth Cycles & Saws (☎ 5728 1402), 17 Camp St, has a limited bike-repair service and parts.

Things to See & Do
Both historical and natural features are part of the attraction of Beechworth. The **Burke Museum** (☎ 5728 1420), on Loch St, is one of Victoria's oldest museums – with probably the most extensive range of memorabilia.

Notable buildings include: those in the **Historic Precinct**, in Ford St; **Murray Breweries**, on Last St; the **Ovens District Hospital** facade, on Church St; and the **Chinese Burning Towers** at the cemetery in Balaclava Rd.

The 5km **Gorge Scenic Drive** twists through the granite hills of the Spring Creek Goldfield past the **Powder Magazine**, designed to reduce destruction in the event of an explosion. The weathered pink granite of the **Cascades** is great place to explore. Alternatively, explore the **Beechworth State Forest** or climb to the nut farms near **Stanley**.

Places to Stay
The *Lake Sambell Caravan Park (☎ 5728 1421, Jarvis Rd)*, relatively

Day 1: Wangaratta to Beechworth

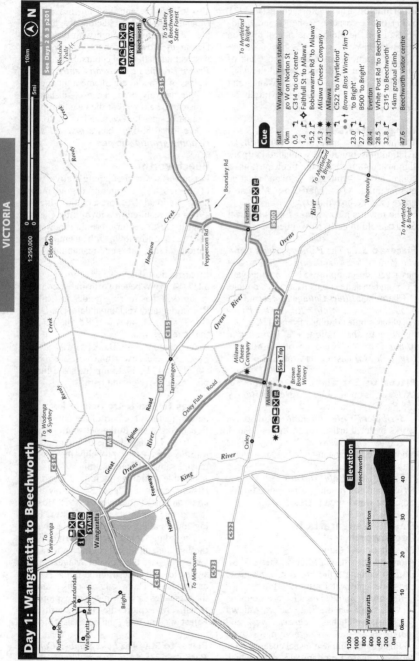

VICTORIA

1:1,250,000

N

See Days 2 & 3 p201

Cue

start		Wangaratta train station
0km		go W on Norton St
0.5	⬅	C314 'to city centre'
1.4	➡	Faithfull St to Milawa'
15.2	➡	Bobinawarrah Rd 'to Milawa'
15.3	✳	Milawa Cheese Company
17.1	✳	Milawa
	➡	C522 'to Myrtleford'
23.0	➡	Brown Bros Winery 1km ↩
27.7	➡	'to Bright'
28.4		B500 'to Bright'
28.5		Everton
	➡	White Post Rd 'to Beechworth'
32.8	➡	C315 'to Beechworth'
	◢	14km gradual climb
47.6		Beechworth visitor centre

Elevation

Rutherglen
Yackandandah
Beechworth
Wangaratta
Bright

close to town, has camp sites for $13, on-site vans from $32, and en suite cabins from $48.

Tanswells Commercial Hotel (☎ *5728 1480, 30 Ford St)* has excellent rooms for $30/50 per single/double ($40/60 weekends), including breakfast. Irish bands are a regular weekend feature.

The *Old Priory* (☎ *5728 1024, 8 Priory Lane)*, a converted historic convent, has rooms from $35/65 ($60 with en suite), including light breakfast.

Quiet *Armour Motor Inn* (☎ *5728 1466, 1 Camp St)*, close to the town centre, has doubles from $86.

Places to Eat The *IGA* supermarket *(Ford St)* is open daily.

The *Beechworth Bakery (27 Camp St)* is famous and worthy of it; the beestings (yeasted, almond-topped custard cakes) are a knockout. Open daily from 6am to 7pm, it is always frenetic at weekends – for quick service, go early.

Victoria's Cafe (☎ *5728 1493, cnr Ford & Camp Sts)*, serves sumptuous breakfasts from 8am, excellent coffee and a range of lunch dishes.

The bistro at *Tanswells Commercial Hotel* (☎ *5728 1480, 30 Ford St)* serves excellent pub meals. Cosy *Pasta Joke* (☎ *5728 2352, 52 Ford St)* has mains with good range of vegetarian options for around $14.

For a special night out *The Bank Restaurant* (☎ *5728 2203, 86 Ford St)* has 19th-century ambience at 21st-century prices: mains from $21.50 to $24.50.

Day 2: Beechworth to Rutherglen

2½–4 hours, 44.6km

This easy ride allows plenty of time to explore the historic gold region.

A gravel-road side trip at 4.8km leads to **Woolshed Falls**, which cascade over exposed granite. The disruption caused by mining can be seen on the **historic walk** at the falls in the intricate network of channels and mullock heaps.

Mt Pilot and the surrounding hills are important sites for the Duduroa people. A side trip at 13.2km to the **Yeddonba Aboriginal art site** at the base of Mt Pilot reveals a painting of a Tasmanian tiger, the Duduroa totem.

Historic Chiltern (25.7km) is quieter, and unfortunately a little more run down, than Beechworth. The main street, with numerous beautiful historic buildings, has been used as a film setting. The old **Bank of Australasia** is now a *cafe*, *restaurant* and *B&B*. The museum in the **Star Theatre** has old photographs of the town and a giant grapevine in the courtyard. In Victoria St, the beautifully restored **Lakeview House** was, briefly, the childhood home of the author Henry Handel Richardson.

The forests of the **Chiltern Box-Ironbark National Park**, once alive with gold diggers, have regenerated and, in spring, are filled with wild flowers and birds.

The site of the gold-rush town of **Christmastown** (34km) has an information board about the region's more populous days. Now it is just part of the quiet rural landscape of the **Rutherglen Wine District**, which initially looks more like grazing country than one of the state's premier wine-growing areas (see the boxed text 'Wineries of the Rutherglen Region' overleaf).

Rutherglen

☎ 02

On the floodplains of the Murray River, Rutherglen is one of the oldest wine-growing areas in Australia. Famous for fortified wines, it also produces a range of quality table wines. Vineyards were planted in the 1860s but the industry declined with the discovery of gold. Later, most vines were devastated by *Phylloxera*, a root disease, while simultaneously ports began to lose favour and the industry slumped. In the 1960s a number of growers organised a wine festival, which re-established the region as a premium wine producer. The vineyards today, mostly small family operations, are scattered around Rutherglen.

Information The visitor centre (☎ 02-6032 9166 or ☎ 1800-622 871), 13–27 Drummond St, in old cellars, has good information on the wineries and the town.

A Commonwealth Bank ATM is on the corner of High and Main Sts. Bike repairs and basic spares are available at the Rutherglen Sports Store (☎ 02-6032 9044), 124 Main St.

Things to See & Do The popularity of Rutherglen as a destination for wine lovers has resulted in a surfeit of activities year-round to indulge wine lovers and gourmands. Most notable is the **Tour de Muscat**,

VICTORIA

a fund-raising cycling tour held each November (contact the visitor centre for details).

There is perhaps no better way to enjoy the wines of Rutherglen than by bike. The region is relatively flat, the roads quiet, and fresh air does wonders for a fuddled brain. Some lovely picnic areas have been created among the red gums on the Murray River floodplains.

Places to Stay The *Rutherglen Caravan Park* (☎ 02-6032 8577, 72 Murray St), on Lake King, has $13 camping sites and cabins from $40.

The National Trust-classified *Victoria Hotel* (☎ 02-6032 8610, 90 Main St) has accommodation, including light breakfast, from $28/55 a single/double (from $66 with en suite).

Most motels are on busy Murray Valley Hwy. In the quieter *Rutherglen Motor Inn* (☎ 02-6032 9776, 10–20 Murray St) rooms cost $55/66 weekdays ($70/85 weekends).

The charming, older-style B&B, *Carlyle House* (☎ 02-6032 8444, 147 High St) has doubles for $120 to $175.

Places to Eat The *IGA* supermarket (95 Main St) stocks most groceries. The *Rutherglen Bakery* (137 Main St), open from 7am, has a great range of breads, cakes and quiches. The *tea rooms* (93 Main St), open from 9am, serves excellent home-made pies and cakes and real coffee.

Poachers Paradise Hotel (☎ 02-6032 7008, 120 Main St) has good pub meals – generous mains cost from $8 to $12 – but limited vegetarian options.

Wineries of the Rutherglen Region

More than a dozen wineries are within striking distance of Rutherglen, which makes for a perfect day or two of wine touring – especially by bike. Mountain bikes can be hired at the visitor centre (the unsealed roads are quite rough). Some of the wineries listed below are passed on Days 2 & 3. An excellent free map and brochure, available from the visitor centre and wineries, details each winery.

Jones Winery, off Chiltern Rd, 3.4km south-east of Rutherglen, is the area's smallest, operating out of a ramshackle collection of sheds and old buildings; try the vintage port. Nearby, the tin shed of Anderson winery houses some of the state's best sparkling wine. Chambers Rosewood Winery, 1km north-west on Corowa Rd, is full of character and history and well known for fortified wines. The first winery west of Rutherglen is Campbells, a modern complex with the sloping roof featured on its label. Across the road is the Stanton and Killeen vineyard; try the reds from the little-grown durif grapes. Further along, on the corner of Three Chain Rd, is Buller's Calliope Winery, which has some great aged fortified and shiraz wines, a picnic area and an interesting aviary.

South of Wahgunyah is Pfeiffer wines' rustic old winery complex. Pre-ordered picnic hampers can be eaten under the red gums on the bridge over the Murray River. St Leonard's vineyard, 1km north-east of Wahgunyah, has a delightful picnic area overlooking the river and an excellent bistro.

East of Rutherglen, on Gooramadda Rd, Mt Prior vineyard has outstanding accommodation and a restaurant. Nearby is the famous Morris Wines, renowned for its fortified wines, in particular its muscats – the glass-sided cellar door looks into the old barrel room. At the edge of the district on the Murray Valley Hwy is Gehrig's winery, Victoria's oldest, set around the historic Barnawartha Homestead (1870). It has picnic facilities and, from Thursday to Sunday, serves wonderful light lunches.

With a couple of exceptions, the wineries in the area open daily from 9am to 5pm (from 10am on Sunday). Most wineries will freight wine and some (eg, Pfeiffers) will deliver wine to Rutherglen. Check with the winery.

NOW THIS IS A RATHER CHEEKY LITTLE NUMBER! ..WHAT A PITY YOU HAVE TO KEEP STEERING!

DON HATCHER

Days 2 & 3: Beechworth – Rutherglen – Yackandandah

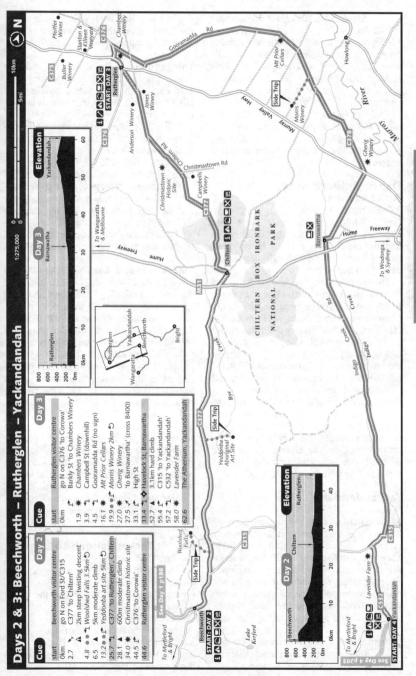

Cue **Day 2**

0km		Beechworth visitor centre
0km		go N on Ford St/C315
2.7		C377 'to Chiltern'
4.8		2km steep twisting descent
6.5		Woolshed Falls 3.5km
13.2		Yeddonba art site 5km
25.7		C377 'to Rutherglen', Chiltern
28.1		600m moderate climb
34.0		Christmastown historic site
44.5		C376 'to Corowa'
44.6		Rutherglen visitor centre

Cue **Day 3**

start		Rutherglen visitor centre
0km		go N on C376 'to Corowa'
		Barkly St 'to Chambers Winery'
1.9		Chambers Winery
3.9		Campbell St (downhill)
4.5		Gooramadda Rd (no sign)
16.1		Mt Prior Cellars
19.9		Morris Winery 2km
27.0		Gherig Winery
27.5		'to Barnawartha' (cross B400)
33.1		High St
33.4		Havelock St, Barnawartha
52.7		3.1km hard climb
55.4		C315 'to Yackandandah'
57.2		C532 'to Yackandandah'
58.0		Lavender Farm
62.6		The Atherium, Yackandandah

See Day 1 p198

VICTORIA

The *Rendezvous Gourmet Restaurant* (☎ 02-6032 9114, 68 Main St) features Mediterranean-style food with an emphasis on gourmet pasta dishes ($12.50–14), well-suited to vegetarians. The up-market *Tuileries (☎ 02-6032 9033, 13–35 Drummond St)*, in the old Seppelts winery, has main courses from $17.50 to $21.

Pfeiffers Winery (☎ 02-6033 2805, Distillery Rd) prepares picnic hampers ($49 for two, including wine; vegetarian available). A number of the wineries have *restaurants* attached.

Day 3: Rutherglen to Yackandandah

3½–6½ hours, 62.6km

Day 3 follows the Murray River before climbing through farming country to Yackandandah. The cycling is easy but there are few facilities after Rutherglen, so carry food and water.

The flat ride along the Murray River has views to the red gums and billabongs of the floodplain and more wineries, including **Chambers Winery** (1.9km), **Mt Prior Cellars** (16.1km), **Morris Winery** (a side trip at 20.2km) and a rough ride up the drive to **Gherig Winery** (27km); see the boxed text on the previous page). **Barnawartha** (33.4km) has little more than a *pub*, *general store* and picnic ground on the Indigo Creek.

It is easier to walk than ride to the shop at the **Lavender Patch Lavender Farm** (58km), which has an amazing array of lavender products and serves Devonshire tea overlooking the Kiewa Valley. The downhill run into Yackandandah through forest and farmland is exhilarating.

Yackandandah

☎ 02

Yackandandah is quiet and picturesque, with its tree-lined main street and 19th-century buildings. The discovery of alluvial gold in Yackandandah Creek in 1852 brought an influx of miners and settlements developed along the creek. Yackandandah survived as a major town but, after the gold rush, fell into decline, supporting a smaller rural population. It has since prospered through tourism.

Information The visitor centre (☎ 02-6027 1988), in the Athenaeum Library, High St, has irregular opening hours.

The post office, in High St, is an agent for the Commonwealth Bank, and the general store and the pub have Eftpos facilities.

Things to See & Do Most of the sites and interesting buildings are associated with gold exploration; the **public buildings** in High St indicate the prosperity and stability the town enjoyed.

A 7km loop around the town includes the **Gorge**, a tail race built to divert water from Yackandandah Creek for sluicing. Yack Track Tours (☎ 02-6027 1757) runs trips down the historic hand-dug Karr's Reef Goldmine.

The **general cemetery**, on the Yackandandah–Wodonga Rd, has imposing gates and the large trees that grace the entrance are classified by the National Trust.

Stanley State Forest has a number of dirt roads worth exploring by mountain bike.

Places to Stay & Eat The *Yackandandah Caravan Park (☎ 02-6027 1380, Dederang Rd)* has camp sites on Yackandandah Creek for $10 and on-site vans for $35.

Yackandandah Motor Inn (☎ 02-6027 1155, 18 High St) has comfortable units from $60/80 a single/double, including breakfast.

Serendipity B&B (☎ 02-6027 1881, 9 Wingham St) has a room for $45 per person (including light breakfast), and a two-room self-contained cottage for $90 a double with breakfast ingredients.

The *Star Hotel (☎ 02-6027 1493, High St)* is recommended for delicious meals, some vegetarian, in its cosy dining room.

Yackandandah Bakery (20 High St) serves an excellent range of cakes and breads and breakfast from 8am. The *supermarket (High St)* is closed Sunday.

Wild on Thyme Tearooms (High St) serves delicious Devonshire teas and displays lots of crafts.

Day 4: Yackandandah to Bright

4–7 hours, 66.3km

Surrounded by the stunning scenery of Victoria's High Country, Day 4 is easy. From Ovens to Bright the route follows the sealed Alpine Rail Trail for 25km; it's perhaps the best rail trail in Victoria.

The ride undulates gently through farming country with views to the High Country and the Kiewa and Ovens Valleys. Passing the granite tors of Nobb Hill, the views

Day 4: Yackandandah to Bright

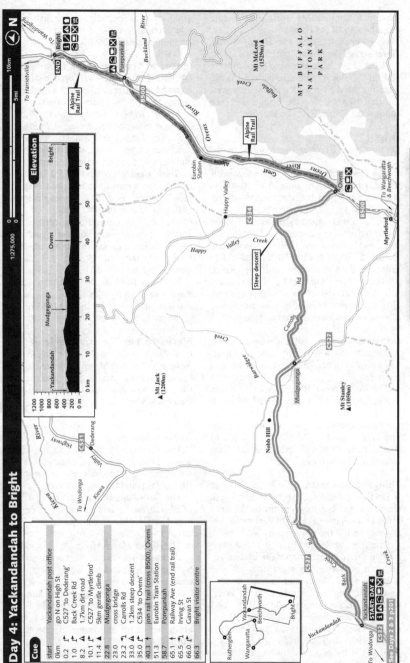

Cue		
start		Yackandandah post office
0km		go N on High St
0.2	←	C527 'to Dederang'
1.0	←	Back Creek Rd
8.2	←	1.7km dirt road
10.1	←	C527 to Myrtleford'
11.4	←	5km gentle climb
22.8		Mudgegonga
23.0		cross bridge
23.2	←	Carrolls Rd
33.0	←	1.2km steep descent
35.0	←	C534 to Ovens'
40.3	←	join rail trail (cross B500), Ovens
51.3		Eurobin Train Station
58.7		Porepunkah
65.1	←	Railway Ave (end rail trail)
65.5	←	Irving St
66.0	←	Gavan St
66.3		Bright visitor centre

VICTORIA

expand to include **Mt Buffalo**, a granite massif south of the Ovens River.

At Ovens (40.3km), the *Happy Valley Hotel* serves fabulous counter meals.

Water is available at the old **Eurobin train station** (51.3km). At **Porepunkah** (58.7km), a town named by a trader in Indian wares, the trail twists under the bridge and then follows the Ovens River to Bright.

Bright

On the Ovens River and surrounded by the foothills of the High Country, Bright is a tourist (and cyclist) mecca. It is busy year-round, particularly in autumn when its deciduous trees turn brilliant shades of red, orange and yellow.

The area was settled by pastoralists in the 1830s but with the discovery of gold in the Buckland Valley in the 1850s the population escalated. Bright became an administrative centre for the surrounding goldfields, which yielded gold until the end of the 19th century; a timber industry subsequently developed. Bright's current prosperity was established after WWII with tourism development.

Information The visitor centre (☎ 5755 2275 or ☎ 1800-813 153), 119 Gavan St, has a display of activities around Bright and the Alps.

The Commonwealth and ANZ banks in Gavan St have ATMs. CyclePath (☎ 5750 1442), 74 Gavan St, run by mountain-bike enthusiasts, does repairs and spares, tours and basic mountain-bike hire from $11 to $17.50 per hour or $22 to $35 per day (serious bikes are also available).

Things to See & Do It is easy just to relax in Bright; browsing the shops and sitting in the cafes. On hot days, **swim** in the cold Ovens River either at Howitt Park or further downstream in the gorge pools.

Bright is surrounded by state forest, with myriad dirt paths to **mountain bike**. CyclePath runs Wednesday night rides.

Many other places can be explored by bike, including the historic town of **Wandiligong** (12km return) and, for a good workout, Mt Buffalo (70km return; 1030m climb), where Devonshire tea is served at the renowned *Mt Buffalo Chalet (☎ 5755 1500)*.

Bright is the base for Audax Australia's **Alpine Classic**, held in January. Around 1000 cyclists participate in this event, which features a 200km, 130km or 100km ride into the High Country.

Places to Stay The *Bright Caravan Park (☎ 5755 1141, Cherry Ave)* has camp sites along Morse's Creek from $17 a double and cabins for $36 ($45 with en suite).

Bright Hikers Backpackers (☎ 5750 1244, e hikers@netc.net.au, 4 Ireland St) has dorms for $17 and doubles from $37. It has Internet access, a comfortable kitchen and lounge, and mountain-bike hire.

Bright Central Motel (☎ 5755 1074, 2 Ireland St) has dorms from $22 per person and motel rooms from $55/65 per single/double.

Bright Motor Inn (☎ 5750 1433, 1 Delany Ave) has comfortable rooms from $50/60, and a wine bar. Self-contained rooms facing a delightful courtyard at the *Coach House Inn (☎ 5755 1475, 100 Gavan St)* cost from $61/77.

In the picturesque Wandiligong Valley, *Knox Farm B&B (☎ 0417-367 494, School Rd)* has one double (with spa) for $120 per night, including breakfast.

Places to Eat The *supermarket (16 Ireland St)* is open until 9pm. The *Bright Bakery (80 Gavan St)* sells a huge range of breads and wonderful pies and pasties. Gavan St also has *takeaways* and a great *ice-cream shop*.

Jackies Tearooms (6 Ireland St) serves delicious breakfasts, wonderful cakes and fabulous damper.

The *Riverview Cafe*, behind the visitor centre, sells great coffee, sandwiches and focaccias on the balcony overlooking Howitt Park and the Ovens River.

The *Cosy Kangaroo Restaurant (☎ 5750 1838, Gavan St)* has pancakes to die for, plus excellent focaccias, pasta and vegetarian fare.

The *Alpine Hotel-Motel (☎ 5755 1366, 7 Anderson St)* serves excellent counter meals for around $14, and has bands most weekends.

The highly regarded, up-market *Simone's (☎ 5755 2022, cnr Great Alpine Rd & Ashwood Ave)* serves modern Italian cuisine. From the same management, the trendy *Caffe Bacco (☎ 5750 1711, 2D Anderson St)* is almost as good, with pasta and noodle dishes for under $20.

VICTORIA

Across the High Country

Duration	3 days
Distance	237.8km
Difficulty	moderate-hard
Start	Bright
End	Bairnsdale

The recent addition of 'Great' to the name of the Alpine Road between Wangaratta and Bairnsdale is apt, and this ride truly is a great one. The Victorian High Country lures cyclists willing to accept the challenge of steep but rewarding climbing and wanting to experience the quiet isolation of the alpine country. The route passes through the largest cattle station in Victoria and into the eastern Gippsland towns of Omeo, Swifts Creek and Ensay. Following the Tambo River to Bruthen, it ends along the recently finished rail trail that runs from Bruthen to Bairnsdale.

HISTORY

Koorie people have been visiting the High Plains for around 5000 years. Traditionally, they travelled to the Alps during summer to feast on the large Bogong moths. Later, Euro-

pean cattlemen used the High Country for summer grazing, and the network of huts and stock routes they established is still used by bushwalkers and skiers. Although overstocking caused considerable damage, the legacy of the cattlemen is an important part of the European cultural history of the high plains.

From the 1850s onwards, gold mining, particularly around Omeo, led to major supply routes being built. In the 1880s a route from the Ovens Valley to Omeo, the present Alpine Road, was built. The route traverses some very exposed areas around the aptly named Mt Blowhard.

The battle over land use in the High Country raged for many years between supporters of an Alpine National Park and cattlemen wanting grazing access to the high plains. While a national park was declared in 1989, ensuring protection of the alpine areas, the increase in year-round tourism and development of resorts could still lead to conflict.

NATURAL HISTORY

The Victorian High Country is a plateau approximately 1800m high extending from NSW to Gippsland. The snow line is at about 1300m in winter. Mt Feathertop is the only significant peak to draw the eye, so the view seems to extend for ever.

Eucalypts dominate, from the dry stringybarks and box forest through stands of towering mountain ash. In colder regions, mountain gum and white sallee – the beautiful and twisted snow gums – occur. Above the snow line, grasses, herbs and shrubs grow in treeless hollows where the wind whips through, and boggy pools are surrounded by sphagnum moss.

Echidnas and wombats live in the alpine areas throughout the year and the endemic mountain pygmy possum is becoming more common (see the boxed text 'The Tunnel of Love'). Cockatoos, pipits, honeyeaters and robins frequent the Alps during the brief summer flowering period.

PLANNING

Camping is not permitted at the ski-resort towns of Mt Hotham or Dinner Plain; bush camping is permitted at JB Plain (see Day 2).

When to Ride

The best time to ride is from early October (spring) to the end of April. In summer the

The Tunnel of Love

Australia's mammals are often small, and usually nocturnal, so the chances of seeing them are fairly remote. But they play an important role in our ecology and their protection is vital. One story about habitat protection is the tale of the mountain pygmy possum (Burramys parvus) of the Australian Alps. This tiny mammal (which can fit into your palm) lives among the rock-stream habitats in alpine and subalpine regions, particularly in the Mt Hotham region. During the non-breeding season adult males disperse to low-altitude areas. They return during the breeding season to the females who have remained at high altitude. Construction of the Alpine Way through Mt Hotham disrupted the route of males during the breeding season. The solution: build a tunnel of boulders under the road. So, when you follow the Alpine Way on your way to Omeo, spare a thought for the male pygmy possum protected below and able to reach his loved one high on the slopes.

ski resorts are deserted, the roads are quiet and the weather is cool. The road, though open in winter, can be snowed in.

Maps
The RACV *North Eastern Victoria* and *Lakes & Wilderness* regional maps cover the ride.

What to Bring
It can snow at Mt Hotham in summer, so be prepared with warm clothing as well as sunglasses and high-strength sunscreen.

Carry spares – the route has no bike shops. Between Bright and Omeo are few facilities; it's important to carry food and drink. You'll need to be self-sufficient to bush camp.

GETTING TO/FROM THE RIDE
The Riches of the North-East ride (earlier in this chapter) ends at Bright. Link to the East Coast Explorer ride (see the Melbourne to the Gold Coast chapter) at Bairnsdale.

Bright
See the Riches of the North-East ride (p195) earlier in this chapter for details on getting to/from Bright.

Bairnsdale
Although Bairnsdale–Sale passenger trains may run again, V/Line (☎ 13 6196) currently operates buses on that route, which connect with the train service to Melbourne ($34.20 plus $3 per bike, four hours, three services per weekday, two at weekends).

THE RIDE
Bright
See Bright (p204) in the Riches of the North-East ride for information about accommodation and other services.

Day 1: Bright to Hotham Heights
3–6 hours, 55km
The 24km to Harrietville provides a warm up for the steep, demanding climb to Mt Hotham. With no shops after Harrietville, you need to carry adequate food, water and warm clothes. Although the ride ends at Hotham Heights, *camping* is possible at JB Plain, 10km on; Dinner Plain, a further 1.5km, has more accommodation (see Day 2).

The gentle climb up the Ovens Valley is dominated by views of Mt Feathertop and

the surrounding mountains. **Lavender Hue Lavender Farm** (22.3km) is a good place for morning coffee accompanied by lavender-flavoured everything!

Small **Harrietville** (24km) has *accommodation*, a *store* and the last toilets before Hotham Heights. The road from Harrietville (500m) to Mt Hotham (1800m) climbs all the way, past the notorious hairpin bend at **The Meg** (28.7km). You have plenty of time to appreciate the changes in vegetation, from stringy bark and box in the valleys to towering mountain ash and finally, beautiful snow gums. The Dargo Rd, built as an alternative access from the south, joins the Alpine Rd at **St Bernards Pass** (44.1km). A number of hotels were built at the pass, most of which were burnt in bushfires in 1939.

Hotham Heights is visible from St Bernards Pass, but there is still almost 12km to go. In good weather, the views from **Danny's Lookout** across the High Plains and to Mt Buffalo in the west are stupendous.

The road into Hotham Heights descends through the garish tunnel under a ski run to Hotham Central.

Hotham Heights
Hotham Heights is a ski resort owned and managed by the Alpine Resorts Commission (ARC). It is spread out for about 5km along the Alpine Rd. While the original resort lodges are an eyesore, the recent ones are more environmentally sensitive. Outside the ski season not much happens in Hotham Heights. Day-trippers from Bright come to walk, but at night it is deserted.

Limited information is available at Hotham Central (☎ 5759 4444 or ☎ 1800-354 555). The Bright visitor centre provides information about walks and accommodation at Hotham Heights.

Things to See & Do Hotham Heights is surrounded by the Alpine National Park. Summer tourism is heavily promoted with activities such as **walking**, **horse riding** and **fishing**. **Mountain biking** is increasingly popular; Adventurama (☎ 1800-801 464) can arrange some pretty exciting downhill biking, returning on the chairlift.

Places to Stay & Eat Accommodation is a bit of a gamble – in summer, it's scarce. Opportunities to eat out are also limited in

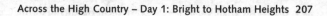

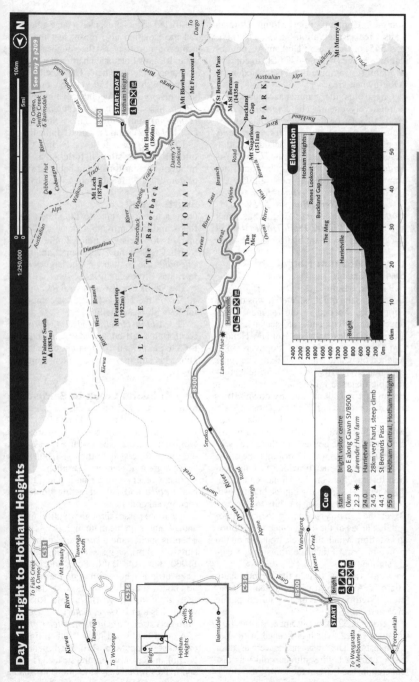

summer. Contact either Mount Hotham Falls Creek Reservation Service (☎ 1800-354 555) or the Mount Hotham Accommodation Service (☎ 1800-032 061) to confirm availability. Camping is not permitted in the ARC-owned area.

On the plus side, summer accommodation is relatively cheap. The *Snowbird Hotel* *(☎ 5759 3503* or ☎ *9889 0647)* has singles from $35 a night and *Lawlers Apartments* *(☎ 5759 3606)* has cheaper accommodation in summer. In Dinner Plain, the *High Plains Lodge (☎ 5159 6455)* has year-round accommodation and serves meals all day.

The Hotham Heights *supermarket* closes at 5pm. *Swindlers Bar (☎ 5759 4421, Hotham Central)* serves pizzas but that's about it. The *Dinner Plain Hotel (☎ 5159 6462)* serves excellent bistro meals.

Day 2: Hotham Heights to Swifts Creek
5–9 hours, 81km

Descend into the quiet, isolated towns of East Gippsland, steeped in the legends of pioneer pastoralists and gold seekers. There are no facilities between Hotham Heights and Omeo, an alternative stopover point, reached on a side trip at 53.2km. The route continues to Swifts Creek to ensure a comfortable distance for the last day (Omeo to Bairnsdale is 130km – mostly downhill).

Development is rife at the **Dinner Plain** ski resort (11.5km) where the housing has won architectural awards. It is worth detouring to see the houses, and there is a *cafe*!

Flourbag Plain was the original site of the Alpine Lodge, which provided accommodation for travellers on the Alpine Rd until in 1928 when it, like many others, burnt down.

As you whiz down the hill to Victoria River the country opens up to the winter grazing areas of the 40,000-hectare **Cobungra Station**. Much of the cleared area on the plateau is part of this, Victoria's largest cattle station.

A side trip at 34km to the **Victoria Falls Historic Area** follows an unsealed road along Victoria River to a beautiful picnic area and *camp site*.

Detour at 52.1km to **Omeo**, on the Livingstone Creek, which is steeped in frontier town history. The grassy plains were used for cattle grazing before alluvial gold was discovered in 1851, when the town was settled.

Restricted access prevented a large gold rush but the isolation also meant that the town achieved notoriety as the roughest in the state. It's now quiet and charming; it's worth spending some time here. The excellent Octagon bookshop (☎ 5159 1411) has numerous local history books unobtainable elsewhere. Omeo has a variety of *accommodation*, *restaurants* and *cafes*. The visitor centre (☎ 5159 1552) is on the Great Alpine Rd.

The back road follows Swifts Creek through the **Cassilis Historic Area**, a reminder of busier times, and between stands of gum trees with a distinct golden bark.

Swifts Creek

Once a town en route to the Omeo goldfields and later providing sheep and cattle markets for the surrounding Tambo Valley, Swifts Creek is now very small and quiet. The *bakery* is popular, and the large *general store* has Eftpos facilities.

The *Swifts Creek Caravan Park (☎ 5159 4272)*, on the Tambo River, has camp sites for $7 with basic facilities.

The *Albion Hotel (☎ 5159 4211)* offers comfortable self-contained accommodation for $20 per person in a small house near the pub. The pub offers an excellent range of meals.

Day 3: Swifts Creek to Bairnsdale
5–10 hours, 101.8km

Day 3 mostly follows the Tambo River as it winds its way downstream towards the Gippsland Lakes. The cycling is easy and the climb to Walsh Cutting (58.3km) precedes a great descent into Bruthen.

Ensay, reached on a side trip at 22.9km, has a *store* and an interesting **bookshop** (open weekends).

The route passes through beautiful forests and, although on the main highway, is quiet. There is shelter and a *camp site* at the **Bark Huts** (49.2km). Signs such as Jews Pinch, £1000 Bend and Battle Point add interest. Their origins can be found on the information board at **Bruthen** (73.4km), at the intersection of the busy Bairnsdale Rd. The village has a *pub*, *store*, *bakery* and Devonshire teas at *Le Cafe at Applespice Cottage*.

A quiet back road from Bruthen links to the **East Gippsland Rail Trail** near the Nicholson River, where the surface is good and makes for an easy ride into Bairnsdale.

Day 2: Hotham Heights to Swifts Creek

VICTORIA

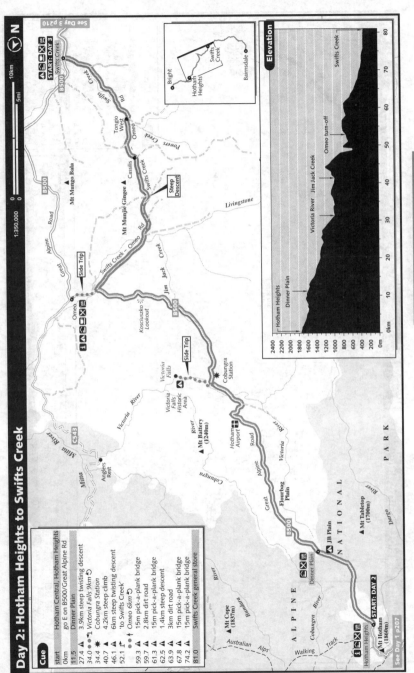

Cue

start	Hotham Central, Hotham Heights
0km	go E on B500/Great Alpine Rd
11.5	Dinner Plain
27.4	3.9km steep twisting descent
34.0	Victoria Falls 9km ↻
34.4	Cobungra Station
40.7	4.2km steep climb
46.1	6km steep twisting descent
52.1	'to Swifts Creek'
	Omeo 6km ↻
59.3	15m pick-a-plank bridge
59.7	2.8km dirt road
61.3	15m pick-a-plank bridge
62.5	1.4km steep descent
63.9	3km dirt road
67.8	15m pick-a-plank bridge
74.2	15m pick-a-plank bridge
81.0	Swifts Creek general store

Elevation

(elevation profile from Hotham Heights to Swifts Creek, showing Dinner Plain, Victoria River, Jim Jack Creek, Omeo turn-off; vertical axis 0m to 2400m, horizontal axis 0km to 80)

Day 3: Swifts Creek to Bairnsdale

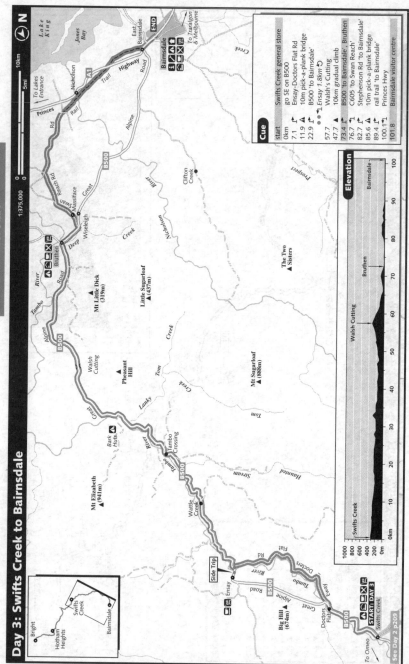

VICTORIA

Cue

start	Swifts Creek general store
0km	go SE on B500
7.1	Ensay–Doctors Flat Rd
11.9	10m pick-a-plank bridge
22.9	B500 'to Bairnsdale'
	Ensay 1.8km
57.7	Walsh's Cutting
47.7	10km gradual climb
73.4	B500 'to Bairnsdale', Bruthen
76.7	C605 'to Swan Reach'
82.7	Stephenson Rd 'to Bairnsdale'
85.6	10m pick-a-plank bridge
89.4	rail trail 'to Bairnsdale'
100:101.?	Princes Hwy
101.8	Bairnsdale visitor centre

Elevation

Bairnsdale

Its skyline dominated by a water tower and the red-brick tower of St Mary's church, Bairnsdale is East Gippsland's commercial centre. The town is on the Mitchell River, which is a few blocks north of the busy, wide boulevard of Main St.

European settlement in Bairnsdale began with cattle. Gold, then crops (hops and grains) and, later, dairying, were important during the 19th century. Primary production remains the town's major industry.

Information The Bairnsdale visitor centre (☎ 5152 3444, 🖳 www.lakesandwilderness.com.au) is at 260 Main St. A block down Main St are the major banks (with ATMs).

Marriots Cycles (☎ 5152 3783) is opposite the visitor centre at 209 Main St. The staff can offer advice about mountain biking in the area (rigid mountain-bike hire costs $15 per day).

Things to See & Do Next to the visitor centre, **St Mary's Catholic Church**, built in 1913, has intricate murals painted in the 1930s by Italian migrant artist Frank Floreani.

Krowathunkooloong (☎ 5152 1891), 37–53 Dalmahoy St, is an Aboriginal cultural centre with interesting displays. The **East Gippsland Historical Museum** is in Macarthur St. Beyond it, the **MacLeod Morass Boardwalk** provides an opportunity to see wetland birdlife.

Places to Stay On the river, the *Mitchell Gardens Caravan Park (☎ 5152 4654,* e *mitchell.gardens@net-tech.com.au, Main St)* has single/double tent sites for $12/14 and cabins ranging from $38 to $92, not including linen.

The *Commercial Hotel (☎ 5152 3031, cnr Main & Bailey Sts)* has singles/twins for $23/44 – weekends can be noisy.

Travelana Motel (☎ 5152 3200, 49 Main St) is good value with singles/doubles from $46/54. Also good value is the quieter *Town Central Motel (☎ 5152 3084, 164 Nicholson St)*.

Henley B&B (☎ 5153 1014, 2 Service St) has comfortable en suite rooms for $95/115 (cheaper midweek); self-catering and evening meals by arrangement.

Places to Eat For East Coast Explorer cyclists, the 24-hour *Coles* supermarket *(96–118 Main St)* is the last serious supermarket before Jindabyne. *Bankers Cafe & Patisserie (146 Main St)* opens from 8am (closed Sunday).

Among the dozens of fast-food joints, *AJ's Pizza (☎ 5152 4845, 87 Main St)* also serves pasta; *Georges (229 Main St)* has good burgers and souvlaki; and *Isleys (235 Main St)* has fish and chips.

The *Commercial Hotel* (see Places to Stay) serves great meals from $12; bar meals cost $7. For cheap pub grub, try the *Grand Terminus (☎ 5152 4040, cnr MacLeod & Service Sts)*. *Oz Mex (☎ 5152 4549, cnr Main & Service Sts)* serves meals ($10–17.50) Wednesday to Sunday evenings. The *Lake of China (☎ 5152 5533)* serves good Cantonese food ($11–13; open late).

Tasmania

Australia's smallest state both in area and population, Tasmania has stunning scenery and good-quality, mostly lightly trafficked roads. These, plus relatively short distances between towns and services, make 'Tassie' the country's best region for cycle touring.

A temperate southerly latitude and long summer days means comfortable cycling conditions and ample time for side trips and sightseeing. The rides in this chapter traverse most of the island's popular routes, along the east and west coasts and through the lake district of the remote central plateau. They visit such tourist 'must-sees' as Cradle Mountain, Macquarie Harbour, Queenstown, Richmond and Port Arthur, plus the largest cities. On the way are lesser-known but equally fascinating places, including Eaglehawk Neck, Bicheno, Sheffield, Great Lake and Bridestowe Lavender Farm.

Always beautiful, often demanding, Tasmania's terrain is renowned among cyclists for its hills, but effort is rewarded. The climb to the east coast's Elephant Pass winds through superb eucalypt forest with frequent coastal glimpses to a most unusual goal – the state's best pancake restaurant. The strenuous ascent of Mt Wellington offers mind-blowing views over Hobart, its suburbs and the Derwent estuary. Both climbs precede memorable downhills. Cyclists seeking easier terrain should start on the east coast.

HISTORY

In 1642, Dutch navigator Abel Tasman discovered and named Van Diemen's Land for the governor of the Dutch East Indies; the name Tasmania has been used since self-government in 1856. Circumnavigating it in 1798, Lieutenant Matthew Flinders showed Tasmania to be an island. In the 19th century, it became a notorious British penal colony.

The recent history of Tasmania's Aboriginal people is more tragic even than that of their mainland relatives – very few records remain of their 40,000-year history, although many traditions, such as mutton-birding, have been retained and are being revived by the Tasmanian Aboriginal community today.

Up to around 10,000 hunter-gatherers lived largely in the more open east when European settlers arrived in 1803. Farming and fencing of Aboriginal lands created conflict. From 1828 martial law meant Aborigines could, in certain places, be shot on sight. Most, including the intact society on the inhospitable west coast, were removed to Flinders Island where their population dwindled through disease, poor food and despair. Recognition of native land title has begun – in 1995 the Tasmanian government returned 12 sites to the Aboriginal community – but there is still much to be reconciled.

Settlements at Hobart and George Town were established in 1804. Penal settlements, for reoffending convicts, were later established on bleak Sarah Island in Macquarie Harbour, then on Maria Island. A third, the 'escape-proof' Port Arthur, replaced the others from 1830.

Gold discoveries in the 1870s attracted settlers from around the world. Massive 1920s mining operations on the west coast brought environmental problems, as did later damming of rivers for hydroelectricity, especially in the south-west. The famous 1980s protest against damming the Franklin River was a landmark conservation victory; see Strahan in the Tassie's West Coast ride.

NATURAL HISTORY

Tasmania separated from mainland Australia between 12,000 and 10,000 years ago when rising seas created stormy Bass Strait. Its highest mountain, Mt Ossa, reaches only 1617m but much of the interior is extremely rugged. The coasts' shallow bays and broad estuaries derive from post-glacial flooding

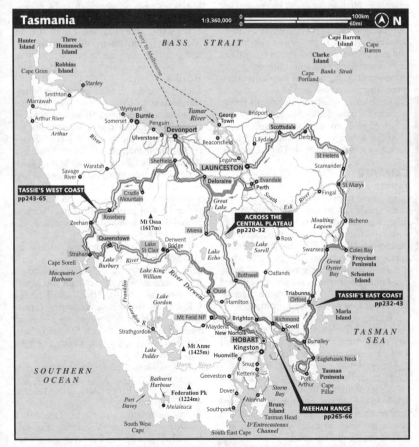

of river valleys. The Central Plateau, covered by an ice sheet during the last Ice age, is a harsh environment unsuited to farming.

Isolation has preserved ancient plants and animals. There are relatively few large mammals; the best-known marsupial, the Tasmanian tiger, is believed extinct since 1936 despite oft-claimed sightings. (Scientists from the Australian Museum now hope to clone the species from a DNA sample.) Common creatures to watch for are echidnas, platypuses, Tasmanian devils, possums, wallabies, wombats and, on the coasts, penguins and even southern right whales.

Many of Tasmania's trees are unique; its native pines are particularly distinctive. The famous Huon pine can live for thousands of years. Others, such as King Billy, pencil and celery-top pines, common in higher regions, live for 500 years. Myrtle beech, similar to European beech, favours wetter forests. Swamp gum (*Eucalyptus regnans* or 'mountain ash' on the mainland) grows up to 100m in Tassie, making it the tallest flowering plant in the world. Along with the state's floral emblem, Tasmanian blue gum, it is common in the south-east. In autumn, deciduous beech, Australia's only deciduous native, adds a splash of gold and red to the forests.

About a quarter of the state is national park, much of it with World Heritage status.

CLIMATE

Tasmania has four distinct seasons but, lying in the path of the Roaring Forties, it can experience wintry conditions at any time. Summer days are generally warm, with mild nights. Ultra-violet radiation can be intense in the middle of the day. Hobart's average January maximum is 22°C while that for Launceston is around 24°C. Average January minimums are about 12°C and 10°C respectively, the wider range at Launceston because of its inland location.

Pleasant conditions continue into autumn – Hobart's March temperatures are generally comfortable, averaging a maximum of 20°C. From April, temperatures plunge.

The prevailing west–east airflow delivers much more rain to the west coast (3000mm annually) than to the east (about 1000mm). The east coast is warmer and milder than elsewhere in the state and boasts the most hours of sunshine of any part of the Australian coast.

Winter (June to August) is wet, cold and stormy, particularly in the west. Hobart's average maximum during its coldest month, June, is 12°C; the minimum is about 3°C. Overcast days are common in the east despite the lower rainfall. Snow lies on the higher peaks but is rarely deep enough for skiing.

Spring is windy and wintry storms can continue into December.

INFORMATION
Maps

Excellent detail, including contours, is shown on the 1:250,000 Tasmania series, published by the state government's Land Information Bureau. Four large sheets cover the state – *North West*, *North East*, *South West* and *South East* (around $9 each, from map retailers).

Navigation is possible with the more compact single-sheet UBD *Tasmania State Map* (1:500,000), widely available at around $8. Most other tourist maps of a similar scale and detail are adequate for sealed road rides.

Books

Lonely Planet's *Tasmania* is an excellent supplement to *Cycling Australia* with detailed sections on plants and animals, activities and accommodation in areas beyond the scope of this guide. Lonely Planet's *Walking in Australia* includes walks in Tasmania, while its Pisces diving and snorkelling guide *Australia: Southeast Coast & Tasmania* covers underwater exploration.

Bookshops and visitor centres have many general travel guides with themes such as colonial accommodation, vineyards or guesthouses.

Recommended background reading includes Lindsay Simpson & Bruce Miller's *Australian Geographic Book of Tasmania*, a travel account with lift-out map and superb photographs. For historical detail peruse L Robson's two-volume *History of Tasmania*, Robert Hughes' best-selling *The Fatal Shore* and Marcus Clarke's *For the Term of His Natural Life*, set in the convict era on Sarah Island.

One of the best books on Aboriginal history is Lyndall Ryan's *The Aboriginal Tasmanians*, while Bruce Elder's *Blood on the Wattle* is fascinating.

Among many guides to Tasmania's wildlife are RH Green's *The Fauna of Tasmania: Birds* and *The Fauna of Tasmania:*

Mammals. On environment, Ralph & Kathleen Gowlland's *Trampled Wilderness* summarises the legacy of European exploration.

Information Sources

The government runs Tasmanian Travel Centres (🖳 www.tourism.tas.gov.au) in Canberra and all Australian mainland capitals, except Perth and Darwin. These can book accommodation, tours and transport tickets.

For useful cycling information, start at the Web site of Bicycle Tasmania (☎ 6226 7168, 🖳 www.netspace.net.au/~dmurphy/bt.htm), 102 Bathurst St, Hobart, 7000 (postal address only).

The Department of Tourism publishes the free bimonthly *Tasmanian Travelways*, containing comprehensive lists of accommodation, activities, public transport and vehicle hire. It's available at visitor centres.

For information on national parks, contact the Tasmania Parks and Wildlife Service (PWS; ☎ 6233 6191, 🖳 www.parks.tas.gov.au). The Tasmanian Environment Centre, 102 Bathurst St, Hobart, is a rich source of environmental information.

Other Information

Internet Access The Tasmanian Government has set up Online Access Centres (🖳 www.tco.asn.au) in towns across the state, which offer email and Internet usage at nominal cost. Most are signposted or can be found via visitor centres.

National Parks A daily fee of $3 per person for entry to National Parks is charged by the Parks & Wildlife Service (☎ 6233 6191, 🖳 www.parks.tas.gov.au). A $12 two-month holiday pass is good value for cyclists spending a few weeks and/or visiting several parks. Passes are available at visitor centres, park entry booths or online.

Bikes on Buses Long-distance coaches carry partly dismantled bicycles any distance for a flat $10.

GETTING TO/FROM TASMANIA

Separated from the mainland by Bass Strait, Tasmania takes a little more effort to reach, but is well worth visiting. From Victoria, taking the ferry is an enjoyable option, while flying will be the easiest way to access Tasmania from the other states.

Air

Hobart, Launceston and Devonport airports receive mainland flights. Fares to Hobart are generally more expensive than to the other cities. Flights from the mainland are cheapest and most frequent from Melbourne. Hobart's 'international' airport doesn't actually receive any international flights. See the Getting There & Away and Getting Around chapters for more information about air travel to and within Australia.

Hobart Airporter Bus Service (☎ 0419-382 240) runs a shuttle service between the airport and the city ($8 plus $7 per bike). A taxi costs around $20. It's an easy 16km ride via the shoulders of the busy Tasman Hwy.

Launceston Redline (☎ 1300-360 000) runs bus services into town ($2.50, plus $10 for the bike, about 30 minutes, twice daily). It's a 15km ride north-west to the town centre, via the Midland Hwy; see Evandale in the Getting to/from the Ride section of the Tassie's West Coast ride for details.

Devonport The airport is about 6km from town via the Bass Hwy and Tarlton St. Fox Coaches (☎ 6424 9112) meets all flights, taking passengers and luggage to Devonport for $6. Phone to arrange transport to the airport. The taxi fare to the city is around $20.

Sea

The overnight *Spirit of Tasmania* ferry (☎ 1800-030 344) crosses Bass Strait between Port Melbourne and Devonport three times weekly each way. Peak season (from December to January) fares range from $136 to $253 per adult and $25 per bicycle.

To reach Launceston, the *Devil Cat* (☎ 13 2010), a fast car-carrying catamaran, links Melbourne with George Town between Christmas and Easter. It runs about every second day each way ($175, plus $27 per bike, six hours). Redline (☎ 1300-360 000) buses ferry passengers between Georgetown and Launceston (around 40 minutes, $10, book a spot for your bike).

GATEWAY CITIES

Tasmania's gateways are Hobart, Launceston and Devonport; see Getting to/from Gateway Cities at the end of this section for details on travelling between each city.

TASMANIA

Hobart

With a population just below 130,000, Hobart is the smallest of Australia's state capitals. It is also the second oldest (after Sydney), second driest (after Adelaide) and most southerly (nearly 43°S).

The first European colony in Tasmania was founded in 1803 on the River Derwent at Risdon Cove, near the present day Bowen Bridge. The site for the future capital was chosen the next year, about 10km south on the opposite bank. Called Hobart Town, until 1881, it became a city in 1842. Development was linked to the Derwent estuary, one of the world's finest deep-water harbours. Early industries like whaling, ship building and produce-export made fortunes for many Hobart merchants.

Information The Tasmanian Travel & Information Centre (☎ 6230 8233) is on the corner of Davey and Elizabeth Sts. It's open daily, but only to 4pm on weekends (to 1pm Sunday in winter). The Transit Centre is at 199 Collins St.

Major banks are near the Elizabeth St mall and ATMs dot the city and suburbs.

Useful bike shops include McBain Cycles (☎ 6234 7594), 132 Bathurst St, and Ray Appleby Cycles (☎ 6234 7644), 125 Elizabeth St.

Cycling Adventures Tasmania (☎ 0412-913 148, e rowanburns@hotmail.com), based outside Salamanca Square's Machine Laundry Cafe, hires out mountain bikes. Good-quality front-suspension models cost $27/105 per day/week, while rigid machines cost $17 per day. Ring to check availability of touring-style bikes. Helmets, accessories, ride notes, maps and advice are supplied.

Derwent Bike Hire (☎ 6268 6161 or ☎ 0419-008 357), at the end of the Inter City Cycleway near the Cenotaph, has hybrid 21-speed touring bikes with a rear rack from $7/20/100 per hour/day/week.

Things to See & Do Sixty of Hobart's 90 National Trust-classified buildings, featuring superb **Georgian architecture**, are on Macquarie and Davey Sts. The visitor centre supplies detailed historic literature for self-guided **walks** around the city, the docks and Battery Point. Ask about times for two-hour guided walks from the centre, from September to May.

Franklin Wharf, close to the city centre, features **Constitution Dock**, where Sydney to Hobart and Royal Hobart Regatta yachts tie up. It has floating seafood stalls as well as sit-down restaurants.

The row of Georgian sandstone warehouses in **Salamanca Place**, once the centre of Hobart Town's trade and commerce, now houses galleries, restaurants, cafes, nightspots and shops selling everything from vegetables to antiques. An open-air craft **market** is held every Saturday morning. Behind, in Salamanca Square, are entertainment venues like **Antarctic Adventure** (☎ 6220 8220). This combined theme park/science centre features exhibits on the exploration of the frozen continent, an exciting skiing simulator and the cold room, for a feel of south polar conditions in minus 15°C temperatures and a 40-knot gale.

The **Tasmanian Museum & Art Gallery** (☎ 6235 0777), 5 Argyle St, entered off Macquarie St, incorporates Hobart's oldest existing building, the 1808 Commissariat Store. Displays include Aboriginal culture and artefacts, colonial art, animals (extinct and prehistoric), and minerals. The **Allport Museum & Library of Fine Arts** (☎ 6233 7484), 91 Murray St, has a collection of rare books on Australasia and the Pacific, antique furniture and fine paintings. **Van Diemen's Land Folk Museum** (☎ 6234 2791), in a Georgian house at 103 Hampden Rd Battery Point, has relics from Tasmania's pioneering days (closed Monday).

Hard to resist is a tour of **Cadbury's chocolate factory** (☎ 6249 0333) at Claremont near Berriedale, north of Hobart. Vistors can sample the wares as they follow the chocolate-making process then buy bargains at the factory shop.

Cycling Adventures Tasmania (see the Information section) offers guided **cycle tours** ranging from early morning in Battery Point, to evening historical explorations, to day trips visiting wildlife parks and wineries. Multi-day packages can be arranged.

Popular places for self-guided cycle exploration include the Inter City Cycleway, which accesses Glenorchy and the 'bike facilities' on Tasman Bridge; and the Rivulet Track to the Cascade Brewery (☎ 6224 1144 for tour bookings), from where you can continue on-road up Mt Wellington (see the boxed text opposite).

TASMANIA

Cycling Mt Wellington

Why would anyone want to cycle *up* Mt Wellington? The answer is obvious (though not original): because it is there. There are other reasons – the challenge, great scenery, light traffic...and it's free.

Those unconvinced of the joys of uphill cycling can take a $35 organised ride *downhill* from the top of Mt Wellington with Brake Out Cycling Tours (☎ 6239 1080).

Mt Wellington (1270m) stands, sentinel-like, on Hobart's back doorstep. It's a hard 21km ride from sea level to the top, but it's easily navigated from the city centre.

There are two road routes to the mountain. The first, more direct route takes busy Davey St west, uphill, from the Hobart visitor centre, becoming Huon Rd as traffic begins to thin. Follow signs to Fern Tree.

For a quieter route out of the city, take Molle St (north off Davey St four blocks west of the visitor centre), and turn left at Collins St onto the Rivulet Track. This bikepath follows Hobart Rivulet to Cascade Brewery. At the brewery turn right onto Strickland Ave and wind gently uphill to join the first route at Huon Rd.

About 10km from the city and at 430m altitude, turn right from Huon Rd onto the C616 to Mt Wellington (detouring first to the Fern Tree General Store, 300m farther along Huon Rd, for a cappuccino booster).

The C616 climbs relentlessly for 11km, zigzagging across the face of the mountain at a punishing average 7.6% gradient. Panoramic views reward a rider's considerable pedalling effort. The rough aggregate road surface in many places adds difficulty to the climb and makes descending uncomfortable, particularly for bikes with skinny, high pressure tyres. The roughness is 'for traction', according to Bicycle Tasmania's Steve Jay: 'in icy conditions you need to beware of out-of-control cars sliding all over the road'. That's something to think about while riding up in winter, but crashing on ice yourself or suffering frostbite on the descent might be greater threats.

On a clear day, as well as a stunning vista of the Derwent Estuary, summit views extend to the South-West Tasmania Wilderness World Heritage Area. Boardwalks lead to viewing points on the very edge of the precipice.

The exposed, rocky summit's next most notable feature is wind. Jutting high into the path of the infamous Roaring 40s, the mountain summit averages only one calm day in 20. June is windiest with nine days of wind in excess of 40km/h and only one likely calm day. Even in summer, January averages only two or three calm days.

The strongest recorded wind gust was 156km/h; a north-westerly wind was once measured averaging 120km/h for a 10-minute period.

In 1895 weather watcher Clement Wragge (unsurprisingly nicknamed 'Inclement') established the first staffed meteorological station on the summit. It now operates automatically.

Aside from a toilet block, the glassed-in shelter/viewing platform is the only public building on top. Unfortunately, there is nowhere to get food or drinks.

The return to Hobart is much faster and easier. Just take care on the mountain road's narrow carriageway, sharp bends, steep grades and rough surface, and in the traffic closer to town.

FUNNY... COULD HAVE SWORN THAT WAS SIR EDMUND HILLARY!

DON HATCHER

Places to Stay The handiest camping ground to the city is the busy but seedy *Sandy Bay Caravan Park* (☎ *6225 1264; 1 Peel St, Sandy Bay)*, uphill off Sandy Bay Rd near the casino. Tent sites cost $9 per person and on-site vans/cabins $44/$66 a double. It's a short ride to Sandy Bay shopping centre's supermarket and cafes.

Around 13km north of town via the Inter City Cycleway, *Elwick Cabin & Caravan Park* (☎ *6272 7115; 19 Goodwood Rd, Goodwood)* is near the Bowen Bridge. Tent sites are $11, on-site vans $35.20, and cabins start at $64.90, all for two people.

Rambling *Central City Backpackers* (☎ *6224 2404, 138 Collins St)*, once the Imperial Hotel, has excellent facilities and spacious communal areas. Dorm beds cost $18, and double rooms $44.

St Ives Motel (☎ *6224 1044, 86 Sandy Bay Rd)* has large, modern rooms with kitchens and balconies for $99 per double.

Friendly *Cromwell Cottage* (☎ *6223 6734, 6 Cromwell St)* offers bed and cooked breakfast in an 1873 two-storey townhouse overlooking the Derwent; doubles cost $125 a double. Opposite, luxurious *Battery Point Manor* (☎ *6224 0888,* e *batteryptma nor@ozemail.com.au, 13 Cromwell St)* has large rooms with views from $125 to $175 a double with a buffet breakfast.

Places to Eat Handy to Sandy Bay and Battery Point accommodation, *Coles supermarket (246 Sandy Bay Rd)* is in the Sandy Bay shopping centre.

Cyclists will find plenty of good food in and near Salamanca Place. Locals recommend *Salamanca Bakehouse* (☎ *6224 6300, Salamanca Square)*, open 24 hours; and, further north, *Mures* (☎ *6231 2121, Victoria Dock)* for good fish and chips, fine dining and sushi.

Dede (☎ *6231 1068, 369 Elizabeth St)* serves Indonesian and Thai vegetarian and meat dishes (around $10–$15). *Queens Head Bar and Cafe* (☎ *6234 4670, cnr Newdegate & Elizabeth Sts)* has a varied cuisine based on seasonally available local produce.

Launceston

Tasmania's second city, at the head of the Tamar Estuary, about 60km from Bass Strait and 200km north of Hobart, was established in 1805. Until 1907 it was known as Patersonia, after its founder, Colonel William Paterson. The name Launceston honours Governor King, who was born in Launceston, in Cornwall, England. A plaque in Batman Fawkner Inn, Cameron St, marks John Batman's 1835 voyage from then Patersonia to found Melbourne.

Now a charming blend of old and new, with around 70,000 people, Launceston is the commercial centre of northern Tasmania.

Information The Tasmanian Travel & Information Centre (☎ 6336 3122) is on the corner of St John and Paterson Sts.

Most banks have branches with ATMs on St John St or Brisbane St near the mall. The post office is in Brisbane St about 100m north-east of the mall.

Well-stocked Rik Sloane Cycles (☎ 6331 9414, e rikbikes@bigpond.com), 10 Paterson St, hires late-model hybrid-style touring bikes for $20/84 per day/week. Panniers are also available.

Things to See & Do View the city's architectural heritage and its many parks and gardens with the aid of the visitor centre's *Historic Walks* brochure. The six-hectare **City Park** is a good example of a Victorian park with fountains, conservatories and animal enclosures.

Cataract Gorge, a couple of minutes ride west of the city centre, is one of Launceston's most popular attractions. Cliffs line the South Esk River and the surrounding area is a wildlife reserve. Walking tracks follow each side of the gorge. Cultural events, including music concerts, take place in the gorge in February and March.

Near Kings Bridge over the South Esk at the gorge's lower end, is **Penny Royal World** (☎ 6331 6699), an expensive entertainment complex with exhibits including various working 19th-century mills and model boats. A restored tram transports visitors between attractions. Also near Cataract Gorge is the 1834 **Ritchies Flour Mill**, originally powered by water piped from the gorge, now housing an art and craft gallery (closed Monday). Leafy grounds contain a huge 160-year-old blue gum and a good restaurant.

Tamar River Cruises (☎ 6334 9900, e tamar@tassie.net.au) offers a choice of **river tours** daily with interesting commentary on history and wildlife.

Places to Stay Being the only one in town, *Treasure Island Caravan Park (☎ 6344 2600, 94 Glen Dhu St)*, 2km south of the city beside the noisy Midland Hwy, can be crowded. Tent sites cost $10/15 for one/two people, cabins start from $63 (for one or two people). More pleasant, but 12km north-west at Legana, is *Launceston Holiday Park (☎ 6330 1714, 711 West Tamar Hwy)*. Tent sites cost $9/13. On-site vans cost $38.50, and cabins $66, both for two people.

Smoke-free *Launceston City Backpackers (☎ 6334 2327, 103 Canning St)* has dorm beds for $14 and doubles for $32. The *YHA summer hostel (☎ 6334 4505, 132 Elizabeth St)*, also known as Metro Backpackers, operates only from mid-December to early February with beds from $16. Book through the Hobart YHA office (☎ 6234 9617).

Batman Fawkner Inn (☎ 6331 7222, 35 Cameron St), an accommodation house since 1822, has $71 doubles, $38 budget singles (noisy on Friday and Saturday) and $50 standard singles. Its restaurant serves meals from $12 and an 'Irish' breakfast for $9.50.

Among B&Bs, the central *Rose Lodge (☎ 6334 0120, 270 Brisbane St)* offers small, comfortable en suite rooms and cooked breakfast for $60.50/77 single/double.

City centre motels are often refurbished old hotels. Most charge between $75 and $95. *North Lodge Motel (☎ 6331 9966, 7 Brisbane St)* is among the cheaper ones, with $71.50 doubles.

In the upper price range is National Trust-listed, Edwardian *Kilmarnock House (☎ 6334 1514, 66 Elphin Rd)*, 1.5km east of the centre. It charges from $85 to $98 a double for lovely nonsmoking rooms with en suite and continental breakfast. The huge *Novotel Launceston (☎ 6334 3434, 29 Cameron St)* has doubles from $176, including buffet breakfast.

Places to Eat A *Roelf Vos* supermarket *(128 Wellington St)* is on the south side of town. Cheap restaurants and cafes abound. *Townsend's Bakery (☎ 6331 5427, 55 George St)* sells standard pastries and drinks. Chinese *Jade Garden (☎ 6331 2535, 64 George St)* offers lunch for $4.50 on weekdays and daily dinner for $6.50, or a $10 all-you-can-eat option. *Arpar's Thai Restaurant (☎ 6331 2786, cnr Charles & Paterson Sts)* is authentic and worthwhile.

The *Happy Pumpkin Vegetarian Kitchen (☎ 6334 6057, 70 Charles St)* serves breakfast for $6.50; and Mexican food and take-away pies and pasties for lunch.

Popular Italian pizza restaurant, *Calabrisella (☎ 6331 1958, 56 Wellington St)* is a good place to go with children (closed Tuesday).

Pierre's (☎ 6331 6835, 88 George St) is a cafe, bar and restaurant serving good meals from $7.50 to $18.50 (closed Sunday, and from 2pm to 6pm Saturday).

Nearby, the more upmarket *Shrimps (☎ 6334 0584, 72 George St)* fish restaurant has an intimate atmosphere and $20 mains.

Devonport

Home to 25,000 people, Tasmania's third-largest city was originally twin towns on flat land either side of the Mersey River. Formby, on the west, and Torquay, on the east bank, merged in 1890. With the arrival of trains, Devonport became the region's port, taking over from upriver Latrobe. The *Spirit of Tasmania* ferry docks on the river's east bank.

Information The visitor centre (☎ 6424 4466), 92 Formby Rd, is between Best and Stewart Sts. The post office, supermarkets and banks are all close by.

Devonport's bike shops are Noel von Bibra Cycles (☎ 6424 7778), 142 William St, and Oliver's Performance Sport & Cycle (☎ 6424 9366), 109 Rooke St.

Things to See & Do The Tasmanian Aboriginal Culture & Art Centre (☎ 6424 8250) known as **Tiagarra**, is north of town at Mersey Bluff, on the lighthouse road. The centre has a rare collection of rock engravings. A walking track leads to Aboriginal rock carvings on the Bluff.

Halfway from town to Mersey Bluff, the **Tasmanian Maritime & Folk Museum** (☎ 6424 7100), off Bluff Rd, has models of sailing ships, old and new, which have visited Tasmania.

Devonport Gallery & Arts Centre (☎ 6424 8296), 45 Stewart St, has a permanent collection and regular special exhibitions.

Home Hill (☎ 6424 8055), 77 Middle Rd, is the National Trust-classified former home of one-time state premier and Australian prime minister Joseph Lyons and his wife Dame Enid (the first woman to become a

TASMANIA

member of the House of Representatives and a cabinet minister).

Most of the city's shoreline is lined with parks and reserves. It's possible to walk from the city along the river shore to **Mersey Bluff**, to **Coles Beach** and along the Don River to the **Don River Railway** (☎ 6424 6335), which is on Bass Hwy, west of the centre. **Steam trains** run on Sunday, public holidays and from Boxing Day to the end of January.

Places to Stay West of the river, the busy *Mersey Bluff Caravan Park* (☎ 6424 8655) is attractively located near beaches, Tiagarra and the lighthouse, 2.5km north of the centre. Tent sites cost $7.15 per person and on-site vans/cabins cost $44/$55 a double.

The YHA hostel is *MacWright House* (☎ 6424 5696, 115 Middle Rd), 3km from the town centre. Beds cost $15.50.

Alexander Hotel (☎ 6424 2252, 78 Formby Rd) is close to the centre and serves good counter meals. Rooms with shared facilities cost from $40/60 for one/two with continental breakfast. Friendly *River View Lodge* (☎ 6424 7357, 18 Victoria Parade) offers en suite rooms and an excellent cooked breakfast from $60 per double.

Among the many motels, convenient *Elimatta Motor Inn* (☎ 6424 6555, 15 Victoria Parade) offers doubles for $65, while upmarket *Gateway Motor Inn* (☎ 6424 4922, 16 Fenton St) charges from $108 for a standard double to $143 for deluxe rooms.

Places to Eat Several supermarkets are on Best St, including *Coles* and *Roelf Vos*.

The mall has plenty of *coffee lounges* and *takeaways,* but, for atmosphere, try *Billabong Cafe* (☎ 6424 3628, 12 Edward St), which has a mainly vegetarian menu.

The *Rialto Gallery Restaurant* (☎ 6424 6793, 159 Rooke St) is moderately priced, with main courses around $11. Chinese food is available at *China Garden* (☎ 6424 4148, 33 King St), *Chinese Chef* (☎ 6424 7306, 4B Kempling St), or *Golden Panda* (☎ 6424 9066, 38 Formby Rd).

Getting to/from Gateway Cities
Bus Redline (☎ 1300-360 000) runs a direct service between the Hobart Transit Centre, 199 Collins St, and Launceston, 18 Charles St ($19.50, 2½ hours, several daily). This service continues to Devonport, 9 Edward

St, and the *Spirit of Tasmania* ferry ($33.20 from Hobart, 4¼ hours). It also operates between Hobart and Launceston via the east coast. Bikes travel for $10 (you must be at the depot with your bike 30 minutes to one hour before departure).

Bicycle Cycle between Launceston and Devonport (about 97km) via Legana, using the West Tamar Hwy (A7), C732 (past Notley Fern Gorge), B71 and River Rd.

Across the Central Plateau

Duration	6 days
Distance	384.2km
Difficulty	moderate–hard
Start	Devonport
End	Eaglehawk Neck

Almost a diagonal crossing of the island, this ride traverses a variety of terrain, from fertile coastal plains to the wild Central Plateau; from the cleared grazing country of the Midlands to the forested, sometimes hilly Forestier and Tasman Peninsulas. The highlight of the journey, in more ways than one, is the climb to and the descent from the central highlands. This expanse is dominated by Great Lake, which can be a magnificent azure blue in sunny weather or a cold steel grey under cloud – conditions which may alternate frequently on the same day (warm and waterproof clothing is essential).

Easy cycling through the Midlands allows you to appreciate the Georgian architecture of the heritage towns, and gives the chance to visit a sanctuary preserving some original vegetation and wildlife. The ride finishes with a circuit of the Tasman Peninsula, visiting historic sites such as Port Arthur and intriguing natural wonders like Tasmans Arch and the Tessellated Pavement.

HISTORY
The first dam in Australia's largest hydroelectric power system was built on Great Lake in 1911. Historic villages along the route are the legacy of early European development. Georgian architecture is especially evident in the Midlands, from the town of Bothwell south.

The Midland Hwy resulted from the need for a land link between Hobart and Launceston. Built by convict gangs, it opened in 1821 and, within two years, a mail coach regularly carryied passengers along the route.

On the Tasman Peninsula, Port Arthur, the state's best known historic site, became a penal colony in 1830 and over the next 47 years about 12,500 convicts served sentences there in hellish conditions. A semaphore system allowed rapid communication with Hobart. In 1996 Port Arthur's notoriety increased when a gunman killed 35 people and injured others before burning down a local guesthouse. He is now in Risdon prison.

NATURAL HISTORY

The thinly populated central lake country comprises steep mountains, hundreds of glacial lakes, heathy vegetation and a variety of wildlife. On the edge of the plateau, the Walls of Jerusalem National Park, a focal point for mountaineers, bushwalkers and cross-country skiers, is accessed by rough roads and tracks west from Liawenee.

Great Lake, the largest natural freshwater lake in Australia, has been a trout fishing area since the release of brown trout there in 1870.

PLANNING
When to Ride

Best in summer, the ride is possible much of the year. Snow, even in summer, can close roads on the plateau and some accommodation also closes from June to August, when maximum temperatures hover around 5°C.

Indoor accommodation may be booked out across much of northern Tasmania in late October/early November for Deloraine's Craft Fair.

Maps

The Land Information Bureau's Tasmania series sheets *North West* and *South East* (both 1:250,000) cover the ride.

GETTING TO/FROM THE RIDE

The Tassie's East Coast ride, described later in this chapter, begins where this ride ends – at Eaglehawk Neck.

Devonport

See the Getting to/from Tasmania (p215) and Gateway Cities (p220) sections for information on getting to/from Devonport.

Eaglehawk Neck

TWT Tassielink (☎ 1300-300 520) runs buses between Hobart and Port Arthur via Eaglehawk Neck ($9.20, 1¼ hours, once each way on weekdays).

THE RIDE
Devonport

See Devonport (pp219–20) in the Gateway Cities section for information about accommodation and other services.

Day 1: Devonport to Deloraine
3½–6 hours, 60.2km

A pleasant, reasonably easy day begins beside the lazy Mersey River. The road stays flat past Latrobe and scoots over a few innocuous undulations to rural Railton. Beyond, the route is hillier with a couple of stiff climbs; one after Kimberley is more than 2km but offers spectacular views. The countryside traversed is mostly grazing land, populated by many more sheep than people. Railton (22.5km), with *supermarket*, *takeaways* and an attractive garden on the defunct train station site, is a convenient lunch spot and the last town with services before Deloraine.

Near Latrobe, the route passes the **Australian Axeman's Hall of Fame** (☎ 6426 2099; 8.2km), celebrating the role of the woodcutter in the country's development. A little further, on the left, is the start of **Sheean Walk** (8.4km), memorial to a local WWII seaman.

Characterful **Latrobe** (side trip at 8.7km) has an historic streetscape dating from the 1830s when the town was the region's port – with ships sailing up the Mersey River to dock. The vibrant business centre, 300m east of the route, has most services. Worth a visit is *La Central Cafe & Bakery* (☎ 6426 2666, 83 Gilbert St) with the 'best coffee in town' plus amazing muffins. Opposite, the original **Kenworthy's Antiques** building still advertises in peeling paint 'Edison phonographs, gramophones & records'. The visitor centre (☎ 6426 2693), 70 Gilbert St, is on the corner of Barclay St.

Each Boxing Day, Latrobe attracts professional cyclists from all over Australia for the **Latrobe Wheel Race**. The town's other main event is the **Henley-on-the-Mersey** carnival on Australia Day (26 January) at the former docks.

TASMANIA

Day 1: Devonport to Deloraine

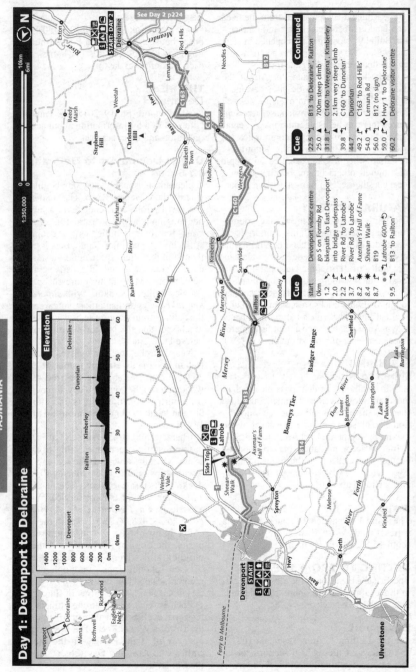

See Day 2 p224

Elevation

Cue	
start	Devonport visitor centre
0km	go S on Formby Rd
1.2	bikepath 'to East Devonport'
2.0	into bridge underpass
2.2	River Rd 'to Latrobe'
3.7	River Rd 'to Latrobe'
8.2	Axeman's Hall of Fame
8.4	Sheean Walk
8.7	B19
	Latrobe 600m ↻
9.5	B13 'to Railton'

Cue		Continued
22.5	B13 'to Deloraine', Railton
25.0	700m steep climb
31.8	C160 'to Weegena', Kimberley
	2.1km very steep climb
39.8	C160 'to Dunorlan'
44.7	Dunorlan
49.2	C163 'to Red Hills'
54.0	Lemana Rd
56.0	B12 (no sign)
59.0	Hwy 1 to Deloraine' ↻
60.2	Deloraine visitor centre

The Gog Range's **Alum Cliffs** rear from the horizon after Kimberley (31.8km). Escarpment views continue on the way to Dunorlan (44.7km); then the route rolls, mostly downwards, in the lee of the **Great Western Tiers**, which rise up to Central Plateau.

Deloraine

With its pleasant site on the Meander River, Deloraine's charm is enhanced by Georgian and Victorian buildings, many of which have been faithfully restored. The town's spring craft fair attracts tens of thousands of visitors who can book out accommodation from Launceston to Devonport.

Information The Deloraine visitor centre (☎ 6362 3471) is in the Folk Museum next to the roundabout on Emu Bay Rd. Banks and the post office are on Emu Bay Rd in the town centre. For camping gas canisters, if neither hardware store on Emu Bay Rd has stock, try Lehner's Home Heating (☎ 6362 2715), 36 Parsonage St.

Things to See & Do Jewellery, art and performing arts are on show at **Gallery 9** (☎ 6362 2005), 2 West Barrack St. Town **history** is depicted in silk at Deloraine Community Complex (☎ 6362 2844), on Alverston Dr east of the river.

St Mark's Church, on high ground east of the river, dates from 1859. It's floodlit at night but closed during school holidays.

Deloraine's four-day October/November **Tasmanian Craft Fair**, claimed to be Australia's largest, has hundreds of stalls at 10 venues around town.

Places to Stay On the river (or, occasionally during floods, *in* the river), *Apex Caravan Park (☎ 6362 2345, West Parade)* tent sites cost $8/10 for one/two. The caretaker lives across the road.

YHA hostel *Highview Lodge (☎ 6362 2996, 8 Blake St)*, safe from flooding up a *steep* hill, has fantastic views of the Tiers. Beds cost $14.

The *Deloraine Hotel (☎ 6362 2022, 144 Emu Bay Rd)*, which is more than 150 years old, has rooms for $30 per person. The *British Hotel (☎ 6362 2016, 80 Emu Bay Rd)* has rooms for $27.50 per person including continental breakfast. Both hotels have counter meals from $12.

On the town's western edge, *Mountain View Country Inn (☎ 6362 2633, 144 Emu Bay Rd)* has $85 doubles.

The child-friendly *Tier View Cottage B&B (☎ 6362 2633, 125 Emu Bay Rd)*, atop the hill, costs $75 for two in a whole house. Enquire at the petrol station opposite. B&B in Deloraine's earliest brick building, the 1830s *Bonneys Inn (☎ 6362 2974)* near the bridge, costs $85 (June–August) to $115 (December–January) per double (it's not suited to children).

Places to Eat Deloraine has plenty of *takeaways* on its main street.

Wholesome House (☎ 6362 3551, 3/53 Emu Bay Rd), which sells bulk and organically grown food, is next to *Crusty's Pizza Bar (☎ 6362 2000)*, open Thursday to Sunday evenings. Opposite, *Deloraine Delicatessen & Gourmet Food (☎ 6362 2127, 36 Emu Bay Rd)* is a coffee shop with good home-made food and pleasant outside tables.

The restaurant at *Mountain View Country Inn* serves main courses from $13 to $18. *Amble Inn (☎ 6362 2142, 144 Emu Bay Rd)*, opposite the post office, makes good stuffed potatoes and toasted snacks. *Sullivan's (☎ 6362 3264, 17 West Parade)*, downhill opposite the park, serves breakfast and snacks from 9am; mains cost from $10.50.

Day 2: Deloraine to Miena
4½–7 hours, 68.6km

Beginning in farming country, the lightly trafficked Lake Hwy winds up the escarpment to above 1200m. Damp, forest-clad slopes are thronged with wildlife and views unfold to the plains below. There's a side trip to Liffey Falls about halfway up. Rocky, dirt road beyond the summit continues most of the way to Miena.

Carry plenty of water and food for lunch – plus, perhaps, for the next three meals, since prices in Miena's sole, poorly stocked shop reflect the elevated altitude.

Quamby Bluff (1228m) looms over Golden Valley village at 15.7km. About 7km farther, a sign marks the start of a five-hour return walk to the Bluff.

About 4km before the top of the escarpment, a **viewpoint** (30.6km; 980m) atop a large boulder provides a panorama to the lowlands eastwards. To the west, crenellated

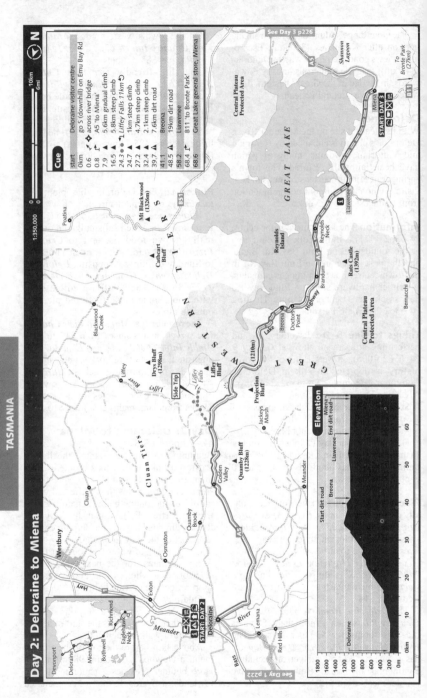

Day 2: Deloraine to Miena

TASMANIA

See Day 1 p222

See Day 3 p226

Cue		
start		Deloraine visitor centre
0km		go S (downhill) on Emu Bay Rd
0.6	◇	across river bridge
0.8	⌐	A5 'to Miena'
7.9	▲	5.6km gradual climb
16.5	▲	5.8km steep climb
24.3	●	Liffey Falls 11km ↻
24.7	▲	1km steep climb
27.2	▲	4.7km steep climb
32.4	▲	2.1km steep climb
39.7	▲	7.6km dirt road
41.1	▲	Breona
48.5	▲	19km dirt road
58.2		Liawenee
68.4	⌐	B11 'to Bronte Park'
68.6		Great Lake general store, Miena

Elevation

bluffs overlook the road. At 34.5km is the highway's **highest point**, 1210m.

Expansive views of the vast Great Lake, 5km later, herald the beginning of intermittent dirt road to Miena. (Five sections of bitumen – the longest 1.3km – interrupt the dirt). Beware of fast traffic flinging stinging stones. Blink-and-miss-it Liawenee (58.2km) is the access point for the Walls of Jerusalem National Park; and has a PWS information office (☎ 6259 8148).

Little shade for most of the final stretch to Miena puts cyclists at the mercy of sun and wind. Forested areas have been affected by the fungal dieback disease, *Phytophthora*, similar to that which has caused major damage in Western Australian jarrah forests (see the 'Warning' boxed text in the Western Australia chapter).

Side Trip: Liffey Falls
11km return
A delightful forest road turning left from Lake Hwy at 24.3km, leads to a walking track (40 minutes return) beside Liffey River as it cascades to pretty falls.

The dirt road gradually rises before suddenly descending steeply on loose gravel to a parking area. The return ride on this section is quite strenuous. The trailhead has picnic tables, a shelter shed and water.

Miena
Miena is a motley collection of holiday shacks whose owners arrive in droves during the summer school holidays. The sprawling settlement's 'business hub' is near the junction of Lake Hwy and the rugged B11 which connects south-westwards to the Lyell Hwy.

Information Great Lake General Store (☎ 6259 8149), on the B11 200m west of the Lake Hwy, is an unofficial visitor centre.

Things to See & Do Sightseeing, swimming, fishing and boating on the lake are the main activities in the area. Rest and relaxation on the lake shore will be many cyclists' favoured option after a tough day.

Places to Stay & Eat The caravan park next to the store has neither on-site vans for hire nor a tent area. The owner advises *camping* is free on the nearby lake shore. Public toilets with water are next to the store.

Great Lake Hotel (☎ 6259 8163), across a car park from the store, has motel units for $66/77 per single/double, including continental breakfast. Self-contained units cost $110 for up to four people, plus $11 for each extra person. Meals are available in the hotel.

The only other accommodation, *Central Highlands Lodge* (☎ 6259 8179, ℮ chl @tassie.net.au), is on the highway 3.5km through town from the store. It charges $150 per person in double or twin rooms ($195 single), including a three-course dinner and full breakfast. A self-contained cabin with cooking facilities sleeps four and costs a flat $100 (open August through April).

Day 3: Miena to Bothwell
3½–5½ hours, 62.8km
This section is a breeze. A 10km length of near-flat or descending dirt road is the only difficulty. After the B51 joins Lake Hwy, sealed road descends almost continuously to Bothwell, a moderate 1.6km climb being the only hiccup. Heathland on the plateau changes to eucalypt forest on the slopes which, in turn, gives way to cleared grazing land at lower altitudes. As there is no town nor anywhere to buy food before Bothwell, carry supplies.

At the edge of the plateau (15.1km), the unsealed C178 diverges, rejoining Lake Hwy at 47km. This could be an adventurous alternative route, adding about 10km, for fat-tyred cyclists who want to visit the Hydro-Electric Commission's **Waddamana Power Museum** (☎ 6259 6175). This former hydro-electricity station, constructed from 1910 to 1916, has operational turbines and a display of the state's hydro-history. It's open daily but ring first to check times.

In a forest clearing at Steppes, a locality in the middle of nowhere, artist Stephen Walker has created the remarkable **Steppes Stones** (27.2km). Life-size bronze figures depict highlands wildlife and scenes of the region's Aboriginal and white settlement.

After the halfway point, forest cover thins and the road emerges into the open expanse of the fertile River Clyde valley.

Across the exposed Ratho Flats and the River Clyde bridge, the route enters historic Bothwell. Attractive stone buildings line its wide avenues.

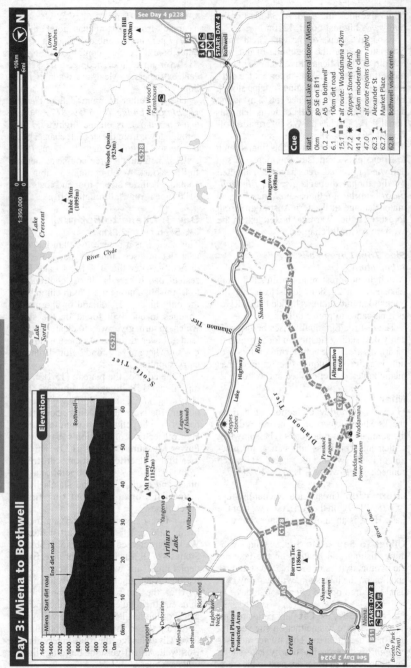

Day 3: Miena to Bothwell

Elevation

Cue

start	Great Lake general store, Miena
0km	go SE on B11
0.2	A5 'to Bothwell'
6.1	10km dirt road
15.1	alt route: Waddamana 42km
27.2	Steppes Stones (RHS)
41.4	1.6km moderate climb
47.0	alt route rejoins (turn right)
62.3	Alexander St
62.7	Market Place
62.8	Bothwell visitor centre

See Day 4 p228

START: DAY 4

Bothwell

Green Hill
(620m)

Lower
Marshes

Mrs Wood's
Farmhouse

Woods Quoin
(923m)

C178

Table Mtn
(1095m)

Lake
Crescent

River Clyde

Dungrove Hill
(698m)

C178

Lake
Sorell

C527

Scotts Tier

Shannon Tier

Shannon

River

Lake Highway

A5

Lagoon
of Islands

Steppes
Stones

Mt Penny West
(1152m)

Yangena

Wilburville

Arthurs
Lake

Alternative
Route

C178

Diamond Tier

Penstock
Lagoon

Waddamana
Power Museum

Waddamana

River Ouse

C178

Barren Tier
(1138m)

A5

Shannon
Lagoon

Miena

START: DAY 3

B11

Great
Lake

See Day 2 p224

To
Bronte Park (27km)

TASMANIA

N

10km
6mi

1:350,000

0

0

**Central Plateau
Protected Area**

Devonport

Deloraine

Miena

Bothwell

Richmond

Eaglehawk
Neck

Bothwell

With more than 50 National Trust recognised buildings, Bothwell is a charming town in a time warp. If not for the occasional car, anyone sitting in the shady central village green could feel transported to the 19th century.

The visitor centre (☎ 6259 4033), in the Golf Museum building in Market Place, opens 10am to 4pm Sunday to Friday.

Things to See & Do The visitor centre supplies a map to buildings of interest; otherwise find them by wandering around town and reading the descriptive plaques on their walls. Notable buildings include **St Luke's Church** and the **Castle Hotel**, both dating from 1821; a **bootmaker's shop** fitted out as it was in the 1890s; and beautifully restored 1830s **slate-roofed cottages**.

The **Australian Golf Museum** is an unusual but appropriate establishment for the home town of Australia's oldest golf course. The course, built by Scottish pioneers in the 1820s, is open to members of any golf club.

Bothwell is also renowned for excellent **trout fishing**.

Places to Stay & Eat The uninspiring vacant lot behind the Golf Museum is *Bothwell Caravan Park (☎ 6259 5503)*. Showers and toilets are in the public amenities block adjacent. Tent sites cost $2.75, and showers 20 cents for three minutes (keys are available from the caretaker's house directly across the village green).

Bothwell Grange (☎ 6259 5556) is a handsome two-storey heritage building on Alexander St. Built in 1836 as a hotel, it now charges $106 per double for B&B and serves guests a la carte meals.

Self-caterers will find a small *supermarket (cnr Patrick St & the B110)* and a quaint country *store (Alexander St)*, which is across from Bothwell Grange. The *Fat Doe Bakery & Coffee Shop (☎ 6259 5551, Patrick St)* does good light meals, cakes and bread. The *Castle Hotel (☎ 6259 5502, Patrick St)* serves counter lunches daily and dinner on Friday and Saturday.

Day 4: Bothwell to Richmond

3½–6 hours, 65.4km
The downhill trend continues with Day 4 finishing virtually at sea level. The lightly trafficked highway south-east of Bothwell descends tortuously for 5km into the Jordan River valley. Past Melton Mowbray (20.6km) the route travels on the busy Midland Hwy. It has a wide shoulder and, at 29km, a gradual 3.6km climb over Constitution Hill. Back on quiet, minor roads after Pontville (47.5km), the rest of the route undulates gently through agricultural country to historic Richmond.

Town names along the Midland reflect a very British heritage. Historic stone buildings recall their former role as bases for garrisons securing the Midlands transport link. **Kempton** (27.5km), founded in 1838, was named for Captain Anthony Kemp, the first recipient of a land grant in the area. Now bypassed by the highway, it's a tranquil oasis where handsome Georgian stone buildings line a wide main street.

Bagdad (37.1km), the turn-off to Chauncy Vale Wildlife Sanctuary (see Side Trip), has two petrol stations with takeaways.

Tiny Mangalore (44km) has the last *food store* before Richmond. Pontville (47.5km), where the route leaves the highway, has accommodation, toilets and views to Mt Wellington, near Hobart.

Side Trip: Chauncy Vale Wildlife Sanctuary

7km return
At 37.6km on the left, take the road signed to Chauncy Vale. It's 3.5km to the sanctuary gate, of which all but 400m is good dirt and virtually flat.

The 400-hectare former property of author Nan Chauncy (1900–70) preserves a valley of eucalypt woodland endemic to the Southern Midlands – the remainder of which are now bare.

It costs $2 to visit the sanctuary, which is home to a large population of wallabies, birds and snakes. Interpretive panels explain features of the vegetation, wildlife and geology; and marked walks visit places of interest, such as the caves which inspired Chauncy's children's stories.

Day Dawn, the house where all her books were written, was built between 1916 and 1918 and is preserved as it was when Chauncy and husband Anton occupied it. It's open from 2pm to 4pm on the first Saturday of each month (veer right inside the gate). Contact Southern Midlands Council (☎ 6259 3011) to visit at other times.

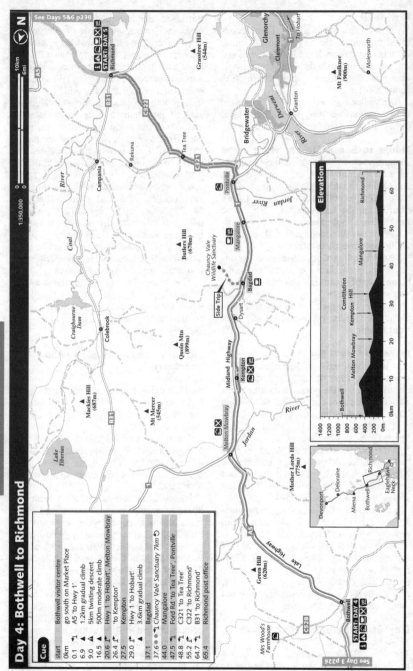

Day 4: Bothwell to Richmond

Cue

start	Bothwell visitor centre
0km	go south on Market Place
0.1	A5 to Hwy 1'
6.9	1.2km gradual climb
9.0	5km twisting descent
16.5	500m moderate climb
20.6	Hwy 1 'to Hobart', Melton Mowbray
26.4	'to Kempton'
27.5	Kempton
29.0	Hwy 1 'to Hobart'
37.1	Bagdad
37.6	Chauncy Vale Sanctuary 7km ↻
44.0	Mangalore
47.5	Ford Rd to Tea Tree', Pontville
48.8	C321 to Tea Tree'
55.2	C322 to Richmond'
64.7	B31 'to Richmond'
65.4	Richmond post office

Elevation

See Days 5&6 p230

START: DAY 5
Richmond

START: DAY 4
Bothwell

See Day 3 p226

TASMANIA

Richmond

Richmond, 25km from Hobart and within sight of Mt Wellington, is renowned for its 1823 **stone bridge**, Australia's oldest. With more than 50 19th-century buildings as well, pretty Richmond is Tasmania's premier historic town.

Beside the Coal River, on the old Hobart–Port Arthur route, Richmond grew as a strategic military post and convict station. With the completion of the Sorell Causeway in 1872, traffic to the Tasman Peninsula and east coast bypassed Richmond and the town changed very little in more than 100 years. It has more recently been discovered by tourists but remains a delightful place to visit.

Information A visitor centre of sorts operates at the Old Hobart Town Model Village (☎ 6260 2502), 30m along a lane opposite Henry St in the town centre.

The post office is in the council chambers building on the south side of Bridge St, the town's main street.

Things to See & Do Straddling the Coal River is **Richmond Bridge**, at the eastern end of town. Walking tracks following the riverbanks under the bridge offer good viewpoints of the fine stonework.

Behind the council chambers, **Richmond Gaol**, built in 1825, is the best preserved convict prison in Australia with original locks, cells and relics.

Other places of historical interest include **St John's Church** (1836), the oldest Catholic church in Australia, up the hill on St Johns Circle east of the bridge; the 1836 **court house** behind the post office; and the 1888 **Richmond Arms Hotel** on Bridge St.

Richmond Historical Walks (☎ 6248 5510) runs daily **guided tours** in January and February (by appointment at other times).

The **Old Hobart Town Model Village** was designed from original plans of 1820s Hobart Town. Superb detail shows how much the city has changed.

Walk along Bridge St to **craft shops** selling locally produced furniture, paintings, carved timber bowls and trinkets, leather goods and books.

Places to Stay & Eat Just 1km from the town centre, *Richmond Cabin & Tourist*

Park (☎ 6260 2192, Tea Tree Rd), has tent sites for $7.50 per person, plus on-site vans for $45, and cabins from $71.50, both for two people.

Richmond Country Guesthouse (☎ 6260 4238, 472 Prossers Rd) is a good value B&B on a dirt road 4km north of town. Singles/doubles cost $61/83, including continental breakfast. *Richmond Antiques B&B* (☎ 6260 2601, 2 Edward St) has rooms above the shop for $15 a single (yes, that's $15) to $85 a double.

Motel units in converted 1830s stables behind *Richmond Arms Hotel* (☎ 6260 2109, 42 Bridge St) cost $99 a double with continental breakfast.

Prospect House (☎ 6260 2207, Main Rd), a two storey Georgian mansion opposite the Cabin & Tourist Park, has rooms around an appealing courtyard. Tariff is $132 a double. It has a quality a la carte restaurant for lunch and dinner.

Bridge St has two *supermarkets*. Those with a weakness for lollies and ice cream will love *Sweets and Treats* (☎ 6260 2395, 50 Bridge St). Tucked around the corner is *Richmond Bakery* (☎ 6260 2628, Edward St), a popular place for croissants and coffee or light meals at indoor or courtyard tables.

The *Richmond Arms Hotel* serves lunch and dinner daily (mains around $15) in its characterful dining room. Meat eaters should try the kangaroo steak.

Day 5: Richmond to Eaglehawk Neck

3½–6 hours, 69.2km

A scenically delightful day begins with one moderate climb before Sorell then an unavoidable section of busy, undulating highway. It's quiet from the Dodges Ferry turn-off through to Dunalley, partly on a good but hilly dirt road along the Frederick Henry Bay shore. The sealed Arthur Hwy winds through bush but is narrow and can be unpleasantly busy to Murdunna. There's a good shoulder for the final 10km.

From Richmond Bridge, the route crosses grazing country to busy Sorell (13.6km), a good stocking-up point – subsequent villages such as Lewisham (22km) and Dodges Ferry (27km) have limited services.

Dunalley (48.3km) has a *supermarket*, plus an excellent *bakery*. The **Denison Canal** is a short cut for small boats between the east

Days 5 & 6: Richmond – Eaglehawk Neck & Tasman Peninsula Circuit

1:350,000

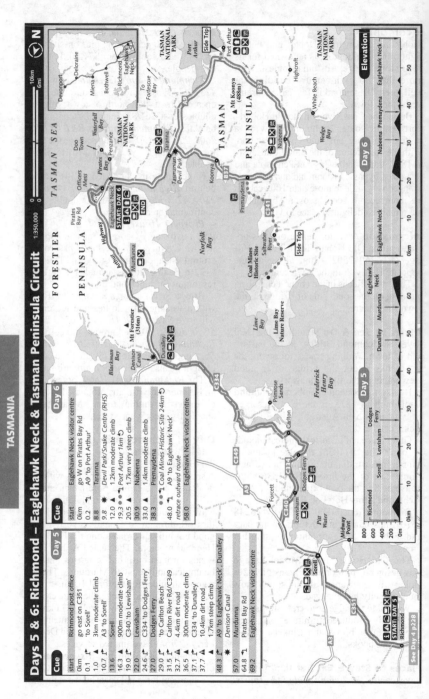

Cue | Day 5

start	Richmond post office
0km	go east on C351 'to Sorell'
0.1	'to Sorell'
1.0	3km moderate climb
10.7	A3 'to Sorell'
13.6	Sorell
16.3	900m moderate climb
19.0	C340 'to Lewisham'
22.0	Lewisham
24.6	C334 'to Dodges Ferry'
27.0	Dodges Ferry
29.0	'to Carlton Beach'
31.5	Carlton River Rd/C349
32.7	4.4km dirt road
36.5	300m moderate climb
37.1	C334 'to Dunalley'
37.7	10.4km dirt road
48.3	1.7km steep climb
	A9 to Eaglehawk Neck', Dunalley
	Denison Canal
57.0	Murdunna
64.8	Pirates Bay Rd
69.2	Eaglehawk Neck visitor centre

Cue | Day 6

start	Eaglehawk Neck visitor centre
0km	go W on Pirates Bay Rd
0.2	A9 'to Port Arthur'
8.8	Taranna
9.8	*Devil Park/Snake Centre (RHS)*
12.0	1.2km moderate climb
19.3	'Port Arthur 1km'
20.5	1.7km very steep climb
30.9	Nubeena
33.0	1.4km moderate climb
38.3	Premaydena
48.0	*Coal Mines Historic Site 24km*
	A9 'to Eaglehawk Neck'
	retrace outward route
58.0	Eaglehawk Neck visitor centre

Elevation

coast and the Derwent; the swing bridge opens often, so you may have time to take in the surroundings. **Dunalley Fish Market** (☎ 6253 5428), south of the bridge, sells oysters, crayfish and other fresh seafood daily. Barbecue and picnic facilities are nearby.

On the timbered Forestier Peninsula, stepping-stone to the Tasman Peninsula, **Murdunna** (57km), with *tearooms* and a *takeaway*, is virtually the only outpost of civilisation.

A **lookout** about 300m along Pirates Bay Rd offers spectacular views over Tasman Peninsula's rugged eastern shore to The Lanterns and Hippolyte Rocks.

Eaglehawk Neck

Eaglehawk Neck is an isthmus connecting the Forestier and Tasman Peninsulas. During convict days, to prevent escape from the penal colony, the 100m-wide Neck had a line of fierce dogs chained across it. A realistic statue of one, teeth bared, straining against its chain, stands beside the road. The Neck is an excellent base for exploring Tasman Peninsula. It has varied accommodation and is less crowded than the more celebrated Port Arthur, an easy 20km ride away.

The visitor centre (☎ 6250 3722), 443 Pirates Bay Rd, is in the Officers Mess restaurant on the north-eastern side of the isthmus.

Things to See & Do Near the Officers Mess, the 1832 **Officers Quarters** is Australia's oldest wooden military building. It's the only remaining structure from convict days and is now a museum.

Rangers give evening slide shows and **nature talks** during summer holidays in the community hall; contact PWS (☎ 6250 3497) or Eaglehawk Neck Backpackers.

A path leads from the Officers Mess along the isthmus past the community hall and the intimidating **Dog Line statue**, and through dunes to Pirates Bay beach.

At the northern end of Pirates Bay, it's a 5-minute walk to the **Tessellated Pavement**, an eroded rock terrace resembling tiled paving. At low tide in calm weather it's possible to continue along the foreshore to **Clydes Island** (25 minutes return) for fine views south to Cape Hauy.

On the south side of the isthmus, Blowhole Rd is signed to **The Blowhole** and **Tasmans Arch**, about 5km away. On the way is

the amusingly kitsch **Doo Town** where each shack is named on a 'Doo' theme. A 4km dirt road signed to Waterfall Bay accesses **walking tracks** to Waterfall Bluff (1½ hours return) and a full day walk to Fortescue Bay, with a shorter option to the viewpoint atop Tatnells Hill. For **guided walks** call Tasman Nature Guiding (☎ 6250 3268).

Explore underwater caves and canyons, **diving** with Eaglehawk Dive Centre (☎ 6250 3566 or ☎ 0417 013 518), on Pirates Bay Rd.

Places to Stay & Eat The small, friendly *Eaglehawk Neck Backpackers* (☎ 6250 3248, Old Jetty Rd), on the northern side of the isthmus, especially welcomes cyclists. Camping costs $6 per person, and beds $15. Canoes are available for guest use.

Lufra Country Hotel (☎ 6250 3262, Pirates Bay Rd), above the Tessellated Pavement, charges $60.50/77 per person for en suite single/double rooms with continental breakfast. The hotel restaurant serves local fish and venison daily. Uphill is *Wunnamurra Waterfront B&B* (☎ 6250 3145, Osprey Rd), which has two en suite double rooms for $99 or $110. *Osprey Lodge Beachfront B&B* (☎ 6250 3629, Osprey Rd) charges $150, including pre-dinner drinks and hors d'oeuvres.

Pirates Bay Motel (☎ 6250 3272, Blowhole Rd) offers dinner, bed and breakfast for $65/80. Its licensed restaurant, open from 6pm (closed Monday), has $15 to $18 mains, including vegetarian; it operates as a tearoom daily until 4pm.

Cafe-style meals and takeaways are available at the *Officers Mess* (☎ 6250 3535, Pirates Bay Rd), which has a small *store*. *Eaglehawk Cafe* (☎ 6250 3331, Arthur Hwy) serves breakfast, lunch and dinner daily in the attractive former post office, on the south side overlooking Norfolk Bay.

Day 6: Tasman Peninsula Circuit

3–6 hours, 58km

Leave your gear at Eaglehawk Neck to explore Tasman Peninsula unladen. While the main route is on sealed roads, the side trip to the site of Tasmania's first coal mine is not. Apart from one moderate climb, the route towards Port Arthur is flat and the wide-shouldered highway traverses dense forest. Hills towards Nubeena and before Premaydena – both offering fine views –

are followed by 10km of undulating country back to the Arthur Hwy.

Sprawling **Taranna** (8.8km), on the shore of Norfolk Bay, was the terminus of Australia's first railway. A convict-powered tramway ran from near Port Arthur to the jetty. There's now an inviting *bakery* and a *store* beside the highway.

If you have time, take a break at the **Tasmanian Devil Park and World Tiger Snake Centre** (9.8km, or 48.2km on the return leg; ☎ 6250 3230), about 200m north of the B37/Arthur Hwy junction. Its sleek, slithering serpents simultaneously attract and repel.

Port Arthur (19.3km), 500m off the highway, has a large visitor centre (☎ 6250 2539) with a *cafe* and *restaurant*. Entry to the penal colony site costs $18 ($40 per family). The ticket, also valid for the following day, includes a guided tour, admission to the museum and a harbour cruise. There is also a *hostel* and *camping ground*.

Nubeena (30.9km; population 230), the peninsula's largest settlement, has a *takeaway*, *bakery*, *supermarkets* and waterside picnic tables.

The hill beyond town offers fine views over Norfolk Bay, Forestier Peninsula and the 'mainland'. Premaydena (38.3km) has a *general store* at the junction with the road to the Coal Mines Historic Site (see Side Trip).

Side Trip: Coal Mines Historic Site
24km return

The C341, signed to Saltwater River and Coal Mines Historic Site, runs north from Premaydena store. After a steep 1km climb (averaging 9%), dirt road begins. At 9.5km, veer right on Coal Mines Rd, riding 2km to the historic site entrance.

Tasmania's first operational mine opened here in 1834. Though of poor quality, the resource lessened the colony's early dependence on coal from New South Wales. Sandy tracks are signed to points of interest, though distances are not always given. The most interesting sight, 500m from the entrance, is the extensive ruin of the main settlement which housed convicts who worked in appalling conditions until 1848. Keep an eye out for wildlife – echidnas are common.

Return to Premaydena via the outward route.

Tassie's East Coast

Duration	6 days
Distance	438.2km
Difficulty	moderate–hard
Start	Eaglehawk Neck
End	Launceston

The east coast is probably the most popular cycle-touring route in Tasmania, offering much to interest cyclists. A tough first day is followed by days of easy, relaxing cycling. Outstanding scenery, fascinating national parks, attractive fishing villages, wildlife spotting, and some more climbing, ensure no cyclist will be bored.

HISTORY
Rapid settlement of the coastal region, highly suited to grazing, occurred after 1803 while, offshore, whaling and fishing became important. Many convicts who served terms in the area stayed to help settlers establish the fishing, wool, beef and grain industries still significant today. Nineteenth-century tin mining brought boom times and many immigrants to the north-east.

NATURAL HISTORY
Tasmania's scenic east coast, with its long, sandy beaches and exceptional peacefulness, is known as the 'sun coast' because of its mild climate. The coast south of St Helens is the state's driest, averaging 2250 hours of sunshine per year, or six hours a day. Attractive red granite peaks on the Freycinet Peninsula are the legacy of ancient volcanic activity while, a little further north, a remnant of the eucalypt forest which once covered the east coast is preserved in Douglas-Apsley National Park. Rainforest, with beautiful myrtle beech, has developed in the wet north-east. Rains also feed 90m St Columba Falls, the state's highest, 10km off the route near Pyengana.

PLANNING
While the ride is described in six days, there's so much to do that adding extra days is advised. Spend them walking in Freycinet National Park (see the Coles Bay section); on Maria Island (see the Orford section); and exploring the side trips and attractions around Bicheno, St Helens and Scottsdale.

When to Ride

A popular holiday spot, the east coast is best avoided at Easter and late December through January, when accommodation and the roads are most crowded. On Day 2, the route requires you use a ferry service that only operates between October and late April – it's a 52km detour if riding outside these months.

Maps

The Land Information Bureau's Tasmania series sheets *North East* and *South East* (1:250,000) cover the ride.

GETTING TO/FROM THE RIDE

Eaglehawk Neck is also the end point for the Across the Central Plateau ride (earlier in this chapter). Launceston is about 20km northwest of Evandale, the start point of the Tassie's West Coast ride (described later in this chapter).

Eaglehawk Neck

Bus TWT Tassielink (☎ 1300-300 520) runs between Hobart's Transit Centre, 199 Collins St, and Port Arthur via Eaglehawk Neck ($9.20, 1¼ hours, once each way weekdays).

Bicycle Ride north from Hobart on the Inter City Cycleway, turning right at Elwick Rd, Glenorchy, and crossing Bowen Bridge. Continue to a roundabout from where the C324, signed to Richmond, rises over the Meehan Range's Grasstree Hill. Wind down to a left turn from where the B31 descends gradually to Richmond. Follow Day 5 (pp229–31) of the Across the Central Plateau ride to Dunalley or Eaglehawk Neck.

Launceston

See the Getting to/from Tasmania (p215) and the Gateway Cities (p220) sections for information on getting to/from Launceston.

THE RIDE
Eaglehawk Neck

See Eaglehawk Neck (p231) in the Across the Central Plateau ride for information about accommodation and other services.

Day 1: Eaglehawk Neck to Orford

4½–7½ hours, 74.2km

The start of this route follows (in reverse) the Day 5 route in the Across the Central Plateau ride, as far as Dunalley (pp229–31). After this,

there are no shops en route so it is essential to carry lunch and plenty of water. Past the Pirates Bay Rd climb (2.2km), terrain is gentle for around 30km. Dirt road begins on the C337, 3km north of Dunalley, at 24km. This lightly trafficked but challenging road enters a superb forest of blue and swamp gums where very steep gradients, with loose, rocky surfaces, make even descents tricky. Keep an ear out for occasional log trucks. The final 9km on bitumen is blessedly easy.

At 37.3km a long steep climb begins to a **lookout** (42.4km) over Marion Bay and the coastline on which Tasman planted the Dutch flag in 1642.

At 48.8km **Sandspit Forest Reserve** protects a valley of tall eucalypt forest and a unique patch of rainforest. The reserve's picnic area is the best place for a lunch break. A 20-minute interpretive rainforest loop walk starts nearby.

The very steep, rough climb out of the valley may require some walking.

At 69.7km, **Spring Beach** is a good surfing location with views of Maria Island – and rather chilly water.

Orford

This low-key resort, population about 500, straddles the Prosser River at the Tasman Hwy bridge. Once an important sea port, it served whalers and the Maria Island garrison. For visitor information, phone the Triabunna visitor centre (☎ 6257 4090), 7.6km north (see Day 2).

Things to See & Do North of the bridge, the remains of an incomplete **convict-built road** now make a pleasant riverside walk upstream for 2km to ruined cells at Paradise Probation Station.

The area has good fishing and Orford's sheltered beaches are ideal for swimming or walking.

Maria Island National Park (see the boxed text 'Maria Island' overleaf) is accessible by ferry (☎ 6257 1589) from Louisville, 5km north of Orford.

Places to Stay & Eat Beside the beach, 1.5km north of the river, *Raspins Beach Camping Park* (☎ 6257 3575 or ☎ 6257 1771) has views of Maria Island. Sandy tent sites cost $11 a double, and showers $1 for three minutes.

TASMANIA

TASMANIA

Day 1: Eaglehawk Neck to Orford

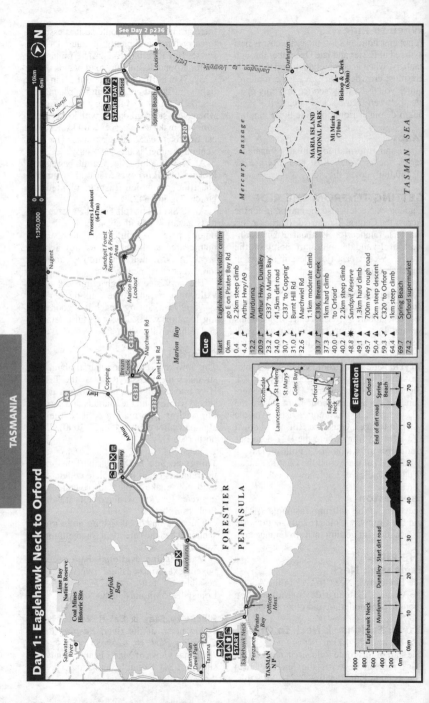

Cue		
start		Eaglehawk Neck visitor centre
0km	◄	go E on Pirates Bay Rd
0.4	◄↗	2.2km steep climb
4.4	◄	Arthur Hwy/A9
12.2		Murdunna
20.9	↘	Arthur Hwy, Dunalley
23.2	◄↗	C337 'to Marion Bay'
24.0	◄	41.5km dirt road
30.7	↗	C337 'to Copping'
31.0	◄↗	Burnt Hill Rd
32.6	◄↗	Marchwiel Rd
		1.1km moderate climb
33.7	◄↗	C336, Bream Creek
37.3		1km hard climb
40.0	◄↗	'to Orford'
40.2	◄	2.2km steep climb
48.8	✳	Sandspit Reserve
49.1		1.3km hard climb
49.7	◄	700m very rough road
50.4	↘	2km steep descent
59.3	↗	C320 'to Orford'
64.4	◄	1km steep climb
69.7		Spring Beach
74.2		Orford supermarket

Elevation

Blue Waters Motor Hotel (☎ *6257 1102*) has doubles for $66; and locals recommend the kitchen's steak and seafood. At the start of the convict road, *Shalom Waterfront B&B* (☎ *6257 1175, 50 Tasman Hwy*) has double rooms with water views from $70, including breakfast. *Riverside Villas* (☎ *6257 1655* or ☎ *1800-817 533)*charges $126 per double for a house-sized, self-contained unit with use of a motorised dinghy.

Riteway supermarket (☎ *6257 1210*) is near the junction of Wielangta Rd and the Tasman Hwy. *East Coast Seafoods* (☎ *6257 1549*), beside the highway, offers both take-away and eat-in meals.

Day 2: Orford to Coles Bay
4½–8 hours, 80.9km

The Tasman Hwy between Orford and Swansea is near dead flat and, with a (common) south-east tailwind and sea views all the way, it's one of the most pleasant day's riding imaginable. After Triabunna, log trucks and other traffic become rarer but

Maria Island

Maria Island (*Toarra Marra Monah* to the Oyster Bay Aborigines, who used it as a safe haven) became a national park in 1972. At various times the island has been a penal settlement (1821–32); a farming district (from 1842); and, between 1884 and 1930, the site of a variety of industries – from silk- and wine-making to cement. Major buildings such as the 1825 Commissariat Store and the 1830 Penitentiary remain as a legacy of early European settlement.

The island can be visited on a day trip, although an overnight stay gives more time to appreciate the plentiful wildlife, historic ruins, pristine forests and superb walks, such as the four-hour return trek to the Bishop & Clerk summit (630m).

The Eastcoaster Express ferry (☎ 6257 1589) departs from Louisville Point three times daily. Return fares for the 20-minute crossing are $19 ($22 if returning on a different day); bikes cost $3.

The island has no shops; and the only accommodation is the *Parks, Wildlife & Heritage Penitentiary Units* (☎ 6257 1420) at Darlington, which cost $8 per adult, and a basic *camping ground* ($4).

there are no more services for 45km to Swansea. The route leaves the highway at 56.8km and minor roads lead to Point Bagot where an informal outboard-dinghy service (☎ 6257 0239) ferries cyclists across to Swanwick for $10 per head, saving a 52km ride around Moulting Lagoon. The service operates between October and late April, weather permitting – phone before starting the level, 20km ride from Swansea. There's emergency camping (no facilities) in the dunes at Pt Bagot. From Swanwick, it's an easy 7km to Coles Bay.

Triabunna (7.6km), commercial centre of the region, has woodchip processing and fishing industries, but it's not an especially attractive place to spend time. The visitor centre (☎ 6257 4090) is on the water's edge at the corner of the Esplanade and Charles St.

At 28.2km is the turn-off to *Gum Leaves Cabins* (☎ *6244 8147*). A 3km dirt road leads to a child-oriented bushland resort, which also has hostel beds.

Cyclists can still ride over the 1843 **Spiky Bridge** (51km), built by convicts with thousands of local fieldstones without mortar.

A popular tourist town, **Swansea** (52.8km) has views to Freycinet National Park. Information is available at the imposing **Wine & Wool Centre** (☎ 6257 8677), 96 Tasman Hwy. Plentiful accommodation includes *camping* (☎ *6257 8177, Shaw St*) and a *youth hostel* (☎ *6257 8367, 5 Franklin St)*, plus *food stores*.

Coles Bay

The spectacular 300m-high red granite range known as The Hazards dominates Coles Bay township's skyline. It also forms the northern boundary of the beautiful Freycinet National Park with its celebrated, much photographed Wineglass Bay.

Information Visitor information is available at the post office/store (☎ 6257 0109) in Garnet St on the south-eastern side of town and at Iluka supermarket (☎ 6257 0383) on the Esplanade. For national park information, contact the PWS ranger station (☎ 6257 0107) inside the park entrance. At the time of writing, a visitor centre was planned for construction near the ranger station during 2001.

Things to See & Do The major attraction is Freycinet National Park. **Bushwalking** on

TASMANIA

Day 2: Orford to Coles Bay

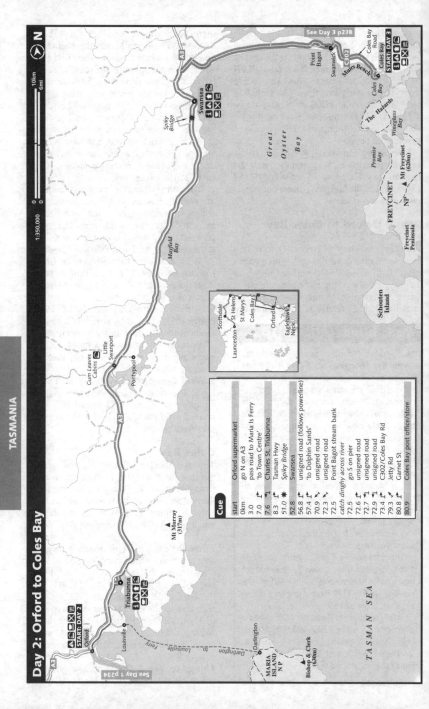

Cue

start		Orford supermarket
0km		go N on A3
3.0		pass road to Maria Is Ferry
7.0	↰	'to Town Centre'
7.6	↰	Charles St, Triabunna
8.3	↱	Tasman Hwy
51.0	✳	Spiky Bridge
52.8		Swansea
56.8		unsigned road (follows powerline)
57.4	↱	'to Dolphin Sands'
70.9	↰	unsigned road
72.3	↱	unsigned road
72.5		Point Bagot stream bank
		catch dinghy across river
72.5		go S on pier
72.6	↰	unsigned road
72.7	↱	unsigned road
72.9	↱	unsigned road
73.4	↰	C302/Coles Bay Rd
79.3	↰	Jetty Rd
80.8	↱	Garnet St
80.9		Coles Bay post office/store

well maintained walking tracks is the only way to see most of it.

The most beautiful walk is to **Wineglass Bay**, a hilly three-hour return journey. An hour return option takes the same track up to a spectacular viewpoint over the bay and to the southern side of The Hazards. Wallabies and echidnas are often seen along the way.

Hire a **boat** from Coles Bay Boat Hire (☎ 6257 0109) at the post office, or **cruise** with Freycinet Sea Charters (☎ 6257 0355 or ☎ 0417-355 524). For thrills very close to the water, Freycinet Adventures (☎ 6257 0500) offers half- or full-day **kayak tours** of Coles Bay or offshore islands, or **abseiling** and **rock climbing** in the national park.

Places to Stay & Eat Inside the national park, *Freycinet Camping Ground (☎ 6257 0107)* has only pit toilets and fresh water. Tent sites cost $5.50 per person. Book at the ranger's office (see Information).

Sites at *Iluka Holiday Centre (☎ 6257 0115 or ☎ 1800-786 512, e iluka@trump .net.au)*, near Muirs Beach, cost $15.40 for two people. The YHA hostel on site has beds for $16.50. On-site vans cost $49.50 per double. Self-contained cabins cost $55 per double for run-down old ones, $71.50 for newer ones, or $99 for 'luxury'.

Big spenders will like *Freycinet Lodge (☎ 6257 0101)*, set unobtrusively inside the national park with views over Great Oyster Bay and The Hazards. Cabins start from $180 for a single or double – though they're not special, the location is. Its restaurant specialises in seafood.

The two *Stores*, at opposite ends of town, one in the post office, the other beside Iluka Holiday Centre, supply self-caterers. The *Freycinet Bakery/Cafe (☎ 6257 0272, the Esplanade)* is highly recommended. Next door, the *Iluka Tavern Bistro (☎ 6257 0429, the Esplanade)* serves lunch and dinner.

Day 3: Coles Bay to St Marys

4½–8½ hours, 84.8km

A quiet, near-level ride beside the sea precedes the only hill of the day. The climb of forested Elephant Pass (68.1km; 8km in total) is a big one. At the summit, the famous Pancake Barn (76.4km) is a compulsory stop. The route's final 8km are downhill. Traffic is hardly a problem all day – the few approaching trucks can be heard and avoided.

Bicheno (39.7km), an attractive fishing village, has all tourist facilities. The visitor centre (☎ 6375 1333) takes bookings for evening **penguin-watching tours** (book well ahead in holiday periods).

North of Bicheno, the **East Coast Birdlife & Animal Park** (45.4km) displays wildlife in 32 hectares of parklands.

Less than a kilometre past the cluster of houses at Chain of Lagoons (67.4km) the highway forks. The left fork begins climbing almost immediately towards Elephant Pass (76km; 400m). At 76.4km, the splendidly isolated *Mt Elephant Pancake Barn (☎ 6372 2263)* is a godsend for cyclists who've struggled up the pass, with fine coffee, a mind-boggling selection of pancakes and great views.

St Marys

Peaceful St Marys, population 630, is a charming town at the head of the Fingal Valley. Its sizeable business area is not very tourist-oriented. Colonial Trust Bank is in the post office on the main street.

There's not a lot to do around town except enjoy peaceful countryside. Wander around the sadly deserted train station at the town's western end or, if you're staying at Seaview Farm, check out the 10-minute walk from South Sister car park to the top of the mountain. Ask for directions at the hostel.

Places to Stay & Eat With magnificent views of coast, sea and mountains, *Seaview Farm (☎ 6372 2341)* is a working cattle station surrounded by state forest, 6.5km up South Sister mountain. Bunks in the cosy cottage cost $16.50; individual en suite units cost $44 a double; and there's a kitchen available. The proprietors can usually offer a lift up the steep, rough road from town; otherwise, ride 200m west from the post office and turn right. After 100m, turn left on Gardiners Creek Rd and, 500m farther, right at a crossroads to grind uphill on dirt. Veer right after 4.4km, following signs.

St Marys Hotel (☎ 6372 2181) offers B&B for $45 a double. It serves counter dinners on Friday, Saturday and Sunday.

Two *supermarkets* serve the town; the one near the post office is better stocked. A *takeaway* and a *coffee shop-bakery* are on the main street.

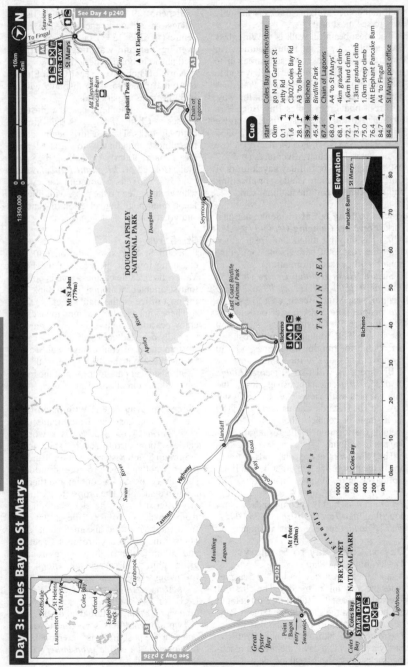

Day 3: Coles Bay to St Marys

TASMANIA

Cue		
0km		Coles Bay post office/store
0km		go N on Garnet St
0.1		Jetty Rd
1.6		C302/Coles Bay Rd
28.1		A3 'to Bicheno'
39.7		Bicheno
45.4		Birdlife Park
67.4		Chain of Lagoons
68.0		A4 'to St Marys'
68.1		4km gradual climb
72.1		1.6km hard climb
73.7		1.3km gradual climb
75.0		1.0km steep climb
76.4		Mt Elephant Pancake Barn
84.7		A4 'to Fingal'
84.8		St Marys post office

Elevation

Day 4: St Marys to St Helens

2–3 hours, 36km

Except for an easy climb from St Marys, this short ride is all downhill or flat. It's big on coastal scenery and so easy, it almost qualifies as a rest day, unless a rare head-wind blows up. Cyclists needing more exercise should have time for the side trip.

After a marvellous 5.5km downhill from forested **St Marys Pass** (5.5km), the level road follows the coast. Lovely white-sand beaches stretch between the sprawling villages of Scamander (16.5km), which has food shops, and Beaumaris (22km).

Approaching St Helens, the narrower road winds around pretty headlands. There is little space in places, so beware of traffic.

Side Trip: Binalong Bay

24km return

This moderate difficulty ride is ideal afternoon entertainment. It uses sealed road to Binalong Bay and returns through coastal forest, partly on hard-packed dirt, with one short, steep hill (mountain bike not essential).

Ride east from the centre of St Helens along Quail St, which zigs left to become Binalong Bay Rd. Binalong Bay township has a shop. Continue to Hilltop Dr and veer left onto the dirt Dora Point road. Follow signs for 5km back to Binalong Bay Rd via Humbug Hill. It's worth detouring to Skeleton Point (signed); a five-minute walk leads to the rocky coast where pelicans soar and sail.

A very steep 300m-long section of sealed road climbs Humbug Hill giving tree-screened ocean, bay and surf views before descending steeply to turn left onto the outward route.

St Helens

From 1830 sealers and whalers used Georges Bay as a base. Farmers, arriving in the 1850s, made St Helens a permanent settlement; and a 'tin rush' in 1874 turned it into an important ore shipping port. Despite mining's demise, the town grew – as a fishing port. Nowadays, with 1145 people, it is the biggest town on the coast and self-proclaimed 'Game Fishing Capital of Tasmania'. The port is east of Golden Fleece River bridge, at the business area's southern end.

Information The visitor centre (☎ 6376 1744), 61 Cecilia St, is in the library build-ing opposite the post office. From October to March, it's open from 9am to 5pm weekdays, to 1pm Saturday, and from 10am to 2pm Sunday; hours are reduced in winter.

Colonial Trust and Westpac banks on Cecilia St have ATMs. The ANZ is in Quail St.

Free hot-water showers are available in the wharf toilet block.

Things to See & Do More historical and town information is available in the library's **History Room**.

Walk across Golden Fleece Bridge into Kings Park recreation area for bay and town **views** plus barbecue facilities.

The bay's flat water is popular for **canoeing** and **windsurfing**. The catamaran *Elektra* (☎ 6372 5342) operates two-hour **cruises**. Professional Charters (☎ 6376 3083) supplies boats and gear for reef, sea and bay **fishing**.

Quiet roads on both sides of Georges Bay offer good cycling to **coastal attractions** like Binalong Bay (see Side Trip) and St Helens Point.

Places to Stay South of the bridge, *St Helens Caravan Park (☎ 6376 1290, Penelope St)* is good value. Tent sites cost $15, on-site vans $38, and cabins $65, all for two people.

St Helens Youth Hostel (☎ 6376 1661, 5 Cameron St), in a quiet spot near the water, charges from $16.

The *Anchor Wheel Motel (☎ 6376 1358, Tasman Hwy)*, at the western end of town, has doubles for $60. One room has cooking facilities and there's a barbecue in the park-like grounds. Its restaurant serves vegetarian and meaty dishes from $10. Opposite, modern self-contained *Kellraine Units (☎ 6376 1169, Tasman Hwy)* charges $40 per double with kitchen.

Bike-friendly *Artnor Lodge (☎ 6376 1234, 71 Cecilia St)* charges $50 per double for rooms with shared facilities (including bath), and $70 for en suite rooms. Cooked breakfast is included.

Places to Eat Head to Cecilia St for *supermarkets*, *takeaways* and *Asian food stores*. *St Helens Bakery (☎ 6376 1260, Cecilia St)* offers a $6 cooked breakfast.

Trimboli's Pizzeria & Coffee Shoppe (☎ 6376 1429, 1B Circassian St) sells large pizzas from $13.

TASMANIA

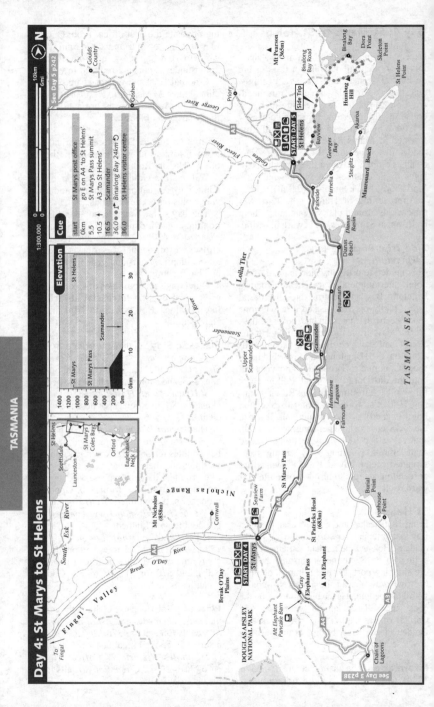

Day 4: St Marys to St Helens

TASMANIA

See Day 5 p242

Cue

start	St Marys post office
0km	go E on A4 'to St Helens'
5.5	St Marys Pass summit
10.5	A3 'to St Helens'
16.5	Scamander
36.0 ●●● ⟲	Binalong Bay 24km ⟲
36.0	St Helens visitor centre

Elevation

St Helens

1400
1200
1000
800
600
400
200
0m

St Marys
St Marys Pass
Scamander

0km   10   20   30

START DAY 5 St Helens
Side Trip
Binalong Bay
Dora Point
Skeleton Point
Bay
Mt Pearson (365m)
Binalong Bay Road
Humbug Hill
St Helens Point
Akaroa
Bayview
Georges Bay
Stieglitz
Maurouard Beach
Goshen
Goulds Country
Priory
George River
Fleece River
Golden
Parmella
Parkside
Dianas Basin
Dianas Beach
Beaumaris
Loila Tier
Scamander River
Scamander
Upper Scamander
Henderson Lagoon
Falmouth
TASMAN SEA

St Helens
St Marys
Coles Bay
Scottsdale
Launceston
Orford
Eaglehawk Neck

Nicholas Range
Mt Nicholas (858m)
Cornwall
Seaview Farm
St Marys Pass
A4
St Patricks Head (663m)
START DAY 4 St Marys
Break O'Day River
South Esk River
Fingal Valley
To Fingal
Break O'Day Plains
DOUGLAS APSLEY NATIONAL PARK
Mt Elephant Pancake Barn
Gray
Elephant Pass
Mt Elephant
A3
A4
Burial Point
Trouthouse Point
Chain of Lagoons

1:300,000
0   10km
0   6mi

See Day 3 p238

Interesting eateries include *Lady Annie Elizabeth Floating Restaurant* (☎ 0419-718 750), a seafood specialist at the wharf near Golden Fleece Bridge. North along the wharf is *Captain's Catch* (☎ 6376 1170), a more traditional seafood restaurant. South of the bridge at Queechy Cottages, award winning *Tidal Water* (☎ 6376 1321) also specialises in seafood with mains from $18.

Day 5: St Helens to Scottsdale

5½–10 hours, 99.4km

Farms give way to forest as the road heads to the hilly inland. The hardest climbing comes with the consecutive 3.8km hauls over Weldborough Pass. After Branxholm, the overall descending route climbs three short, steep hills. Food is available at several places en route.

Opportunity for a break comes at *St Columba Falls Tearooms* (26.7km), just past the Falls/Pyengana turn-off. The proprietor is obsessive about where bikes are *not* to be left, but provides no bicycle parking facility.

Serious climbing begins at 30km to rainforested **Weldborough Pass** (38.2km; 590m). Beyond the summit is **Myrtle Rainforest Walk** (41km), a 10-minute easy interpretive circuit through damp jungle.

Weldborough (45km), once a busy tin-mining town, now has only a *camping ground* and the *Weldborough Hotel* (☎ 6354 2223), which serves meals – don't be deterred by the 'Irish menu' displayed outside featuring such delicacies as 'maggot mornay', 'ant rissoles' and 'leeches and cream'. Rooms cost $35, and tent sites $10, both for two people.

Derby (66.8km), a classified historic town, preserves its old mine buildings in the **Derby Tin Mine Centre** (☎ 6354 2262) on Main Rd. The town comes alive in late October when up to 10,000 people flood in for the annual **Derby River Derby** – many take to rafts of every description on the Cascade River. Derby has a *general store* (☎ 6354 2324), accommodation at the *Dorset Hotel* (☎ 6354 02360) and free *camping* at the riverbank recreation reserve.

The gently rolling highway plunges suddenly into **Branxholm** (73.8km), which has a *tearoom* and *store*. Passing Tonganah (91.7km) on a 4km straight, the route grinds uphill into Scottsdale, passing the turn-off to the Bridestowe Lavender Farm (see the Day 6 Side Trip).

Scottsdale

The largest town in the north-east, with just over 2000 inhabitants, Scottsdale is a good base for exploration. It has fantastic scenery and wildlife spotting in the forests and off the main roads. Farming is still important role to the area: poppy and hop growing employ many locals. Frozen-food processing, timber plantations and sawmilling are other economic mainstays. A new forest interpretive centre is being planned (to be located on the road towards Launceston).

Information The visitor centre (☎ 6352 2263), 65 King St, 500m west of the post office, is also the Bellow's Backpacker reception.Banks are on King St in the town centre; Westpac and Commonwealth have ATMs.

The nearest thing to a bike shop is Toy Kingdom (☎ 6352 3100) behind Good Sports on King St, opposite the Roelf Vos supermarket.

Things to See & Do The easy way into the hilly hinterland forests is with Pepper Bush Peaks Tours (☎ 6352 2263), operating out of Bellow's Backpacker. Wildlife and scenic **tours** include fishing, cruising and food.

Bridestowe Lavender Farm (see the Day 6 Side Trip) is well worth the ride, which can be extended to Bridport, a beach resort popular with Tasmanians. Sprawling on the shore of Anderson Bay, Bridport – about 20km from Scottsdale – is an easy, mostly downhill ride on the B84; riding back is a little more strenuous.

Places to Stay & Eat On the highway south-east of town, camping is rather noisy at *North-East Park Camping Ground* (☎ 6352 2017). Sites cost $5 per person and hot showers operate with 20-cent coins. Check in at the house opposite.

Bellow's Backpacker & Budget Accommodation (☎ 6352 2263, e pepper@microtech.com.au, 65 King St) charges $10 per person for camping with use of good facilities, $19.80 for a dorm bed, including linen, and from $49.50 for single or double rooms.

Scottsdale Hotel/Motel (☎ 6352 2510, e kendalls@microtech.com.au, 18 George St) is the better located of two hotels. Older style, well-equipped rooms cost $43/54 per single/double. Continental ($8) or cooked ($12) breakfasts are good value.

TASMANIA

TASMANIA

Day 5: St Helens to Scottsdale

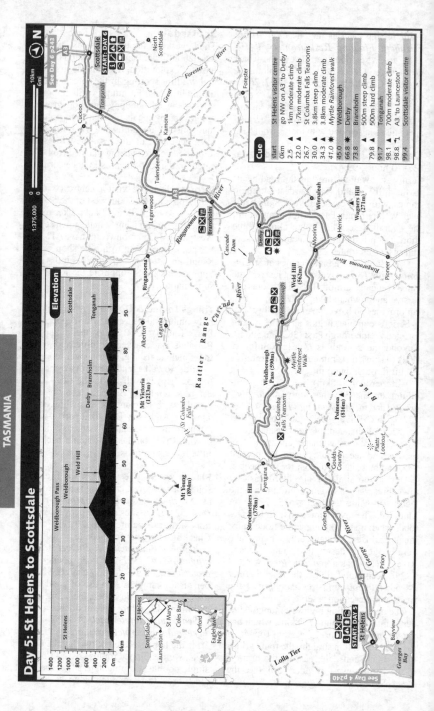

Elevation

Cue

start		St Helens visitor centre
0km		go NW on A3 to Derby
2.5	▲	1km moderate climb
22.0	▲	1.7km moderate climb
26.7	▲	St Columba Falls Tearooms
30.0	▲	3.8km steep climb
34.3	▲	3.8km moderate climb
41.0	✱	Myrtle Rainforest walk
45.0	✱	Weldborough
66.8	✱	Derby
73.8	▲	Branxholm
79.8	▲	500m steep climb
91.7	▲	500m hard climb
98.1	▲	Tonganah
98.8	↰	700m moderate climb
98.8		A3 to Launceston
99.4		Scottsdale visitor centre

See Day 6 p243

1:375,000

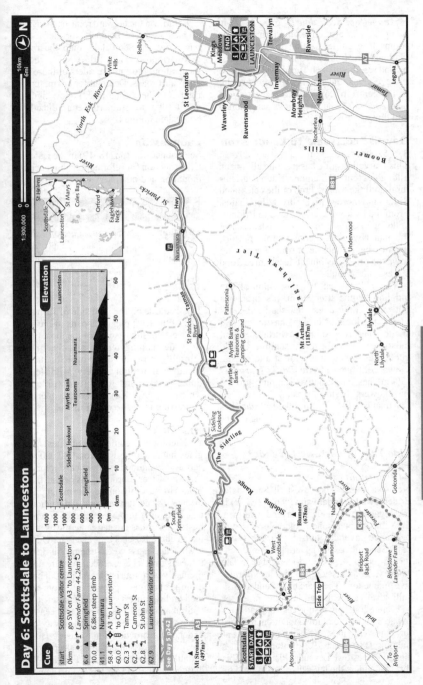

Day 6: Scottsdale to Launceston

Cue

start		Scottsdale visitor centre
0km		go SW on A3 'to Launceston'
	⚲	Lavender Farm 44.2km ↻
6.6	▲	Springfield
10.0	✳	6.8km steep climb
41.1		Nunamara
58.4	↰	A3 'to Launceston'
60.0	↱	'to City'
62.3	↰	Tamar St
62.4	↱	Cameron St
62.8	↱	St John St
62.9		Launceston visitor centre

See Day 5 p242

START DAY 6

Elevation

TASMANIA

Anabel's of Scottsdale (☎ 6352 3277, 46 King St) has attractive, modern en suite rooms in a garden setting from $99. The National Trust-classified main building has a good restaurant open Tuesday to Saturday.

Several *takeaways* and *supermarkets* are in the centre of town and a *pizza shop* is near Anabel's. The two *hotels* serve lunch and dinner daily.

Day 6: Scottsdale to Launceston

3½–6½ hours, 62.9km

This marvellous ride has just one climb and a long descent. The countryside is agricultural until the tough climb of the celebrated Sideling where native forest dominates. From the lookout, views extend to Bridport and Cape Barren and Flinders Islands. The Tasman Hwy, wide enough for comfort, usually has moderate traffic. There's no town of any size but at least three food stores dot the route.

The 6.8km steep, twisting climb of **The Sideling** begins after 10km. It's strenuous but overarching trees offer shade. Besides views, the **lookout** (16km) has toilets and shelter. The road climbs a further 3.8km, mostly easily, to the 496m summit. On the gentle descent, pleasant forest and coastal views continue. *Myrtle Bank Tearooms* (30km) has an attractive camping ground (no showers) beside a stream.

Nunamara (41.1km) has the last *store* before Launceston. At 52km a sweeping downhill leads to Launceston's suburbs.

Side Trip: Bridestowe Lavender Farm

44.2km return

Near Nabowla, 22km west of Scottsdale, **Bridestowe Lavender Farm** (☎ 6352 8182) is the biggest oil-producing lavender farm in the southern hemisphere and sole source of perfumed lavender outside Europe (open daily September–May). During the spectacular flowering season, mid-December to late January, $3 admission includes an informative guided tour. There are toilets and a kiosk selling refreshments and lavender products.

From Scottsdale visitor centre, head back towards the centre of town for 100m and turn left onto William St, which becomes the undulating B81. After 19.1km, turn right at a sign to Bridestowe Lavender Plantation. This dirt road enters the lavender farm after 3km.

Return via the outward route or, to visit the popular resort of Bridport, turn left 6.8km back towards Scottsdale, onto the rough, dirt Bridport Back Rd (C827), recommended only to fat-tyre riders or those who enjoy dirt roads. Descend for 16km, turning right onto the coastal B82. Follow signs for about 10km to Bridport. Return directly to Scottsdale on the B84.

Launceston

See Launceston (pp218–19) in the Gateway Cities section for information about accommodation and other services.

Tassie's West Coast

Duration	10 days
Distance	669.5km
Difficulty	hard
Start	Evandale
End	Hobart

This is a ride on the wild side of Tasmania. One of the least populous parts of the state, the west coast has some of the most physically demanding terrain and the highest rainfall. Attractions for cyclists include spectacular natural scenery, wildlife, national parks, quiet roads (two sections of which are unsealed), as well as plenty of interesting things to do off the bike.

HISTORY

Archaeological evidence indicates Aborigines inhabited the west coast 20,000 years ago, surviving the Ice age in caves along the Franklin River. European history in the region is inextricably linked with mining. Since the late 19th century, mineral exploitation has taken the area through cycles of boom and bust. Mining has created large towns – Zeehan, Tullah, Rosebery, Strahan and Queenstown – and massive environmental damage (Queenstown's bare, eroded hills are now in themselves a tourist attraction). Though mining continues, populations have dwindled and rainforest is reclaiming territory.

Strahan boomed as a port for Queenstown ore, transported via the Abt Railway (now under reconstruction for tourists). But the town went bust and became a sleepy village – until the blockade of the Franklin River during the 1980s. Protesters against damming the Franklin for hydroelectricity set off from Strahan in boats to stop construction. At the protest's height, in the summer of 1982–3, 1400 people were arrested. But, in a coup for conservationists, the Federal Government eventually overrode the state (paying it millions of dollars in compensation) and the Franklin still runs free.

NATURAL HISTORY

King William Saddle between Queenstown and Derwent Bridge divides Tasmania into two regions contrasting in geology, topography, vegetation and rainfall. East of the saddle, the King William Range's red dolerite crags cap mudstone and sandstone laid down up to 300 million years ago. Typical of mountains rising from the Derwent and Tamar catchments, they support open savanna woodland. Peaks to the west like Frenchmans Cap are mostly ancient quartzite. In the surrounding valleys, cut into schists or limestone between 750 and 370 million years ago, dense rainforest and buttongrass moors dominate the vegetation. Glaciation between 30,000 and 10,000 years ago extended to much lower levels on the west of the divide than on the east.

PLANNING

This ride can also be done as a three-day jaunt to Cradle Mountain National Park (allow at least another day there for walking and sightseeing). See Getting to/from the Ride for transport details.

On the full ride, extra days are recommended at Strahan, Lake St Clair and Mt Field National Park.

This is the place to combine cycling with rafting. For multi-day Franklin River trips, contact Rafting Tasmania (☎ 6239 1080, 🖳 www.view.com.au/raftingtas/) or Tasmanian Expeditions (☎ 6334 3477 or ☎ 1800-030 230, 🖳 www.tas-ex.com/tas-ex/).

When to Ride

The best periods are late October to mid-December and February to mid-April. Winter (and sometimes summer) snows on the highlands and extreme wind/rain on the west coast limit good riding times. January school holidays may make roads busier and fill accommodation. Accommodation in the north is also heavily booked in late October/early November for Deloraine's Craft Fair.

Maps

The Land Information Bureau's Tasmania sheets *North East*, *North West*, *South West* and *South East* (1:250,000) cover the ride.

What to Bring

Be prepared for wet and cold weather even in summer. Waterproofed panniers are recommended.

GETTING TO/FROM THE RIDE

The Tassie's East Coast ride (earlier in this chapter) ends at Launceston, 19.6km northwest of Evandale. Alternatively, follow this ride with the Tassie's East Coast ride, linking to Dunalley from Hobart.

Evandale

The Midland Hwy links Evandale to Launceston airport (4.6km north-west) and Launceston city (19.6km north-west).

Bus Redline (☎ 1300-360 000) runs from Launceston (18 Charles St) to Evandale via the airport ($2.50, plus $10 for the bike, about 30 minutes, twice daily).

Bicycle From Launceston visitor centre, go south-east on St John St, turning right into York St after 300m. After 500m, go left on Wellington St which becomes the Midland Hwy. An 11km moderate uphill follows on a sealed shoulder. At a roundabout (12.9km), veer left following signs to the airport. The airport entry road is at 15km; Evandale visitor centre is 4.6km farther along.

Hobart

See the Getting to/from Tasmania (p215) and Gateway Cities (p220) sections for information on getting to/from Hobart.

Cradle Mountain

Bus TWT TassieLink (☎ 1300-300 520) runs an afternoon service (between December and March) from the visitor centre to Launceston ($36.50, about 3¼ hours) via Devonport ($23.50, about 1½ hours).

Bicycle To reach Launceston, retrace the outward route and use the directions for cycling to Evandale in reverse. To Devonport, head back to Deloraine before riding Day 1 (in reverse) of the Across the Central Plateau ride (earlier in this chapter).

TASMANIA

THE RIDE
Evandale

National Trust-classified Evandale is known to cyclists as the venue for the National Penny Farthing Championships (☎ 6391 8223), part of the February village fair. For the rest of the year, its narrow streets, flanked by 19th-century buildings and cottage gardens, give it the atmosphere of an English village. Penny farthings lean nonchalantly against shop door-ways and murals depict cycling amid a variety of village activities. It's well worth spending at least a night in the town.

Information The visitor centre (☎ 6391 8128), 14 High St, is open from 10am to 3pm. Historic displays include photographs of the village fair and penny farthing races. *Evandale Heritage Walk* ($2) is a guide to the town's main features.

The handsome post office is on the corner of High & Russell Sts.

Things to See & Do Places worth seeing include the brick **water tower**, the two **churches**, and historic houses such as **Solomon House**, **Ingleside** and **Fallgrove**. The **Clarendon Arms Hotel**, built in 1847 and continuously licensed since 1849, has interesting historical murals in its hall.

Off Nile Rd 8km south of Evandale, the National Trust property **Clarendon** (☎ 6398 6220) is one of Australia's grandest Georgian mansions. It is the destination of a penny farthing race during the championships.

Craft galleries on Russell St cater to tourists. **Michael Papas' Tile Creations** (☎ 6391 8031) makes wall and novelty tiles illustrated with Evandale scenes.

A popular **market**, with children's steam train rides, is held every Sunday morning on Logan Rd.

Places to Stay & Eat The nearest place for *camping* is 11km south at Nile cricket oval. With only water and pit toilets, it's free.

At the *Clarendon Arms Hotel* (☎ 6391 8181, 11 Russell St) basic double rooms cost $60. Its dining room serves adequate meaty fare from $10 (except Sunday evening).

Greg & Gill's Place (☎ 6391 8248, 35 Collins St), next to the market site, is a child-friendly establishment with B&B for $75 per double. The elegantly renovated, two-bedroom *Solomon Cottage* (☎ 6391 8331,

1 High St) is a converted bakery which sleeps four. A huge cooked breakfast makes the place good value at $80/105 per single/double. *The Stables* (☎ 6391 8048, 5 Russell St)*, behind the general store, is run by the store proprietors. Modern self-contained units cost $120 per double, including breakfast provisions.

Ingleside Bakery (☎ 6391 8682, 4 Russell St), in the spacious historic council chambers, serves light meals and snacks.

Counter meals are available from the *Prince of Wales Hotel* (☎ 6391 8381, 2 Nile Rd). The only true restaurant in town, the excellent *Russells Restaurant* (☎ 6391 8622, 3 Russell St)* serves main meals from around $18 and lunches for $9 (closed Monday and Tuesday, and Sunday evenings).

Day 1: Evandale to Deloraine

4½–8 hours, 81.1km

The ride begins through open, level grazing country with views to the Great Western Tiers. An English landscape is created by hedgerows lining the quiet, narrow roads. After Bracknell (39.5km), the route heads for the hills and there's a long moderate to steep climb on dirt, eventually reaching a high point just above 600m. The route descends for the final 20km to Deloraine.

Historic **Longford** (18.7km) dominates the plains which originally provided good hunting for the Aborigines. Now the centre of a rich pastoral area watered by the South Esk and Macquarie Rivers, the town has many 19th-century farmhouses and grand estates. Its *cafes*, *food stores* and pleasant central park make it an ideal rest stop.

Tiny Bracknell (39.5km), a convenient lunch stop, has a *pub*, a *general store* and a *takeaway shop*. The town is on the 'Tasmanian Trail', a walking, mountain-biking and horse-riding route across the state (for more information, look up the Web site 🖳 www.tassie.net.au/~kwhite/).

Hills begin as the route skirts the Cluan Tiers beside the Liffey River. *Liffey Valley Tea Gardens* (51km; ☎ 6397 3213 or ☎ 6397 3437), a fernery and tearoom, opens at 11am on weekends and public holidays (November–May). The dirt road starts 2km later.

Beyond a bridge (56.5km) is the access road to **Liffey Falls** lower car park-picnic area, from which a one-hour uphill forest walk leads to the impressive falls. (The

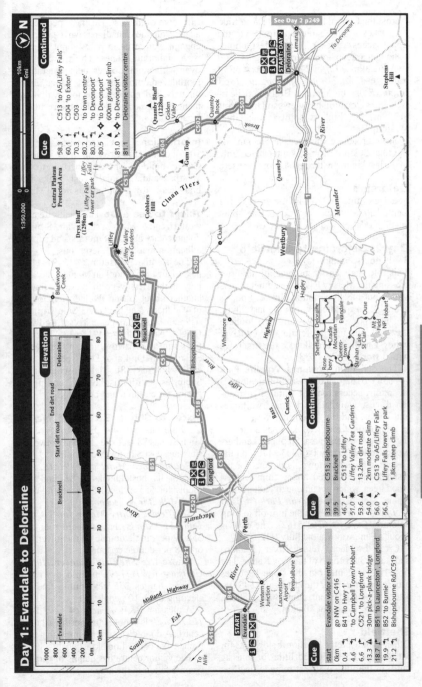

Day 1: Evandale to Deloraine

Elevation

TASMANIA

See Day 2 p249

To Devonport

Cue

58.3		C513 'to A5/Liffey Falls'
60.1		C504 'to Exton'
70.3		C503
80.2		'to town centre'
80.3		'to Devonport'
80.5		600m gradual climb
81.0		'to Devonport'
81.1		Deloraine visitor centre

Central Plateau Protected Area

Drys Bluff (1298m) ▲

Liffey Falls lower car park

Liffey Valley Tea Gardens

Liffey

Cobblers Hill ▲

Cluan Tiers

Gum Top ▲

Quamby Bluff (1228m) ▲
Golden Valley

Quamby Brook

Deloraine
START DAY 2

Lemana
To Devonport

Stephens Hill ▲

Bracknell

Bishopsbourne

Cluan

Westbury

Hagley

Whitemore

Highway

Carrick

Exton

Quamby

Brook

River

Meander

Blackwood Creek

Longford

Perth

Macquarie

Western Junction

Launceston Airport
Breadalbane

START
Evandale

Midland Highway

River

Esk

South

To Nile

Roseberry
Sheffield • Cradle Mountain • Deloraine • Evandale
Queens-town • Ouse
Strahan • Lake St Clair • Mt Field NP • Hobart

Cue

33.4		C513: Bishopsbourne
39.5		Bracknell
46.7		C513 'to Liffey'
51.0		Liffey Valley Tea Gardens
53.6		13.2km dirt road
54.0		2km moderate climb
56.0		C513 'to A5/Liffey Falls'
56.5		Liffey Falls lower car park
		1.8km steep climb

Continued

Cue

start		Evandale visitor centre
0km		go NW on C416
0.4		B41 'to Hwy 1'
4.6		'to Campbell Town/Hobart'
6.6		C521 'to Longford'
13.3		30m pick-a-plank bridge
18.7		B51 'to Launceston', Longford
19.9		B52 'to Burnie'
21.2		Bishopsbourne Rd/C519

1:350,000

0   10km
0   6mi

N

Continued

Across the Central Plateau ride's Day 2 Side Trip takes a more strenuous route via the upper access track.) The hardest climb, 1.8km on a steep, loose surface, begins here.

At 61.3km is *Liffey Falls Lodge* (☎ 6369 5363, e liffall@southcom.com.au, 1363 Bogan Rd). This modern B&B in a near-wilderness location has views to Drys Bluff (1298m), the highest point in the Great Western Tiers.

Sealed road recommences at 66.8km and the final 20km downhill is interrupted only in the last kilometre through Deloraine itself.

Deloraine

See Deloraine (p223) in the Across the Central Plateau ride for information about accommodation and other services.

Day 2: Deloraine to Sheffield
3–5½ hours, 53.8km

This ride starts easily, but gets hillier after crossing the Mersey River. The quiet road is sealed but has three tough climbs. Food is available en route but not in the last 30km.

The striking Great Western Tiers loom to the south, through the fertile Mersey River valley. Chudleigh (16.4km) is the first town with a *store* (☎ 6363 6138).

The delightful **Trowunna Wildlife Park** (☎ 6363 6162; 19.6km) is 400m along a steep, dirt access road. It features Tasmanian devils, wombats, echidnas, wallabies and koalas, and runs nocturnal tours.

Little **Mole Creek** (23.6km) has a surprisingly large business area. **Stephens Leatherwood Honey Factory** (☎ 6363 1170), on the eastern approach to town, is famous for the distinctively flavoured honey from leatherwood trees, which are unique to western Tasmania. *Mole Creek Caravan Park* (☎ 6363 1150) is 4.4km farther, at the turn-off to **King Solomon Cave** (☎ 6363 5182). The cave is about 14km away via the hilly B12.

Cross the black Mersey River (33.8km) and start a 3km climb of the Gog Range. The first 1km is gentle but the slope becomes gruesomely steep for the last 2km. At 43km, after a winding descent, climb 80m in 800m. A third slog begins at 50.6km.

Sheffield

Other than a pretty location below 1234m Mt Roland, Sheffield had little for tourists until, in the mid-1980s, it remade itself as 'the town of murals'. Business people took a lead from the Canadian town, Chemainus, engaging an artist to paint about 30 walls with elaborate scenes. The trend carried over with mural scenes being lucratively reproduced onto souvenirs – which, unfortunately, did not translate to royalty payments for the original artist; the result was legal action in 2000.

Information The visitor centre (☎ 6491 1036), on Pioneer Crescent in the Bluegum Gallery building, opens from 10am to 4pm. Westpac and Colonial Trust banks have branches in town but there is no ATM.

Things to See & Do The theatrette at the western end of Main St shows an 18-minute documentary about the **murals**, and supplies a location map with descriptions.

The **Kentish Museum** (☎ 6491 1180), next to the high school on Main St, has a display on the Mersey-Forth hydro scheme and another about Gustav Weindorfer, founder of Waldheim (see the Day 3 Side Trip).

Steam fans can get a fix at **Redwater Creek Steam Rail** (☎ 6491 1613). Locomotives run on a narrow track at the eastern end of town. On Labor Day weekend at the end of February, Sheffield hosts an annual Steamfest, with displays of equipment, games for children and craft stalls.

Places to Stay & Eat Central *Sheffield Caravan Park* (☎ 6491 2364, Albert St), off High St, has $8 tent sites for one or two; on-site vans cost $25 for two people.

Roland Rock Motel (☎ 6491 1821, 47 Main St) has hostel bunks for $17 and motel rooms for $55 a double; it's behind *Sheffield Milk Bar & Tearoom*.

Sheffield Country Motor Inn (☎ 6491 1800, 51 Main St) has standard rooms for $58/82 per single/double on the lower level or $68 per double upstairs.

Smoke-free *Sheffield Pioneer Holiday Units* (☎ 6491 1149), behind the visitor centre, charges $75 per double for units sleeping up to 10 people.

A pleasant B&B, *Acacia* (☎ 6491 2482, 113 High St) is about 800m north-east of the centre. A double en suite room with a comprehensive cooked breakfast costs $80.

The visitor centre has details of rural accommodation in the area.

Day 2: Deloraine to Sheffield

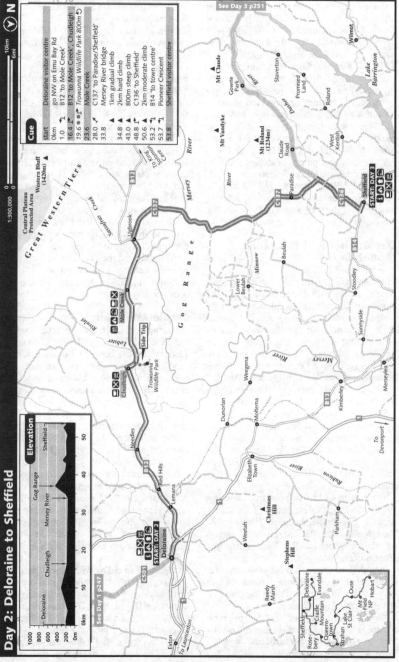

Cue

0km		Deloraine visitor centre
		go NW on Emu Bay Rd
1.0		B12 'to Mole Creek'
16.4		B12 'to Mole Creek'; Chudleigh
19.6		Trowunna Wildlife Park 800m ↺
23.6		Mole Creek
28.0		C137 'to Paradise/Sheffield'
33.8		Mersey River bridge
34.8		1km gradual climb
43.0		800m steep climb
48.8		C136 'to Sheffield'
50.6		2km moderate climb
53.2		B14 'to town centre'
53.7		Pioneer Crescent
53.8		Sheffield visitor centre

See Day 3 p251

See Day 1 p247

Elevation

TASMANIA

Sam's Cut Price Supermarket (59 Main St) is opposite Murray's. *Binny's Food Store & Tobacconist (☎ 6491 1709, 76 Main St)* offers country fried chicken. The Irish-style *Red Rose Cafe (☎ 6491 1866, 49 Main St)* is open for lunch and dinner.

For years, Sheffield's most famous eating place was Flo's Country Kitchen, established by former Queensland senator, Florence Bjelke-Petersen, whose husband, Sir Joh, was a controversial Queensland premier. It's now *Murray's Scottish Scone Shop (☎ 6491 1077, cnr Main St & Pioneer Crescent)* but pumpkin scones and Joh-and-Flo memorabilia still feature.

Sheffield Hotel (☎ 6491 1130, Main St), 100m west of High St, serves counter lunches and dinners with meaty mains for around $11.

Day 3: Sheffield to Cradle Mountain

3½–6 hours, 57.2km

The route, all sealed and very lightly trafficked, heads into superb forests on the slopes of the central highlands and into world-renowned Cradle Mountain National Park. The pattern of previous days continues: starting easily, getting harder – much harder, in this case. At first flat-to-gently-undulating, the road passes pleasant farms beneath sentinel-like Mt Roland. Climbing begins at Gowrie Park (15.5km) and continues after Lake Cethana (24.8km) with a 5.5km grind. Beyond Moina gradients ease but the upward trend continues.

Food is available at both tiny towns en route and near the Cradle Mountain National Park entrance, but the budget conscious would be well advised to stock up at Sheffield.

Gowrie Park (15.5km) has free *camping* (water, toilets, tables, shed) at its sports ground. The rustic, licensed *Weindorfers Restaurant (☎ 6491 1385)* is well signed off the road behind *Mt Roland Budget Backpackers*.

At 20.7km, the road reaches 400m after a 2km winding climb through forest, before losing 250m in switchbacks to the dammed River Forth's Lake Cethana.

On a hot day, the shadeless 5.5km climb to **Moina** (30.3km; 530m) is tough. The village *guesthouse and tearooms (☎ 6492 1318)* serve takeaway food.

Undulating across the Middlesex Plains, the route reaches 790m at the turn-off to Cradle Mountain (51.7km). Most supply and accommodation options are around the 55km mark, before the visitor centre.

Side Trip: Waldheim and Dove Lake
15km return

A trip to Waldheim and Dove Lake – for the famous postcard views of Cradle Mountain – is practically imperative.

Waldheim (forest home) was the name Austrian Gustav Weindorfer gave to the chalet in which he lived from 1916. It now refers to the locality, 500m along a rugged dirt road, where the chalet (rebuilt after fire) has been joined by eight bushwalkers huts (see Places to Stay).

The road is unsealed from the visitor centre to the Waldheim turn-off (5km) and continues on dirt to Dove Lake.

Walks around the lake and beyond leave from the car park and Waldheim.

Return to the visitor centre via the outward route.

Cradle Mountain

Towering over Dove Lake, spectacular Cradle Mountain (1545m) lends its name to Tasmania's best known wild place, Cradle Mountain-Lake St Clair National Park. The park, one of Australia's most glaciated areas, stretches from the Great Western Tiers in the north to Derwent Bridge in the south. Containing deep gorges, lakes, tarns and wild open moorland, it owes its preservation to Gustav Weindorfer, who fell in love with and lived in the area.

Information At the northern park boundary, beside a rainforest boardwalk, the visitor centre and ranger station (☎ 6492 1110) opens year-round (until 7pm in summer) and has good static and audio-visual displays. Rangers can advise on weather conditions, walking gear, bush safety and bush etiquette.

Things to See & Do With many signed and well-defined tracks, **walking** is the area's main activity. Most walks start from Waldheim (see Day 3 Side Trip) and maps are available at the visitor centre. The famous **Overland Track** from Waldheim to Lake St Clair's Cynthia Bay takes self-sufficient walkers about five days, though detours, for

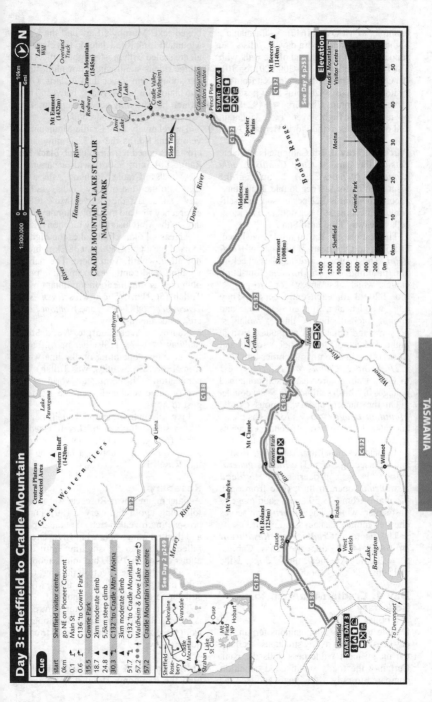

Day 3: Sheffield to Cradle Mountain

Cue

start		Sheffield visitor centre
0km		go NE on Pioneer Crescent
0.1	↰	Main St
0.6	↱	C136 'to Gowrie Park'
15.5	▲	Gowrie Park
18.7	▲	2km moderate climb
24.8	▲	5.5km steep climb
30.3	↰	C132 'to Cradle Mtn', Moina
	▲	3km moderate climb
51.7	↰	C132 'to Cradle Mountain'
57.2 ●●●	↰	Waldheim & Dove Lake 15km ↺
57.2		Cradle Mountain visitor centre

TASMANIA

Elevation

See Day 2 p249

START: DAY 3

See Day 4 p253

START: DAY 4

Cradle Mountain Visitor Centre

example, to Mt Ossa (1617m) – Tasmania's highest peak – adds extra days. Cyclists can send a bike to the other end of the walk with TWT TassieLink (☎ 1300-300 520) for $10. An Overland Track Information Kit from the visitor centre costs $20 (plus $5 if posted).

Seair Adventure Charters (☎ 6492 1132) operates **scenic flights** over Cradle Mountain and other places in the World Heritage Area.

Places to Stay & Eat Camping is available outside the park at *Cosy Cabins Cradle Mountain* (☎ *6492 1395*), 2.5km from the visitor centre, for $10 per double. Bunkhouse accommodation is $22 per person, and self-contained cabins $90 per double. The kiosk sells takeaway food until 8pm.

The best place to stay, if fully provisioned, is 5.5km into the heart of the park at *Waldheim*. The visitor centre handles check-in and bookings for comfortable four-bunk cabins, which cost $60.50 for two people, plus $20.90 for each extra person. They have wood heater, kitchen, gas stove and cooking utensils, but no linen. (Wallabies, possums and other wild marauders visit at night, so keep *all* food inside.) Toilets and showers are in a nearby amenities block.

Highlanders Cabins (☎ *6492 1116*), next to Cosy Cabins, are rustic, self-contained cottages in a bush setting from $90 a double.

On the park boundary, famous *Cradle Mountain Lodge* (☎ *6492 1303*) has pleasant but undistinguished self-contained cabins from $186 per double. It has good facilities and organises abseiling, canoeing, fishing and sightseeing tours. The lodge's *general store* sells basic groceries. Its *Highland Restaurant*, open to the public from 6pm, has mains from $18.50 and a good range of Tasmanian wines. The *Tavern Bar* serves cheaper, mundane snacks and meals.

The licensed *Cradle View Restaurant* (☎ *6492 1400*), opposite Cosy Cabins, serves home-style meals until 7.30pm daily, and sells takeaway food.

Day 4: Cradle Mountain to Rosebery

4–7 hours, 71.4km

Despite traversing mountainous terrain, the day does not seem overly strenuous – perhaps the magnificent wilderness dulls the pain. Certainly the roads are in good condition compared to only a few years ago (see the

boxed text 'Murphy's Law and the Cradle Mountain Link Road' later in this chapter) – all are sealed with mostly light traffic. Overall the ride is significantly downhill, finishing about 750m lower than it starts. Of the two major climbs, Mt Black, between Tullah (which has the only services en route) and Rosebery, is the more strenuous.

The relatively new Cradle Mountain Development Rd, as the C132 is now called, crosses exposed terrain to climb **Black Bluff Range** (14.5km; 930m) with a panoramic view back to Cradle Mountain. After a descent onto the First of May Plains, gradients stay gentle past the Hellyer Mine (28km; emergency first aid available Monday to Friday) to the Murchison Hwy junction (32km).

An easy 4.6km climb takes the highway to its highest point, 690m at 38.2km, but it's not all downhill from there. The narrow, winding road continues to undulate before plummeting into the former mining town of Tullah (56.1km). The town's *Bush Nook Tearoom* (☎ *6473 4252*) and *Wombat Lodge* are beside the highway.

Nearby is **Wee Georgie Wood Steam Railway** (☎ 6473 4289 after 6pm), named for an engine operating on the line which, from 1908 to the 1960s, was Tullah's sole connection with the outside world. It runs two or three weekends a month from August to April.

Five kilometres beyond Tullah, begin a 4.4km steep climb of thickly forested Mt Black (66.2km) – you'll reach 355m on the 929m mountain – before a headlong dive into Rosebery.

Rosebery

Another mining town, Rosebery was founded following a gold discovery in 1891. Further prospecting revealed rich sulphide deposits and the first mines opened in 1896. Ore was railed to Zeehan for smelting until operations closed in 1913, but mines reopened in 1936 when the Electrolytic Zinc Company built a new mill in the town. Mining still supports the town's economy.

There is no official visitor centre. On Agnes St, the Colonial Trust Bank operates from the post office, and the ANZ from the newsagency.

Things to See & Do The high school, behind the Plandome Hotel, has interesting

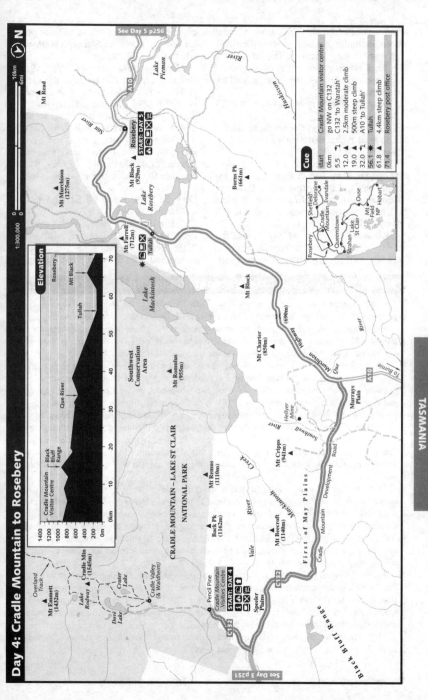

Day 4: Cradle Mountain to Rosebery

Cue

start	0km	Cradle Mountain visitor centre
	5.5	go NW on C132
	12.0	C132 to Waratah'
	19.0	2.5km moderate climb
	32.0	500m steep climb
	56.1	A10 'to Tullah'
	61.8	Tullah
	71.4	4.4km steep climb
		Rosebery post office

Elevation

TASMANIA

remnants from the old mines along its front fence, including a water wheel and railway carriage for steep inclines. The school also houses a **mining museum** displaying artefacts and old photos – ask at the school office to visit it.

Two-hour **Rosebery Mine Tours** (☎ 6473 1247) run daily.

The picnic area on the southern side of the town is the start of a **walk** along the Stitt River.

Places to Stay & Eat With views of the mountains and the nearby mine, *Rosebery Caravan Park* (☎ 6473 1366, Park Rd) has $11 tent sites, on-site vans for $30, and $60 cabins, all for two people.

Plandome Hotel (☎ 6473 1351), in the middle of town, has reasonable rooms at $27.50/41.80 for one/two people, and self-

contained units sleeping up to three people for $63.80. It houses *Shanny's Restaurant* which serves $12 steaks.

Miss Murchison (☎ 6473 1366, 2 Park Rd) is a six-bed cottage near the caravan park, charging $65 a double. *Miners Cottage* (☎ 6473 1796, Karlson St) charges $90 a double, with breakfast provisions included, or $55 for a flat with two single beds.

A number of *snack bars* and *general stores* on the main street serve takeaways. *Rosebery Cake Shop* (☎ 6473 1329) is at the entrance to town on the left – brake hard.

Day 5: Rosebery to Strahan
4–7 hours, 72.4km

This is a ride to be savoured. It's relatively easy, but traverses isolated, wild terrain. After Zeehan, it's as near flat and traffic-free as is possible on the west coast. Three short

---

Murphy's Law & the Cradle Mountain Link Rd

The 'link road' as it was originally called, from Cradle Mountain to the Murchison Hwy, was completed in 1988, creating a convenient short cut for cyclists. But some of us couldn't wait.

In February 1986, when the road was a muddy construction site between Cradle Mountain and the Black Bluff Range – and little more than a line of surveyors' pegs after that – my wife, Alethea, and I became the first cyclists (we reckon) to use the 'road'. It was a nightmare.

Days of heavy rain and massive earthmoving equipment had churned the surface to treacle into which bikes simply sank. The workmen we met were not optimistic about our chances; somewhere between Buckley's and none was the consensus. And, they said, we were certain to get hopelessly lost in the labyrinth of 'pulp' roads if we made it past where construction ended. Armed with our naive sense of pioneering adventure and a vague map, we would not be deterred. Besides, turning back now would seem a cowardly admission of defeat and we'd still have to slog back through mud.

Our decision appeared vindicated – the road soon improved, along with the capricious weather. The pulp roads, so called because of the imminent fate of the beautiful forests they traversed, proved firm and rideable. They just didn't agree with our map. The solution was to follow the power lines westwards.

Fine...until we ran into a swamp, unable to reach the road on the other side. Sudden rain swept over us as we procrastinated, then back-tracked to the previous intersection. At another unbridged waterway, the discovery of a well-used road nearby led us to believe we were out of trouble – until it swung north for undulating kilometres, through dripping, primeval, apparently deserted forest. 'Who'd be out here in this lousy weather?' I thought. 'Oh, the driver of that approaching utility is!' Unable to accept a lift (our bikes wouldn't fit), we at least found – to our amazement – that we were going the right way after all.

Excited, I shot off while Alethea, unable to keep up, watched me disappear into a curtain of drizzle. On a rocky descent, an ominous rattling brought her to a shuddering halt. Somewhere on the slope behind lay the rack bolts which, on abandoning their posts, had allowed her pannier rack to collapse into her cluster. Unfortunately, I was carrying the spares and tools – though even had she any, her freezing fingers rendered her incapable of using them.

I found her eventually. Both of us (even the marriage) survived. We have never been so wet, dirty or tired after a day of cycle touring. But it was great!

Neil Irvine

climbs, two of them steep, punctuate the first third of the ride but, after leaving the highway, there are just two moderate climbs in 49km. After Henty River, rainforest forms a tunnel for the road. Zeehan, the only town en route, is a convenient lunch stop. The final 20km meanders easily through forest thick with flowering ti-tree and bottlebrush.

The first steep climb emerges from forest at the operating **Renison Bell tin mine** (11.7km), which revitalised the Zeehan economy when it reopened in the late 1960s. The next steep section ends at the mine boundary, the subsequent downhill arriving at the highway's junction with the B27 (23.6km).

Zeehan (28.4km) was founded in the 1880s around rich silver and lead deposits and grew rapidly. By 1900 it boasted a population of 8000, 26 hotels and a 1000-seat theatre. By 1960, the major mines had closed.

The town, population now about 1100, has *supermarkets* and *tearooms* off-route near the historic part of town. The excellent **West Coast Pioneers' Memorial Museum** (☎ 6471 6225) is in the 1894 School of Mines building on Main St. Entry fees ($5) go to restore the **Grand Hotel-Gaiety Theatre** building farther along Main St. When opened in 1899, the Gaiety was one of the biggest, most modern theatres in the world. The West Coast Heritage Authority intends to restore the town's other historic buildings, including the **post office** (still in use), the **old bank** and **St Luke's Church**.

Skirting Mt Zeehan (702m), the road stays flat or descends gently through sparsely treed country. A moderate climb over the Professor Range (40.8km) precedes another to a **lookout** (52km). On a clear day, the views extend to the restless Southern Ocean.

Strahan

Since shooting to prominence in the 1980s as the centre for protest against proposed hydroelectricity dams on the Gordon and Franklin Rivers, spectacularly located Strahan has developed its tourist potential. As a base for cruises on vast Macquarie Harbour, it is now reputedly the state's second most popular tourist destination after Port Arthur.

Information The visitor centre (☎ 6471 7488) is on the Esplanade, 200m west of the town centre. The post office and a PWS office (☎ 6471 7122) are in the Customs House building, 100m further west. The newsagency is an ANZ agency. Eftpos is available, but there's no ATM.

Things to See & Do The visitor centre's museum, **West Coast Reflections**, displays all aspects of south-west Tasmanian history, including the Franklin River issue. Outside, a covered amphitheatre often hosts live performances. The imposing **Customs House** is probably the west coast's finest old building.

Spectacular **Water Tower Hill lookout** is less than 1km walk or ride from the village along Esk and Tamar Sts. Swim at sandy **West Strahan Beach** near the caravan park.

Cruises leave Strahan wharf daily. Gordon River Cruises (☎ 6471 7187) runs half- or full-day trips to Sarah Island and up the Gordon River to Heritage Landing. Family-run World Heritage Cruises (☎ 6471 7174) takes six-hour cruises to Sarah Island, Hell's Gates (Macquarie Harbour's entrance) and Heritage Landing.

West Coast Yacht Charters (☎ 6471 7280) makes two-night **sailing trips** up the Gordon River. For those with less time, 80-minute **seaplane flights** with Wilderness Air (☎ 6471 7280) leave the wharf from 9am daily to fly up the Gordon, setting down for a rainforest walk before returning over Sarah Island and Cape Sorell.

Places to Stay Advance booking is essential in summer. Much of the accommodation in the town centre can be booked through the Strahan Village reservation office (☎ 6471 7191), corner of the Esplanade and Esk St. Some other accommodation, including the hostel, is handled by Strahan Central (☎ 6471 7612), on the corner of the Esplanade and Harold St.

Unexciting *West Strahan Caravan Park* (☎ 6471 7239) charges $14 a double for tent sites.

Strahan Youth Hostel (☎ 6471 7612, Harvey St), a 10-minute walk from the town centre, charges $18 for YHA members. Twin rooms cost $46 and tiny cabins are $47 per double.

Strahan Cape Horn Accommodation (☎ 6471 7169, Frazer St), scenically perched above Strahan Point, is an easy walk from town. The plain, comfortable self-contained unit costs $65/85 per single/double. *Strahan Inn* (☎ 6471 7191), managed by Strahan

TASMANIA

Days 5 & 6: Rosebery – Strahan – Queenstown

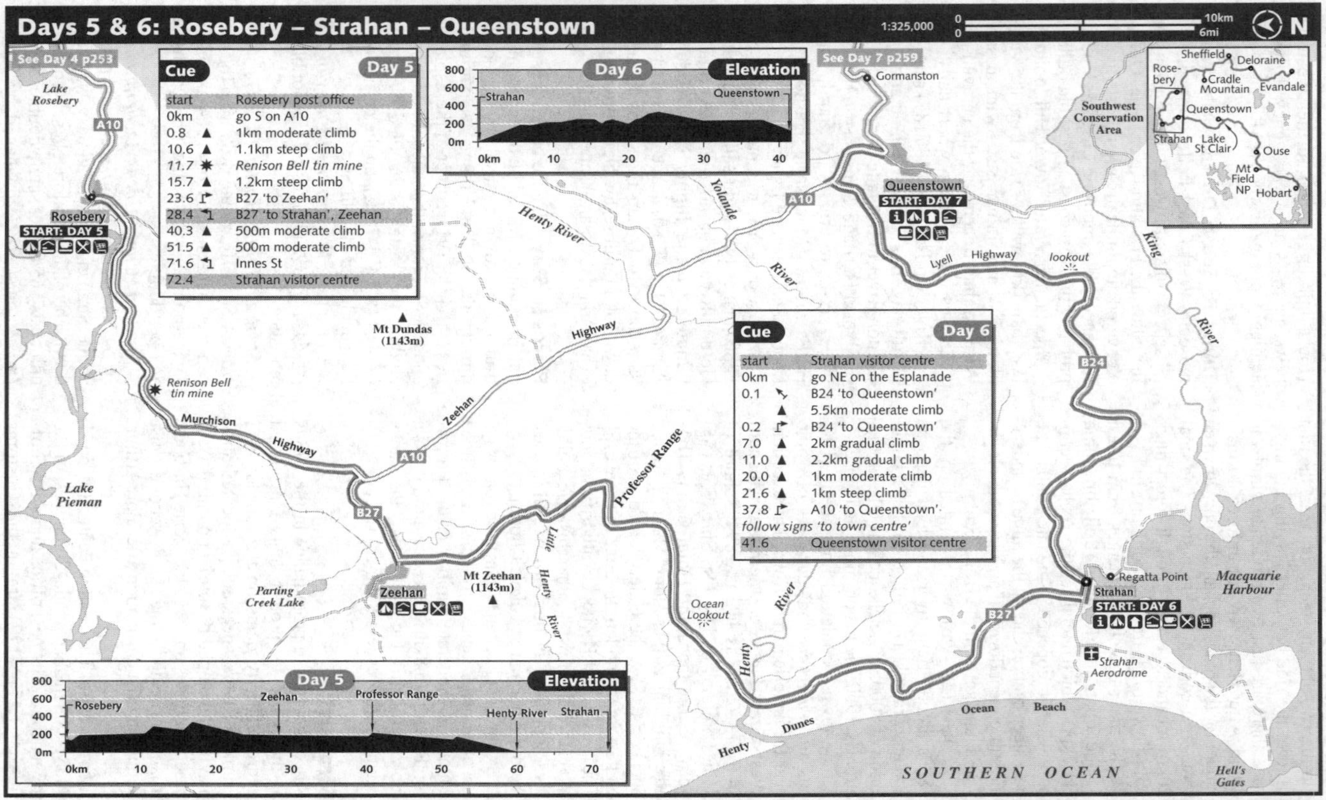
1:325,000
0 10km
0 6mi
N
See Day 4 p253
See Day 7 p259
Lake Rosebery
A10
Rosebery
START: DAY 5
Renison Bell tin mine
Murchison
Highway
Zeehan
Highway
A10
B27
Mt Dundas (1143m)
Henty River
Yolande
River
Gormanston
Queenstown
START: DAY 7
Lyell
Highway
lookout
King
River
B24
Southwest Conservation Area
Lake Pieman
Parting Creek Lake
Zeehan
Mt Zeehan (1143m)
Little
Henty
River
Professor Range
Ocean Lookout
Henty
River
Henty
Dunes
Ocean
Beach
SOUTHERN OCEAN
Hell's Gates
B27
Regatta Point
Strahan
START: DAY 6
Strahan Aerodrome
Macquarie Harbour
Sheffield
Deloraine
Rose-bery
Cradle Mountain
Evandale
Queenstown
Strahan
Lake St Clair
Ouse
Mt Field NP
Hobart
Day 6
Elevation
800
600
400
200
0m
Strahan
Queenstown
0km
10
20
30
40
Day 5
Elevation
800
600
400
200
0m
Rosebery
Zeehan
Professor Range
Henty River
Strahan
0km
10
20
30
40
50
60
70

Cue — Day 5

start		Rosebery post office
0km		go S on A10
0.8	▲	1km moderate climb
10.6	▲	1.1km steep climb
11.7	✷	*Renison Bell tin mine*
15.7	▲	1.2km steep climb
23.6	↱	B27 'to Zeehan'
28.4	↰	B27 'to Strahan', Zeehan
40.3	▲	500m moderate climb
51.5	▲	500m moderate climb
71.6	↰	Innes St
72.4		Strahan visitor centre

Cue — Day 6

start		Strahan visitor centre
0km		go NE on the Esplanade
0.1	↖	B24 'to Queenstown'
	▲	5.5km moderate climb
0.2	↱	B24 'to Queenstown'
7.0	▲	2km gradual climb
11.0	▲	2.2km gradual climb
20.0	▲	1km moderate climb
21.6	▲	1km steep climb
37.8	↱	A10 'to Queenstown'
follow signs 'to town centre'		
41.6		Queenstown visitor centre

Tasmania's Great Western Tiers.

The 300m-high granite Hazards dominate the Coles Bay skyline.

Studying the map outside Bishopbourne, near Bracknell.

Conquer Mt Wellington, Hobart.

Visit historic Port Arthur, Tasmania's famous penal colony site, on the Across the Central Plateau ride.

The spectacular 40m Russell Falls in Mt Field National Park.

Queenstown's stark mining landscape.   Mt Roland looms above the road to Sheffield from Paradise.

Combine walking with cycling in Tasmania's spectacular Cradle Mountain–Lake St Clair National Park.

Village, is on a hill and many of its rooms, priced from $92 per double, have harbour views (from $72 with shared facilities).

Harbour Views (☎ 6471 7143, cnr Charles St & Lyell Hwy), nearly 1km out of town, offers B&B from $70 per double with en suite.

In the top price bracket, B&B at luxurious 1899 *Ormiston House* (☎ 6471 7077 or ☎ 1800-634 663, the Esplanade), towards West Strahan Beach, starts at $185 (double).

Places to Eat Most places are in the strip of shops across from the harbour shore. There's a *Riteway* supermarket and *Strahan Bakery*, open from 7.30am to 8pm, serving pizza and pasta after 5.30pm. *Strahan Fresh Seafood* (☎ 6471 7209) sells fish and chips from $7. *Hamers Hotel* (☎ 6471 7191) serves breakfast, lunch and dinner, with mains from $11.

Day 6: Strahan to Queenstown
2½–4 hours, 41.6km

While it's not far to Queenstown, it *is* hilly as the road winds up onto a ridge separating the north-west-flowing tributaries of the Henty River from the south-flowing tributaries of the King. The heavily forested route is lightly trafficked outside school holiday times. A high point at about halfway offers fine views of Queenstown's denuded hills. There are no services from start to finish.

The first climb, from the centre of Strahan, continues at a moderate grade for 5.5km. Climbing continues fairly easily until 13km, from where the road undulates gently before the last steep climb (21.6km). At 23km, pull into the gravel car park on the right for **views** of Queenstown's yellow, white and purplish-orange rocky hills poking above an otherwise all-pervading green carpet.

Queenstown

With nearly 3400 people, Queenstown is the west coast's largest town. It is famous for (and proud of) its bare, multicoloured hills. First gold extraction, then copper and silver mining powered the area's economy. Copper smelting began in 1895 and, by 1900, Queenstown was Tasmania's third largest town, with 28 mining companies and 11 smelting furnaces.

By the 1920s, the surrounding rain-forested hills had been stripped of three million tonnes of timber to feed the furnaces,

while uncontrolled pollution from smelters killed what little vegetation hadn't been cut. Bushfires wiped out regrowth and the rain washed away the topsoil, leaving bare rocks.

Since the smelters closed in 1969, slow natural scrub recolonisation has begun. The landscape is becoming less stark, but some townsfolk worry this will reduce tourism.

Information The visitor centre is Lyell Tours (☎ 6471 2388) in the basement of the Empire Hotel, corner Driffield and Orr Sts. Colonial Trust Bank is on Orr St opposite the post office. There is no ATM.

Things to See & Do The visitor centre supplies an attractive free brochure, *Walk-about Queenstown*, showing the way to 30 points of interest.

High on a Queenstown 'to do' list, according to the visitor centre, should be an underground **mine tour** – a 3½ hour, 340m-deep odyssey into a working copper mine ($50) – which, it is claimed, only one other mine in the world conducts. If going underground doesn't appeal, try the $13.20, hourlong surface tours of the 105-year-old Mt Lyell mine. Book at the visitor centre.

The **chairlift** (☎ 6471 2338) beside Penghana Rd, built on the site of a former aerial ropeway to the smelters, rises 369m up the valley to a viewing platform. From here, short walks lead to old mine sites.

The Miner's Siding park on the site of the former train station features a restored **Abt steam locomotive**.

Bushwalking and **prospecting** are also popular. Ask the visitor centre for details.

Places to Stay The cramped and gravelly *Queenstown Cabin & Tourist Park* (☎ 6471 1332, 17 Grafton St), about 1km south of town, has unappealing tent sites for $8/12 for one/two people, hostel accommodation for $20/27, on-site vans for $27/33, and self-contained cabins with linen for $50/60.

Alternative *camping* is at Linda (see Day 7), 7.6km east of Queenstown, beside the *Royal Hotel Restoration Tearooms* (☎ 6471 1441). Only water and toilets are available and the cost is a donation to the restoration of the historic hotel. The tearooms' proximity is a bonus.

On the approach to Queenstown, *Mountain View Holiday Lodge* (☎ 6471 1163,

TASMANIA

1 Penghana Rd) has backpacker accommodation in two-bed rooms for $14 per person. Four-share rooms with en suite, TV and kitchen are $14 per person.

The lovely old *Empire Hotel (☎ 6471 1699, 2 Orr St)* has a superb National Trust-classified blackwood staircase in its foyer. Clean, comfortable singles/doubles cost $25/40 with shared facilities, or $50 for a double with en suite. Sometimes backpacker accommodation at $15/20 is available; ring to check. Meals are served in the dining room.

Centrally located but unattractive, *Mt Lyell Motor Inn (☎ 6471 1888, 1 Orr St)* has basic suites for $44/50 and serves meals. Uphill on the corner of Bowe St, *Queenstown Motor Lodge (☎ 6471 1866, 54 Orr St)* has small rooms for $60/72 while *Silver Hills Motor Inn (☎ 6471 1755)* has traditional units with views for $80.80/88. Its *Smelters Restaurant*, probably the most expensive in town, has mains from $13.50 or a set three-course menu for $27.50.

The priciest option is *Penghana Guesthouse (☎ 6471 2560)*, former residence of the geological manager of Mt Lyell Mining. It stands grandly above town on the western side of the river off Preston St. B&B costs $110 per double.

Places to Eat Self-caterers can buy supplies at *Riteway* supermarket (*Orr St*). *JJ's Coffee Lounge (☎ 6471 1793, 13 Orr St)* serves tasty light meals. For a fresh cake feast, call at the *Mixing Bowl Bakery (☎ 6471 1526, Batchelor St)*. *Axel's Takeaway (☎ 6471 1834, 7 Orr St)*, famed for its monster burgers, also serves cakes and light snacks. *Filis Pizza (☎ 6471 2661, 21 Orr St)* has takeaway pizzas from $10.

Day 7: Queenstown to Lake St Clair
5–9½ hours, 92.1km

More than half of Day 7 is through magnificent World Heritage Area. It's packed with climbing, though after an early steep grind most of it is moderate. There are walking opportunities in the wilderness around Franklin River, plus lookouts to famous peaks such as Frenchmans Cap and fascinating geological features at King William Saddle.

Great views unfold as the quiet highway winds up and around Queenstown's bare hills. Life is returning to the ghost town of **Linda** (7.6km). The *Royal Hotel Restoration Tearooms (☎ 6471 1441)* provide welcome refreshment and, by 2004, the proprietors hope to offer accommodation in the hotel, relic of a once bustling town.

Beyond Bradshaw Bridge (18km), the terrain is hillier with more trees. At 25km the **World Heritage Area** begins.

A 20-minute return walk to **Nelson Falls** (27.8km) starts at the base of the climb up forested Victoria Pass (31.9km; 530m). A PWS *camping ground* on the Collingwood River (48.4km) is shortly before moderate-to-steep Donaghy's Hill. The 40-minute return Donaghy's Hill Wilderness Walk (52.2km) goes to a lookout over the south-west wilderness.

At 55km, the white peak of **Frenchmans Cap** (1445m) appears on the right, about 2km before the multi-day walking trail to the mountain starts.

On the right at the **Franklin River** crossing (61.2km) is a nature trail and picnic area.

The climb of **King William Saddle**, the geological divide between east and west Tasmania, begins at 62.5km. After 5.9km, views are complemented by a **geological history plaque**. Atop the **saddle** (70.8km; 805m), another interpretive panel describes the south-west wilderness.

Descending gently, and leaving the World Heritage Area at 79.4km, the highway has lost only 95m by Derwent Bridge (86.4km). The final 5km, beside the broad, shallow River Derwent, are barely noticeably uphill.

Lake St Clair
Australia's deepest natural freshwater lake is at the southern boundary of the Cradle Mountain-Lake St Clair National Park, and of the Overland (walking) Track. Accommodation and other services are on the shore of Cynthia Bay, at the lake's southern end.

Information The large visitor centre and ranger station (☎ 6289 1115) has walking maps and informative, interactive displays on the park and wildlife. There's plenty to entertain kids on a wet day.

Things to See & Do The main activity is **walking**. Besides the Overland Track to Cradle Mountain, there are many shorter well-marked trails. A one-hour walk to

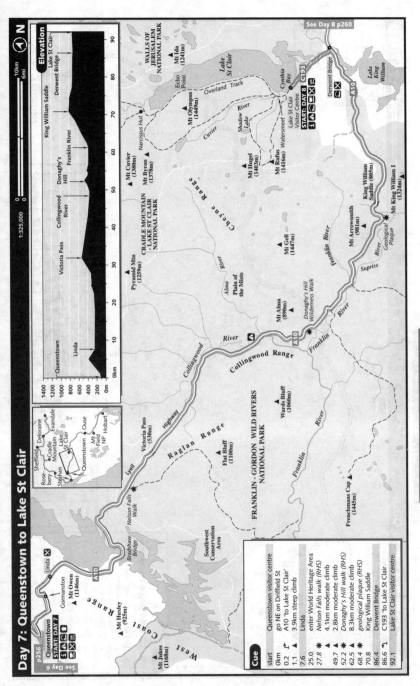

Day 7: Queenstown to Lake St Clair

See Day 6 p256

Elevation

	Cue
start	Queenstown visitor centre
0km	go NE on Driffield St
0.2	A10 'to Lake St Clair'
1.1	3.9km steep climb
7.6	Linda
25.0	enter World Heritage Area
27.8	Nelson Falls walk (RHS)
49.7	4.1km moderate climb
52.2	2.8km moderate climb
62.5	Donaghy's Hill walk (RHS)
68.4	8.3km moderate climb
70.8	geological plaque (RHS)
86.4	King William Saddle
86.6	Derwent Bridge
92.1	C193 'to Lake St Clair'
	Lake St Clair visitor centre

See Day 8 p260

START: DAY 7 Queenstown

START: DAY 8 Lake St Clair Visitor Centre

TASMANIA

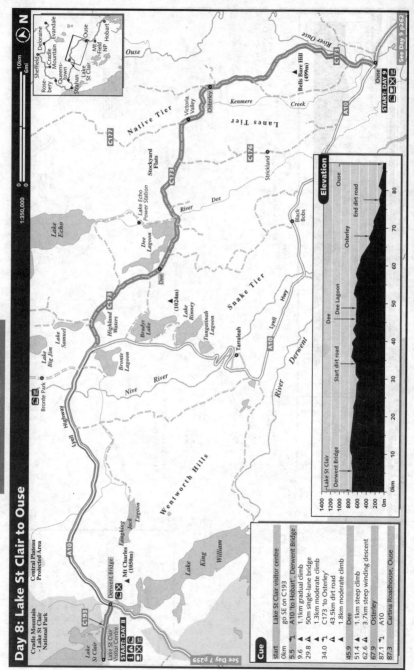

Day 8: Lake St Clair to Ouse

TASMANIA

See Day 7 p259

Cue

start	Lake St Clair visitor centre
0km	go SE on C193
5.5 ←	A10 'to Hobart', Derwent Bridge
9.6 ▲	1.1km gradual climb
29.8 ▲	50m single-lane bridge
	1.3km moderate climb
34.0 →	C173 'to Osterley'
▲	43.5km dirt road
	1.8km moderate climb
45.9	Dee
51.4 ▲	1.1km steep climb
62.6 ▲	3.7km steep winding descent
67.9	Osterley
87.1 →	A10
87.3	Cartina Roadhouse, Ouse

Elevation

See Day 9 p262

Watersmeet returns via a nature trail. The **Shadow Lake** walk takes about four hours return, a circuit over **Mt Rufus** seven hours. Alternatively, take the **ferry** across the lake and walk back along the shore from Echo Point (about three hours) or Narcissus Hut (five to six hours). Ferry times are posted at the Lakeside St Clair kiosk (☎ 6289 1137) at Cynthia Bay.

Scenic flights operate over Lake St Clair (see Things to See & Do in the Cradle Mountain section).

Places to Stay & Eat About 10 minutes' walk along the Overland Track, you'll find free *camping* at Fergy's Paddock. At *Lakeside St Clair* (☎ *6289 1137,* ⓔ *lakestclair @trump.net.au),* tent sites cost $6 per person. Backpacker beds in poorly ventilated, cell-like cubicles, which barely accommodate two people and their bikes, cost $25 per person. Campers pay extra to use the spacious shared kitchen and dining area at one end of the accommodation building. The *cafeteria-kiosk*, a short walk from the accommodation, has food supplies and takeaways plus a good sit-down eating area. A separate cabin with its own kitchen costs a minimum $50. Self-contained huts cost $180 a double.

Back on the highway, the *Derwent Bridge Wilderness Hotel* (☎ *6289 1144)* has hostel-standard individual rooms in huts for $20 a person. B&B costs $75 per double with shared facilities or $85 in en suite. The lounge bar serves hearty meals from $11.

Day 8: Lake St Clair to Ouse
5–8½ hours, 87.3km

Most of Day 8 is downhill but the degree of difficulty is increased by a long stretch of dirt road where, of course, the worst climbs are. The terrain is still easier, and the traffic lighter, than on the alternative sealed Lyell Hwy. Buttongrass plains, thick eucalypt forest and grazing land on the highlands changes to open forest on the descent, then back to grazing country on the lower slopes. There are no services after Derwent Bridge, so carry plenty of water and food.

Ouse has limited accommodation with equally limited appeal. For those with the energy to tackle an extra 20 or 27km with steep hills, Ellendale or Fentonbury have attractive alternative B&B options (see Day

9). Alternatively, continue all the way to Mt Field National Park (38.5km).

Mt Olympus (1427m) floats above buttongrass and distant tree tops on the left after about 7km, but the only notable climb in the first 29km is a gradual 1.1km rise at 9.6km.

At 34km the route turns onto dirt Victoria Valley Rd/the C173, rising moderately on a loose surface for 1.8km between peppermint-scented gums. Sealed surface returns momentarily through the tiny settlement of Dee (45.9km). Skirting Dee Lagoon, the road climbs steeply past the Lake Echo Power Station turn-off (51.4km). At 56.2km, another brief sealed section passes the only house since Dee; snow retainers on its roof give a clue to the climatic extremes here.

A sign (62.6km) warns of a twisting, rocky downhill – caution is required!

Osterley (67.9km) is a 'town' of one house opposite the remains of several others. The sealed road returns at 77.5km.

Ouse
A convenient place to break the journey, Ouse (pronounced 'ooze') is an otherwise fairly charmless collection of weatherboard buildings bisected by the highway.

Cartina Roadhouse (☎ 6287 1337), on Main St, is the town's visitor centre, bank, post office, takeaway and restaurant. It has Eftpos.

Places to Stay & Eat Opposite the petrol station, the *Lachlan Hotel* (☎ *6287 1215)* offers B&B for $25/55 per single/double. Counter meals are available from Wednesday to Saturday. The only other places to stay are B&B cottages: *Rosecot* (☎ *6287 1222, the C173),* about 600m from the highway, charges $90 per double; and *Sassa-del-Gallo* (☎ *6287 1289* or ☎ *6287 1263),* beside the petrol station, costs $70 per double.

Besides *Cartina Roadhouse*, the town has a *supermarket* and *takeaway* near the hotel. The riverside picnic area by the roadhouse is a good place to eat or rest.

Day 9: Ouse to Mt Field National Park
2–4 hours, 38.5km

The short, mostly easy ride undulates through agricultural land with two steep climbs before Ellendale. The final 9km is a

TASMANIA

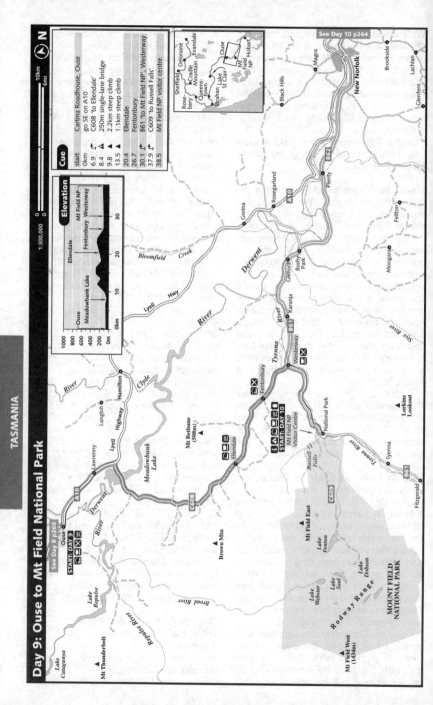

TASMANIA

Day 9: Ouse to Mt Field National Park

Cue

start	Cartina Roadhouse, Ouse
0km	go SE on A10
6.9	C608 'to Ellendale'
8.4	250m single-lane bridge
9.8	2.2km steep climb
13.5	1.1km steep climb
20.4	Ellendale
26.7	Fentonbury
30.1	B61 'to Mt Field NP'. Westerway
37.9	C609 'to Russell Falls'
38.5	Mt Field NP visitor centre

Elevation

See Day 10 p264

See Day 8 p260

lovely gentle rise through forest between a disused railway and the Tyenna River.

The 250m-long, single-lane Meadowbank Lake bridge (7.9km) has a passing bay. At its eastern end is a reserve with picnic tables while, beyond its western end, the first steep climb begins. The second follows after a descent.

Ellendale (20.4km), a village in a former hop-growing area, has a *general store* and *Hopfield Cottages* (☎ 6288 1223, the C608) charges $110 for B&B in en suite doubles. Pre-arranged evening meals cost $22.50.

At Fentonbury (26.7km) is delightful *Hamlet Downs* (☎ 6288 1212, Gully Rd), a characterful, restored 1860s farmhouse, uphill from the main road. B&B costs from $85 per double. Delicious home-cooked meals are available.

Mt Field National Park

Mt Field is well known for spectacular mountain scenery, alpine moorlands, rainforest, lakes, wildlife and waterfalls – of which Russell Falls are the most famous. Most services are in the adjacent village of National Park.

The PWS office (☎ 6288 1149), inside the national park near the Russell Falls car park, has informative brochures on park history and walks.

Things to See & Do The major attraction of the park is magnificent 40m **Russell Falls**, an easy 15-minute walk from the park entrance. It's well worth continuing along the **Tall Trees Circuit**, about another 45 minutes, past towering swamp gums. The signed detour to **Lady Barron Falls** adds a further two hours (return). For walks on top of the range and around **Lake Dobson**, get further information from PWS.

In summer school holidays, rangers organise free activities such as slide shows and after-dark walks to Russell Falls to see the nightlife (wallabies, possums, quolls and glow worms).

Places to Stay & Eat Just inside the national park, *Mt Field Caravan Park* (☎ 6288 1526) has tent sites for $5.50 per person. It's usually booked out in high-season holiday periods and at all times it's essential to keep food secured from animals.

National Park Youth Hostel (☎ 6288 1369, Gordon River Rd), 200m west of the turn-off to Russell Falls, charges $16 per person.

In the township, the *National Park Hotel* (☎ 6288 1103) has rooms with shared facilities, and a cooked breakfast, for $60 per double. It serves counter meals nightly.

Russell Falls Holiday Cottages (☎ 6288 1198), next to the bridge at the park entrance, consists of four one- or two-bedroom self-contained cottages, which cost $66 per double.

The national park *kiosk* serves takeaways.

Day 10: Mt Field National Park to Hobart
4–7½ hours, 74.1km

The all-sealed route rolls gently past opium poppy and other crop fields in its first half then turns up a long, steep hill west of the Derwent. It takes near-deserted forest roads before dropping back to the water's edge to follow cycleways and suburban byways into Hobart. Several towns along the way have food shops.

The petrol station at Bushy Park (19.3km) has a *takeaway* shop and toilets.

New Norfolk (39.2km), the largest centre since Devonport with nearly 6,000 people, offers all services, including banks (with ATMs) in High St and a bike shop, Norfolk Cycles (☎ 6261 2201), on Richmond St. The town, developed since 1808 in lush country, straddles the Derwent less than 40km from Hobart. Old oast houses, used for drying hops, and rows of tall poplars, used to shield the hop gardens from wind, are distinctive features. **Pulpit Rock Lookout**, 1km north-east of the bridge and 2km up a steep dirt side road, offers fine views over the town and sweeping river bend.

While it's physically easier to follow main roads along the valley to Hobart, it's far more pleasant to ride via **Molesworth** (46km), climbing over a spur of the Wellington Range and descending to suburban Berriedale (61.2km).

In Berriedale, ride the highway's dirt shoulder for 1km before veering left into a waterside park and onto the Montrose Bay Cycleway. Rejoin the highway for another 370m, before turning right into Elwick Rd (64.3km). Join the Inter City Cycleway, which follows the railway line between Glenorchy and Hobart. South of the Tasman Bridge, it climbs a hill near the Cenotaph,

TASMANIA

Day 10: Mt Field National Park to Hobart

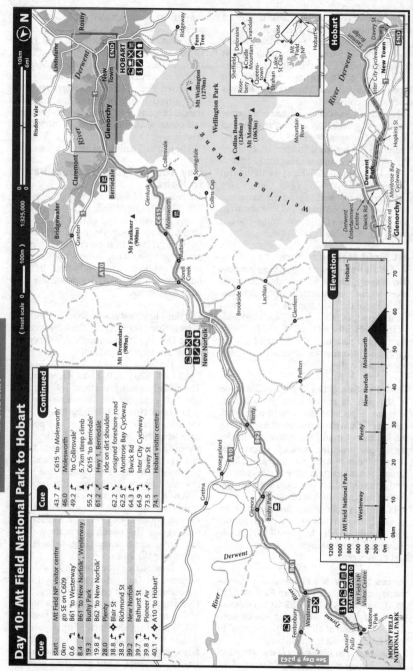

(Inset scale 0 ——— 100m 1:325,000 0 ——— 10km 6mi)

N

Cue

start		Mt Field NP visitor centre
0km	↗	go SE on C609
0.6	↰	B61 to Westerway'
8.4	↱	B61 to New Norfolk', Westerway
19.3	↑	Bushy Park
19.8	↱	B62 to New Norfolk'
28.0	↑	Plenty
38.8	↰ ◆	Blair St
38.9	↱	Richmond St
39.2	↱	New Norfolk
39.7	↰	Bathurst St
39.8	↱	Pioneer Av
40.1	↗ ◆	A10 to Hobart'

Cue **Continued**

43.7	↰	C615 to Molesworth'
46.0		Molesworth
49.2	↰ ◀	'to Collinsvale'
		5.7km steep climb
55.2	↱	C615 'to Berriedale'
61.2	↱ ◀	Hwy 1, Berriedale
	◀	ride on dirt shoulder
62.2	↘	unsigned foreshore road
62.5	↰	Montrose Bay Cycleway
64.3	↰	Elwick Rd
64.9	↱	Inter City Cycleway
73.5	↱	Davey St
74.1		Hobart visitor centre

Elevation

zigs right across a road and joins the footpath of Tasman Hwy to reach the eastern end of Davey St.

Hobart
See Hobart (pp216–18) in the Gateway Cities section for information about accommodation and other services.

Meehan Range

MOUNTAIN-BIKE RIDE
Duration .... 2½–3½ hours
Distance 25km
Difficulty .... hard
Start/End .... Hobart

The Meehan Range rises on the east bank of the Derwent estuary, running from near Rokeby in the south to Brighton in the north. The attractions of this challenging ride are the views – to Bridgewater in the north and to the Iron Pot at the estuary mouth in the south – plus wildlife and solitude. Further exploration of the myriad of tracks on the range is definitely recommended.

HISTORY
The summit of the Meehan Range north of Mornington was the location of one of the former semaphore stations, which allowed fast communication using coded flags (wittily dubbed, in modern times, 'convict fax') between Hobart and the penal colony at Port Arthur.

NATURAL HISTORY
The vegetation on the range reflects the low rainfall of the area; it's mostly dry, open, eucalypt woodland, typical of that which covered much of eastern Tasmania before white settlement. The area is now a reserve controlled by the PWS.

PLANNING
When to Ride
The ride should be possible year-round except when heavy rain makes trails impassable or fire bans close the area.

Maps
A useful map for the ride is Tasmap No 5225 *Hobart* (1:25,000), which costs $9

from Service Tasmania (☎ 1300-366 773), 134 Macquarie St, Hobart.

What to Bring
Carry sufficient food and drink as there is no water nor any shop on the mountain.

GETTING TO/FROM THE RIDE
See the Getting to/from Tasmania (p215) and Gateway Cities (p220) sections for information on getting to/from Hobart.

THE RIDE
Meehan Range Mountain-Bike Ride
2½–3½ hours, 25km
Ride from Hobart visitor centre north-east along the shared footpath of Davey St/ Tasman Hwy to the Inter City Cycleway. Follow directional signposting onto the northern shared footway of the Tasman Bridge then use the Tasman Hwy shoulder, where it exists, to the Mornington exit – where the off-road circuit begins.

On the right of the looping exit road is a white gate marked with a PWS sign. Go around it onto an abandoned railway embankment. This runs north-east, parallel to the highway, to where the stone footings of an old rail bridge stand forlornly amid scrub. A path runs to the left along a grassy gully onto a gravelled fire trail. This climbs the steep, forested scarp in a series of zigzags. The loose surface makes it a very tough climb but some, at least, is rideable. Take the left or uphill fork at each trail junction. On the level section atop the range, one of these junctions is an inverted Y. Take a hard left here to complete the circuit or continue on the tracks ahead, which beg to be explored, for as long as time and energy hold out.

The downward track suddenly becomes precipitous and rutted. At the bottom, it parallels the power lines. Follow these through another white gate to the sealed Flagstaff Gully Link. Turn left to return to the highway and follow the outward route back to Hobart.

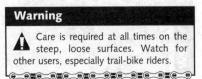

Warning
⚠ Care is required at all times on the steep, loose surfaces. Watch for other users, especially trail-bike riders.

TASMANIA

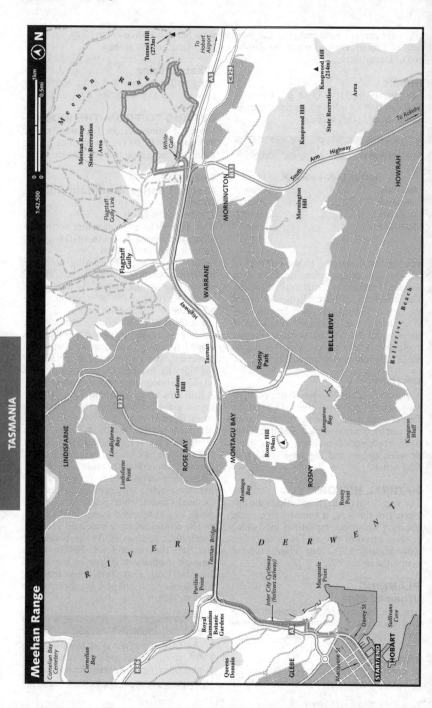

Meehan Range

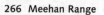

South Australia

Less hectic (although no less scenic), than the eastern states, South Australia (SA) is in many ways a cycle tourist's paradise. The capital – Adelaide – enjoys a relaxed lifestyle with an arts and cultural scene that is second to none, while less than a day's pedalling away, historic townships, wine-growing regions, spectacular coastlines and rolling hills await discovery.

The diversity of terrain and range of scenic attractions ensures the cycle tourist is spoilt for choice in SA. Rather than including every possible itinerary, this chapter details two rides that are particularly cycle-friendly.

Both rides start and finish in Adelaide. The first explores the rolling hills and spectacular coastline of the Fleurieu Peninsula. The ride winds along the coast before returning to Adelaide through the Southern Vales wine-growing district.

The second ride offers the chance to experience something of SA's German heritage. The historic settlement of Hahndorf, the former copper mining town of Kapunda, and the vineyard-studded Barossa Valley are visited on this circuit. The ride returns to Adelaide along part of the Mawson Trail, a long-distance cycle route.

For the serious expedition cyclist, the rugged isolation of Kangaroo Island and the full Mawson Trail are recommended but not included in this edition of *Cycling Australia* (see the boxed texts 'Kangaroo Island' and 'The Mawson Trail' later in this chapter).

HISTORY

Archaeological evidence dates the Aboriginal occupation of SA to as far back as 43,000 years ago. Most Indigenous inhabitants lived between Gulf St Vincent and the Victorian border. At the time of European settlement, an estimated 15,000 Indigenous people lived in SA. Many were killed by white settlers or died from introduced diseases, and many more were forced from their traditional lands in order to make way for farming. Of the country covered by the rides in this chapter, the northern Mt Lofty Ranges and the Barossa Valley are Kaurna and Ngadjuri lands, and the Fleurieu Peninsula is Ngarrinjeri and Kaurna land.

The European settlement of SA was somewhat hit-and-miss. In 1802, the English explorer Matthew Flinders sighted Mt Lofty in the Adelaide Hills. However, it was not until 1836 that the inaugural governor, Captain John Hindmarsh, and the first settlers arrived at Holdfast Bay (now the suburb of Glenelg).

Unlike most Australian colonies, SA began as a 'convict-free zone'. Small blocks of land were sold at low prices to attract workers from Britain, keeping the colony free of convict labour. By 1840, a wave of German farmers and artisans had arrived, and copper discoveries in the mid-1800s drew Cornish settlers.

SA has a distinguished cycling history. As well as being the base for the Australian Institute of Sport track cycling program, Adelaide is home to European-based professional cyclists Stuart O'Grady, Patrick Jonker and Jay Sweet; Australian coach Charlie Walsh; and Mike Turtur, a member of the gold medal-winning pursuit team at the 1984 Los Angeles Olympics. The state also hosts the Tour Down Under (see the boxed text of the same name opposite).

NATURAL HISTORY

The fourth-largest state or territory, SA covers 984,400 sq km of Australia. While the vast plains of the interior are spanned by the Flinders Ranges, most of SA is undulating terrain, with few mountains of any note. The highest is Mt Woodroffe (1435m) in the Musgrave Ranges in the north-west of the state.

Two-thirds semi-desert, SA is Australia's driest state. The Adelaide Hills, with a relatively high rainfall, are a lush contrast to the Outback. SA's main watercourse is the Murray River, which supplies 90% of the state's population with water for drinking and irrigation.

Hardy eucalyptus thrive in SA's heat and aridity. Around Adelaide, blue gums and candlebarks are common, while the coolibah

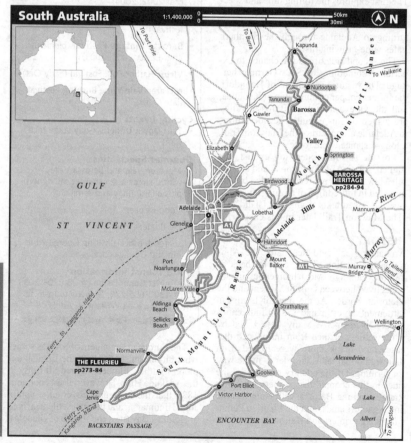

SOUTH AUSTRALIA

can be found in the dry north. Salt bushes, saw banksias and acacias (wattles) grow in the interior; in the Adelaide Hills, orchids and paper daisies line roads in spring. SA's most distinctive plant is probably salvation Jane (or Patterson's curse), a purple-flowered weed poisonous to stock and humans.

Koalas are common in the Adelaide Hills, and several species of kangaroo (euros, reds and western and eastern greys) roam the state. Much of the bird life in SA is migratory, and includes tiny dotterels and cranes who have headed south to kick back during the northern winter. The rainbow lorikeet is found in

The Tour Down Under

First staged in 1999, the Tour Down Under was an overwhelming, if unexpected, success. For six days, South Australia (SA) was alive with the colour, drama and excitement of (mens) European professional cycling. Thanks to the commitment of a major corporate backer in Jacob's Creek wines, the Tour Down Under is now held annually in January.

The brain child of Olympic gold medallist Mike Turtur, the race attracts many of the sport's biggest teams. The legal requirement to wear a helmet catches many of them unaware, with the police issuing many 'friendly' warnings – as a humble amateur, don't expect to escape so lightly!

The race follows a similar format to that of the biggest European races such as the Tour de France. It is contested over six days, the first kicking off with a *criterium* (circuit race) through the streets of the Adelaide city centre. From here, the tour heads through the countryside of SA, serving as the ideal 'postcard' for the regional attractions of SA. Destinations have included the Adelaide Hills, the Fleurieu Peninsula and the Barossa Valley, and several of the stages feature circuits through a region, giving spectators the chance to see the riders more than once.

Other attractions include the Tour Village. Based in the heart of Adelaide, the village gives spectators the chance to mingle with the riders and their mechanics. Few other sports give their fans a chance to see up close what happens behind the scenes.

The race also uses a jersey system similar to the Tour de France. At the end of each stage, the overall leader gets to wear the coveted yellow jersey. The best sprinter is awarded a green jersey, while the best climber wears the polka dot jersey of the 'king of the mountains'.

While the terrain is comparatively flat when compared with the towering French Alps or the Pyrenees, the Tour Down Under is still a gruelling test of a rider's fitness. The infamous Willunga Hill, to the south of Adelaide, and Menglers Hill, in the Barossa Valley, certainly sort out the contenders.

RUSSELL MOUNTFORD

the Adelaide Hills, and pelicans are common along the Fleurieu Peninsula.

CLIMATE

With its Mediterranean climate, SA's weather is generally reliable and temperate. Rainfall is minimal, with most falling between May and October. Winters are short and temperatures are rarely below freezing, although maximum temperatures can be as low as 12°C between June and September.

The main consideration for cyclists is the heat, with summer (January, February and occasionally March) temperatures often too high for cycling. Daily maximums of 35°C or more are common in Adelaide (higher in the interior where there is also a bushfire risk).

Cyclists will also need to watch out for 'northerlies', blisteringly hot winds from the north. The dust and pollen they stir up will have hay fever sufferers reaching for their hankies. For these reasons, the best seasons for cycling in SA are autumn and spring.

The coastal Fleurieu Peninsula is cooled by sea breezes, and temperatures tend to be lower than elsewhere in the state.

INFORMATION
Maps

The SA Tourist Commission (☎ 8303 2033), 18 King William St, puts out the *Barossa Secrets* and *Fleurieu Peninsula Secrets* colour brochures (free), featuring 1:200,000 maps.

The Royal Automobile Association (RAA; ☎ 8202 4538), 41 Hindmarsh Square, has a good range of 1:200,000 regional maps (free for members/$1.50 for nonmembers). Otherwise, try Europa Bookshop (☎ 8223 2289), 238 Rundle St or the Map Shop (☎ 8231 2033), 16A Peel St.

Information Sources

Bicycle SA (☎ 8410 1406, 🖳 www.bikesa .asn.au), 1 Sturt St, sells some maps and can

Warning

⚠ South Australia's 'hard' drinking water is something of an acquired taste. If it's not to your liking, bottled water is readily available.

Many of SA's back roads are unsealed and, for the most part, well maintained. While our rides stick mainly to sealed roads, heading briefly onto dirt is sometimes unavoidable.

offer advice on all aspects of cycling and cycle touring.

GATEWAY CITIES
Adelaide

With the beaches of Gulf St Vincent to the west, the Mt Lofty Ranges to the east, and split down the middle by the meandering River Torrens, the 'City of Churches' is a pretty place indeed. Often likened, somewhat unfairly, to a big country town, Adelaide is in fact an enchanting mix of cosmopolitan bars, cafes and galleries. The city takes its wining and dining seriously, and is home to many superb restaurants, sophisticated wine bars, throbbing nightclubs and pubs full of eccentric characters and infinitely drinkable Coopers beer.

In 1836, the surveyor-general, Captain William Light, designed Adelaide as a city of green spaces and ordered streets. 'Light's Vision', as this grand plan for the settlement of Adelaide was known, saw the city develop around a grid of wide streets, graced by five main squares and completely enclosed by an extensive tract of parklands. The resulting layout is a grand, spacious city that is remarkably easy to navigate by bike (see the boxed text 'Adelaide City Day Ride' opposite).

Adelaide's main drag is Rundle Mall, where department stores, fast food restaurants, fruit and flower stalls and a series of endearing pig sculptures can all be found. East along Rundle Mall is the hip and happening 'East End' – home to book stores, restaurants, groovy clothing shops and several pubs and wine bars. To the west is Hindley St, with its somewhat rougher pubs and less than salubrious collection of sex shops and amusement arcades.

Information The tourist office (☎ 8303 2033, 🖳 www.tourism.sa.gov.sa) is at 18 King William St; an information kiosk is at the western end of Rundle Mall.

Several ATMs are in Rundle Mall and others are throughout the city centre. For currency exchange, the Adelaide Casino, on North Terrace, is open 24 hours (you'll need a passport or a current driver's license to exchange money).

For sales and repairs, go to Super Elliot Cycles (☎ 8223 3946), 200 Rundle St, or Bikesmart (☎ 8223 3946), 43 Rundle Mall.

Mountain Designs (☎ 8232 9690), 203 Rundle St, stocks some Ortlieb gear.

Things to See & Do Lined with elegant buildings, the grand boulevard of North Terrace has several galleries and museums and the city's **Botanic Gardens**. The main stretch starts outside the Lion Arts Centre, home to the **Jam Factory**, a design and craft centre exhibiting works from some of SA's most innovative artists, and finishes with the **University of Adelaide**.

The **Adelaide Casino**, on North Terrace, is set inside the grand central train station, near **Parliament House** and **Government House**. Nearby, the **State Library of SA** (☎ 8207 7250) has a permanent exhibition of memorabilia from local hero and cricket legend Sir Donald Bradman.

The **Migration Museum** (☎ 8207 7580), 82 Kintore Ave, houses an excellent display of SA's rich multicultural heritage. The **Museum of SA** (☎ 8207 7500) houses the Sir Douglas Mawson Gallery and has an impressive new Aboriginal Cultures Gallery; the **Art Gallery** (☎ 8207 7000), with its enormous collection of predominantly colonial art, is next door.

Tandanya (☎ 8224 3200), 253 Grenfell St, is an Aboriginal cultural institute containing art and craft galleries, performance spaces, a cafe and a gift shop.

Known as the 'Festival State', Adelaide plays host to the **Festival of Arts** (biennial; 2002, 2004) and the world music feast **Womadelaide** (biennial; 2001, 2003).

While in Adelaide, wolf down a **pie floater**. A local culinary institution, it is definitely not for the faint hearted (see the boxed text later in this chapter).

Venture down Hindley St to visit **Imprints Booksellers**, a literary oasis in the heart of the forgotten West End.

Places to Stay The *Adelaide Caravan Park* *(☎ 8363 1566; 8 Bruton St, Hackney)* has tent

Adelaide City Day Ride

With its flat wide streets and network of bikepaths, Adelaide is something of a cyclist's paradise. Many of Adelaide's attractions are found in the suburbs, which can be visited on a day ride from the city centre.

Most of the attractions can be reached using the extensive network of 'Bike Direct' bikepaths that run throughout the Adelaide suburbs. Free maps are available from the State Information Centre (☎ 8204 1900), 77 Grenfell St, or the information kiosk in Rundle Mall.

From the tourist office, head west along North Terrace to West Terrace, marked by the impressive, heritage-listed **Newmarket Hotel**, on the corner. At West Terrace, the Westside bikepath takes you from the city to the sea, to finish in Glenelg. It was Glenelg where the HMS Buffalo delivered the inaugural governor, Captain John Hindmarsh, and the first settlers at Holdfast Bay in December 1836. These days Glenelg has a buzzing cafe scene. En route, the **Old Gum Tree** is where the colony of South Australia was proclaimed.

From Glenelg, continue north along the foreshore to reach **Henley Square**. Overlooking the white sand and long jetty of Henley Beach, the square has several restaurants and wine bars. Throughout the summer, the Square plays host to a number of jazz concerts and wine-tasting events, usually on a Sunday afternoon. Film buffs can visit **Henley on Sea**, where the piano recital scene in the Oscar-winning movie Shine was filmed. Continuing north takes you to the arty beachside suburb of **Semaphore**. An up-and-coming suburb of Adelaide, it has an eclectic mix of interesting restaurants and cafes, antique shops, galleries, bookshops and plenty of friendly pubs.

SA's maritime history is alive and well in this **Port Adelaide**. Watch the ships load and unload at the working port, or visit the **Maritime Museum**, which includes the Nelecebee, the third-oldest ship on Lloyd's Register. Just down the street is the **Port Dock Station Railway Museum**, which houses an impressive collection of locomotives, passenger carriages and freight vehicles. Port Adelaide also has a great food market early on Sunday morning. **Ozone Fish Cafe**, in Commercial Rd, first opened in 1884 and is SA's oldest fish shop.

As you head back to Adelaide, pick up the bikepath along the River Torrens. Close to town, you pass the **original jail**, from where the bikepath continues along the river to finish outside the Festival Centre.

sites for $23 and is the closest camping ground to the city centre. *Levi Caravan Park* (☎ *8344 2209, 69 Landsdowne Terrace*), visible, to the right, from the bikepath of Day 6 of the Barossa Heritage ride, charges $17.

Adelaide has a huge range of backpacker accommodation, particularly along Gilles St. *Rucksack Riders* (☎ *8232 0823, 257 Gilles St*) is a good place to meet fellow cycle tourists. Dorm beds cost $14.50; twins cost $15.50 per person. The brand-new *Adelaide Central YHA* (☎ *8414 3010, 135 Waymouth St*) charges $22 in dorms; twins with en suite cost $66. *Sunny's Backpackers Hotel* (☎ *8231 2430* or ☎ *1800-225 725, 139 Franklin St*) is clean and quiet. Dorm beds cost $18; twins and doubles cost $42.

Several city pubs provide accommodation. *The Nomads Cumberland Arms Hotel* (☎ *8231 3577, 205 Waymouth St*) has dorm beds for $15, or twin and double rooms for $36. The *Austral Hotel* (☎ *8223 4660, 205 Rundle St*) charges $35/55 for singles/doubles. The bar downstairs is excellent, as are the meals. *Moore's Brecknock Hotel* (☎ *8231 5467, 401 King William St*) has rooms from $40/55, which includes a light breakfast. A popular Irish pub, traditional bands usually play on Friday nights.

Kent Town Lodge (☎ *1800-806 059; 22 Wakefield St, Kent Town*) is a basic motel with a pool and rooms from $39/72.

Adelaide has several gorgeous, if expensive, B&Bs. *Allison's Apothecary* (☎ *8271 1435; ⓔ tcosh@iaccess.com.au; 21 Albert St, Mitcham Village*) has single/double rooms for $65/125. The *North Adelaide Heritage Group* (☎ *8272 1355; ⓔ heritage@senet .com.au; office: 109 Glen Osmond Rd, Eastwood*) manages 19 beautifully restored cottages with B&B prices from $158 to $348.

Places to Eat For self-catering, try the bustling *Central Market*, near Victoria Square; a *Coles* supermarket is in the market complex. The food hall at *David Jones* (*100 Rundle Mall*) sells a range of gourmet supplies.

Adelaide has three main food strips: Gouger St, Rundle St and Hutt St, with everything from pizzerias to tapas bars to 'pub grub'.

Gouger St Come here for several great seafood places and a host of Asian restaurants; *Ying Chow* (☎ *8211 7988, 114 Gouger St*) serves fantastic northern Chinese food. *Talbot Hotel* (☎ *8231 9780, 104 Gouger St*) serves good pub food – check out its kitsch cocktail bar.

Rundle St Try the *Exeter* or *Austral* hotels. *Cafe Michael* (☎ *8223 3519, 204 Rundle St*), across the road from the Austral Hotel, is an exceptionally good, reasonably cheap, Thai restaurant. The stylish *Koko* (☎ *8223 2243, 187 Rundle St*) has an interesting menu, including various pasta and risotto dishes, and also does a great breakfast.

Hutt St A small but lively restaurant, cafe and pub scene centres on Hutt St between Wakefield and Halifax Sts, particularly on Friday and Saturday nights. For Malaysian hawker food and stir fries, try *Woks Happ' Ning* (☎ *8232 1625, 174A Hutt St*). Several cafes in the strip also open for breakfast.

Getting There & Away Adelaide is reached by the Western and Dukes Hwys from Melbourne and the Hume and Sturt Hwys from Sydney. The Great Eastern and Eyre Hwys span the Nullarbor to Perth in the west.

Air Adelaide airport has international and domestic terminals, both of which are 7km east of the city centre. See the Getting There & Away chapter for more information on fares and carriers.

A bus service carries passengers and their bikes into the city. If riding to the city, join the bikepath along the River Torrens at the end of Airport Rd.

Bus Adelaide is well serviced from Sydney, Melbourne, Perth, Alice Springs and other

---

The Pie Floater

The meal of choice for drunks, impoverished students and politicians alike, South Australia's most famous culinary contribution is not for the faint-hearted. A meat pie turned upside down in a bowl of garish green-pea soup and topped with a liberal dose of 'dead horse' (tomato sauce), the pie floater is best approached when you've had a skinful. Tuck into a floater at one of the pie carts outside the Casino or nearby on Victoria Square.

main centres. The two main bus companies – McCafferty's (☎ 13 1499, 🖳 www.mccaffertys.com.au) and Greyhound Pioneer Australia (☎ 13 2030, 🖳 www.greyhound.com.au) – have services to Adelaide. (See the Getting Around chapter for information on fares and conditions.) The bus terminal is at 101–111 Franklin St.

Train Trains arrive at the desolate Keswick Terminal, 1.5km south-west of the city centre. The airport bus stops at the terminal.

Great Southern Railway (☎ 13 2147) runs direct services from Melbourne on the *Overland* ($60, 13½ hours). Catch the *Ghan* from Alice Springs ($197/624 for a seat/sleeper, including meals; 20 hours) or the *Indian Pacific* from Perth ($283/879 for a seat/sleeper, including meals; 37 hours).

If travelling from Sydney, the fastest way is with Speedlink – Sydney to Albury on the XPT train, then a V/Line Bus ($105, 20 hours) to Adelaide on a V/Line Bus. However, places for bikes on the XPT are limited; see the Getting Around chapter for details of bike carriage on all train services.

Bicycle It is a long, long (boring) way from Adelaide to anywhere else. Mt Gambier is 459km to the east, Port Augusta is 311km to the north and Perth is 2624km to the west.

Nonetheless, many cyclists make the journey across the Nullabor between Adelaide and Perth; more do the trip from Adelaide to Melbourne, generally via Victoria's Great Ocean Road (see the Great Ocean Road ride in the Victoria chapter).

Fleurieu Peninsula

This undulating peninsula incorporates conservation reserves, pretty seaside hamlets and one of SA's finest stretches of sand and sea, from Normanville to Port Willunga.

HISTORY
The Fleurieu Peninsula was first visited by Europeans in 1802. The French expedition, led by Nicholas Baudin, named the Peninsula after Charles Pierre Claret, Comte de Fleurieu, an eminent 19th-century French explorer. Baudin played a key role in much of the Peninsula's history. When cruising the coastline of SA, he met Matthew Flinders in

the waters off Victor Harbor; Encounter Bay was named to commemorate the meeting.

In 1837, whalers set up stations at Encounter Bay to hunt Southern right whales. From the 1850s until the 1880s, Goolwa, at the Murray mouth, was SA's major port. In the 1880s, however, a new railway line linking Adelaide and Melbourne via Murray Bridge was established, spelling the end for this once-bustling port.

Inland, much of the Peninsula's history is linked to wine making. The first winery in the region was established in 1838 by John Reynell at Reynella, now part of Adelaide's southern suburban sprawl. These days, most of the Peninsula's 70 or so wineries are concentrated around McLaren Vale, and produce outstanding shiraz, cabernet sauvignon and varietal whites.

NATURAL HISTORY
Stretching south from the Southern Vales wine district, the Fleurieu Peninsula is bordered on three sides by the sea – Gulf St Vincent, the Backstairs Passage, Encounter Bay and Lake Alexandrina. Featuring some of Australia's most stunning coastline, the distinctive landscape of the Peninsula includes extensive sand dunes, off-shore reef systems and towering cliffs that drop into inviting, crystal-clear waters.

Inland, rolling hills, vineyards and orchards comprise the more rural centre of the Peninsula, while in the Adelaide Hills, gold was mined from 1852 until as late as 1930 in the area around Echunga and Macclesfield.

Southern right whales, which come in close to shore to breed, had been harpooned to near-extinction by the 1930s. However, their numbers are on the rise, and between June and September they make a spectacular sight frolicking off Encounter Bay.

The Fleurieu

Duration	5 days
Distance	289km
Difficulty	moderate
Start/End	Adelaide

This ride takes in the superb coastal scenery, surf beaches, rolling hills, historic townships and orchards, and vineyards that are characteristic of the Fleurieu Peninsula.

It is a reasonably tough stretch in the saddle, particularly the very hilly, exposed section from Victor Harbor to Normanville.

PLANNING
When to Ride
Any time, except for the depths of winter, is good for exploring the region, although accommodation can be extremely hard to find in January.

To catch the Peninsula in party mode, try May, when 'From the Sea and the Vines' showcases local seafood and wine, or October, for the Wine Bushing Festival.

Maps
Cartographics' *The Fleurieu* (1:200,000) or the RAA's *Central-South* (1:200,000) maps both provide adequate detail of route.

The initial section out of metropolitan Adelaide is detailed on the free No 7 *Bike Direct* map.

What to Bring
Sunglasses and sunscreen are a must – even in winter. Insect repellent is useful year round.

GETTING TO/FROM THE RIDE
See the Adelaide Getting There & Away section (pp272–73).

THE RIDE
Day 1: Adelaide to Strathalbyn
3½–5 hours, 60.7km
This scenic and vertically challenging first day heads out of the city on a quiet cycling route before climbing the Adelaide Hills and (except for a 10km gradual uphill) then descends for much of the day (later, along the Angas River) to Strathalbyn.

After the initial climb up **Old Belair Rd**, the route flattens out through the peaceful **Belair National Park**, where a challenging climb finishes off the day's major obstacles.

Stirling (21km), with its grand manors and extensive plantation of deciduous trees, is particularly attractive. Stop for a smoothie at the *organic market* in the main street.

Shortly before reaching Mylor, the ride passes by **Warrawong Sanctuary** (26.8km) – just look for the feral-animal-proof fence to your left.

From Mylor, a pretty stretch heads through the area known as **Biggs Flat** and into the

former gold mining towns of Echunga (37.8km) and Macclesfield (47.6km). Both very pretty towns, **Macclesfield** is a particularly nice place to stop for lunch. Try the 1841 *Three Brothers Arms*. Serving filling fare, the pub is run by a friendly fellow – he'll even let bikes into the front bar!

Strathalbyn
'Strath' (as the locals call it) is in many ways a quintessential country town, with its wide streets and friendly folk who'll chew the ear off a passing cycle tourist.

Settled by Scottish immigrants in 1839, much of the town centre has been preserved and heritage-listed.

Information The tourist office (☎/fax 8536 3212) is inside the train station on South Terrace. Bank SA, 7 Dawson St, is opposite the Foodland supermarket (which has an ATM inside).

Things to See & Do Stroll along the **Angas River** or pick up a **walking tour** brochure,

Warrawong Sanctuary

Covering 14 hectares of revegetated bushland, Warrawong Sanctuary was originally a working dairy farm. Earth Sanctuaries – the company founded by committed environmentalist John Wamsley – bought the land in 1969 and the property has since been progressively re-established and replanted with native Australian trees and plants. The result is the recreation of an entire ecosystem, nestled safely behind a feral-animal-proof fence. Here, kangaroos, wallabies, pademelons, bandicoots, bettongs and many other rare and endangered native animals roam freely.

The sanctuary runs guided walks at dawn, 2pm and sunset, which are an entertaining, educational and environmentally-sensitive way to appreciate some of Australia's endangered animals. The dawn and sunset walks are the best for animal watching. Thanks to the sanctuary's successful breeding program, it is even possible to glimpse the elusive platypus.

The sanctuary runs 'dinner, walk & breakfast' packages that include overnight accommodation in the tent-like bush cabins. Bookings (☎ 8370 9422) are essential for all walks and accommodation.

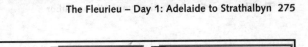

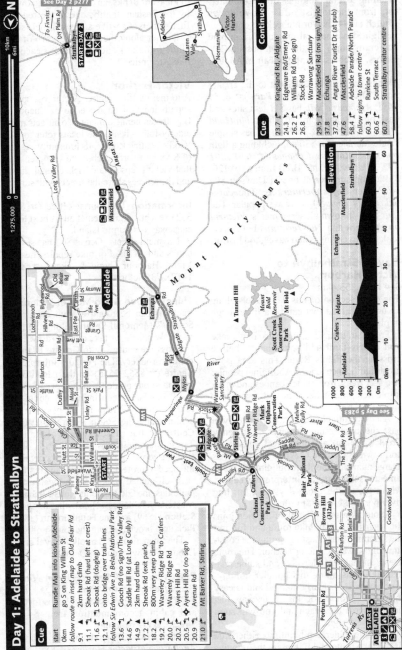

Day 1: Adelaide to Strathalbyn

Cue

start	Rundle Mall info kiosk, Adelaide
0km	go S on King William St
	follow route on inset map to Old Belair Rd
9.1	2km hard climb
11.1	Sheoak Rd (hard left at crest)
11.6	Sheoak Rd (dogleg)
12.1	onto bridge over train lines
	follow Sir Edwin Ave in Belair National Park
13.6	Gooch Rd (no sign)/The Valley Rd
14.6	Saddle Hill Rd (at Long Gully)
14.9	2km hard climb
17.2	Sheoak Rd (exit park)
18.2	800m very steep climb
19.2	Waverley Ridge Rd 'to Crafers'
20.0	Waverley Ridge Rd
20.2	Ayers Hill Rd
20.5	Ayers Hill Rd (no sign)
20.9	Avenue Rd
21.0	Mt Barker Rd, Stirling

Cue — Continued

23.7	Kingsland Rd, Aldgate
24.3	Edgeware Rd/Emery Rd
26.2	Williams Rd (no sign)
26.8	Stock Rd
29.5	Warrawong Sanctuary
	Macclesfield Rd (no sign), Mylor
37.8	Echunga
37.9	Angas River Tourist Dr (at pub)
47.6	Macclesfield
58.4	Adelaide Parade/North Parade
	follow signs 'to town centre'
60.3	Rankine St
60.6	South Terrace
60.7	Strathalbyn visitor centre

Elevation

See Day 2 p277

See Day 5 p283

SOUTH AUSTRALIA

detailing several buildings of historic interest, from the tourist office. **St Andrews Church** (1844) is worth checking out.

High St has several antique, bric-a-brac and craft shops, and the town hosts a **Collectors, Hobbies & Antique Fair** in August.

Places to Stay & Eat Next to the cricket pitch, *Strathalbyn Caravan Park* (☎ 8536 3681, Ashbourne Rd), has $11 tent sites and basic on-site vans from $20. The *Robin Hood Hotel* (☎ 8536 2608, 18 High St) has simple singles/doubles for $30/45, including a light breakfast. *Railway Cottages* (☎ 0407-601 692, 5 Parker Ave) has B&B from $110/120.

Pick up supplies at one of Dawson St's two seven-day *supermarkets*. The *cafe-bakery (24 High St)* is always popular. The four pubs in town all serve meals; *Victoria on the Park* and *The Terminus* both overlook the River Angas and have good bistros.

Day 2: Strathalbyn to Victor Harbor

3–4 hours, 53.4km
The early section of this day travels along an unsealed road that can be a little rough in places.

From Strathalbyn, quiet back roads take you across farm and scrub lands, before crossing the Finnis River. This area is of great significance to local Aboriginal people; two **scar trees**, from which canoes and other implements have been carved, are either side of the route.

A comparatively lush stretch takes you past the picturesque winery at **Currency Creek** (23.3km) and into the former river port town of **Goolwa** (32km). The town has a large number of **heritage buildings**, a **maritime museum** and an **interpretive centre**, where the town's glory days as a bustling river port are brought to life.

About 5km out of Goolwa the ride joins the **Ngarrinjeri Way bike route** and follows the stunning 'surf coast', hugging the coastline all the way to Victor Harbor. The route uses designated cycle ways and some residential streets along this popular holiday-home strip. It is clearly marked and is easy to follow. Should you lose your way, just head towards the beach and you will soon find the next sign.

A couple of derelict buildings either side of the bike route at 44.5km are the remains of **Pleasant Banks**, an old homestead owned by the Basham family, one of the region's first settlers. Creative signs tell their story.

Further along the coast the town of **Port Elliot** (46.5km) and its quaint beach are likely to entice.

Victor Harbor

A former whaling centre, 'Victor' occupies a superb location on the edge of Encounter Bay. Its temperate climate also attracts many elderly folk – hence the locals refer to it as 'God's Waiting Room'. Its proximity to some of SA's best surf beaches, however, ensures that Victor keeps its laid back, coastal charm, and the retirees share the streets with surfers.

Information The tourist office (☎ 8552 5821, @ vhtic@granite.net.au) is next to the causeway to Granite Island.

The main street – Ocean St – has several banks and ATMs. For bike repairs, head to Victor Harbour Cycle & Skate (☎ 8552 1417), 73 Victoria St.

Things to See & Do Most of Victor's attractions can be found around the grassy **Soldier's Memorial Reserve** along the foreshore. Wander – or take a horse-drawn cart – across the causeway to **Granite Island**, a penguin rookery. The **Penguin Interpretive Centre** (☎ 8552 7555) on the island operates one-hour guided walks every evening.

Whales have been intimately connected to the history of Victor for the best part of a century, and the **South Australian Whale Centre**, at the causeway end of Railway Terrace, has an interesting collection of old flensing tools, as well as displays detailing the need to protect these majestic creatures.

A self-guided walk takes in local historic buildings: the **Old Customs House & Station Master's Residence** (1866), the **Telegraph Station** (1869) and the **Fountain Inn** (1838). Pick up a brochure from the tourist office.

The town also hosts a **folk festival** on the Labour Day weekend in October.

Places to Stay & Eat The *Victor Harbor Beachfront Caravan Park* (☎ 8552 1111, 114 Victoria St) has shady tent sites for $18, and cabin accommodation from $47 to $69.50. BYO bedding.

A range of accommodation is available at *Anchorage at Victor Harbor* (☎ 8552 5970,

Day 2: Strathalbyn to Victor Harbor

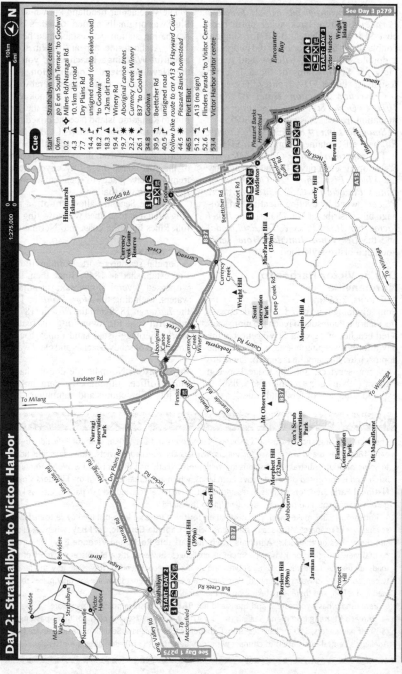

Cue

start		Strathalbyn visitor centre
0km		go E on South Terrace 'to Goolwa'
0.2	◇	Milnes Rd/Narragi Rd
4.3	↰	10.1km dirt road
7.7	↱	Dry Plains Rd
14.4	✳	unsigned road (onto sealed road)
18.2	↱	'to Goolwa'
18.3	↰	1.2km dirt road
19.4	↱	Winery Rd
19.7	✳	Aboriginal canoe trees
23.2	↰	Currency Creek Winery
26.1	↱	B37 'to Goolwa'
34.8		Goolwa
39.5	↰	Boettcher Rd
40.5	↱	unsigned road
44.5		follow bike route to cnr A13 & Hayward Court
46.5		Pleasant Banks homestead
51.2	↰	Port Elliot
52.6	↱	A13 (no sign)
53.4	↰	Flinders Parade 'to Victor Centre'
		Victor Harbor visitor centre

SOUTH AUSTRALIA

@ *victor@anchorage.mtx.net, 21 Flinders Parade)*. Seafront backpacker dorm beds cost $17. In the hotel, B&B for singles/doubles costs $40/65, or blow the budget on a double with a spa, balcony and ocean view for $140. Mains at the a la carte restaurant start at $11.50, or try the cafe.

Grosvenor Junction Hotel (☎ 8552 1011, 40 Ocean St) has backpacker accommodation from $22; rooms cost $30/55.

Smugglers Inn (☎ 8551 5200, 16 Crozier Rd) has self-contained rooms from $110.

The *supermarket (cnr Ocean & Torrens Sts)* is open seven days. For takeaways, try the *Victor Fish Shop (20 Ocean St)* or *Nino's Pizzaria (☎ 8552 3501, 16 Albert Place)*, owned by cycling identity and Colnago bike distributor Nino Salari. The *Hotel Victor (cnr Albert Place & The Esplanade)* and the *Grosvenor Junction Hotel* serve good pub bistro-style food.

Day 3: Victor Harbor to Normanville
4–5 hours, 75.9km

Some climbing is involved as the ride crosses the Fleurieu Peninsula to reach the more sheltered beaches along Gulf St Vincent, but the day affords sweeping coastal views and the approach to Normanville is superb. There are very few services, and the ridge between Parawa (39km) and Delamere (55.9km) is exposed. Take lots of food and water!

The spectacular headland known as **The Bluff** was originally named Rosetta's Head. A whaling station was established here in 1837. A short side trip at 16.2km to the beautiful **Waitpinga Beach** takes you into the **Newland Head Conservation Park**, which has bush *camping* and several walks.

At Delamere, it is possible to hook left to Cape Jervis (15km), from where the ferry runs to **Kangaroo Island** (see the boxed text).

It's worth detouring to visit either **Rapid Bay** (10km return) or **Second Valley** (4km return). A far cry from the pounding beaches of the surf coast, these tiny coves are extremely pretty places to spend an afternoon splashing in the shallows.

From the Second Valley turn-off, a stunning stretch of road lined with towering Norfolk Pines hugs the coast into Normanville.

Normanville
A popular seaside resort, Normanville was first established in 1849. Since then, it has witnessed several shipwrecks in adjacent waters, including the *Mary Smith* in 1856, the *Teaser* in 1859 and the *Rose* in 1875. A beautiful bay for swimming, it features World Heritage-listed sand dunes backing onto miles of sandy beaches and clear waters.

Information Normanville doesn't have a tourist office, although the caravan park has lots of brochures and pamphlets.

Kangaroo Island

The third-largest island off Australia's shores, Kangaroo Island sits 120km south of Adelaide. In the early 1880s, the island was a base for sealers, whalers and escaped convicts. Nowadays, it is home to some of South Australia's most pristine wilderness. Nearly half of the island is World Heritage-listed, and is comprised of dense native bush lands, which are contained within the **Flinders Chase National Park**. Predators such as foxes and rabbits have never reached 'KI', so natives such as kangaroos, bandicoots and possums are plentiful on the island.

Kangaroo Island makes an idyllic destination for the hard-core long-distance cycle tourist with several weeks to spare. Must-see destinations include **Cape de Couedic**, **Seal Bay**, where sea lions sun themselves on the rocks, **Admirals' Arch**, **Remarkable Rocks** and **Vivonne Bay**, for superb coastal views. Cycling on KI is not without its challenges, however. It's a big place and most of the roads are unsealed and very rough. Fat tyres and shocks are recommended. Towns are few and far between, so food and water are limited. Parndana, Kingscote and Penneshaw are the only places to reload and refuel, and there is no bike shop on the island.

Penneshaw has two hostels, and the island has B&Bs and bush camping spots galore.

To reach KI, Kangaroo Island Sealink (☎ 13 1301, @ kiexpert@sealink.com.au) takes passengers ($60 for passengers, $10 for bicycles) from Cape Jervis to Penneshaw. Sealink has a bus service from Adelaide's central bus station to connect with ferry departures ($14). Bookings are essential.

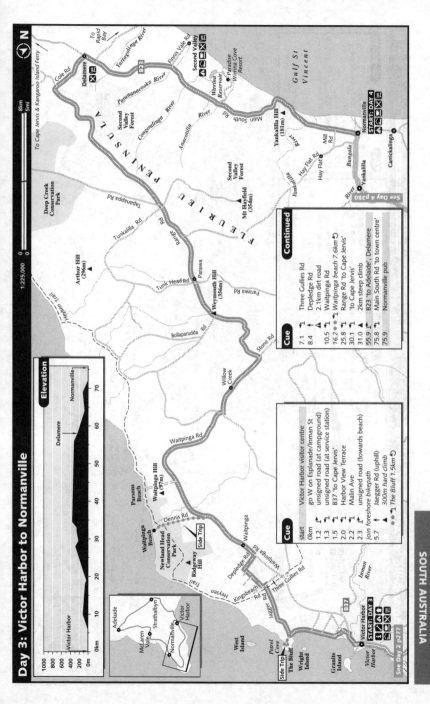

Day 3: Victor Harbor to Normanville

Elevation

1000
800
600
400
200
0m

Victor Harbor — Delamere — Normanville

0km 10 20 30 40 50 60 70

1:225,000

0   5mi   8km

N

To Cape Jervis & Kangaroo Island Ferry

Cue

start		Victor Harbor visitor centre
0km		go W on Esplanade/Inman St
1.2		unsigned road (at campground)
1.3		unsigned road (at service station)
1.5		B37 'to Cape Jervis'
2.0		Harbor View Terrace
2.2		Malin Ave
2.3		unsigned road (towards beach)
		join foreshore bikepath
5.7		Jaeger Rd (uphill)
		300m hard climb
	● ● ●	*The Bluff 1.5km* ↺

Cue Continued

7.1		Three Gullies Rd
8.4		Depledge Rd
		2.1km dirt road
10.5		Waitpinga Rd
16.2	● ● ●	*Waitpinga beach 7.6km* ↺
25.8		Range Rd 'to Cape Jervis'
		'to Cape Jervis'
30.1		2km steep climb
31.0		B23 'to Adelaide', Delamere
55.9		Main South Rd 'to town centre'
75.8		Normanville pub
75.9		

SOUTH AUSTRALIA

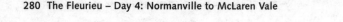

SOUTH AUSTRALIA

Day 4: Normanville to McLaren Vale

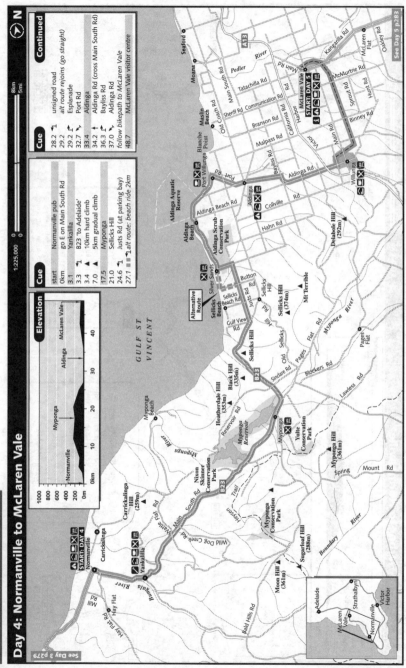

Cue (Continued)

28.2	↰	unsigned road
29.2		alt route rejoins (go straight)
29.2	↰	Esplanade
32.7	↱	Port Rd
33.4		Aldinga
34.2	↱	Aldinga Rd (cross Main South Rd)
36.3	↱	Bayliss Rd
37.0	↰	Aldinga Rd
		follow bikepath to McLaren Vale
48.7		McLaren Vale visitor centre

Cue

start		Normanville pub
0km		go E on Main South Rd
3.1		Yankalilla
3.3	↱	B23 'to Adelaide'
3.4	▲	10km hard climb
7.0	▲	5km gradual climb
17.5		Myponga
21.0		Sellicks Hill
24.6	↰	Justs Rd (at parking bay)
27.1	■■■	↰ *alt route: beach ride 2km*

Elevation

Normanville — Myponga — Aldinga — McLaren Vale

The chemist has a sub-branch of Bank SA. The newsagent is an agent for the Commonwealth Bank. Yankalilla Cycles & Mowers (☎ 8558 2507), 204 Main Rd, is 1.5km east of Normanville (on the Day 4 route).

Things to See & Do Take the plunge at Normanville **beach** – a glorious stretch of clean, white sand. High Country Trails (☎ 8558 2507) offers **horse rides** from an hour to a full day. The **'pub ride'** (☎ 8558 3200), which finishes with lunch at the Normanville Hotel (established in 1851), is an extremely decadent way to spend a morning.

Just up the road, Yankalilla's claim to fame is the tiny **Anglican church**. In 1994, mysterious images, believed to be of Jesus and the Virgin Mary, first appeared on the walls of the church, leading to the 140-year-old building becoming known as 'Australia's Lourdes'.

Places to Stay & Eat The beachside *Normanville Beach Caravan Park (☎ 8558 2038, Jetty Rd)* has tent sites for $14.85 and cabins for $44 to $73.70). *Normanville Hotel (☎ 8558 3200, cnr Main Rd & Cheeseman St)* has $80 self-contained cabins.

Yankalilla has several B&Bs – none of which are particularly cheap. Try *Meander Cottage (☎ 8558 3139, 161 Main South Rd)*, where a self-contained cottage costs $140.

The *supermarket (cnr Main Rd & Andrew Ave)* is open seven days. The *bakery (89 Main Rd)* has the usual, as well as superb sandwiches. The *Normanville Beach Cafe (Jetty Rd)* does simple meals and takeaways. Otherwise, try the *pub* for filling counter meals.

Min Palace (☎ 8558 2422, cnr Mary & Edwards St) is a Chinese and Thai restaurant just behind the supermarket; mains from $10.

Day 4: Normanville to McLaren Vale

3–4 hours, 48.7km

Day 4 heads inland across the Peninsula, before following the coast to reach the postcard-perfect bay of Port Willunga. From here, the route winds through the almond blossoms and the vineyards of the Southern Vale wine growing district, to finish at the wine growing (and drinking) hub of McLaren Vale.

From Yankalilla (3.1km), the road climbs slowly but steadily to reach **Myponga** (17.5km). Surrounded by lush hills, this is prime dairy land, and until 1980 produced most of the milk consumed in SA.

Sellicks Hill, of Tour Down Under fame, affords spectacular views of the azure waters of Gulf St Vincent. An alternative onto Button Rd allows you to take a short ride along the beach – watch out for cars.

From here, the road hugs the coast past Aldinga, where an **aquatic reserve** protects a rare reef formation offshore. The protected beach of **Port Willunga** is home to the simple kiosk-style restaurant *The Star of Greece*, which overlooks the wreck of the same name (it ran aground in 1888).

If the weather's fine, stop and take a swim. Or, if you want to go the 'Full Monty', **Maslins nudist beach** is 12km further up the main road.

The road heads inland after the town of Port Willunga through the vineyards to reach the outskirts of the pretty town of **Willunga**. Slate was discovered here in 1840 – check out the slate footpaths, gutters, roofs, bridges and even fence posts that adorn the town. At the turn of the century, almonds were introduced, and the roads around 'Willy' are lined with pretty pink blossoms in July and August.

At Willunga, a bikepath follows a disused railway line to McLaren Vale, the main centre of the Southern Vales wine district.

McLaren Vale

At last, some gastronomic indulgence! As the buzzing hub of the Southern Vales, McLaren Vale has several wineries and first-class restaurants located in the main street. The town also enjoys a superb setting, nestled in a valley of the Mt Lofty Ranges and surrounded by vineyards.

Information The visitor centre (☎ 8323 9944), Main Rd, has winery brochures, a wine bar for tastings, and also books accommodation. Main Rd has several banks and ATMs.

Things to See & Do Wine is the staff of life in McLaren Vale – most activities are wine related.

Whether you fancy yourself a bit of a wine buff, or have absolutely no idea what you're quaffing, then the **wine-tasting trial** offered at the visitor centre is bound to please and inform. Under the watchful eye

SOUTH AUSTRALIA

of an expert wine maker, tasters can sample various whites and reds, picking up some clues to prevent embarrassment when they hit the cellar door.

Spend an extra day in McLaren Vale to do the **winery tour** side trip – a leisurely, winding route through the vineyards and almond groves of the Southern Vales (see the boxed text 'Southern Vales Winery Tour' for side trip details).

The region has several conservation parks, including the **Onkaparinga River National Park**, which has several good **walking trails** (no bikes) – see the boxed text 'Southern Vales Winery Tour'.

Meet the locals at McLaren Vale's **Bushing Festival**, a week-long booze up in late November, which culminates with an enormous feast using regional produce.

Places to Stay & Eat Set among the vines, the ***McLaren Vale Lakeside Caravan Park*** (☎ 8323 9255, *Field St*) has tent sites for $15 and self-contained cabins from $55. Eight kilometres west at Maslins Beach the ***Beachwood Eco Tourist Park*** (☎ 8556 6113, *2 Tuit Rd*) has tent sites for $12.10.

Other accommodation options tend to be on the pricey side. ***McLarens on the Lake*** (☎ 8323 8911, *Kangarilla Rd*), which shares its quarters with the Serafino Winery; has singles/doubles for $99/121.

McLaren Vale is particularly well served by B&Bs: rooms at ***Southern Vales B&B***

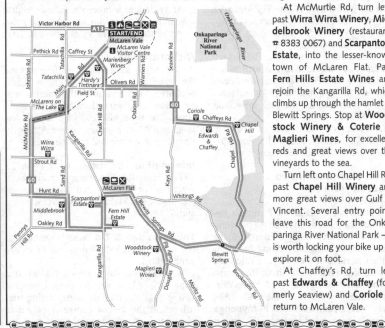

Southern Vales Winery Tour

1:120,000

With most wineries only a couple of kilometres apart on this 27km circuit, the chance to dawdle between cellars is too good to miss! Most open between 9am and 10am and close between 4pm and 5pm from Monday to Saturday; Sunday hours are usually from 11am to 4pm.

Far less developed than the Barossa Valley, it is not uncommon for the wine makers to greet you at the cellar door.

From the visitor centre, head back through town, past **Marienberg Wines**, **Hardy's Tintinara Winery**, **Tatachilla Winery** and out along the Kangarilla Rd past **McLarens on the Lake**. Hop onto the bikepath that you took into town and head towards Willunga.

At McMurtie Rd, turn left, past **Wirra Wirra Winery**, **Middelbrook Winery** (restaurant: ☎ 8383 0067) and **Scarpantoni Estate**, into the lesser-known town of McLaren Flat. Pass **Fern Hills Estate Wines** and rejoin the Kangarilla Rd, which climbs up through the hamlet of Blewitt Springs. Stop at **Woodstock Winery & Coterie** or **Maglieri Wines**, for excellent reds and great views over the vineyards to the sea.

Turn left onto Chapel Hill Rd, past **Chapel Hill Winery** and more great views over Gulf St Vincent. Several entry points leave this road for the Onkaparinga River National Park – it is worth locking your bike up to explore it on foot.

At Chaffey's Rd, turn left past **Edwards & Chaffey** (formerly Seaview) and **Coriole** to return to McLaren Vale.

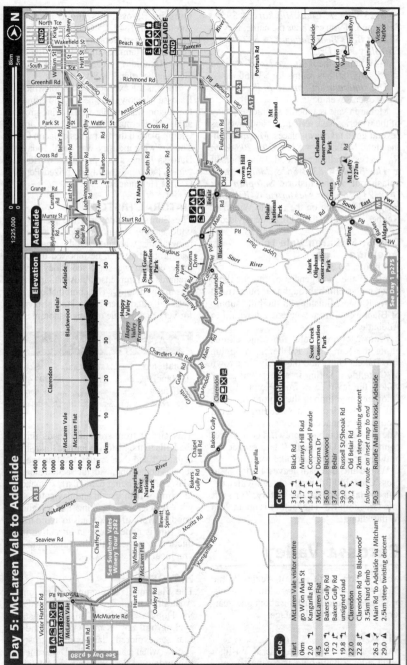

Day 5: McLaren Vale to Adelaide

SOUTH AUSTRALIA

Elevation

McLaren Vale	
McLaren Flat	
Clarendon	
Blackwood	
Belair	
Adelaide	

Adelaide

1:225,000

Cue

start		McLaren Vale visitor centre
0km	↑	go W on Main St
2.0	↱	Kangarilla Rd
4.5	↰	McLaren Flat
16.0	↱	Bakers Gully Rd
17.2	↰	Bakers Gully Rd
19.8	↱	unsigned road
22.0		Clarendon
22.8	↰	Clarendon Rd 'to Blackwood'
26.3	↗	3.5km hard climb
29.0	◁	Main Rd 'to Adelaide via Mitcham'
		2.5km steep twisting descent

Cue · Continued

31.6	↰	Black Rd
31.7	↱	Murrays Hill Rad
34.3	↰	Coromandel Parade
35.1	✧	Diosma Dr
36.0		Blackwood
37.4		Belair
39.0	↱	Russell St/Sheoak Rd
39.2	↰	Old Belair Rd
	◁	2km steep twisting descent
		follow route on inset map to end
50.3		Rundle Mall info kiosk, Adelaide

(☎ 8323 8144, 13 Chalk Hill Rd) cost $95 to $105; and, if you can *bear* the name, they're $120 at *Bev's Bear Cottages* (☎ 8323 9351, 56 Valley View Dr).

In Willunga, the *Willunga Hotel* (☎ 8556 2135, High St) has rooms for $30/60.

The *supermarket (cnr Main Rd & Field St)* is open seven days.

McLaren Vale is a foodie's paradise. Many of the wineries have restaurants and town has several good *takeaway* places. *Magnum's* in the Hotel McLaren (☎ 8323 8208, 208 Main Rd) serves excellent pub food. Treat yourself at *The Barn* (☎ 8323 8618, Main Rd), or splash out at the historic *Salopian Inn* (☎ 8323 8769, cnr McMurtrie & Willunga Rds), 2.5km south on the road to Willunga. Neither is cheap and bookings are advised.

Day 5: McLaren Vale to Adelaide
3–4 hours, 50.3km
Work off the indulgences of the Southern Vales with a climb through the southern Mt Lofty Ranges, finishing in the hills suburb of Blackwood, from where it's downhill to Adelaide.

From McLaren Vale, the route climbs along the Kangarilla Rd before dropping into Bakers Gully and the pretty little town of **Clarendon**. Sitting in a deep and pretty valley, the town dates from around 1880s. Another long climb to the top of Chandlers Hill is rewarded by a sweeping descent though Coromandel Valley and the start of Adelaide's suburban sprawl. The ride reconnects with Old Belair Rd, to retrace the outward route along the bike route.

Where the bikepath leaves Porter St to cross Greenhill Rd, treat yourself with a detour to **Haighs chocolate factory**. Turn left into Greenhill Rd. The factory is about 20m further along.

Barossa Valley

About 55km north-east of Adelaide, the Barossa is Australia's best known wine-producing district, crushing about one quarter of Australia's total vintage.

HISTORY
Named by the surveyor-general William Light after a battlefield in Spain, the pic-turesque Barossa sits about 75km from Adelaide. In 1842, 25 German families settled the town of Bethany, and the following year, more families moved into Langmeil (now Tanunda), creating something of a German heartland in SA.

But it is the excellent wines for which the Barossa is renowned. The soil and climate of the region was similar to the wine-growing areas of Germany and in 1847, Johann Gramp planted the first vines at Jacob Creek. The SA wine industry was born! Today, the Barossa vineyards produce world-class wines, including the highly prized Penfolds Grange Hermitage.

NATURAL HISTORY
The Barossa's vineyards are nestled in a wide valley. Johann Menge, the German mineralogist who surveyed the area in 1838, was prophetic when he reported that 'I am quite certain we shall see vineyards and orchards and immense fields that are matchless in this colony'. The combination of valleys, hills and open-range land also makes for very picturesque cycling panoramas.

Barossa Heritage

Duration	6 days
Distance	301.4km
Difficulty	moderate
Start/End	Adelaide

This circuit from Adelaide heads through the Hills to the historic German township of Hahndorf and then around the Barossa. The route is undulating, with the section along the Mawson Trail being particularly demanding, in terms of both terrain and navigation. But, with its German-speaking history and its good network of back roads to avoid traffic, this ride is nonetheless an attractive introduction to some of the historical and geographical riches of SA.

HISTORY
The Mawson Trail commemorates one of Australia's greatest explorers. Named after Sir Douglas Mawson, this long-distance cycling trail covers much of the land that Mawson explored – largely on his trusty bicycle – when teaching in the Department of Mineralogy at the University of Adelaide.

NATURAL HISTORY

Stretching north from Adelaide, the terrain of the Mt Lofty Ranges and Barossa Valley is best described as steeply undulating. The area through Eden Valley is noted for its towering river red gums, while the Barossa Valley is noted for, well, its vineyards.

Unfortunately, the hills have seen more than their fair share of bush fires. The most tragic were the Ash Wednesday fires, which swept though the hills on February 16, 1983. The ferocity of the fires took most people by surprise, and they razed several historic homesteads, as well as claiming 28 lives.

PLANNING
When to Ride

While spring and autumn are the most picturesque (and temperate) seasons to cycle, it is worth trying to be in the Barossa in September for the Spring into the Barossa food and wine festival.

Avoid the Barossa from December to February as it gets incredibly hot – days frequently hit 40°C.

Accommodation can be extremely hard to find in January; also avoid the Easter long weekend, when roads are especially busy because of the popular Oakbank racing carnival.

Maps

The RAA's *Central-North* (1:200,000) map covers the region adequately. The final section of Day 6 along the Linear Park bikepath is detailed on the free No 5 *Bike Direct* map, available from the State Information Centre.

GETTING TO/FROM THE RIDE

See the Gateway Cities section (pp272–73) for information on getting to/from Adelaide.

THE RIDE
Day 1: Adelaide to Hahndorf

3–4 hours, 45.4km

Although not *too* long distance-wise, your legs will still feel the pain of the short, sharp climbs in the undulating Adelaide Hills. This is serious lactic acid territory. Fortunately, you can stop and stretch at several places along the way.

The ride climbs out of Adelaide along the western scarp of the Mt Lofty Ranges to Norton Summit – a popular training spot for Australian Institute of Sport and local cyclists.

Cleland Wildlife Park, a 3km return side trip (downhill, in; uphill, out) at 23.5km, is where you can cuddle a koala, view numerous species of Australian fauna or get a coffee at the *cafe*. It's open from 9.30am to 4.30pm; adult entry costs $9.50.

The Mawson Trail

The Mawson Trail is a true long-distance cycling challenge. Extending from Adelaide through the Hills and mid-north to Blinman in the Flinders Ranges, the route offers more than 800km of car-free cycling.

Named after Sir Douglas Mawson (1882–1958), the British-born geographer, geologist and Antarctic explorer who led the first expedition to reach the south magnetic pole (1907–09), as well as the first Australian Antarctic expedition (1911–14), the trail winds through the heart of South Australia.

Developed by the Adelaide Mountain Bike Club and the SA Touring Cyclists' Association, among others, the trail follows minor roads, dirt tracks, stock routes, forest trails and vacant Crown land. The route is marked at intersections, turn-offs and at 1km intervals. Excellent topographical strip maps of the route are also available from the Map Shop (☎ 8231 2033), 16A Peel St.

The Mawson Trail is an arduous but rewarding cycling undertaking. Completing the full Mawson Trail would take the best part of a fortnight, and much of the route is very remote. You're likely to encounter few people or facilities along the way, and bush camping is the order of the day. It is possible to restock food supplies every few days.

The Mawson Trail should not be undertaken lightly. The trail can be very rugged, not to mention steep, in places. Be prepared to push your bike on the climb from Castambul, near Adelaide, and up onto the southern Flinders Ranges in the Wirraara Forest. Still, the rugged remoteness and the spectacular views of an ever-changing landscape more than compensate for the effort.

While a touring bike could possibly negotiate the full trail, a mountain bike is by far your best option. If you want to hire a mountain bike, try Flinders Outdoor Leisure (☎ 8359 3344), 235 Pirie St, where you'll pay $14 per day or $70 for a week.

SOUTH AUSTRALIA

Day 1: Adelaide to Hahndorf

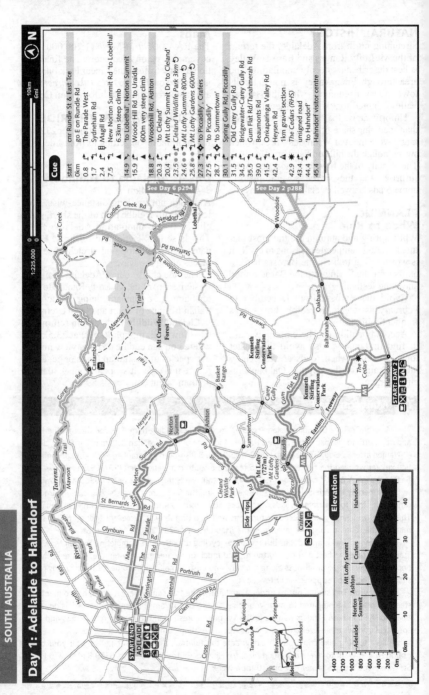

Cue		
start		cnr Rundle St & East Tce
0km		go E on Rundle Rd
0.8		The Parade West
1.7		Sydneham Rd
2.4		Magill Rd
7.5		New Norton Summit Rd 'to Lobethal'
		6.3km steep climb
14.9		'to Lobethal', Norton Summit
15.9		Woods Hill Rd 'to Uraidla'
		600m very steep climb
18.8		Woodshill Rd, Ashton
20.3		'to Cleland'
20.4		Mt Lofty Summit Dr 'to Cleland'
23.5		Cleland Wildlife Park 3km
24.6		Mt Lofty Summit 800m
25.8		Mt Lofty Gardens 600m
27.3		'to Piccadilly', Craters
27.5		'to Piccadilly'
28.7		'to Summertown'
30.1		Spring Gully Rd, Piccadilly
31.5		Old Carey Gully Rd
34.5		Bridgewater-Carey Gully Rd
35.5		Gum Flat Rd/Tanahmerah Rd
39.0		Beaumonts Rd
41.5		Onkaparinga Valley Rd
42.4		Heysen Rd
42.9		1km gravel section
		The Cedars (RHS)
43.4		unsigned road
44.4		'to Hahndorf'
45.4		Hahndorf visitor centre

See Day 6 p294

See Day 2 p288

Mt Lofty summit, a side trip at 24.6km, also has a *cafe* and great views back over Adelaide. Don't miss the display of newspaper articles, detailing the bush fires of Ash Wednesday. Shortly after, another side trip (at 25.8km) leads to the picturesque **Mt Lofty Botanic Gardens**.

On the outskirts of Hahndorf is **The Cedars** (42.9km; ☎ 8388 7277), the original house and studio of famed artist Hans Heysen. Tours are conducted daily, except Saturday.

Hahndorf

Meaning 'Hahn's village' in German, Hahndorf was named after the captain of the immigrant ship *Zebra*, which delivered the first wave of Lutheran settlers to the hills in 1839.

With many antique and other interesting shops to be found along the tree-lined main street, Hahndorf is a delightful, if touristy, cycling destination.

Information The tourist office (☎ 8388 1184) is at 41 Main St. Bank SA has a branch at 62 Main St; an ANZ ATM is outside the tourist office.

Things to See & Do Wall to wall with craft shops, art galleries, gift shops, a leathersmith and restaurants, **Main St** is truly a wanderer's paradise. A **heritage walk** links several of the original German buildings, including the incredibly-friendly **German Arms Hotel**. Pick up a free brochure from the tourist office.

To commemorate the arrival of the first settlers in 1839, Hahndorf holds several German-style festivals throughout the year, including **Founders Day** in January.

Places to Stay & Eat The *Hahndorf Resort Caravan Park* (☎ 8388 7921, 145A Main St), about 1.5km out of town, charges $14.30 for a tent site, but the 'resort' is really not geared for tent camping, with rock-hard ground (and the ever-present power lines).

Warning

⚠ Some care will need to be taken during Days 5 & 6, where the ride follows the unsealed Mawson Trail. A touring bike should have no problems negotiating the surface, but carry at least one extra tube.

Several cabin options, from $60.50 to $165, are also available.

Chamomile Cottage (☎ 8388 7079, 54 English St) can accommodate one or two cyclists. The $20 per-person tariff includes linen and breakfast.

Hahndorf Inn Motor Lodge (☎ 8388 1000, 35 Main St) has rooms for $87. *Zorro Hacienda* (☎ 8388 1309, 60 Main St) has motel units starting at $93.50 or self-contained apartments for $143.

The *supermarket (Main St)* is open seven days. Otherwise, go German! Try the *German Arms Hotel* (69 Main St) or *Karl's German Coffee House Restaurant* (☎ 8388 7171, 17 Main St).

Day 2: Hahndorf to Springton
2½–4 hours, 55.7km

Gentle climbs and sweeping descents through expansive, tree-lined valleys can't help but win you over to the quiet charm of the Adelaide Hills. The terrain is gently undulating until the final 10km or so, where a 'false flat' makes the run into Springton harder on your legs than it appears.

The ride starts by following the line of the **Onkaparinga River** through the towns of Balhannah, Oakbank and Woodside, where it cuts through lush, green countryside (on some dirt roads) to reach Mt Torrens and the pretty town of **Mt Pleasant** (46.6km).

A short side trip (on dirt) before the final drop into Springton leads to **Grand Cru Winery** (☎ 8568 2378), set in a pleasant courtyard surrounded by several restored old buildings. Tastings are held daily from 10am to 5pm.

Springton

At the top of the River Torrens, Springton is a pretty, if uneventful, place to spend the night. It has no tourist office, bank or bike shop. In fact, the town's main attraction is the **Herbig Tree**, a river red gum that Frederich & Caroline Herbig used as their home for two years in the late 1850s.

Springton Herb Haus Gallery (☎ 0500-800 552), 10–12 Miller St, is interesting for its herb gardens and crafts.

Places to Stay & Eat The nearest camping is at *Murray Recreation Park* (☎ 8564 1107), 6km north on the main road in Eden Valley; sites cost $3.30 per person.

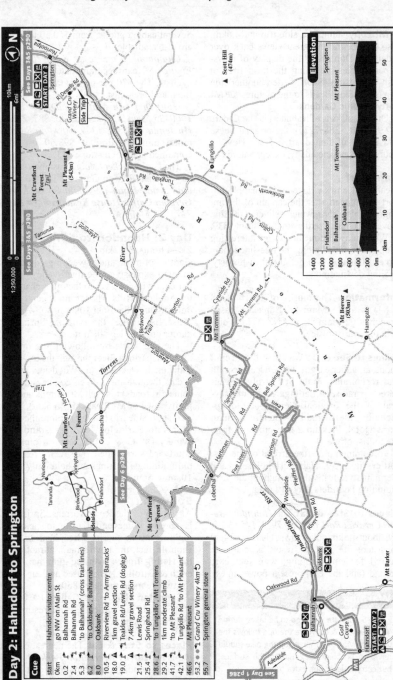

SOUTH AUSTRALIA

Day 2: Hahndorf to Springton

Elevation

Cue	
start	Hahndorf visitor centre
0km	go NW on Main St
0.2	Balhannah Rd
2.4	Balhannah Rd
5.3	'to Balhannah' (cross train lines)
6.2	'to Oakbank', Balhannah
8.0	Oakbank
10.5	Riverview Rd 'to Army Barracks'
18.0	1km gravel section
19.0	Teakles Rd/Lewis Rd (dogleg)
	7.4km gravel section
21.5	Lewis Road
25.4	Springhead Rd
28.6	'to Tungkillo', Mt Torrens
29.2	1km moderate climb
41.7	'to Mt Pleasant'
42.1	Tungkillo Rd 'to Mt Pleasant'
46.6	Mt Pleasant
53.2	Grand Cru Winery 4km
55.7	Springton general store

See Day 1 p286

Wouldn't *you* be content if you lived in the Barossa Valley, one of Australia's premier wine regions?

Tour McLaren Vale vineyards.

Or get back to nature on Kangaroo Island, not far from Adelaide.

Strathalbyn, outside Adelaide, is the quintessential country town, with wide streets and laid-back pubs.

Perth's a great city for cycling (Narrows Bridge).

Nearby Fremantle has a heritage feel.

See unusual Australian plants close up (grass trees).

Introduced paddymelons line the roads.

Wild flowers carpet WA in spring (copper cups).

Glide through the karri forest on Caves Road.

Other accommodation options tend to be limited (if everything is full continue cycling to Angaston) and on the upmarket side. Try the *Springton Herb Haus Gallery*, for B&B at around $125 a double; book ahead.

In Mt Pleasant, the *Talunga Hotel-Motel* (☎ *8568 2015, 43 Melrose St*) has units from $55/71.50, including light breakfast.

You don't have many options on the food front. There's a small *general store* and Springton Herb Haus Gallery has a pleasant *cafe* serving coffee and light snacks.

Cafe C Restaurant (☎ *8568 2633, Main St*), in the town's old blacksmith shop, is open Friday night and for lunch and dinner over the weekend. The *Springton Hotel* (☎ *8568 2290, cnr Miller & Main St*) may be your best bet for evening meals.

Day 3: Springton to Nuriootpa
3–4 hours, 43.9km

A short day in the saddle, Day 3 winds through Eden Valley to reach Nuriootpa, in the Barossa Valley. As well as passing several wineries, the route does take in some Barossa landmarks that aren't wine-related.

Kaiser Stuhl Conservation Park is a short, good side trip at 18.8km. Two walks start from the Tanunda Creek Rd entrance.

Collingrove Homestead (26.5km; ☎ 8564 2061), built in 1856, comes after a sweeping descent through Flaxmans Valley. Once the home of George Fife Angas, the founder of Angaston, Collingrove is now owned by the National Trust, and is furnished with many of George's original antiques. The homestead is also a *B&B* and has a *restaurant*.

The route passes through the middle of **Lindsay Park Stud** (32km), home of the Hayes horse-racing dynasty, winners (so far) of three Melbourne Cups. Just after the stud is the **Yalumba Winery**; a short side trip at 34.7km.

Angaston (36.6km), a thriving little town with quaint shops with crafts, antiques and bric-a-brac lining its main street (Murray St), is blessed with plenty of *accommodation*, *takeaways*, *cafes* and *restaurants*.

Nuriootpa
As the commercial centre of the Barossa Valley, 'Nuri' perhaps lacks some of the quaint Germanic charm of other parts of the valley. It is still a pretty place, however, with the Para River winding through its centre.

Information Tourist brochures are available from several businesses in Murray St

Wines of the Barossa Valley

The Barossa is different from any other Australian wine region. Settled by German families, the vineyards were planted in small plots on family farms. Even today, the vineyards are still small, which makes for a veritable patchwork of different varieties, from light rieslings to full-bodied shirazes.

Some of the better-known wineries are:

Basedow Wines (Murray St, Tanunda) Its cavernous wine tasting area is bursting with atmosphere.

Bethany (Bethany Rd, Bethany) Perhaps the most scenic of all Barossa wineries, this winery sits in the shadow of the infamous Menglers Hill (see the boxed text 'Tour Down Under' earlier in this chapter).

Chateau Dorrien (Seppeltsfield Rd, Dorrien) This small winery produces a range of mead and 'stickies' – try the quandong liqueur.

Orlando Wines (Rowland Flat; see Day 5) Home of Jacob's Creek, the site of South Australia's very first vineyard, planted in 1847 by the early Lutheran settler Johann Gramp.

Peter Lehmann Wines (Para Rd, Tanunda) The patriarch of the valley, the wines produced at this family-owned winery have an enviable reputation both locally and internationally.

Rockford Wines (Krondorf Rd, Bethany) Small and intimate, its tasting room is a cosy old stable.

Seppelts (Seppeltsfield; see Day 4) This enormous complex looms large on the palm-fringed road between Greenock and Marananga.

Yalumba (Angaston; see Day 3) Dating back to 1849, it is still owned and managed by relatives of the original Yalumba family.

Stop by the tourist office in Tanunda, which has a brochure listing addresses and opening times, as well as other wineries in the region.

SOUTH AUSTRALIA

SOUTH AUSTRALIA

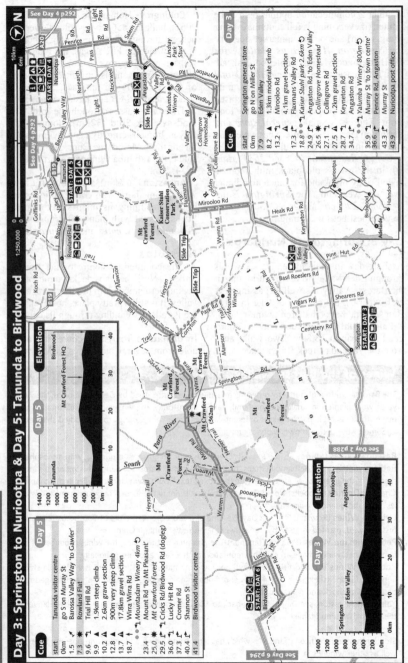

Day 3: Springton to Nuriootpa & Day 5: Tanunda to Birdwood

Day 5

Cue

start	Tanunda visitor centre
0km	go S on Murray St
1.5	Barossa Valley Way 'to Gawler'
7.3	Rowland Flat
9.6	Trail Hill Rd
9.9	1.9km steep climb
10.2	2.6km gravel section
12.8	900m very steep climb
13.7	17.8km gravel section
18.7	Wirra Wirra Rd
23.4	Mountadam Winery 4km ↰
25.0	Mount Rd 'to Mt Pleasant'
29.5	Mt Crawford Forest
36.0	Cricks Rd/Birdwood Rd (dogleg)
37.3	Lucky Hit Rd
40.4	Cromer Rd
41.4	Shannon St
	Birdwood visitor centre

Day 3

Cue

start	Springton general store
0km	go N on Miller St
7.9	Eden Valley
8.2	1.3km moderate climb
13.2	Mirooloo Rd
17.3	4.1km gravel section
18.8	Flaxmans Valley Rd
	Kaiser Stuhl park 2.6km ↰
24.9	Angaston Rd 'to Eden Valley' ↰
26.5	Collingrove Homestead
27.1	Collingrove Rd
27.5	1.2km gravel section
28.7	Keyneton Rd
34.7	Angaston Rd
	Yalumba Winery 800m ↰
35.9	Murray St 'to town centre'
36.6	Penrice Rd, Angaston
43.3	Murray St
43.9	Nuriootpa post office

Elevation

Day 5

Day 3

(try the BP service station), or call the Tanunda visitor centre (☎ 8563 0600, ⓔ bwta @dove.net.au) for information.

For bike repairs head to Barossa Lawnmowers (☎ 8562 2139), 49 Railway Terrace.

Places to Stay & Eat The shady *Barossa Valley Tourist Park (☎ 8562 1404, ⓔ barp ark@dove.net.au, Penrice Rd)* has tent sites for $13.50 and cabins from $32.50. *Bunkhaus Travellers Hostel (☎ 8562 2260, Barossa Valley Way)*, about 1.5km towards Tanunda (look for the keg), has $15 dorm beds or doubles in a quiet cottage for $44.

Nuriootpa has plenty of B&Bs. *Karawatha Guest House (☎ 8562 1746, cnr Greenock Rd & Stonewall St)* is 3.5km west (take Gawler St). A basic single costs $45, doubles cost $70. The *Nuriootpa Vine Court Motel (☎ 8562 2111, 49 Murray St)* charges $71/82 B&B for singles/doubles.

The *supermarket* (Murray St) opens daily. Many of the butchers and bakers in Nuriootpa still use traditional methods. *Linke's butcher (27 Murray St)* is famous for its *jaegerbraten* (stuffed pork belly) and *lachshinken* (smoked pork fillet), both prepared in smokehouses out the back (which they are often happy to show visitors). *Linke's Bakery & Tearooms (40 Murray St)* is another tradition in Nuri.

Murray St has several takeaways, including *Nuriootpa Pizza (☎ 8562 1896, 51 Murray St)*. The *Angas Park Hotel (☎ 8462 1050, 28 Murray St)* and the *Vine Inn (☎ 8562 2133, 14 Murray St)* have good pub meals.

Shangri-La Thai (☎ 8562 3559, 31 Murray St) has green curry chicken for $10.50 (closed Tuesday). While *Kaisler Estate Restaurant (☎ 8562 2711, Barossa Valley Way)*, on the outskirts of town towards Tanunda, serves regional dishes from $16.

Day 4: Nuriootpa to Tanunda

3½–4½ hours, 52km

A relatively easy day, the route presents no navigational challenges. The terrain is undulating, but has no climbs of any real note.

A **cairn** (11.6km) marks the spot where Captain Charles Sturt's party rested in 1844 on its central Australian expedition.

The former copper-mining town of **Kapunda** (22km) is where, in 1842, a rich copper deposit was found. At its peak in 1861,

the town was the colony's largest commercial centre outside Adelaide. A side trip at 22.9km marks the location of the **original mine**. A monument to **Cornish miners** is on the way out of town.

The **Seppelts Winery** (40.9km) and the **Seppelt family mausoleum** (42.4km), where generations of this famous wine-making family have been buried, follow in quick succession on the winding road through the hamlet of Seppeltsfield.

Tanunda

Originally named Langmeil, Tanunda was one of the first Lutheran settlements in the Barossa Valley. The town still retains much of its German heritage – the Tanunda *liedertafel* choir is legendary.

Murray St is the main drag, where most services can be found.

Information The tourist office (☎ 8563 0600, ⓔ bwta@dove.net.au) is at 66–68 Murray St. Murray St has several banks and ATMs. Tanunda doesn't have a bike shop; the nearest is in Nuriootpa.

Things to See & Do As befitting one of the earliest settlements in the valley, Tanunda has several **historic buildings**, including the early cottages around Goat Square on John St – the original market centre of Tanunda. **Brauer Biotherapies** (☎ 8563 2932), 1 Para Rd, can offer just the pick-me-up for a weary cyclist; it produces natural homeopathic medicines and remedies. Weekday tours are available.

For a true taste of the Barossa, join the locals in a 'schluck' of port at the **Tanunda Club**, 45 MacDonnell St. Widely regarded as the 'soul' of the Barossa, you'll need to find someone to sign you in to the club, but the bar will be packed and the atmosphere friendly.

Places to Stay & Eat The *Tanunda Caravan & Tourist Park (☎ 8563 2784, Barossa Valley Way)*, 1.4km south of town, has tent sites for $14, on-site vans for $35, and cabins from $45.

Tanunda Hotel (☎ 8563 2030, 51 Murray St) has $60 self-contained doubles ($70 with en suite).

About 3.5km north of town, the *Barossa Junction Resort (☎ 8563 3400, Barossa Valley Way)* has a pool, spa, tennis courts

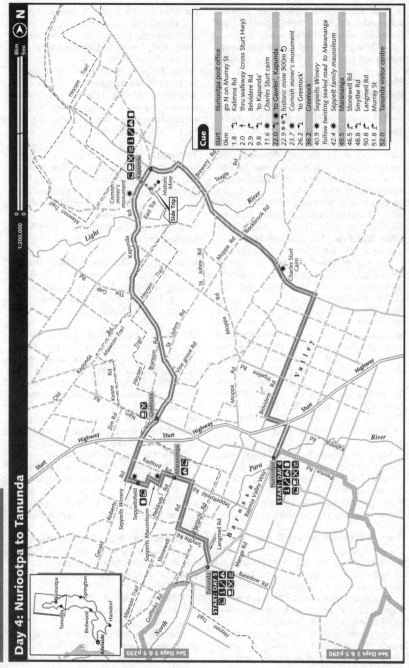

SOUTH AUSTRALIA

Day 4: Nuriootpa to Tanunda

N
8km
5mi

1:200,000

Cue		
start		Nuriootpa post office
0km		go N on Murray St
1.8		Kalimna Rd
2.0		thru walkway (cross Sturt Hwy)
2.9		Belvidere Rd
9.8		'to Kapunda'
11.6	✱	Charles Sturt cairn
22.0		'to Gawler', Kapunda
22.9		historic mine 900m
23.7	✱	Cornish miner's monument
26.2		'to Greenock'
36.2		Greenock
40.9	✱	Seppelts Winery
42.4		follow twisting sealed road to Marananga
45.5		Marananga
46.5		Stonewell Rd
48.8		Smythe Rd
50.8		Langmeil Rd
51.8		Murray St
52.0		Tanunda visitor centre

START: DAY 4
Nuriootpa

START: DAY 5
Tanunda

See Days 3 & 5 p290

and a train theme. 'Carriages' cost $76/87 for a single/double.

The Victorian *Paranook B&B* (☎ *8563 0208, 6 Murray St)* is conveniently central; singles/doubles cost $100/150.

The *supermarket (Murray St)* is open seven days. *Apex Bakery (Elizabeth St)* has sensational local breads and pastries. Built in 1924, the bakery still uses its original wood-fired ovens and recipes.

There are several eateries in Murray St. The *Tanunda Hotel (51 Murray St)* serves good pub meals, or *1918 Bistro & Grill* (☎ *8563 0405, 94 Murray St)* is the place for a more upmarket feed. *Cafe Heidelberg* (☎ *8563 2151, 8 Murray St)* does traditional German fare with mains starting at $12 (closed Tuesday).

Day 5: Tanunda to Birdwood

2½–3½ hours, 41.4km

Today's map is combined with that for Day Day 3, on p290. A tough stretch, this section follows the Mawson Trail out of the Barossa and into Mt Crawford Forest. There are lots of short, steep climbs, and some not so short, on the way back into the Mt Lofty Ranges and the historic finish town of Birdwood.

Much of the ride is on unsealed forest roads. They are in very good condition, just a little bumpy in places! However, the tranquillity and solitude of pedalling car-free through thick forest more than compensates.

Orlando Wines, the home of the Jacob's Creek label, is in the hamlet of Rowland Flat (7.3km). Another winery, **Mountadam** (☎ 8564 1101) is a 4km side trip off the route at 18.7km. Its chardonnay is highly regarded and tastings are available from 11am to 4pm.

Mt Crawford Forest (25km) is a popular recreation and picnic area. The arboretum walk (20 minutes) takes in many of its highlights. Bush *camping* costs $5; permits are available at forest headquarters (☎ 8524 6004), off Murray Vale Rd.

Birdwood

Originally called 'Blumberg' (the hill of flowers), Birdwood is a pretty town, nestled in the heart of the Mt Lofty Ranges. Like nearby Lobethal, Lutheran families settled Birdwood in the 1840s.

The Top of the Torrens Galley (☎ 8568 5577), Shannon St, acts as the town's visitor centre. Other than that the town is decidedly lacking in facilities; it doesn't have a bank or bike shop. It is really just an attractive and convenient place to catch your breath before the final run into Adelaide.

Things to See & Do Several National Trust-listed **buildings** are now home to art and crafts shops. The impressive **Flour Mill**, built in 1852, is a reminder of Birdwood's former glory as an agricultural powerhouse.

The **National Motor Museum**, which traces the motoring history of Australia, occupies part of the Mill. Featuring everything from FJ Holdens to vintage motorbikes, the museum is the finish point for the annual Bay to Birdwood Run, a vintage car rally that begins in suburban Glenelg.

Places to Stay & Eat Like most places in the hills, accommodation options are mostly luxurious B&Bs.

Mud-brick *Birdwood B&B* (☎/*fax 8568 5444, 38 Olivedale St)* offers cottage accommodation from $85 for two ($160 for four). At *Blumberg Mews* (☎ *8568 5551, 7 Cromer Rd)*, single/double rooms cost $104.50/121.

The *supermarket (Shannon St)* is open seven days. The *Blumberg Tavern (Shannon St)* serves lunches and dinners, or there's always the *takeaway* selling the usual greasy stodge – perfect after a hard day on the bike!

Day 6: Birdwood to Adelaide

3–4 hours, 63km

Day 6 follows a combination of unsealed roads, sealed roads and bikepaths through steeply undulating terrain. The section out of Lobethal is particularly hard on the legs.

The ride heads out of Birdwood along the unsealed Mawson Trail, passing through pretty **Lobethal** (16.2km). One of the original Lutheran settlements, the town takes its name from the German for 'valley of praise'.

At the Lenswood Rd, the route leaves the trail (which gets very rough) to follow the sealed Fox Creek Rd and Gorge Rd to the outskirts of Adelaide. Those riding well-equipped mountain bikes can continue along the Mawson Trail into town.

From **Linear Park** (44.3km), a dual bikepath follows the River Torrens into the centre of Adelaide. It's not well signposted, but if you keep the river in sight (except for a short section beside the bus route) and to your left you won't have any problems.

SOUTH AUSTRALIA

SOUTH AUSTRALIA

Day 6: Birdwood to Adelaide

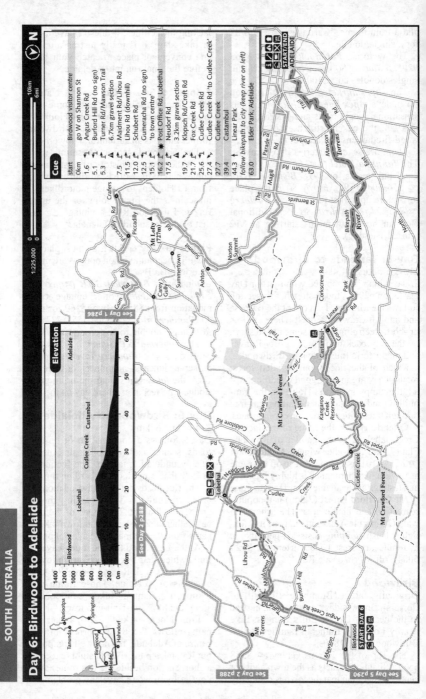

Cue

start	Birdwood visitor centre
0km	go W on Shannon St
1.6	Angus Creek Rd
5.1	Burford Hill Rd (no sign)
5.3	Turner Rd/Mawson Trail
	6.7km gravel section
7.5	Maidment Rd/Lihou Rd
11.5	Lihou Rd (downhill)
12.0	Schubert Rd
12.5	Gumeracha Rd (no sign)
15.1	'to town centre'
16.2	Post Office Rd, Lobethal
17.5	Neudorf Rd
	3.2km gravel section
19.7	Klopsch Rd/Croft Rd
21.7	Fox Creek Rd
25.6	Cudlee Creek Rd
27.4	Cudlee Creek Rd 'to Cudlee Creek'
27.7	Cudlee Creek
39.4	Castambul
44.3	Linear Park
	follow bikepath to city (keep river on left)
63.0	Elder Park, Adelaide

Elevation

Birdwood — Lobethal — Cudlee Creek — Castambul — Adelaide

1:225,000

Western Australia

Western Australia's vast land mass accounts for one third of the entire country. While much of the state is inhospitable desert, the small coastal strip in the south-west corner is green, fertile and popular for cycling.

The south-west's bright-green vegetation against wide, deep-blue skies and sparkling water gives an impression of looking through a polarising filter. During spring, the landscape is enlivened by the marvellous floral displays that have made Western Australia (WA) famous.

The warm climate, beautiful surrounds and sandy soil (which gives a beachy impression, even away from the beach) creates a laid-back, barefoot atmosphere and strong outdoors culture.

With such huge distances, it's no surprise that WA is very car-oriented. However, the population is small enough to have good, lightly-trafficked roads.

HISTORY

It's believed Aboriginal people first landed in the north of Western Australia, perhaps 60,000 years ago. Near Perth, stone tools have been found, along with charcoal from a campfire made about 39,500 years ago.

The region's position near the Indian Ocean trading routes led to early European contact. Dutch and English ships explored sections of the coast during the 17th century.

The French showed interest in the early 1800s and an outpost was established at Albany in 1826.

Captain James Stirling began a second, English, settlement (Perth) in 1829. Enthusiastic and ambitious, he spoke of lush country, convincing the British government to grant land and financial aid to settlers.

Aboriginal–European relations soured during the early years as the Europeans moved into the hunting grounds of the Nyoongar people. In 1834, Stirling led an expedition to eliminate Nyoongar resistance, ambushing and killing around 50 Nyoongar people in 1½ hours. Aboriginal people were also hit hard by European diseases.

Life for new settlers was hard and lonely. Mail to England took a year; ships were infrequent and supplies ran out. With labour

---

In Brief

Area Code: ☎ 08

Highlights
- limestone caves, wild flowers and beaches in the **Capes region**
- **Margaret River** wines and vibe
- giant trees, unspoilt coastal parks and laid-back towns on the **south coast**
- **Avon Valley** historic towns and spring wild flowers

Special Events
- **Kings Park Wildflower Festival** (Sep)
- **Festival Fremantle** (Nov)
- **York Jazz Festival** (Sep)

Cycling Events
- **On Your Bike Tour** nine-day supported ride (Oct); contact the Cycle Touring Association
- **Karri Cup** mountain-bike race (Mar), Northcliffe; contact the Northcliffe visitor centre

Gourmet Specialities
- marron (freshwater crayfish) and seafood
- Margaret River cabernet sauvignon
- Watsonia cheese

State Tourist Information
Western Australian Tourist Centre
(☎ 1300-361 351, 🖳 www.westernaustra lia.net) cnr Forrest Place & Wellington St, Perth

---

in short supply, the new colony requested convicts, who built public buildings and roads from 1850 to 1868.

It was not until the gold rushes of the 1890s that the colony really began to progress. Today, a larger and far more technologically advanced mineral boom forms the basis of the state's prosperity – and WA is deeply embroiled in the native-title debate on Aboriginal land rights because of conflicting mining interests.

NATURAL HISTORY

The environment of the south-west is very different from most of the state. This tiny pocket has large tracts of forest intersected by waterways. Much is the drier, jarrah-marri forest; taller karri grows in wetter areas.

Large areas of the scenic coast are protected in parks and reserves. Inland is lush farmland and plenty of wine growing.

Ranges in the south-west include the Darling Range east of Perth; the hills around Pemberton and Walpole; and the Porongurup and Stirling Ranges north of Albany (which occasionally receive light snow).

Wild flowers are plentiful in areas of the south-west, particularly in the jarrah forests east of Perth and in the Leeuwin-Naturaliste National Park.

WA's faunal emblem is the numbat – a pretty, rabbit-sized, striped marsupial. Like other small mammals (dunnarts, honey possums and phascogales) it's elusive and is dwindling in numbers because of introduced foxes and cats and habitat destruction.

More commonly seen is the wallaby-like, small quokka, especially on Rottnest Island (see the boxed text on the island later in this chapter). On the road, you may also see kangaroos, wallabies, possums, emus, echidnas, goannas, snakes, black swans, cockatoos and parrots and eagles. Whales swim off the southern coast during winter.

CLIMATE

Western Australia has several climate zones, the main three being the tropical north, the semi-arid interior and the Mediterranean south-west.

Hot, dry summers and cool, wet winters typify the south-west. Little rain falls between November and March; most of it falls between May and September. Perth's average annual rainfall is 975mm.

In Perth the average maximum temperature is above 30°C in summer, February being the hottest month. It's generally warmer further inland (the Avon Valley reaches 40°C) and several degrees cooler in the south-west; Albany's maximum during January and February averages 25°C.

Perth's winds are predictable from late spring to mid Autumn. Morning winds are easterly, with the westerly 'Fremantle Doctor' sea breeze blowing during the afternoon.

Afternoon sea breezes are common down the coast to Cape Naturaliste. Further south, south-westerly winds predominate during winter and spring, but during summer and autumn they're more likely to be southeasterly. Autumn is generally calmest.

INFORMATION
Maps

The RAC maps are best for road touring. The standard, regional Tour Planner maps (about 1:250,000) are available from the RAC (☎ 9421 4444 or ☎ 1800-807 011), 228 Adelaide Terrace; petrol stations; and tourist bureaus ($1.50/3 for members/nonmembers). Popular areas are also covered by larger-scale tourist maps, ($3/6) which include town maps, accommodation and attractions.

Auslig publishes Natmap topographic maps ($7.70 each) in several scales. Try Perth Map Centre (☎ 9322 5733), 891 Hay St.

In Perth, Bikewest's excellent Perth Bike Map series (1:30,000) is invaluable for cycling around Perth and Fremantle. Maps ($3.95) are available from visitor centres, bike shops and some bookshops.

The state-government body TrailsWest (☎ 9387 9740) is working on an 804km mountain-bike trail from Perth to Albany; contact them to see which sections are open.

Bikewest's *Ride Around the Rivers* booklet maps more than 60km of bikepaths (available free from Bikewest and bike shops).

Books

Lonely Planet's *Western Australia* guide provides additional detail. The *Free Camping* guide, by S&S Collis, is handy. Jane Scott's *Walking the Capes* provides excellent detail of Leeuwin-Naturaliste National Park geology and natural history.

Novelist Tim Winton vividly portrays Perth and south-west WA in novels such as *Cloudstreet* and *An Open Swimmer*.

Warning

Dieback disease, caused by the soil-borne pathogen *Phytophthora cinnamomi*, has decimated jarrah forests in the south-west. Help prevent its spread by observing quarantine restrictions (mud on tyres is a major cause). For more information contact the Department of Conservation and Land Management (CALM).

Information Sources

The Bicycle Transportation Alliance (☎ 9420 7210, 🖳 sunsite.anu.edu.au/wa/bta), 2 Delhi St, West Perth, has useful touring information on its Web site.

The Cycle Touring Association (CTA; 🖃 cta_wa@yahoo.com), PO Box 174, Wembley, WA 6014, runs regular social rides and the annual spring On Your Bike WA touring event. Find the CTA's current telephone number in the Perth *Yellow Pages* directory.

Bikewest (☎ 9216 8000, 🖳 www.transport.wa.gov.au/metro/bikewest), 441 Murray St, Perth, is a section of the state government Transport department and can provide a list of WA cycling clubs.

Contact the Department of Conservation & Land Management (CALM) for information

about national parks. CALM has offices in Perth (☎ 9334 0333, 🖳 www.calm.wa.gov.au), Technology Park, Western Precinct, 17 Dick Perry Ave, Kensington; and Fremantle: WA Naturally (☎ 9430 8600), 47 Henry St.

Other Information

Community telecentres in country towns provide Internet and email, fax and photocopying facilities. Opening hours vary.

GATEWAY CITIES
Perth

This shiny, modern city claims to be the sunniest Australian capital and the world's most isolated.

It was founded in 1829 on the banks of the Swan River. The river is very much a focal

point – and an excellent network of well-maintained bicycle paths run along its banks.

Another highlight is magnificent Kings Park, a 4-sq-km area of botanic gardens and natural bushland, near the heart of town.

Practically a suburb of Perth, but with a definite character of its own, is the city's port, Fremantle, around 20km downstream. Charming, historic 'Freo' accommodates healthy arts and 'alternative' communities, a significant migrant population, good eateries – and tourists. With a good train link to the city, it's a popular base.

Information Perth's busy Western Australian Tourist Centre (☎ 1300-361 351, 🖳 www.westernaustralia.net), Forrest Place, corner Wellington St, opens daily. Next door is the GPO. Currency exchange is available at the Nationwide Bureau de Change, 639A Hay St Mall (open daily), American Express and Thomas Cook offices and city banks.

Fremantle's visitor centre (☎ 9431 7878, 🖲 holzwart@wantree.com.au), old Town Hall, Kings Square, opens daily (Sunday afternoon only) and books accommodation. Currency exchange is next door and the major banks are on Adelaide and High Sts.

Gordonsons Cycles (☎ 9321 6412, 🖲 gordonsoncycles@bigpond.com), 374 Murray St, operates a 50% buy-back scheme for bikes. About Bike Hire (☎ 9221 2665, 🖲 lhoffman@cygnus.uwa.edu.au), No 4 Car

Park, Riverside Dr; hires rigid and suspension mountain bikes for $30 to $55 per week. Panniers cost extra. In Fremantle, Fleet Cycles (☎ 9430 5414), 66 Adelaide St, has good workshop service. Bike hire costs $20/100 per day/week; it has a buy-back scheme and second-hand bikes.

Citiplace Rest Centre, Perth train station, has toilets, showers and luggage lockers.

Things to See & Do In spring, **Kings Park** has magnificent wild flower displays and superb views.

The **Art Gallery of WA** (☎ 9328 7233) is in the Perth Cultural Centre behind the train station. Close by, the **Perth Institute of Contemporary Art** (☎ 9227 6144), 51 James St, promotes new and experimental arts.

Exhibitions at the **Museum of Western Australia** (☎ 9328 4411), Francis St, Northbridge, include Aboriginal culture, marine life, meteorites and Perth's original prison.

Perth's **historic buildings** are hidden in the modern city. The Department for Sport & Recreation's *Pedal Through the Past* brochure describes many of them. Alternatively, get the free *What's On* tourist guide from the Tourist Centre.

Don't leave without visiting the sparkling sandy **beaches**. Cottesloe Beach, about 14km from the city via the river bikepath, has good swimming and is also accessible by train. A bikepath runs along the ocean.

Western Australian Place Names

In laconic Australian style, Western Australian place names are rarely heard in full. Rather than mumble through a jumble of syllables, locals substitute an 'o' or a 'y': Peppermint Grove becomes 'Peppy Grove'; Pemberton is 'Pemby' and the beach at Margaret River gets 'Margie's'. Fremantle is, of course, Freo, and Rottnest Island, Rotto. Curiously, Cottesloe becomes simply 'Cot'.

In the south-west place names often end in 'up', which means 'place of' in the regional Aboriginal language. Thus, Yallingup means 'place of love', Meelup is 'place of the moon', and Cowamarup, 'place of the parakeet'. 'Up' names are generally associated with water – for nomadic Aborigines, watering places were important to know.

YEP! YOU'LL HAVE A WHALE OF A TIME AT MARGIES!

THIS 'MARGIE' SOUNDS ALRIGHT!

DON HATCHER

Explore the excellent network of bikepaths along the Swan and Canning Rivers; see Maps under Information earlier.

Fremantle is the quickest and cheapest port from which to catch ferries to **Rottnest Island** (see the boxed text below). The town also has plenty of interesting history to discover. Free attractions include the fascinating **Maritime Museum** (☎ 9431 8444, ☐ www.mm.wa .gov.au), corner Cliff St and Marine Terrace, with the Dutch ship *Batavia*, which sank in

1629; the **Fremantle History Museum & Arts Centre** (☎ 9430 7966), corner Ord and Finnerty Sts; and WA's oldest public building, the 1831 **Round House**, High St.

The **Fremantle Market**, corner South Terrace and Henderson St, is a prime attraction (open Friday to Sunday).

Tours shed light on the dark history of the **Fremantle Prison** (☎ 9430 7177), 1 The Terrace, which operated until 1991. **Aboriginal-heritage walking tours** run Wednesday,

Rottnest Island

Cycling is the time-honoured mode of transport on 'Rotto', a sandy island – 11km by 5km – off the coast of Fremantle. Bikes can be hired on the island (☎ 9292 5105), or you can take your own.

Dutch explorer Willem de Vlamingh named the island 'Rotte-nest' (rats nest), after the king size 'rats' (quokkas, wallaby-like marsupials) he saw there, but the Nyoongar people knew it as 'Wadjemup' (thought to mean 'place across the water'). Although 7000-year-old evidence of occupation has been found, the island was uninhabited when Europeans arrived.

The Rottnest settlement, established in 1838 as an Aboriginal prison, was occupied until 1920 (it's considered a sacred site by the Noongar, because hundreds of their people died there). Later Rottnest became an escape for Perth society and has become a popular day trip in the last 30 years.

Rottnest Island is the only place in Australia where you can see quokkas in the wild.

Overnight accommodation includes camping, a youth hostel and upmarket hotel or resort accommodation – telephone the visitor centre for details.

Information The visitor centre (☎ 9372 9752) is north of the jetty at the Thomson Bay Settlement. The free *Welcome to Rottnest Island* visitor information booklet is also available from mainland visitor centres.

Things to See & Do The excellent **Rottnest Museum** includes exhibits about Aboriginal incarceration and European settlement on the island, wildlife and shipwrecks. Walking-tour leaflets direct you around interesting old convict-built buildings.

Rottnest is a great spot for **wildlife spotting**. **Cycling** is popular – carry water. You can also **swim**, **snorkel**, or **surf**.

Getting There & Away Three companies run services to Rottnest:

- The Rottnest Express (☎ 9335 6406) departs Fremantle from C Shed Victoria Quay ($34/39 for same-day/extended return, plus $5 per bike).
- Oceanic Cruises (☎ 9430 5127) departs Fremantle from East St Jetty (same fares); or Perth, from Barrack St Jetty ($47 plus $5 for bikes).
- Boat Torque (☎ 9430 7644) departs from Rous Head, North Fremantle ($35/40 same day/extended return); or Barrack St Jetty, Perth ($50). Bikes cost $7.

Friday and Sunday (book through the Maritime Museum).

Places to Stay Perth and Fremantle have accommodation for all tastes and budgets.

Perth The caravan parks are outside the centre. The closest, ***Perth Central Caravan Park*** *(☎ 9277 1704; 34 Central Ave, Redcliffe)*, is near the airport. Tent sites cost $17 for one/two people, budget on-site vans cost $38 to $44 and en suite cabins, $77 to $88.

Northbridge, north of the Perth train station, is Perth's hostel, restaurant and nightclub district. Quiet and well-run ***Coolibah Lodge*** *(☎ 9328 9958, ☺ mail@coolibahlodge*

.com.au, 194 Brisbane St) has $18.50 dorm beds and doubles from $48. Also popular is central ***Northbridge YHA*** *(☎ 9328 7794, ☺ yhanb@hotmail.com, 46 Francis St)*. Dorm beds cost $20.50 and doubles, $55.

In the city, ***YMCA Jewell House*** *(☎ 9325 8488 or ☎ 1800-998 212, 180 Goderich St)* has singles/doubles with shared facilities for $37.40/48.40 (limited bike-storage).

Spacious en suite rooms at the ***Perth City Hotel*** *(☎ 9220 7000, ☺ info@perthcityhotel.com.au, 200 Hay St)* cost $82.50.

Airport B&B *(☎ 9478 2923 or ☎ 1800-447 000; 103 Central Ave, Redcliffe)* will meet you at the airport. Rooms start at $55/75.

Cycling to/from the Airport

1:150,000   0 —— 5km / 3mi   Ⓝ N

The scenic route to the city centre from Perth airport to the city (to the WA Tourist Centre) is largely traffic free. It's 26.6km from the international terminal and 19.3km from the domestic terminal. Most of the generally flat journey can be undertaken along the scenic Swan River bikepath and quiet streets.

The river route is reasonably well signed; the bikepath is 3.9km from the domestic terminal, via quiet streets; from the international terminal it's 11.2km, including a 4.8km stretch along the Tonkin Hwy. The highway is busy, but has a wide shoulder (all bikes must leave the highway at 8.6km, where a signed bikepath links to Stanton Rd).

About Bike Hire (16.4/23.7km) sells Perth Bike Maps and the free *Ride Around the Rivers* booklet.

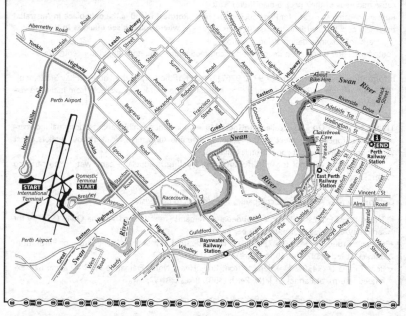

Fremantle The closest camping is 2.5km south at *Fremantle Village Caravan Park* (☎ *9430 4866, cnr Cockburn & Rockingham Rds)*. Tent sites cost $18 and self-contained accommodation starts at $65 for two people. Backpacker accommodation includes the well-run *Backpackers Inn-Freo YHA* (☎ *9431 7065, 11 Pakenham St)*. Dorm beds cost $18 and doubles, from $46.

Clean rooms at the *Fremantle Hotel* (☎ *9430 4300, 6 High St)* cost from $55/80.

The lovely *Port Mill Bed & Breakfast* (☎ *9433 3832, 3/17 Essex St)* is an extension of the 1836 flour mill. Rooms cost from $130/140.

Places to Eat Buy good-value bulk food at *Kakulas Bros (183 William St)*. Supermarkets include *City Fresh Fruit Co (375 William St)* and, in the city, *Foodland (556 Hay St)*.

Northbridge This area is chock-a-block with eating places. For budget meals, try the *Old Shanghai Food Hall (123 James St; closed Monday)*, or *Hans Cafe (cnr William & Francis Sts)* for noodles. *Il Padrino Caffe* (☎ *9227 9065, 198 William St)* has Italian meals from $10 (closed Monday). The renovated pub, *The Brass Monkey* (☎ *9227 9596, cnr James & William Sts)* has modern Australian mains from $14.50 to $22. *The Fishy Affair* (☎ *9328 3939, 132 James St)* has massive seafood platters for $33 per person (minimum two people). Stylish *Valentinos* (☎ *9328 2177, cnr Lake & James Sts)* has good food and great coffee.

Perth Centre Try *Fast Eddys (cnr Murray & Milligan Sts)* for burgers and breakfast. The English-style pub *Moon and Sixpence (300 Murray St)* has counter meals, mostly around $14. *Cino to Go (36A King St)* has excellent coffee.

Fremantle Head to South Terrace, dubbed the 'Cappuccino Strip'. The *Fremantle Market (cnr South Terrace and Henderson St)* has fresh produce Friday to Sunday. *The Mill Bakehouse* is at No 52, but the kilometre-or-so ride south to *Abhi's Bread (270 South Terrace)* is worth the effort (closed Monday).

Italian *Old Papa's* (☎ *9355 4655, 17 South Terrace)* is a cyclists' meeting point

for weekend morning rides. *Nick's Place (2 South Terrace)* has shish kebabs, souvlaki and felafel from $5, and *Pizza Bella Roma* (☎ *9335 1554, 14 South Terrace)* is reasonably priced. For a pleasant meal, try the brasserie in the renovated *Sail & Anchor* (☎ *9335 8433, 64 South Terrace)*.

Getting There & Away Although a long way from the populous eastern states, Perth is a popular entry point for overseas visitors. It is connected by a regular train service to Fremantle.

Air Perth's international airport receives direct flights from Britain, Asia and Africa (see the Getting There & Away chapter). Qantas (☎ 13 1313) and Ansett (☎ 13 1300) fly between Perth and Australia's other capitals (see the Getting Around chapter for more information).

The domestic terminal is 11km east of the city; the international terminal, 16km. It's a pleasant ride, mostly along the Swan River, to the city (see the boxed text 'Cycling to/from the Airport' opposite).

Feature Tours (☎ 9479 4131 or ☎ 0417-959 691) runs an airport shuttle to city and inner-suburban accommodation. It costs $10; bikes (preferably boxed) may cost a few dollars. Fremantle Airport Shuttle (☎ 9383 4115) charges $12 from the domestic terminal and $15 from the international terminal, plus $5 per bike, to Fremantle and other western suburbs. A taxi to the city costs $15 to $20 from the domestic terminal and about $5 more from the international terminal.

Bus Greyhound Pioneer (☎ 13 2030) buses connect Perth with Adelaide ($225), via Kalgoorlie, and Darwin ($504.90) via the coast; see the Getting Around chapter for bike-carriage rules. Westrail and Greyhound operate out of the Westrail Centre, West Parade, East Perth (Interstate Railway Station).

South West Coachlines (☎ 9324 2333) is very accommodating when it comes to cyclists; see the Tall Trees & High Seas ride later in this chapter for details of buses to the south-west. Their buses leave from the City Busport, 3 Mounts Bay Rd. (Enter via the ramp just north of Mounts Bay Rd on George St).

Train Perth is the start and end point of one of the world's great train journeys – the 65-hour trip between the Pacific and Indian oceans (see the Getting Around chapter). Within WA, Westrail's (☎ 13 1053 in WA or ☎ 1800-099 150) country trains and buses are not particularly bike-friendly. Information on services is provided in the Getting to/from the Ride sections of this chapter and in the Getting Around chapter. The Westrail Terminal in West Parade, East Perth, is for all WA rail services and Westrail buses, and trains arriving from the east coast.

Transperth (☎ 13 6213) runs an efficient metropolitan train service, with lines heading south-west to Fremantle, south-east to Armadale, east to Midland and north-west to Joondalup. Bikes travel free on weekends and outside peak periods (7am–9am and 4.30pm–6pm weekdays).

Tall Trees & High Seas

Duration	9 days
Distance	611.4km
Difficulty	moderate–hard
Start	Bunbury
End	Albany

The far south-west region appeals for its attractive and varied natural environment. From the rare Tuart Forest and deep-blue Geographe Bay near Busselton, the ride takes in premium wine districts, wild flower-rich jarrah forests and limestone caves, before rolling through to the magnificent tall forests and unspoilt coastal parks, inlets and beaches of the southern coast.

While sections of the ride are peppered with things to explore, other days involve just riding through the lightly trafficked forest.

HISTORY

Evidence of Aboriginal occupation in the south-west dates back 40,000 years. Many Aboriginal place names are still used (see the boxed text 'Western Australian Place Names' earlier in this chapter).

European expansion into the south-west began at Augusta in 1830. The hardship of establishing farms was enough to drive many away. The development of timber industries during the 1880s brought infrastructure to the region.

The Group Settlement Scheme, designed by Premier Sir James Mitchell in the 1920s, was a second attempt to open up the region and establish a dairy industry. A joint venture between the WA, Federal and British Governments, it offered land at attractive rates to settlers. The scheme was eventually abandoned as 'a glorious failure'.

Since the early 1960s wine production has become a major regional industry.

NATURAL HISTORY

Rich coastal heath and jarrah-marri forests cover the ancient granite-limestone ridge between Capes Naturaliste and Leeuwin. Limestone caves are hidden beneath its surface, while white, sandy beaches, world-renowned surf and rugged coastal cliffs lie at its edge.

Further inland are dry jarrah forests and, in the south-coast hinterlands, tall karri and tingle forests.

The southern coastline features a series of inlets, wonderful coastal parks and more beautiful beaches.

The rare red-tailed tropicbird is found at Cape Naturaliste. Unique to the south-west is marron, a freshwater crayfish, regarded as a delicacy and available in restaurants from January to March.

PLANNING
When to Ride

While this ride can be done all year, the best months are March and April, when the weather is calm, or October and November, when spring flowers are out (winds are more likely to be south-westerly). Rainfall is highest between May and August; summer is dry, and hot weather encourages bush and march flies. Avoid holiday periods (mid-December to the end of January, and Easter).

Days 6 and 7 could be combined into a very long day to make this an eight-day ride. If you're short of time, you can also skip Day 1.

Maps

The RAC tour-planner maps *Lower South West* and *Albany Region* (approximately 1:250,000) cover the ride. However, more useful are the RAC's larger-scale *Cape to Cape*, *Tall Timbers* and *Great Southern* maps (all approx 1:130,000), which include town maps, accommodation and attractions.

What to Bring
Camping gear increases your options between Pemberton and Walpole (see Days 6 and 7). In summer, pack insect repellent and/or a fly net.

GETTING TO/FROM THE RIDE
Bunbury
Train Westrail (☎ 13 1053 in WA or ☎ 1800-099 150) runs the *Australind* service from Perth to Bunbury ($18 plus $8 per bike, 2¾ hours, twice daily). An additional bus service runs Monday to Thursday. Bikes are discouraged, but space is available for two – you need to book.

Bus This is the best transport from Perth to Bunbury. South West Coachlines (☎ 9324 2333) run three services daily ($16 plus $10 for bikes).

Most services continue to Busselton and Dunsborough, which are alternative starting points.

Bicycle It's possible to ride south from Fremantle, but not recommended – traffic is heavy and the scenic reward, light.

Albany
Bus Westrail (☎ 13 1053) is the only operator between Albany and Perth ($35.10, plus $8 per bike, six hours, one or two daily). Book places for bikes in advance. Carriage of bikes is not guaranteed – avoid peak season and weekends. Generally the service via the wheatbelt (same fare, eight hours) has fewer passengers.

Bicycle Some cyclists continue from Albany, either north to the Stirling Ranges, or east across the Nullarbor Plain. The Great Southern Bicycle Company (see Information under Albany later) is a good place for advice. Be aware that distances are very much greater between services past Albany.

THE RIDE
Bunbury
WA's second-largest town (population 28,000) lies in a region which, according to scientists, has Australia's 'most comfortable climatic environment for human existence'.

Information The visitor centre (☎ 9721 7922), at the old railway station on Carmody

Place, opens daily (until 4.30pm on Sunday). The main banks (with ATMs) are mostly on Victoria St.

City Cycles (☎ 9721 6438), 15 Princep St, is near the visitor centre. Fitzroys Cycles (☎ 9721 8600) is at 110 Blair St.

Things to See & Do Bunbury is known for the 100 or so **dolphins** in Koombana Bay. The best chance of seeing them is at the beach by the **Dolphin Discovery Centre**, Koombana Dr from early morning or on a **dolphin cruise**. Also off Koombana Dr, is a short **mangrove boardwalk**.

Places to Stay At the central **Koombana Bay Holiday Resort** (☎ 9791 3900, Koombana Dr) tent sites cost a steep $16.50 for one or two people; self-contained cabins/chalets cost $55/132.

The clean and well-run **Wander Inn Backpackers** (☎ 9721 3242, 16 Clifton St) charges $18 in dorms and from $28/45 for singles/doubles.

The best motels have great views. Bright, clean, air-conditioned **Ocean Drive Motel** (☎ 9721 2033, 121 Ocean Dr) has rooms from $60/66.

Homely **Aran Brae B&B** (☎ 9721 2177, 5 Sherry St) has one self-contained double unit – good value at $50/77 for one/two people.

The **Prince of Wales Hotel** (☎ 9721 2016, 41 Stephen St) has standard rooms for $35/55 or slightly newer rooms for $49.50/66, including cooked breakfast. Bands play Thursday to Saturday nights.

Places to Eat Many of Bunbury's eateries are on Victoria St's 'cappuccino strip'. Locals favour **Sibs Restaurant** (☎ 9791 5886, 52 Victoria St) – it does pastas from $11.90 to $18.90. The **Rose Hotel** (cnr Wellington & Victoria Sts) has counter meals under $10 and pricier meals in the Art Deco bistro. For a big steak, try the **Hog's Breath Saloon, Bar & Grill** (☎ 9791 7177, 5 Victoria St). With Indian Ocean views,

> ## Warning
> ⚠ Beware of freak king waves on exposed sections along the coast, which can come without warning. Every year, people are washed off rocks.

WESTERN AUSTRALIA

Ex-tension Cafe (☎ 9791 2141, Ocean Dr) opens at 7am – a continental buffet breakfast costs $8.80.

Day 1: Bunbury to Dunsborough
3½–5 hours, 80.8km

The flat and easy ride begins with 32km on the busy Bussell Hwy, which has a good shoulder. Traffic is still fast (though light) on the narrower Tuart Drive through the lovely Tuart forest – one of the only stands of its type – and the Vasse Estuary wetlands.

By the Tuart forest (45km) is the 1834 **Wonnerup House Settlement** (☎ 9752 2039), a restored example of early farm pioneering in WA.

Busselton's 150-year-old **jetty** (56km) is the longest of its kind in the Southern Hemisphere, stretching almost 2km into Geographe Bay. The nearby beachfront kiosk, *Cafe Nautical*, sells Simmo's Ice Cream – a regional favourite. Town has a few *cafes*; the *Busselton Fresh Market (33 Queen St)* sells groceries and bread.

Busselton's visitor centre (☎ 9752 1288) is 130m off the route, on the corner of Bussell Hwy and Peel Terrace; Busselton Bikery (☎ 9752 2887) is at 88 Queen St.

After 65.2km, the route continues on Caves Rd, along which lie a series of youth camps nestled among the peppermints.

Side Trip: Cape Naturaliste
33km

The road rolls to the cape, starting with a moderate climb around 1.5km from town. Take Naturaliste Terrace, which enters Cape Naturaliste Rd after 2.3km.

Heading through coastal forest, a right turn (4.2km) drops to lovely **Meelup Beach** (6.3km), a well known swimming bay (no camping) and climbs out through Eagle Bay's burgeoning real estate development. The only *store* is at 9.6km.

At Sugarloaf Rock, 2.6km off Cape Naturaliste Rd at 17.3km, is the southernmost **nesting colony** of the rare red-tailed tropicbird. The best time to see the birds is between December and April, but don't disturb them by walking onto the rock.

It costs $5 to go inside the Cape **Naturaliste lighthouse** (20.1km); take valuables with you on the signed **walks** around the Cape. Drinking water from the complex is not advised; bottled water and snacks are on sale.

Return via the outward route, skipping the detour to Meelup Beach.

Dunsborough
This beach town, built for tourism and expanding fast, has an air of newness. Its hub is a group of modern shopping centres built around the intersection of Naturaliste Terrace and Dunn Bay Rd. However, there's still plenty of bushland and the perfect blue of Geographe Bay is never far away.

Spend time hanging out at the **beach** or ride out to the **Cape** (see the Day 1 side trip).

Information The visitor centre (☎ 9755 3299, 🖳 www.downsouth.com.au) is in the Dunsborough Park Shopping Centre, Seymour Blvd.

The National bank, at the Forum Naturaliste shopping centre, opens only on Monday and Wednesday (10am to 1pm) and Friday (until 4.30pm). Bank West has similar hours. A Commonwealth ATM is in the Dunsborough Park shopping centre.

Places to Stay The plain *Dunsborough Lakes Holiday Resort (☎ 9756 8300, Commonage Rd)* is 2km south-east, just off Caves Rd. Tent sites cost $9 per person ($10 in school holidays) and self-contained units start at $88 (BYO linen).

It's nicer camping (also $8) at the *Three Pines Beach Resort YHA (☎ 9755 3107, Geographe Bay Rd)* on the beach 2.5km south-east of town. Dorm beds cost $20.50; double rooms, $47.50. Dorm prices (including bedding) are similar at the central *Dunsborough Inn (☎ 9756 7277, Dunn Bay Rd)*; spacious, self-contained units cost $95.

Self-contained multishare units ($38 per person) offer the best deal at the otherwise pricey *Dunsborough Bay Village Resort (☎ 9755 3397, 26 Dunn Bay Rd)*. Other accommodation starts at $145 for two people; all includes spa, sauna and linen.

Have a massage ($45/hour) at *Seagrass Cottage (☎ 9756 7957, 3 Seagrass Cove)*, where B&B costs $85a double. *Grevillea Cove B&B (☎ 9756 7861, 5 Grevillea Cove)*, has private units from $85.

Places to Eat The *Newmart* supermarket inside the Forum Naturaliste Shopping Centre opens until 6.30pm (9pm Thursday). *Dunsborough Health Food (Shop 2, The*

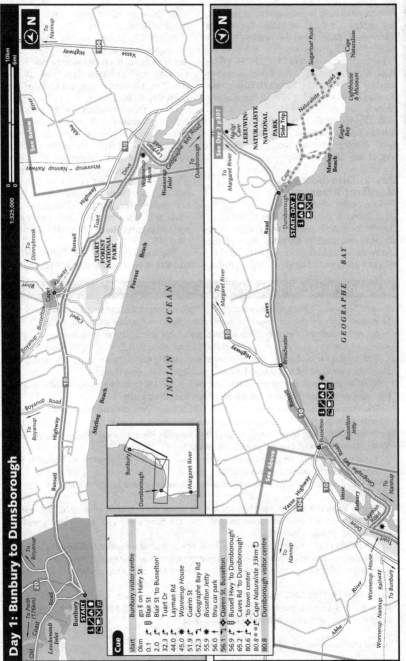

Day 1: Bunbury to Dunsborough

Cue

start	Bunbury visitor centre
0km	go E on Haley St
0.1	Blair St
2.0	Blair St 'to Busselton'
32.3	Tuart Dr
44.0	Layman Rd
45.0	Wonnerup House
51.9	Guerin St
52.3	Geographe Bay Rd
55.9	Busselton Jetty
56.0	thru car park
56.1	Queen St, Busselton
56.9	Bussell Hwy 'to Dunsborough'
65.2	Caves Rd 'to Dunsborough'
80.6	'to town centre'
80.8	Cape Naturaliste 33km ↺
80.8	Dunsborough visitor centre

WESTERN AUSTRALIA

Terrace) has bulk foods, vegetarian lunches and snacks. Of the three bakeries, the most renowned is *Dunsborough Bakery (☎ 9755 3137, The Terrace)*, open from 6.30am.

Funky, licensed *enJoia (☎ 9756 7997, Seymour House, Dunn Bay Rd)* has imaginative meals from $13 to $24. Italian *Domenic's on the Bay (☎ 9756 8866, 13 Dunn Bay Rd)* has pasta for around $11 to $15.

In Dunsborough Park Shopping Centre, *Adrian's Seafood Grill (☎ 9756 7777, Seymour Blvd)* is an attractive licensed place with mains from $17.50.

Day 2: Dunsborough to Margaret River

2½–3½ hours, 47.6km

Undulating Caves Rd makes a pleasant change from the Bussell Hwy. Traffic is not intrusive and much of the ride is through the Leeuwin-Naturaliste National Park, broken by vine paddocks. The day's highlight for wine drinkers is, of course, the Margaret River wineries.

Along with grapevines, the area between the capes is riddled with limestone caves. Several have been developed for public viewing, such as **Ngilgi Cave**, just off-route at 7.7km. However, most are south of Margaret River (see Day 3).

Most of the **vineyards** are about halfway between Dunsborough and Margaret River, along Caves, Metricup, Harmans Mill and Harmans South Rds. It's worth visiting a couple to taste wine from the cellar door. Some have restaurants and picnic areas where you can bring your own food and buy a glass or bottle of wine (see the boxed text below for details). The alternative route at 25km also takes in the European-style **Margaret River Chocolate Company** (☎ 9755 6555).

The main route passes **Cullen Winery** and **Vasse Felix** (see the boxed text below).

Margaret River Wineries

Despite Governor Stirling's enthusiasm for the agricultural potential of the south-west, it was not to be realised in his lifetime; the dreams of early settlers faded as they faced years of hardship.

But when studies in the early 1960s showed favourable soil conditions for viticulture and a climate similar to that of Bordeaux, it seemed that fortune was at last to shine on the region.

Trial plantings around Margaret River showed encouraging results. These, along with subsequent plantings, eventually led to a regional reputation as a premium-wine producer.

Now vineyards exist all over the south-west, though the Margaret River region – home to more than 40 – remains most famous, notably for its full-bodied cabernets.

The *Margaret River Regional Vineyard Guide* ($1.50) and *The Complete Guide to the Margaret River Wine Region* ($5.95) are available from the Margaret River Tourist Bureau. The bureau also has information about winery tours, as does the Margaret River Regional Wine Centre (☎ 9755 5501), Bussell Highway, Cowaramup (closed Sunday).

If you do go tasting, remember that about five standard 20ml tastes within an hour puts you close to the legal blood-alcohol limit (0.05%).

For a selection of contrasting wineries between Dunsborough and Margaret River, try:

Willespie Wines (☎ 9755 6248) Harmans Mill Rd, opens daily. Established in 1976, and nestled among bushland, it's small and down-to-earth. You can bring a picnic or, except during vintage (March to May), buy a cheese platter.

Cullen (☎ 9755 5277) Caves Rd, open daily. It was one of the first wineries established. Diana Cullen made history as the first woman to win a trophy at the Royal Show (for her flagship Cabernet Sauvignon Merlot). Picnicking is allowed providing you buy a drink – or you can buy lunch (mains around $16–20).

Vasse Felix (☎ 9755 5242) corner Caves Rd and Harman's Rd South. One of the better known wineries, vines were first planted here in 1967. The excellent restaurant (around $20 for mains) has delightful views, and a breathalyser by the cellar door.

Several other wineries are close to Margaret River township.

Day 2: Dunsborough to Margaret River

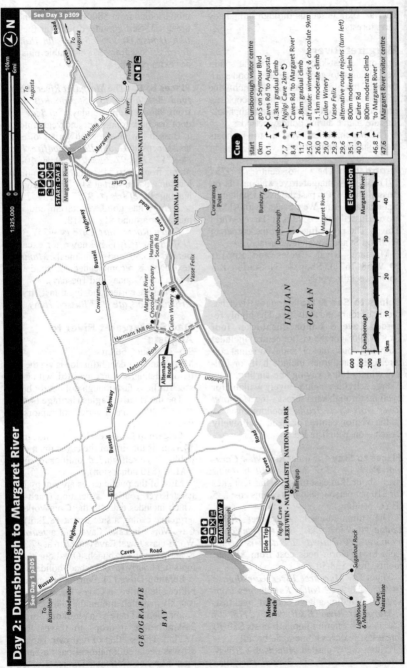

Cue

start		Dunsborough visitor centre
0km		go S on Seymour Blvd
0.1		Caves Rd 'to Augusta'
7.7		4.3km gradual climb
8.4		Ngilgi Cave 2km ⟳
11.7		Caves Rd 'to Margaret River'
25.0		2.8km gradual climb
26.0		alt route: wineries & chocolate 9km
29.0		1.1km moderate climb
29.3		Cullen Winery
		Vasse Felix
29.6		alternative route rejoins (turn left)
35.1		800m moderate climb
40.9		Carter Rd
46.8		800m moderate climb
47.6		'to Margaret River'
		Margaret River visitor centre

Elevation

The last 5km descends through tall, shady karri forests.

Margaret River

One of the best-known towns in the southwest, thanks to good wine and good surf, 'Margie' has plenty to do, even for non-wine drinkers. As for any tourist town, book accommodation well ahead. Single-night bookings are scarce during holiday periods.

The beach, 11km west of town, hosts major surfing competitions.

Information The visitor centre (☎ 9757 2911, ☐ www.margaretriverwa.com) is on Bussell Hwy, 350m past the river. Challenge, National and Bank West banks (with ATMs) are on Bussell Hwy; ANZ is at Harvey World Travel. The post office is on the corner of Willmott St and Townview Terrace.

Margaret River Cycles and Repairs (☎ 9758 7671), Shop 4, 31 Station Rd, opens weekdays only.

Things to See & Do Margaret River has plenty of tours and activities. The highly regarded **Cave & Canoe Bushtucker Tour** (☎ 9757 9084 or the visitor centre) includes canoeing, 'bush tucker' and Aboriginal culture. Other activities include half- or full-day **winery tours**, **caving** and **surfing**.

Free activities include lovely **walking** (or cycling) through karri forest – the *Margaret River Walk/Cycle Trails* brochure costs $1 at the visitor centre, or head to **Prevelly Beach** – on Walcliffe Rd.

Places to Stay The quiet *Riverview Caravan Park* (☎ 9757 2270, 8–10 Willmott Ave), about 1km east of town, has tent sites for $10 per person; standard cabins cost $55 (BYO bedding).

The rammed-earth *Margaret River Lodge* (☎ 9757 9532, ☐ stay@mrlodge .com.au, 220 Railway Terrace) is 2.5km from town. Dorm beds cost from $17.60; rooms, from $38.50.

The 1928 *Margaret River Guesthouse* (☎ 9757 2349, 22 Valley Rd) charges from $60/80, including a large cooked breakfast.

Margaret River B&B (9757 2118, 28 Fearn St) is a family home. It costs $50/70 (breakfast features homemade bread).

With a pretty garden, *Adamson's Riverside* (☎ 9757 2013, 71 Bussell Hwy) has

motel rooms from $80/85, with continental breakfast. Self-contained units at the *Station House* (☎ 9757 3175, 208 Railway Terrace) cost from $78 a double plus $10 per extra person.

Places to Eat The *Margaret River Wholefood Bakehouse* (31 Station Rd) opens from 9am, except Sunday. *ZarBzar* next door has bulk food, fruit and vegetables.

Bussell Hwy has a good variety of eateries. Licensed *Goodfellas Woodfire Pizza* (☎ 9757 3184, 97 Bussell Hwy) has 10-inch pizzas from $9 to $13; other modern mains, including pasta, start at $14. The alternative-leaning *Arc of Iris* (☎ 9757 3112, 151 Bussell Hwy) has good vegetarian and meat mains for around $12 to $18.

Green Room Surf Cafe (☎ 9757 3644, 113B Bussell Hwy) is known for excellent burgers ($5.50) and cheap meals. *Mammas*, next door, is recommended for good value (both close Monday and Tuesday).

For great coffee and breakfast, try the *Urban Bean Cafe* (157 Bussell Hwy).

Day 3: Margaret River to Augusta

2½–3½ hours, 56km

Most of today's delightful ride is via the gently undulating, scenic Caves Rd, with lots to see. Traffic is fast, though not overly heavy.

The informative **Eagles Heritage** (4.6km; ☎ 9757 2960) has a variety of raptors and free flight displays.

Calgardup Cave (reached on a side trip at 14.1km) is the first of the caves open to the public. It's a self-guided, unlit cave, run by CALM ($10 admission).

Most of the public caves are run by Margaret River Tourist Association (each $13, which includes entry to the **CaveWorks** interpretive centre, a side trip at 18.2km). By CaveWorks is **Lake Cave** and a *tearoom*. World-class **Jewel Cave** (side trip at 47.3km) is the pick of the bunch. One-hour guided tours run hourly (avoid school holidays).

Boranup Drive (21.3km) is an unsealed, hillier alternative to Caves Rd, which runs roughly parallel; mountain bikes are recommended. There's a **lookout** around 2.5km before it drops to Caves Rd at 32.2km. This section of regrowth karri forest was declared a national park a century after Maurice Coleman Davies created a

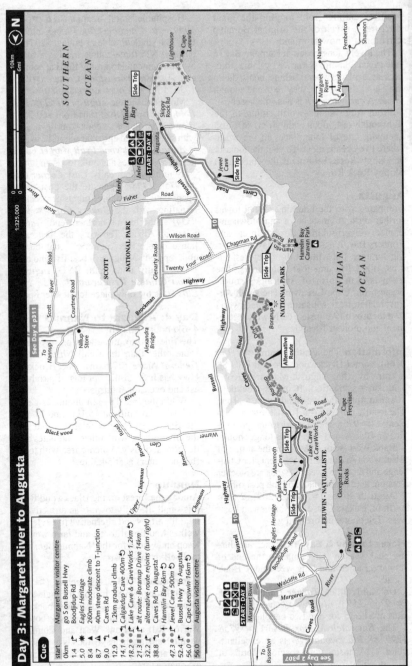

Day 3: Margaret River to Augusta

Cue	
start	Margaret River visitor centre
0km	go S on Bussell Hwy
1.4	Boodjidup Rd
5.0	Eagles Heritage
8.4	260m moderate climb
8.7	40m steep descent to T-junction
9.0	Caves Rd
12.9	1.2km gradual climb
14.7	Calgardup Cave 400m
18.2	Lake Cave & CaveWorks 1.2km
21.3	alt route: Boranup Drive 14km
32.2	alternative route rejoins (turn right)
38.8	Caves Rd to Augusta'
47.3	Hamelin Bay 6km
52.4	Jewel Cave 500m
56.0	Bussell Hwy to Augusta
56.0	Cape Leeuwin 16km
56.0	Augusta visitor centre

business empire from logging the giant karri trees. Much of the original Boranup karri forest is now farmland.

The lovely, long beach at **Hamelin Bay** (a side trip at 38.8km) is known by some stingrays as a place where fishing boats dump tasty morsels. Word is, they're placid enough to pat. A *caravan park* is near the beach.

From Augusta it's worth riding to the **lighthouse** ($4, open 9am–4pm) at **Cape Leeuwin**, one of four places in the world where two oceans meet. To visit the lookout at **Skippy Rock**, return on the (unsealed) Skippy Rock Rd.

Augusta

Compared with the booming tourist towns further north, Augusta has a small-town ambience. Overlooking Hardy Inlet and Flinders Bay, it's a beach-holiday spot during summer, but without the fancy restaurants, night life and tour companies. The town is 8km north of Australia's southwestern tip, Cape Leeuwin. The small **Augusta Historical Museum** on Blackwood Ave focuses on Augusta's early white settlement and pioneer lifestyle.

Information The visitor centre (☎ 9758 0166), corner Blackwood Ave and Ellis St, is run by the Augusta-Margaret River Tourism Association. It opens weekdays 10am to 4pm, and weekends 9am to 1pm. The locally run Augusta Tourist Information Centre (☎ 9758 1695), next to the post office on Blackwood Ave, keeps longer hours.

Bank West (with ATM) is on the corner of Blackwood Ave and Ellis St; agents for Challenge and Commonwealth Banks are Stocker Preston, across the road, and the post office.

Augusta Bikes (☎ 9758 1269), 2.5km north on Bakers Close, is a home-run business. Telephone before you go.

Places to Stay & Eat Prices increase during peak season (Christmas to the end of January, Easter, and long weekends). Book ahead.

On Hardy Inlet, *Turner Caravan Park* (☎ 9758 1593, *Blackwood Ave)* has tent sites at $12/15 for one/two people.

The *Baywatch Manor Resort* (☎ 9758 1290, 88 Blackwood Ave) is an excellent, quiet YHA hostel with spacious dorms at $19, doubles from $50.

Hospitable, small *Maria's B&B* (☎ 9758 1049, 20 Chamberlain Place) charges $45/75 a single/double or budget $20 (room only). A $25 three-course meal is available by arrangement. Homestay B&B at comfortable *Augusta Warmstone Cottage* (☎ 9758 1036, 5 Parry Court) costs $40/80.

Motel units at the *Augusta Hotel* (☎ 9758 1944, Blackwood Ave) start from $60/71. Its Jimmy's Grill has a cook-your-own affair with salad bar and chips (around $12 to $15).

Augusta Blackwood Fruit Market, opposite the post office, has bulk foods and opens early until 5.30pm daily. *Cosy Corner Cafe* (☎ 9758 1408), opposite the post office, opens until 7.30pm three nights per week, alternating with the *Bakery Cafe* (☎ 9758 0554) at the town's northern end. *Colourpatch* on Albany Terrace – the 'last eating house before the Antarctic' – has burgers and, reputedly, Augusta's best fish and chips – open daily until 7pm. BYO *August(a) Moon Chinese Restaurant* (☎ 9758 1322, Ellis St) is the only place to eat after 8pm.

Day 4: Augusta to Nannup
4–6½ hours, 90.2km
The ride has no attractions or services en route other than the small *Nillup Village General Store* (27.6km). The Brockman Hwy has little traffic but lots of jarrah forest and occasional farms.

While the first 18.9km undulates gently, with two short hills at 15.1km and 17.4km, the Brockman Hwy is relatively flat until the final 30km, which then undulates a little more seriously. A **picnic area** with toilets (but no water) is at 54.3km.

Nannup

Among the forest on the Blackwood River, this small, friendly town is an attractive retreat for artists and alternative lifestylers, as well as traditional forest and farm workers. Keep an eye out for the 'Nannup tiger' said to dwell in these parts.

Information The visitor centre (☎ 9756 1211), Brockman St, just off the main street (Warren Rd) handles caravan park bookings.

LJ Hooker and the post office (both on Warren Rd) are Bank West and Commonwealth Bank agencies; Eftpos is available at the BP and Ampol service stations and the 4-Square store.

Day 4: Augusta to Nannup

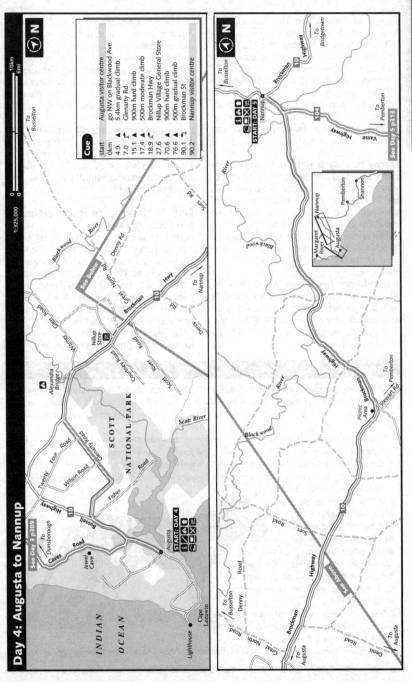

Cue		
start		Augusta visitor centre
0km		go NW on Blackwood Ave
4.9	◀	5.4km gradual climb
7.0	↲	Glenarty Rd
15.1	◀	900m hard climb
17.4	◀	500m moderate climb
18.9	↲	Brockman Hwy
27.6		Nillup Village General Store
70.6	◀	900m hard climb
76.6	◀	500m gradual climb
90.1	↱	Brockman St
90.2		Nannup visitor centre

1:325,000

See Day 3 p309

See Day 5 p313

START: DAY 4

START: DAY 5

WESTERN AUSTRALIA

Things to See & Do The visitor centre feeds the **birds** around 9am.

The **Blackwood Winery** (☎ 9756 0077), Kearney St, is a young and – according to the locals – improving winery. Overlooking a wetland less than 1km from town, it's a pleasant lunch spot.

The **Nannup Heritage Trail** brochure from the Information Centre details some of the town's historical buildings; or you can walk in the local **forest**.

Places to Stay & Eat On the river, *Nannup Caravan Park* (☎ 9756 1211, Brockman St) charges $6.60 per person in tents and $44 for two people in the only cabin. It's operated by the visitor centre; phone ahead for keys if arriving after 5pm.

The relaxing hostel, the *Black Cockatoo* (☎ 9756 1035, 27 Grange Rd), oozes ambience. Dorm beds cost $17 or it costs $10 to pitch a tent.

Family-run *Dry Brook B&B* (☎ 9756 1049, 25 Grange Rd) is more a homestay. It costs $30 per person, with evening meals by arrangement. *Argyll Cottage* (☎ 9756 3023, e argyll@comswest.net.au, 121 Warren Rd) charges $80/90.

There's a *bakery (Warren Rd)* and *4-Square* grocery store *(Warren Rd)*, which closes Sunday.

The *Blackwood Cafe* (☎ 9756 1120, 24 Warren Rd) opens to 8pm daily for country-style mains for around $12 or takeaways. Standard counter meals at the *Nannup Hotel (Warren Rd)* are mostly around $12.50 to $14.50.

For good eating, try the *Mulberry Tree Restaurant* (☎ 9756 3038, cnr Warren Rd & Cross St), Wednesday to Sunday; or *Hamish's Cafe* (☎ 9756 1287, 1 Warren Rd), Wednesday to Saturday (evenings Friday and Saturday).

Day 5: Nannup to Pemberton
4–6 hours, 78.8km

Again, there's little to break today's ride through jarrah and tall karri forest. The Vasse Hwy carries little traffic, though it undulates all the way, making it relatively strenuous.

A hall at Carlotta (14.2km) has toilets and water. Pretty **Donnelly River Winery** (42.5km; ☎ 9776 2052) has picnic tables. The expensive *Karri Valley Resort* (57.5km; ☎ 9776 2020) has a shop for snacks. The wonderful **karri forest** begins just past the resort.

Nannup Tiger

The thylacine (Tasmanian tiger) is widely believed to be extinct, the last known animal having died in captivity in 1936. Though Europeans only saw it in Tasmania, fossils indicate that the thylacine was once widespread throughout Australia. It's thought to have disappeared from the mainland around 2000 years ago, with the arrival of the dingo.

The 'extinct' classification is not bought by everyone, however. Unconfirmed sightings have been reported in various parts of Australia, including the forests around Nannup.

Locals tell of the furore created in the late 1970s when the scientific journal *Nature* received a paper, accompanied by clear photographs, claiming the thylacine was alive in Nannup. The 'tiger' turned out to be the authors' dog, painted with thylacine stripes. But the prank only strengthened support for the creature and, despite no concrete evidence (other than the odd footprint in fresh pavement), the tiger has apparently been spotted by plenty of 'clear thinking people' – before the ingestion of Nannup weed...

Keep your eyes peeled and your camera handy; the Black Cockatoo hostel is offering a $25 reward for an authenticated photograph.

MARTIN HARRIS

Extinct or not? Ask a local if the Nannup tiger exists.

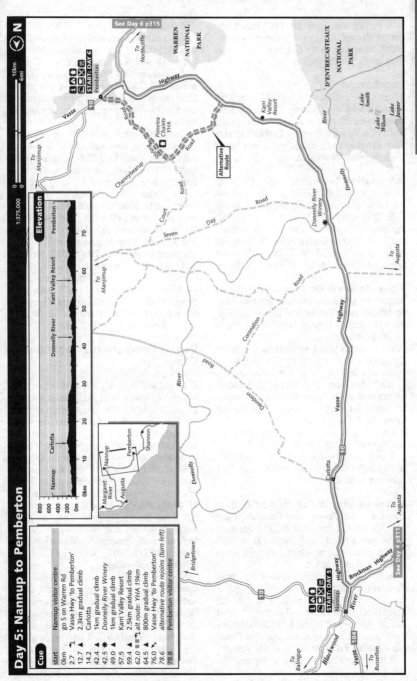

Day 5: Nannup to Pemberton

Cue		
start		Nannup visitor centre
0km		go S on Warren Rd
2.7		Vasse Hwy 'to Pemberton'
12.7		2.3km gradual climb
14.2		Carlotta
42.4		1km gradual climb
42.5		Donnelly River Winery
49.0		1km gradual climb
57.5		Karri Valley Resort
59.4		2.5km gradual climb
62.0		alt route: YHA 19km
64.5		800m gradual climb
76.0		Vasse Hwy 'to Pemberton'
78.6		alternative route rejoins (turn left)
78.8		Pemberton visitor centre

Elevation

If you're staying at the YHA (see Pemberton Places to Stay), it's more direct to take Channybearup Rd (left at 62km) rather than going via Pemberton.

Pemberton

There's no mistaking timber as this town's industry, with the clanking mill and permeating smell of sap and wood smoke. In the heart of hilly karri country, Pemberton also attracts artists and tourists, and is making its mark in wine production.

Information The visitor centre (☎ 9776 1133 or ☎ 1800-671 133) is 200m past the tram line on Brockman St. Showers cost $2.

BankWest (with ATM) is on Brockman St; the post office, on the corner of Brockman and Ellis Sts, is a Commonwealth Bank and ANZ agent. CALM (☎ 9776 1207) is on Kennedy St (en route to the Gloucester Tree).

Things to See & Do The visitor centre incorporates the **pioneer museum and karri forest discovery centre**. The award-winning **Fine Woodcraft Gallery** (☎ 9776 1399), is on Dickinson St.

Pemberton's best-known attraction is the **Gloucester Tree**, a giant karri, which brave souls climb 61m to a fire lookout. It's around 3km from town and is signposted. Signposted **walks** leave from the Gloucester Tree, including a 10km loop via the **Lavender & Berry Farm**.

Or, in hot weather, swim in the **Pemberton pool** on Swimming Pool Rd.

The free *Pemberton Karri Country* booklet lists Pemberton's **wineries**. Some of them serve food.

Places to Stay & Eat Only 500m from Brockman St, *Pemberton Caravan Park* (☎ 9776 1300, 1 Pumphill Rd) has tent sites at $8 per person, and cabins from $50 (higher prices during school holidays, when you'll need to book).

Opposite the clanking mill is the basic *Pemberton Backpackers* (☎ 9776 1105, 7 Brockman St). Dorm beds – which fill quickly during vintage (harvest) – cost $16.50 per person; twins, $18.50. In the forest 9km north-west of town, peaceful *Pimelea Chalets YHA* (☎ 9776 1153) charges $19.50 for dorm beds and $46.60 for doubles. Bring food – there are no shops.

Gloucester Motel (☎ 9776 1266, Ellis St) has nice views; nonsmoking singles/doubles cost $55/71.50. The restaurant alternates bar meals with a smorgasbord.

Pemberton Old Picture Theatre Apartments (☎ 9776 1513, cnr Ellis & Guppy Sts) have smoke-free, self-contained apartments from $110. Ask them about mountain-bike trails.

The *Pemberton Hotel* (☎ 9776 1017, Brockman St), north-east of the shops, has basic single rooms for $25. New luxury motel units cost $80/110. The bistro serves good country-style mains from $11 to $14.50.

The *Supa Valu* supermarket (Dean St) opens until 6.30pm. The olde worlde *Shamrock Restaurant* (☎ 9776 1186, Brockman St) serves seafood and chicken ($15.50 to $18.50) until 9pm (high-carb and vegetarian meals on request). *2 Jay's Cafe* (☎ 9776 1433, Brockman St) has takeaways (closed Monday). *Pemberton Chinese Restaurant* (☎ 9776 1514, Dean St) closes Tuesday. For breakfast (from 8.45am, except Thursday) or cake, try *Gryphons Garden Cafe* (☎ 9776 1159, Dickinson St).

Day 6: Pemberton to Shannon Camp Site

3–4 hours, 64.6km

The long and relatively strenuous stretch between Pemberton and Walpole is through gorgeous countryside, which again is fairly isolated. The roads are fairly quiet, but watch for logging trucks. Days 6 and 7 could be done as one strenuous leg. Northcliffe could be an alternative overnight stop for Day 6.

Soon after Pemberton, the road winds up and down through tall, shady karri forest, opening out before the small service town of **Northcliffe** (30.7km), the last chance to buy food before Walpole. Try *The King Karri* (☎ 9776 7112, Wheatley Coast Rd) for coffee and meals. Northcliffe visitor centre (☎ 9776 7203), Wheatley Coast Rd, adjoins a small museum.

Northcliffe has a purpose-built, 7km **mountain-bike track**, where the **Karri Cup** – one of WA's biggest prize-money events – is held every March Labour Day weekend (for more details check 🖳 www.wantree.com .au/~pimms/northcliffe/karricup or phone the Tourist Centre). The track is near the *Round Tu-it Caravan Park* (☎ 9776 7276, Muirillup Rd), which also offers

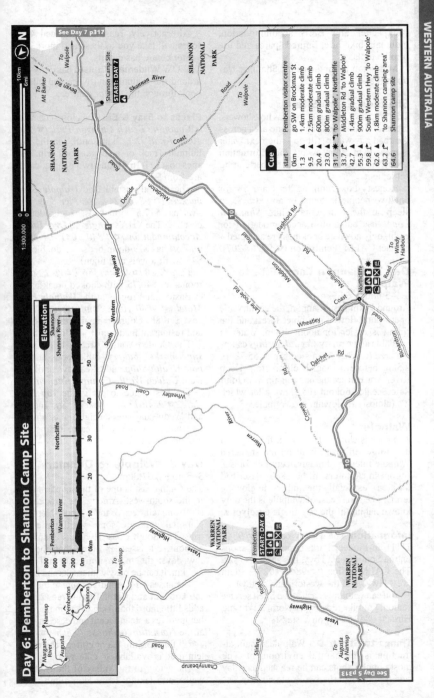

Day 6: Pemberton to Shannon Camp Site

See Day 7 p317

Cue

start	Pemberton visitor centre
0km	go SW on Brockman St
1.3	1.4km moderate climb
9.5	2.5km moderate climb
20.4	600m gradual climb
23.0	800m gradual climb
31.7	'to Walpole', Northcliffe
33.7	Middleton Rd 'to Walpole'
42.7	1.4km gradual climb
55.3	900m gradual climb
59.8	South Western Hwy 'to Walpole'
62.6	1.8km moderate climb
63.2	'to Shannon camping area'
64.6	Shannon camp site

Elevation

See Day 5 p313

backpacker and B&B accommodation, mountain-bike hire, limited spares and use of bike tools.

Middleton Rd undulates to **Shannon National Park**.

Shannon Camp Site

This attractive camping area has hot showers, tables and firewood. The picnic area across the road has water (fill up – the next water is more than 50km away) and information about the original Shannon timber-cutting settlement.

Honesty-box camping fees are $8 for one/two people in tents; or an extra $5 to sleep in the rudimentary hut. *Shannon Lodge* has bunkhouse accommodation for eight; only advance bookings are accepted – contact CALM, Pemberton (☎ 9776 1207).

Day 7: Shannon Camp Site to Walpole

3½–5 hours, 68.9km

Around 17km past Shannon, the countryside opens out to lower, scrubbier forest and the riding is easier for about 40km. Water is available at the pretty *Crystal Springs* camping area (reached on a side trip at 55.7km), 2.5km before a longish climb from Deep River. You can see the coast again from **John Rate Scenic Lookout** (63.3km), after which it's (almost) all downhill to Walpole.

Walpole

The pace is slow in this small, friendly and down-to-earth town, built on the sheltered Walpole Inlet amid magnificent tall forests. European explorers in the 1830s described the area – especially the timber – in glowing terms. The forest east of Walpole is the only known habitat of the rare tingle eucalyptus.

Information The visitor centre (☎ 9840 1111), in Pioneer Park, opposite the shops on the South Coast Hwy, has showers ($2). The CALM office (☎ 9840 1027), South West Hwy, is at the western end of town.

You can withdraw cash at the Shell service station. For bike repairs, try Norm's Tyre and Hire (☎ 9840 1297) on Vista St.

Things to See & Do Walpole's main attraction is the natural environment. The most popular spots can be reached as a day ride (see the Alternative Route on Day 8).

Alternatively, reasonably priced **4WD tours** will take you to these and more – the visitor centre has details.

WOW **Wilderness Cruises** has daily trips around the Walpole and Nornalup inlets – book through the visitor centre.

Places to Stay & Eat The closest camping is *Coalmine Beach Caravan Park* (☎ 9840 1026, Knoll Dr), 3km south, via the Bibbulmun Track or a longer road trip. Tent sites cost $11/16 for one/two people; cabins are from $55.

The recently established *Walpole Backpackers* (☎ 9840 1244, cnr Pier St & Park Ave) has $17.5 dorm beds; singles/doubles cost $42. The YHA's *Tingle All Over Budget Accommodation* (☎ 9840 1041, 61 Nockolds St) has $19 dorm beds and doubles for $45 (with towels and linen).

Vista B&B (☎ 9840 1386, 94 Vista St) has rooms for $40/75 with cooked breakfast.

Basic motel rooms at the *Walpole Hotel Motel* (☎ 9840 1023, South Western Hwy) cost $70/80. Counter meals start at $4.50 and restaurant meals cost $14 to $18.50.

The Golden Wattle Arcade has a small *supermarket*, *bakery*, bulk foods at *Walpole Health Shop* and takeaways until 7pm from *Golden Wattle Country Kitchen*.

The best place to eat is the *Top Deck Cafe* (☎ 9840 1344, Nockolds St). Tuesday and Wednesday are special nights; on Friday and Saturday a la carte mains cost around $17 to $20.

Day 8: Walpole to Denmark

3–5 hours, 67.8km

The south coast is one of the loveliest areas in the south-west. Among the low coastal scrub and tall trees of the Walpole-Nornalup National Park are some worthwhile side trips. The South Coast Hwy has undulating sections, but is easier riding than the past few days; the most significant hill is at 52.7km. It can be busy with trucks and buses.

The unsealed alternative route to the **Hilltop Lookout** and **Giant Tingle Tree** (2.5km) adds little more than 1km to the main route, but involves a steep ascent and descent. Stop at the *Nornalup Teahouse (9.8km, ☎ 9840 1422)* for morning tea or coffee. The excellent food is available to take away.

The detour to the Valley of the Giants is well worth taking. It's a 5km climb to the

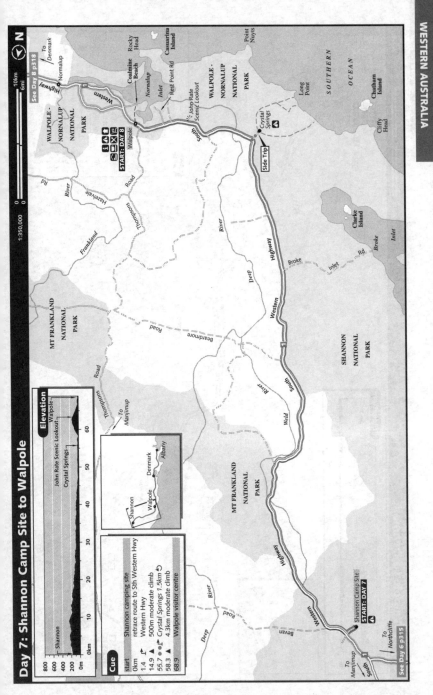

WESTERN AUSTRALIA

Day 7: Shannon Camp Site to Walpole

Elevation

John Rate Scenic Lookout
Walpole
Crystal Springs
Shannon

800
600
400
200
0m

0km 10 20 30 40 50 60

Cue

start	0km	Shannon camping site
	1.4	retrace route to Sth Western Hwy
	14.9	Western Hwy 500m moderate climb
	55.7	Crystal Springs 1.5km
	58.3	4.3km moderate climb
	68.9	Walpole visitor centre

To Manjimup
Walpole
Denmark
Albany
Shannon

N

1:350,000

0 6mi 10km

See Day 8 p318

WESTERN AUSTRALIA

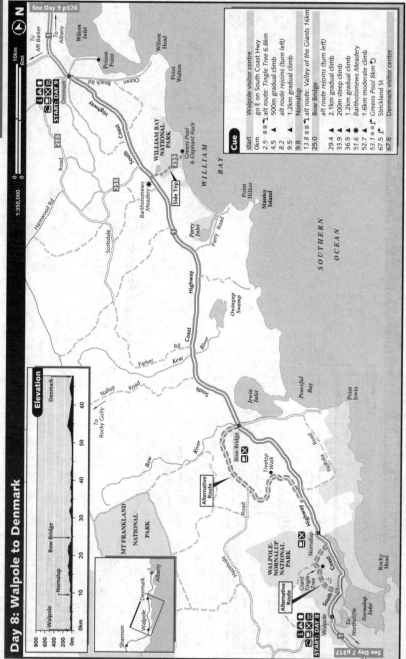

Day 8: Walpole to Denmark

See Day 9 p320

N

To Mt Barker
To Albany

START DAY 9

Wilson Inlet

Poison Point

Wilson Head

Denmark

Ocean Beach Rd

Point Walton

Harewood Rd

Scotsdale

Highway

South Coast

Road

Road

Bartholomews Meadery

Side Trip

WILLIAM BAY NATIONAL PARK

Greens Pool & Elephant Rock

WILLIAM BAY

Point Hillier

Stanley Island

SOUTHERN OCEAN

Parry Road

Parry Inlet

Owingup Swamp

Parker

Kent

River

Rd

Coast

Highway

South

River

To Rocky Gully

Nullup Road

Peaceful Bay

Irwin Inlet

Point Irwin

Eidolfa

Road

Bow River

Bow Bridge

Treetop Walk

Alternative Route

MT FRANKLAND NATIONAL PARK

Shannon

Denmark

Albany

Walpole

Road

Hazelvale

Nornalup

WALPOLE-NORNALUP NATIONAL PARK

Giant Tingle Tree

Alternative Route

START DAY 8

Walpole

To Northcliffe

South Coast

Highway

Nornalup Inlet

Rocky Head

See Day 7 p317

Cue

start	Walpole visitor centre
0km	go E on South Coast Hwy
2.5	alt route: Tingle Tree 6.8km
4.5	500m gradual climb
8.2	alt route rejoins (turn left)
9.5	1.2km gradual climb
9.8	Nornalup
13.8	alt route: Valley of the Giants 16km
25.0	Bow Bridge
	alt route rejoins (turn left)
29.4	2.1km gradual climb
33.9	200m steep climb
36.9	1.2km gradual climb
51.6	Bartholomews Meadery
52.7	1.6km moderate climb
53.1	Greens Pool 8km
67.5	Strickland St
67.8	Denmark visitor centre

Elevation

Walpole — Nornalup — Bow Bridge — Denmark

800
600
400
200
0m

0km   10   20   30   40   50   60

Scale 1:350,000

0   10km
0   6mi

Tree Top Walk turn-off – a 600m bridge through the forest's canopy ($5) – and free **Ancient Empire** boardwalk. From the Bow Bridge Roadhouse, the country opens into farmland, swampy wetland and low scrub.

For a change from wine, visit **Bartholomews Meadery** (51.6km, ☎ 9840 9349), as the road starts climbing to Denmark.

Another side trip (53.1km) goes through the William Bay National Park to the clear, sheltered **Greens Pool** and nearby **Elephant Rock**. It's the shortest distance to the coast from the highway.

Denmark

Compared with Walpole's laid-back ambience, attractive Denmark is a touch more vibrant. Home to a significant arts and alternative population, its main industries are tourism and wine.

Information The visitor centre (☎ 9848 2055, ⊖ touristb@denmarkwa.net.au) is at 60 Strickland St. Across the road are Bank West (with ATM) and National banks and the post office (Commonwealth Bank agent). Challenge Bank operates from Harman Ricketts, 22 South Coast Hwy. Rabbit Bicycle Repairs (☎ 9848 1513) is a home-operated business 5km south-west of town on Ocean Beach Rd.

Things to See & Do Ask for the visitor centre's free **Discover Denmark** brochure, which lists local attractions.

The visitor centre has details of walks around Denmark, including the 6km **Wilson Inlet Heritage Walk Trail**, an old rail route, with information on Aboriginal heritage, railway construction and natural history. You can cycle the trail (which runs from the old railway bridge on Inlet Dr to the highway west of Denmark) as an alternative, flat route out of town on Day 9.

Places to Stay & Eat In a pleasant spot 1.5km from town on Wilson Inlet, **Rivermouth Caravan Park** (☎ 9848 1262, Inlet Dr) has tent sites for $9/12.50 for one/two people, on-site vans at $28/34 and cabins at $34/44 (BYO linen). Book ahead (even tents) during school holidays.

Excellent **Denmark Waterfront** (☎ 9848 1147, 63 Inlet Dr), 3km from town, has $17 backpacker accommodation and motel suites for $80/90 (more during holidays).

Smoke-free **Waters Edge B&B** (☎ 9848 1043, 9 Inlet Dr) has great views and comfy rooms for $55/77. Central **Edinburgh Guest House** (☎ 9848 1477 31 South Coast Hwy) has en suite rooms for $60/85. Book ahead.

Denmark's **Cooperative** supermarket (*cnr South Coast Hwy & Strickland St*) is closed Sunday afternoon. Buy bulk foods at **Denmark Fruit & Veg** (*South Coast Hwy*); it's closed Sunday. For good bread and award-winning pies, go the popular **Denmark Bakery** (*Strickland St*). **Food Haven** (☎ 9848 1636, cnr Holling & South Coast Hwy), has takeaways.

The **Denmark Waterfront Restaurant** (*Inlet Dr*) serves modern cuisine (pasta from $12.50, mains around $18.50). Backpacker specials cost around $7. **Denmark Tavern's** restaurant (☎ 9848 1084, South Coast Hwy), at the western end of town, has good mains from $14 to $17. The **Blue Wren Cafe** (☎ 9848 1365, 21 South Coast Hwy) has $15 curry nights Wednesday, and a-la carte (from $16.50) Thursday to Sunday.

Day 9: Denmark to Albany

2½–4 hours, 56.7km
The final day is probably the easiest. Apart from a couple of gradual hills leaving Denmark, the route is more or less flat, heading through open scrub and farmland north of Wilson Inlet before turning on to the quieter Lower Denmark Rd (17.7km). This route, through pleasant agricultural land, is flatter and more scenic than the highway.

Young's Siding (19.2km) has a *store*, as does Elleker (40.2km). To swim, take the flat side trip (31.2km) to the beach at **Cosy Corner**, which is just north of West Cape Howe National Park.

Albany

Albany sits on Princess Royal Harbour, within King George Sound. Established in 1826 as a military outpost, it was the state's first European settlement. Albany's harbour has been a major asset and the town retains a maritime feel. Within a few hours' ride are pristine beaches and impressive coastal scenery.

Information The visitor centre (☎ 9841 1088 or ☎ 1800-644 088, ⊖ atb@albanytourist.com.au) and the Westrail office (☎ 13 1053) are at the Old Railway Station on

WESTERN AUSTRALIA

Day 9: Denmark to Albany

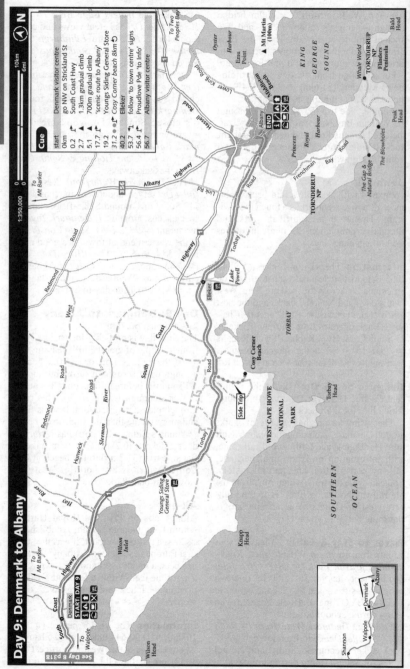

Cue

start	Denmark visitor centre
0km	go NW on Strickland St
0.2	South Coast Hwy
2.7	1.3km gradual climb
5.1	700m gradual climb
17.7	'scenic route to Albany'
19.2	Youngs Siding General Store
31.2	Cosy Corner beach 8km
40.2	Elleker
53.7	follow 'to town centre' signs
56.4	Proudlove Pde 'to Info'
56.7	Albany visitor centre

N

1:350,000

0   10km
0   6mi

To Mt Barker

To Two Peoples Bay

KING GEORGE SOUND

Oyster Harbour

Emu Point

▲ Mt Martin (100m)

TORNDIRRUP NP Flinders Peninsula

Bald Head

Whale World

Lower King Road

Middleton Beach

Albany
END

Princess Royal Harbour

Frenchman Bay

Peak Head

The Blowholes

The Gap & Natural Bridge

TORNDIRRUP NP

Peak Head Road

Albany Highway

356

Hassell Road

Link Rd

Highway

Redmond Road

West Road

Redmond Road

Sleeman River

Hay River

To Mt Barker

Torbay Highway

Elleker

Lake Powell

South Coast Road

Torbay Road

Torbay

Youngs Siding General Store

Cosy Corner Beach

TORBAY

Torbay Head

WEST CAPE HOWE NATIONAL PARK

Side Trip

Knapp Head

SOUTHERN OCEAN

Wilson Inlet

Wilson Head

Denmark
START DAY 9

South Coast Highway

To Walpole

See Day 8 p318

Shannon

Walpole

Denmark

Albany

Proudlove Parade at the southern end of town. Ask for the free *Andimap Street & Locality Guide*. Showers at the complex cost $2.

The major banks and ATMs are on York St. The Great Southern Bicycle Company (☎ 9841 7031), 47A Sanford Rd, off Albany Hwy, is excellent for touring advice and offers discounts to YHA members.

Things to See & Do Albany has some fine colonial buildings, some of which are now museums. Near the water, **Albany Residency Museum** (☎ 9841 4844), Residency Rd, covers early exploration and industry, and natural history. The **Old Gaol Museum**; is opposite; a full-scale replica of the **Amity brig,** which carried Albany's founding party, is adjacent. The tourist bureau has more information on the town's historic buildings.

The **coastal shared path** from the western end of Princess Royal Dr to Emu Point goes via **Middleton Beach**, the closest swimming beach. Walk or ride up **Mt Clarence** (overlooking the town) for great **views**.

It's well worth visiting **Flinders Peninsula**, south of Albany. The wonderful coastline in **Torndirrup National Park** includes **The Gap**, **Natural Bridge** and **The Blowholes** rock formations (beware of theft and vandalism at remote car parks). **Whale World** (☎ 9844 4021) was the whaling station at Flinders Bay (21km from Albany). Closed in 1978, it is now an excellent museum (adults $11, last entry 4.30pm).

Take care at the dangerous exposed sections of coast on the peninsula: **swim** at the sheltered beaches inside Princess Royal Harbour.

Places to Stay The well-equipped *Mt Melville Caravan Park* (☎ 9841 4616, 22 Wellington St) is around 2.5km north-west of town. Tent sites cost $14 for two people; on-site vans $44, park homes and chalets (both with linen) from $50 and $60. *Middleton Beach Holiday Park* (☎ 9841 3593 or ☎ 1800-644 674, Middleton Rd) is a little pricier.

Bright and cheery *Albany Backpackers* (☎ 9842 5255, cnr Spencer St & Stirling Terrace)* charges $19/46.20 for dorm beds/doubles, which includes light breakfast, coffee and cake. Friendly *Albany Bayview YHA* (☎ 9842 3388, 49 Duke St) has dorm beds/doubles at $17/40.

At the *Discovery Inn* (☎ 9842 5535, 9 Middleton Rd) at Middleton Beach (3.5km from town), B&B costs $41/65 for singles/ doubles.

Guests are greeted with cake at the small, homely *Oakview Cottage B&B* (☎ 9841 4538, 34 Fredrick St)*; rooms cost $55/66.

My Place Colonial Accommodation (☎ 9842 3242, 47–61 Grey St East) has self-contained quarters, built between the 1890s and 1940s, from $65/85 (no single-night bookings during holidays).

Places to Eat The *Foodland* supermarket *(York St)* opens until 9pm.

Eat great curry and surf the web at the cheap and cheerful *Yak Bar* (☎ 9842 8343, 38 Stirling Terrace)*. *Dylans* (☎ 9841 8720, 82 Stirling Terrace)* has good burgers (around $8 with chips); and the *Shamrock Cafe* (☎ 9841 4201, 184 York St)* does full Irish (or vegetarian) breakfast for just $6.50.

Al Fornetto (☎ 9842 1060, 132 York St)* is good for pizza (from $13.50). Locals recommend *Bangkok Rose* (☎ 9842 2366, 112 York St)* – Thai mains cost mostly $12.50 to $14 (closed Monday).

Avon Valley

Duration	3 days
Distance	272km
Difficulty	hard
Start/End	Midland train station

Rich in wild flowers, the forest of the Perth Hills is spectacular in spring, and lovely even when the flowers aren't out. Heading east through Chittering Valley's rural idyll, the ride also features the Avon Valley's charming towns, their 19th-century streetscapes still intact. The return journey's highlight is the hill forest around Mundaring Weir and fabulous city views down the Zig Zag Scenic Drive.

HISTORY

Within a year of European settlement in WA, food shortage forced a search for more arable land. Over the Darling Range, Ensign Dale found the Avon Valley, green and pastoral, in August 1830. A settlement was established at York the following year. Other town sites, including Northam and Toodyay, were selected downstream. Convicts were used to build public buildings, bridges and roads.

York flourished during the gold rush as a commercial centre, equipping miners en route to diggings further east. However, Northam was chosen as the main rail link to the goldfields in 1891, leading to its development as the region's major service town.

NATURAL HISTORY

Between the gently rolling farmland of the Avon Valley and Perth's coastal plain lies the Darling Range – an ancient, creased plateau, which ends abruptly at the western scarp. The Avon River winds northward around the range through York, Northam and Toodyay and – unbeknownst to the early explorers – south again, where it was known as the Swan.

The flora of the Darling Range is dominated by jarrah and marri forest. Towards the east, wandoo (white gum) is dominant. Mid-storey species include banksias, grass trees and acacias (wattles). This area is also rich in wild flowers, such as kangaroo paws, hakeas, grevilleas, orchids and more, most of which flower in spring.

Animals include kangaroos, wallabies, emus, possums, echidnas and harder-to-spot small mammals such as dunnarts; plus a variety of lizards, frogs and snakes. Some of the more obvious of the many bird species are cockatoos and ringback parrots, known in this area as 'twenty-eight' parrots because that's what their call sounds like.

PLANNING
When to Ride

Spring is best, with its abundant wild flowers and greenery. Avoid the dry, hot summer. Autumn and late winter are also pleasant.

Summer is low season in the Avon Valley. Booking accommodation is wise through spring and essential for Easter and festival weekends.

Maps

The RAC's *Perth Region* map (approx 1: 250,000) is adequate, but lacks detail close to town. It can be supplemented with the *Swan-Stirling Perth Bike Map* ($3.95 from bike shops and tourist centres).

What to Bring

Carry plenty of water, especially on Days 1 and 3, which have limited services.

GETTING TO/FROM THE RIDE

Train Metropolitan commuter trains to Midland leave regularly from Perth train station on Wellington St (25 minutes, $2.50 plus $1.70 for bikes on weekdays). See Perth's Getting There & Away section for peak-hour travel.

Bicycle Bikepaths exist most of the way from the city to Midland (around 24km). Bikewest's *Ride Around the Rivers* booklet describes the route to Garvey Park. Continue to the Great Eastern Hwy and follow it north-east to Midland train station (around 7km).

THE RIDE
Midland

Midland, on the metropolitan train line, is a retail centre 24km east of central Perth. The shopping centre opposite the train line has a *supermarket* and *bakery*. Midland Cycles (☎ 9250 6330) is at 214 Great Eastern Hwy.

Day 1: Midland to Toodyay
4½–6½ hours, 97.9km

Today's ride is demanding for its length. While two thirds is flat – with one short hill (27.7km) – the final 38km rolls more strenuously. The ride is quiet and scenic after the first 26.5km of flat, busy Northern Hwy (beware of trucks).

After **Bullsbrook** (26.3km), which has a *store*, *cafe* and *bakery*, freshly squeezed orange juice at the *Golden Grove* orange orchard (40.6km) is the only service.

Once over the climb out of Bullsbrook, it's easy riding through the Chittering Valley, dotted with orange orchards, sheep and vineyards.

From Julimar Rd (60km), the road undulates to Toodyay, climbing gradually. It's a lovely ride, most of it through the **Julimar Conservation Park**, filled with wild flowers in spring. Towards Toodyay, clearings offer vistas of the Avon Valley.

Toodyay

Declared an historic town by the National Trust in 1980, Toodyay has a friendly village atmosphere and its fair share of historic buildings. Europeans first settled the area in the late 1830s and within a few decades the town (then called Newcastle) had a wild

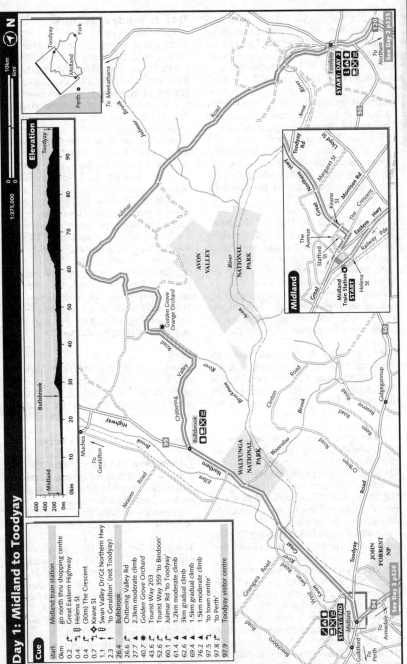

Day 1: Midland to Toodyay

Cue		
start		Midland train station
0km		go north thru shopping centre
0.2	⌐	Great Eastern Highway
0.4	⌐	Helena St
0.4	⌐	(30m) The Crescent
0.7	⌐	Keane St
1.1	✦	Swan Valley Dr/Gt Northern Hwy
2.3	⌐	'to Geraldton' (not Toodyay)
26.4		Bullsbrook
26.6	⌐	Chittering Valley Rd
27.7	▲	2.3km moderate climb
40.7	✳	Golden Grove Orchard
43.6	⌐	Tourist Way 203
52.6	⌐	Julimar Way 359 'to Bindoon'
60.1	⌐	Julimar Rd 'to Toodyay'
61.4	▲	1.2km moderate climb
62.6	▲	3km gradual climb
69.4	▲	1.5km gradual climb
76.2	▲	1.5km moderate climb
97.5	⌐	'to town centre'
97.8	⌐	'to Perth'
97.9		Toodyay visitor centre

Elevation

Midland — Bullsbrook — Toodyay

N

10km
6mi

1:375,000

reputation, with the likes of WA's most famous bushranger, Moondyne Joe, roaming around. Joe escaped from the Toodyay jail in 1861 and, after several more escapes, achieved infamy for his Houdini-like abilities rather than for his crimes.

Information The visitor centre (☎ 9574 2435, ⓔ toodyay@gidgenet.com.au) is in Connors Mill, Stirling Terrace, which houses 19th-century flour-milling machinery.

Bendigo Bank is on Stirling Terrace; the Commonwealth and Challenge Bank agents are the post office and Ray White Real Estate. Eftpos is available at the Foodland supermarket.

Things to See & Do The 1862 **Old Newcastle Gaol** (☎ 9574 2435), Clinton St, is now a museum of the colonial and convict era and features Moondyne Joe.

An **historic buildings** guided walk is described in the free *Toodyay* booklet.

Toodyay hosts several special events, including the **May Moondyne Festival** and others, mostly held in spring. Telephone the visitor centre for details.

Places to Stay & Eat Book ahead for green tent sites ($6.60 per person) at the *Avonbanks Toodyay Caravan Park (☎ 9574 2612, Railway Rd)*, 1.5km from town. Onsite vans cost $38.50 and fully self-contained chalets, from $60.50 a double.

Freemasons Hotel/Motel (☎ 9574 2201, 125 Stirling Terrace) has pleasant, smoke-free rooms for $33 per person, with continental breakfast. New motel units cost $71.50/82.50 for one/two people (without breakfast). Counter meals (from around $10) are smallish. Toodyay's *B&Bs* are all several kilometres from town – contact the visitor centre for details.

Foodland supermarket *(Stirling Terrace)* opens daily. *Toodyay Bakery (123 Stirling Terrace)* is closed Sunday.

Stirling House Cafe Restaurant (☎ 9574 4407, 122B Stirling Terrace) opens Friday nights only for a three-course, $21.50 steak grill (vegetarian available). The *Victoria Hotel/Motel (Stirling Terrace)* has restaurant mains from $15 and counter meals from $8. After 8pm, there's only truckies' food at the *Toodyay Roadhouse (143 Stirling Terrace)*: last orders at 8.45pm.

Day 2: Toodyay to York
3–4½ hours, 68.9km
Today's route largely follows the Avon Historic Tourist Drive via Northam, the region's largest town. The route has no real hills, and little traffic after the first 13.6km (during which trucks may be encountered).

The 15km Northam/Katrine Heritage Trail (13.6km) passes ruins and significant sites from early colonial settlement, including **Katrine historic complex** (☎ 9622 3790), open April to October (14.6km). Historical leaflets for the trail are available from the Toodyay and Northam visitor centres.

Northam (28.6km) is a regional service centre rather than tourist town. However, its interesting history is worth discovering at the Avon Valley Visitor Centre (☎ 9621 1062), 2 Grey St. A bike shop is in the main street, Fitzgerald St.

After Northam, the railway line and Avon River are followed through flat wheat and sheep country to York. Late afternoon is perhaps the nicest time to ride this section, as the sinking sun softens the colours (but don't miss closing time at York!).

York
Classified by the National Trust, York, settled in 1931, is WA's oldest inland town. It's just as delightful as Toodyay, though a little more touristy. York has earned a 'festival town' reputation; the Jazz Festival (October) and the Veteran Car Rally (August), in particular, have the town packed out.

Information The tourist office (☎ 9641 1301, 🖳 www.YorkWA.com.au/Tourist.Bureau/default.htm) is in the grand old town hall on Avon Terrace (corner Joaquina St).

Commonwealth (with ATM) and Challenge banks are on Avon Terrace.

Things to See & Do The **York Motor Museum** (☎ 9641 1288), 116 Avon Terrace, has a wonderful collection of old cars and motorbikes. For expensive hand-made furniture and other arts and crafts, check out **The Mill Gallery** (☎ 9641 2522), Broome St.

Many of York's **historic buildings** and **churches** are marked on the tourist bureau's free *York Living History* town map and in the $3.50 *Heritage Trail York* booklet, which also includes historical commentary.

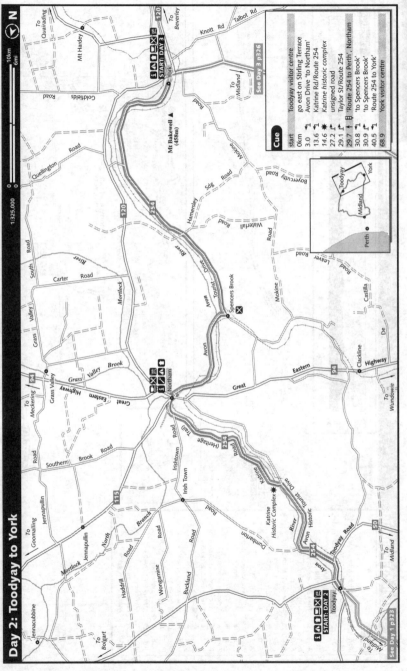

Day 2: Toodyay to York

Cue

start		Toodyay visitor centre
0km		go east on Stirling Terrace
3.0	⌐ ⌐	Avon Drive 'to Northam'
13.6	⌐	Katrine Rd/Route 254
14.6	✳	Katrine historic complex
27.2	⌐ ⌐	unsigned road
29.1	⌐ ⤚⌐	Taylor St/Route 254
29.7	⌐ ⤚⌐	'Route 254 to Perth', 'Northam'
30.8	⌐ ⌐	'to Spencers Brook'
30.9	⌐ ⌐	'to Spencers Brook'
40.5	⌐	'Route 254 to York'
68.9		York visitor centre

WESTERN AUSTRALIA

Day 3: York to Midland

Cue		
start		York visitor centre
0km	⤵	go S on Avon Terrace
0.2	⬎	Henrietta St/Great Southern Hwy
31.7	◀	3.4km moderate climb
46.9	◀	1.7km gradual climb
59.8		The Lakes Roadhouse
		Sawyers Valley
63.0	⬎	800m no shoulder & grates
63.6	⬎	Hodgson St, Mundaring
		follow signs to Mundaring Weir
69.2	✳	Lavender Patch Tearooms
		'to Kalamunda'
70.0	⬎	Djarli-Mari YHA
70.8	● ●	O'Connor Museum 200m ↻
71.7	◀	dam wall
71.8	◀	2km hard climb
72.6	✳	
74.5	◀	1.5km gradual climb
84.0	◀	2.3km moderate climb
86.7	◀	1.3km moderate climb
88.0	⬧⬎	Railway Rd, Kalamunda
		Gooseberry Hill Rd
90.4	⬎	(50m) Williams St
90.4	⬎	Ridgehill Rd
96.0	⬎	grates at road edge, 1.5km
97.8	⬧⬎	Helena Valley Rd
101.6	⬎	Military Rd 'to Midland'
103.1	⬎	Clayton St
104.1	⬎	Great Eastern Hwy
105.2		Midland train station

See Above

See Below

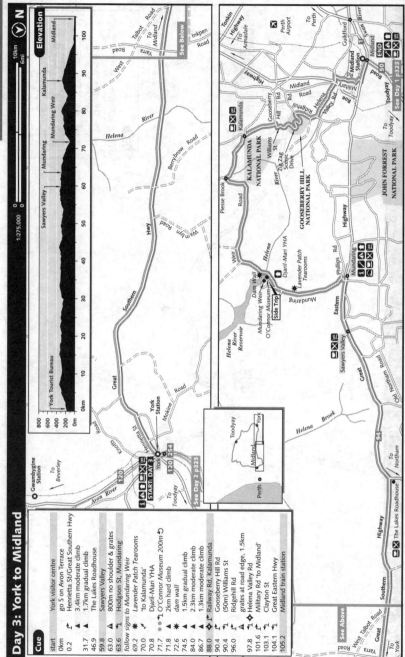

Places to Stay Under the mount's shadow, the *Mt Bakewell Caravan Park (☎ 9641 1421, Eighth Rd)* is 3km from town. Tent sites cost $10/15.50 for one/two people and on-site vans $33/38.50.

The *Castle Hotel (☎ 9641 1007, 97 Avon Terrace)* can be impersonal, but the rooms aren't bad for $35/65 per single/double. Spacious motel rooms cost $80/110 for one/two people, with B&B.

Avon Motel (☎ 9641 2066, 10 William St) has rooms for $60/88, including a light breakfast.

Wansbrough House (☎ 9641 2887, 22 Avon Terrace) does B&B in a charming 1859 cottage; it costs $125 a couple. The *King's Head (☎ 9641 1234, 37 Avon Terrace)* is plainer, but better value at $50/75.

Places to Eat The *Supa Valu* supermarket *(138 Avon Terrace)* opens at least until 5.30pm weekdays and 1pm Saturday; for fresh bread and cakes, go to the *York Village Bakehouse & Tearooms (82 York Terrace)*.

The main eating in York is on Avon Terrace, but few places open every night. Two that do are the *Castle Hotel* bistro, for standard pub mains (slim vego pickings) from $11.50; and *York Deli*, for takeaways. Italian, family-run *Cafe Bugatti (☎ 9641 1583, 104 Avon Terrace)* opens Thursday to Saturday, as does *Goodtimes Pizza (☎ 9641 1222, 135 Avon Terrace)*. *Happy Valley Chinese Restaurant (☎ 9641 2888, 143 Avon Terrace)* has mains from $8.

Day 3: York to Midland
5–8 hours, 105.2km

Another strenuous day, ending closer to sea level than it begins, but with a few ups and downs in between – plus some rewarding views. Traffic on the Great Southern Hwy is not too intrusive, but swells after joining the Great Eastern (47.1km). It's a relief to turn on to quiet roads again after **Mundaring** (63.6km).

After climbing gradually for the best part of 7km, the southern highway continues to roll through pleasant forest and farmland. At Mundaring Village shopping centre (200m west of the turn-off) is the Mundaring visitor centre (☎ 9295 0202), Mundaring Cycles (☎ 9295 2042) and the well-stocked *Clarkes Bread & Patisserie*.

The Mundaring Weir road to Kalamunda involves scenic forest, two terrific long descents and two long (though not steep) hills.

Attractions and services include the *Lavender Patch Tearooms (69.2km; ☎ 9295 1665)*; the *Djaril-Mari YHA (70.8km; ☎ 9295 1809)*; the **Mundaring Weir Gardens** and **O'Connor Museum** (71.7km), which shows how water was pumped to the gold fields a century ago; and walking along the **dam wall** (72.6km).

Kalamunda has shops and *cafes* (88km), after which the road is downhill, via the one-way **Zig Zag Scenic Drive** – originally a railway line – through the Gooseberry Hill National Park.

The great descent continues on Ridgehill Rd – but watch for gutter grates.

Queensland

Twice the size of Texas, Queensland still has something of a frontier feel about it. The population is heavily concentrated in the south-east, around the capital Brisbane. This leaves a lot of space for cycling. Much of the state is dry and very wide open, with 100km or more between towns. This can make good touring for the determined and well equipped, but most people will find the east coast more interesting. Those riding from Brisbane to Cairns should avoid, where possible, the Pacific Hwy, which is often narrow and heavily trafficked.

HISTORY
Queensland was home to a third of Australia's Aboriginal population in pre-European times. A penal colony was established in Moreton Bay in 1822 to take Port Jackson's overflow of hard-core convicts. Exploration and settlement by pastoralists, loggers and gold miners soon followed. The Aborigines were gradually displaced; resistance to the white invasion was countered by massive reprisals. More recently, Queensland's Murray Islands were the subject of a significant legal victory for Eddie Mabo and his fellow inhabitants. The Mabo decision recognised Native Title over the islands and led to the federal *Native Title Act* being established in 1993.

The 1860s gold rushes and separation from New South Wales (NSW) heralded a time of growth and prosperity. In the 1890s, depression hit, fostering strong unions and, in 1899, the world's first Labour government. State politics in the latter half of the 20th century were dominated by conservatives, including Sir Joh Bjelke-Petersen, who ruled Queensland in an autocratic fashion for 19 years.

NATURAL HISTORY
The spine of the Great Dividing Range separates a narrow, wet, coastal plain from the great, dry expanse known generally as 'the Outback'. All of the rides described are east of the divide, where towns are closer together and the landscape more lush and varied.

Much of Queensland's fauna, apart from its colourful birds, is shy or nocturnal. Western regions are the domain of the superbly athletic red kangaroo. Cyclists in

In Summary

Area code ☎ 07

Highlights
- snorkelling, sailing and diving on the **Great Barrier Reef**

- coastal and hinterland forest in the **Wet Tropics World Heritage Area**

- cycling through the **Tweed Caldera**

- great **coastal scenery** on the Captain Cook Hwy north of Cairns

Special Events
- **surf life-saving events** (Mar) Gold Coast and Sunshine Coast beaches

- **Brisbane International Film Festival** (July)

- **The Royal Brisbane Show (The Ekka)** agricultural and family show (Aug)

- **Woodford Folk Festival** (Dec)

Cycling Events
- **Bike Week** – including the Great Brisbane Bike Ride (mid-Oct); contact Bicycle Queensland

- **Brissie to the Bay** state's biggest one-day fun ride (early May); contact Bicycle Queensland

Gourmet Specialities
- seafood, especially mud crabs, Moreton Bay bugs, reef fish and barramundi

- Bowen mangoes

- macadamia nuts

- XXXX and Powers beers

State Tourist Information
Queensland Tourist and Travel Corporation (☎ 3874 2800 or ☎ 13 1801, 💻 www.qttc.com.au) 243 Edward St, Brisbane

eastern coastal regions are more likely to encounter the eastern grey kangaroo.

North Queensland, connected to New Guinea during the Ice age, has some rather special and dangerous wildlife, including estuarine crocodiles (known as 'salties'). Normanton boasts a life-sized model of an 8.4m specimen hunted nearby. The other one to watch is the taipan – not only does this 4m snake have world-beating venom, it's one of Australia's few aggressive snakes and is unlikely to bite you just once. However, it's not too hard to keep out of the way of both of these – see the Health & Safety chapter.

Two species of bizarre tree kangaroo inhabit the tropical rainforests of far-north Queensland. Another notable inhabitant is the cassowary. A flightless bird growing to 2m, it has a heavy casque on its head to help it push through the viny undergrowth.

CLIMATE

Much of Queensland lies in the tropics so summers are hot or, in coastal areas, humid. North Queensland has a pronounced wet season (January to March) that delivers well above half the annual rainfall, which is 2220mm in Cairns, for example. South-east Queensland has a less-pronounced wet season (Brisbane's average annual rainfall is 1150mm), but winter (June to August) is markedly drier than the summer. December (with an average temperature of 29°C in Brisbane, 32°C in Cairns) is one of the hottest months, and enough rain falls statewide to drive the humidity up to sauna levels.

The combined sea breeze and trade wind give the state a predominantly south-easterly airflow. This makes for a good run if you are heading up the coast.

INFORMATION
Maps & Books

The Queensland Department of Natural Resources (☎ 3896 3216, 🖳 www.dnr.qld .gov.au), at the Land Centre, corner Main and Vulture Sts, Coorparoo, produces the Sunmap topographic maps and the Tourist Map series (at varying scales, $6.25); the latter is very good for cycle touring. Maps are available from Department centres around the state, book stores and map stockists, such as World Wide Maps and Guides (☎ 3221 4330), 187 George St, Brisbane.

The Royal Automobile Club of Queensland (RACQ; ☎ 13 1905, 🖳 www.racq.com .au) produces a series of road maps covering the whole state, but at 1:1,250 000 they can lack detail, South-east Queensland is better covered at three times this scale. The maps are available from RACQ offices (mostly free to members or around $4 to the public).

Hema (☎ 3340 0000) city and regional maps (1:250,000) are widely available from newsagents and book stores.

Lonely Planet's *Queensland* guide makes a useful companion for tours beyond those described here.

Information Sources

Bicycle Queensland is the volunteer-run state lobby group (☎ 3844 1144, 🖳 www .uq.net.au/~zzbikeq), PO Box 8321, Woolloongabba 4102; the Web site has details of organised fun rides in Brisbane.

The Queensland Parks and Wildlife Service is part of the Environment Protection Agency (EPA). Information on all of the state's national parks is available online at 🖳 www.env.qld.gov.au.

If you are spending some time in Brisbane, the Brisbane Bicycle Touring Association (BBTA; 🖳 www.bbta-au.org), PO Box 286, Ashgrove 4060, runs day rides every weekend and overnight tours at least monthly.

GATEWAY CITIES
Brisbane

Queensland's capital has an enviable subtropical climate and remains more laid-back than its southern counterparts. The city heart is neatly contained in a bend of the Brisbane River. Beyond this radiates a vast, suburban sprawl, a product of the claustrophobic and acquisitive Australian lifestyle. Brisbane streets are not overly bike-friendly, but facilities and attitudes are slowly improving. There is, however, some great riding in the south-east, accessed by a growing suburban/inter-urban rail network.

Information The Queen St Mall visitor centre (☎ 3229 5918), on the corner of Queen and Albert Sts, is particularly helpful with ideas for things to see and do. It also has free *Bikeway* maps of Brisbane (closed Sunday afternoon).

In the Transit Centre on Roma St, the Visitors Accommodation Service (☎ 3236 2020) is a free booking service for hostels and other budget accommodation.

All the major banks have branches throughout central Brisbane, many with foreign exchange sections.

QUEENSLAND

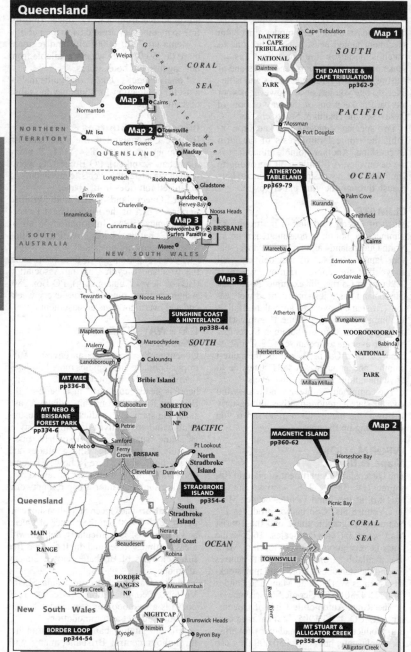

Queensland

Map 1

DAINTREE › CAPE TRIBULATION NATIONAL PARK

Cape Tribulation

SOUTH

Daintree

THE DAINTREE & CAPE TRIBULATION
pp362-9

PACIFIC

Mossman

Port Douglas

OCEAN

ATHERTON TABLELAND
pp369-79

Palm Cove

Kuranda

Smithfield

Cairns

Mareeba

Edmonton

Gordanvale

Atherton

Yungaburra

WOOROONOORAN

Babinda

Herberton

NATIONAL

Millaa Millaa

PARK

Weipa

Great Barrier Reef

CORAL

SEA

Cooktown

Normanton

Map 1

Cairns

NORTHERN TERRITORY

Mt Isa

Map 2

Townsville

Charters Towers

Airlie Beach

QUEENSLAND

Mackay

Longreach

Rockhampton

Gladstone

Birdsville

Charleville

Bundaberg

Hervey Bay

Noosa Heads

Innamincka

Cunnamulla

Map 3

Toowoomba

BRISBANE

SOUTH AUSTRALIA

Surfers Paradise

Moree

NEW SOUTH WALES

Map 3

Tewantin

Noosa Heads

SUNSHINE COAST & HINTERLAND
pp338-44

Mapleton

Maroochydore

SOUTH

Maleny

Caloundra

Landsborough

Bribie Island

MT MEE
pp336-8

Caboolture

MORETON ISLAND NP

MT NEBO & BRISBANE FOREST PARK
pp334-6

Petrie

PACIFIC

Samford

Ferny Grove

BRISBANE

Mt Nebo

Pt Lookout

North Stradbroke Island

Cleveland

Dunwich

STRADBROKE ISLAND
pp354-6

Queensland

South Stradbroke Island

OCEAN

MAIN

Nerang

Gold Coast

RANGE

Beaudesert

NP

Robina

BORDER RANGES NP

Gradys Creek

Murwillumbah

New South Wales

NIGHTCAP NP

Brunswick Heads

BORDER LOOP
pp344-54

Kyogle

Nimbin

Byron Bay

Map 2

MAGNETIC ISLAND
pp360-62

Horseshoe Bay

Picnic Bay

CORAL

SEA

TOWNSVILLE

Ross River

78

MT STUART & ALLIGATOR CREEK
pp358-60

Alligator Creek

City bike-shop prices tend to reflect their overheads. Brisbane Bicycle Sales & Hire (☎ 3229 2433), 87 Albert St, has a good range and hires bikes, charging from $9 per hour to $160 per month. Ridgway's Cycles (☎ 3355 9653), 629 Stafford Rd, Stafford Heights, is 8km north of the city centre. Despite its tiny shopfront, it stocks an amazing range of spares and will track down the unusual.

Things to See & Do Next to the city are the **botanic gardens**, a great place for a mid-day stroll.

Opposite, the floodlit cliffs of **Kangaroo Point** are a favourite haunt of rock climbers. Upstream is the **Queensland Maritime Museum** (☎ 3844 5361, Sidon St), where the steam tug *SS Forceful* makes occasional pleasure cruises. Next are the **Southbank Parklands**, which feature a fantastic inland beach and lagoon, and a weekend craft market. Further upstream, the **Queensland Cultural Centre** incorporates the state's Performing Arts Complex, Museum, Gallery and Library. The **Queensland Museum** (☎ 3840 7555) has free admission; displays include state history, and current and prehistoric Australian animals. The **Queensland Art Gallery** is also free, apart from visiting exhibitions, and has an impressive collection of Australian art, including many Aboriginal paintings.

One of the best ways to visit all of these sights – and see Brisbane – is by the **City Cat** ferry. The Cats ply a 19km route from The University of Queensland in St Lucia past the city to Bretts Wharf in Hamilton. The round trip takes about two hours. A Day Rover card ($8) allows all-day travel on the Cat, as well as buses and the small, cross-river ferries. The Off-Peak Saver ticket ($4.40) allows the same travel between 9am and 3:30pm and after 7pm. The only catch is that this fare must be bought from a ticket agency (most newsagents). Bikes are carried free.

At 300m elevation, **Mt Coot-tha** is a popular and scenic training ride, while the **Moreton Bay foreshore** around Manly, Redcliffe and the Boondall Wetlands Reserve provides good recreational rides.

Places to Stay At the *Newmarket Gardens Caravan Park* (☎ 3356 1458; 199 Ashgrove Ave, Ashgrove)*, 4km north of the city, camp sites cost $17.60, on-site vans $33, and cabins $58.30 (all for two people).

Palace Backpackers (☎ 3211 2433 or ☎ 1800-676 340, cnr Ann & Edward Sts) is the city centre's only hostel. The facilities are excellent, but it can be noisy. Dorm beds cost from $17; doubles are $45.

Upper Roma St, near the city and the Transit Centre, is a burgeoning hostel precinct. The modern *Brisbane City YHA* (☎ 3236 1060, 392 Roma St) has dorm beds at $21 and doubles for $55. The *City Backpackers Hostel* (☎ 3211 3221, 380 Roma St) has dorm beds for $18 and doubles for $44.

The *Annie's Shandon Inn* (☎ 3831 8684, 405 Upper Edward St) is a friendly guesthouse with immaculate singles/doubles from $44/55 (including light breakfast). The *Acacia Inner City Inn* (☎ 3832 1663, 413 Upper Edward St) offers a similar deal, charging from $40/50. Both are a short walk from the city. The *Explorer's Inn* (☎ 3211 3488, 63 Turbot St) is a modern, three-star hotel with good-value, if a little tight, doubles for $75.

The central five-star *Stamford Plaza Brisbane* (☎ 3221 1999, cnr Edward & Margaret Sts) combines understated luxury with excellent facilities. All rooms overlook the river, and doubles start from $185 (more midweek).

Places to Eat For self-caterers, a handy *Coles* supermarket is at the northern end of the Queen St Mall. A lot of Brisbane's best eating is in the inner suburbs of West End, Fortitude Valley, New Farm and Paddington.

West End For a bargain, head across the river to West End. The Vietnamese-Chinese *Kim Thanh* (93 Hardgrave Rd) is well known. The soups, around $7, are a meal in themselves, while mains cost $6 to $13. The *bakery* by the same name (81 Vulture St) has dirt-cheap pastries to tempt hungry cyclists. *Lefkas Taverna* (☎ 3844 1163, 170 Hardgrave Rd) serves great Greek food, with mains from $6. Boundary and Mollison Sts have a dozen or so good cafes – try *Cafe Babylon* (142 Boundary St) or the *Three Monkeys Coffee House* (58 Mollison St) for a cultural and culinary experience.

Fortitude Valley & Newfarm Home to Brisbane's China Town, Fortitude Valley – The Valley – also has a burgeoning alternative cafe scene. *McWhirters Marketplace (cnr Brunswick & Wickham Sts)* has a produce market and foodhall. Go to Duncan St, between Anne and Wickham Sts, for Asian meals. *The Enjoy Inn (167 Wickham St)* is widely regarded as the best Cantonese restaurant in town, and has meals from $8 to $16. Go to *Lucky's Trattoria (683 Ann St)* for Italian cooking, with pasta mains from $9.

More mainstream cafes are in Newfarm, south-east of the Valley, along Brunswick St. The *New Farm Deli & Cafe (900 Brunswick St)* serves award-winning deli lunches.

Paddington For a budget feed, try the *City YHA hostel cafe (392 Upper Roma St)*; you don't have to be staying at the hostel. Most other good places are on Given Terrace, about 1km east of Petrie Terrace. Try the *Paddo Tavern* for cheap mid-week lunches; *Kari Tandoori (235 Given Terrace)* for great tandoori; and the Brisbane institution, *Le Scoops (283 Given Terrace)*, for ice cream and crepes.

Getting There & Away Brisbane's Transit Centre (☎ 3236 2020) on Roma St is the terminus and booking centre for all long-distance buses and trains, and the airport bus. See the Getting There & Away and Getting Around chapters for more information about air, train and bus travel to and/or within Australia.

Air Brisbane airport is 16km north-east of the city, with the international and domestic terminals about 2km apart. Regular domestic services fly to the other state capitals, as well as Townsville ($441) and Cairns ($492). A shuttle bus (☎ 3236 1000) runs from the domestic and international terminals to the city every 45 minutes ($7.50). At the time of publication, a rail line was being built to both terminals, making city access quick and easy (due to be opened May 2001).

Train Queensland Rail (QR; ☎ 13 2232 or ☎ 1800-806 468, 🖳 qroti.bit.net.au/travel train/) operates long-distance train services in Queensland and takes bookings for the XPT to Sydney. The Citytrain network is the best way of getting to, or through, Brisbane from nearby centres. Trans Info (☎ 13 1230) provides fare and timetable information.

Cairns

Cairns, gateway to the tropical north, is an international tourist mecca – I once heard a frustrated drunk shouting in the main street, 'I want to meet an Australian. Are you an Australian?'. Visitors shouldn't expect to meet too many locals, but they will be well catered for.

Information The rides which travel to/from Cairns in this book use the Wet Tropics Information Centre as a base, on the Esplanade near Shields St. It combines information with displays on the environment of the far north. For phone queries call Tourism Tropical North Queensland (☎ 4051 3588). The Cairns visitor centre (☎ 4031 1751) is across the road. The EPA (☎ 4052 3096) is at 10–12 McLeod St.

All the major banks are in central Cairns, and many have foreign exchange sections.

The Bike Man (☎ 4051 7135), 310 Mulgrave Rd, is a friendly and helpful store.

Internet 2000 (☎ 4041 0388) on Grafton St opens daily.

Things to See & Do The **Great Barrier Reef** is Cairns' must-see. On every corner, dive companies advertise the **snorkelling** and **diving** trips that depart daily from Trinity Wharf. Check at the visitor centres or your accommodation for good deals.

Dan's Mountain Biking (☎ 4033 0128) offers a range of half- and full-day **rides**, including the course used for the 1996 UCI World Mountain-Bike Championships. Prices start from $59 and include bike hire.

Can I Bring My Bike?

Queensland Rail trains have space for bikes on *most* services. Front wheels and pedals must be removed and handlebars turned; and they're loaded by rail staff. Bikes are charged 20% of the adult economy fare.

On Brisbane's Citytrain network, bikes are carried free but cannot be taken through the city centre or in the peak-flow direction during peak times (weekdays 7am–9am and 3pm–6.30pm).

Standard charges and packing conditions also apply to transporting bikes on buses; see Carrying Your Bicycle in the Bus section of the Getting Around chapter.

White-water rafting along the Tully River is very popular; ask at the tourist office.

Browse the **Pier Marketplace** for a good range of speciality shops. **Flecker Botanic Gardens**, 3km north-west of the centre, show how Aborigines used native plants.

The award-winning **Tjapukai Aboriginal Cultural Park** (☎ 4042 9900) has three theatres displaying Aboriginal history, the creation story and a corroboree performance. Aboriginal people tell about their traditional food and medicines and demonstrate the use of the spear, boomerang and didjeridu. See Day 1 of The Daintree & Cape Tribulation ride for directions; admission costs $24.

The adjacent **Skyrail** (☎ 4038 1555) is a spectacular 7.5km gondola ride over the Barron Gorge National Park to the hill town of Kuranda. **Kuranda** has a vibrant craft and gift market and every tourist attraction from butterfly park to shooting gallery. The **Kuranda Scenic Railway** (☎ 4031 3636) passes through cane fields before grinding its way up the track perched precariously above the Barron Gorge.

Places to Stay The most central camping is at the *City Caravan Park (☎ 4051 1467, cnr Little & James Sts)*, 2km north-west of the city. It's well set-up, if a little cramped. Tent sites cost $15 for two people; on-site vans cost $35 and cabins $45.

A number of small, personal hostels are west of the rail station. *Ryan's Rest (☎ 4051 4734, 18 Terminus St)* is a breezy, converted Queenslander (traditional Queensland house) with a pool. Singles/doubles cost $35/40; there are no dorms. The *Captain Cook Backpackers Hostel (☎ 4051 6811, 204 Sheridan St)*, with two pools, a bar and cheap meals, is a good stand-by in busy periods. Dorm beds cost from $15, and doubles $35.

Costa Blanca Apartments (☎ 4051 3114, 241 Esplanade) provide affordable waterfront accommodation. The one-bedroom units are clean, have kitchens and good views from upstairs. Their double units cost from $66. *The Country Comfort Outrigger (☎ 4051 6188, cnr Abbott & Florence Sts)* has a pool and restaurant. Air-conditioned doubles cost from $134.

Cairns' most impressive five-star hotel is the *Cairns International Hotel (☎ 4031 1300, 17 Abbott St)*. Rooms start at $315 and suites, from $640.

Places to Eat The *Bi-Lo* supermarket is in the Central Shopping Centre on McLeod St.

Many backpackers end up eating in bars and nightclubs, lured by free or heavily discounted meal vouchers from their hostel. The Esplanade, between Shields and Aplin Sts, has every sort of eatery, operating at all hours.

Barnacle Bill's (☎ 4051 2241, 65 Esplanade) is a casual seafood restaurant. Mains ($23–$30) are discounted by 30% if you eat between 5.45pm and 7pm.

Yama (☎ 4052 1009, cnr Spence & Grafton Sts) is one of Cairns' best Japanese restaurants. Lunch specials cost around $7, and evening mains from $17.

The smart *Red Ochre Grill (☎ 4051 0100, 43 Shields St)* uses indigenous plants, animals and herbs in mains ranging from $17 to $25.

Getting There & Away Firmly established on the backpacker circuit, Cairns is a popular international entry point to Australia.

Air Flights link Cairns to only a few international destinations, but there are plenty of flights within Queensland and to interstate capitals.

The airport is a flat and easy 7km ride north of the city – just turn left from Airport Ave onto the highway.

Alternatively, taxis to/from the airport cost around $13. You may need to hail a maxi cab to fit your bike.

Train QR (☎ 13 2232) runs the *Sunlander* service three times a week to and from Brisbane. An economy sleeper costs $193.60 for the 32-hour journey. The luxury *Queenslander* runs weekly from Brisbane ($503.80, including all meals).

Bus Greyhound Pioneer (☎ 13 2030) and McCafferty's (☎ 13 1499) offer frequent bus services linking Cairns with Brisbane ($167, 27 hours) and Townsville ($44, six hours). Buses depart from the Transit Centre at Trinity Wharf.

Bicycle Plenty of cyclists ride the main highway from Brisbane to Cairns but it is generally uninspiring and unpleasant. Riding in the other direction, into the wind, would be even worse.

The South-East

While rapidly developing and growing in population, the 'Great South-East' has some fine attractions and great cycling. The beach strips of the Gold and Sunshine Coasts (south and north of Brisbane respectively) are justly famous for their white-sand beaches and clear waters. Their hinterlands ranges are cloaked in vestiges of the Gondwana rainforests, and offer a cool respite from the summer heat. Enclosing Moreton Bay are the great sand islands Moreton and Stradbroke, while further north is the World Heritage-listed Fraser Island. The sand tracks offer little joy to the cyclist, but Stradbroke Island's roads are paved.

HISTORY

The Brisbane area was first occupied by Aboriginal people of the Turrbal language group. The first white settlement was a penal colony, established in the 1820s under Captain Logan, who became notorious for flogging his charges. Free settlement slowly followed, spurred on by the discovery of gold around Gympie (170km north of Brisbane) in 1867.

Brisbane once had a reputation as a 'big country town' and for many years the city hall was the largest building in town. During World War II, Brisbane was home to a large garrison of US troops who came to be jealously referred to as 'overpaid, oversexed and over here'. The controversial Brisbane Line cordoned off the south-east corner of Australia – the most that was believed defendable in the case of invasion.

The 1982 Brisbane Commonwealth Games and 1988 World Expo marked a coming of age for Brisbane. It now has a thriving metropolitan heart, and the region enjoys a steady population growth at the expense of the southern states.

PLANNING
When to Ride

Most of the rides described involve significant climbs so it's best to get out early and, if possible, avoid the humid summer months (December to February). Coastal areas are inundated with tourists over the summer holidays, particularly the two weeks after Christmas, and for the Easter break.

Mt Nebo & Brisbane Forest Park

Duration ....3–5 hours
Distance..52.1km
Difficulty ....moderate–hard
Start/End ....Ferny Grove train station

This easily accessible ride in the D'Aguilar Range north of Brisbane can be ridden as a weekend escape, a picnic jaunt or hard training session.

NATURAL HISTORY

Much of the D'Aguilar range is in Brisbane Forest Park – a management umbrella for 28,500 hectares of national park, state forest and water catchment reserve. Some parts are subtropical rainforest while most of the park is open eucalypt forest.

PLANNING

The Brisbane Forest Park headquarters (☎ 3300 4855), 60 Mt Nebo Rd, The Gap, has information on activities in the park and issues permits for camping at Manorina; fees are $3.50 per person.

When to Ride

Starting later, after 9am, makes train travel easier, but avoid the peak hour (5pm) traffic on Settlement Rd at the end of the day.

Maps

The ride is covered by the RACQ *Brisbane–Sunshine Coast* map.

What to Bring

Overnight riders need to be equipped for bush camping at Manorina; day riders should bring lunch. Carrying insect repellent is recommended.

GETTING TO/FROM THE RIDE

Citytrain (☎ 13 1230) services run to Ferny Grove from Brisbane's Roma St Station ($5.40 return, 25 minutes, half-hourly).

It's possible to finish in the city by continuing from The Gap along Waterworks Rd for a further 10km, though traffic will become progressively heavier on this route.

Mt Nebo & Brisbane Forest Park

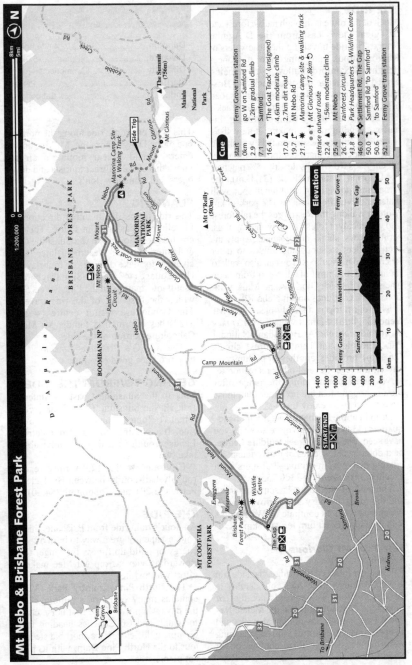

1:200,000

N

8km
5mi

QUEENSLAND

Cue

start		Ferny Grove train station
0km		go W on Samford Rd
2.9	▲	1.2km gradual climb
7.1		Samford
16.4	↑	'The Goat Track' (unsigned)
17.0	▲	4.6km moderate climb
17.0	▲	2.7km dirt road
19.7	↑	Mt Nebo Rd
21.7	✴	Manorina camp site & walking track
21.7	↰	Mt Glorious 17.8km ↺
		retrace outward route
22.4	▲	Mt Nebo
25.4	✴	1.5km moderate climb
26.7	✴	rainforest circuit
43.8	◈	Park Headquarters & Wildlife Centre
46.0	↑	Settlement Rd, The Gap
50.0	↱	Samford Rd 'to Samford'
50.6	↲	'to Samford'
52.1		Ferny Grove train station

Elevation

Ferny Grove

Manorina Mt Nebo

Ferny Grove

Samford

Samford

The Gap

1400
1000
800
600
400
200
0m

0km   10   20   30   40   50

QUEENSLAND

THE RIDE

Much of the route is through native forest and has great views east from the D'Aguilar Range. The ride travels up the headwaters of Kedron Brook, dropping into the once-delightful Samford Valley – now being carved into acreage lifestyle blocks for Brisbane commuters – and up an anonymous road affectionately known as 'The Goat Track'. The authorities sternly warn drivers off this narrow, winding road – making it a cyclist's haven. It's intimately surrounded by bush and nicely graded, in sharp contrast to the main Mt Glorious Rd with its deadly 15% pinches.

Manorina National Park (21.1km), the turnaround point, is an ideal lunch spot, with water and even flush toilets! The park's 6km **Morelia walking track** explores the rainforest and wet eucalypt forest, alive with songbirds, scrub turkeys, skinks and goannas. Apply insect repellent to shoes and ankles to deter leeches and mosquitoes. You can also walk to the indistinct summit of Mt Nebo from here. The side trip to Mt Glorious and Maiala National Park continues on Mt Nebo Rd.

The return trip is a steady push up to **Mt Nebo** (25.4km), a small village with a *takeaway* and *tearoom*. At Boombana National Park, the pleasant 1km **rainforest circuit** (26.1km) provides another opportunity to stretch the legs. Several other recreation reserves and lookouts along the range offer views, though most are no better than those from the road, so enjoy the ride.

Drop in at the **Brisbane Forest Park headquarters** (43.8km) to learn more about all you have seen. **Walkabout Creek Wildlife Centre**, next door, has 80 species of native fauna, including platypus, in captivity. Upstairs is an excellent *restaurant* (☎ 3300 2558).

The rest of the route is semi-suburban and the roads are busy and narrow in parts. An alternative is to continue on Waterworks Rd to the city (don't turn left at 46km).

Side Trip: Mt Glorious
17.8km

Following a roller-coaster ridge, the side trip to Mt Glorious village adds considerably to the day's effort. The rewards are the *tea rooms* and **craft cottages** and the **Maiala National Park**, which has rainforest walks and an open, grassy picnic area with commanding views to the east. To get there, continue on Mt Nebo Rd, which becomes Mt Glorious Rd.

Mt Mee

Duration	4–7½ hours
Distance	75.9km
Difficulty	moderate–hard
Start	Petrie
End	Caboolture

This is an energetic ride along the northern end of the D'Aguilar range. Mt Mee has the emerald fields, clear mountain air and views that should attract tourists and developers, but somehow don't.

PLANNING

This ride is possible in either direction, but the climb is easier from Petrie. This also creates scope to link to the Sunshine Coast & Hinterland ride (described later in this chapter) to make a three- or four-day trip. Hay Cottage (☎ 3425 1788) in Dayboro has useful information on the Pine Rivers Shire, which the first half of the ride traverses. The Caboolture visitor centre (☎ 5495 3122) has information for the Mt Mee to Caboolture portion of the ride.

The RACQ's *Brisbane–Sunshine Coast* map provides good coverage.

GETTING TO/FROM THE RIDE

Link to the Sunshine Coast & Hinterland ride via the Sunshine Coast Link (see Alternative Route), which joins Day 1 of that ride. It's possible to ride from Petrie to Landsborough in a day, but advisable to take two.

Citytrain (☎ 13 1230) runs services roughly half-hourly between Brisbane and Petrie ($3.20), and Caboolture ($4.30).

THE RIDE

An hour's train ride from Brisbane, this bucolic escape is a great way to burn off some energy or build up fitness for longer tours. Rewarding views from Mt Mee make the effort worthwhile.

The **North Pine Country Park** (3.2km) contains many of Petrie's buildings from the days when it was the first horse change for Cobb and Co Coaches heading to the Gympie goldfields. It's a short but steep detour to the **North Pine Dam**, with its pleasant picnic area.

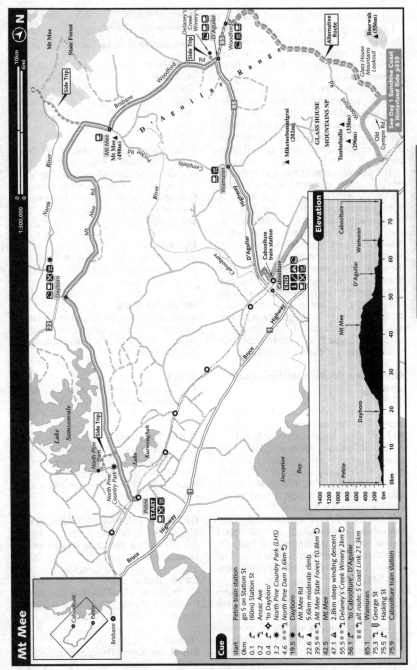

QUEENSLAND

Mt Mee

Elevation

1400						
1200						
1000						
800						
600						
400						
200						
0m						
0km	10	20	30	40	50	60	70

Cue

start	Petrie train station
0km	go S on Station St
0.1	(60m) Station St
0.2	Anzac Ave
0.4	'to Dayboro'
3.2	North Pine Country Park (LHS)
4.6	North Pine Dam 3.6km
19.5	Dayboro
22.6	Mt Mee Rd
39.5	5.6km moderate climb
42.5	Mt Mee State Forest 10.8km
47.1	Mt Mee
55.5	2.8km steep winding descent
56.1	Delaney's Creek Winery 2km
	'to Caboolture', D'Aguilar
	alt route: S Coast Link 21.3km
65.1	Wamuran
75.3	George St
75.5	Hasking St
75.9	Caboolture train station

QUEENSLAND

At **Dayboro** (19.5km), history and local information are available from **Hay Cottage** (☎ 3425 1788), built in 1872 from local red cedar. The *Crown Hotel* is a genuine country pub with broad verandahs shaded by old fig trees.

The climb to Mt Mee is long but never difficult. A side trip (at 39.5km) to **Mt Mee State Forest** adds 170m of steep climbing to the day, so shouldn't be taken lightly. However, the forest's 1km **Piccabeen walk** among the palms and forest giants is well worth doing.

The colonial-style *Munchkins* restaurant (☎ *5498 2244*; closed Monday and Tuesday) is the only business taking advantage of the outstanding location at Mt Mee.

Campbells Pocket Rd (43.4km) is a potential shortcut home, but the descent to Wamuran is very steep and has a few tight bends and narrow bridges, so beware. On the main route, great views to the Glass House Mountains precede a fast descent to D'Aguilar (56.1km). If you still have the energy to tackle 2km of dirt road, a detour at 55.5km leads to **Delaney's Creek Winery**, which offers tastings daily until 5pm.

The D'Aguilar Hwy back to Caboolture is fairly quiet, but has little shoulder.

Alternative Route: Sunshine Coast Link
21.3km
This scenic and mostly unsealed back route connects to the Sunshine Coast & Hinterland ride about halfway through Day 1.

The full Petrie to Landsborough journey is a hard 78km. A better alternative may be to stay at the *D'Aguilar Motel* (☎ *5496 4060*) or 4km further at the *Woodford Country Motel* (☎ *5496 1122*), both of which have doubles for around $50.

Woodford's *bakery* sells wickedly delicious *beestings* (yeasted, almond-topped custard buns) and the bizarre *Elvis Parsley's Grapeland* fruit shop is hard to miss. The renowned **Woodford Folk Festival** runs after Christmas.

Sandy surfaces make the riding tough, but the **lookout** has magnificent views over the Glass House Mountains – the erosion-resistant cores of extinct volcanoes. Turn left at Old Gympie Rd and then follow the Day 1 cues for the Sunshine Coast & Hinterland ride.

Sunshine Coast & Hinterland

Duration	3 days
Distance	135km
Difficulty	moderate
Start	Caboolture
End	Noosa Heads

Ride among ancient volcanic plugs then up to the lush Blackall Range with its thriving arts scene and expansive views. Descend to rich sugar- and ginger-growing valleys and explore the historic village of Eumundi. The destination, Noosa, is renowned for its surf and coastal scenery.

PLANNING
The National Parks office (☎ 5494 3983) for the Sunshine Coast hinterland is at 61 Bunya St, Maleny.

When to Ride
Avoid, if possible, the December to January summer holiday peak: accommodation prices can double and traffic volumes go through the roof.

Maps
The Sunmap *Sunshine Coast and Hinterland Tourist Map* (1:130,000) covers the ride with good detail.

What to Bring
The challenge is to carry walking shoes for scrambling up mountains, something respectable for the cafe and gallery scene, and beach gear, all the while keeping the bike light.

GETTING TO/FROM THE RIDE
It's possible to follow on from the Mt Mee ride, described earlier in this chapter, to make a four-day trip.

Caboolture
Citytrain (☎ 13 1230) services connect Brisbane's Roma St station with Caboolture, 50km north ($4.30, half-hourly).

Noosa
Bus Buses stop at the corner of Noosa Dr and Noosa Parade. Suncoast Pacific Coaches

(☎ 5449 9966) runs services to Brisbane ($22, eight daily); bikes cost $15.50, or $10.50 boxed.

Greyhound Pioneer (☎ 13 2030) runs to Brisbane ($15, one daily) and Cairns ($161, two daily); bikes cost $22.

Train The nearest train station is Cooroy, a scenic 20km ride inland on the Cooroy–Noosa Rd. Citytrain (☎ 13 1230) runs services to Brisbane ($13.40; two daily on weekdays, one daily on weekends).

THE RIDE
Caboolture
Caboolture (population 17,500) is a modern centre with all amenities. The visitor centre (☎ 5495 3122) is in the council buildings on King St.

Big and well stocked, Caboolture Cycle Sports (☎ 5495 7499) is at 31 Morayfield Rd, south of the centre; and Morayfield Road Super Cycles (☎ 5499 3655) is at 126 Morayfield Rd.

Travel from Brisbane rather than stay overnight here.

Day 1: Caboolture to Landsborough
2½–4 hours, 38.5km
This is a short, mostly flat day allowing plenty of time to explore the striking peaks of the Glass House Mountains. Twenty million years of erosion have left the cores of these 13 volcanoes standing out from the coastal plane. Their Aboriginal names are as striking as the land forms – try Tibberoowuccum or Miketeebumulgrai.

The **Caboolture Historical Village** (☎ 5495 4581; 2.7km) is an extensive museum of pioneering cottages, commercial buildings and machinery, with a few vintage bikes. The side trip to the **Glass House Mountains Lookout** (20.8km), the ride's only real hill, is a worthwhile detour. From here you can easily understand the Aboriginal legend of the mountains as a family frozen in stone. The pleasant picnic area has toilets and water. A couple of basic *cafes* are passed on the way.

A side trip at 23.9km leads to a walk up **Mt Ngungun**, the easiest climb of the main peaks, yet with superb views of its neighbours. The 700m walking track is steep, and in places loose, but not difficult. Allow an

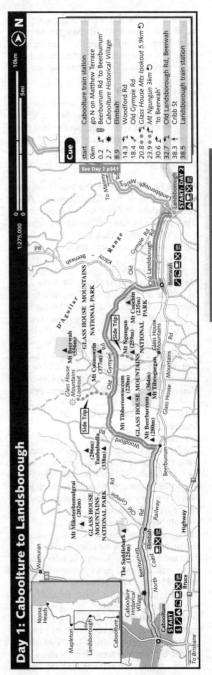

Cue		
start	0km	Caboolture train station
		go N on Matthew Terrace
0.2	↰ ╬	Beerburrum Rd to Beerburrum'
2.7	✱	Caboolture Historical Village
8.9		Elimbah
14.3	↱	Woodford Rd
18.4	↰	Old Gympie Rd
20.8	↰ ↰	Glass House Mts lookout 5.9km ↻
23.9	↰ ↱	Mt Ngungun 3km ↻
30.6	↰ ↱	to Beerwah'
32.7	↱ ↰	Old Landsborough Rd, Beerwah
38.3	↱	Cribb St
38.5		Landsborough train station

See Day 2 p341

Day 1: Caboolture to Landsborough

QUEENSLAND

hour or two for the return walk. Climbing Mt Beerwah and Mt Tibrogargan requires more time, confidence and experience while Coonowrin is recommended only for those with rock-climbing experience.

Landsborough

This is one of those towns where even the takeaways shut at 8pm. Landsborough has a small **museum** and a pub, but the best thing to do is get up the road early to make the most of the Blackall Range. An information board is in the park just east of the railway line.

Places to Stay & Eat The town's only accommodation is the *Landsborough Pines Caravan Park (☎ 5494 1207, 1 Eudlo St)*, off Glass House Mountains Tourist Rd, abutting a rainforest creek. Tent sites cost $13, and cabins with kitchen facilities are $42.50.

Those seeking greater comfort will have to push another 20km uphill to Maleny. The *Maleny Lodge Guest House (☎ 5494 2370, 58 Maple St)*, a B&B in a magnificent old Queenslander, has en suite doubles for $145.

Landsborough's *IGA supermarket*, off Mill St, opens until 7pm, the *7 to 7 (Cribb St)* until 8pm. *Fu Tasia (Cribb St)* has typical Chinese fare with dishes from $5 to $8. *Mellum Munchies (cnr Cribb St & Maleny Rd)* is the place for a burger. The *Landsborough Hotel* does the standard run of counter meals.

Day 2: Landsborough to Mapleton

2½–4½ hours, 43.5km

The Blackall Range – including its waterfalls – is cool, fresh, inviting and utterly deserved after the hard grind up from Landsborough. The route undulates, sometimes steeply, between the towns along the range, but the views over the Sunshine Coast will keep your spirits high. The towns are packed with cafes, restaurants and galleries. Avocadoes and macadamia nuts are often available fresh from roadside stalls. Though heavily cleared, some small national parks preserve the area's original beauty. The route mostly follows the Blackall Range Tourist Drive, through a variety of name changes.

Mary Cairncross Park (11.3km), 52 hectares of rainforest preserved by the philanthropic Thynne family, has a *kiosk*, an **education centre**, a **tree identification walk** – and great views of the Glass House Mountains. At 14km, *Malcolm's* restaurant (14.2km; open Wednesday to Sunday) has a super location on the range's edge.

Maleny (19.5km) is a laid-back place with a superb local art scene. The **Bold in Gold** gallery at the top end of Maple St displays the lifelike, ceramic rainforest scenes of Lindsay Muir. Vegetarians can rejoice at the *Up Front Club (31 Maple St)*.

Gardiners Falls (a side trip at 22.5km) aren't particularly grand, but on a hot day the plunge pool below is well worth missing school for – as the local truants will attest.

Montville (34.6km) is busier and glitzier than Maleny, with even more galleries. **Gallery D**, in a dome building just north of town, has everything from textiles to oil paintings and a gallery glass studio.

It's a steep climb back out, but the diversion (at 37.3km) to the 80m-high **Kondalilla Falls** is worth it. You can swim at the top of the falls, and walk a 4.8km circuit to the rainforest at their base. Thieves have been known to work the car park, so be especially careful securing your gear before walking.

Mapleton Falls are wonderful to visit at the quiet end of the day. Continue on the Blackall Range Tourist Dr, turning left at 0.3km into Obi Obi Rd, and right to the falls at 3.3km. Bikes can be wheeled into the picnic area, from where it's a 200m walk to view the 120m plunge of Pencil Creek.

Mapleton

Mapleton is another pretty village on the edge of the range and the extensive Mapleton State Forest. It's a small place, so the stage start/finish is simply the shopping strip on the left as you enter 'town'. A small information stand is kept here, so you can read about the local attractions while you stock up.

Things to See & Do The **Mapleton Forest Drive** traverses some lovely eucalypt forest. Ride west for 100m along Obi Obi Rd then turn right onto Delicia Rd, where the Forest Drive signs begin. The pretty **Mapleton Day Use picnic area** is 3km from town and the Forest Drive, though dirt, has a good surface thus far.

Places to Stay & Eat The friendly *Lilyponds Caravan Park (☎ 5445 7238, 26 Warruga St)* has camp sites in an old avocado grove for $14 and cabins from $43.

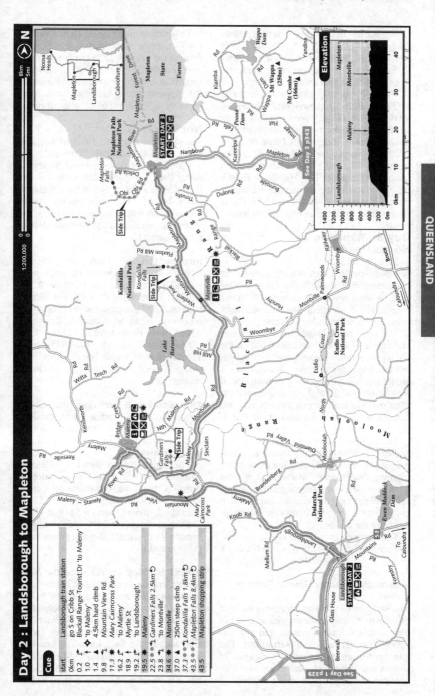

Day 2 : Landsborough to Mapleton

QUEENSLAND

Cue

start		Landsborough train station
0km	⬆	go S on Cribb St
0.2	⬅	Blackall Range Tourist Dr 'to Maleny'
1.0		'to Maleny'
1.4	⬆	4.5km hard climb
9.8	✳	Mountain View Rd
11.3	✳	Mary Cairncross Park
16.2	⬅	'to Maleny'
18.9		Myrtle St
19.2	⬅	'to Landsborough'
19.5	✳	Maleny
22.5	⬅	Gardiners Falls 2.5km ↻
23.8	⬅	'to Montville'
34.6		Montville
37.0	⬆	250m steep climb
37.3	⬅	Kondalilla Falls 1.8km ↻
43.5	⬆	Mapleton Falls 8.4km ↻
43.5		Mapleton shopping strip

Elevation

Side Trip

START DAY 2 Landsborough

START DAY 2 Mapleton

See Day 3 p343

See Day 1 p339

Good B&Bs in the area include *Obilo Lodge (☎ 5445 7705, Obi Obi Rd)*, 2km west of town, which offers a pool, spa, rainforest surrounds and gourmet breakfast from $115 to $135 a double midweek.

The shopping strip contains a *bakery* and a *Food Barn* supermarket. *Mapleton Seafoods (Obi Obi Rd)* does a full takeaway selection topped by the generous $9.80 fisherman's basket. *Lilypond's Pizza (☎ 5445 7722, cnr Post Office & Obi Obi Rds)* does pasta for $7, and standard pizzas with imaginative names. The *Mapleton Tavern (Mapleton Rd)* has a good menu at reasonable prices. *Piccabeens Cafe (1 Post Office Rd)* is the place for breakfast or coffee from 9am.

Day 3: Mapleton to Noosa Heads

3–5½ hours, 53km

A gravity-charged start sets the pace for an undulating ride through the green hinterland to the coastal resort town of Noosa Heads. The descent, in two stages, allows some appreciation of the scenery.

The route skirts **Nambour**, the commercial centre of the region, before hitting the old highway north. Recent road building has left this carriageway almost abandoned – a great place for cycling, if a little dull. One of the casualties of the highway diversion is the **Big Cow** (17.4km). Once a dairy theme park where children could shudder at the feel of an udder, it's now abandoned and fading.

The tranquil Bunya Rd leads past ginger and cane fields to the historic village of Eumundi (31.7km), scene of a huge Saturday-morning **craft market**. Midweek it is a lot quieter, but it's worth stopping at the *Imperial Hotel* for a pot of Eumundi Lager and to check out the antique Penny Farthing hanging from the ceiling.

The camping ground and one of the hostels are in Noosaville, 5km before the day's end.

Alternative Route: Ginger Factory

1.7km

The **Buderim Ginger Factory** churns out half of the world's confectionery ginger. Entry is free to this unique operation and the surrounding *restaurants* and **craft shops**. The gardens feature more than 100 varieties of ginger and heliconias, and every conceivable form of ginger product is for sale.

To get there, turn right at 19.6km and follow Fleming St under the train line. Continue through the roundabout to the factory on Pioneer Rd. On the return go right at the roundabout (Coulson Rd) and right again on School Rd. Another underpass leads back to the highway, 1.5km north of the original turn.

Noosa Heads

Noosa is the northern limit of Sunshine Coast development, and it goes out with a bang. The vast Cooloola–Great Sandy National Park stretches 50km north from the river. Generations of surfers have ridden the point breaks, and enjoyed the natural scenery. Today this chic resort is home to as many fine restaurants and boutique stores as grungy surfers.

Information The visitor centre (☎ 5447 4988) is at the junction of Hastings St and Noosa Dr. The National Parks office (☎ 5447 3243) is at the end of Park Rd. The Westpac bank and ATM is handy at 40 Hastings St; otherwise head to Sunshine Beach Rd where all the banks have branches.

Mammoth Cycles (☎ 5447 3845), corner Thomas St and Gympie Terrace, Noosaville, stocks a good range and runs mountain-biking tours.

Things to See & Do Noosa National Park covers the entire headland area and has a network of **trails** up to 7km long – collect a map from the park office and keep an eye out for **koalas**.

The sandy **Noosa Beach** is lifesaver-patrolled and most surf shops hire out boards. Granite and Alexandria Bays are the spots for secluded sunbathing.

Fraser Explorer Tours (☎ 5449 8647) and Trailblazer Tours (☎ 5449 8151) run **4WD trips** to World Heritage-listed **Fraser Island** (80km north).

Places to Stay On the river, the *Noosa River Caravan Park (☎ 5449 7050; Russell St, Noosaville)* has tent sites for $14.50. Also in Noosaville, the *Noosa Backpackers Resort (☎ 5449 8151, 9–13 William St)* is pleasantly relaxed with dorm beds for $19 and doubles for $42, including breakfast. The YHA *Halse Lodge (☎ 5447 3377, 2 Halse Lane)*, a former 1880s guesthouse, has a tremendous location a stone's throw

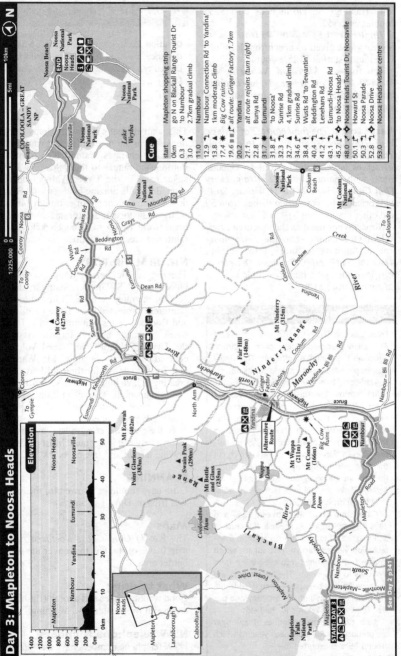

Day 3: Mapleton to Noosa Heads

Elevation

Cue	
start	Mapleton shopping strip
0km	go N on Blackall Range Tourist Dr 'to Nambour'
0.3	◀
3.0	2.7km gradual climb
11.0	Nambour
12.9	Nambour Connection Rd 'to Yandina' ◀
13.8	1km moderate climb ◀
17.4	*Big Cow ruins*
19.6	alt route: Ginger Factory 1.7km
20.2	Yandina
21.1	alt route rejoins (turn right)
22.8	*
31.7	Eumundi
31.8	'to Noosa' ◀
32.3	Sunrise Rd
32.7	4.1km gradual climb
34.6	Sunrise Rd ◀
38.4	Wusts Rd 'to Tewantin'
40.4	Beddington Rd
41.2	Lenehans Rd
43.1	Eumundi-Noosa Rd ◀
45.7	'to Noosa Heads' ◀
48.0	◇ Noosa Heads Tourist Dr, Noosaville
50.1	Howard St
50.3	◇ Noosa Parade
52.8	◇ Noosa Drive
53.0	◇ Noosa Heads visitor centre

QUEENSLAND

from Hastings St. Dorm beds cost $23; doubles cost $52.

Tingirana *(☎ 5474 7400, 25 Hastings St)* is great value given its beachfront location. Motel units start at $125 a double.

The five-star **Sheraton Noosa Resort** *(☎ 5449 4888, Noosa Parade)* has doubles from around $410, with cheaper advance-purchase rates.

Places to Eat The *food court (Bay Village Mall, Hastings St)* allows you to eat well from around $6. **Cafe Le Monde** *(Hastings St)* serves large portions from an eclectic menu with mains from $12. **Bratpackers Thai Cafe** *(☎ 5474 1844, 11 William St)* is well priced with vegetarian dishes from $9 and other mains from $10 to $14.

Noosa hypes itself as the epicurean capital of Queensland, and there are many fine restaurants to support this claim. **Artis** *(☎ 5447 2300, 8 Noosa Dr)* serves terrific meals, but a hungry couple will get no change from $100.

Sugar Cane

From Grafton (NSW) north along the east Australian seaboard, sugar cane is grown wherever the rainfall is sufficient. This vigorous, tropical grass can grow as tall as 4m.

Traditional harvesting involved burning the field to remove the 'trash' of dead leaves and scare off rats and snakes, before cutters moved in. The fires were spectacular, but the coastal skies would be grey for months in some areas. Now more common 'green cutting' uses million-dollar harvesters, which cut the cane into 40cm lengths for transport to the mill. In many regions a light-gauge rail network links the mill with farms, but, sadly, road transport is increasing.

Cane stem contains between 12% and 14% sucrose (sugar). At the mill, it is crushed and washed to extract the sugar juice. Crystallisation yields a brown 'raw sugar', which can be further refined into everything from molasses to icing sugar. The by-products are dry cane fibres – bagasse – often used to fire mill boilers; and mill mud – a pongy and potent fertiliser that returns to the fields.

More than five million tonnes of raw sugar are produced in Australia each year, of which around 85% is exported.

Border Loop

Duration	5 days
Distance	338.9 km
Difficulty	hard
Start	Robina
End	Nerang

This is an energetic ride with plenty of options for variations off the main route. The landscape changes dramatically from the rainforested ranges to the fields of waving sugar cane in the Tweed Valley and the open, dry cattle grazing lands around Beaudesert. Allow a couple of extra days if you really want to explore the area or take a break from riding to wind back beside a rainforest creek for a while.

NATURAL HISTORY
The rugged McPherson Range marks the Queensland–NSW border. Rising to almost 1200m, the range is cloaked in subtropical rainforest, protected now in the Lamington and Border Ranges National Parks. To the south, the range plunges into the basin of the Tweed Caldera. The Tweed Volcano, centred on what is now Mt Warning (1157m) was active for three million years, creating a lava shield 5000 sq km in area and 2000m high. Twenty million years of erosion have created the southern hemisphere's largest caldera.

To the north the erosion has carved deep valleys between long spurs. Most roads follow the terrain and few cross it.

PLANNING
Extra days should be allowed for the longer side trips on Days 1, 2 and 5.

Maps
The RACQ *Gold Coast–Northern Rivers* map is one of the few that cover the whole border area.

What to Bring
Good walking shoes and a torch (flashlight) are useful for climbing Mt Warning.

NSW Telephone Numbers
NSW telephone numbers have an ☎ 02 area code.

GETTING TO/FROM THE RIDE

On the Gold Coast (Robina) Citytrain line (☎ 13 1230), services run between Brisbane's Roma St station and Nerang/Robina ($7.80/8.30, 65/70 minutes, half-hourly). The Robina train station is off Robina Town Centre Dr.

THE RIDE
Robina

Robina and nearby Mudgeeraba have a full range of banking and shopping services. Rebel Sports (☎ 5578 8666), at the Robina Town Centre, Bazaar St, has a cycle section. Stay overnight in Brisbane.

Day 1: Robina to Murwillumbah

4–7½ hours, 76.2km

The road to Springbrook National Park is part of an Olympic cycle-training route – with a total of 11.2km of climbing, it's no picnic, but it is a shortcut to the delights of the Gold Coast hinterland. Cresting the Wunburra Range you have the option of climbing further along Springbrook Rd (see Side Trip) or descending directly to **Numinbah Valley**, in arguably the most beautiful valley in South-east Queensland. The road winds through verdant pastures as the valley closes in beneath the buttresses of Turtle Rock and Ship's Stern.

Natural Bridge is an impressive formation, where Cave Creek plunges into an underground pool. It's a short side trip at 44.9km in the Springbrook National Park; with hundreds of thousands of visitors a year, though, the **1km circuit walk** is no wilderness experience.

The **border gate** (48.3km) is at the cusp of a 6km climb up the McPherson Range. The mesh fence is to try to stop interstate travel by feral rabbits, while the border guard's job is to prevent the spread of agricultural diseases, so cyclists attract only a wave.

As the exhilarating descent starts to ease, the route passes a **banana stall** (52km), where the wonderful, fresh fruit is dirt cheap. The stately **Lisnagar Homestead** (73.7km), on the Rous River opens Sundays only.

Side Trip: Purling Brook Falls
11.8km

A whole day could easily be spent exploring the lush Springbrook Plateau, fringed with delightful waterfalls and lookouts to the coast and beyond. The plateau rises to 900m, but is, fortunately, closer to 600m at the falls.

Continue along Springbrook Rd, climbing steeply up an intriguing one-way section. After 900m, the road passes **Wunburra lookout**. Also on the way is *Springbrook Homestead*, a cafe and good source of local info. After 5.4km turn left on Forestry Rd and follow it to the park entrance. It is only 100m to a lookout above the falls, or walk the 4km circuit track to the rainforest at their base.

Camping is allowed at *Gwongorella (☎ 5533 5147)*, next to the falls. The *YHA Springbrook Mountain Lodge (☎ 5533 5366, 317 Repeater Station Rd)* has budget beds. A range of *B&Bs* are on the plateau.

Murwillumbah

☎ 02

Murwillumbah, on the banks of the Tweed River, is a laid-back cane- and banana-growing centre. It's by no means touristy but makes a good base for visiting the World Heritage rainforests of the Tweed Caldera.

Information The visitor centre (☎ 6672 1340), on the corner of Alma St and the Pacific Hwy, displays a model of the caldera and information on the rainforest areas. The town's main street is called just that, or by its alternate name of Murwillumbah St.

The big banks are all in town; Westpac, on the corner of Brisbane and Murwillumbah Sts, has an ATM. Jim's Cycle Centre (☎ 6672 3620), 58 Wollumbin St, does spares and repairs.

Things to See & Do The **Tweed River Regional Art Gallery**, 5 Tumbulgum Rd, is excellent. The century-old **Condong Sugar Mill**, 5km north-east of town, runs weekday tours during the crushing season (July–November).

Places to Stay The *Greenhills Caravan Park (☎ 6672 2035, Pacific Hwy)*, 2km south of town, has sites for $11 and cabins from $37.40.

The associate YHA *Mt Warning Backpackers (☎ 6672 3763, 1 Tumbulgum Rd)* is right on the river. The owners run a daytime shuttle service to **Mt Warning** (see the Day 2 Side Trip) and can recommend local rides. Dorm beds cost $20, doubles $44.

The strikingly pink *Imperial Hotel (☎ 6672 1036, Main St)* has doubles from

QUEENSLAND

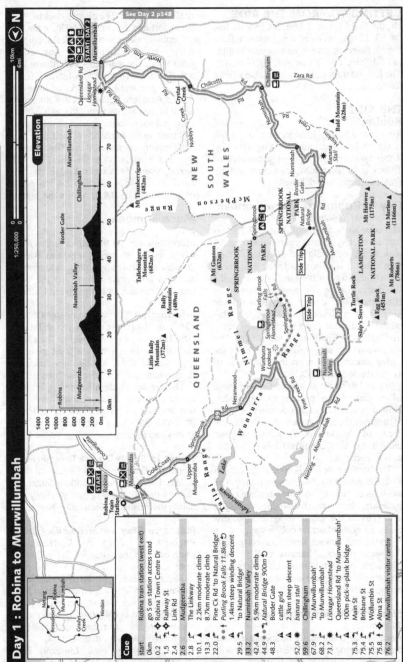

Day 1: Robina to Murwillumbah

Cue		
start		Robina train station (west exit)
		go S on station access road
0.2	⌐↑◆	Robina Town Centre Dr
1.5	↑	Railway St
2.4	↑	Link Rd
2.6		Mudgeeraba
2.8	↑	The Linkway
10.1	↑	2.2km moderate climb
13.3	↑	8.7km moderate climb
22.0	⌐↑	Pine Ck Rd 'to Natural Bridge'
		⚡ Purling Brook Falls 11.8km ↻
		1.4km steep winding descent
29.5	↑	'to Natural Bridge'
33.2		Numinbah Valley
42.4	↑	5.9km moderate climb
44.9	↑⌐	Natural Bridge 900m ↻
48.3		Border Gate
		cattle grid
		2.3km steep descent
52.0	✳	banana stall
59.6		Chillingham
67.9	↑	'to Murwillumbah'
68.2	↑	'to Murwillumbah'
73.7	↑✳	Lisnagar Homestead
		Queensland Rd 'to Murwillumbah'
		100m pick-a-plank bridge
75.3	↑	Main St
75.4	⌐	Brisbane St
75.5	⌐	Wollumbin St
75.8	⌐◆	Alma St
76.2		Murwillumbah visitor centre

$339. The bright and clean *Town Motel* (☎ *6672 8600, 3 Wharf St*) has air-con doubles for $55. The *Murwillumbah Motor Inn* (☎ *6672 2022* or ☎ *1800 023 105, 17 Byangum Rd*) overlooks Mt Warning and has a pool. Doubles start from $72.

Places to Eat Go to Wollumbin St for *supermarkets*. The hangar-like *Austral Cafe and Bakery* (*88 Main St*) opens for breakfast; its good-value coffee, cakes and light meals make it a cyclist's favourite. The eclectic *Riverside Pizza Cafe* (☎ *6672 1935, 4 Commercial Rd*) serves delicious salads, plus Thai, pasta and pizza dishes. The *Hung Too Chinese Restaurant* (☎ *6672 2349, 6 Commercial Rd*) has a $7 evening buffet. *Karni's Middle Eastern Vegetarian Cafe* (☎ *6672 8590, 2 Wharf St*) serves dinner Wednesday to Saturday. The 'large Mediterranean platter' ($17.50) would feed two.

Day 2: Murwillumbah to Nimbin
3–5½ hours, 51.4km
This is a day of gentle climbing up the rural Tweed Valley before clambering out of the caldera and into the catchment of the Richmond River. Mt Warning dominates the first half of the route and the Tweed Range forms an impressive backdrop to the west. It's a short but steep detour to climb Mt Warning (see Side Trip). Pick-a-plank bridges spot the route but most are shorter than 50m.

You can't escape the publicity machine of the *fruit stall* at Snake Creek – a trail of handmade signs that stretches for kilometres. The fruit stall is indeed good, and there is also a small *store*, picnic area and caravan park.

The route partly circles the Nightcap Range, the scene of unprecedented environmental protests in 1979. Terania Creek's stand of massive brush box trees were saved in a campaign that led to the creation of a national park and eventual World Heritage listing.

The area around Nimbin is the 'Rainbow District' – transformed from a declining dairy district to a region of hippy communes, spiritual retreats and 'high' society by the Aquarius Festival of 1973. The road into Nimbin – Rainbow District's capital – is bumpy and potholed, a reflection, perhaps, on the local culture. Are its maintainers distracted by the beauty of the area, cash-strapped, or just stoned?

Side Trip: Mt Warning
12.5km
The Mt Warning summit has a certain mysticism, being the first mainland point struck by the sun. The walk is best at pre-dawn. Botanist Michael Guilfoyle's party were the first whites to climb Mt Warning in 1871, taking 3½ days. 'When we reached the top we were so enchanted with the glorious view that we quite forgot the inner man, remaining on top all night without food.'

Turn right on to Mt Warning Rd (unsigned at 10.5km). Camping in the national park is not allowed, but the *Mt Warning Caravan Park* (☎ *6679 5120, Mt Warning Rd*), on the side trip, makes a great stopover. Shady tent sites cost $14; on-site vans, $33; and cabins, $44. From the caravan park, it's a 4.7km ride uphill to the walk, which is a hefty 350m ascent. It's mostly on a graded track through rainforest, but the last section is a rocky scramble. To be at the summit at dawn, start walking two to three hours before sunrise (allow five hours in total); take a good torch, some energy food and dress warmly.

Nimbin
☎ 02
This village has a reputation far bigger than its size. The hippy movement transformed it from an obscure country town to a thriving centre of alternative culture. It is home to the Hemp Embassy – a lobby centre for cannabis law reform – and the annual Mardi Grass street parade in the first week of May.

Information The Nimbin Neighbourhood Centre (☎ 6689 1847), Cullen St, opens weekdays and has information for tourists. The *Nimbin and Environs* booklet ($3 from Perceptio Books, 47 Cullen St) explains local history and services. There are no banks but a number of traders have Eftpos facilities.

Things to See & Do The cosmic **Nimbin Museum** (☎ 6689 1123), at 62 Cullen St, offers a legal trip through Nimbin's post-Aquarius history. The **Nimbin School of Arts Gallery** (☎ 6689 1444), 47–49 Cullen St, is a good gallery, while **Djanbung Gardens** (☎ 6689 1755), 74 Cecil St, is a working permaculture showcase.

Nimbin Explorer (☎ 6689 1557) **tours** of the region take in the **Rainbow Power**

QUEENSLAND

Day 2: Murwillumbah to Nimbin

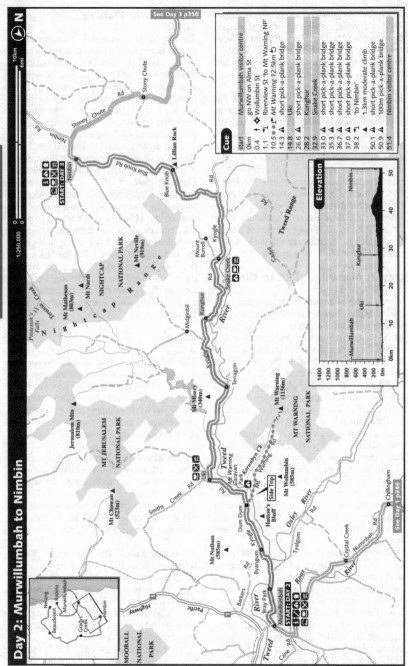

See Day 3 p350

Cue		
start		Murwillumbah visitor centre
0km		go NW on Alma St
0.4	◇	Wollumbin St
1.1	↑⌐	Riverview St 'to Mt Warning NP'
10.5	●●↗⌐	Mt Warning 12.5km ↺
14.3	▲	short pick-a-plank bridge
14.8		Uki
26.6	▲	short pick-a-plank bridge
28.2		Kunghur
32.9		Snake Creek
33.0	▲	short pick-a-plank bridge
35.3	▲	short pick-a-plank bridge
36.7	▲	short pick-a-plank bridge
37.0	▲	short pick-a-plank bridge
38.2	⌐	'to Nimbin'
		1.3km moderate climb
50.1	▲	short pick-a-plank bridge
50.9	▲	100m pick-a-plank bridge
51.4		Nimbin visitor centre

Elevation

MOORANBAH NATIONAL PARK

Company, which sells sustainable energy solutions. The **Bush Theatre** (☎ 6689 1111), Cullen St, shows films Friday to Sunday evenings.

Places to Stay & Eat The creek-side *Granny's Farm* (☎ *6689 1333, 110 Cullen St*) has sites at $10 per person, dorm beds for $18 and doubles for $40. *Rainbow Retreat* (☎ *6689 1262, Thorburn St*), just outside town, has dorm beds and doubles, when available, for $13 per person. *Grey Gum Lodge* (☎ *6689 1713, 2 High St*) is a big, renovated house. Doubles are cheap, from $40; breakfast is an extra $5 per person.

Nimbin Emporium carries a great range of organic groceries and health foods. The *Rainbow Cafe* (*64 Cullen St*) has delicious cakes and light meals – and claims to have had more than a million joints smoked on-site (though signs ask you to refrain from dealing on the premises). The *Nimbin Pizza & Trattoria* (☎ *6689 1427, 70 Cullen St*) has pastas from $9.50 and large pizzas from $11, including a good vegetarian range. *Mulgum Cafe* (☎ *6689 1427, Cullen St*), on the northern approach to town, is the place to eat before the movies.

Day 3: Nimbin to Gradys Creek
3½–6 hours, 68.1km

This is a tough day with three ranges of hills and some gravel road to negotiate before Kyogle. It is wonderful countryside, however, and the views of the Tweed Range make it all worthwhile. The second half is straightforward and picturesque.

The striking **Nimbin Rocks** (1.9km) are an important part of the Bundjalung Aboriginal folklore. One story tells of Nimbun, who was imprisoned in a cave in the rock known as the Cathedral. He escaped by charging through the wall, creating a hole visible today. In 1990 the site was handed back to the traditional owners.

Take care at the bottom of the first dirt descent where the bridge approach (12.2km) can be gouged out. **Cawongla** (18.9km), part way up the longest climb, is an easy place to pause. The *Cawongla Store* serves espresso coffee and has a small gallery, but its real highlight is the **rustic building**.

Kyogle (32.9km) has *supermarkets*, banks and a National Parks office (☎ 02-6632 1473) in Geneva St. Stock up on food here – options

are limited at Gradys Creek. The closest thing to a bike shop is Doug Campbell Saw Works (☎ 02-6632 1619) at 12 Geneva St. The *Box & Dice (137 Summerland Way)* is popular for coffee or locally made ice cream.

The Lions Clubs of Kyogle and Beaudesert combined forces in the early 1970s to join existing roads along Gradys and Running Creeks. The whole route is often referred to as The Lions Tourist Rd, though the original road names persist.

Gradys Creek
☎ 02

The beautiful Gradys Creek valley is surrounded by the Border Ranges National Park. The park can be accessed from The Lions Rd, but it's a major undertaking. The best thing to do locally is laze in or beside the creek and hope to spot an elusive platypus. There is no real town and services are very limited. It's best to stock up on food and cash in Kyogle. The accommodation places listed will be able to serve most information needs, and there is a National Parks office in Kyogle (☎ 6632 1473, @ kyogle@npws.nsw.gov.au).

Places to Stay & Eat There are two accommodation options in the Gradys Creek valley. The lovely *Rainforest Gateway Van Park* (☎ *6636 6114, Gradys Creek Rd*) is at the junction of Gradys and Cedargetters Creeks. Camping costs $5.50 per person and self-contained motel units cost $55. A renovated timbergetter's hut ($65) makes a romantic alternative. *Hidden Valley* (☎ *6636 6140, The Lions Rd*), is 7km further up the valley on a bend in Gradys Ck. Camping costs $5; a self-contained cabin costs $55.

A *shop* 6km north of Rainforest Gateway carries necessities. Both accommodation venues have *tea rooms* open in the day, but bring your own food for solid meals.

Day 4: Gradys Creek to Beaudesert
4–7½ hours, 69km

After some solid climbing early on and a whooping descent into Queensland, this day's route becomes mostly flat. The main feature is the border railway loop – designed to reduce the length of tunnel required through the McPherson Range. The tight loop gains 20m in elevation and makes an ideal train spotting venue for those so inclined. You'll become

QUEENSLAND

Day 3: Nimbin to Gradys Creek

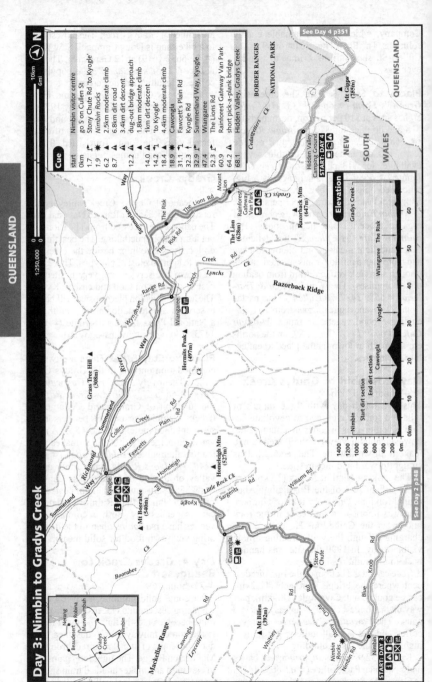

Cue

start		Nimbin visitor centre
0km		go S on Cullen St
1.7	⌐	Stony Chute Rd 'to Kyogle'
1.9	☀	Nimbin Rocks
6.2	◄	2.5km moderate climb
8.7	◄	6.8km dirt road
12.2	◄	3.4km dirt descent
		dug-out bridge approach
14.0	◄	1.8km moderate climb
14.2	⌐	'to Kyogle'
		1km dirt descent
18.4	◄	4.4km moderate climb
18.9	☀	Cawongla
31.1	⌐	Fawcett's Plain Rd
32.3		Kyogle Rd
32.9	⌐	Summerland Way, Kyogle
47.4		Wiangaree
52.3	⌐	The Lions Rd
60.9		Rainforest Gateway Van Park
64.2	◄	short pick-a-plank bridge
68.1		Hidden Valley, Gradys Creek

Elevation

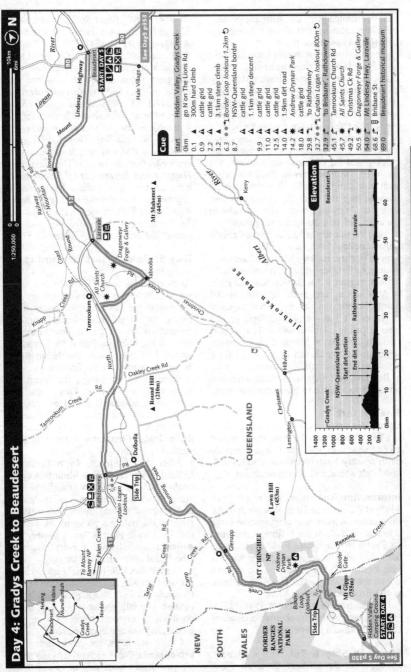

well acquainted with the Brisbane–Sydney train line, crossing it 10 times between Kyogle (Day 4) and Beaudesert.

The side trip to the **Border Loop Lookout** (at 6.3km) is one of those heart-sinking descents, but there are good views and historical information, plus water and a 1.6km walking trail. The XPT train (☎ 6662 0222) from Brisbane passes at around 9am (summer time); the first town stop is Kyogle.

The **border** at the head of Running Creek Valley is a great vantage point. Height is lost quickly, and the country becomes quite flat and open. *Andrew Drynan Park* (14.2km), with basic camping for $3.50, is about the last place to stop and enjoy the scenery of lush valley and gurgling stream. Have a **swim** in the creek before tackling the hot plains.

Take the side trip at 32.7km to the **Captain Logan Lookout** for a view of Mts Lindesay, Ernest, Barney, Ballow, May and Maroon – collectively Queensland's premier bushwalking region, in Mt Barney National Park.

At 45.7km, the beautiful, timber **All Saints Church** was built in 1915 in memory of Robert Collins – a philanthropic grazier who helped to establish national parks, particularly Lamington National Park. Inspections of the church can be arranged for a donation (if the caretaker's there).

Dragonweyr (50.5km) provides a rare opportunity to see artisan blacksmiths at work.

Beaudesert

Beaudesert's main pastime seems to be driving V8s up and down the main street. It's no entertainment capital, but it is a down-to-earth country town (population 5000) with good-value food and accommodation.

Information The visitor centre (☎ 5541 4495) at 2 Enterprise Dr is 3km north of the town centre. A more convenient option is the information desk at the **historical museum** (☎ 5541 3740) in Jubilee Park, which opens daily to 4pm. The museum itself is worth a visit for the 1875 timber-slab hut. Beaudesert is well served with banks. The Westpac bank at 103 Brisbane St has an ATM.

Beaudesert Motorcycles (☎ 5541 1322), 108 Brisbane St, has a reasonable range of bike spares and a competent staff.

Places to Stay & Eat With a friendly atmosphere, *Beaudesert Caravan Park*

(☎ 5541 1368, Albert St) has tent sites for $14, and on-site vans for $27.50. The *Logan & Albert Hotel* (☎ 5541 1107, 12 Brisbane St) is a nice old pub at the quiet end of town. Single/double rooms with shared bathrooms are good value at $10/20 – as are their meals, at $7 to $9. The *Kerry Court Motel* (☎ 5541 1593, cnr Brisbane & Albert Sts) is clean and quiet with air-con doubles for $50.

Beaudesert has a *Coles supermarket (cnr Anna & William Sts)*. The glistening new *Beaudesert RSL (William St)* serves attractive mains from $9 to $16. The inexpensive *Happy Valley Restaurant (115 Brisbane St)* has a lengthy Chinese menu, but nothing for vegetarians. The surprise package is *Everydays Cafe (105 Brisbane St)*. It's hard to beat for breakfast, with good coffee and light meals, and also opens for dinner on Friday.

Day 5: Beaudesert to Nerang
4–7½ hours, 74.2km

Another day, another 500m climb. Cycling via Mt Tamborine is certainly not the easiest way to the coast, but this oasis of galleries, cafes and resplendent rainforest remnants is its own reward. An exciting descent on the infamous 'goat track' past the army's live-firing range should supply the adrenalin needed for the final miles.

Winding up the range, the forest suddenly canopies the road. This magnificent grove of piccabeen palms and towering rose gums *(Eucalyptus grandis)* is **Joalah National Park**. Explore the park by walking the 4.2km **Joalah Circuit** that starts at the intersection at 33km.

After the climb, at North Tamborine (34km), is the **Tamborine Mountain visitor centre** (☎ 5545 3200) in Dougherty Park, which has free tourist maps of the plateau and loads of natural history information. Besides the national parks in the vicinity, the Tamborine Plateau has a **winery**, and **galleries** specialising in everything from Aboriginal art to cuckoo clocks.

The **Witches Falls National Park** (35.3km), declared in 1908, has the distinction of being Queensland's first national park – albeit fairly modest. The falls are an anticlimax, but the one-hour circuit walk traverses some great piccabeen palm and cycad patches.

Check out more ancient cycads at the **Lepidozamia Grove** (39km). If your schedule permits an extra day or two, it's well

The 'Grand Arbour' at Brisbane's Southbank.

Zoom down Mt Tamborine's narrow 'Goat Track'.

Beerwah (L) and Coonowrin (R), Glasshouse Mtns.

It's a beautiful ride up the rural Tweed Valley towards Mt Warning, on the Border Loop ride.

PETER HINES

Near Yungaburra, visit Lake Barrine, with its elegant old teahouse and wildlife cruises.

MARTIN COHEN

Mangrove seedling, Cape Trib.

PETER HINES

Nth Queensland – avoid the wet.

RICHARD I'ANSON

Mossman Gorge rainforest.

SALLY DILLON

The Atherton Tableland – famous waterfalls, crater lakes and lush farming country.

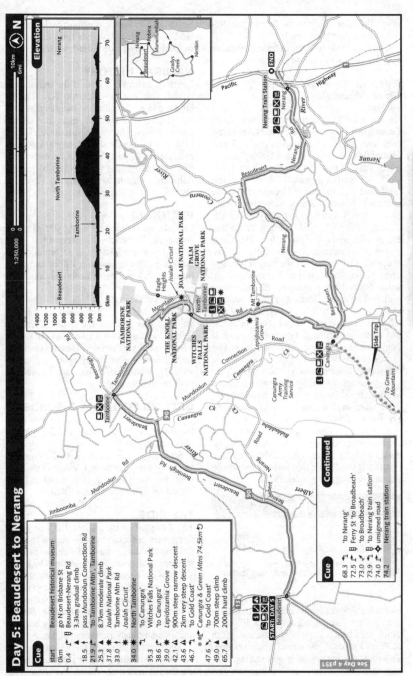

Day 5: Beaudesert to Nerang

Cue

0km		Beaudesert historical museum
0.4	↰	go N on Brisbane St
		Beaudesert-Nerang Rd
	◀	3.3km gradual climb
18.5		pass Mundoolun Connection Rd
21.9	↳	'to Tamborine Mtn', Tamborine
25.3	◀	8.7km moderate climb
31.8	✳	Joalah National Park
33.0		Tamborine Mtn Rd
	✳	Joalah Circuit
34.0	✳	North Tamborine
	↰	'to Canungra'
35.3		Witches Falls National Park
38.6	↱	'to Canungra'
39.0	✳	Lepidozamia Grove
42.1	◀	900m steep narrow descent
43.6	◀	2km very steep descent
46.7	↱	'to Gold Coast'
		Canungra & Green Mtns 74.5km ↺
47.6	↱	'to Gold Coast'
49.0	◀	700m steep climb
65.7	◀	200m hard climb

Continued

Cue

68.3	↰	'to Nerang'
72.5	↰	Ferry St to Broadbeach'
73.0	↱	'to Broadbeach'
73.9	↱	'to Nerang train station'
74.0	◇	unsigned road
74.2		Nerang train station

worth the long climb to the Lamington National Park (see Side Trip).

The ride leads to Nerang train station, so cyclists can head back to Brisbane.

Side Trip: Canungra & Green Mountains
74.5km

It's less than 1km to the rustic township of **Canungra** if you can face the steep climb back out. The real attraction is the **Green Mountains** section of the Lamington National Park. A tree-top walk and a vast network of walking tracks show off the rainforest and rugged landscape, while the abundant birdlife draws naturalists from around the world. The highest parts of the park contain pockets of Antarctic beech forest, isolated since the last Ice age. The climb to Green Mountains is beautifully graded, averaging 3.5% most of the way. There are great views, tall forest and some emerald dairy fields before entering the rainforest proper. The return descent is simply magic.

In Canungra there's a *hotel*, a *motel* and a *B&B*. A shuttle bus (daily except Saturday, $11 each way) runs to Green Mountains if you can't face the long climb on a bike. The visitor centre (☎ 5543 5156) on Kidston St can supply information on all these options.

If you are planning to stay at Green Mountains it is essential to book ahead. Tent sites in the national park *camping ground* (☎ 5544 0634) cost $3.50 per person. *O'Reilly's Guesthouse* (☎ 5544 0638) charges from $114 per person, including all meals and activities. *Gran O'Reilly's* is a bistro/gift shop/store that sells a limited and expensive range of groceries.

Stradbroke Island

Duration	3–5hours
Distance	46.8km
Difficulty	easy
Start/End	Cleveland Train Station

North Stradbroke Island has some of the region's best coastal scenery and 50km of sandy surf beach stretching west and south of Point Lookout, the island's tourism hub. The physical barrier of Moreton Bay isolates the island from over-development and

heavy traffic. Public transport makes the island accessible to cyclists for a day outing or longer, staying at Point Lookout.

NATURAL HISTORY

North Stradbroke is one of the major sand islands that enclose Moreton Bay. The island has been linked to the mainland at various stages, so it has rich plant and animal communities. The marine life around Point Lookout is spectacular. Humpback whales migrate north past the point between June and November and year-round, bottlenose dolphins, loggerhead turtles, manta rays and sharks swim in the clear waters.

PLANNING

Contact the visitor centre (☎ 3409 9555) on Junner St, Dunwich, for information about activities on the island and accommodation bookings. Point Lookout offers camping, hostel, hotel and rental accommodation.

What to Bring

'Straddie' has good diving and snorkelling; you can hire gear at the Scuba Centre in Point Lookout but it's easiest to pack your own mask if you're keen. Beach gear is essential, and binoculars are good for spotting wildlife. Banking services are limited, so cash up in Cleveland.

GETTING TO/FROM THE RIDE

Citytrain (☎ 13 1230) services run from Brisbane's Roma St station ($3.30, 50 minutes, half-hourly).

Stradbroke Ferries (☎ 3286 2666) operate ferry services from Cleveland to Dunwich on the island's west coast ($10.50 including bike, one hour, 11 daily).

THE RIDE

The day starts with a short, flat ride to the ferry, then a scenic voyage across the bay, passing the large mass of Peel Island and the specks that are Bird and Goat Islands.

Dunwich, originally a quarantine station, is the commercial centre of the island. It is also the home of many of the island's Noonuckle Aboriginal people. The *Straddie Bakery (Ballow Rd)* does a magnificent opera slice and a dangerously rich caramel tart.

The main road across the island is known variously as Ballow Rd in Dunwich, Mooloomba Rd in Point Lookout, and Dixon Way

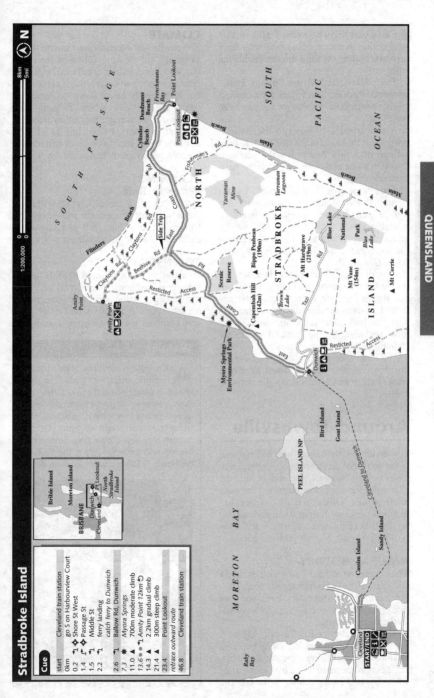

Stradbroke Island

Cue

start	Cleveland train station
0km	go S on Harbourview Court
0.2	Shore St West
1.4	Passage St
1.5	Middle St
2.2	ferry landing
	catch ferry to Dunwich
2.6	Ballow Rd, Dunwich
7.3	Myora Springs
11.0	700m moderate climb
13.6	Amity Point 12km ↺
14.3	2.2km gradual climb
21.4	300m steep climb
23.4	Point Lookout
	retrace outward route
46.8	Cleveland train station

QUEENSLAND

or East Coast Rd in between. Traffic on this road comes in bursts, coinciding with ferry arrivals. Pulling off for a minute avoids the rush.

The pocket-sized **Myora Springs Environmental Park** is a good place for a cooling freshwater dip, and habitat for the rare false water-rat.

A side trip (at 13.6km) to the island's north-west tip heads to the laid-back fishing village of **Amity Point**. It's the place to throw in a line and commune with the pelicans and dolphins.

The township of Point Lookout (23.4km) is spread out along the main road. It's mostly quiet, but well serviced with a dive operator, The Scuba Centre (☎ 3409 8888), and a range of shops and eateries, including the excellent *Blue Water Bistro (☎ 3409 8300, Galeen St)*.

A variety of clean, sandy beaches are within walking distance of the town. Cylinder Beach has safe swimming and is patrolled on summer weekends. Main Beach is also patrolled, while Frenchmans Bay is the most secluded, but not generally safe for swimming.

The route ends at one of the islands must-dos: the one-hour **Point Lookout headland walk**. Return to Cleveland via the outward route.

Around Townsville

Townsville, 1400km north-west of Brisbane, is the unofficial capital of north Queensland. Convincingly tropical, the sun is hot, the beer cold, the characters large and the cane toads prolific. Offshore is the 2000km expanse of the Great Barrier Reef, and the city is the headquarters of the authority (GBRMPA) charged with protecting it.

NATURAL HISTORY
The vegetation around Townsville is hardy and sparse, unlike the rainforests found further north. Many migratory birds and vast flocks of magpie geese visit the seasonal wetlands in the area.

The Great Barrier Reef quells any surf, but there are still some nice, sandy beaches. Diving and snorkelling trips are available, but it may be better to take a trip from Cairns where the reef sweeps closer to the coast.

CLIMATE
Townsville has a monsoonal climate with a summer wet season followed by nine months of much drier weather. The annual rainfall is not particularly high (1100mm), but it can really heave down, as happened one February day when 290mm were recorded. The average maximum temperature ranges from 24°C in July to 31°C in January. Winds tend to be south-easterly sea breezes, which strengthen as the day warms.

PLANNING
When to Ride
From April to November, cyclists will avoid the extremes of temperature and most of the wet season rains. June, July and August are definitely the coolest and driest months.

TOWNSVILLE
Townsville (population 130,000) is the main centre of north Queensland, servicing the mining, grazing and sugar industries of a vast region. It is also a university town and home to a large military contingent.

> ### Warning
>
> ⚠️ The tropical north has some particular hazards: estuarine **crocodiles** (also known as salties) inhabit the coastal rivers and streams – heed warning signs and check with locals before swimming. **Box jellyfish** (stingers), which appear from October through May, have a lethal sting. Swim only at beaches with protective nets at this time; see the Health & Safety chapter for more details.

MARINE STINGERS ARE PRESENT IN THESE WATERS DURING SUMMER MONTHS

PETER HINES

Townsville is often overlooked by travellers; it has its ugly, industrial aspects, but this laid-back northern city boasts a delightful island retreat and some great recreational riding. Despite the heat Townsville is a 'bike city' with a good network of lanes and paths and a young, fit population.

Information

Townsville's main visitor centre (☎ 4778 3555) is 8km south of town on the Bruce Hwy. A more convenient information kiosk (☎ 4721 3660) is in the Flinders St Mall (closed weekend afternoons).

The EPA information office (☎ 4721 2399) is in the Reef HQ building on Flinders St.

Most of the banks have branches in the mall or on the adjacent Sturt St. Top Brand Cycles (☎ 4725 4269), 200 Charters Towers Rd, is well stocked and in touch with the local cycling clubs.

Things to See & Do

Townsville's premier attraction, **Reef HQ** (☎ 4750 0800), 2–68 Flinders St, has a walk-through aquarium with a carefully cultivated coral reef and an impressive predator tank.

In the mall, the **Perc Tucker Gallery** is always interesting, and free! A three-minute ride north of the city centre, **The Strand** features a great kid's water playground, stinger enclosures and attractive parklands.

It's an easy ride to the old quarantine station at **Cape Pallarenda**, 10km north-west of town. The picnic area is alive with native birds and it's a good swimming spot outside the stinger season. For a work-out, and great **views**, pedal 4.5km to the top of **Castle Hill** (286m).

Places to Stay

Just off the beach, *Rowes Bay Caravan Park (☎ 4771 3576, Heatley's Parade)*, 3km north of town, has tent sites for $16 and air-con cabins for $48.

Transit Centre Backpackers (☎ 1800-628 836, cnr Palmer & Plume Sts) is a large hostel, convenient for travellers. Dorm beds cost $13.50 and doubles, $37.50 ($45 with en suite). The *Reef Lodge (☎ 4721 1112, 4 Wickham St)* is central, has a garden and some rooms have balconies. Dorm beds cost from $14; doubles cost $36.

The *Beach House Motel (☎ 4721 1333, 66 The Strand)* is a renovated budget motel

with doubles from $77. *The Rocks (☎ 4771 5700, 20 Cleveland Terrace)* is a renovated 1880s home with ocean views. Doubles are great value at $99, including breakfast; booking is recommended. *Aquarius on the Beach (☎ 4772 4255, 75 The Strand)* is an excellent all-suite hotel. Self-contained units, with air-con and great views, cost from $115.

Places to Eat

The *Woolworths supermarket (126 Sturt St)* is the most central. The bistro of the imposing *Great Northern Hotel (cnr Flinders & Blackwood Sts)* has mains from $12 to $15; generous bar meals cost $5 to $8. The hugely popular *Franks Pizza Napoli (☎ 4725 5181, 3 Ross River Rd)*, a few kilometres out, serves a full Italian menu. Prices are cheap, the helpings generous, and the service abrupt (closed Tuesday).

Flinders St East has plenty of cafes, including the modern *Heritage Cafe & Bar (141 Flinders St)*, which serves light meals from $8. The *Thai International Restaurant (235 Flinders St)* has imaginative vegetarian dishes from $6 and other mains from $10.

Getting There & Away

Air Townsville airport is 7km north-west of the city centre. Ansett (☎ 13 1300) and Qantas (☎ 13 1313) fly regularly between Townsville and major domestic centres. The regular fare to Cairns is $220; to Brisbane, it's $441. To cycle to the city follow John Melton Black Dr and then Bundock and Warburton Sts around the northern side of Castle Hill. Shuttle buses (with luggage trailer) meet all the capital city flights and charge $6. A taxi (☎ 13 1008) will cost around $12.

Bus Greyhound Pioneer (☎ 13 2030) and McCafferty's (☎ 13 1499) each run frequent services to Cairns ($44, six hours) and Brisbane ($143, 20 hours). All buses depart from the transit centre on Palmer St.

Train QR (☎ 13 2232 or ☎ 1800-806 468, ⌨ qroti.bit.net.au/traveltrain/) runs the *Sun-lander* train three times a week between Brisbane and Cairns via Townsville's station on Flinders St (☎ 4772 8546). An economy sleeper to Brisbane (22 hours) costs $173.80. The seven-hour journey to Cairns costs $43, but stand-by fares ($29) are usually available.

Mt Stuart & Alligator Creek

Duration...2 days
Distance 64.6km
Difficulty ....easy
Start/End ....Townsville

This is an easy primer to self contained touring; or, by including the Mt Stuart Side Trip and the Alligator Falls hike, a tough weekend outing. Either way, you will appreciate the cool, clear water and lush surrounds of Alligator Creek, which, despite its ominous name, has no alligators (or crocodiles).

NATURAL HISTORY

The 1234m granite peak of Mt Elliot dominates the local landscape and creates its own weather – its upper slopes having Australia's most southerly tropical rainforest. The lower slopes and coastal plains around Mt Elliot, in Bowling Green Bay National Park, are forested with species resistant to, and dependent on, fire – eucalypts, acacias, cycads, grass trees and native kapok.

PLANNING
When to Ride

Townsville weather is rarely cool, so get on the road early, especially if you are climbing Mt Stuart. Alligator Creek camping area can be popular on weekends and holidays, so book ahead.

What to Bring

Camping and cooking gear is needed at Alligator Creek. Bring enough food for all meals.

THE RIDE
Day 1: Townsville to Alligator Creek
2–3½ hours, 33.6km

Riding the broad shoulder of the Flinders Hwy the scene changes from suburban to industrial to rural. The *Stuart Snack Bar* (12.3km) sells good burgers and is your last chance to take on water before the Mt Stuart Side Trip (at 12.8km). A corned beef fritter the size of your face costs only $2, comes with enough oil to do your chain and tastes as good as it is bad for you. **Country Collectables**, next door, have a bizarre

range of curios, including a ship's binnacle – just the souvenir for a cycling trip.

The route to the Bruce Hwy skirts the copper refinery and a prison farm. As you pedal south-east on the highway you may well encounter a headwind and some traffic, but it's all behind you the next day. Alligator Creek Rd meanders quietly through mango and pawpaw farms. The *Alligator Creek General Store* has takeaways, basic commodities and some fresh goods. To the rear is the quaint but friendly *Melville's Tavern and Pioneer Farm* where a few locals will be enjoying a beer. Continue to the camping ground.

Side Trip: Mt Stuart
24km

About 1.5km along the side trip route is the Mt Stuart turn-off and the start of a 10km climb. Watch for a timber bridge and then a cattle grid near the beginning. The gradient averages 5.5% – including several dips and compensating steep bits. A dilapidated, waterless picnic area at the summit looks down on Lavarack Army Barracks and north-east to Townsville, Cape Pallarenda and Magnetic Island.

On the return, after 250m, turn left down a small road to a telecommunications tower. There, a rough track leads to a scenic reserve at the top of the cliffs. This popular rock-climbing area is much more attractive than the summit lookout.

Alligator Creek

Alligator Creek is a popular day use and camping area in the Bowling Green Bay National Park. The stream, fed by the clouded upper slopes of Mt Elliot, rarely stops flowing. Agile wallabies and scrub turkeys roam freely around the camping area.

Things to See & Do Cooling off in the **rock pools** of the creek and watching wildlife are the essentials here.

The 17km (return) walk to **Alligator Creek Falls**, apart from the last kilometre, is rather dull but the falls themselves are spectacular.

Places to Stay & Eat Camping is the only option at *Alligator Creek*; showers, picnic shelters and wood-fired barbeques are available. Bring food and cooking gear for all meals. Book sites ($3.85 per person) with the park ranger (☎ 4778 8203).

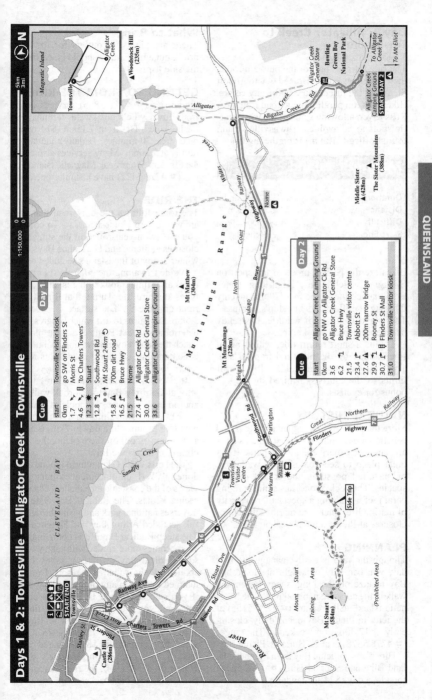

Days 1 & 2: Townsville – Alligator Creek – Townsville

1:150,000

Day 1

Cue		
start		Townsville visitor kiosk
0km		go SW on Flinders St
1.7	↘	Morris St
4.6	↘ 🚉	'to Charters Towers'
12.3	✳	Stuart
12.8	● ↑	Mt Stuart 24km ↺
15.8	● ▲	700m dirt road
16.5	↑	Southwood Rd
21.5		Nome
27.4	↱	Alligator Creek Rd
30.0		Alligator Creek General Store
33.6		Alligator Creek Camping Ground

Day 2

Cue		
start		Alligator Creek Camping Ground
0km		go NW on Alligator Ck Rd
3.6		Alligator Creek General Store
6.2	↱	Bruce Hwy
21.5	↱	Townsville visitor centre
23.4	↰	Abbott St
27.6	▲	200m narrow bridge
29.9	↑	Rooney St
30.7	↱ 🚉	Flinders St Mall
31.0	🚉	Townsville visitor kiosk

QUEENSLAND

Day 2: Alligator Creek to Townsville

1½–3 hours, 31km

The ride retraces half of the outward route, then continues on the Bruce Hwy to Abbott St, taking the direct route to the city centre. Bikepaths run parallel to the road from near Ross River, allowing some of the worst traffic spots to be avoided. Townsville's main **tourist office** (21.5km) is on the highway.

Magnetic Island

Duration	1½–2½ hours
Distance	22.6km
Difficulty	easy–moderate
Start/End	Picnic Bay

Bikes are the perfect mode of transport on 'Maggie', which is only 11km long. James Cook named the island in 1770, mistakenly thinking it influenced his ship's compass. The island teems with wildlife, has sandy beaches and good snorkelling.

This is a short return ride, with a bit of spice added by the hills and tropical sun. The West Point and Radical Bay Rds are off limits to the tourists in hired mokes – a bonus for cyclists.

NATURAL HISTORY

More than half of this rugged granite island is national park and five of the island's bays are zoned as marine national park. It's a great place to see koalas, rock wallabies, brush-tailed possums and a host of bird species. The rocky coast has some fringing coral reef, attracting a spectacular diversity of marine life. There are marine stinger enclosures at Picnic and Horseshoe Bays.

PLANNING

Though the ride is easily manageable in a day, you can stay overnight at Horseshoe Bay to laze on the long, sandy beach and walk in the adjacent national park. The Magnetic Island visitor centre (☎ 4778 5155) at the jetty in Picnic Bay opens daily, closing early at 12.30pm on weekends. The ranger (☎ 4778 5378) is at 22 Hurst St, Picnic Bay.

Hire bikes at Picnic Bay from Magnetic Island Bike and Snorkel Hire (☎ 4778 5411) for $12 a day ($24 for tandems).

What to Bring

There are plenty of outlets for food and drink, but ample water should be carried on the side trips.

GETTING TO/FROM THE RIDE

SunFerries (☎ 4771 3855) services depart from Townsville's breakwater terminal (Sir Leslie Thiess Dr) from 7.15am ($14 return, bikes free, 30 minutes, 11 daily); the last return is at 7.20pm. Many services also call at the Flinders St terminal. Magnetic Island Ferries (☎ 4772 5422) have a similar operation.

THE RIDE

The route follows the only road that goes anywhere – to Horseshoe Bay. To cool off you can swim year-round in the stinger enclosures at Picnic and Horseshoe Bays, or in winter at any of the island's secluded coves.

A side trip along the quiet West Point Rd gives an intimate look at the island's forest types and bird life. Turn left at Birt St, then right on Yule St. The surface is paved for 3.5km, then turns to dirt which progressively deteriorates. **West Point** is a great place to watch the sunset over the mainland, but there is no camping, so you'll need lights for the return journey.

It's worth detouring (at 6.5km) to the jetty at **Geoffrey Bay** to see rock wallabies and, in the clear water, schools of diamond scale mullet – all waiting for a feed from the next tour group. **Alma Bay** (6.7km) is an absolute gem – cool off there before the 100m climb to Horseshoe Bay.

The **Forts Walk** (3km return) around abandoned WWII emplacements offers good views of the coast and an excellent chance of seeing koalas. The Radical Bay Side Trip traverses national park and visits the delightful, secluded **Arthur Bay** and **Florence Bay**. The steep Radical Bay Rd is not maintained and becomes more eroded with each wet season. **Radical Bay** itself is a sandy beach spoiled by the ruins of a resort. Don't be tempted to ride on any of the walking paths; if you're caught, your bike will be confiscated and you'll be left with a steep fine!

Accommodation at Horseshoe Bay includes *Geoff's Place* (☎ 1800-285 577), which has camping for $8 and shared cabins from $17.60 per person. *Maggie's Beach House* (☎ 4778 5144), the ride's turnaround point, is a large backpackers with dorm beds

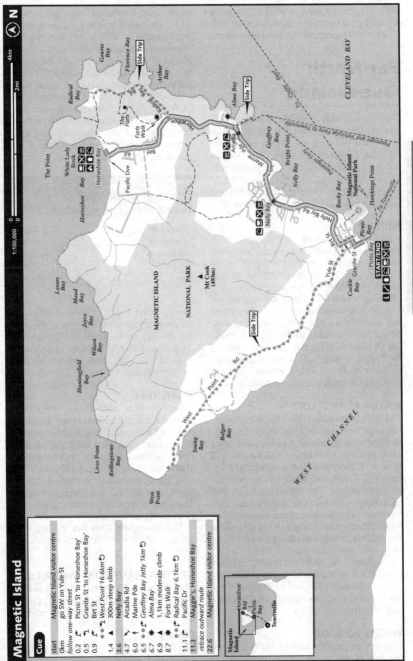

QUEENSLAND

Cue		
start		Magnetic Island visitor centre
		go SW on Yule St
0km		follow one-way street
0.2	↰	Picnic St 'to Horseshoe Bay'
0.5	↰	Granite St 'to Horseshoe Bay'
0.9	↱	Birt St
1.4	↱	West Point 16.6km ↺
3.6	▲	300m steep climb
		Nelly Bay
4.7	↖	Arcadia Rd
6.0	↑	Marine Pde
6.5	↰	Geoffrey Bay Jetty 1km ↺
6.7	▲	Alma Bay
6.9	▲	1.1km moderate climb
8.7	✳	Forts Walk
	↱	Radical Bay 6.1km ↺
11.1	↱	Pacific Dr
11.3		Maggie's, Horseshoe Bay
		retrace outward route
22.6		Magnetic Island visitor centre

from $21. *Myra's B&B (☎ 4758 1277)* on the national park boundary has doubles for $60.

Return to Picnic Bay via the outward route.

Far North Queensland

The region is blessed with lush tropical rainforests, the wonders of the Great Barrier Reef, and the cool lush hinterland of the Atherton Tableland. Cairns and Port Douglas are the tourism hubs, and in recent decades tourism has eclipsed sugar growing as the far north's principle industry. But it's beyond these centres that the true attractions exist.

HISTORY

Far North Queensland's colonial history is similar to other areas in the state. Initial exploitation was of red cedar and gold on the Palmer and Hodgkinson Rivers in the 1870s. Overland routes were developed, allowing access for grazing and agriculture. Much of the lowland rainforest was slashed and burned for sugarcane growing, and little account was taken of the original inhabitants. More recently, the economic value of the region's biological wonders and Aboriginal culture are being realised and exploited in a much more sustainable way.

NATURAL HISTORY

The 900,000-hectare Wet Tropics World Heritage Area was declared in 1998 to protect and manage remnant forest areas from Townsville to Cooktown. Spectacular and diverse, it incorporates coastal mangroves, eucalypt forest and some of the world's oldest rainforest. The region is so rich that an average two hectares of Daintree rainforest contains more tree species than either North America or Europe. Also diverse is the wildlife, which includes remarkable tree kangaroos and cassowaries.

Offshore, the 2000km Great Barrier Reef, is one of the world's natural wonders – to which tour operators in every coastal centre run diving, snorkelling and glass bottom boat trips.

WHEN TO RIDE

The wet season (December–April) changes the face of the region. Rivers swell, minor roads flood and major roads get potholed. The clear blue Coral Sea becomes increasingly turbid with run-off and rainforest streams turn to torrents. Add to this the likelihood of tropical cyclones and the threat of box jellyfish and you will understand that this is the absolute bottom of the tourism season.

Many tourism ventures, particularly north of Port Douglas, close or reduce services in this period. That said, if you can cope with being drenched daily, you will have an adventure, experiencing the other side of life in paradise.

The Daintree & Cape Tribulation

Duration	3 days
Distance	181.7km
Difficulty	moderate
Start	Cairns
End	Cape Tribulation

The sparkling blue Coral Sea contrasts with the deep greens of the Daintree rainforest on this journey to the frontier of the far north. Also in contrast are the various communities – cane growers, Aborigines and back-to-nature ferals.

PLANNING

A popular route with cyclists is the 106km Bloomfield Track between Cape Tribulation and Cooktown, which could add an extra day to this tour. Buses and local aircraft depart from Cooktown to Cairns, making it a good alternative end to the ride. Seek advice on the road condition before proceeding. Most of the route is dirt and is very steep in sections. There are several major river crossings, including of the Bloomfield River.

The *Bloomfield River Inn (☎ 4060 8178)*, 37km north of Cape Tribulation, sells takeaways and some groceries.

GETTING TO/FROM THE RIDE

The Atherton Tableland ride (Kuranda–Cairns) could precede (or follow) this ride to make an eight-day tropical adventure.

Cairns

See the Gateway Cities section (p333) for information on getting to/from Cairns.

Cape Tribulation

Rum Runner (☎ 1800-656 211) runs services to Cairns ($39, three daily). It's the only service that takes bikes, which travel for free.

THE RIDE

Cairns

See Cairns (pp332–33) in the Gateway Cities section for information on accommodation and other services.

Day 1: Cairns to Port Douglas

4–7 hours, 71.2km

Cairns is a busy hub, and the highway north reflects this. Things are quieter beyond the airport and there is a generous shoulder as far as Ellis Beach.

The road to the airport skirts a large mangrove flat. This muddy, unglamorous habitat is the breeding ground for many commercial fish species, and home to Queensland's culinary icon, the mud crab. A side trip at 4.3km leads to a **mangrove boardwalk**, with excellent interpretive signs explaining the ecology.

At 13.7km, two of Cairns' best commercial attractions lie together just off the route. The **Tjapukai Aboriginal Cultural Park** (☎ 4060 8178) features live performances of the Tjapukai tribe's corroboree dances. The cultural displays and chilling historical video are excellent. The **Skyrail** (☎ 4038 1555) gondola gives a bird's-eye view of the tropical rainforest and visits the impressive display centre at Barron Falls Station.

The undulating World Heritage section of the Captain Cook Hwy north of Buchan Point (28km) is a noted accident zone: those drivers not gawking at the scenery are rushing to ferry another load of tourists to Port Douglas or beyond, so beware. The scenery is indeed superb and there are plenty of quiet beaches to stop at. The last stinger enclosure for summer swimming is at **Ellis Beach** (31km).

The **Hartleys Creek Reptile Park** (☎ 4055 3576; 44.3km) is one of the better parks of its type. The highlight is the daily crocodile feeding at 3pm.

The palm-lined road into Port Douglas gives a distinct sense of 'arriving'. This is a town focused on making people feel good about themselves, and spend a lot of money.

Port Douglas

Port Douglas was a gold-rush port that lay dormant for almost a century. In the 1980s, entrepreneur Christopher Skase recognised the town's potential – ready access to the reef and rainforest, and a sandy beach that Cairns could only ever wish for – and turned it into a five-star playground.

Information There's no independent visitor centre in town, but the Port Douglas Tourist Information Centre (☎ 4099 5599) at 23 Macrossan St is a helpful tour booking office.

ANZ, National and Westpac banks all have branches with ATMs on Macrossan St. Port Douglas Bike Hire (☎ 4099 5799), 42 Macrossan St, carries a basic range of parts and has competent mechanics.

Things to See & Do The **lookout** on Island Point Rd has great views along the coast. Exclusive boutiques fill the glamorous **Marina Mirage** shopping and restaurant complex.

The sandy **Four Mile Beach** just east of town has a stinger enclosure. **Snorkelling and diving** trips to the reef are popular, with prices dependent on how far and fast you go.

Places to Stay Central to town and the beach, *Tropic Breeze Van Village* (☎ 4099 5299, 24 Davidson St) charges $17 for tent sites. Cabins sleeping up to four people cost from $63.50 a double.

The YHA-associate hostel, *Port O'Call Lodge (☎ 4099 5422, Port St)*, is 1km south of the centre. Dorm beds cost $21; doubles are $65. The *Coconut Grove Motel (☎ 4099 5124, 58 Macrossan St)* is central, with doubles from $85. Beds in dingy six-bed dorms cost $21.

The *Archipelago Studio Apartments (☎ 4099 5387, 72 Macrossan St)* are well equipped with air-con, kitchen and laundry facilities. Prices range from $89 to $159 for rooms with a sea view.

Places to Eat There are stacks of high quality restaurants in 'Port', with correspondingly high prices. Most eateries are along or near Macrossan St.

The *SPAR* supermarket *(6 Macrossan St)* opens 24 hours; nearby is *Coles (11 Macrossan St)*. Grant St has a couple of *takeaways* and the *Port Douglas Pantry (Shop 4, Grant St)* with sandwiches, pies, pastries and coffees.

For a $10 pub meal try the *Court House Hotel (cnr Macrossan & Wharf Sts)* or the

QUEENSLAND

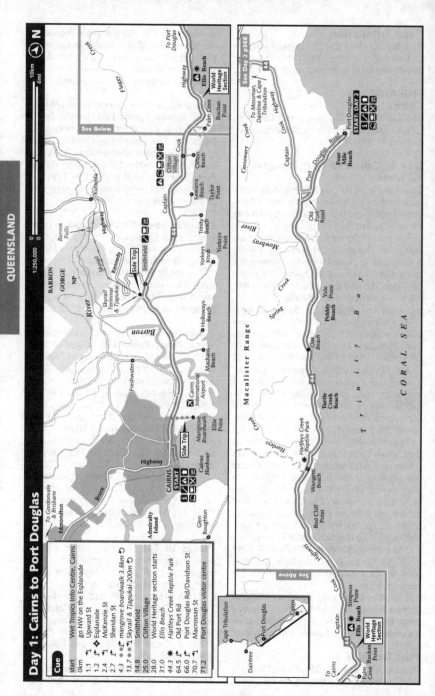

Day 1: Cairns to Port Douglas

Cue	
start	Wet Tropics Info Centre, Cairns
0km	go NW on the Esplanade
1.1	Upward St
1.2	Esplanade
2.4	McKenzie St
2.7	Sheridan St
4.3	mangrove boardwalk 3.8km ↻
13.7	Skyrail & Tjapukai 200m ↻
14.8	Smithfield
25.0	Clifton Village
28.0	World Heritage section starts
31.0	Ellis Beach
44.3	Hartleys Creek Reptile Park
64.5	Old Port Rd
66.0	Port Douglas Rd/Davidson St
70.7	Macrossan St
71.2	Port Douglas visitor centre

Combined Services Club near the Marina. The funky *Mango Jam Cafe (24 Macrossan St)* features live bands on Friday and Saturday nights and does gourmet pizzas, pastas and salad. *Nautilus (☎ 4099 5330, 17 Murphy St)* has a magical open-air setting and a great reputation. Mains cost $24 to $30 and bookings are advised.

Day 2: Port Douglas to Daintree

3½–6 hours, 58.9km

Much of the day is spent among the patchwork of cane fields that feed the Mossman sugar mill. Depending on the season you can be walled in by mature, 4m-high cane or between ploughed fields. There are glimpses of the rainforest to come when the road skirts parts of the Daintree National Park.

Mossman (21km) is an unpretentious working town, largely unaffected by the frenzied tourist activity which surrounds and passes through it. As you approach, look out for the coloured array of **wind toys** in a front garden. From Mossman, detour to walk though Mossman Gorge in the Daintree National Park (see Side Trip).

Scommazon's fruit shed (26.1km) is a treasure trove of locally grown coffee, honey and tropical fruit. Apart from delicious lychees and papaya, try such exotics as sour sop, mangosteen, durian and the cosmic-looking rollinia.

Wonga (38.1km) has a nice **beach**, but no stinger enclosure.

Winding through rainforest up the Daintree Valley, a real sense of the wild north begins. The birdlife is prolific and you'll be unlucky not to see the dazzling blue **Ulysses butterfly**.

Side Trip: Mossman Gorge

11km

From Mossman, turn left on Johnston Rd (signed to Mossman Gorge), which climbs gently up the river valley – watch the slippery cobbles at the entrance to Daintree National Park.

The term 'gorge' is a bit exaggerated, but the fast, clear water has cut a valley through the granite. Beneath the surface turtles clamber, while jungle perch hover mid-current and Ulysses butterflies flutter above the river. A short **walk** links river bank lookouts and a 2.7km rainforest loop just scratches the surface of this 56,000-hectare park.

Kuku Yalanji Dreamtime Walks (☎ 4098 2595), at the park entrance, offers 1½-hour walks guided by local Aborigines. Walks run weekdays, and weekends by arrangement.

Daintree

The land around Daintree village is surprisingly open. Early settlers cleared the rainforest for dairying and then faced the daunting prospect of getting fresh butter to distant markets. Today the economy relies heavily on ecotourism, which usually consists of a quick wildlife cruise followed by a feed of barramundi before reboarding the bus.

Information Almost every business in town advertises itself as a visitor centre and books tours. The private Daintree Tourist Information Centre (☎ 4098 6133) at 5 Stewart St is the start/end point for the ride. The Daintree store has Eftpos facilities.

Things to See & Do The **river** is really Daintree's key attraction. Chris Dahlberg's Specialised River Tours (☎ 4098 7997) are informative and first out, catching the peak of bird activity. Electric Boat Cruises (☎ 1800-686 103) run throughout the day.

Wet Tropics World Heritage Area

Most of Australia was covered in rainforest 50 million years ago, but climate change dwindled this to about 1% of the continent by the time Europeans arrived. After 200 years of logging, clearing for farms and settlement, less than a third of that remains, half of which is in Queensland.

Despite strenuous resistance from the timber industry and state government the Wet Tropics World Heritage Area was declared in 1988. The area, stretching from Townsville to Cooktown, covers 900,000 hectares of the coast and hinterland and includes Queensland's highest peak, Mt Bartle Frere, the 305m Wallaman Falls and the Daintree-Cape Tribulation National Park.

Local residents now overwhelmingly support the World Heritage listing, with ecotourism easily eclipsing sugar as Far North Queensland's biggest industry. For more information on the wet tropics, visit the Web site 🖳 www.wettropics.gov.au.

QUEENSLAND

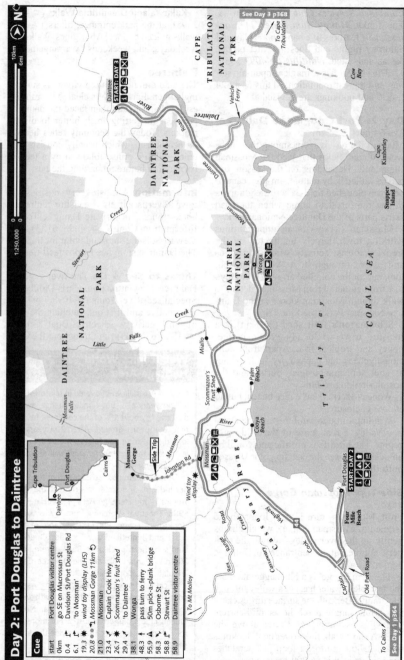

Day 2: Port Douglas to Daintree

Cue		
start		Port Douglas visitor centre
0km	↰	go SE on Macrossan St
0.4	↱	Davidson St/Port Douglas Rd
6.1	✳	'to Mossman'
19.3	✳	wind toy display (LHS)
20.8	●⤺	Mossman Gorge 11km ↻
21.0		Mossman
23.4	↗	Captain Cook Hwy
26.7	✳	Scommazon's fruit shed
29.4	↗	'to Daintree'
38.1		Wonga
48.3	←	pass turn to ferry
55.9	⚠	50m pick-a-plank bridge
58.3	↘	Osborne St
58.8	↰	Stewart St
58.9		Daintree visitor centre

See Day 3 p368

See Day 1 p364

Places to Stay The *Daintree Riverview Caravan Park (☎ 4098 6119, 2 Stewart St)* is handy, but short of shade. Tent sites cost $12. *Daintree Kenadon Homestead Cabins (☎ 4098 6142, Dagmar St)* overlook green pastures and the river. Cabins cost $80 a double, including bathroom, limited cooking facilities and light breakfast.

Excellent *Red Mill House (☎ 4098 6233, Stewart St)* is a breezy Queenslander; B&B costs from $66 a double (shared bathroom). *Billirene B&B (☎ 4098 6199)* has cosy rooms with bathrooms for $75. The *Daintree Eco Lodge (☎ 4098 6100, Daintree Rd)*, 3km south, has stylish timber cabins facing the rainforest canopy. The well-equipped rooms fetch $476 a double (including breakfast).

Places to Eat Daintree village caters mostly to day visitors, so is very quiet at night. The *Daintree Store (☎ 4098 6146, 1 Stewart St)* opens daily. Adjoining it, *Jacanas Restaurant* serves sandwiches, burgers and main meals until 8pm.

Baaru House (☎ 4098 6100), the restaurant at the Eco Lodge, is open to the public for breakfast, lunch and dinner. Mains include vegetarian and start at $17.

Day 3: Daintree to Cape Tribulation
3–5 hours, 51.6km

Retracing the Day 2 route for 10km, the ride then continues north, crossing the Daintree by ferry. The 200m Heights of Alexandra range is the physical challenge of the day. From here the scenery alternates between cleared freehold blocks and dense rainforest. Three floodway crossings can prove barriers during heavy rains. If in doubt wait a few hours as the waters usually subside quickly.

The $1 ferry trip is the cheapest cruise on the Daintree. The river really is a frontier. Beyond it there is no sugar cane, fewer cars and more rainforest. It's no wilderness, with 1000 freehold properties, but development is certainly low-key and many rainforest blocks are being bought back for conservation.

A side trip (at 19.6km) to **Cape Kimberley** is typically Daintree – a gravel road leads to a quiet resort and an almost deserted beach. It's on roads like this that you may just happen upon a magnificent cassowary.

A very worthwhile side trip (at 24.5km) is the **Daintree Rainforest Environment Centre**. The $8 entry includes displays on rainforest animals and Gondwanan history, a canopy-viewing tower and guided walks.

The **Daintree Ice-Cream Company** (at 29.5km) makes an amazing range of exotic fruit flavours; black sapote (chocolate-pudding fruit) is a popular favourite (closed mornings and Sundays).

The **Maardja boardwalk** (43.6km) takes advantage of its 'where-rainforest-meets-the-sea' geography to show off three distinct plant communities. The amazing fan palms are an icon of Cape Tribulation. From Cape Tribulation is a side trip to Emmagen Creek.

Side Trip: Emmagen Creek
14km

Emmagen Creek, 7km north of Cape Tribulation, is a beautiful example of the wild streams that flow from the rainforest wilderness. This was the end of the road until 1983 when the Bloomfield Track (still unsealed and very steep) was pushed through to link with Cooktown. Vigorous environmental protests were overcome by pro-development local and state governments.

From PK's Jungle Village, the road to Emmagen Creek is unsealed. After 1.3km is the turn-off to the **Kulki** picnic area, where the postcard view of the cape unfortunately draws crowds of visitors. The road then becomes rough and steep, but levels near an enormous **strangler fig**. Having germinated from a bird dropping high in a host tree, this fig would have dropped root tendrils to the forest floor, used its host for support in the sunlit canopy and, eventually, enveloped it – ungratefully killing it.

There is the great temptation to swim at Emmagen Creek – but the possibility, too, of meeting a crocodile.

Cape Tribulation

There is no real town, but the Cape has a range of accommodation, and a few eateries. The ranger station (☎ 4098 0052), 1.4km north, opens from 9am to 11am. Most accommodation places offer information and can book activities. *PK's Jungle Village* has Eftpos facilities.

Things to See & Do The **Dubuji** picnic area, next to Cape Tribulation Village, features another very good boardwalk through the swamp and palm forest of Myall Creek.

QUEENSLAND

Day 3: Daintree to Cape Tribulation

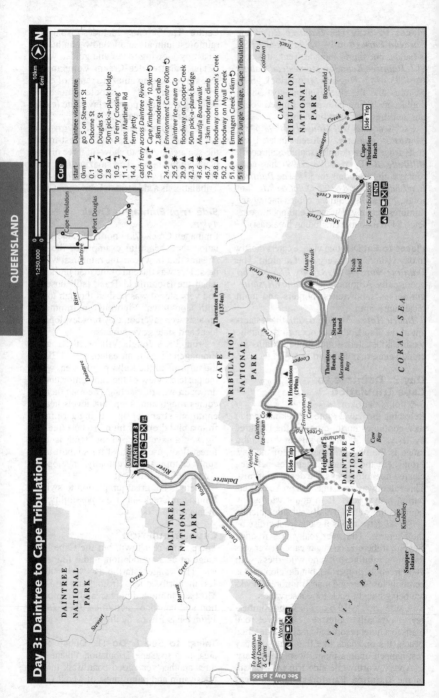

Cue		
start	Daintree visitor centre	
0km	go S on Stewart St	↰
0.1	Osborne St	↱
0.6	Douglas St	↲
2.8	50m pick-a-plank bridge	↲
10.5	'to Ferry Crossing'	↱
11.1	pass Martinelli Rd	
14.4	ferry jetty	
	catch ferry across Daintree River	
19.6 ●	↰↱ Cape Kimberley 10.9km ↻	
	▲	
	▲ 2.8km moderate climb	
24.5 ✳	↱ Environment Centre 600m ↻	
29.5	✳ Daintree Ice-cream Co	
29.9 △	floodway on Cooper Creek	
42.3 △	50m pick-a-plank bridge	
43.6 ✳	Maardja Boardwalk	
45.7 △	1.3km moderate climb	
49.8 △	floodway on Thomson's Creek	
50.2 △	floodway on Myall Creek	
51.6 ←	Emmagen Creek 14km ↻	
51.6 ●	PK's Jungle Village, Cape Tribulation	

N

1:250,000

0   6mi

0   10km

See Day 2 p366

A rainforest **walking track** links the Dubuji with the Kulki picnic area, north of the cape.

Swimming, snorkelling and **fishing** are all good dry-season activities. **Sea kayak** trips are run by PK's Jungle Village (☎ 4098 0040). Paul Mason's Guided Rainforest Walks (☎ 4098 0070) are one of the most experienced for day and night **rainforest walks**.

Places to Stay The *Cape Tribulation Beach House (☎ 4098 0030)*, 2km north of the cape, is amid lovely rainforest. Tent sites cost $8 per person and dorm beds, $25. Doubles with en suite cost $99.

PK's Jungle Village (☎ 4098 0040, Cape Tribulation Rd) is a comfortable hostel, with a pool, bar and restaurant. There's a party atmosphere and activities include horse riding and sea kayaking. It offers camping ($11 per person), dorm beds ($24) and doubles ($65).

Rainforest Hideaway (☎ 4098 0108, 19 Camelot Close) is surrounded by rainforest. B&B costs $90 a double.

Ferntree Rainforest Resort (☎ 4098 0000, Camelot Close) has luxury cabins in a landscaped garden ($280 a double), suites overlooking the pool ($320) and bungalows ($230); all include breakfast.

Places to Eat A small *general store* is just north of Myall Creek on the approach to the village. The *Boardwalk Cafe (Cape Tribulation Rd)*, serves good breakfasts, burgers and meals at reasonable prices (open 7.30am–7pm). Over the road, *PK's Jungle Village* restaurant opens to the public, serving simple meals (evening roast or BBQ costs $9). The restaurant at *Ferntree Rainforest Resort* serves light lunches and dinner mains cost from $20.

Atherton Tableland

Duration	5 days
Distance	252.4km
Difficulty	moderate
Start	Kuranda
End	Cairns

The cool clime, waterfalls, crater lakes, rainforest giants and historic towns all beckon the cyclist. The tablelands are a rich agricultural region, and there's plenty of opportunity to sample the produce. This tour goes to the highest point in the Queensland road system, so it has some great downhills.

HISTORY
The coastal ranges provided a formidable challenge to white settlers trying to the work the rich Atherton Tableland. The Gillies Hwy has the most fascinating history. Originally a mule-train route, a single-lane road was cut, largely by hand, over a three-year period. There were 611 bends in the range section and the one-way traffic was controlled by a gate system that remained in place until 1959.

PLANNING
What to Bring
At elevations of up to 1100m, the Tableland is a welcome relief from the muggy tropical coast. Many visitors find themselves unprepared, however – a good raincoat and warm clothes are useful even in summer. A great alternative to staying in Mareeba on the first night is Granite Gorge (see Day 2 Side Trip); bring a tent and food supplies to stay there.

When to Ride
The Tableland has a much milder climate than the neighbouring coast, and in parts a lower average rainfall, but the comments in the Far North Queensland When to Ride section still apply.

GETTING TO/FROM THE RIDE
Link this ride with The Daintree & Cape Tribulation ride, described earlier in this chapter, which starts from Cairns.

Kuranda
Train The Kuranda Scenic Railway (☎ 4036 9249) is justly famous. Trains depart Cairns daily at 8.30am and 9.15am ($25, bikes $7, 1½ hours).

Bicycle Kuranda is 27km north-west of Cairns. Follow Day 1 of The Daintree & Cape Tribulation ride (described earlier in this chapter) to Smithfield, and turn left onto the Kennedy Hwy. It's busy but scenic, steadily climbing 400m before descending 100m to Kuranda.

Cairns
See the Gateway Cities section (pp332–33) for details on getting to/from Cairns.

THE RIDE
Kuranda

Kuranda (population 750), famed for its craft market, is a major day-trip destination from Cairns. A host of tourism ventures and some pleasant walks can fill a day, or you can push straight through. The place reverts to a laid-back mountain village at night.

Information The Kuranda visitor centre (☎ 4093 7570), on the highway 2km west of town, opens daily from 9am to 8pm. The artistically inspired public toilet building in the park on Therwine St houses a town map and information board.

There is an ATM at the Northern Building Society at 19 Coondoo St.

Things to See & Do The **Kuranda markets**, on Rob Vievers Dr, run Wednesday, Thursday, Friday and Sunday mornings. Attractions near the market include **Birdworld** (☎ 4093 9188), the **Australian Butterfly Sanctuary** (☎ 4093 7575) and, for bungy jumpers, **Sky Screamer** (☎ 4041 3280). The **Kuranda Arts Co-op** (☎ 4093 9026), 7/24 Coondoo St, sells some of the best local works.

Barron Falls Rd passes a large flying fox colony and leads to a lookout over the falls.

Places to Stay The *Kuranda Van Park* (☎ 4093 7316, Kuranda Heights Rd) is north of the highway. Tent sites cost $15; cabins start at $66. Beds in twin-share, backpacker-style rooms cost $15 per person.
Kuranda Backpacker's Hostel (☎ 4093 7355, 6 Arara St) is relaxing – with big communal areas, gardens and a pool. Dorm beds cost $16 and doubles cost $38.

Places to Eat Kuranda has plenty of daytime eating options, but evenings are quieter. *Kuranda Foodstore (Coondoo St)* is open 7am to 7pm weekdays and until 6pm on weekends.

At the 'top pub', *Billy's Garden Bar & BBQ (Coondoo St)* is a pleasant bistro with mains from around $10 (or attack the salad bar for $7). *The Garden Bar & Grill (Arara St)* in the 'bottom pub' serves burgers for $5 and grills from around $8.
Monkey's Cafe/Restaurant (☎ 4093 7451, 1 Therwine St) is a good BYO place with an outdoor deck, open all day. Evening mains start from $18.

Day 1: Kuranda to Mareeba
2–4 hours, 38.4km

This easy, undulating ride has a gradual overall climb. It's remarkable how quickly the rainforest is left behind and open eucalypt forest takes over. Around Mareeba the ride enters irrigated farmland growing a rich variety of crops. The ride ends at Mareeba, but Granite Gorge camping ground, 15.8km further, is a very attractive alternative stopover for self-sufficient cyclists (see the Day 2 Side Trip).

Detour (at 23.9km) to **Davies Creek** where the granite bed runs with cool, clear water year-round. Lace monitors (goannas) and birds are common. There is a picnic area near some nice swimming holes, and camping costs $3.50 per person. The 75m-high Davies Creek Falls are 2km further along the road.

A faded 'coffee' sign on a drum lid by the highway is the only sign of the **Tablelands Coffee** plantation (side trip at 28.5km), accessed by Kovacic Rd. You might catch the family roasting, grinding and packing the beans in the kitchen. Tablelands are just one of the producers in a growing local industry. The quality is good and you can't buy fresher.

Mareeba

This busy agricultural and pastoral hub (population 17,000) hosts one of Australia's largest rodeos in July each year. The town was once the centre of a major tobacco industry, but production is now shifting to fruit, coffee and sugar cane.

Information The visitor centre (☎ 4092 5674), 345 Byrnes St, is also the Mareeba Heritage Museum (see Things to See & Do).
The big banks are all along Byrnes St, and both the Westpac and National have ATMs. Eddleston Super Cycles (☎ 4092 1517) is at 39 Constance St.

Things to See & Do Displays at the **Mareeba Heritage Museum** range from local Aboriginal artefacts to white settlement and the rural industries.
Opposite the museum is **Ant Hill Park**, devoted to the termites whose enormous homes dot the savanna landscape. **Coffee Works** (☎ 4092 4101), on Mason St, has guided tours and tastings during the week.

Day 1: Kuranda to Mareeba

Cue

start	0km	Therwine St Park, Kuranda
		go SE on Therwine St
0.0		(70m) Coondoo St
0.2	←	Rob Vievers Dr
1.4	←	Kennedy Hwy 'to Mareeba'
19.5		cross Davies Creek
23.9	● ● ←	Davies Creek 12.1km ↻
28.5	● ● ←	Tablelands Coffee 600m ↻
37.2	↑	'to Town Centre'
38.1		Byrnes St
38.4		Mareeba visitor centre

Bird-watching tours of the **Mareeba Wetlands Reserve** (☎ 4093 2304) depart from the visitor centre.

Places to Stay & Eat At the *Riverside Caravan Park* (☎ 4092 2309, Egan St), tent sites cost $11 on-site vans cost $27.50.

The *Highlander Hotel* (☎ 4092 1032, Byrnes St) has backpacker beds for $13 and the renovated *Ant Hill Hotel* (☎ 4092 1011, 79 Byrnes St) has classic pub rooms for $36 a double.

Motels include the *Jackaroo* (☎ 4092 2677, 340 Byrnes St), which has air-con doubles from $60; and the smaller *Golden Leaf Motel* (☎ 4092 2266, 261 Byrnes St), which charges $65 a double.

Mareeba has **supermarkets** and a range of *cafes* and *takeaways* along Byrnes St. Farm work, like cycling, must generate some big appetites. *Curcio's Bakery (313 Byrnes St)* is an amazing drive-through bakery that bakes loaves of incredible size. The *Ant Hill Hotel* serves good counter meals.

Day 2: Mareeba to Herberton
3½–6 hours, 63.9km
The route climbs almost imperceptibly, initially through rich agricultural land. Some farms along Chewko Rd still have tobacco-drying sheds, but mostly now the crops are avocadoes, macadamias, mangoes, coffee and sugar cane. An interesting indigenous crop is ti-tree, grown for its antiseptic oil.

Tolga Woodworks (☎ 4095 4488; 38.4km) features an exceptional range of bowls, furniture and other pieces. The adjoining *cafe* serves light meals.

Atherton (44.3km), population 6000, is a large centre with all facilities. The popular *Cafe Culture*, in the main street, makes a good lunch stop, particularly for vegetarians. The **Railco historic steam train** (☎ 4091 4871) runs from Atherton to Herberton and back every Wednesday, Saturday and Sunday. The **Hou Wang Temple** (45.5km) is a rare reminder of the Chinese contribution to North Queensland's early settlement – in spite of discrimination against them. When they were banned from reef mining at the Hodgkinson goldfield they established market gardens at Atherton. Ineligible for freehold title, the Chinese tenant-farmed so successfully that they produced 80% of the Tableland's crops. After WWI, their leases were given to returned servicemen, and Chinatown, once home to 1100 people, simply died.

The Herberton Range is a solid climb, but the reverse is good fun, especially if you are early enough to race the steam train. It's not all downhill though – a crazy swoop to the Wild River precedes a hard grind up to the centre of town at the end of the day.

Side Trip: Granite Gorge
8.2km
The route to the popular Granite Gorge is signed all the way along Paglietta Rd, at times on beaten up old car hoods – it's a good prelude to this quirky camp site, which is owned by Jack Bryde, son of Charlie Bryde – one of the area's first settlers and author of a colourful autobiography *From Chart House to Bush Hut*. The facilities are fairly basic, but at $2 per person, nobody complains. You'll need to be self sufficient. The area backs onto Granite Creek – a scenic jumble of granite boulders – and is famous for its rock wallaby population, which forages at dusk in the camping area. A marked walk around Granite Gorge takes an hour, and the swimming hole is permanent, but it can get pretty soupy.

Herberton
Herberton was established almost overnight when tin-mining leases were pegged in 1880. A rail link from Cairns began construction in 1886, but it took 24 years to reach the town. Mining and smelting ceased in 1978. Tourism and the catholic boarding school now maintain the town's economy. There is no visitor centre nor any banks in town, but several businesses have Eftpos facilities.

Things to See & Do Many of the fine, timber **buildings** remain in this attractive town. An impressive **mural** in John St depicts the town's past. By the bridge there is a tranquil **walking track** along the bank of the (not so) Wild River. Some people collect antiques, the Skennars collect entire buildings of them – of the 28 buildings in the wonderful **Herberton Historical Village** (☎ 4096 2271), 18 are open for display.

Places to Stay & Eat The friendly and quiet *Wild River Caravan Park* (☎ 4096 2121, Holdcroft Dr) has camp sites for $10 and units for $38.

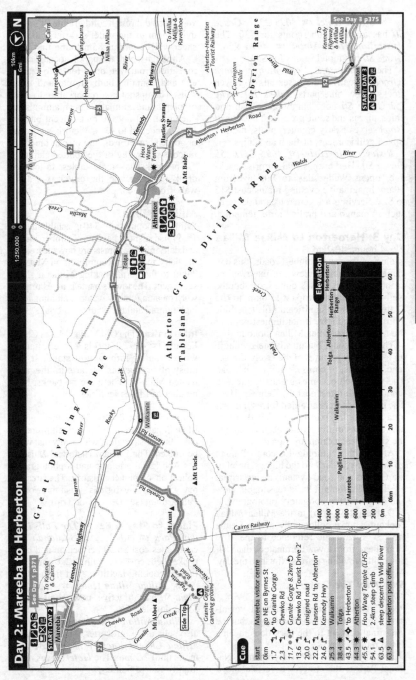

Day 2: Mareeba to Herberton

QUEENSLAND

Elevation

Cue	
start	Mareeba visitor centre
0km	go NE on Byrnes St
1.7	'to Granite Gorge'
2.3	Chewko Rd
11.7	Granite Gorge 8.2km ↻
13.6	Chewko Rd 'Tourist Drive 2'
20.0	unsigned road
22.6	Hansen Rd 'to Atherton'
24.6	Kennedy Hwy
25.3	Walkamin
38.4	Tolga
43.5	'to Herberton'
44.3	Atherton
45.5	Hou Wang Temple (LHS)
54.1	2.4km steep climb
63.5	steep descent to Wild River
63.9	Herberton post office

QUEENSLAND

The **Royal Hotel** (☎ 4096 2231, Grace St) has average pub rooms for $30. The **Australian Hotel-Motel** (☎ 4096 2263, Grace St) has motel rooms for $50.

The **Herberton Convenience Store** (Grace St) carries the essentials and even stocks a few bike parts. **Jake's Takeaway** (52 Grace St) does hamburgers, fish and chips, pizzas and some groceries. The **Royal Hotel** serves hearty counter meals; the $11 mixed grill is a feast of flesh and chips.

Risley's a la carte (☎ 4096 2111, 55 Grace St), Herberton's real surprise package, opens Wednesday to Sunday from 10am. Imaginative evening mains cost $15 to $21. Servings are generous and desserts, such as mango and praline torte, tempting.

Day 3: Herberton to Millaa Millaa

2½–4 hours, 40.2km

Riding on the state's highest roads, this day can give spectacular views, or may well be spent inside a cloud. It's quite short, but the well-worthwhile side trip (at 15.6km) to **The Crater** adds some significant hills (see Side Trip). The highlight, if not highest point of the route, is the Millaa Millaa lookout.

There is a long, but mostly steady climb up to the dairy pastures of the Evelyn Tableland, which is, of course, anything but flat. The vegetation becomes gradually greener, tending to rainforest near the Kennedy Hwy. The tablelands were an **allied forces training area** and staging post during WWII. There are few relics of the former occupation, but the sites of each camp are signed.

After all this climbing it is compelling to go that extra distance to the highest point of the Queensland road system, a side trip at 18.2km. The summit has a reasonable view and a sign for the obligatory photograph.

Detour (at 33.4km) to the **Millaa Millaa Lookout**, known colloquially as the Gentle Annie – a sarcastic reference to the 10% climb there from town. Fortunately, that's all downhill, providing a cruisy finish to the day.

Side Trip: The Crater

10.2km

Pedalling through superb rainforest, you almost forget the steep ups and downs, but the long final descent to the park does mean a 150m return climb.

The key feature of Mt Hypipamee National Park is the crater – a vertical-sided

vent blasted through solid granite. It's a giddying 58m to the water's surface, and the sheer walls continue 85m to the first bend.

Although small, the park is located on the transition from wet, open forest to rainforest, and contains both granite and basalt soils. The upshot is a remarkable diversity of plants and animals. The mammals are nocturnal, but not the magnificent birdlife. Luck is needed to see a Victoria's riflebird or golden bowerbird, but you can't miss the raucous miaowing of the spotted catbird.

The park has picnic tables, toilets and drinking water and the crater is a 400m walk from the car park.

Millaa Millaa

'Millaa' (population 340), established in 1909, had a short heyday of timber milling and dairying. The forests are now cleared and the dairy industries centralised on Malanda, 24km to the north, making Millaa a sleepy settlement. The town's name is an Aboriginal word meaning 'many waters'; alluding to the high rainfall and the nearby waterfalls.

Information The Old Millaa Millaa Cheese Factory (☎ 4097 2509) is a cafe/restaurant with a tourist information stand. It, and most other businesses, are in the aptly named Main St. There are no banks, but a number of Eftpos facilities.

Things to See & Do The northern end of Main St has a life-sized comic **sculpture** of a dairy farmer struggling with a cow that won't be milked. The **Eacham Historical Museum** has Aboriginal artefacts and a photographic collection of pioneer history. The area has many beautiful **waterfalls** – visit three on the Falls Circuit (see Day 4 Side Trip).

Places to Stay & Eat At **The Falls Holiday Park** (☎ 4097 2290, Malanda Rd), camp sites cost $6.50 per person and backpacker beds cost a bargain $12. Cabins with limited cooking facilities start from $26.

The **Millaa Millaa Hotel** (☎ 4097 2212, Main St) has attractive, new motel units at $55 a double.

Millaa Millaa Takeaway (61 Main St) also sells a few groceries. The **Old Millaa Millaa Cheese Factory** has a cafe-style menu until 7.30pm. The **Hotel** serves meals nightly except Sunday.

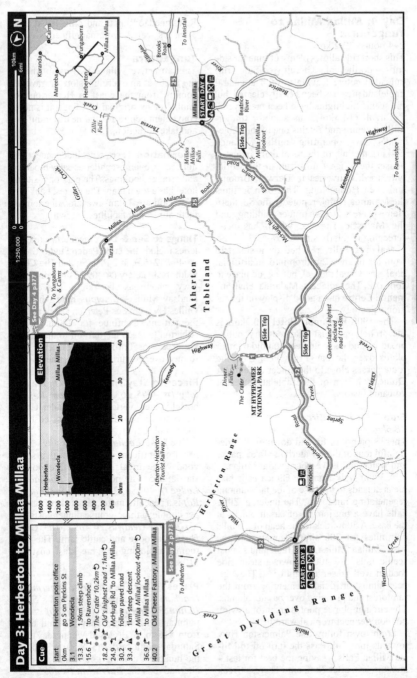

Day 3: Herberton to Millaa Millaa

Cue		
start	Herberton post office	
0km	go S on Perkins St	
3.1	Wondecla	
13.3	1.9km steep climb	
15.6	'to Ravenshoe'	
18.2	The Crater 10.2km ↻	
24.9	Qld's highest road 1.1km ↻	
30.2	McHugh Rd 'to Millaa Millaa' follow paved road	
33.4	1km steep descent	
36.9	Millaa Millaa lookout 400m ↻ 'to Millaa Millaa'	
40.2	Old Cheese Factory, Millaa Millaa	

Elevation

QUEENSLAND

Day 4: Millaa Millaa to Yungaburra

2–4 hours, 39.2 km

This short ride allows plenty of time for side trips – do the Falls Circuit (see Side Trip) unloaded before leaving town. The central Tableland area has been heavily cleared, but the scenic highlights have been preserved.

Tarzali (14.5km) was a major timber-milling centre and retains one of the Tableland's few operating mills. Malanda (24km), the hub of the local dairy industry, boasts the longest milk run in the world, with fresh deliveries to Darwin, Broome and even Hong Kong. The town features the **Malanda Hotel**, reputedly the Southern Hemisphere's largest timber building, and the **Majestic Theatre**, which has been screening regularly since 1928.

Malanda Falls, reached on a side trip from town, are a 2m drop into an artificial pool – no visual marvel, but a good place to cool off. The adjacent **Malanda Environmental Centre** has a good display on the region's geology.

The 1908 **Peeramon Hotel** (30.9km) is the archetypal Australian country pub – broad verandahs, cold beer and old number plates over the bar. From Peeramon the route passes close to the cinder cone of **Mt Quincan**, a sign of the Tableland's recent volcanic history.

Side Trip: Falls Circuit

18.5km

There's plenty of up and down on this delightful tour of three waterfalls. Take snacks and water, and leave your gear at Millaa.

A 300m walk from the **Elinjaa Falls** picnic area leads to the base of the falls, among regenerating rainforest. The undercut **Zillie Falls** have a big jumble of basalt blocks at the base. A 50m track to the head of the falls continues for 200 slippery metres to the base. **Millaa Millaa**, the Tableland's most scenic falls, are 400m down a steep side road in well-preserved rainforest. They appear almost artificial – emerging from the rainforest and plunging over basalt columns. The circular plunge pool is great for a swim, but don't expect tropical warmth.

From town follow the Palmerston Hwy towards Innisfail. Pass the turn-off to Millaa Millaa Falls – saving the best for last – and turn left, after 2km, onto Theresa Creek Rd (signed to Elinjaa and Zillie Falls). After 30m, it's sealed, with magnificent views.

Yungaburra

This attractive village was established in the 1880s as an overnight stop for travellers coming from the coast to Herberton. Retaining many original buildings, it is now a convenient centre for the nearby rainforest and lake attractions (see Day 5).

Information There's no independent visitor centre, but most galleries carry brochures and arrange bookings. The park opposite the hotel has a town map. The nearest banks and bike shop are 13km away in Atherton and there are Eftpos facilities in town.

Things to See & Do Yungaburra's fine galleries include the **Ludij Peden Studio Gallery** (☎ 4095 2160), at 2 Pine St; and **The Chalet Rainforest Gallery** (☎ 4095 2144), on Gillies Hwy, which has clay rainforest scenes by Lindsay Muir. A **platypus hide** where the Gillies Hwy crosses Peterson Creek rewards the patient. Continue for 200m towards Atherton to reach the turn-off to the **Curtain Fig Tree** – a 50m-high veil of aerial roots formed over centuries – 2km further.

Places to Stay The excellent *On the Wallaby* (☎ *4095 2031, 34 Eacham Rd)* is a hostel in a converted Queenslander. Camping costs $8 per site, dorm beds cost $18, and doubles, $40.

The *Lake Eacham Hotel* (☎ *4095 3515)* has a magnificent dining room that serves good-value meals. Comfortable doubles start at $55. The nonsmoking *Kookaburra Lodge* (☎ *4095 3222, cnr Oak St & Eacham Rd)* is a peaceful motel. Units start from $65 per double; a three-course dinner costs $20.

Gumtree Getaway (☎ *4095 3105, Gillies Hwy)* is a lodge and cattle farm. The 'king rooms', including light breakfast, cost from $108.

Places to Eat The *Cut Price Supermarket* (*Eacham Rd)* is open daily. *Nick's Swiss-Italian Restaurant* (☎ *4095 3330)* is ever-popular, with pasta from $11 and mains from $16 to $23 (closed Wednesday). The Saturday-night buffet ($28.50) will satisfy the hungriest cycling gourmand. A quieter alternative is the *Burra Inn* (☎ *4095 3657,*

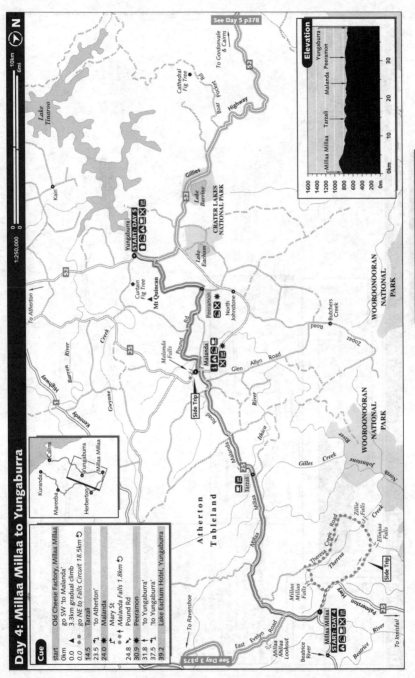

Day 4: Millaa Millaa to Yungaburra

Cue

start		Old Cheese Factory, Millaa Millaa
		go SW 'to Malanda'
0km	▲	3.3km gradual climb
0.0	●●●	go NE to Falls Circuit 18.5km ↻
14.5		Tarzali
23.5	↱	'to Atherton'
24.0	✳	Malanda
	↰	Mary St
	●●	Malanda Falls 1.8km ↻
24.8	↱	Pound Rd
30.9	✳	Peeramon
31.8	↱	'to Yungaburra'
37.5	↰	'to Yungaburra'
39.2		Lake Eacham Hotel, Yungaburra

QUEENSLAND

Elevation

QUEENSLAND

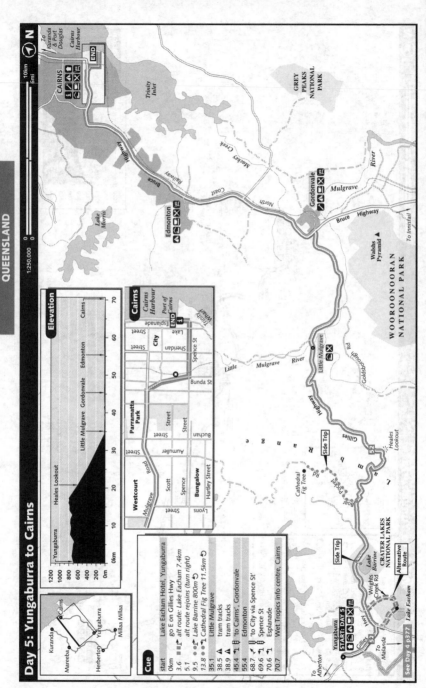

Day 5: Yungaburra to Cairns

Elevation

1200
1000
800
600
400
200
0m

Yungaburra | Heales Lookout | Little Mulgrave | Gordonvale | Edmonton | Cairns

0km 10 20 30 40 50 60 70

Cairns

Cairns Harbour / Port of Cairns

City
Sheridan Street
Spence St
Street
Bunda St
Parramatta Park
Westcourt
Buchan Street
Street
Aumuller Street
Bungalow
Scott Spence
Hartley Street
Lyons Street
Mulgrave Road

Cue

start		Lake Eacham Hotel, Yungaburra
0km		go E on Gillies Hwy
3.6		alt route: Lake Eacham 7.4km
5.1		alt route rejoins (turn right)
9.5		Lake Barrine 800m ↻
13.8		Cathedral Fig Tree 11.5km ↻
35.1		Little Mulgrave
38.5		tram tracks
38.9		tram tracks
45.4		to Cairns', Gordonvale
55.4		Edmonton
68.7		to City via Spence St'
69.6		Spence St
70.6		Esplanade
70.7		Wet Tropics info centre, Cairns

See Day 4 p377
START DAY 5
Yungaburra

To Malanda
To Atherton

Lake Eacham
Wrights Creek Rd
CRATER LAKES NATIONAL PARK
Alternative Route
Side Trip
Lake Barrine

Cathedral Fig Tree
Side Trip
Boar Pocket Rd

Heales Lookout
Gillies Highway

R a n g e
L a m b

Little Mulgrave River
Little Mulgrave
Goldsborough Rd

WOOROONOORAN NATIONAL PARK

Walshs Pyramid ▲
To Innisfail

Gordonvale
Mulgrave
Bruce Highway

GREY PEAKS NATIONAL PARK

Mackay Creek
North Coast Railway
Mulgrave River

Edmonton

Bruce Highway
Lake Morris

Trinity Inlet

CAIRNS
END

To Kuranda & Port Douglas
Cairns Harbour

N

1:250,000
0   10km
0   5mi

1 Cedar St), a charming BYO restaurant serving excellent mains from around $18.

Day 5: Yungaburra to Cairns
4–7 hours, 70.7km

All that hard-earned elevation is lost in one dream-like descent. It's preceded by some of the Tableland's finest attractions (see Alternative Route and Side Trip) – this really is a case of saving the best for last.

The Yungaburra area is famous for its crater lakes, Eacham and Barrine. They were formed by a huge volcanic explosion when hot magma met ground water. Now they are tranquil pools surrounded by lush rainforest. A side trip at 9.5km leads to **Lake Barrine**, which is larger, and in some ways less disturbed than **Lake Eacham** (see Alternative Route). An elegant old *teahouse* overlooks the lake and regular cruises give commentary on the forest and animals. You can swim; and a 6.5km walking track passes 50m-tall bull kauri pines – estimated to be more than 1000 years old – 100m east of the teahouse.

A side trip to an incredible fig tree is at 13.8km. The descent of the Lamb Range, through World Heritage-listed park, is a definite highlight of this tour. It's almost 20km and 260 bends before you need to touch the pedals. A quick stop at **Heales Lookout** (20.8km) is worthwhile for the views south over the Mulgrave Valley.

Once on the valley floor traffic gets heavier because of to local quarrying industries.

Watch for the two acute-angled **tram tracks** at 38.5km and 38.9km.

On the Bruce Hwy heat and humidity will strike again, but the road is flat, has a good shoulder, and there's usually a tailwind.

Alternative Route: Lake Eacham
7.4km

Lake Eacham is a great place for a swim or a picnic and there's a 4.5km walk around the lake. Saw-shelled turtles and water dragons are common.

At 3.6km take the right turn signed to Malanda and Lake Eacham. Turn left after 50m, again following signs to Lake Eacham. To return, backtrack 300m from the lake's edge and veer right on the road signed to Cairns (Wrights Creek Rd). Go right when you hit the highway.

Side Trip: Cathedral Fig Tree
11.5km

Is it worth pedalling 11.5km over hilly terrain, three of those on dirt, just to see another tree? The Cathedral Fig Tree makes an impression that outlasts the extra leg pain. This banyan, or green fig, is immense. The network of roots that support it has a girth of 43m. The canopy, 50m overhead, has the same area as two Olympic swimming pools, and the limbs support epiphyte colonies the size of small cars.

To get there, turn left on Boar Pocket Rd (13.8km) and follow it for 5.7km, the last 1.5km of which are good dirt.

Melbourne to the Gold Coast

From Victoria's Snowy Mountains to the golden sands of Queensland's resort capital, Surfers Paradise, the East Coast Explorer travels Australia's most populous region: the coast beside the Great Dividing Range.

Despite the romanticised notion of the Outback as the 'real' Australia, the overwhelming majority of Australians live in urban areas on the country's coastal fringe – and most of them in the east. For cyclists, this means plenty of towns, from tiny hamlets to glitzy tourist towns and busy regional centres, and three major cities: Melbourne, Sydney and Brisbane. Among them, there's opportunity to mingle with all manner of Australians – laconic farmers and fishers, tanned and tousled surfers, suburban mums and dads, and 'round-Oz-in-a-caravan' retirees.

The ride begins on Phillip Island, southeast of Melbourne. A brief flirtation with the south coast ends with a parting glance at Wilsons Promontory, and the cold waters of Bass Strait are jilted as the route – in the manner of many Victorians in winter – heads north to bask by the Pacific.

The main inland foray heads through Gippsland's coal-mining and farming regions before climbing over the Australian Alps – within a few hours' ride of Mt Kosciuszko (2228m), the country's highest peak.

East of the Divide, the ride rolls through the green, cow-pocked hills of the New South Wales (NSW) southern cheese district to the coast. If you're not yet acquainted with that recreational bastion of Australian life – the beach – you soon will be: apart from two brief inland stretches, the Tasman Sea (South Pacific Ocean) sits at your right hand all the way to Queensland.

Unfortunately for cyclists another great bastion of Australian life is the motor car and, with it, highway travel. While the east coast is more generous than much of Australia in its offering of quiet, scenic roads, it also hosts greater traffic volumes on Hwy One (known in the south as the Princess Hwy; the Pacific Hwy north of Sydney), sections of which are unavoidable on the route.

However the highway is avoided at times, by taking the ferries which bridge coastal inlets, including the obligatory crossing of Sydney Harbour on a Manly ferry.

Thirty-one days are recommended to do the ride's 2320km – which, incidentally, covers less than half of Australia's east coast: it's another 2750km from Brisbane to Queensland's northern tip, Cape York. The ride's average daily distance is 75km; four days are 50km or less, while three just tip over 100km.

HISTORY

The east coast has long been a popular cycling route. In 1893, the first north-to-south crossing of the continent was made (although the route was predominantly inland on this occasion). Riding between Sydney and Brisbane or Sydney and Melbourne was common – though again, not necessarily via the route in this book. Sydney to Melbourne, for example, was often covered more directly, via what is now the Hume Hwy. Touring in the Alps was also very popular with cyclists from Sydney and Melbourne. (See the History of Cycling in Australia section in the Facts about Australia chapter.)

NATURAL HISTORY

Except when crossing the Great Dividing Range – the highest parts of which could almost be called subalpine – the route stays by the coast, occasionally deviating into the foothills.

The traverse of the Divide begins in the Strzelecki Ranges, featuring temperate rainforest, and after a return to the lowlands climbs again through partially forested foothills. Through the Alpine and Kosciuszko National Parks, dry sclerophyllous forest is punctuated by stands of white cyprus pine alongside the Snowy River. North of Jindabyne are the Monaro's rolling grassy plains.

The NSW coastal stretch has considerable diversity. The lovely sclerophyllous coastal heath typical of the southern areas gives way to lusher subtropical vegetation north of Coffs Harbour. You'll see plenty of mangrove-fringed inlets along the north-east coast – there's an excellent interpretive walk at the Coffs Harbour Botanic Gardens. Between Port Stephens and Forster is a network of coastal lakes, sealed off from the ocean thousands of years ago. A little further north are the wide rivers of the floodplain.

There's a variety of wildlife to be seen. Don't miss the penguin colony at Phillip Island at the very beginning. Keep your eyes peeled along the coast for dolphins, even whales (from July to November). Pedal softly through the Strzeleckis and you might encounter (or at least hear) lyrebirds: the masters of mimicry whose repertoire has been known to include chainsaws and mobile phones. The male's lyre-shaped tail is magnificently displayed during courtship. Other birds include pelicans, eagles, kookaburras, cockatoos, rosellas, magpies and gulls. Sharp eyes are not so necessary for spotting the ubiquitous kangaroos, wallabies and brushtail possums; snakes and lizards are also relatively common. Less widespread are koalas and wombats, inhabiting only specific areas.

CLIMATE
Starting in temperate Victoria, the ride crosses into NSW via the Australian Alps (where the weather is far less predictable than in lower-lying areas) and ends in subtropical southern Queensland.

Broadly, the climate becomes warmer (and a little more humid) as the ride progresses, the one exception being the higher, cooler section through the Alps (Days 6–9).

Climate is discussed in further detail in the relevant regional chapters.

INFORMATION
Maps
To see the whole route, you'll need a map such as the NRMA's (NSW's motoring organisation; ☎ 13 2132) *South East Australia*

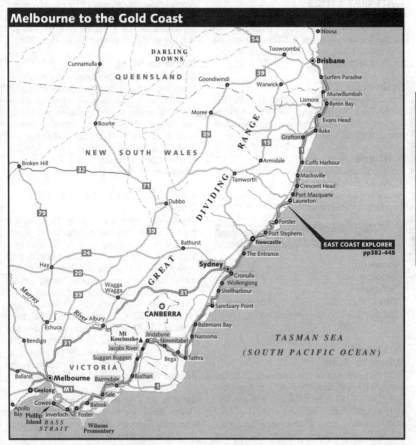

Melbourne to the Gold Coast

EAST COAST EXPLORER
pp382–448

TASMAN SEA
(SOUTH PACIFIC OCEAN)

MELBOURNE TO THE GOLD COAST

(1:1,800,000); it's free to members or $5 from NRMA outlets. Needless to say, the detail isn't great; and a number of roads on the route are not shown. For navigational purposes, the best bet is to use the smaller-scale maps produced by state automobile associations (in NSW, there's also the series of free Cartoscope tourist maps). For topographical information, the Auslig Natmap series (1:250,000) is useful. See the Maps sections of relevant regional chapters for details.

INFORMATION SOURCES

The ride takes in three states – Victoria, NSW and Queensland – information sources for which can be found in the relevant regional chapters.

GATEWAY CITIES
Melbourne

See the Gateway Cities section (pp164–66) of the Victoria chapter for information on accommodation, other services and getting to/from Melbourne.

Sydney

See the Gateway Cities section (pp115–19) of the New South Wales chapter for information on accommodation, other services and getting to/from Sydney.

Brisbane

See the Gateway Cities section (pp329–32) of the Queensland chapter for information on accommodation, other services and getting to/from Brisbane.

East Coast Explorer

Duration	31 days
Distance	2319.9km
Difficulty	hard
Start	Cowes, Victoria
End	Surfers Paradise, Qld

PLANNING
When to Ride

Different sections of the ride vary as to the best (and worst) times to ride. The Alps section (Days 6–9) is best ridden between December and March, before the onset of cold weather (and snow). Conversely, the northern NSW and southern Queensland section

is best avoided during this period, which is its most humid. Traffic and holiday crowds – at their worst from mid-December through January, Easter and on long weekends – are also important to take into account. Expect higher-than-listed accommodation prices during school holidays and long weekends, particularly along the NSW coast.

A good option is to begin the ride from Victoria around late February/early March, when the summer heat through Gippsland lessens, but there's little chance of snow through the mountains; the holiday crowds disappear from the east coast beach towns; and by the time you reach the north, it's April/May – still great for the beach, but not too humid.

Avoid cycling Days 7 to 9 from June to August, when roads may be blocked by snow.

Consider scheduling rest days to avoid travelling on busy highway stretches (or staying at tourist towns) on weekends.

What to Bring

Some extended dirt sections make mountain bikes the best choice (though not essential) for this ride. Camping equipment, food supplies and water-purifying tablets are highly recommended for the remote and strenuous section (Days 7–9) between Buchan and Jindabyne (see the 'Warning' boxed text in that section): camping is the only accommodation option for Days 7 and 8.

GETTING TO/FROM THE RIDE
Cowes

Train From Melbourne, take the suburban train to Frankston and transfer to the Stony Point line. The Zone 1, 2 & 3 fare costs $5.50 one-way (plus $2.70 for bikes during peak hours: 7am–9am and 4pm–6pm). For train times contact Bayside Trains (☎ 13 1638, ☐ www.baysidetrains.com.au).

The train links with Inter Island Ferries' (☎ 03-9585 5730, ☐ www.interislandferries .com.au) Phillip Island service. Fares are $7.50 one-way and $2 for the bike. The 30-minute trip runs twice daily (8.30am and 5pm), with a noon service on Tuesday, Thursday and weekends and a 7pm Friday service.

Bicycle To join this ride from The Great Ocean Road ride (see the Victoria chapter), ride from Torquay (Day 5) to Queenscliff. It's 37km via Barwon Heads: take Torquay

Rd north and follow the signs. A regular ferry service (☎ 03-5258 3244) runs between Queenscliff and Sorrento. Ride across the beautiful Mornington Peninsula from Sorrento to Stony Point (66km): take the Point Nepean Rd to Rosebud and then follow the C777 (Boneo Rd/Rosebud–Flinders Rd) to Stony Point, via Flinders. Stony Point has a caravan park. See the Train section for details on the ferry to Cowes.

Surfers Paradise

The simplest option to Brisbane is via train from Nerang. Cycling along the busy Pacific Hwy to Brisbane is not recommended.

Train It's a 10km ride from Surfers Paradise to Nerang train station, from where the City-train (☎ 13 1230) semi-express service to Brisbane takes 65 minutes ($7.80). Bikes are free but restrictions apply in peak hours.

The route from Surfers to the train station is mapped on Day 31 of the ride. Head north from the mall on the Esplanade to the next left, Elkhorn Ave, following it through various name changes until turning left on Camellia Ave at 3.1km. Heeb St (3.2km) is closed to through traffic, but on a bike you can cut through the closed section and continue to the true end of Heeb St. At 5.2km, turn right onto Ashmore Rd, then left onto Ross St 400m on. Nerang–Broadbeach Rd is a right turn at 7.2km and from there the navigation is straightforward; follow the 'Nerang Station' signs.

THE RIDE
Cowes (Phillip Island)
☎ 03

The main town on Phillip Island, Cowes is predominantly a holiday town with the population swelling during the peak holiday season from January to Easter. But the holiday homes and caravan parks are unobtrusive and during the off-peak season Cowes has a lovely atmosphere.

Look out for seals playing in the water on the ferry from Stony Point.

Information The visitor centre (☎ 1300-366 422, 🖳 www.phillipisland.net.au) is at Newhaven (28.2km on the Day 1 route); however, accommodation can be booked by email or phone. Maps and information are available at most accommodation places.

The post office is at 77 Thompson Ave. The Commonwealth and ANZ banks, in Thompson Ave, have ATMs.

The Cowes Sports Store (☎ 5952 3178), Thompson Ave, sells tubes and puncture-repair kits. The bike shop Ride on Bikes (☎ 5956 7740), 24 Boys Home Rd, Newhaven (opposite the skate park), is the only place on the island to do repairs.

Things to See & Do Cowes is a base to explore Phillip Island, where Grand Prix motorcycling meets nature tourism.

The major attraction is the **Penguin Parade**. Every evening little (fairy) penguins gather on the shore of Summerland Bay before waddling to their nests on the cliffs. It's quite a sight, attracting more than half a million people a year. In high season, you may need to book at the visitor centre or the Phillip Island Nature Park (☎ 5956 8300, 🖻 penguins@penguins.org.au); admission costs $12.50. Although it is possible to cycle to the Penguin Parade (see the Day 1 map), the return trip in the dark along a busy, narrow road can be dangerous. Duck Truck Tours (☎ 5952 2548, 🖻 amaroo@waterfront.net.au) runs trips from the youth hostel; the $22 price includes admission.

The Nature Park also runs the **Koala Conservation Centre**, the **Seal Rocks Sea Life Centre** and **Churchill Island**; discount passes to all four venues are available.

The beaches around Cape Woolamai are renowned for their **surf**; the quieter ones on the north coast have excellent **swimming**.

Places to Stay & Eat Accommodation can be scarce and expensive during peak periods. The busy, friendly *Amaroo Park Caravan Park (☎ 5952 2548, 97 Church St)* is an associate YHA hostel. Dorm beds cost $21, doubles cost $24 per person and tent sites, $11 per person. Breakfast and dinner are also available.

The *Isle of Wight Hotel (☎ 5952 2301, 9 The Esplanade)* faces the bay and has reasonable motel rooms from $71.50 a double.

The 1880s *Rhylstone Park B&B (☎ 5952 2730, 190 Thompson Ave)* is well away from the crowds of Cowes and has elegantly restored rooms. Prices start from $110 per double. The owner is happy to arrange transport (including for bikes) from the Penguin Parade.

MELBOURNE TO THE GOLD COAST

The *Phillip Island Bakery (cnr Thompson Ave & Chapel St)* is open from 7am and the licensed *IGA* supermarket *(cnr Settlement Rd & Thompson Ave)* opens until 10pm.

A number of restaurants on The Esplanade have beautiful views across the bay. A great place for breakfast from 7am is *Madcowes Cafe & Foodstore (☎ 5952 2560, 4/17 The Esplanade)*. The *Clock Cafe by the Bay (☎ 5952 2856, 4 The Esplanade)* serves large breakfasts from 7.30am; its vegetarian noodle dishes are great for cyclists. Pasta and pizza is available from *Cafe Terrazo (☎ 5952 3773, 5 Thompson Ave)*.

Day 1: Cowes to Inverloch
4–7 hours, 74km

Follow the Gippsland coastline through the historic coal-mining area around Wonthaggi. The cycling is easy, giving ample time to enjoy side trips to The Nobbies, Churchill Island and the State Coal Mine. The Hub Bicycle Centre (☎ 5672 1415), 7 McBride Ave, Wonthaggi, is the last bicycle shop before Sale (Day 4).

The road to **The Nobbies** (see Side Trip 1) affords fine views of the Mornington Peninsula. Cross Phillip Island on a rollercoaster road, passing the **Grand Prix motor-racing circuit** and its **museum**.

The turn-off to **Churchill Island** (see Side Trip 2) at 27.2km is just before Newhaven and The Narrows bridge to San Remo (29.5km). From here, enjoy superb views of Western Port Bay to the north, and of the surf crashing along the coastline from Phillip Island to Cape Paterson.

At Kilcunda (40.2km), spanning Bourne Creek, is a large **trestle bridge**. This is a relic of the railway, now being converted into a rail trail, which transported coal from Wonthaggi to Melbourne. At the **No 20 Coal Mine** (49.4km), 13 miners were killed when a shaft collapsed in 1937; however, operations continued until 1962.

Wonthaggi (53.8km), once the busy centre of the black-coal-mining industry, is now a quiet service town with *accommodation*, *cafes* and a large *supermarket*.

The **State Coal Mine** (turn off at 55.4km) is Victoria's last black-coal mine. The mine closed in 1968 but now has a **museum** and hourly **tours** to the coalface.

The **Cape Paterson** side trip provides an alternative stopover; the lovely *camping ground* (☎ 5674 4507) has views across rocky beaches to the surf, and there's a *tavern* and *cafe*.

The coast road from Cape Paterson to Inverloch follows the cliff tops, with views to Cape Liptrap and, in the distance, Wilsons Promontory. Closer, spectacular coastal formations, such as the basalt stack of the **Eagles Nest** (67.4km), and beaches and rock pools can be explored. This section of coast is famous for the discovery of **dinosaur bones**.

Side Trip 1: The Nobbies
10km

The Nobbies and **Seal Rocks** are eroded remnants of basalt flows. Seal Rocks boast the remaining fur seal colony in Victoria, a sad reminder that in the early 19th century sealers decimated the population in the area.

The **Seal Rocks Sea Life Centre** claims to be 'the Zoo of the Future'. Seals can be viewed via a TV/laser beam link and the history of exploration of the coast can be obtained through a virtual 'Voyage' of discovery. It also has a *cafe* and *restaurant*.

Away from the piped muzak which surrounds the Sea Life Centre are **boardwalks** and, depending on the season, it is possible to walk to The Nobbies.

A gravel road leads from The Nobbies car park around the east coast of the peninsula. Along this flat road, with sweeping views down the coast, it is possible to quietly appreciate the surrounding landscape. The route passes the **Penguin Parade** complex (see the Cowes Things to See & Do section); you're unlikely to see penguins during the day, but the museum can be visited.

Side Trip 2: Churchill Island
10km

In 1802 James Grant, exploring the southern coast of Victoria, settled on Churchill Island, built a small cottage and planted crops. Even though the site was abandoned soon after, the island is renowned for having the first farm in Victoria.

Access is via a small bridge which can be covered in extremely high tides.

A bikepath around the island passes a stand of rare 400- to 500-year-old **Moonah trees** *(Melaleuca lanceolata)*, some excellent **short walks** to look at the **bird life**, and a number of **historic buildings**.

See the best of Australia on the East Coast Explorer ride: see the little penguins at Phillip Island; detour to the wild beaches of magnificent Wilsons Prom National Park; explore Gippsland's rural idyll; walk in the rainforest of the tiny, exquisite Tarra-Bulga National Park; and swim in the famous Snowy River...

MARK KIRBY

RICHARD I'ANSON

PETER HINES

...explore the bays and inlets of the New South Wales coast (St Georges Basin, Jervis Bay); cross Sydney Harbour on one of the famous ferries; then beach hop your way to Surfers Paradise, tourism mecca and the hub of Queensland's Gold Coast.

Day 1: Cowes to Inverloch

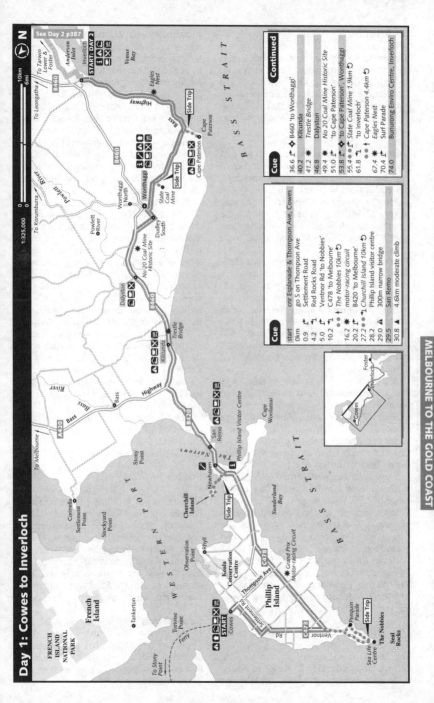

MELBOURNE TO THE GOLD COAST

Cue		
start		cnr Esplanade & Thompson Ave, Cowes
0km	↱	go S on Thompson Ave
0.9	↱	Settlement Road
4.2	↰	Red Rocks Road
5.0	↱	Ventnor Rd 'to Nobbies'
10.2	↱	C478 'to Melbourne'
16.2	●	*The Nobbies 10km* ↻
20.2	✱	*motor-racing circuit*
27.2	●	B420 'to Melbourne'
28.2	●	Phillip Island visitor centre
29.0	●	*Churchill Island 10km* ↻
29.5		300m narrow bridge
30.8		San Remo
		4.6km moderate climb

Cue		
36.6	↱ ◇	B460 'to Wonthaggi'
40.2		Kilcunda
41.2		Trestle Bridge
46.8		Dalyston
49.4		No 20 Coal Mine Historic Site
51.0	↱	'to Cape Paterson'
53.8	◇	'to Cape Paterson', Wonthaggi
55.4	● ↱	*State Coal Mine 1.9km* ↻
61.8	↰	'to Inverloch'
67.4		Eagles Nest
70.4	↱	Surf Parade
74.0		Bunurong Enviro Centre, Inverloch

Continued

Inverloch
☎ 03

This small holiday town, spread out around the entrance to Andersons Inlet, is perfect for swimming and fishing. The South Gippsland Conservation Group runs the **Bunurong Environment Centre** (☎ 5674 3738), which has a **shell museum**, brochures on walks and can arrange tours to the dinosaur dig.

Information The visitor centre (☎ 5674 2706) is in the council offices, corner of A'Beckett and Reilly Sts (open weekdays, closed between noon and 1pm).

Most shops are in A'Beckett St. The post office, 12 William St, is an agent for the Commonwealth Bank. The National Bank is at 3 A'Beckett St but has no ATM.

Places to Stay & Eat The *Inverloch Holiday Park (☎ 5674 1447, Cuttriss St)*, at the east end of town, has shaded sites from $22 and cabins from $70. It also manages the adjacent *Foreshore Camping Reserve*, which has tent sites close to the beach for $15.

The *Inverloch Central Motor Inn (☎ 5674 3500, 32–34 A'Beckett St)* has clean, basic rooms from $82.50 double. It is quiet and close to town.

A'Beckett St has a number of *takeaways* and a *supermarket (5 A'Beckett St)* that opens daily.

Slightly out of town, *The Kiosk Cafe (☎ 5674 3611, The Boulevard)* has fantastic views of the beach and surf (open for breakfast and lunch from 8am, and for dinner from Thursday to Saturday).

The *Esplanade Hotel* (☎ 5674 1432, cnr A'Beckett St & The Boulevard) has a good range of typical pub food.

In the eastern section of town, the *Rippleside Cafe-Bar (☎ 5674 3066, cnr The Esplanade & Cuttriss St)* has meals and great desserts (closed Monday).

Bistro Blue (☎ 5764 3339, 23 A'Beckett St) has main courses, mainly seafood, from $17, plus an excellent vegetarian curry for $15 (open Wednesday to Saturday). Booking is essential.

Day 2: Inverloch to Foster
4–7 hours, 75.7km

The ride across the coastal plains around Inverloch crosses the Hoddle Range to Foster. It features stunning views of Wilsons

Promontory and **Waratah Bay**, one of Victoria's most beautiful beaches. To extend the trip, an overnight stop at Walkerville is recommended. There are few shops on this ride, so you must carry sufficient food and water.

The road skirts Anderson Inlet to Tarwin Lower (21.1km), noted for its fishing and birdlife, which can be seen from the **boardwalk** along the Tarwin River. At the turn-off to the Cape Liptrap lighthouse (40km), magnificent views stretch back to Phillip Island and east to Wilsons Promontory. The road to the lighthouse is corrugated and sandy – and isn't recommended for loaded touring bikes.

The beach at **Walkerville** (a side trip at 43.1km) is reached after a steep 2km descent through beautiful forest. It is hard to imagine that Walkerville was once one of the busiest towns in Gippsland, manufacturing quicklime for Melbourne's booming building industry. It is now a beautiful, quiet spot; the *camping reserve* (☎ 5663 2224) has tent sites, on-site vans and a *kiosk* with very limited supplies. A short walking track visits the historic **lime kilns** at Walkerville South.

The gently undulating road travels alongside the **Cape Liptrap Coastal Park** before heading inland across green hills to **Fish Creek** (a side trip at 62.5km), where you should sample the enormous Devonshire teas at *The Flying Cow Cafe* (open Wednesday to Sunday).

The climb over the Hoddle Range passes a **lookout** with stunning views of Wilsons Promontory and Corner Inlet before a magical descent into Foster.

Foster
☎ 03

Nestled in the foothills of the Strzelecki Ranges, close to Wilsons Promontory, Foster is a small service town for south Gippsland and it has most facilities. Foster was one of the few areas in south Gippsland where gold was mined and some excellent photographs from the gold-mining days can be seen at the **museum** next to the **Stockyard Gallery and Craft Shop**, which sells lovely local craft.

Information The visitor centre (☎ 5682 1125) in the Stockyard Gallery (open Thursday to Saturday) has good maps and information. If closed, lists of accommodation and activities are posted on the notice board outside.

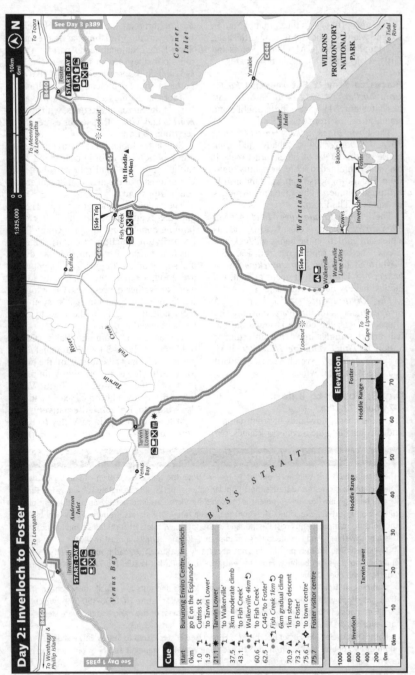

Day 2: Inverloch to Foster

MELBOURNE TO THE GOLD COAST

Elevation

Cue		
start		Bunurong Enviro Centre, Inverloch
0km		go E on the Esplanade
1.0	↰	Cuttriss St
1.9	↳	'to Tarwin Lower'
21.1	✳	Tarwin Lower
37.5	▲	3km moderate climb
43.1	↱	'to Fish Creek'
	↳	⟳ Walkerville 4km
60.6	↱	'to Fish Creek'
62.5	↳	C445 'to Foster'
	●	⟳ Fish Creek 1km
70.9	▲	6km gradual climb
73.2	▼	1km steep descent
75.6	↳	'to Foster'
75.7	◇	'to town centre'
	↰	Foster visitor centre

The post office is on the corner of Station Rd and Main St. The Commonwealth Bank, 27 Main St, has an ATM. Glenns Sports and Gifts, 41 Main St, has basic bike spares.

Places to Stay & Eat The quiet *Foster Caravan Park (☎ 5682 2440, 38 Nelson St)* has sites for $11/15 a single/double and standard cabins from $50.

The *Foster Backpackers Hostel (☎ 5682 2614, 17 Pioneer St)* is a shady mud-brick house on the banks of Stockyard Creek. It has self-contained double or family units from $50, dorm beds from $17, and a fully equipped kitchen. The manager arranges transport to The Prom.

The *Wilsons Promontory Motel (☎ 5682 2055, 26 Station Rd)* is close to town and has a pleasant garden on the banks of Stockyard Creek. The basic rooms cost from $60/85.

Main St has two *supermarkets* and a *bakery (18 Main St)* that opens at 7am; it's the last bakery before Rosedale (Day 4).

The Rhythm Cafe (☎ 5682 1612, 3/5 Bridge St) opens for lunch and morning and afternoon teas; the coffee is great and the fish entertaining! Almost the only dinner option is *The Exchange Hotel (☎ 5682 2377, 43 Main St)*, which serves standard pub fare with local wines.

Day 3: Foster to Balook
4–7 hours, 72.7km
Leave the coastal lowlands of south Gippsland and head into the Strzelecki Ranges. On a 37km dirt road, the climbing is challenging but rewarding, finishing at the exquisite Tarra-Bulga National Park. Apart from a *cafe* at Balook, there are no stores between Toora (13.5km) and Gormandale (Day 4) so it is important to have sufficient food and drink.

Toora is a quiet, charming town, at the base of the Strzelecki Ranges, with a *supermarket* and a *hotel* that serves espresso coffee from 10am.

Stop at the **lookout** (15.2km) on the steep climb out of Toora for gobsmacking views to the south. The road follows rolling hills characteristic of the high country all around south Gippsland.

The sealed road ends at Wonyip (31.9km) and the road winds up through cleared farming country and joins the **Grand Ridge Rd** at **Ryton Junction** (40.3km). Much of this land is used for commercial hardwood and softwood plantations. The distant views are good, even if the immediate logged areas are rather depressing. A few logging trucks use this road but it is easy to hear them coming – get off the road to avoid being encased in dust.

The section from **English's Corner** (49.3km) to **Tarra-Bulga National Park** is perhaps the most beautiful of the whole route, with towering eucalypts lining the road. At the turn-off to Tarra Valley (68.3km) the road becomes sealed and gently winds to Balook. Alternatively, turn right for camping at Tarra Valley (see Side Trip and Balook Places to Stay & Eat).

Cycling Wilsons Promontory

The granite peaks of Wilsons Promontory tower above the flat, coastal plain of South Gippsland. This peninsula is one of the state's most popular national parks; affectionately known as The Prom, its emphasis on low-key development is treasured by Victorians who fiercely opposed recent plans to develop resort-style facilities. The Prom features a range of habitats, from mangrove colonies in the north to rainforest and coastal heathland in the south, with lots of secluded swimming beaches. It is a bushwalker's and wildlife lover's paradise and, if time permits, a must to visit.

Cycling to The Prom is possible but not necessarily pleasant. The road is exposed and at weekends and holidays can be busy. From the entrance to the Park it is 30km to Tidal River, including a lengthy climb over Darby Saddle.

Camping at Tidal River is the best option as the lodges and huts are usually fully booked. Tidal River has shops with basic supplies (no alcohol) and a visitor centre (☎ 1800-350 552), which has excellent maps of the region. Cycling is not permitted in most of the park, and there are steep fines for being caught. But a bike is a great way to get to the start of walks.

Rather not cycle? The Foster Backpackers Hostel (see Foster Places to Stay & Eat) will drive a minimum of two people to The Prom for $15 each one way. The manager also hires out camping gear (even a backpack) and fits bikes in her van.

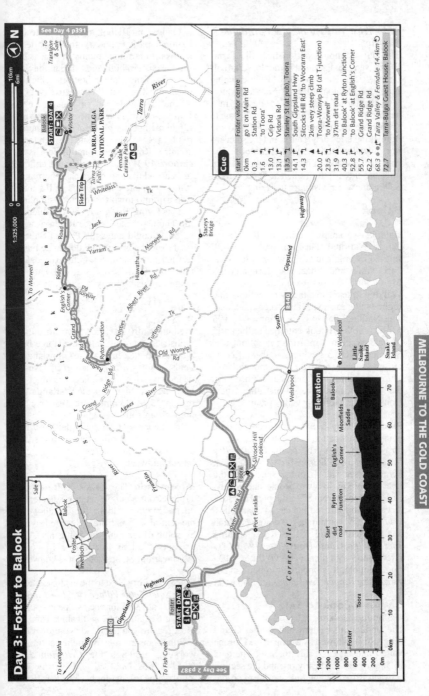

Day 3: Foster to Balook

See Day 4 p391

MELBOURNE TO THE GOLD COAST

1:325,000

| | 0 | 10km |
| | 0 | 6mi |

N

See Day 2 p387

TARRA-BULGA NATIONAL PARK

Tarra-Bulga National Park

To Traralgon & Sale

To Morwell

To Leongatha

To Fish Creek

Cue

start	Foster visitor centre
0km	go E on Main Rd
0.3	Station Rd
1.6	'to Toora'
13.0	Grip Rd
13.1	Victoria Rd
13.5	Stanley St (at pub), Toora
14.1	South Gippsland Hwy
14.3	Silcocks Hill Rd 'to Woorara East'
	2km very steep climb
20.0	Toora-Wonyip Rd (at T-junction)
23.5	'to Morwell'
31.9	37km dirt road
40.3	'to Balook at Ryton Junction
52.8	'to Balook at English's Corner
55.7	Grand Ridge Rd
62.2	Grand Ridge Rd
68.3	Tarra Valley & Ferndale 14.4km
72.7	Tarra-Bulga Guest House, Balook

Elevation

```
m
1400
1200
1000
 800
 600
 400
 200
  0m
     0km   10        20        30        40        50        60        70
    Foster      Toora   Start      Ryton      English's   Moorfields  Balook
                        dirt road  Junction   Corner      Saddle
```

Side Trip: Tarra Valley & Ferndale
14.4km

The only camping option near the Tarra-Bulga National Park is at **Ferndale**, 7.2km off Grand Ridge Rd. The road to the camping ground (see Balook Places to Stay & Eat) follows the Tarra River; while the descent may be fast, the slower climb back allows time to appreciate the **rainforest** and listen to the mimicking cries of **lyrebirds** and the screeching of **yellow-tailed black-cockatoos**. The entrance to **walks** in the Tarra Valley is 3km after the side trip turn-off. The **Tarra Falls** at 3.5km are worth visiting after rain.

Balook
☎ 03

Balook is a small locality next to Tarra-Bulga National Park, a park recently formed by amalgamating two smaller ones: Tarra Valley and Bulga. They form an oasis of Victoria's most exquisite rainforest. **Walking tracks** link the two sections and night walks are especially recommended. The National Park Visitor Centre (☎ 5196 6166) is at the Balook entrance to the park; it has excellent information about the Strzelecki Ranges which, if the office is closed, can be read through the window. Maps of walking tracks can be obtained from the visitor centre, the Tarra-Bulga Guest House and at the Tarra Valley picnic area.

Places to Stay & Eat You need to choose your accommodation before the Tarra Valley turn-off (68.3km). The pretty *Tarra Valley Caravan Park & Tearooms (☎ 5186 1283)* at Ferndale (see Side Trip) has sites along the river from $13 for two people and lovely, basic log cabins from $50 a double. The kiosk serves Devonshire tea and has basic supplies.

One of few remaining guest houses which once dotted Grand Ridge Rd, charming *Tarra-Bulga Guest House (☎ 5196 6141)* offers B&B with dinner (BYO) for $67/125 single/double. It is important to book in advance. The *Balook Tea Rooms* are also here.

Day 4: Balook to Sale
4–8 hours, 83.4km

The undulating eastern end of the Grand Ridge Rd is followed by a drop to the Latrobe Valley and an easy ride to Sale. There is 15.5km of dirt road early on, and the section between Rosedale and Sale can be exposed.

On leaving Balook, the route follows the national park boundary for a while then opens into farming country. It is possible to see the eastern highlands and, in the valley, the Loy Yang Power Station, which produces most of Victoria's electricity.

The unsealed road finishes at 16.9km, followed by a descent to **Gormandale** (25.6km) and its *general store*. The quiet roads to Rosedale undulate through farming country. Rosedale is famous for its **train station** (49.1km), with its bizarre collection of bears, dolls and other paraphernalia the station manager has salvaged. It's a short side trip into town for lunch or supplies.

The **Swing Bridge** at the confluence of the Thomson and Latrobe Rivers was built so boats could enter the Port of Sale. The road from the bridge to Sale can be busy, as traffic from Yarram, Seaspray, Rosedale and the Gippsland Lakes National Park converge on this highway.

Sale
☎ 03

Predominantly a service town for the local industries – gas, oil and the airforce base – Sale is also the centre of the Gippsland Wetlands, a sprawling collection of lakes and waterways that are home to many waterbird species. Maps for the **Wetlands Walk** through **Sale Common** are available from the visitor centre.

It's a friendly town with plenty of places to stay and eat. Unlike tourist towns, however, accommodation (especially motels) is busier midweek.

Information The visitor centre (☎ 5144 1108, ℮ toursale@i-o.net.au), 8 Foster St, is on the highway, about 1km south-west of the central shopping area. Head to Raymond St, south of the mall, for banks and ATMs. Friendly Mallard Cycles (☎ 5144 6566), 89 Macarthur St, has good local knowledge.

Places to Stay Next to the visitor centre, the clean *Sale Motor Village (☎ 5144 1366)* has tent sites at $8/14 for one/two people, on-site vans at $35 a double, and cabins from $61. Most require you to provide your own linen.

Pub rooms are mostly pitched at transient workers, although the *Criterion Hotel (☎ 5144 2031, cnr York & Macalister Sts)* is refurbishing to cater for backpackers. Expect

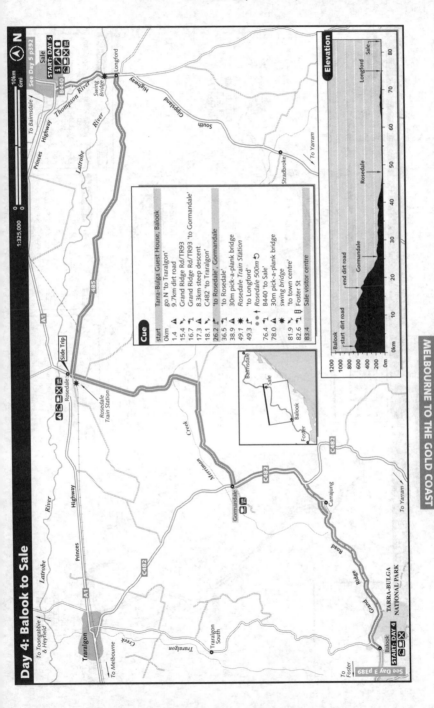

Day 4: Balook to Sale

N 1:325,000

See Day 5 p392

START DAY 5 Sale

MELBOURNE TO THE GOLD COAST

Cue

start	Tarra-Bulga Guest House, Balook
0km	go N 'to Traralgon'
1.4	9.7km dirt road
15.4	Grand Ridge Rd/TR93
16.7	Grand Ridge Rd/TR93 'to Gormandale'
17.3	8.3km steep descent
18.1	C482 'to Traralgon'
26.2	'to Rosedale' Gormandale
36.5	'to Rosedale'
38.9	30m pick-a-plank bridge
49.7	Rosedale Train Station
49.3	'to Longford'
	Rosedale 500m
76.4	B440 'to Sale'
78.0	30m pick-a-plank bridge
81.9	swing bridge
82.6	'to town centre'
83.4	Sale visitor centre

Elevation

Balook — start dirt road — end dirt road — Gormandale — Rosedale — Longford — Sale

START DAY 4 See Day 3 p389

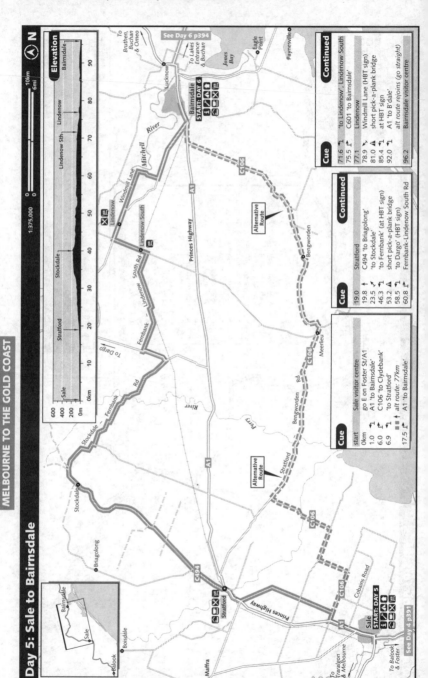

MELBOURNE TO THE GOLD COAST

Day 5: Sale to Bairnsdale

Elevation

Sale	Stratford	Stockdale	Lindenow Sth	Lindenow	Bairnsdale

Cue	
start	Sale visitor centre
0km	go E on Foster St/A1
1.0	A1 'to Bairnsdale'
6.0	C106 to Clydebank'
6.9	'to Stratford'
	alt route: 77km
17.5	A1 'to Bairnsdale'

Cue	
19.0	Stratford
19.8	C494 'to Briagolong'
23.5	'to Stockdale'
46.3	'to Fernbank' (at HBT sign)
53.2	short pick-a-plank bridge
58.5	'to Dargo' (HBT sign)
60.8	Fernbank-Lindenow South Rd

Continued	

Cue	
71.6	'to Lindenow, Lindenow South
75.5	C601 'to Bairnsdale'
77.1	Lindenow
78.9	Windmill Lane (HBT sign)
81.0	short pick-a-plank bridge
	at HBT sign
85.4	A1 'to B'dale'
92.0	alt route rejoins (go straight)
96.2	Bairnsdale visitor centre

Continued	

Alternative Route

Alternative Route

See Day 6 p394

See Day 4 p391

Bairnsdale
START: DAY 6

Sale
START: DAY 5

to pay around $15 in basic dorms and $25/35 for singles/doubles (kitchenette only).

The *Midtown Motel* (☎ *5144 1444, 91 York St*) has a pool and plain but good rooms from $65/71.50. The *Sale Motel* (☎ *5144 2744, 271 York St*) has similar rooms from $55/65.

For an atmospheric treat, the gracious 1860s *Bon Accord B&B* (☎ *5144 5555*) is Sale's oldest habitable house, set in lovely gardens. Stay inside or in the rustic 'Old Schoolhouse' or 'Milk Separator Room', which have been beautifully converted into comfortable, en suite bedrooms. B&B is $121/154.

The *Creek B&B* (☎ *5144 4426, 3 Foster St*), opposite the visitor centre, offers self-contained accommodation in a three-bedroom Californian bungalow. It costs $85 per room, including continental breakfast, or $160 for the whole house.

Places to Eat The *Country Bakehouse* is one of two bakeries on Raymond St, south of the mall. In the Gippsland Centre, off the mall, *Coles* supermarket opens late, daily.

With groovy artwork, *Catchadeli House* (☎ *5143 1911, 192 Raymond St*) advertises 'filling stuff', including pasta and crepes from $11 (closed Monday). For Asian food, *Gippsland Dragon* (☎ *5144 7088*), at the mall's western end, charges around $9.50 for most mains. In the takeaway strip, *Sale Pizza & Pasta House* (☎ *5144 4775, 251 York St*) has a good selection. The smoke-free Gaslight Bistro at *The Gippy Hotel* (☎ *5144 4003, cnr York & Cunninghame Sts*) has pasta from $8 and meat mains from $11.80. Bar meals are a bargain at $4.

A chic, licensed espresso bar, *Post* (☎ *5144 3388, cnr Foster & Raymond Sts*) has modern cuisine on the pricey side, but the coffee is good, as is breakfast ($5–10; open 9.30am–9pm weekends).

Day 5: Sale to Bairnsdale
5–9½ hours, 96.2km

This day offers two alternatives, but the Stockdale route is the prettier – if not the most direct – way to Bairnsdale. It's predominantly via quiet roads, joining the Howitt Bicycle Trail (HBT) at Stockdale locality (40.2km), then following it most of the way to Bairnsdale. A shorter, flat alternative route is also described.

Avoid highway traffic 6km north of Sale by travelling via quiet and flat local roads to Stratford (19km). Services, including *cafes*, a *bakery* and *store*, are the last (including water) until Lindenow South (71.6km).

From Stratford the road undulates gently, approaching the foothills of the Great Dividing Range with a long, gradual climb through attractive, dry eucalypt forest, to Stockdale. Thereafter, the country opens out, with pleasant, gently undulating farmland to Bairnsdale.

After Lindenow South, the road drops to the fertile valley of the Mitchell River. Lindenow (77.1km), the largest village on the route, has a **scenic lookout** over the valley.

After the fields of vegetables on the river flats, the road climbs briefly and eventually rejoins the Princes Hwy at West Bairnsdale.

Alternative Route: To Bairnsdale
77km

To conserve energy for the tough ride through the mountains (Days 6–9), go via the localities of Meerlieu and Bengworden. Remain on the C106 when the main route turns off it at 6.9km, then follow the C106 as it turns left (13km), right (16km), left (18km), and then right (25km) onto the Stratford–Bengworden Rd. Continue for 45km, turning right at the Princes Hwy, 7km west of Bairnsdale.

Bairnsdale
☎ 03

See Bairnsdale (p211) in the Across the High Country ride in the Victoria chapter for information about accommodation and other services. Bairnsdale is the end point for that ride, a journey through alpine country.

Day 6: Bairnsdale to Buchan
4½–7½ hours, 78.1km

As you head towards the mountains, riding becomes reasonably strenuous, though increasingly pretty, with the second half of the route mostly amid forest. After Nicholson (10.3km), the only services are at **Bruthen** (a side trip at 30.2km). This pleasant little spot has a **store**, **bakery** and a **pub** serving meals.

With a sealed shoulder (albeit rough, at times), traffic is not too worrying during the first 12km. Once off the Princes Hwy, there's little traffic, but some undulation on the attractive Tambo Upper Rd, which crosses a couple of small valleys.

MELBOURNE TO THE GOLD COAST

MELBOURNE TO THE GOLD COAST

Day 6: Bairnsdale to Buchan

Elevation

Bairnsdale · Tambo River · Bruthen – Nowa Nowa Road · Buchan Road · Buchan

▲ Mt Little Dick (319m)

1:375,000

See Day 7 p396

Buchan   START DAY 7

To
Suggan Buggan
& Jindabyne

C608

Bogey Creek

Harris Creek

Mt Nowa Nowa ▲

Nowa Nowa   Boggy Creek

Nowa Nowa Road

Nowa Road

Princes Highway

Lake Tyers

Lakes Entrance

Kalimna West

BASS STRAIT

Bruthen

B500   Wiseleigh   C620   Side Trip

Tambo Upper

Tambo Upper Rd

Swan Reach

Metung

Lake King

Lake Victoria

Lakes Entrance

Stephensons Rd

Johnsonville

Nicholson

Nicholson River

Princes Highway

Eagle Point

Paynesville

B500   Lucknow

Bairnsdale   START DAY 6

To Sale &
Melbourne

See Day 5 p392

Cue

start		
0km		Bairnsdale visitor centre
		go E on Main St
2.4	↰	A1 'to Lakes Entrance'
10.3	◈	Nicholson
12.6	◀	'to Tambo Upper'
13.8	◀	1.1km gradual climb
15.6	◀	300m moderate climb
17.7	◀	10m pick-a-plank bridge
	◀	1.1km moderate climb
23.5	◀	30m pick-a-plank bridge
23.6	↰	Tambo Upper Rd (no sign)
26.9	◀	1.3km gradual climb
30.2	↲	C620 'to Buchan'
	•	2.5km moderate climb
	↱	Bruthen 4km ↰
33.1	◀	2.4km moderate climb
49.3	◀	400m moderate climb
50.6	↘	C608 'to Buchan'
54.6	◀	2.2km moderate climb
58.0	◀	1.7km hard climb
78.1		Buchan General Store

0   10km
0   6mi

N

Things warm up a little on the rolling C620/Bruthen–Nowa Nowa Rd (30.2km), beginning with around 5km of fairly steady climbing. Although relatively light at the time of research, traffic on this road includes some fast log trucks. It's to become the main heavy vehicle route in 2003; however, the new shoulder is wide and smooth.

After the Buchan turn-off (50.6km), climbing out of Boggy Creek (54.6km) and Harris Creek (58km) is hard work. There's nothing too taxing after that and the final descent is a welcome, picturesque end to the day.

Buchan
☎ 03

The last town until Jindabyne, 176km away, Buchan is a pretty village, settled around the Buchan River. It's chiefly known for the spectacular **limestone caves** in the reserve west of town.

Information The Buchan General Store (☎ 5155 9202), Main St, offers limited tourist information (closes at 1pm on weekends).

The Parks Victoria office (☎ 5155 9264; open 9am–4pm daily,) in the Caves Reserve, has information about the reserve and the general area. The post office opposite the store is a Commonwealth Bank agent.

Things to See & Do Don't miss **Buchan Caves Reserve**, an enchanting spot with **walking tracks**, kangaroos, a **swimming pool** fed by an underground spring, and a timeless air. Guided **cave tours** run daily. It's also possible to explore undeveloped caves in the area. Contact Parks Victoria for permission and advice on guides.

Other activities around Buchan and the Snowy River National Park include rafting, horse riding, walking, mountain biking, fishing and abseiling. Ask at the Parks Victoria office for more information.

Places to Stay & Eat A tent site at the *Buchan Caves Campground (☎ 5155 9264, Caves Rd)* in the Caves Reserve costs $11 for one to three people. Self-contained cabins cost from $50.50 – BYO linen.

Warning

⚠ Between Buchan and Jindabyne you're in remote country. After the few, limited services north of Buchan, a handful of cars (if that) is likely to be the only human activity for more than 100km. Make sure your bike is in good working order, carry tools and spares, a tent, water-purifying tablets, plus three days' of food. Travel with a friend if possible and should you break down, *don't* leave the road – a passing vehicle is your only chance of avoiding a looong walk.

Having said that, the ride is a highlight of Australian cycling. A tough 176km section, with some long climbs and 78km of unsealed road, it travels through classic Australian mountain wilderness within the beautiful Alpine and Kosciuszko National Parks, and alongside the legendary Snowy River – on what, incredibly, was once the main route south from Sydney.

Despite the unsealed surface, it's a reasonably good road, best tackled on a mountain bike (but manageable on touring and hybrid bikes). The section can be covered in two days, breaking at Suggan Buggan. However, we recommend taking three, breaking again at Jacobs River, to properly enjoy the area – and rest before the final tough leg.

Camping areas in the national park have pit toilets, fireplaces and tables. Water, available from rivers, should be filtered or sterilised before drinking. *Don't* use fire or stoves during fire-risk conditions; check the fire status with a local before entering the area.

The only services in this section are within 69km of Buchan: *Karoonda Park* (☎ 5155 0220), 40km north of Buchan at Gelantipy, is a youth camp and horse-riding ranch, with YHA-hostel and motel accommodation. Dorm beds cost $22, hostel doubles $27 per person, and motel doubles $55 each; and you can order good-value meals. It also offers group activities such as rafting and abseiling, and has a limited store. Local advice is not to rely on the *Seldom Seen Roadhouse* (55km), which infrequently has basic supplies. More welcoming is *Springs* (☎ 5155 0263), at 69km, which has coffee and light refreshments most days, offers B&B accommodation ($50/90), plus a self-contained, gas-powered stone cottage ($27.50 per person). Meals are available by arrangement. The adjacent Eagle Loft gallery displays local arts and crafts.

Day 7: Buchan to Suggan Buggan

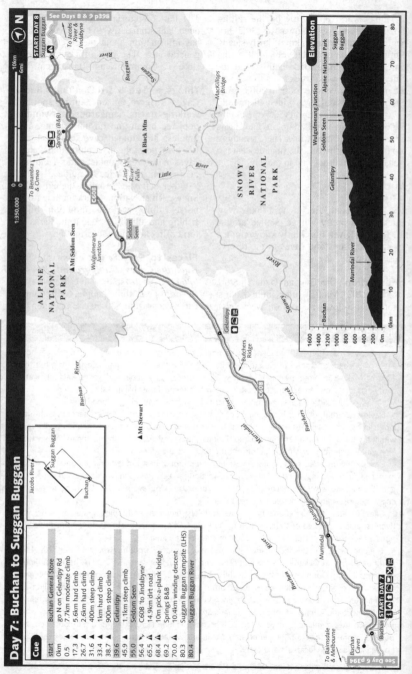

Cue

start		Buchan General Store
0km		go N on Gelantipy Rd
0.5	▲	
17.3	▲	7.7km moderate climb
26.7	▲	5.6km hard climb
31.6	▲	2.6km hard climb
33.4	▲	400m steep climb
38.7	▲	1km hard climb
39.6		900m steep climb
45.9	▲	Gelantipy
55.0		1.1km steep climb
56.4	↘	Seldom Seen
65.5	▲	C608 to Jindabyne'
68.4	▲	14.9km dirt road
69.2		10m pick-a-plank bridge
70.0	▲	Springs B&B
80.3		10.4km winding descent
80.4		Suggan Buggan campsite (LHS)
		Suggan Buggan River

START: DAY 8
Suggan Buggan

To Jacobs
River &
Jindabyne

Buggan River

Springs (B&B)

To Benambra
& Omeo

Little River Falls

Little River

MacKillops Bridge

▲Mt Seldom Seen

C608

Wulgulmerang Junction

Seldom Seen

▲Black Mtn

S N O W Y   R I V E R

N A T I O N A L   P A R K

Gelantipy

Butchers Ridge

▲Mt Stewart

C608

Snowy River

Buchan River

Murrindal River

Butchers Creek

Murrindal

Gelantipy Rd

Buchan River

START: DAY 7
Buchan

Buchan Caves

To Bairnsdale
& Melbourne

See Day 6 p394

See Days 8 & 9 p398

1:350,000

0 — 10km
0 — 6ml

Elevation

Buchan — Murrindal River — Gelantipy — Seldom Seen — Wulgulmerang Junction — Alpine National Park — Suggan Buggan

1600
1400
1200
1000
800
600
400
200
0m

0km 10 20 30 40 50 60 70 80

Jacobs River

Suggan Buggan

Buchan

The *Buchan Lodge Backpackers* (☎ 5155 9421, Saleyards Rd), just across the river, is spacious and well run, and has dorm beds for $17.

Buchan Motel (☎ 5155 9201, Main St), 500m uphill behind the store, has great views. Singles/doubles cost $50/61.

Buchan Valley Log Cabins (☎ 5155 9494, Main Rd), 300m north of the river, offers self-contained accommodation (including bedding and laundry) from $60/77; meals are by arrangement.

The small *General Store* is the last reliable chance for supplies before Jindabyne. For takeaway, try the *Buchan Valley Roadhouse* (☎ 5155 9484). *Willow Cafe* serves delicious home-made pies and other mains from $6.50 every night (doesn't open late). Across the road, the *Caves Hotel* serves meals from 6pm to 7.30pm (8.30pm Friday and Saturday).

Day 7: Buchan to Suggan Buggan
5½–8½ hours, 80.4km
The climb out of the Buchan Valley sets the tone for this day: it's predominantly up – though it's not gut-bustingly steep. The quiet road carries some trucks in the first half, but after Wulgulmerang Junction

(56.4km) it's virtually deserted. The road is sealed until the final 14.9km.

After a drop and a couple of false starts, the climbing starts again in earnest at the Murrindal River (17.3km), with little relief for 9km. By Gelantipy (39.6km), the hardest slog is over, though the road continues to roll all day. The final 10km is an exhilarating and wonderfully scenic descent through the Alpine National Park, the unfolding mountains an indication of the height gained over the day.

The official Suggan Buggan *camp site* is just before the river, but for a more secluded spot, cross the river and, at the School House sign, turn right and follow the dirt track for 240m (in front of the house) to the river.

Day 8: Suggan Buggan to Jacobs River
3–4½ hours, 40.8km
After Day 7's thrilling descent, the only way out is up – at least to begin with. The climb to Monaro Gap (3.9km) is the toughest for the day – despite the sealed road. Enjoy the views before a steepish, unsealed descent and some short climbs through the beautiful, open forest of white cypress pine.

MELBOURNE TO THE GOLD COAST

The Wild Snowy River – Forever Tamed?

Rising within sight of Mt Kosciuszko, the Snowy River once carried thundering high-country meltwater across southern NSW and eastern Victoria to the sea near Orbost. But the Snowy Mountains Hydro-Electric Scheme, an ambitious post-WWII engineering project to provide electricity and irrigation water, has changed the river forever. Since the 1960s, about 99% of the Snowy River's average natural flow has been captured at Jindabyne Dam and pumped west of the Great Divide into the Murray and Murrumbidgee River systems.

Below Jindabyne, the Snowy is today a small, weed-infested stream meandering along a wide, sandy river channel. Changes to the river and surrounding environment are profound. Siltation has reduced populations and diversity of fish and other animals, altered vegetation and allowed weeds to take hold. Reduced flows near Orbost allow seawater to intrude many kilometres upstream from the river mouth, affecting local landholders.

After years of lobbying by people of the Monaro in NSW and the Orbost district in Victoria, the Federal and New South Wales and Victorian State Governments formed an independent panel to assess the river's condition and suggest ways to improve it. The panel's 1996 report recommended increasing flows at Jindabyne from the current annual average of about 1% to a minimum of 28% of natural flows.

In 1998, the Snowy Water Inquiry began investigating ways to satisfy the requirements of all stakeholders – Snowy region landholders, the hydro-electric scheme (owned by NSW, Victorian and Federal governments, but likely to be privatised), Murray and Murrumbidgee River irrigators, and conservationists. In late 2000, the Victorian and NSW state governments pledged to increase the flow to 21% over the following decade. However, it's unclear whether the flow will be extended to the 28% level required to redress environmental damage.

Days 8 & 9: Suggan Buggan Jacobs River Jindabyne

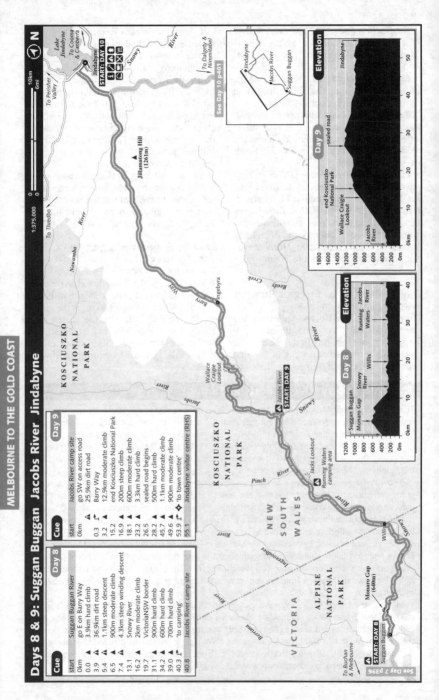

1:375,000

0 — 10km
0 — 6mi

N

Cue | Day 8

0km		Suggan Buggan River
0.0	◣	go E on Barry Way
3.9	◣	3.9km hard climb
5.4	◣	36.9km dirt road
6.5	◣	1.1km steep descent
7.4	◣	900m moderate climb
13.1		4.3km steep winding descent
16.2	◣	Snowy River
19.7	◣	2km moderate climb
31.1	◣	Victoria/NSW border
34.2	◣	900m hard climb
39.0	◣	600m hard climb
40.3	↳	700m hard climb
40.8		'to camping'
		Jacobs River camp site

Cue | Day 9

start		Jacobs River camp site
0km	△	go SW on access road
0.3	↳	25.9km dirt road
3.2	◣	Barry Way
15.2	◣	12.9km moderate climb
16.9	◣	end Kosciuszko National Park
18.1	◣	200m steep climb
23.2	◣	600m moderate climb
26.5		3.3km hard climb
28.2	◣	sealed road begins
45.7	◣	500m hard climb
49.6	◣	1.1km moderate climb
53.9	↳	900m moderate climb
55.1	⬦	'to town centre'
		Jindabyne visitor centre (RHS)

Elevation | Day 8

Suggan Buggan
Monaro Gap
Snowy River
Willis
Running Waters
Jacobs River

Elevation | Day 9

Jacobs River
Wallace Craigie Lookout
end Kosciuszko National Park
sealed road
Jindabyne

See Day 10 p401

START: DAY 10

Jindabyne

To Perisher Valley
To Thredbo
To Cooma & Canberra
Lake Jindabyne
Snowy River
To Dalgety & Nimmitabel

Jilamatong Hill (1261m)

KOSCIUSZKO NATIONAL PARK

Nowamba River
Barry Way
Ingebyra
Reedy Creek
River

Wallace Craigie Lookout

Jacobs River

START: DAY 9

Snowy River

Jacks Lookout
Running Waters camping area

Pinch River
River

KOSCIUSZKO NATIONAL PARK

NEW SOUTH WALES

Ingeegoodbee River

Willis

Snowy River

VICTORIA

ALPINE NATIONAL PARK

Monaro Gap (640m)

Berrima River

To Buchan & Melbourne

START: DAY 8
Suggan Buggan

See Day 7 p396

After descending to the Snowy River – broad, shallow and begging to be swum in – things remain relatively strenuous until Willis, at the Victoria–NSW border (19.7km). The Snowy is followed to its junction with Jacobs River, with gentle undulations heating up a little after *Running Waters camping area* (30.9km). Seven designated *camping areas* lie between Willis and Jacobs River; then there's nothing until Jindabyne. The pleasant *Jacobs River* camping area is 200m off the road, by the river.

Day 9: Jacobs River to Jindabyne
3½–6 hours, 55.1km

Three kilometres into this section is a good reason to break the journey at Jacobs River: around 15km of (almost) solid climbing. Cooler and shadier in the morning, the climb from Jacobs River has a fairly gradual gradient and the views just keep getting better; seeing the road far below is a reward for all that effort. At 12.8km is **Wallace Craigie Lookout**, 2.4km beyond which the countryside opens out, as Kosciuszko National Park is left for grazing country. The road undulates some more – the highest point (1343m) is reached at 26.5km after a tough 3.3km climb. From here the road is sealed and, despite a couple of short ups, it's comparatively easy. Towards Jindabyne are a few more homesteads and a little traffic, but it's still pretty quiet.

Jindabyne
☎ 02

The Snowy region's principal tourist town is also one of its newest – at least in this location. Old Jindabyne disappeared under the waters of Lake Jindabyne when, in the 1960s, the Snowy River was dammed as part of the Snowy Mountains Hydro-Electric Scheme. 'New' Jindabyne is a neat, busy town of about 2000 permanent residents, but it swells to more than 20,000 during the ski season.

Information The impressive visitor centre (☎ 6450 5600) is on Kosciusko Rd in the centre of town. It's in the same building as the regional National Parks and Wildlife Service headquarters (and is run by the NPWS), providing information on accommodation and a variety of attractions as well as those in Kosciuszko National Park.

The long-established Paddy Pallin shop (☎ 6456 2922, e paddys@jindabyne.snowy .net.au) near the Thredbo turn-off has a range of bicycle spares, rents mountain bikes and does repairs (open daily). Most of the major banks have branches (with ATMs) in the Nugget's Crossing commercial centre, just west of the visitor centre. The post office is behind Nugget's, fronting Gippsland St.

Things to See & Do As a gateway to the Snowy Mountains, Jindabyne is something of an adventure-sport destination. In summer, people flock to the region for **bush walking, camping, horse riding, fly fishing, mountain biking, abseiling, rock climbing** and **whitewater rafting**. The visitor centre has contact details for the many operators. The main winter attractions are **skiing** and **snowboarding** (although winter is a bit chilly to be cycling through the region and roads may be closed by snow).

A lovely lake-front **bikepath** runs for about 3km from Bay St (near the bowling club) to Snowline Caravan Park. There, Snowline Boat Hire (☎ 6456 2099) rents power boats and three-person canoes. To explore the lake with less effort, take a **cruise** on the MV Kalinga (☎ 6456 1195). There's a **cinema** (☎ 6450 5609) at the visitor centre and a heated **swimming pool** at Nugget's Crossing.

The three-day **Kosciuszko High Country** mountain-bike ride starts in nearby Perisher Valley (see the New South Wales chapter).

Places to Stay The *Jindabyne Holiday Park (☎ 6456 2249, Kosciusko Rd)* offers the closest camping to the centre of town; a site (for two people) costs $15. If you're cycling in a group, on-site vans here are a bargain in summer – as little as $35 for a five-berth van.

The *Snowy Mountains Backpackers (☎ 6456 1500, e backpackers@snowy.net .au, 7–8 Gippsland St)*, near Nugget's Crossing, has dorm beds for $22.50 and double rooms with/without en suite for $50/70; it's brilliantly equipped – cafe, laundry, Internet access etc – and also offers B&B or dinner and B&B packages.

Jindabyne's variety of hotel, motel, lodge and apartment accommodation is staggering and its (multi-season) price structure confusing. The *Alpine Resort Travel Centre (☎ 6457 1124 or ☎ 1800-802 315, Nugget's Crossing)* is the best place to begin inquiries.

The *Jindy Inn* (☎ 6456 1957, 18 Clyde St) offers great value in summer – a room to yourself (with linen) costs from \$20. The Jindy has a self-catering kitchen, laundry facilities, and is a hop from the town centre. In the middle of town, the *Lake Jindabyne Hotel/Motel* (☎ 6456 2203 or ☎ 1800-646 818, Kosciusko Rd) does B&B in summer from \$65 for singles (much cheaper if you're sharing).

Places to Eat You're unlikely to go hungry in this town, whatever the season. *Supermarkets* are in both the 'old' shopping centre and at Nugget's Crossing; the latter, *IGA*, is the biggest, and is near the visitor centre.

Wilfred's (☎ 6457 2111), in the visitor centre, serves all-day breakfasts, burgers and intriguing dinners such as trout sushi. At Snowy Mountains Plaza, try *Angie's Italian Kitchen* (☎ 6456 2523) for pasta and *Walita's Coffee Shop* for hot drinks and cakes. At Nugget's Crossing, *Il Lago* (☎ 6456 1171), facing Snowy River Ave, and *Bacco's* (☎ 6456 1420, Shop 10) do pasta and pizza. *Noodles Cafe* (☎ 6457 1130, Snowy River Ave) does tasty laksa and stir-fried noodles from \$11. Head to *Chit Thai* (☎ 6456 2052, Snowline Caravan Park) for Thai curries.

Day 10: Jindabyne to Nimmitabel

6–7 hours, 82km

After a few days of huge, grinding climbs, it's something of a relief to tackle this rolling day in the Monaro high country. Bring enough water for the stretch from Dalgety (34.8km) to Nimmitabel, as there are no shops. Late in the day is a good 17km dirt road.

If it's tackled midweek, the route to Dalgety is quiet and there's plenty of time to take in the rural sights. The climb to the top of Guys Range passes isolated paddocks dotted with sheep and somewhat ratty-looking gum trees; just before the descent (starting at 17.8km) come the first views of the wide Monaro tableland.

The Monaro, a vaguely defined region stretching from south of Canberra to nearly the NSW–Victoria border, is characterised by natural grasslands at about 1000m altitude. It's very open country, prone in winter to frosts and occasional snowfalls, and raked by southerly and south-westerly winds. It's prime fine-wool sheep country

and, just before Dalgety, the **Ag Barn** (33.1km; ☎ 6456 5102) provides a chance to see a shearing demonstration. Dalgety straddles the banks of the once mighty Snowy River – now, tragically, a rather shallow and disappointing stream (see the boxed text 'The Wild Snowy River – Forever Tamed?', earlier).

There's an exhilarating feeling of isolation after Dalgety, especially once the route turns onto the dirt section at 53.1km. This is classic Monaro country – wide vistas with the Snowy Mountains in the distance, sheep (and the odd jumble of granite boulders) in paddocks and, almost always, wind-bending pasture grass. Frequent pauses to enjoy the views are recommended – shortly the route will descend to the coast and hug it for most of the way to Queensland.

Nimmitabel

☎ 02

There's a lot of spirit about this quiet stop on the Snowy Mountains Hwy. Nimmitabel is only 37km south of Cooma, the regional centre, but the two are worlds apart. It's tiny, quiet and friendly, with a nice pub and an easy-going air. The local point of interest is the **Old Mill**, built in the 1860s by a German settler and restored in the 1960s. Nimmitabel itself dates back to the 1840s.

Information The Royal Arms Guest House (☎ 6454 6422) and Anything Goes store (☎ 6454 6372), both on Bombala St/Snowy Mountains Hwy, are good sources of local and regional information. The Nimmitabel General Store (☎ 6454 6237), Bombala St, is also the post office and a Commonwealth Bank agent.

Places to Stay & Eat The delightfully casual *Nimmitabel Caravan Park* (☎ 6454 6484, Bombala St) is on the way to Cooma; sites cost \$5/7 for one/two people. The friendly *Tudor Inn* pub (☎ 6454 6204, Bombala St) is good value for \$25/40 per single/double; it's also a fair place for dinner, with classic pub counter meals at rock-bottom prices. The *Royal Arms Guest House* (☎ 6454 6422) is pricier, with B&B at \$53/93, while the small *Nimmitabel Motel* (☎ 6454 6387, Snowy Mountains Hwy) has rooms for \$46/57; both serve evening meals.

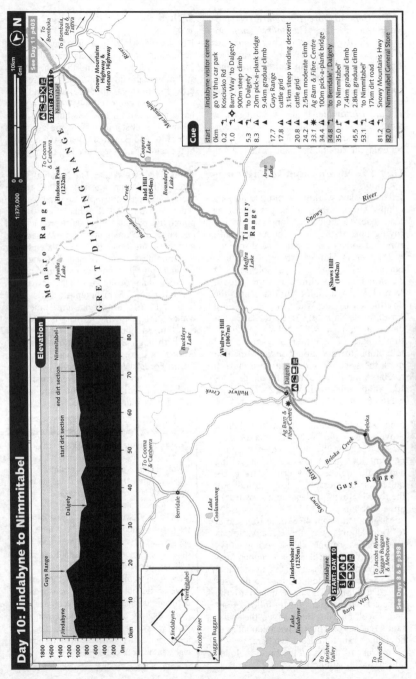

Day 10: Jindabyne to Nimmitabel

Cue		
start		Jindabyne visitor centre
0km	↱	go W thru car park
0.2	↰	Kosciusko Rd
1.0	◇	'Barry Way to Dalgety'
	◄	900m steep climb
5.3	↱	'to Dalgety'
8.3	◄	20m pick-a-plank bridge
	◄	9.4km gradual climb
17.7		Guys Range
17.8	⊞	cattle grid
	◄	3.1km steep winding descent
20.8	⊞	cattle grid
24.2	◄	2.5km moderate climb
33.1	✳	Ag Barn & Fibre Centre
34.4	◄	100m pick-a-plank bridge
34.8	↰	'to Berridale' Dalgety
35.0	↱	'to Nimmitabel'
45.5	◄	7.4km gradual climb
53.1	◄	2.8km gradual climb
	↰	'to Nimmitabel'
81.2	↱	17km dirt road
82.0		Snowy Mountains Hwy
		Nimmitabel General Store

Elevation — Day 10: Jindabyne to Nimmitabel

Jindabyne Guys Range Dalgety start dirt section end dirt section Nimmitabel

MELBOURNE TO THE GOLD COAST

The **General Store** *(Bombala St)* can provide basic groceries. The **Bakery Shop**, opposite the Royal Arms *(Snowy Mountains Hwy)*, is open very early. It's a great place for breakfast, morning coffee and other meals, all of which can be enjoyed with local radio in the background – whoever said Rick Astley is gone forever?

Cafe Inimitable, in the Anything Goes store, is good for breakfast and lunch Thursday to Monday and dinner on Friday and Saturday; try the home-made pasta ($9.50).

Day 11: Nimmitabel to Tathra
7–8 hours, 103.4km

After this day, working at altitude on long climbs will be a thing of the past: the route leads back to the coast, along the way enjoying one of the ride's longer downhill runs and some of its prettiest rural scenery.

Another 15.5km of dirt opens the day, but it's easy going and very pleasant. At 16.3km the road climbs towards **Brown Mtn** (1390m), a high point that marks the confluence of the Wadbilliga and South East Forests National Parks – the latter, declared in January 1997, NSW's 100th national park. The rather ugly radio and telephone towers atop Brown Mtn also mark the start of the descent: near enough to 20km, the first 2.5km of it on a delightful, smooth dirt road. At the 28.7km mark is **Fred Piper Lookout**, a perfect spot to take in the view across the verdant Bega Valley (and to rest your braking hands). Fred Piper drove a bus on the Bega to Cooma route six days a week for 28 years; he died at a point near the lookout in 1947 while shovelling a path through a snow drift. Care is required on the descent below the lookout; the road is rough in places and slow trucks are a problem.

Mogilla Rd (from 46.8km to Candelo at 67.1km) shows why the Bega Valley is renowned as 'rolling'. This is prime dairying country (Bega Cheese is a famous Australian brand) that has a reliable rainfall and lush pastures – quite a contrast to the usually dry Monaro. From Candelo to the Princes Hwy the route mostly follows Candelo Creek and the Bega River, the wide, sandy reaches of which leave no doubt as to how much rain tumbles down here.

Be wary of traffic on the Snowy Mountains Hwy into Tathra.

Tathra
☎ 02

Best known for its historic wharf, Tathra is becoming more popular as a holiday town for city folk from the north, although it's still mostly the domain of the more relaxed crowd from Bega, about 12km inland.

The visitor centre (☎ 6494 4062), a fairly basic affair with a few brochures, is at the wharf. The post office is at the corner of Wharf Rd and Beach St. There are no banks, but several businesses have Eftpos facilities.

Things to See & Do The National Trust-listed **Tathra Wharf** was built in 1862 for the then-vital coastal supply steamer service (known as the 'Pig & Whistle' as it transported live pigs, as well as dairy products and passengers). A small **Maritime Museum** is upstairs in the wharf building. **Water sports** – swimming, surfing, diving and fishing – are popular; you'll often see fisherfolk practically shoulder-to-shoulder on the wharf.

A pleasant 2.5km **bikepath** leads north from Tathra to Mogareka and some nice **walks** start in town: the best is probably the 9km Kangarutha Track, which leads south through **Bournda National Park** to Wallagoot Lake. A 3km loop goes through **Tathra Forest Wildlife Reserve**, home to a variety of furry and feathered Australian animals, including the lyrebird and threatened glossy black-cockatoo.

The East Coast Price Hike

When you hit the New South Wales coast, get ready for beautiful beaches, sunny days and – if you're riding during the Christmas school holidays (mid-December to late January), Easter holidays or on long weekends – a big jump in accommodation prices.

In hugely popular Byron Bay, a caravan park we've listed as charging $17 for a tent site for two charges $30 during school holidays. What's more, many coastal-town parks only take week-long bookings over the holidays, making things tough for the passing traveller. It's not only the caravan parks or big-name destinations where you'll feel the pinch. As early on as Tathra, for example, a motel will charge $135 for a standard double in January, a significant hike from the normal high-season price of $83.

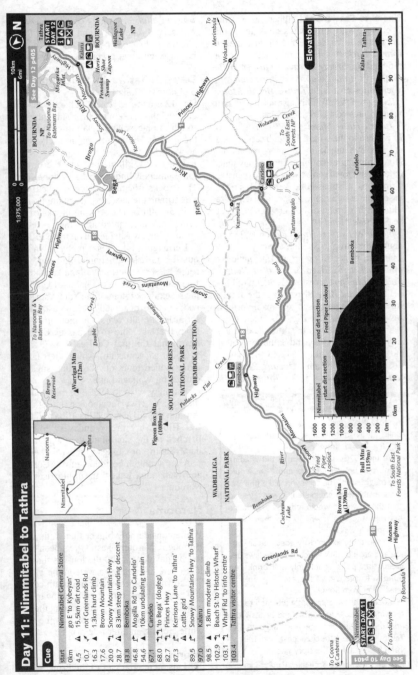

Day 11: Nimmitabel to Tathra

Cue		
start		Nimmitabel General Store
0km		go E 'to Kybeyan'
4.5	◄	15.5km dirt road
10.7	◄	*not* Greenlands Rd
16.3	◄	1.3km hard climb
17.6	◄	Brown Mountain
20.0	↱	Snowy Mountains Hwy
28.7	◄	8.3km steep winding descent
43.8		Bemboka
46.8	↳	Mogilla Rd 'to Candelo'
54.6	◄	10km undulating terrain
67.1		Candelo
68.0	↱↱	'to Bega' (dogleg)
82.7	↳	Princes Hwy
87.3	↳	Kerrisons Lane 'to Tathra'
	◄	cattle grid
89.5	↳	Snowy Mountains Hwy 'to Tathra'
97.0		Kalaru
98.5	◄	1.8km moderate climb
102.9	↱	Beach St to Historic Wharf'
103.1	↱	Wharf Rd 'to info centre'
103.4		Tathra visitor centre

MELBOURNE TO THE GOLD COAST

Places to Stay & Eat Campers have plenty of choice, with three parks on Andy Poole Dr. In the town centre are *Tathra Beach Tourist Park* (☎ 6494 1302), with sites for $16, and *Seabreeze Caravan Park* (☎ 6494 1350, e info@seabreezetathra.com.au), where sites cost $19; *Tathra Beach Motor Village* (☎ 6494 1577) is just north and a bit quieter; sites cost $16 and cabins, $48.

Tathra Hotel Motel (☎ 6494 1101, Bega St) is close to the wharf. The pub serves food and has live music in summer; rooms are $40/65 for singles/doubles. The holiday units dotted about town can be wickedly expensive during the Christmas-holiday period but quite reasonable at other times, especially if you're riding with a friend or in a group. Rooms at the *Surfside Motel* (☎ 6494 1378, cnr Andy Poole Dr & Francis Hollis Dr) cost $135 in January, but drop to $83 in February.

On the route, stock up at *McCormacks supermarket (32 Bega St). Tathra Bakery (Andy Poole Dr)* serves a decent cup of coffee. The *Ocean Blue Brasserie* at the Tathra Hotel has filling meals at reasonable prices. Down at the wharf, the *Pig 'n' Whistle Cafe* (☎ 6494 4062) serves breakfast and lunch daily and dinner Friday and Saturday; you'll find great seafood in the $12 to $15 range. Closer to the beach, *Ocean Paradise Restaurant* (☎ 6494 1280; Tathra Beach

Of Roads, Bends & Beers

A story that's entered far-south-coast lore brilliantly illustrates a small-town solution to a silly legal conundrum.

In the 1920s, it was decided the winding 12mi road between Tathra and Bega would be straightened. The surveyors did a fine job: when plans were completed, it was revealed that the new road would reduce the distance between the two towns to less than 10mi. Brilliant. Or was it?

At this time, so the story goes, the charming and arcane NSW liquor-licensing laws decreed that pubs could only sell drinks on Sunday to 'genuine travellers' – people at least 10mi from home.

Road plans were promptly returned to the drawing board, a few twists and bends were added, and the distance from Bega to the Tathra pub was stretched past that thirsty, 10mi barrier. Or so the story goes...

Bowling Club, cnr Andy Poole Dr & Dilkera Rd) serves Asian food and *Mimosa Rocks Restaurant* (☎ 6494 1483, Andy Poole Dr) has tasty gourmet pizzas from $12.

Day 12: Tathra to Narooma
6–7 hours, 78.8km

Day 12 is a mixed bag, with the first half including about 12km of dirt road that can be rough in places. At 58.9km, the route joins the Princes Hwy – the major artery in this neck of the woods.

Just a few kilometres into the day the route enters **Mimosa Rocks National Park**. The 'rocks' themselves are reached via a side trip on the unsealed Aragunnu Rd (turn right at 24km). The striking blocks of volcanic rock are named after the vessel *Mimosa*, which was wrecked on them in 1863.

Bermagui (44km) is a pretty town famous for its fishing. About 10km north, the route passes beautiful **Wallaga Lake**, also a fine fishing spot and the home of Umbarra, the black duck totem of the Yuin Aboriginal people, who occupied these coastal lands for at least 6000 years. On the climb away from the lake, the route passes **Umbarra Aboriginal Cultural Centre** (☎ 4473 7232, e umbarra@acr.net.au), which offers fascinating guided tours of Aboriginal sites and cruises on Wallaga Lake.

You may wish to take a 3km detour off the Princes Hwy (at about 61km) to ride through the villages of **Tilba Tilba** and **Central Tilba**, very pretty and very touristy, perched on the side of striking Mt Dromedary (806m), or Gulaga to the Yuin people.

After a stretch beside beautiful Corunna and Nangudga Lakes, the route rises into Narooma.

Narooma
☎ 02

While considerably bigger than Tathra and Bermagui, Narooma hasn't (yet) been overrun by developers and the tourists that follow them, and retains a welcoming charm. The town occupies one of the south coast's most attractive settings, on Wagonga Inlet, and its main-street pubs rate among the best places south of Sydney to take in the view while sipping an after-ride drink.

Information The visitor centre (☎ 4476 2881) is on the flat part of the Princes Hwy

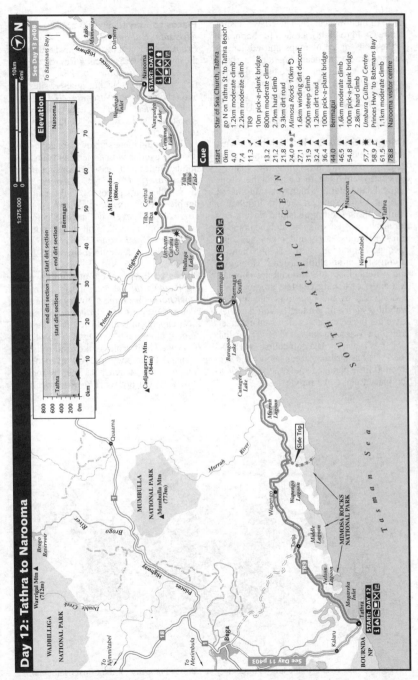

Day 12: Tathra to Narooma

Elevation

Cue

start		Star of Sea Church, Tathra
		go N on Tathra St to 'Tathra Beach'
4.0	▲	1.2km moderate climb
7.4	▲	2.2km moderate climb
11.3	↗	TR9
13.2	▲	10m pick-a-plank bridge
21.2	▲	800m moderate climb
21.8	▲	2.7km hard climb
24.0 ●●↰		9.3km dirt road
27.1	▲	*Mimosa Rocks 10km* ↩
31.9	▲	1.6km winding dirt descent
32.4	▲	500m steep climb
36.4	▲	1.2km dirt road
44.0		100m pick-a-plank bridge
46.5	▲	Bermagui
54.8	▲	1.6km moderate climb
57.7	✳	100m pick-a-plank bridge
58.9	↰	2.8km hard climb
61.5	▲	Umbarra Cultural Centre
78.8		Princes Hwy to Batemans Bay'
		1.1km moderate climb
		Narooma visitor centre

MELBOURNE TO THE GOLD COAST

SOUTH PACIFIC OCEAN

Tasman Sea

north of the town centre. The NPWS visitor centre (☎ 4476 2888), a touch further north, is the best source of maps and advice for visits to the several nearby national parks or nature reserves. The big banks all have branches with ATMs on Wagonga St (the Princes Hwy). Go to Narooma Squash & Fitness Centre (☎ 4476 4821), 8 Hopkins Place, for bicycle spares.

Things to See & Do The **Lighthouse Museum** at the visitor centre has interesting displays covering local maritime history, especially anything to do with the Montague Island light, which was automated only in 1986. You can see the lighthouse while visiting **Montague Island Nature Reserve**, about 10km offshore and the home of fairy penguins, seals and many sea bird species; book tours at the NPWS centre. **Diving** and **snorkelling** around Montague and waters closer to Narooma are popular. A number of **fishing charters** are available and several of the operators run **whale-watching** tours in winter. If you'd rather leave the finned creatures alone, take a quiet cruise on Wagonga Inlet and River on the *Wagonga Princess*. The **golf course** (☎ 1800-105 000) has striking ocean views and the **cinema**, little changed since the 1920s, is a fun place to take in a movie.

Places to Stay Camp sites are $20 at *Easts Riverside Holiday Park* (☎ 4476 2046, *Princes Hwy*), near the takeaway food strip in the north of town. *Surfbeach Resort* (☎ 1800-762 275, *Ballingalla St*), near Narooma Beach, is further out but quieter; sites cost $16. The renovated *Narooma YHA* (☎ 4476 4440, 8 Princes Hwy) is getting good reports. A standard bed costs $18; double and twin rooms cost $40.

The several motels in town are good value if you're cycling with a friend and outside of holiday times. Off-season, rooms at *Whale Motor Inn* (☎ 4476 2411, *Wagonga St*), in the middle of town, cost $80/90 for singles/doubles. The *Farnboro Motel* (☎ 4476 4611, 206 Princes Hwy) charges $55 for one or two people, but it's a bit further out.

Lynch's Hotel (☎ 4476 2001, 135 Wagonga St) has older-style rooms for $35/45.

Places to Eat On the route into town is a big *Woolworths (Princes Hwy)*; a smaller *supermarket* is on the highway in the town centre. *Casey's Cafe (Wagonga St)* serves great cappuccinos and killer lentil burgers, among other tasty treats. Go to *A&K's (Campbell St)* for pies, cakes and rolls.

Spend the money you've saved on accommodation at Lynch's Hotel by tucking into tasty seafood at *The Restaurant at*

Forget skimpy lycra – in the late-19th Century you dressed properly for the beach (Narooma).

MELBOURNE TO THE GOLD COAST

NATIONAL LIBRARY OF AUSTRALIA

Lynch's (☎ *4476 3022)*, where mains are mostly less than $15.

The bistro in *O'Brien's Hotel* (☎ *4476 3691, Princes Hwy)* serves good-value pub dinners from 6pm; the ocean and inlet views from the outdoor tables give the meals a gourmet flavour. You'd expect to find good seafood in Narooma and *Rockwall Restaurant* (☎ *4476 2040, 107 Campbell St)* does not disappoint, although with mains from $14 to $19 it's pricey by local standards.

Day 13: Narooma to Batemans Bay

6–7 hours, 82.2km

As of this morning, the honeymoon is over as far as traffic is concerned. From Narooma to Moruya, the next major town to the north, there are no viable alternatives to the Princes Hwy. After Moruya, the route follows secondary roads to Batemans Bay, providing relief from trucks and semi trailers. The area around Batemans Bay is popular and populated, and there's a lot of traffic compared to further south.

There's no doubting the beauty of the forests the route passes through from Narooma to **Bodalla** (17.2km). The town was once central to the vast south-coast landholding of colonial-era businessman Thomas Mort. Mort (1816–78) established dairy co-operatives in the area and the Bodalla cheese factory; his grave is in the yard of Bodalla's historic **All Saints Church**.

Moruya (42.7km) was starting to establish itself as the regional centre at about the time gold was discovered, in the 1850s. From the river flats around the Moruya River there are stirring views of **Deua National Park**, a rugged wilderness park about 10km west of the route that unfortunately, owing to lack of roads, cannot be explored by bike.

At about 46.5km, the route passes the long-disused quarry from which granite was cut for the Sydney Harbour Bridge pylons. About 90 Scottish stonemasons were brought to the district to complete the work, and they lived here in the purpose-built settlement of Granitetown from 1925 to '32.

Broulee (pronounced 'brow-lee'), at 56.1km, was established before Moruya. Although 25km south of Batemans, Broulee is practically an outer suburb, and traffic can be intense during holiday periods. North of Broulee, a string of beachside 'suburbs' –

Rosedale, Malua Bay, Lilli Pilli and Batehaven – provide plenty of opportunity for refreshment stops on a warm afternoon.

Batemans Bay

☎ 02

This busy town sits handsomely on, and shares the name of, the wide bay where the Clyde River estuary meets the sea. The bay was 'named' by James Cook in 1770 during his voyage up the east coast. It's a full-on tourist-and-retiree town, attractive for its natural assets (lovely beaches, excellent fishing) and proximity to land-locked Canberra.

Information The visitor centre (☎ 4472 6900 or ☎ 1800-802 528), on the Princes Hwy close to the town centre, has a huge range of maps, books and brochures and will help with accommodation and tour bookings. The post office and branches of all the big banks (with ATMs) are on Orient St. Go to Sportscene (☎ 4472 5033, 43 Orient St) for spares and repairs.

Things to See & Do The **Old Courthouse Museum** (☎ 4472 8993), on the corner of Orient and Beach Sts, is small but a fair starting point to learn about local history.

The **Eurobodalla Native Botanic Gardens**, off the Princes Hwy about 5km south of Batemans bay, are worth a look (open school holidays, and Wednesday and Sunday).

Water sports loom large here: the visitor centre can reserve Clyde River cruises, deep-sea fishing charters, river-fishing boat hire and sundries such as canoeing, kayaking and (if you must) jet skiing. The Dive Shop (☎ 4472 9930), 5/33 Orient St, offers a great variety of off-and near-shore **guided dives**; they also run courses and hire gear.

Places to Stay Like most popular tourist towns, Bateman's Bay has abundant accommodation. The area has several caravan parks, most of which have cabins. *Easts Riverside Holiday Park* (☎ *4472 4048, Wharf Rd)*, just north of the bridge, has sites for $19.70 for two people. *Pleasurelea Caravan Park* (☎ *4472 4258, 438 Beach Rd)*, south-east of the town centre, charges $18 per site; its cabins start at $55 most of the year.

Shady Willows Holiday Park (☎ *4472 4972, cnr Old Princess Hwy & South St)* has tent sites from $11 and is also home to the *Batemans*

MELBOURNE TO THE GOLD COAST

Day 13: Narooma to Batemans Bay

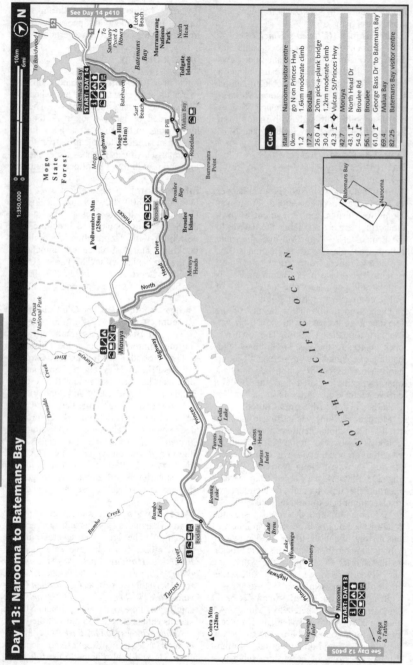

Cue		
start		Narooma visitor centre
0km		go N on Princes Hwy
1.2	▲	1.6km moderate climb
17.2		Bodalla
26.0	▲	20m pick-a-plank bridge
30.4	▲	1.2km moderate climb
42.3	↶	Vulcan St/Princes Hwy
42.7	◇	Moruya
43.1	↶	North Head Dr
54.9	↶	Broulee Rd
56.1	↶	Broulee
61.0	↶	George Bass Dr to Batemans Bay
69.4		Malua Bay
82.25		Batemans Bay visitor centre

Bay YHA, where you'll pay $21.50 for a dorm bed and $46 per person for a double/twin.

Zorba Motel (☎ 4472 4804, Orient St), close to the waterfront in the town centre, charges $95 to $100 a double. The *Clyderiver Motor Inn* (☎ 4472 6444, 3 Clyde St) is also close to the central restaurants; rooms cost $70 to $110. Closer to the beach, the self-catering units at *Tollgate Lodge* (☎ 4472 5843, 374 Beach Rd) start at $55, while *Taliva Holiday Lodge* (☎ 4472 4904, 236 Beach Rd) has singles/doubles for $60/68.

Places to Eat Bateman's Bay has good food and plenty of choice. For self-caterers, a *Woolworths* supermarket (cnr Orient St & Flora Crescent) is close to the majority of accommodation.

In Bay Centre Plaza, the *Bakehouse & Patisserie* is great for a bargain focaccia and good coffee. Try *Mexican Munchies* (☎ 4472 8746; Annetts Arcade, Orient St) for a spicy fill-up and the *Vietnamese, Thai & Malaysian Restaurant* (☎ 4472 7274), across Orient St in the plaza, for Asian flavours. *Skippers Bistro* at the Batemans Bay Soldiers Club (☎ 4472 4117, 2 Beach Rd) has big mains from $12 to $15.

The *Starfish Deli* (☎ 4472 4880; The Promenade, 2 Clyde St) gets good reviews and big crowds; the seafood is great but not cheap ($20–25 for a couple of courses) and the pizzas mighty fine. Nearby, on The Promenade, *Aussie Pancakes* (☎ 4472 5727) opens at 7am daily for big breakfasts. Also nearby, on the waterfront, *The Boatshed* (☎ Clyde St) is great for fresh-as-fresh seafood; eat fish and chips there or take away.

Day 14: Batemans Bay to Sanctuary Point
7–8 hours, 103.2km

There isn't another day on the ride – certainly not on the NSW coast – that's as hard work as this one. It's not that the territory covered isn't worthwhile; indeed, this single day takes you from Batemans Bay, the gateway to the 'far' south coast, nearly to Nowra. But for the entire day, owing to a lack of alternatives, the route follows the Princes Hwy, and the traffic isn't always fun.

In the first 20km north of Batemans Bay, the route passes a signed turn-off to Pebbly Beach, backed by Murramarang National Park. A 16km return journey, it has a *camp-*

ing ground and is renowned for its kangaroos (*don't* feed them!), which often wander down to the surf to cool off on a hot day.

Ulladulla (52.5km), the day's halfway point, is a pleasant place to stop. It's a fairly busy town, but hasn't been overrun by tourists. It is, however, a popular place with visiting surfers, none of whom (to the vast amusement of everyone else) regards him or herself as a 'tourist'. In Ulladulla, the local Aboriginal Land Council has established the **Coomie Nulunga Cultural Trail**, which starts near the lighthouse oval, off Deering St.

In the 25km north of Ulladulla, the route has more climbing – about 12km in total – than at any other point on the NSW coast. It's a long, gradual uphill from Ulladulla to Milton (59.5km), which predates 'Ulla' as a regional centre. The toughest ascent – and it's pretty soft compared to the big climbs on Days 8 and 9 – comes at 72.3km, between Milton and Wandandian. From there it's an easy run to St Georges Basin and Sanctuary Point, the last 10km, happily, off the highway.

Sanctuary Point
☎ 02

On a peninsula on the north of St Georges Basin, Sanctuary Point is in a pretty setting, but isn't the prettiest of towns: there's a jarring suburban ordinariness about the street layout and many of the houses. It's saved by a laid-back coastal feel and proximity to two attractive bodies of water – St Georges Basin and Jervis Bay (Booderee).

It's a small place and locals are happy to give directions. There's no visitor centre. The post office is in the strip of shops on Paradise Beach Rd. A Colonial State Bank branch is among the shops, but it doesn't have an ATM. Several businesses have Eftpos facilities.

Things to See & Do The best swimming spot is **Palm Beach**, off Greville Ave. A variety of **watercraft** – catamarans, canoes, sailboards – is for hire at Sanctuary Point Sail Centre (☎ 4443 0205), 272 Greville Ave. A pleasant **walking track** linking Palm and Paradise Beaches takes about 40 minutes.

It's about 12km from Sanctuary Point to lovely **Huskisson**, on Jervis Bay, the place to come for a rest day hereabouts. 'Husky' has a great pub, cinema, dive centres, dolphin watching and the **Lady Denman Heritage Complex** (☎ 4441 5675), which includes a

Day 14: Batemans Bay to Sanctuary Point

Cue		
start		Batemans Bay visitor centre
0km		go N on Princes Hwy 'to Nowra'
41.0		Tabourie Lake
48.5		Burrill Lake
52.5	✳	Ulladulla
53.3	◄	6km gradual climb
59.5		Milton
65.6	◄	2.1km moderate climb
71.1	◄	400m hard climb
72.3	◄	3.2km hard climb
90.0		Wandandian
92.5		Bewong
93.5	↰	The Wool Rd 'to Basin View'
95.4	↗	The Wool Rd 'to St Georges Basin'
96.5	↗	'to St Georges Basin'
99.0	↰	Island Point Rd 'to Sanctuary Point'
99.2		St Georges Basin
99.9	↰	Meriton St 'to Sanctuary Point'
101.9	↰	Walmer Ave 'to Sanctuary Point'
102.8	↰	Paradise Beach Rd 'to Sanctuary Point'
103.2		Sanctuary Point shops

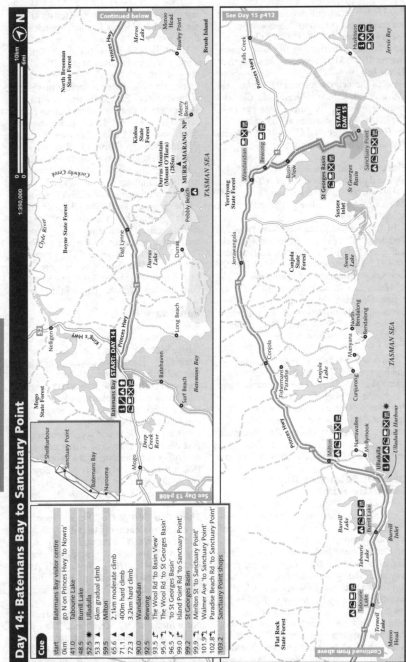

maritime museum, a boardwalk through mangroves and **Laddie Timbery's Aboriginal Art and Craft Centre** (☎ 4441 5999).

Places to Stay & Eat The *Palm Beach Caravan Park* (☎ 4443 0356, Greville Ave) has sites for $17.60 and cabins from $49. The *Golf View Motel* (☎ 4443 9502, 49 Paradise Beach Rd) has singles/doubles for $94/99.

If you're cycling in a group, try *South Coast Holiday Cottages* (☎ 4443 7665, e dave@machelp.com.au); rates are $80 to $150 (for two), depending on which cottage you choose, plus $16 per extra adult.

In the shopping strip on Paradise Beach Rd you'll find the *supermarket*, *bakery* and, for dinner, *Sanctuary Point Chinese Restaurant* (☎ 4443 9138) and *Sanctuary Point Pizza Paradise* (☎ 4443 9578). Across the road, *Pelican's Brasserie* in the St Georges Basin Country Club (☎ 4443 0666) is open for lunch and dinner daily; roasts, chicken and seafood mains cost from $11.

The *Sanctuary Restaurant* (☎ 4443 0603, 4 Paradise Beach Rd) has bistro-style mains for $4 to $7; it's in a motel but the owners don't appear too keen for cyclists to stay.

Day 15: Sanctuary Point to Shellharbour

6–7 hours, 86.4km

It's a pleasant enough start to this day, with the first 18km covering quieter roads in the Jervis Bay area. After that the route follows the Princes Hwy to Bomaderry, then back roads to Gerringong and Werri Beach, then mostly the highway to the Shellharbour turn-off. The mostly dead-flat terrain is broken by a couple of short, but intense, climbs.

Nowra (30km) is the NSW coast's largest town south of Wollongong–Port Kembla, and sprawls a long way south of the town centre. It's a busy service centre; take particular care on the Shoalhaven River bridge

and as you negotiate the right turn onto Bo-long Rd (32.6km).

Coolangatta Historic Village (45.5km; ☎ 4448 7131) at is a good place for a break. This is the site of one of the south coast's first European settlements. Pioneer Alexander Berry selected the site in 1822; today, convict-era buildings are used for accommodation.

For most of the next 10km the route runs through **Seven Mile Beach National Park** and, while the ocean is out of sight, the breakers on the beach make for nice background noise. The best views come on the climb out of **Gerroa** (58.4km).

It's well worth a look at the **Kiama Blowhole** and nearby **Pilots Cottage Museum** (☎ 4232 1001), both on a short side trip at 72.7km. With big surf, the blowhole is spectacular (and scary), spurting foaming seawater up to 60m into the air. The Princes Hwy between Kiama and the Shellharbour turn-off is narrow in parts and can be quite busy on weekends, but the final 5km covers quieter roads and has wonderful views.

Shellharbour

☎ 02

One of the longest-settled localities on the south coast, Shellharbour has been a popular holiday destination for decades. Its name apparently comes from the large shell middens (remnants of Aboriginal feasts) in the area; Dharawal Aboriginal people called the harbour Yerrowah.

Information The visitor centre (☎ 4221 6169) is inconveniently located a couple of kilometres from the 'old' town centre, in the Shellharbour Square shopping complex on Lake Entrance Rd. The post office, on Addison St (the main street), is a Commonwealth Bank agent, and several Addison St businesses have Eftpos facilities. The nearest bike shop is CMW Cycle Specialists

MELBOURNE TO THE GOLD COAST

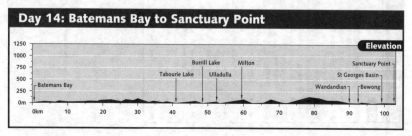

Day 14: Batemans Bay to Sanctuary Point

Elevation

1250
1000
750
500
250
0m

Batemans Bay

Tabourie Lake

Burrill Lake

Ulladulla

Milton

Wandandian

Bewong

St Georges Basin

Sanctuary Point

0km   10   20   30   40   50   60   70   80   90   100

Day 15: Sanctuary Point to Shellharbour

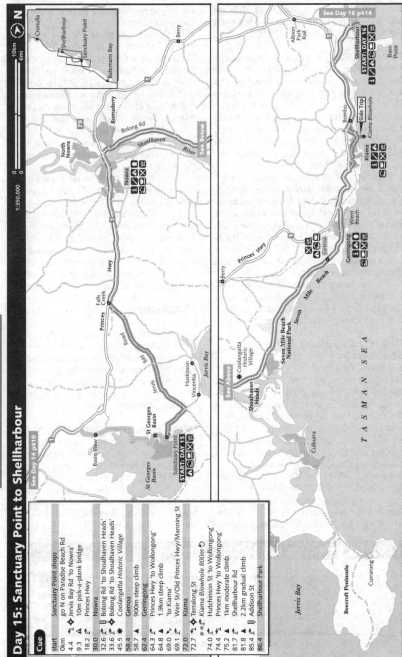

Cue

start	Sanctuary Point shops
0km	go N on Paradise Beach Rd
4.4	Jervis Bay Rd 'to Nowra'
9.3	10m pick-a-plank bridge
18.2	Princes Hwy
30.0	Nowra
32.6	Bolong Rd 'to Shoalhaven Heads'
33.6	Bolong Rd 'to Shoalhaven Heads'
45.5	Coolangatta Historic Village
58.4	Gerroa
58.7	900m steep climb
62.4	Gerringong
64.3	Princes Hwy 'to Wollongong'
64.8	1.9km steep climb
69.0	'to Kiama'
69.1	Weir St/Old Princes Hwy/Manning St
72.0	Kiama
72.7	Terralong St
	Kiama Blowhole 800m ↺
74.0	Hutchinson St 'to Wollongong'
74.4	Princes Hwy 'to Wollongong'
75.2	1km moderate climb
81.7	Shellharbour Rd
81.8	2.2km gradual climb
85.4	Addison St
86.4	Shellharbour Park

(☎ 4256 6872), about 7km from Shellharbour in Kanahooka St, Albion Park Rail (Cityrail trains go hourly from Shellharbour to Albion Park Rail; the fare is $2.40).

Things to See & Do The **Bass Point Reserve**, 5km south of Shellharbour, is one of the most important archaeological sites on the NSW coast – Aboriginal people began using the area at least 16,000 years ago. The reserve also protects the best remaining example of coastal heath flora in the region. **Bay Marine Reserve**, offshore, is a great spot for diving and snorkelling.

Closer to Shellharbour, the 100-hectare **Blackbutt Forest Reserve** has native gardens and natural bushlands crossed by walking tracks and bikepaths. **Fishing** and **diving** are popular; Leisure Coast Dive (☎ 4296 3644), 2/17 Addison St, rents snorkel and dive gear and offers guided dives from shore and boat.

A little further afield, at Albion Park, the **Tongarra Bicentennial Museum** (☎ 4256 6698) has displays on European-Australian and Aboriginal history (open Wednesday and Sunday afternoons). From Illawarra Regional Airport at Albion Park, there are scenic **flights** in microlights (☎ 4294 1031), with Sydney Microlight Centre, and larger aircraft (☎ 4257 2000), with South Coast Aviation.

Places to Stay & Eat The *Shellharbour Beachside Tourist Park (☎ 4295 1123, John St)* has sites for $16.50 and cabins for $88. About 5km north, the large *Windang Beach Tourist Park (☎ 4297 3166, Fern St)* is a good back up, with $16 sites.

Right across from Shellharbour itself, the *Ocean Beach Hotel (☎ 4296 1399, 2 Addison St)* has singles/doubles for $60/85. The hotel bistro serves standard pub fare at reasonable prices. Just up the road, pretty *Windradene Seaside Guest House (☎ 4295 1074, 29 Addison St)* offers B&B for $85/100 midweek.

Shellharbour Convenience Store (Addison St) is closest to the route. *Coles* and *Franklins* are both in Shellharbour Square shopping mall. *Shellharbour Country Kitchen (☎ 4296 3205, cnr Addison & Wentworth Sts)* serves great coffee and big breakfasts. *Shelly's Pizza Cafe (☎ 4297 0020, 1/19 Addison St)* has pizza and pasta from $8. *Tang's Chinese Seafood Restaurant (☎ 4296 3900, 31 Addison St)* has filling, if slightly predictable, fare. By the harbour, *Shellhar-*

bour Fish & Chips and *Salvatore's Cafe* have standard, filling-but-greasy takeaway.

Day 16: Shellharbour to Bundeena/Cronulla

6½–7½ hours, 88.2km

Given the largely urban/industrial territory it passes through, this day is a revelation, thanks mainly to the truly wonderful system of bikepaths the Wollongong City Council has created. The best-known of these follows the coast for nearly 16 glorious, traffic-free kilometres (another 6.2km are on roadside paths), from just south of central Wollongong nearly to Thirroul. Farther north, the route hugs the coast as far as Stanwell Park then spears through lovely Royal National Park to Bundeena and Cronulla, on Sydney's fringe.

BHP's giant **Port Kembla Steelworks** are a dominating presence in this part of the world and the route runs beside them for about 5km. The visitor centre is just inside the complex's north gate, on Springhill Rd (at 19.6km), from which tours (☎ 4275 7023) depart on Wednesday and Friday. It's a fascinating look at heavy industry.

In central Wollongong, it's worth going slightly off-route (go west on Burelli St) to the to visit the **Wollongong City Gallery** (☎ 4228 7500), corner Kembla and Burelli Sts, Australia's largest regional art museum with a collection concentrated on Aboriginal and 20th-century Australian art. The nearby **Illawarra Museum** (☎ 4228 7770), 11 Market St, is also worth a look.

With the bikepath sadly left behind, the route rolls up and down through the coast-hugging northern Wollongong suburbs. From 53.1km the route rises sharply, passing **Bald Hill Lookout** at 54.7km. Views from here are stunning, but the site is more interesting for its memorial to aeronautical engineer Lawrence Hargrave.

The remaining 30km of the day is spent in **Royal National Park**, one of the world's first two national parks (the other is Yellowstone, in Wyoming, USA). About 95% of the park was burnt during the awful 1994 bushfire season, but one can hardly tell riding through it now – a brilliant testimony to Australian flora's adaptations to fire. High points in the park provide the first big views of Sydney – on a clear day, it stretches wide to the north. Savour these last few kilometres on quieter roads as you approach Bundeena!

MELBOURNE TO THE GOLD COAST

Day 16: Shellharbour to Bundeena/Cronulla

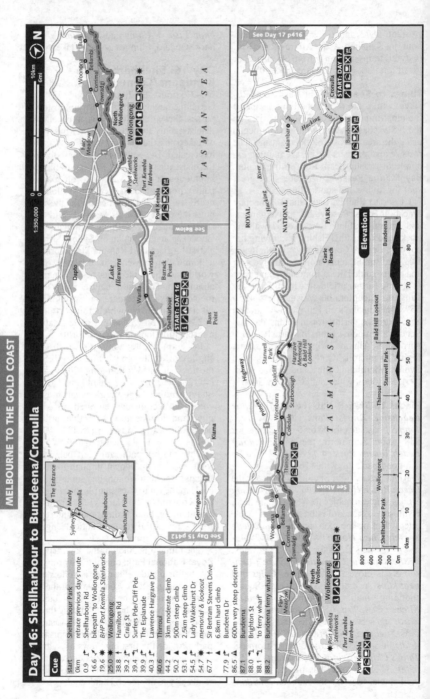

Cue		
start		Shellharbour Park
0km		retrace previous day's route
0.9	⌐	Shellharbour Rd
16.6		bikepath to Wollongong'
19.6	✳	BHP Port Kembla Steelworks
25.0		Wollongong
38.8	⌐	Hamilton Rd
39.2	⌐	Craig St
39.4	⌐	Surfers Pde/Cliff Pde
39.9	⌐	The Esplanade
40.3	⌐	Lawrence Hargrave Dr
40.6		Thirroul
44.2	◄	3km moderate climb
50.2	◄	500m steep climb
53.1	◄	2.5km steep climb
54.5	⌐	Lady Wakehurst Dr
54.7	✳	memorial & lookout
67.7	⌐	Sir Bertram Stevens Drive
	◄	6.8km hard climb
77.9	⌐	Bundeena Dr
86.5	◄	600m very steep descent
87.1		Bundeena
88.0	⌐	Brighton St
88.1	⌐	'to ferry wharf'
88.2		Bundeena ferry wharf

Cronulla National Park Ferries (☎ 9523 2990) run from Bundeena Wharf, at the bottom of Brighton St, to Tonkin St Wharf in Cronulla (weekdays on the hour 6am–7pm; weekends on the hour 9am–7pm/6pm in summer/winter). The one-way fare is $3.10; bikes cost $1.55. The next day's ride into central Sydney isn't strenuous, so staying in Bundeena is a good option (Cronulla has a far greater choice of places to eat).

Bundeena/Cronulla

☎ 02

Bundeena pretty much has the best of both worlds. The small town is surrounded by Royal National Park, but you can jump on a ferry here and you're soon in Cronulla and a stroll away from a Sydney suburban train station. While it's self-contained, with its own small supermarket and other shops, Bundeena is a far cry from Cronulla, which is being swamped, especially along its beachfront, by high-rise developments.

Information There's no visitor centre in Bundeena or Cronulla. Drop into the post office, on Brighton St not far from the ferry wharf, for advice on getting around. The ferry crews can help you get your bearings upon reaching Cronulla. All the big banks, with ATMs, are found Cronulla's Cronulla St and the mall, as is the post office. Chain Reaction bike shop (☎ 9544 1066), 25–35 The Kingsway, is big and well stocked (open daily).

Things to See & Do If you opt to stay in Bundeena, the **Jibbon Aboriginal Rock Engravings Walk** is a must; the track starts at the eastern end of Jibbon Beach. The engravings, the work of the Dharawal people, are thought to represent food and possibly a mythical spirit, and could be up to 5000-years-old. Charcoal found in a rock shelter nearby has been dated at about 8000-years-old, but no one's really sure how long the Dharawal occupied these lands; estimates go as high as 30,000 years. Swimming is pleasant at Jibbon, Gunyah and Horderns **Beaches**.

Cronulla's **beaches** are also very pleasant, and a fantastic **walking track** almost circles the peninsula, from Dunningham Park (North Cronulla) to Gunnamatta Bay. Legitimately an outer suburb of Sydney, Cronulla offers the full range of secular madness – pubs, clubs, oodles of restaurants, cinemas and so on.

Places to Stay The *Bundeena Caravan Park* (☎ 9523 9520, 74 Scarborough St) has sites for $15. *Bundeena Bed & Breakfast* (☎ 9527 2605, 2 Crammond Ave) and *Beachhaven Bed & Breakfast* (☎ 9544 1333, 13 Bundeena Dr) offer fairly pricey B&B for $170 a weekend (no single rates).

In Cronulla, the new *Cronulla Beach YHA* (☎ 9527 7772, 40 The Kingsway) has dorm beds from $23, and double en suite rooms for $30 per person. Nearby, *Rydges Cronulla Beach* hotel (☎ 9527 3100, 20–26 The Kingsway) has doubles from $180 and suites from $245. *Cronulla Motor Inn* (☎ 9523 6800, 85 The Kingsway) has single/double rooms at $89/154.

Places to Eat Bundeena's *IGA supermarket (Brighton St)* is on the route. The bistro at *Bundeena RSL Memorial Club* (☎ 9523 2115, 71 Loftus St) serves dinner Wednesday to Sunday, with mains from $5. The *Bundeena Bowling & Sports Club* (☎ 9523 7292, Liverpool St) serves dinner Thursday to Sunday.

In Cronulla, the sheer volume of eateries in the vicinity of The Kingsway, Gerrale St, Surf Rd and Cronulla St/Mall makes 'shop around' the best recommendation. A big *Franklins* supermarket *(Cronulla St)* is close to most of the accommodation. Try *Jetz Cafe (6 Surf Rd)* for great smoothies and fresh juices, and the *Bakerway Bakery*, at the Kingsway end of Cronulla Mall.

At *Nulla Nulla Cafe* (☎ 9544 3239, 75 Cronulla St), $3.50 buys a coffee and 15 minutes on the Internet. Go to legendary *P Michael's Seafood (The Kingsway)* for fish and chips. The *Best Noodle Inn* (☎ 9523 8188, 105 Cronulla St) has cheap rice and noodle dishes.

Cronulla Mall is a mass of cafes with outdoor tables; *Strawberry Fair* has nice pizzas, while *Ness's Patisserie & Cafe* has big breakfasts for $11 and pastas from $9.

Day 17: Cronulla to Centennial Park (Sydney)

2–3 hours, 32.7km

Given that Sydney is a city where the car reigns unchallenged, this is a surprisingly fun day, with quite a lot of time spent on minor roads or bikepaths. (The moments that are unavoidably on busier roads are, er, 'lively'.) It's a very exciting day, with the mass of

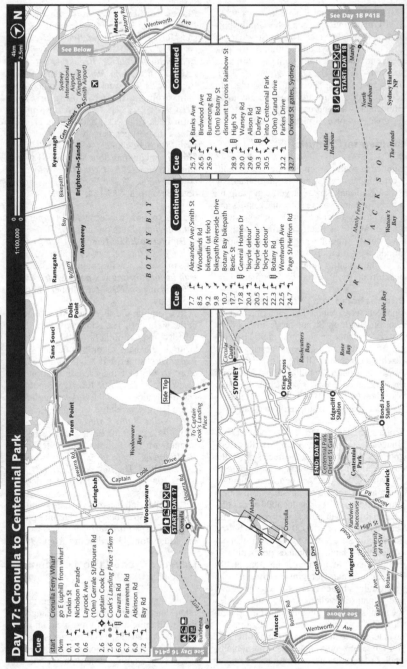

MELBOURNE TO THE GOLD COAST

Day 17: Cronulla to Centennial Park

Cue

start		Cronulla Ferry Wharf
0km		go E (uphill) from wharf
0.1		Tonkin St
0.4		Nicholson Parade
0.6		Laycock Ave
		(10m) Gerrale St/Elouera Rd
2.6		Captain Cook Dr
2.6		Cook's Landing Place 15km ↺
6.0		Cawarra Rd
6.7		Parraweena Rd
6.9		Atkinson Rd
7.2		Bay Rd

Cue   **Continued**

7.7		Alexander Ave/Smith St
8.5		Woodlands Rd
9.2		bikepath (at fork)
9.8		bikepath/Riverside Drive
10.7		Botany Bay bikepath
17.7		Bestic St
17.8		General Holmes Dr
20.4		'bicycle detour'
20.5		'bicycle detour'
22.1		'bicycle detour'
22.3		Botany Rd
22.5		Wentworth Ave
24.7		Page St/Heffron Rd

Cue   **Continued**

25.7		Banks Ave
26.5		Birdwood Ave
26.9		Bunnerong Rd
		(10m) Botany St
		dismount to cross Rainbow St
28.9		High St
29.0		Wansey Rd
29.6		Alison Rd
30.3		Darley Rd
30.5		into Centennial Park
		(30m) Grand Drive
32.2		Parkes Drive
32.7		Oxford St gates, Sydney

See Day 18 P418

START: DAY 18   Manly

N   4km   2.5mi

1:100,000

0   0

Mascot

Wentworth   Ave

Sydney International Airport (Kingsford Smith Airport)

See Below

Gen Holmes Dr

Kyeemagh

Brighton-le-Sands

bikepath

bikepath

Bay

B O T A N Y   B A Y

Botany

Ramsgate

Monterey

Dolls Point

Sans Souci

Taren Point

Woolooware Bay

Cawarra Rd

Caringbah

Captain   Cook   Drive

Elouera Rd

Side Trip

To Captain Cook's Landing Place

Wooloware

START: DAY 17   Cronulla

See Day 16 p414

Bundeena

Circular Quay

SYDNEY

Kings Cross Station

Edgecliff Station

Rushcutters Bay

Rose Bay

Double Bay

P O R T   J A C K S O N

Middle Harbour

North Harbour

Sydney Harbour NP

The Heads

Watson's Bay

Manly Ferry

Bondi Junction Station

END: DAY 17
Centennial Park
Oxford St Gates

Centennial Park

Randwick

Randwick Racecourse

Alison   Rd

High St

University of NSW

Cross   Dve

Bunnerong   St

Kingsford

Botany   St

Southern

Banks   Ave

Mascot

Botany   Rd

Wentworth   Ave

See Above

Manly

Sydney

Cronulla

Sydney city ever-closer, planes roaring over Botany Bay and that 'city-rush' feeling.

The suggested side trip (at 2.6km) to Botany Bay National Park (☎ 9668 9111), and **Captain Cook's Landing Place Historic Site**, is almost compulsory. Although best known as English navigator James Cook's first landfall in Australia (on 29 April 1770), it's fittingly a place where Aboriginal Australia also has a presence. There's a small museum here with Cook and *Endeavour* relics; and you can wade to the rock onto which the first Englishman ashore, young midshipman Isaac Smith, is thought to have leapt. Aboriginal rock engravings and middens in the area – some of the latter ruined by sand mining and 4WD vehicles – are a reminder of the land's original custodians.

From 10.7km, the Botany Bay bikepath provides another perspective of the bay, this time from the busy suburban strip on its western shore. Once the airport tunnel has been negotiated, it's a straightforward run towards the city, past the University of NSW and that great Sydney place of worship, the Randwick Racecourse.

Sydney
☎ 02

See Sydney in the Gateway Cities section of the New South Wales chapter (pp115–18) for information about accommodation and

Not Cycling through Sydney?

If you'd prefer to get to, or past, central Sydney without cycling, Cronulla train station is just up the hill from the Tonkin St Wharf.

From Cronulla, trains go direct to Sydney's Central station. From there, pick up the route at Circular Quay (Day 18; the ferry ride to Manly is highly recommended) and head north from there. Alternatively, continue by train from Central station to Woy Woy on the NSW central coast, which is about 5km from the Day 18 route (rejoin at the 32.8km mark).

Bikes are welcome on Sydney's suburban Cityrail (☎ 13 1500) trains at any time; they travel free off-peak; but are charged a child's fare in peak periods (outside 6am–9am and 3.30pm–7.30pm).

The adult fare from Cronulla to Sydney Central is $4. Cronulla to Woy Woy (change trains at Central) costs $9.80.

other services. The **Sydney Olympic Explorer** ride is detailed that chapter.

From Centennial Park, it's a short ride (in traffic) to each of the areas we've favoured for food and accommodation suggestions. We haven't mapped routes to these; if you intend to cycle around central Sydney, buy a clear, up-to-date city map (Lonely Planet's *Sydney*, $7.80, will do nicely). They're all reasonably close to suggested attractions.

Day 18: Manly to The Entrance
4½–5 hours, 67.8km

Make your way to Circular Quay and take a ferry to Manly. Manly ferries (☎ 13 1500) leave the Quay regularly from 6am on weekdays and from 8am on weekends ($5, bikes free outside peak hour, ½ hour).

A couple of lovely ferry rides and a route that's rarely out of sight of the ocean are features of this mostly flat day. The route from Manly to Palm Beach follows mainly quiet minor roads and is sublime on a mild day. With the exception of Whale and Palm Beaches to the far north, you can see every one of Sydney's famed northern beaches. Beyond Ettalong, the route passes through areas as yet unspoilt by development, although NSW Central Coast towns are these days mostly dormitory suburbs of Sydney.

After a cruise along the beachfront at world-renowned **Manly**, the route rolls along the northern headland of Freshwater Beach and past a statue of Hawaiian surfing champion **Duke Kahanamoku**, whose 1914 demonstration at Freshwater is credited as the starting point of Australian surfing. The bronze Duke is depicted on his board, handsomely poised atop a weathered lump of Sydney sandstone; the sandstone path leading to his statue is inlaid with tile plaques listing the surfing champions of various eras.

From Mona Vale (18.2km) north, the route follows busy Pittwater and Barrenjoey Rds and care is required, especially on the tight 'Bilgola bends' section (at 23km).

Call ahead to Palm Beach Ferries (☎ 9918 2747) to tell them you'll be taking the boat to Ettalong ($7 plus $1 for the bike, about 30 minutes). The trip is delightful, passing beautiful Barrenjoey Head (and its 30m-tall 1881 lighthouse) and Lion Island, both in **Ku-ring-gai Chase National Park** (☎ 9472 8949).

From Ettalong, the route again follows mainly minor roads and, north of Terrigal,

MELBOURNE TO THE GOLD COAST

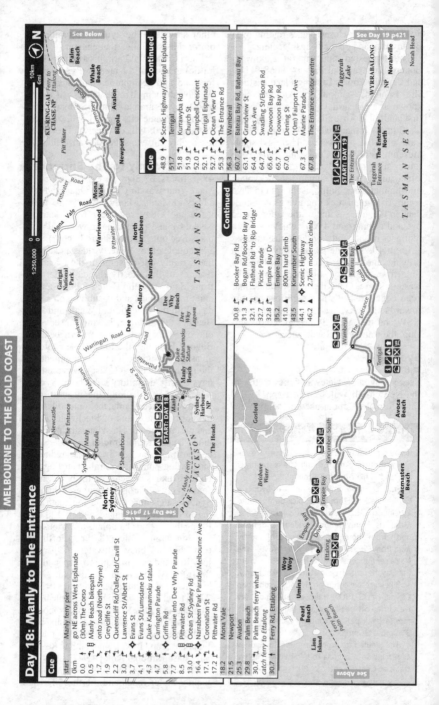

Day 18: Manly to The Entrance

Cue

start	Manly ferry pier
0km	go NE across West Esplanade
0.0	(30m) The Corso
0.5	Manly Beach bikepath
1.7	onto road (North Steyne)
1.9	Greycliffe St
2.2	Queenscliff Rd/Dalley Rd/Cavill St
3.0	Lawrence St/Albert St
3.7	Evans St
4.1	Evans St/Lumsdane Dr
4.4	Duke Kahanamoku statue
4.7	Carrington Parade
5.8	Griffin Rd
7.7	continue into Dee Why Parade
8.5	Pittwater Rd
13.0	Ocean St/Sydney Rd
16.4	Narrabeen Park Parade/Melbourne Ave
17.1	Coronation St
17.2	Pittwater Rd
18.2	Mona Vale
21.5	Newport
25.3	Avalon
29.8	Palm Beach
30.7	Palm Beach ferry wharf
	catch ferry to Ettalong
30.7	Ferry Rd, Ettalong

Continued

30.8	Booker Bay Rd
31.3	Bogan Rd/Booker Bay Rd
32.1	Flathead Rd 'to Rip Bridge'
32.7	Picnic Parade
32.8	Empire Bay Dr
35.2	Empire Bay
41.0	800m hard climb
43.5	Kincumber South
44.1	Scenic Highway
46.2	2.7km moderate climb

Cue / Continued

48.9	Scenic Highway/Terrigal Esplanade
51.7	Terrigal
51.8	Kurrawyba Rd
51.9	Church St
52.0	Campbell Crescent
52.1	Terrigal Esplanade
52.7	Ocean View Dr
55.3	The Entrance Rd
56.3	Wamberal
60.7	Bateau Bay Rd, Bateau Bay
63.1	Grandview St
64.4	Oaks Ave
64.7	Swadling St/Eloora Rd
65.6	Toowoon Bay Rd
65.7	Toowoon Bay Rd
67.0	Dening St
	(10m) Fairport Ave
67.3	Marine Parade
67.8	The Entrance visitor centre

START & DAY 19 — The Entrance

this requires a bit more navigation. You can save a few kilometres and several twists and turns by just remaining on The Entrance Rd from 55.3km all the way to The Entrance.

The Entrance
☎ 02
Long a popular holiday destination, The Entrance doesn't quite live up to its brochure hype. The good points are fine – the lake and beaches are pretty and the locals mostly friendly. The bad points come down, as is so often the case, to poor planning fuelled probably by greed – the developers have well and truly got a grip on The Entrance foreshore.

Information The visitor centre (☎ 4385 4430 or ☎ 1800-151 699) is on Marine Parade. The town centre is compact, stretching up the hill from the waterfront on The Entrance Rd. All the big banks have branches with ATMs on The Entrance Rd. The post office is in the Lakeside shopping complex, on the corner of The Entrance Rd and Dening St. The Bike Shop The Entrance (☎ 4332 1392, 31 Coral St) is just off the main drag; it carries all the basics and is open daily (closes early on wet weekends).

Things to See & Do The big activities close to town are **fishing** and **swimming**; Entrance Boathouse (☎ 4332 2652) rents canoes, rowing and motor boats. The daily **pelican feeding** (3.30pm on the plaza near the visitor centre) is an event. The visitor centre has maps for the 3.5km **Coast Walking Track** in Wyrrabalong National Park (☎ 4324 4911).

Of the pay-for attractions, the best is the cinema, on The Entrance Rd.

Places to Stay You guessed it, The Entrance Rd is also the place to head for food and a bed. *Pinehurst Caravan Park (☎ 4332 2002, 11, The Entrance Rd)* has sites for $22 and cabins from $50 (both for two people); it's the closest park to the town centre. One place that's off the main road, *Dunleith Caravan Park (☎ 4332 2172, Hutton Rd)* is just over the bridge; sites cost $23 and cabins, from $80 midweek.

The Entrance Hotel (☎ 4332 2001, 87 The Entrance Rd) does B&B for singles/doubles for $38.50/77 and its bistro is good value for dinner. *Sapphire Palms Motel (☎ 4332 5799, 180 The Entrance Rd)* is the best value of the many motels in town, charging $79/89.

Places to Eat Coles supermarket *(The Entrance Rd)* has a big range. *Kam's Tea House (☎ 4332 0038, 40–48 The Entrance Rd)* has fair vegetarian choices and is good value. *Maxwell's Mexican Cantina (☎ 4332 5682, 107 The Entrance Rd)* serves a variety of nachos from $5.50 to $11. Down by the lake, *Pree Cha Thai Takeaway (☎ 4334 3193, No 147)* is a good alternative to fish and chips.

Side-by-side on the waterfront plaza, *Fonzirelli's (☎ 4334 4315, 113 The Entrance Rd)*, serving gourmet pizza and pasta, and *Old Bank Waterfront Restaurant (☎ 4333 4422, 115 The Entrance Rd)* are worth a try. The Old Bank has innovative Modern Australian mains in the $19-plus range.

Day 19: The Entrance to Newcastle
4½–5 hours, 64.5km
There's three distinct stages to this fairly easy day. The first, lasting nearly 24km, covers quiet and quieter roads between The Entrance and the turn onto the old Pacific Hwy. For about 25km afterwards, good bike lanes make the going comfortable, even though the highway is a major road. Over the last 15km or so, the route edges closer to central Newcastle and, in parts, the traffic is quite heavy.

A bike lane for nearly 10km north of The Entrance is a great way to start the day, but beware the lane's abrupt end at the 9.7km mark. For most of the way between Norahville (11.2km) and Budgewoi you can opt to follow the **Darren Smith Memorial Cycleway**; Smith, a superb road racer and central coast resident, was killed when struck by a vehicle while training in this area in the early 1990s.

From 19km to 23km the route passes through **Munmorah State Recreation Area**. From high points, stunning views stretch east to the sea (tiny Bird Island lies just offshore) and south towards The Entrance. Once on the old Pacific Hwy, a brilliant bike lane features frequent views of **Lake Macquarie** all the way to Swansea (36.8km), which is effectively the southern limit of Greater Newcastle.

It's a slog in traffic up to the turn onto Scenic Dr (57.6km), but views of (and the rollercoaster descent to) lovely **Merewether Beach** make up for it. The final kilometres are flat and include a run along **Darby St**, one of Newcastle's main 'eat streets'; take your time and browse for dinner venues.

Newcastle
☎ 02

Australia's sixth largest city is a lively and unexpectedly attractive place: easy to get around; and close to lovely beaches, the extensive waterways of Port Stephens and the Hunter Valley wineries. (As the route passes close by the city's CBD, our suggestions for Places to Stay & Eat are concentrated here.)

Information The visitor centre (☎ 4974 2999 or ☎ 1800-654 558), 363 Hunter St, near Civic train station, is open daily. Newcastle is quite decentralised, and banks with ATMs are common in the city centre (the main drag is Hunter St, a pedestrian mall between Perkins & Newcomen Sts) and throughout the metropolitan area. The main post office is on the corner of Hunter and Bolton Sts. The Bicycle Centre (☎ 4929 6933), corner King and Darby Sts, has a big range (closed Sunday).

Things to See & Do In summer, a swim in the ocean is a must: **Newcastle Beach** is a stroll from Hunter St. The **Newcastle Region Art Gallery** (☎ 4974 5100), Laman St, has an interesting collection. Just east of the main train station, the **Convict Lumber Yard**, Scott St, was the centre of convict-era

Newcastle. It's an evocative site filled with sculptures and interpretive signs, and superb views. East again, off Nobbys Rd, the **Newcastle Region Maritime Museum** is housed at historic Fort Scratchley; the fort's gun returned fire on a Japanese submarine in June 1942. The **Christ Church Cathedral**, Church St, is a graceful building with a long history. It was dedicated in 1902 but not completed until 1979, then damaged in the 1989 earthquake and restored. It received a heritage award in 1997.

Places to Stay The *Stockton Beach Tourist Park* (☎ 4928 1393, Pitt St) is a five-minute ferry ride across Newcastle Harbour (the ferry trip is part of the Day 20 route) and right on the beach. For two, sites cost $15, cabins from $44.

The lovely *Newcastle Beach Backpackers YHA* (☎ 4925 3544, @ yha@hunterlink .net.au, 30 Pacific St) is near the route and CBD. Dorm beds are $23.50 and double/ twins $61. *Backpackers by the Beach* (☎ 4926 3472, 34–36 Hunter St), a near neighbour of the YHA; and *Backpackers Newcastle* (☎ 4969 3436, 42–44 Denison St), a bit further out in inner-western Hamilton, are good back-ups.

Hotels and guesthouses near the CBD are very pleasant but they're not cheap. The best deal is probably at the *Novocastrian Motor Inn* (☎ 4926 3688, 21 Parnell Place), where rooms cost $135 (singles and doubles).

Newcastle Rising

What is NSW's city of the future? Sydney? Take a sedative! As any Novocastrian can tell you, bigger isn't necessarily better.

Newcastle was a major industrial centre from the 1930s to the '80s, thanks mainly to the giant BHP company, owner of the huge steelworks and the city's largest employer. Then the city ran out of luck.

The 1980s saw the loss of many jobs in steel making and related industries. In December 1989, an earthquake struck Newcastle, killing 13 people; it was the first 'quake in Australian history known to have claimed lives. Capping off the run of outs, in April 1997 BHP announced the closure of its steelworks, resulting in the direct loss of 2500 jobs (and up to 8000 in allied industries) over a three-year period.

So is Newcastle shattered? Dream on. Far from slipping away quietly, Newcastle has a burgeoning reputation as a happening place. The local arts scene is lively (but then it always has been), unemployment is falling, civic and business leaders have been taking can-do pills by the handful and there are big hopes for tourism in the future. In the year to June 2000, the City Council fielded more than 2800 development applications (value: $273.5 million) and more than 1000 new projects were completed, begun or approved.

The only thing that's not changing is the vibe. Newcastle remains a friendly place. It might lag Sydney for size, but it's a mile ahead for smiles.

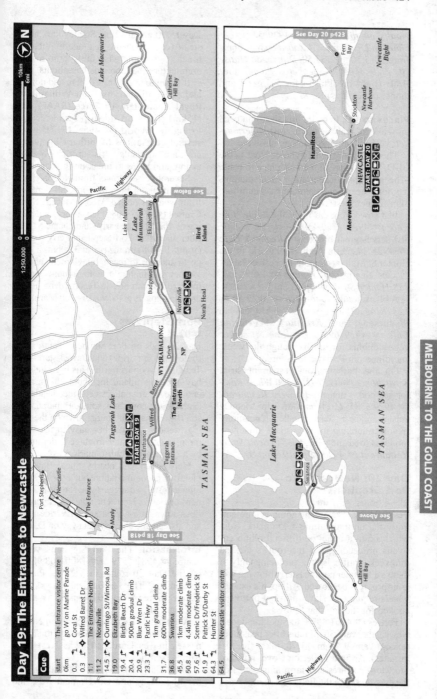

Day 19: The Entrance to Newcastle

Cue

start	The Entrance visitor centre
0km	go W on Marine Parade
0.1	Coral St
0.3	Wilfred Barret Dr
1.1	The Entrance North
11.2	Norahville
14.5	Ouringo St/Mimosa Rd
19.0	Elizabeth Bay
19.4	Birdie Beach Dr
20.4	500m gradual climb
20.9	Blue Wren Dr
23.3	Pacific Hwy
31.7	1km gradual climb
36.8	600m moderate climb
45.5	Swansea
45.5	1km moderate climb
50.8	4.4km moderate climb
57.6	Scenic Dr/Frederick St
61.9	Patrick St/Darby St
64.3	Hunter St
64.5	Newcastle visitor centre

MELBOURNE TO THE GOLD COAST

Noahs on the Beach (☎ *4929 5181, cnr Shortland Esplanade & Zaara St*) has rooms from $115.50 to $137.50. *Dunvegan House* (☎ *4929 4103, 4 Shepherds Place*) does B&B (light breakfasts) for $115/162 and dinner (weekdays) for $25.

Places to Eat In a city this size, you need only ask a local for the nearest *supermarket*; you're bound to find one close by.

There's a lot of dining choice close to the CBD, with Darby St the best place to head. (The greatest concentration of restaurants has long been in Beaumont St, Hamilton, 5km further west).

Just down from the YHA, the *Bogie Hole Cafe* (☎ *4929 1790, cnr Hunter & Pacific Sts)* serves great breakfasts. *Reader's Cafe* (☎ *4925 3422)*, in A&R Bookworld in the Hunter St Mall, is pleasant for coffee and focaccias. Nearby *Cafe Plumes* (☎ *4929 7333, 188 Hunter St)* is also pleasant for a snack.

A block south, *Topo-Nico* (☎ *4929 5148, 123 King St)* has $4 pastas Monday to Wednesday; and *Krishna's Vegetarian Cafe* (☎ *4929 6900, 110 King St)* serves vego delights for lunch through the week, and dinner on Friday and Saturday.

On the harbour-front restaurant strip, *Scratchley's* (☎ *4929 1111, 200 Wharf Rd)* – for seafood – and the *Brewery Restaurant* (☎ *4929 6333, 150 Wharf Rd)* – for Mod Oz cuisine and beer – have excellent reputations. If you're looking to blow some money on top-class food and wine, head to *Scott Street Restaurant* (☎ *4920 0107, 19 Scott St)*.

Day 20: Newcastle to Port Stephens

3½–4 hours, 49.7km

Yes, this day is easy. The going is unrelentingly flat until about the 45km mark, from which point a none-too-difficult climb enlivens proceedings. If the route's tackled midweek, traffic isn't a problem. Only if there's a summer north-easterly blowing will your progress be slowed. All up, it's exactly what's required to stay warm but not overcooked for the day that follows.

Ferries (☎ *4961 8930)* to Stockton depart Newcastle every 30 minutes after peak hour (except 9am–9.45am; $1.70, bikes free, 10 minutes). Around Fullerton Cove, north of Stockton, pastures and farm animals catch the eye: these are the first rural scenes since

Day 15. At about 12km, Stanley Park homestead (c. 1897) adds a graceful Victorian touch to the otherwise fairly drab modern architecture that abounds hereabouts.

It's rare to cycle around here and not hear and see military jets from **Williamtown Royal Australian Air Force (RAAF) Base** (15km). The short side trip 2km later leads to **Fighter World** (☎ 4965 1717), where several generations of military fighter aircraft are on display. It's surprisingly interesting, and helps to break up the day.

Several vessels travel from Nelson Bay to Tea Gardens in the afternoon, all departing from wharves near d'Albora Marina. Simba Cruises (☎ 4997 1084) has a service departing at 4pm (but be early) and charge $10 for rider and bike. Port Stephens Ferry Service (☎ 4981 3798) do the run at 3.30pm. It takes up to an hour to reach Tea Gardens and the journey is a highlight, with dolphins sighted more often than not. In Tea Gardens, ferries drop passengers at the wharves on Marine Dr.

Port Stephens

☎ 02

Day 20 ends on Port Stephens' south shore (before the ferry ride) and Day 21 starts from Tea Gardens on its north. This big, sheltered bay stretches inland for about 20km; at its entrance are dramatic, steep-sided heads: Yacaaba to the north and, south, Tomaree. Nelson Bay is the main tourist town on the port; it's friendly enough, but busy in the warm months, and its water frontage is dominated by a consumer-paradise marina.

Nelson Bay and nearby Shoal Bay have plentiful accommodation but unless you're after a hostel, we suggest you stay at Tea Gardens or Hawks Nest. The quiet and unpretentious towns are a pleasant ferry ride away, and also enable an early getaway on Day 21.

Information The Port Stephens visitor centre (☎ 4981 1579 or ☎ 1800-808 900) is on the Day 20 route, in Victoria Parade, Nelson Bay. The Tea Gardens/Hawks Nest visitor centre (☎ 4997 0111) is on Myall St, Tea Gardens.

A greater range of services are in Nelson Bay, especially banks. Most of the businesses in Tea Gardens/Hawks Nest have Eftpos facilities.

Shoal Bay Bike Hire (☎ 4981 4121), corner Shoal Bay and Government Rds, and

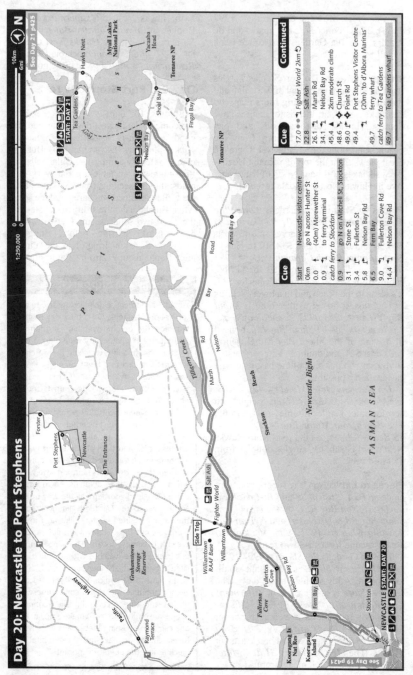

Day 20: Newcastle to Port Stephens

1:250,000

0   10km
0   6ml

N

See Day 21 p425

Myall Lakes National Park

Hawks Nest

Yacaaba Head

Tea Gardens
START DAY 21

Port   Stephens

Shoal Bay

Tomaree NP

Nelson Bay

Fingal Bay

Tomaree NP

Anna Bay

Nelson   Bay   Road

Tilligerry Creek

Marsh   Nelson   Rd

Salt Ash

Fighter World

Williamtown

Side Trip
Williamtown RAAF Base

Fullerton Cove

Nelson Bay Rd

Fern Bay

Kooragang Island

Kooragang Is Nat Res

Grahamstown Storage Reservoir

Pacific Highway

Raymond Terrace

Fullerton Cove

Stockton   Beach

Newcastle Bight

TASMAN SEA

Stockton
START DAY 20

NEWCASTLE
START DAY 20

See Day 19 p421

Cue	
start	Newcastle visitor centre
0km	go N across Hunter St
0.0	(40m) Merewether St
0.9	to ferry terminal
	catch ferry to Stockton
0.9	go N on Mitchell St, Stockton
3.1	Stone St
3.4	Fullerton St
5.8	Nelson Bay Rd
6.5	Fern Bay
9.0	Fullerton Cove Rd
14.4	Nelson Bay Rd

Cue	Continued
17.0	*Fighter World 2km*
22.8	Salt Ash
26.1	Marsh Rd
34.1	Nelson Bay Rd
45.4	2km moderate climb
48.6	Church St
49.0	Point Rd
49.4	Port Stephens Visitor Centre
	(20m) 'to d'Albora Marinas'
49.7	ferry wharf
	catch ferry to Tea Gardens
49.7	Tea Gardens wharf

MELBOURNE TO THE GOLD COAST

Hawks Nest Mowers & Hire (☎ 4997 1133), 2/71 Booner St, carry spares and do repairs. The Tea Gardens post office is on Myall St.

Things to See & Do Port Stephens styles itself as 'the dolphin capital of Australia' and has more **dolphin-watching tours** than you can poke a stick at; the visitor centres have details. Hawks Nest has surf and bay **beaches**; there's good **fishing** from the beaches and along the Myall River. There are great views from the top of **Yacaaba Head** – the walk takes ¾–1 hour. North of Kingfisher Ave in Hawks Nest is a **koala reserve**.

Places to Stay In Tea Gardens, *Lone Pine Caravan Park* (☎ 4997 0207, 93 Marine Dr) is close to the ferry wharves; a site costs $16.50 and on-site vans, $38.50. In Hawks Nest, *Jimmys Beach Caravan Park* (☎ 4997 0466, Coorilla St) has tent sites for $17.60, cabins from $49.50 and on-site vans for $33; it's close to the beach and in a lovely setting.

The closest hostel to the route is *Shoal Bay YHA* (☎ 4981 0982, e shoalbay.yha@castle.net.au, 59–61 Shoal Bay Rd), housed in a wing of the Shoal Bay Motel. Dorm beds cost $21 and doubles, $26 per person. If you stay on this side of the bay, catch the earliest ferry possible.

Tea Gardens Hotel Motel (☎ 4997 0203, cnr Marine Dr & Maxwell St) is friendly and comfortable; singles/doubles cost $45/65. The *Beachfront Motor Inn* (☎ 4997 0324, 15 Beach Rd), across the road from Hawks Nest's surf beach, has singles/doubles from $59 midweek.

Places to Eat Nelson Bay supermarkets include an *IGA (Austral St)* and *Bi-Lo (Stockton St)*. *Nelson Bay RSL* (☎ 4981 1344, cnr Shoal Bay Rd & Dixon Dr)* and *Nelson Bay Bowling Club* (☎ 4981 4906, Stockton St) are best value for a sit-down feed.

The Tea Gardens *Pie Shop* (☎ 4997 1922; Myall Plaza, Myall St) is a brilliant small-town oddity – it's open 24 hours daily. The *General Store* is on Marine Dr. *Tillermans Cafe Restaurant* (☎ 4997 0138, 77 Marine Dr) does a mean fetta & veggie pizza for $11.50. *Lake's Rest Cafe* (☎ 4997 0138, 69 Marine Dr) does huge cooked breakfasts for $10.50. The *Tea Gardens Hotel Motel bistro* has big seafood meals from $12.

In Hawks Nest, the *supermarket* is on Booner St. *Myall Country Bakery (Tuloa St)* is open daily. Try *Hawks Nest Chinese (☎ 4997 0662, Booner St)* or *Fairways Restaurant (☎ 4997 0980)* at the golf club.

Day 21: Port Stephens to Forster
7–8 hours, 107.6km
Welcome to the longest day of the ride. The good news is it is easier than the other two 100km-plus days (Days 11 and 14). But for a couple of teensy climbs near Bulahdelah, the first 44km are on table-top flat, very quiet roads; the dirt sections (only 8.1km in total) are well maintained and barely reduce speed. After Bulahdelah, the traffic is busier and there are two solid ascents (between 48km and 58km). Starting before Bungwahl (71.8km), there's a string of smaller climbs; after Tiona (about 91km) it's flat to Forster.

A Frenzy for Flipper(s)

About 140 bottlenose dolphins are said to reside in Port Stephens. On a busy day in midsummer, the dolphin-watchers outnumber their quarry by a very, very wide margin.

From the shoreline, watching the watchers is something akin to a free screening of *Keystone Captains*. A variety of big cruise vessels packed with rubbernecking tourists motor about. A dolphin pod is sighted. Boats in the vicinity converge (with due regard and care for the animals, it must be emphasised). Vessels slow. Dolphins go about their business. Cameras click and flash at sun-bright water: a thousand over-exposed images are born.

Then there's the brisk autumn afternoon when a pod of three dolphins – two adults and a calf – lead your ferry all the way up the Myall River to Tea Gardens, gliding through the tannin-stained waters like a trio of teenagers out for a Friday-night lark. You're the only passenger aboard. The skipper throttles back and he watches with as much excitement as any first-time tourist.

It's hard to be cynical when you see this elemental human delight in connecting with nature and, the fact is, in this economy people are entitled to try to make a dollar. But one can't stop wishing that profits were used to enrich the animals and their habitat as much as line the operators' pockets.

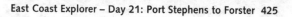

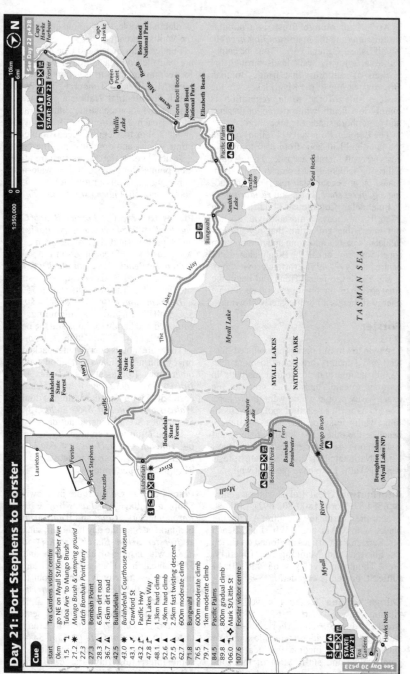

MELBOURNE TO THE GOLD COAST

Day 21: Port Stephens to Forster

Cue		
0km		Tea Gardens visitor centre
		go NE on Myall St/Kingfisher Ave
1.5		Tuloa Ave 'to Mungo Brush'
21.2	☀	Mungo Brush & camping ground
27.3		catch Bombah Point ferry
27.3		Bombah Point
28.3	▲	6.5km dirt road
36.7	▲	1.6km dirt road
42.5		Bulahdelah
43.0	☀	*Bulahdelah Courthouse Museum*
43.1	↰	Crawford St
43.2	↱	Pacific Hwy
47.8	↱	The Lakes Way
48.1	▲	1.3km hard climb
52.6	▲	4.9km hard climb
57.5	▲	2.5km fast twisting descent
62.7	▲	600m moderate climb
71.8		Bungwahl
76.5	▲	600m moderate climb
79.7	▲	1km moderate climb
84.5		Pacific Palms
89.8	▲	800m gradual climb
106.0	✦	Mark St/Little St
107.6		Forster visitor centre

At 21.2km **Mungo Brush** is a popular destination (and the main *camping area*) in Myall Lakes National Park. From the camping area, a lovely walk leads through the pockets of rainforest that fringe Bombah Broadwater, one of the Myall lakes. On the eastern side of the route vegetation is mainly low heath, while ti-tree, casuarinas and angophora shade the lake shore.

The Bombah Point ferry (27.3km) runs on the hour and half-hour from 8am to 6pm; it costs 60 cents for bike and rider. There's quite a thriving settlement at Bombah Point, dominated by an 'ecotourism resort' and including a *general store*, *kiosk* and *restaurant*.

Bulahdelah Courthouse (43km), built in 1886, is these days a museum with a small but interesting collection that reveals Bulahdelah's past as a logging and mining town (open Saturday; or call the Bulahdelah visitor centre on ☎ 4997 4981 to arrange a viewing).

It's a relief to reach Tiona and begin the final stretch on the flat, but you'll need some energy if there's a north-easterly blowing.

Forster
☎ 02

The twin towns of Forster (pronounced 'foster') and Tuncurry are home to more than 14,000 people and are tourist magnets in summer. Outside busy times you can see exactly why people would want to live here. The towns are in a beautiful spot, with 20km-long Wallis Lake on one side and lovely beaches, the other. The surfing, fishing and water sports are excellent and nearby Booti Booti National Park and the State forests west of Wallis Lake have pleasant walks.

Information Great Lakes visitor centre (☎ 6554 8799 or ☎ 1800-802 692), Little St, is near the Forster town centre. All the big banks, with ATMs, are in Wharf and Beach Sts, Forster. Post offices are found on Beach St, Forster, and Manning St, Tuncurry. Steve Thompson Cycles (☎ 6554 9180), 44 Little St, Foster, is excellent.

Things to See & Do It's well worth visiting **Tobwabba Art** (☎ 6554 5755), 10 Breckenridge St. The Aboriginal-owned studio/gallery provides a valuable source of employment and income for local Aboriginal artists and staff. Most of the Tobwabba artists are descendants of the Wallamba people, the original custodians of the Wallis Lake area.

Forster Main Beach and One Mile Beach are patrolled during holidays and are best for **swimming**; the **surf** is generally better at Nine Mile Beach, Tuncurry. The **Pebbly Beach Bicentennial Walk** is a great way to explore the local coastline. Starting at the Main Beach swimming pool, it runs for about 2.5km to Bennett Head Lookout, a prime whale- and dolphin-watching point.

A flotilla of **watercraft** is for hire at various points along the Little St waterfront. For a guided, two-hour tour of Wallis Lake, book a spot on *Amaroo II* (☎ 6554 7743).

Places to Stay The *Forster Beach Caravan Park* (☎ 6554 6269, *Reserve Rd*) is right on Main Beach and close to the town centre. A site costs $17.60; cabins cost from $38.50. *Tuncurry Beach Caravan Park* (☎ 6554 6440, *Beach St*) is also close to the surf; a site costs $17.50 and en suite cabins, $52.80.

Dolphin Lodge (☎ 6555 8155, *43 Head St*), a YHA affiliate, is welcoming, well equipped and handy to shops and the beach. Dorm beds cost $20 and doubles, from $44.

There are motels everywhere, packed and pricey during holidays but good value at other times. Rooms at *Great Lakes Motor Inn* (☎ 6554 6955, *cnr West & Head Sts*) cost $50/55 for standard singles/doubles. *Wallis Lake Motel* (☎ 6555 5600, *5 Wallis St*) charges $70/75 outside holidays.

If you're up for a splurge, try the lovely old *Tokelau Guest House* (☎ 6557 5157; *2 Manning St, Tuncurry*), where B&B costs $154 to $176 per double.

Places to Eat On the route into town, the Shopping Village (*cnr Lakes Way & Breese Parade*) includes *Coles* and *Woolworths* supermarkets. Start the day bathed in sunshine at *Forster Main Beach Kiosk* (☎ 6555 8582) with a mug of black coffee and big $5.40 breakfast. For lunch, attack any of the countless takeaway joints about town; our pick is the *Wallis Lake Fisherman's Co-op* (☎ 6554 6402; *1 Wharf St, Tuncurry*), home of the freshest local seafood.

Wharf St, Tuncurry, caters to a range of tastes. The *Fat Ant Cafe* (☎ 6555 3444, *32 Wharf St*) has great balcony views and some interesting flavours. *El Barracho Mexican* (☎ 6554 5573, *12 Wharf St*) does the cheerful salsa thing: big nachos cost $12.50 and fajitas, $16.50. *Pelican Pizza (☎ 6555 6633, 25 Wharf St)* has a range of pastas from $8. Go to *Casuarina (☎ 6555 6522; 8 Little St, Forster)* for Asian flavours.

The *Forster-Tuncurry Memorial Services Club (☎ 6554 6255, Strand St)*, its affiliated *Sports Club (☎ 6554 9270; Beach St, Tuncurry)*, and the *Forster Bowling Club (☎ 6554 5488, Strand St)* are open for dinner every night.

Day 22: Forster to Laurieton
6½–7 hours, 83.9km

For the first time since Day 15, the route spends some serious time (about 35km) on the new Pacific Hwy, though there's mostly a decent (sealed) verge. The last 27km are virtually traffic-free, as the route traverses rural lands and Crowdy Bay National Park on very quiet roads (21km is on good dirt roads).

The Lakes Way north of Forster can be busy and isn't fun to cycle on a weekend; it's almost a relief to turn onto the Pacific Hwy and its wide bike verge. From about the 32km mark come wide views of the **Manning Valley**, one of the wide, big-river floodplains for which northern NSW is renowned. The valley's main town is **Taree**, reached via a turn west at 30.7km. Until re-cently, the Pacific Hwy went through Taree, but extensive road- and bridge-works now sees most traffic crossing the Manning River on bridges east of the town. Following the old highway through Taree will add 6km to the day's total.

The route is flat as a pancake from 32km to nearly 52km, when a couple of easy climbs break the monotony. Fortunately, there's nothing monotonous about the route after the turn east at 57km. After a few kilometres in rural flatlands, the road passes into the western fringe of Crowdy Bay National Park. The park protects a variety of coastal habitats, including freshwater wetlands and old-growth eucalypt communities; birdlife seen here includes huge, noisy flocks of lorikeets and, occasionally, a soaring osprey. The rich variety of marsupials includes koalas and rufous bettongs, and it isn't unusual to disturb eastern grey kangaroos grazing by the road.

The last stretch from Diamond Head to Laurieton is flat and easy, and cars are rare.

Laurieton
☎ 02

Laurieton is the main centre in the quartet of settlements – the others are Dunbogan, North Haven and West Haven – that comprise

Slow Down Pleas

Only the new or large roadside memorials to car crash victims are obvious from motor vehicles; the slower pace of bicycle travel allows time to see them all – and there are many to see. Their appearance focuses the mind wonderfully...'The traffic's really whooshing along here. Maybe I should look at the road, not the map.'

Outside of cities and larger regional centres, Australia is thinly populated, and towns and settlements are widely spaced. People, especially country people, will drive great distances for a special occasion, or sometimes just for company. They often travel at night, in all weather, sometimes after drinking alcohol. And they often drive too fast.

A 1997 Monash University report noted that, overseas, excessive speed was a definite cause in 8% of car crashes and a probable cause in up to 16%. In Australia, excessive speed is a contributing factor in up to 30% of fatal crashes. Monash reckoned speed-related road trauma cost the Australian community up to A$1 billion annually.

After a time, one realises that people have erected roadside memorials to honour a lost loved one and, additionally, to plead and warn. Take care and slow down, is the plea: this happened to our Mum and it could happen to you.

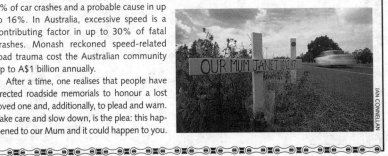

MELBOURNE TO THE GOLD COAST

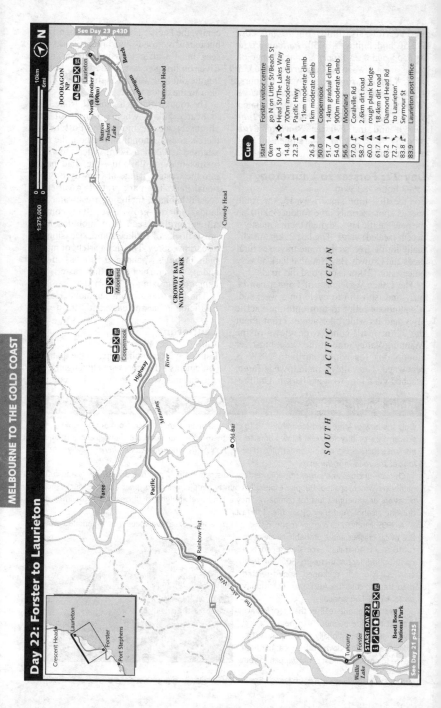

Day 22: Forster to Laurieton

Cue		
start	Forster visitor centre	
0km	go N on Little St/Beach St	◆
0.4	Head St/The Lakes Way	
14.8	700m moderate climb	◀
22.3	Pacific Hwy	⌐
26.3	1.1km moderate climb	◀
50.0	1km moderate climb	◀
51.7	Coopernook	◀
54.0	1.4km gradual climb	◀
56.5	900m moderate climb	◀
57.0	Moorland	
58.7	Coralville Rd	⌐
60.0	2.6km dirt road	◀
61.7	rough plank bridge	◀
63.2	18.4km dirt road	⌐
72.7	Diamond Head Rd	↘
83.8	'to Laurieton'	⌐
83.9	Seymour St	
	Laurieton post office	

Scale 1:375,000

0 — 10km
0 — 6mi

See Day 23 p430

See Day 21 p425

Camden Haven. Dooragan National Park and its towering peak, North Brother, create a backdrop; Camden Haven Inlet and Stingray Creek provide the water frontages.

Information There's no visitor centre in the Camden Haven area, but it falls into the ever-widening orbit of Port Macquarie visitor centre (☎ 6581 8000 or ☎ 1800-025 935). The Laurieton post office, on Seymour St, is a good starting point for local orientation. The main drag, Bold St, has several bank branches, most of which have ATMs.

Things to See & Do Swimming is best near the surf club at Grants Beach, North Haven, but Dunbogan Beach is also nice. Walking tracks in **Kattang Nature Reserve**, east of Dunbogan, lead to the Pilot Station and Charles Hamey Lookouts on Perpendicular Point and Camden Head. These are excellent vantage points for shore-based **whale watching** from June to October. It's a steep and twisting ride up Captain Cook Bicentennial Rd to **North Brother Lookout** but the view is stunning; the return ride from central Laurieton is about 14km. Try Dunbogan Boatshed & Marina (☎ 6559 9713) if you keen to hire a runabout for **fishing**. The Plaza Theatre (☎ 6559 8755), Bold St, screens current **movies**.

Places to Stay Close to the river and Laurieton shops, *The Haven Caravan Park (☎ 6559 9584, Arnott St)* has sites for $13.20 and cabins from $33. *Beachfront Caravan Park (☎ 6559 9193; The Parade, North Haven)* is a stone's throw from the surf beach; a site costs $14.30.

Laurieton Hotel Motel (☎ 6559 9004, Bold St) is in the middle of town; singles/doubles cost $35/45 and you can grab a decent pub dinner in the bistro from Tuesday to Saturday. The *Mariner Motel (☎ 6559 9398; 12 Kew Rd, Laurieton)* has rooms for $49.50/58.50. *North Haven Motel (☎ 6559 9604, 506 Ocean Dr)* charges $55.

Dunbogan B&B (☎ 6559 6222, 64 Camden Head Rd) is a bit further out; B&B costs $50/80.

Places to Eat Stock up on starch at *Scotts Plaza Bakehouse*, in the Laurieton shopping centre off Bold St; a *Bi-Lo* supermarket is there too.

For reliable meals at reasonable prices, try *Dolphins Family Restaurant (☎ 6559 9110, cnr Seymour & Lake Sts)* in the Laurieton United Servicemens Club ($6.95 pastas on Tuesday nights); or the bistro at *North Haven Bowling Club (☎ 6559 9150, 1 Woodford Rd)*, with $8 roasts. In Laurieton, *Golden Inn Restaurant (☎ 6559 9754, 62 Bold St)* serves Chinese food every night and *Big Brother Pizza (☎ 6559 9118, 463 Ocean Dr)* does pizza, ribs and pasta.

Day 23: Laurieton to Crescent Head
5–6 hours, 70.7km

This is a day of two greatly contrasting parts. From Laurieton to Port Macquarie the route follows well-used sealed roads through the seaside communities of Bonny Hills (8.5km) and Lake Cathie (15.1km; pronounced 'cat-eye'). This is one of the mid-north coast's most popular holiday areas, and cyclists should anticipate a lot of traffic in midsummer. North of Port Macquarie, it's dirt roads and prime surfing destinations most of the way to lovely Crescent Head.

Port Macquarie is a large, developed centre (population about 40,000) that has managed to retain a relaxed feel. It's worth considering staying overnight here as there's a lot to see and do; the visitor centre (☎ 6583 1293 or ☎ 1800-025 935) is right on the route (34.3km), at the corner of Clarence and Hay Sts.

Port was the third town established on the Australian mainland and has a rich European-Australian history. The **Maritime Museum** (☎ 6583 1866), 6 William St; and the **Port Macquarie Museum** (☎ 6583 1108), on Clarence St, between Murray & Hay Sts, reveal much of colonial life in Port; the latter is in an 1830s convict-built storehouse.

There's no charge to use the Settlement Point **ferry** (at 39.6km), which runs 24 hours daily (except for the fourth Wednesday of each month). North of the ferry, the route includes a 5.7km track, small parts of which are impossible to ride. It's worth the walk: the track runs through lovely **Limeburners Creek Nature Reserve**, and at several points it's easy to divert to the beach for wonderful views north to Queens Head and south to Port. (If the track sounds too scary, take the Maria River Rd, just west, which adds about 6km to the day.)

MELBOURNE TO THE GOLD COAST

Day 23: Laurieton to Crescent Head

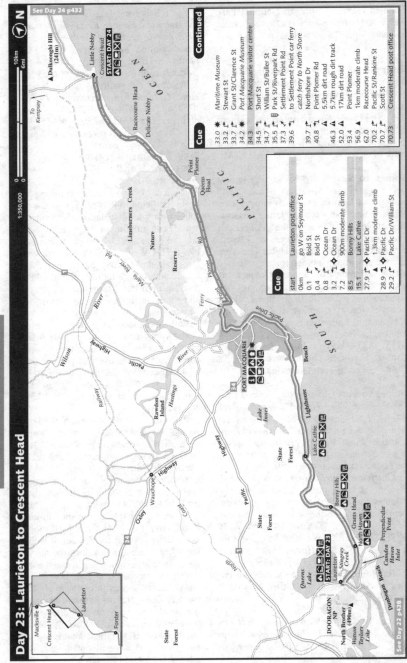

See Day 24 p432

▲ Dulkoonghi Hill (241m)

Crescent Head
START DAY 24
Little Nobby
Racecourse Head
Delicate Nobby

To Kempsey

OCEAN

Point Plomer

Queens Head

Limeburners Creek

Nature Reserve

Maria River Rd

Plomer Rd

PACIFIC

Ferry

Pacific Drive

SOUTH

Wilson River

Hastings River

Rawdon Island

Pacific Highway

River

Wauchope

Oxley Highway

Railway

Pacific Highway

North Coast Highway

PORT MACQUARIE
※ 👁 ⊞ ✕ 🅿
🛈 🏕 🛏

Lake Innes

Lighthouse Beach

State Forest

Lake Cathie
👁 ⊞ ✕ 🅿

State Forest

Bonny Hills
👁 ⊞ ✕ 🅿

Grants Head

North Haven
👁 ⊞ ✕ 🅿 🛏

Stingray Creek
START DAY 23
Laurieton
👁 ⊞ ✕ 🅿 🛏

Perpendicular Point

Camden Haven Inlet

Queens Lake

DOORAGON NP
North Brother (490m)
Watson Taylors Lake

Dunbogan Beach

See Day 22 p428

Inset map:
Macksville
Crescent Head
Laurieton
Forster
State Forest

N
1:350,000
0 — 10km
0 — 6mi

Cue		
0km		Laurieton post office
0.1	⬏	go W on Seymour St
0.4	⬐	Bold St
0.8	⬏	Bold St
3.2	⬏	Ocean Dr
7.2	◆	Ocean Dr
		900m moderate climb
8.5	◀	Bonny Hills
15.1	◀	Lake Cathie
27.9	⬏ ◆	Pacific Dr
		1.3km moderate climb
28.9	◆	Pacific Dr
29.2	⬏	Pacific Dr/William St

Cue		Continued
33.0	✳	Maritime Museum
33.2	⬏	Stewart St
33.7	⬏	Grant St/Clarence St
34.2	✳	Port Macquarie Museum
34.3		Port Macquarie visitor centre
34.5	⬏	Short St
34.7	⬏	William St/Buller St
35.5	⬏	Park St/Riverpark Rd
37.3	🚢	Settlement Point Rd
		to Settlement Point car ferry
39.6	⬏	catch ferry to North Shore
		Northshore Dr
39.7	⬏	Point Plomer Rd
40.8	⬏	Point Plomer Rd
		5.5km dirt road
46.3	◀	5.7km rough dirt track
52.0	◀	17km dirt road
53.4	◀	Point Plomer
56.9	◀	1km moderate climb
62.0		Racecourse Head
70.2	⬏	Pacific St/Rankine St
70.7	⬏	Scott St
70.73		Crescent Head post office

Between **Point Plomer** (53.4km) and **Racecourse Head** (62km) – legendary surfing point breaks – there's a moderate, 1km climb. Make the most of it – it's the only worthwhile rise until about halfway through Day 24.

Crescent Head
☎ 02

One of the legendary surfing destinations on the NSW north coast, Crescent Head is (sadly) starting to catch on as a holiday destination, and development looks set to expand. But it's still an attractive place with a laid-back atmosphere, lovely beaches and friendly locals (unless you 'drop in' on them in the surf).

Information There's no visitor centre in Crescent, but Kempsey visitor centre (☎ 6563 1555), about 20km west, is a good information source and has an accommodation booking service (☎ 1800-642 480). Crescent is fairly compact, centred on the Pacific–Rankine–East Sts roundabout. The post office on Scott St is a Commonwealth Bank agent and there are ATMs in the Crescent Head Country Club and the Tavern.

Things to See & Do Crescent Head and, to the south, Racecourse Head and Point Plomer, are brilliant for **surfing**. **Swimming** is best at Killick Front Beach. Nice **walks** lead to Little Nobby and Big Nobby, the prominent headlands east of the town; Little Nobby is good for whale watching in the cooler months. The lookout at the water tank on Skyline Crescent offers fantastic **views**. The **golf course** overlooks the ocean and hit-and-giggle standard isn't frowned upon on quiet days.

Places to Stay & Eat The *Crescent Head Holiday Park* (☎ 6566 0261 or ☎ 1800-006 600, Pacific St) is right on the beach. It's hard to get a site for a night during holidays (weekly bookings dominate); at all other times a site costs $16.50.

The *Mediterranean Motel* (☎ 6566 0303, 35 Pacific St) has rooms for $88, dropping to $55 outside peak times. *Bourne's Holiday Flats* (☎ 6566 0293, 1 Baker Dr) are $75 (dropping to $55).

Crescent is packed with *holiday cottages*, some of which are available by the night outside peak times. Either of the local estate agents (☎ 6566 0306 or ☎ 6566 0500) can assist with bookings.

The *Crescent Head Foodstore (Rankine St)* is on the route. *Barnett's Bakery (East St)* is open early daily. *Malibu Munchies (Rankine St)* is great for daytime snacks and *Crescent Head Seafoods* (☎ 6566 0672, East St) is the place for takeaway fish and chips. Head to the *Odd Sock Coffee Shop* (☎ 6566 0172, Main St) and you can sip a tasty cappuccino while doing your laundry. The restaurant in *Crescent Head Country Club* (☎ 6566 0551, 1 Rankine St) serves great seafood. Across the road, the *Crescent Head Tavern* (☎ 6566 0166, 2 Main St) has restaurant meals upstairs and pizzas downstairs (in the bottle shop).

Day 24: Crescent Head to Macksville
6½–7½ hours, 87.6km

Charming riverside roads, rolling green coastal hinterland and magnificent beaches – this is the day that shows the best of the NSW mid-north coast in one pleasant ride. The route is so flat up to about the 44km mark that you risk falling asleep on a windless day. The second half of the day has a lot more action, and takes in some busier road sections (on the Pacific Hwy).

From 11km to nearly 40km, the route follows the Belmore River and then the wide and mighty Macleay River. This is mostly dairy country, and paddocks full of quizzical cows are the main feature.

At 37.7km (and at a couple of points before), signs indicate a right turn to **South West Rocks**. While 22km is a long side trip on an 88km day, this is one place worth the effort (see the boxed text 'Jewel of the (Mid) North?'overleaf). If you're keen to visit South West Rocks but want a shorter day, stay on the Pacific Hwy (rather than turning onto Stuarts Point Rd) at 55.1km: this will take about 10km off the mapped route.

That said, the route past Stuarts Point and through Grassy Head is a cracker. Grassy (a side trip at 67.7km) is the most beautiful of beaches, quiet as a whisper midweek and out of season; it's legal to swim or sunbake nude at the southern end of the beach.

Take care on the final section on the Pacific Hwy: semitrailers seem particularly close here.

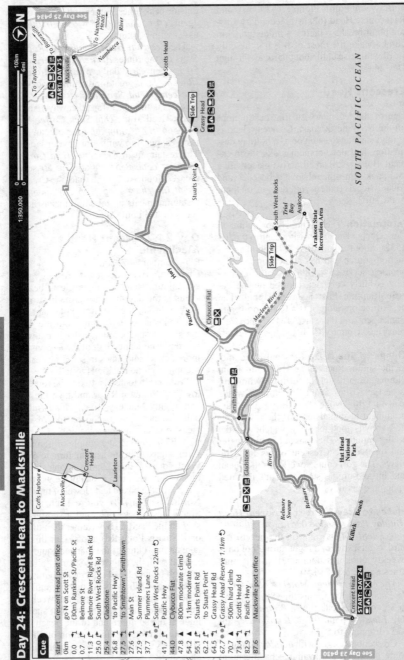

MELBOURNE TO THE GOLD COAST

See Day 25 p434

See Day 23 p430

1:350,000

0 ———— 10km
0 ———— 6mi

N

SOUTH PACIFIC OCEAN

To Taylors Arm
To Bowraville
To Nambucca Heads
Nambucca River
Macksville
START: DAY 25
Scotts Head
Side Trip
Grassy Head
Stuarts Point
South West Rocks
Trial Bay
Arakoon
Arakoon State Recreation Area
Macleay River
Side Trip
Clybucca Flat
Pacific Hwy
Smithtown
Gladstone
River
Belmore
Belmore Swamp
Hat Head National Park
Killick Beach
Crescent Head
START: DAY 24

Coffs Harbour
Macksville
Crescent Head
Laurieton
Kempsey

Day 24: Crescent Head to Macksville

Cue		
start		Crescent Head post office
0km		go N on Scott St
0.0	⌐⌐	(30m) Rankine St/Pacific St
0.7	⌐⌐	Belmore St
11.3	⌐	Belmore River Right Bank Rd
25.0	⌐	South West Rocks Rd
25.4		Gladstone
26.8	⌐	'to Pacific Hwy'
27.5	⌐	'to Smithtown', Smithtown
27.6	⌐	Main St
27.9	⌐	Summer Island Rd
37.7	⌐	Plummers Lane
		South West Rocks 22km ↺
41.7	⌐	Pacific Hwy
44.0		Clybucca Flat
47.8	◄	800m moderate climb
54.2	◄	1.1km moderate climb
55.1	⌐	Stuarts Point Rd
62.2	⌐	'to Stuarts Point'
64.5	⌐	Grassy Head Rd
67.7	↺	*Grassy Head Reserve 1.1km* ↺
70.7	◄	500m hard climb
73.4	◄	Scotts Head Rd
82.9	⌐	Pacific Hwy
87.6		Macksville post office

Macksville
☎ 02

This old town on the wide Nambucca River services the local fishing, oyster-farming, tropical fruit, vegetables, grazing, dairy and timber industries. It's bigger than a blink-and-you'll-miss-it proposition, but tends to be neglected because of its proximity to popular Nambucca Heads. That's a shame, because Macksville is neat and friendly and has some nice pubs and places to eat.

Information There's no visitor centre in town; the Nambucca Valley visitor centre (☎ 6568 6954), on the Pacific Hwy about 10km north, can help with information, and the map/signboard on River St (opposite the post office) will help with orientation.

Bank and credit-union branches (a couple with ATMs) are in the town centre on the highway; there's a third ATM in Wallace St (outside the supermarket). The post office is on the corner of Pacific Hwy and Cooper St.

Things to See & Do The charming **Star Hotel**, on River St, was built in 1885. It's one of the area's oldest surviving buildings and still a great place for a beer and a yarn. The bar and staircase are made of local red cedar and there are great 1950s beer advertisements on the walls. Two kilometres further east on River St is **Mary Boulton's Cottage** (☎ 6568 1457), a fair replica of the rough-sawn wooden homes of early settlers. Old furniture, clothing, tools and other memorabilia are on display (open by appointment).

At Taylors Arm, 25km west of Macksville, is the former Cosmopolitan Hotel (built 1903) – immortalised in song as (and now officially called) **The Pub with No Beer**. This old timbergetters' watering hole is great fun and has plenty of beer (it did, in fact, run out in the 1950s during a flood). A feature of friendly Bowraville, 11km north-west of Macksville, the **Bowraville Folk Museum** (☎ 6562 7251) is worth the ride; call ahead to check opening times or arrange a viewing.

Places to Stay & Eat The nearest camping ground is at **Nambucca River Tourist Park** (☎ 6568 1850, 999 Nursey Rd), about 3km south of town; a site costs $17.60, and cabins $75.90 for up to seven people.

The **Star Hotel** (☎ 6568 1008, River St) has singles/doubles for $22/40. You can also stay at the **Nambucca Hotel** (☎ 6568 1033, cnr Wallace St & Pacific Hwy) for $20/33, although it's a bit noisier. Both pubs serve good bistro meals. The **Mid Coast Motor Inn** (☎ 6568 3544, Pacific Hwy) is on the route about 1km south of the town centre; rooms cost $55/70.

An **IGA supermarket** (Wallace St) is just off the route. On the Pacific Hwy, grab bread and pastries at **Peter Pan Bakery**; take away or eat-in at the **Macksville Chinese Restaurant** (☎ 6568 2291); or enjoy club bistro standards at great prices at

---

Jewel of the (Mid) North?

Several towns on the NSW mid-north coast claim to be 'the best'. Port Macquarie has its history, Crescent Head its beaches. And South West Rocks? A visit will reveal it has history *and* beaches, and something far more valuable: obscurity.

South West Rocks is just far enough off the Pacific Hwy – about 15km by the most direct route – to be bypassed by most holiday-makers. The township, in a handsome location on Trial Bay, was established in 1896, but the name South West Rocks wasn't adopted until 1910.

Today the town's main attractions are peace and quiet, nice beaches, fishing and the nearby Arakoon State Recreation Area, site of Smoky Cape lighthouse and Trial Bay Gaol. The gaol was built between 1877 and 1886, primarily to house prisoners put to work on the 1.6km long breakwater around the bay. In 1903 a storm wrecked the 300m of breakwater then completed; the project was abandoned and the prison closed. It was used again in WWI to house German detainees. Fish Rock Cave, about 2km offshore, is one of the largest ocean caves in the southern hemisphere. The 120m-long chamber is a wonderland of coral, cowries and fish species, including wobbegong sharks and stingrays.

Tempted? To do South West Rocks justice you'll need to add a day to the route, but it's worth it. Just don't tell too many of your friends about it. There's camping and other accommodation in town; you can't miss the visitor centre (☎ 6566 7099) on Gregory St as you enter town.

MELBOURNE TO THE GOLD COAST

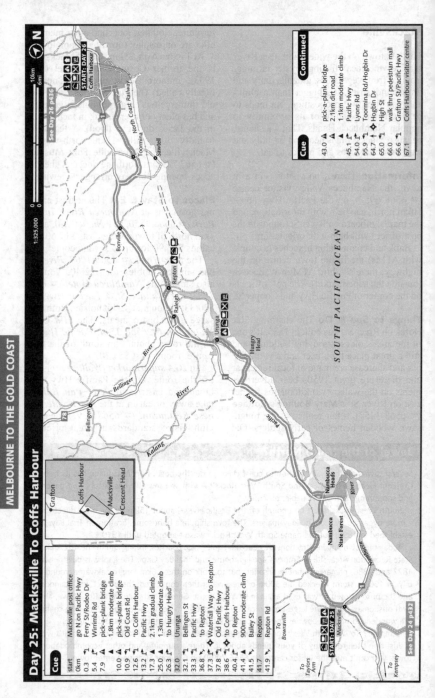

MELBOURNE TO THE GOLD COAST

Day 25: Macksville To Coffs Harbour

Cue

start		Macksville post office
0km		go N on Pacific Hwy
0.3	↱↰	Ferry St/Rodeo Dr
5.4	↱↰	Wirrimbi Rd
7.9	◄	pick-a-plank bridge
	◄	1.8km moderate climb
10.0	◄	pick-a-plank bridge
10.9	↱↰	Old Coast Rd
12.6	↱↰	'to Coffs Harbour'
13.2	↱↰	Pacific Hwy
17.3	◄	2.1km gradual climb
25.0	◄	1.3km moderate climb
26.3	↱↰	'to Hungry Head'
32.0		Urunga
32.1	↱↰	Bellingen St
33.3	↱↰	Pacific Hwy
36.8	↱↰	'to Repton'
37.3	↱◆	Waterfall Way 'to Repton'
37.8	↱↰	Old Pacific Hwy
38.6	↱◆	'to Coffs Harbour'
40.4	↱↰	'to Repton'
41.4	◄	900m moderate climb
41.5	↰	Bailey St
41.7		Repton
41.9	↱	Repton Rd

Cue — Continued

43.0	◄	pick-a-plank bridge
	◄	2.1km dirt road
45.1	◄	1.1km moderate climb
54.0	↱↰	Pacific Hwy
55.9	↱↰	Lyons Rd
64.7	↱◆	Toormina Rd/Hogbin Dr
65.0	↱	Hogbin Dr
66.0	↱	High St
		walk thru pedestrian mall
66.6	↱↰	Grafton St/Pacific Hwy
67.1		Coffs Harbour visitor centre

Macksville Ex-Services Club (☎ *6568 1344, cnr Winifred St*). A meal at *Salz Gourmet Pizzeria* (☎ *6568 2494, 14 River St*) is a must. The pizzas and pastas are yummy, the $5.50 salads are brilliant, and they make – as the blackboard proclaims – 'rather good coffee'.

Facing the river just west of the highway, *The Bridge Cafe* (☎ *6568 1028, River St*) is a trip back to cafe glory days – seating in booths, piles of fudge in the window. It's great for coffee and a burger.

Day 25: Macksville to Coffs Harbour

4½–5½ hours, 67.1km

Very much like Day 14, this is a day on which you'll make important progress but it won't be the best fun, mainly because of traffic. Coffs Harbour is big and getting bigger, and with growth comes a general buzz of people and traffic. So busy is the highway hereabouts that it's something of a surprise to realise only 25.5km of the day are actually spent on it.

The main features of the day are the twisty sections that avoid the highway. For 13km north of Macksville, the route follows quiet back roads and passes through Nambucca State Forest. Further along (from 26.3km to 33.3km), a diversion leads past Hungry Head and through Urunga, where the Kalang and Bellinger Rivers flow to sea. Yet another 'back way' (36.8km to 45.1km) leads over the Bellinger on the old Pacific Hwy bridge. It isn't all that many years ago that summer traffic choked the old highway, slowing for kilometres around here. These days there's a new, freeway-style highway section to the west, and cyclists on these good, flat roads are barely disturbed by traffic.

There's a pleasant off-road bikepath from Toormina (58km) to the big roundabout at 64.7km. The route then passes Coffs Harbour airport and the university, and it can get pretty hectic on the road.

Coffs Harbour

See Coffs Harbour (pp141–42) in the Coffs & Dorrigo Circuit in the New South Wales chapter for information on accommodation and other services. The **Coffs & Dorrigo Circuit** is a two-day ride that starts/ends at Coffs Harbour.

Day 26: Coffs Harbour to Grafton

4½–8½ hours, 83.5km

The ride starts by climbing the banana-plant-clad hills behind Coffs Harbour, affording good views early on. From there the road gently undulates down the rural Orara Valley. The wet, closed forest of the upper valley gradually becomes drier and the lower valley is more cleared. Around the 50km mark, a change to sandstone soils creates an understorey of flowering shrubs and banksias beneath the spotted gums.

On a good day the side trip to the **Ferndahl Swedish Restaurant and Coffee House** (☎ 6653 8448), with its magnificent views and art gallery, is well worthwhile (open 10am–4pm Wednesday–Sunday).

An old sawmill painted bright yellow is the first sign of Coramba. Opposite is the **Coffs Harbour Craft Village** (15.5km), specialising in wool-spinning wheels and other timber products. The road then dives under the rail line before crossing the delightful Orara River. Coramba has a general store and a couple of other galleries, but little else to hold you. Entering **Nana Glen** (26.7km) look out for the wonderful **wildlife mural** on the wall of the preschool.

The Glenreagh district has a history of cattle, gold mining and timber getting. The rustic 1912 **general store** has everything from fruit to fencing wire and hay bales. Opposite, the cubicle-sized **post office** is reputed to be the smallest in NSW. The *Golden Dog Hotel* (☎ *6649 2162*) serves counter meals from noon to 2pm. Behind the pub is the town pool, picnic area and playground – a quiet spot for lunch. *Glenreagh Bakery*, 150m past the store, is the home of the Bobcat – beef, onion, bacon, cheese and tomato – pie.

The approach to Grafton past timber mills, cattle saleyards and the abattoir belies the beauty of this historic river port. From the visitor centre, cross the Clarence River to reach the main part of town. The 700m-long bridge is narrow and constantly trafficked; a footpath on the bridge's lower (railway) deck provides a safe alternative.

Grafton

☎ 02

Grafton is the big city on the 'big river', a major port from the early days (1830s) of exploitation of the precious rainforest red

MELBOURNE TO THE GOLD COAST

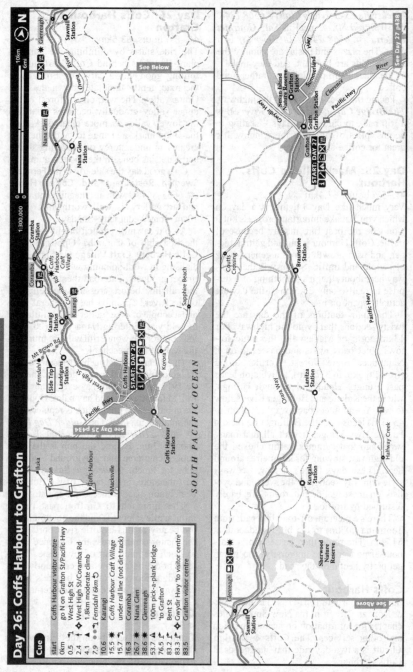

Day 26: Coffs Harbour to Grafton

Cue		
start	ℹ	Coffs Harbour visitor centre
0km		go N on Grafton St/Pacific Hwy
0.5	↰	West High St
2.4	◆	West High St/Coramba Rd
4.1	▲	1.8km moderate climb
7.9	●	Ferndahl 6km ↰
10.6	🏠	Karangi
15.5	✳	Coffs Harbour Craft Village
15.7		under rail line (not dirt track)
16.3		Coramba
26.7	✳	Nana Glen
38.6		Glenreagh
53.7	↰	100m pick-a-plank bridge
		'to Grafton'
76.5	↱	Bent St
83.2	↰	
83.3	◆	Gwydir Hwy 'to visitor centre'
83.5	ℹ	Grafton visitor centre

cedar. Dairying and sugar-cane growing followed the land clearing and, along with fishing, are still the principal industries of the Clarence Valley. The city's early wealth is evidenced in the architecture, much of it heritage listed, and the broad, tree-lined streets.

Grafton proper is north of the river, centred on Fitzroy and Prince Sts.

Information The excellent Clarence River visitor centre (☎ 6642 4677), on the Pacific Hwy in South Grafton, has brochures on the Clarence's history and natural attractions. They sell Craig Bellamy's (1988) book *Cycling Around Grafton & the Clarence Valley Area*. The NPWS office (☎ 6642 0613) is at 50 Victoria St.

Banks are concentrated around Prince St in the city. Southside Cycle Centre (☎ 6642 3352), 49 Skinner St, South Grafton, is well stocked and very helpful. The Grafton Internet Cafe (100 Queen St, ☎ 6642 1304) is closed Sunday.

Things to See & Do Grafton is a great place to enjoy a beer or one of the delicious local Zietsch Brothers soft drinks while watching the lazy waters drift by, and the **Crown Hotel**, 1 Prince St, is a great place to do just that. At dusk witness the exodus of the southern hemisphere's largest fruit bat colony from Susan Island.

The acclaimed **Grafton Regional Art Gallery** (☎ 6642 3177), 158 Fitzroy St, is in the heritage-listed **Prentice House**. The **Schaffer House Museum**, 192 Fitzroy St, occupies another fine heritage homestead.

The tourist centre has a brochure for the **heritage trail**, exploring the many heritage-listed Victorian buildings. Another brochure covers **Ulmarra**, a side trip on Day 27. The country-styled **Saraton Theatre** (☎ 6642 2727), in Prince St, has nightly screenings.

In November, the **Jacaranda Festival** show off the trees in full violet bloom. The annual 228km **Grafton–Inverell Classic** cycling race is in September.

Places to Stay & Eat The charmless *Glenwood Tourist Park & Motel* (☎ 6642 3466, Heber St), 500m south of the visitor centre, has camping sites/cabins for $13.50/45. The pleasant *Gateway Village* (☎ 6642 4225, 598 Summerland Way), 4km north of the town centre, charges $15.50/50.

The *Crown Hotel Motel* (☎ 6642 4000, 1 Prince St) has twin-share backpacker rooms at $20 a head, doubles from $35, and motel rooms from $50. A block away, *Roches Family Hotel* (☎ 6642 2866, 85 Victoria St) has singles/doubles for $27/35. The *Clarence Motor Inn* (☎ 6643 3444, 51 Fitzroy St) is Grafton's top-shelf option, with standard rooms from $99/104 (cottages from $99) and a good restaurant.

Woolworths supermarket *(42 Duke St)* is on the Day 27 route. The *Crown Hotel* has better-quality pub meals, but they are not exactly hearty. Try *Big River Pizzas* (☎ 6643 1555, 100 Fitzroy St) for Italian. The *Grafton District Services Club* (☎ 6642 2066, 105 Mary St) has a good-value $13 dinner buffet.

Day 27: Grafton to Iluka
4–7 hours, 68.3km

This is one of the flattest day's riding to be found anywhere, to the twin towns of Yamba and Iluka at the mouth of the Clarence. Iluka is the quieter of the two; you may prefer to stay in the bustling seaside resort of Yamba, and take the first ferry (☎ 6646 6423) north at 9.30am. The last ferry service is at 4.45pm, except for 26 December to 26 January, when an extra service operates at 6.15pm.

On the quiet back roads of the Clarence delta, it's easy to lose track of what is mainland and what is island. Egrets, ibis and swamphens strut the marshes around Lawrence (34.7km), while pelicans and sea-eagles soar over mangroves downstream.

The imposing, heritage-listed **Grafton Gaol** (4.1km) looms over the route out of town. Within Lawrence the road passes a small wetland teeming with nesting **water birds** (35.8km).

Beware the slippery steel rails embedded in the Bluff Point Ferry landing ramps. This is one of two remaining vehicular ferries on the Clarence – there were once 19! On alighting, welcome yourself to Woodford Island – reputed to be the largest inland island in the southern hemisphere. Downstream of the ferry and offshore the (shrimp) trawler fleet works incessantly. The best places to buy fresh seafood are the fisherman's cooperatives – good value for prawns and outstanding value for the fish that are simply considered 'by-catch'.

The **McFarlane Bridge** (47.4km) into Maclean was built with a raising section to

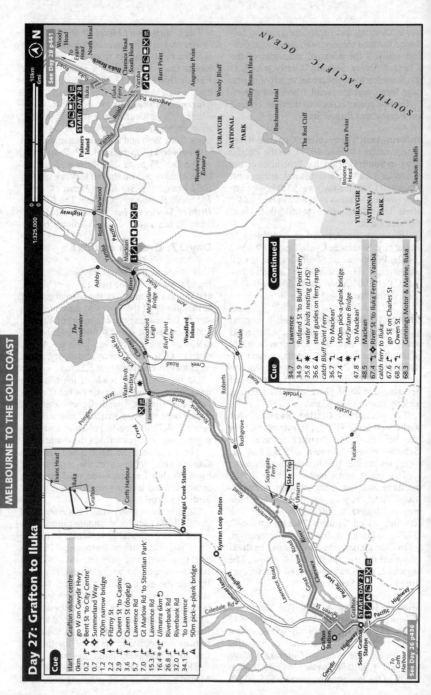

MELBOURNE TO THE GOLD COAST

Day 27: Grafton to Iluka

1:325,000

	0		6mi
	0		10km

N

South Grafton Station

START: DAY 27

Grafton Station

Cue

start		Grafton visitor centre
0km	⌐	go W on Gwydir Hwy
0.2	◆ ⌐	Bent St 'to City Centre'
0.7	⌐	Summerland Way
1.2	◆ ⌐	700m narrow bridge
2.2	⌐	Fitzroy St
2.9	◆ ⌐	Queen St 'to Casino'
3.6	⌐	Queen St (dogleg)
5.7	⌐	Lawrence Rd
7.0	⌐	Gt Marlow Rd 'to Strontian Park'
15.3	⌐	Lawrence Rd
16.4	⊕ ⊕	Ulmarra 6km ↻
26.8	⌐	Riverbank Rd
32.0	⌐	Riverbank Rd
34.1	⌐	'to Lawrence'
	△	50m pick-a-plank bridge

Continued

Cue

34.7		Lawrence
34.9	⌐	Rutland St 'to Bluff Point Ferry'
35.8	✱	water birds nesting (LHS)
36.6	△	steel guides on ferry ramp
		catch Bluff Point Ferry
36.7	⌐	'to Maclean'
47.4	△	100m pick-a-plank bridge
		McFarlane Bridge
47.8	⌐	'to Maclean'
48.5		Maclean
67.4	⌐ ◆	River St 'to Iluka Ferry', Yamba
		catch ferry to Iluka
67.6	⌐	go SE on Charles St
68.2	⌐	Owen St
68.3		Gennings Motor & Marine, Iluka

START: DAY 28

See Day 28 p441

See Day 26 p436

allow ships to pass. Maclean has a proud, if incongruous, Scottish heritage, set as it is amid sugar-cane fields. It's a nice place to stop for lunch on the riverbank, or at the *Skye Coffee Lounge* for its gourmet sandwiches and tasty vegetarian burgers. The *Clarence Hotel* does a $4 lunch Monday to Friday.

Mangrove channels dissect the route to Yamba (67.4km). Allow time to explore the beaches and check out the superbly located *Pacific Hotel (☎ 6646 2466, 18 Pilot St)*. Stock up here if you need cash or a bike shop – Yamba Squash and Cycle Centre (☎ 6646 2237), 35 Coldstream St. The ferry operators are very accepting of bikes and the winding half-hour chug to Iluka is an enjoyable way to end the day.

Side Trip: Ulmarra
6km
The entire town of **Ulmarra** is heritage listed, but rather spoilt by the fact that it straddles the busy Pacific Hwy. The town now boasts a number of antique stores and galleries, but nothing opens before 10am, so don't be too eager. Turn into Southgate Ferry Rd and, after 100m, take the left turn marked 'Ferry'. A kilometre on, beware the pick-a-plank wheel tracks of the small bridge. The ferry is free, and runs on demand. Beware the slippery steel rails that guide the ferry's ramp up the bank. On alighting, turn right and ride 1km to town on the Pacific Hwy.

Iluka
☎ 02
Referred to in Yamba as Siberia, Iluka is a delightfully sleepy enclave. Development stops short of the ocean-front, which is World Heritage-listed, littoral rainforest. The ocean beaches are superb, the fishing good and the bird life vibrant. Most people are there for the fishing, many are retired, and everyone has time for a chat.

Information Charles St runs south-east from the ferry jetty, and the junction with Young St is the commercial hub of town. The town garage, Gennings Motor & Marine (☎ 6646 6165), on the corner of Spenser and Owen Sts, doubles as the visitor centre.

Things to See & Do A walk through the **Iluka Nature Reserve** (south-east end of Spenser St) is a must – take insect repellent.

Yellow robins and Lewin's honeyeaters abound; if you're lucky you might spot a goanna. There is safe **swimming** in the north end of Iluka Bay, or good **surf** on Iluka Beach, but no lifesaver patrol. The social focus of town are the Iluka Bowls Club and Sedgers Reef Hotel – it is joked that fishermen often get stranded on Sedgers Reef on the way home. Hire **fishing** dinghies from Iluka Boatshed & Marina (☎ 6646 6106), 1 Charles St.

Places to Stay & Eat The *Iluka Riverside Tourist Park (☎ 6646 6060, 4 Charles St)* has a superb riverfront location and lots of trees. A site costs $14.85 and cabins cost $38.50 to $66. Next to the rainforest is the *Clarence Head Caravan Park (☎ 6646 6163, 113 Charles St)*, with $9.90 tent sites and on-site vans from $25. Six kilometres north of town, the *Woody Head Camping Area (☎ 6646 6134)*, nestled in Bundjalung National Park, has sites for $5 per person.

In a central, if not stunning, location, *Iluka Motel (☎ 6646 6288, 47 Charles St)* has doubles with cooking facilities from $62.

A *Five Star supermarket* is at 4A Young St. Head to the *Iluka Fish Co-op (☎ 6646 6116)* for fresh fish and prawns, or a selection of deep-fried takeaway (open until 7pm, or 8pm on weekends). For a morning coffee, try the *Pelican's Pouch Delicatessen (Charles St)*.

Sedgers Reef (☎ 6646 6122, 5 Queen St) has standard pub counter meals. The *Bowls Club (☎ 6646 6188, Spencer St)* serves a $5 buffet lunch; its *Master Wok* restaurant is probably the pick of Iluka's eats, with its Chinese, Thai and Australian menu. Mains range from $7 for vegetarian dishes to $17 for the chef's seafood specialities.

Day 28: Iluka to Evans Head
4–6½ hours, 66.5km
It's an easy day between these delightful coastal towns, the only detraction being the unavoidable highway kilometres. As you ride through **Bundjalung National Park** you may well encounter the enormous, flightless emu, one of the park's 200 recorded bird species. The inky **Esk River** is one of the state's best preserved river ecosystems. Woombah (14.4km) is home to the **Woombah Coffee Plantation** (the world's southernmost plantation), a pie factory and little else.

On weekends you can sample the local brew at dirt-cheap prices and buy beans.

The highway is not unpleasant, with a smooth shoulder up to 3m wide. Some amusement can be drawn from the waterways crossed. First Tabbimoble Creek, then Tabbimoble Overflow, followed by Tabbimoble Floodway No 3, Tabbimoble Floodway No 2 and finally, but inconsistently, Tabbimoble Overflow No 1, none of which are anything more than muddy creeks.

A side trip at 44km, the **New Italy** complex (☎ 6682 2622) has a picnic area, cafe, a useful information stand and a museum depicting the life of the district's Italian settlers. Adjacent is Gurrigai Aboriginal Art and Crafts, selling work by local artists.

Tuckombil Canal (53.7km) was blasted more than a century ago to allow the floodwaters of the Richmond River to escape down the more direct Evans River. Woodburn's Riverside Park, on the bank of the flood-prone Richmond, is a nice place for a picnic. The Woodburn Newsagency (☎ 6682 2459), opposite, doubles as the bike shop. From Woodburn the route passes **Broadwater National Park** – a coastal heath environment very different from the forested Bundjalung area. The flowering banksias and shrubs are alive with rainbow lorikeets, noisy friar birds and yellow-tailed black-cockatoos.

Side Trip: South Evans Head
5km
Continuing through town on Woodburn St, veer right into Elm St and cross the Evans River. Here, a fork gives you two options for exploration. To the right is Bundjalung Rd – 2km of dirt road to the national park of the same name. Short walks explore the different forest types and a midden – an accumulation of thousands of shells from generations of feasting by the Bundjalung Aborigines.

Travelling left on Ocean Dr (this is the 5km side trip), you pass the harbour and a 17m-high, pole-top platform provided for ospreys to nest on. The road overlooks the cosy Shark Bay, then rises very steeply to Razorback Lookout, with its superb views north to Ballina. Complete the circuit by turning right at Wirraway Ave, passing Anson Ave and Chinamens Beach Rd (both lead to walking trails in the Goanna Headland area), and turning right on Evans Rd.

Evans Head
☎ 02
Now very much a holiday retreat, the area was settled in the 1870s when prospectors found gold on nearby beaches. During WWII, **RAAF Station Evans Head** was home to the No 1 Bombing and Gunnery School and later the No 1 Air Observers School, as well as an antisubmarine squadron. These days the town is home to a prawning and tuna long-lining industry.

Information The Professionals Real Estate (☎ 6682 4611), 9 Oak St has an information stand (closed Sunday). A small information bay is on Woodburn Rd 1km before town. A Westpac Bank branch is at 8 Oak St.

Things to See & Do The **Paperbark Gallery** (☎ 6682 5188), 11–15 Canberra Rd, has some fine works by local artists. The Illawong Hotel has **live music** three nights a week. A **market** is held in the caravan-park reserve on the fourth Saturday of each month. Evans Head Fishing and Sea Cruises (☎ 6682 4827) runs **fishing trips** and **scenic cruises**.

Places to Stay & Eat The enormous *Silver Sands Caravan Park* (☎ 6682 4212, Park St)* has some choice camping sites near the adjoining rainforest for $12, and a big range of cabins from $35. The scruffy but friendly *Illawong Hotel* (☎ 6682 4222, cnr Park & Oak Sts)* has singles and en suite doubles for $20/40. The *Pacific Motor Inn* (☎ 6682 4318, 38 Woodburn St)* has spacious, newly fitted doubles from $49.50.

A *Five Star supermarket* (7 Oak St) is on the route. *Evans Head Fish Centre* (☎ 6682 4366, Oak St)* does a roaring trade in all things fried and other takeaways, while the *Riverfront Kiosk* (☎ 6682 5845, Caravan Park Reserve)* serves coffee, snacks and meals. The *Illawong Hotel* bistro has pub meals with a nightly $6 special. *Heng Lees* (☎ 6682 4658, 22 Woodburn St)* serves cheap, Cantonese-style Chinese; it has a big range of seafood dishes but few vegetarian options.

Day 29: Evans Head to Byron Bay
4–7 hours, 71.1km
The day starts by cutting inland to the Richmond River, where two short highway stretches are balanced by sleepy back-road

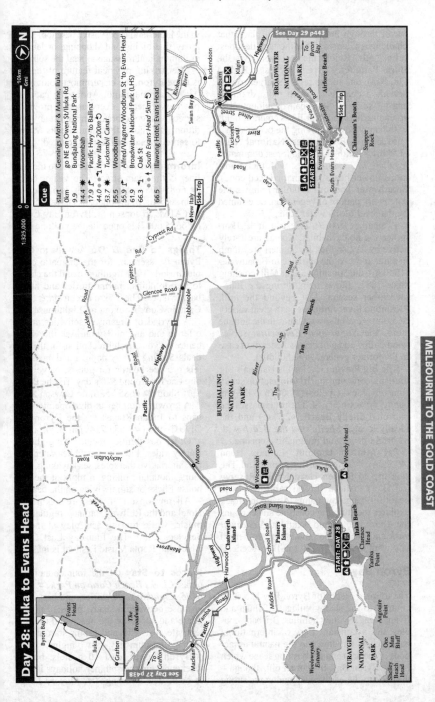

Day 28: Iluka to Evans Head

See Day 27 p438

See Day 29 p443

Cue		
start		Gennings Motor & Marine, Iluka
0km		go NE on Owen St/Iluka Rd
9.9		Bundjalung National Park
14.4	✳	Woombah
17.9	↱	Pacific Hwy 'to Ballina'
44.0	●●●↰	New Italy 200m ↻
53.7	✳	Tuckombil Canal
55.5		Woodburn
55.9	↱	Alfred/Wagner/Woodburn St 'to Evans Head'
61.9		Broadwater National Park (LHS)
66.3	↰	Oak St
	●●	South Evans Head 5km ↻
66.5		Illawong Hotel, Evans Head

MELBOURNE TO THE GOLD COAST

travel through **Empire Vale** – a place that challenges Glenreagh for the 'smallest post office' title. Rejoin the real world via the Burns Point ferry (free for cyclists). Ballina (38.7km), one of the region's larger towns, heralds a change to much more dramatic coastal scenery. Suburban development is spreading here, but it still has emerald fields with happy cows enjoying the ocean view.

Much of **Broadwater National Park** (3.9km) is heath or stunted forest dominated by *Banksia serratus* trees, with their enormous flower heads and gnarled seed cones. **Broadwater Lookout** (10.6km) shows the patchwork pattern of vegetation, determined by the level of the water table.

A small reserve (a side trip at 13.1km) protects a **koala** habitat. Koalas are rarely active by day, so look for an inert grey lump in a tree fork. At the entrance to Broadwater (13.8km), the **Sunshine Sugar Mill**, crushing since 1881, allows tours during the June–December season. Just beyond the mill, **Richmond River Antiques** has a great variety of tools, axes and saws. Opposite the antique store, the *Sugartown Emporium* serves good coffee and a delicious Federation cake in the former general store building.

The **Big Prawn** (35.5km) is Ballina's big tourism icon-cum-tourist information stand. Ransom Jack Cycles (☎ 6686 3485) is handy, at 16 Cherry St. The route passes the patrolled **Shelly Beach** (42.7km) and the ideally located *Shelly's on the Beach* with its bright decor and imaginative cuisine.

Pat Morton Lookout, Lennox Head (49.9km), is a great surfing grandstand. The side trip to **Broken Head Nature Reserve** (64.5km) visits a littoral rainforest with beautiful bangalow palms. A walking track explores the stunning coastline and explains the Aboriginal legend behind it. A *caravan park* and other accommodation are here if you want to avoid the Byron Bay 'scene'.

Byron Bay
☎ 02

The tourism mecca of Byron Bay is a stark contrast to the sleepy villages of Iluka and Evans Head. Sydney families, Brisbane couples and a constant flow of international backpackers are drawn to the natural attractions of the area and the bustling scene which is now Byron Bay. It's not all glitz though – the back-to-the-earth counterculture so strong

in the hinterland is pervasive here too. Spend a day fine dining and shopping, or learning drumming and massage to heal the spirit.

The striking physical feature of the area is **Cape Byron**, the easternmost point of the Australian mainland. About the cape are beaches of nearly every aspect, providing surfers with good breaks in almost any condition. Off shore, the **Julian Rocks Marine Reserve** is renowned for its scuba diving.

Information Jonson St, parallel to the train line, is the main street. The visitor centre (☎ 6685 8050), 80 Jonson St, is outside the train station. All the big banks have branches and ATMs in Jonson St. Byron Bay Cycles (☎ 6685 6067) is opposite the visitor centre.

Things to See & Do A walk to **Cape Byron** is essential, for the dramatic coast, picturesque 1901 lighthouse and the chance to see dolphins, marine turtles and humpback whales. The 3.5km circuit starts at the Captain Cook Lookout on Lighthouse Rd.

A myriad of organised activities are on offer in and around Byron. Ask the visitor centre or your hostel reception for the best deals. **Surfing** is very popular and most hostels provide boards for guests, or you can hire one for around $20 a day. Try the Byron Surf Shop (☎ 6685 7536) on Lawson St.

A growing number of **dive** operators run trips to Julian Rocks; try the Byron Bay Dive Centre (☎ 6685 7149) in Bay Lane.

Other possibilities include hang-gliding, Harley rides, kite flying, white-water rafting, alternative therapies, sea kayaking, bush tours, mountain biking, a night at the Pighouse Flicks or simply lying on the beach.

All on Jonson St, the Great Northern Hotel and the Railway Bar have **regular live music**, while touring acts play at the Ex Services Club. The four-day East Coast Blues and Roots Music Festival is in April.

Places to Stay Of the four council-run parks, *Clarks Beach Caravan Park (☎ 6685 6496, Lighthouse Rd)* offers the best compromise between a shady, pleasant atmosphere and access to the beach and town. A tent site costs $17 and cabins start at $69, with a minimum stay of two nights.

Byron has at least 10 hostels, but on weekends and the summer holidays it pays to book. The amazing *Arts Factory Lodge*

MELBOURNE TO THE GOLD COAST

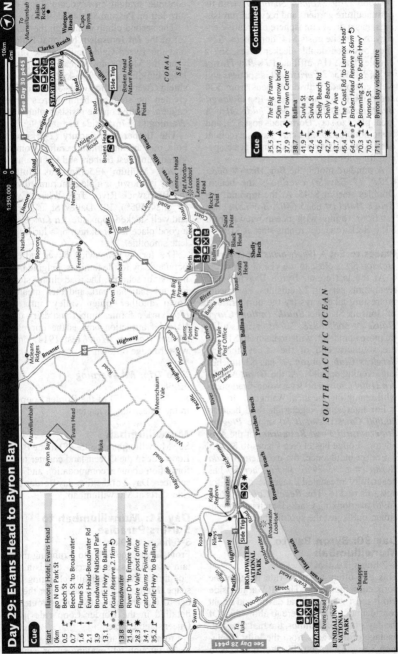

Day 29: Evans Head to Byron Bay

Cue		
start		Illawong Hotel, Evans Head
0km	↑	go N on Park St
0.5	↱	Beech St
0.7	↰	Beech St to Broadwater'
1.6	↑	Flame St
2.1	↑	Evans Head-Broadwater Rd
3.9		Broadwater National Park
13.1	↱	Pacific Hwy 'to Ballina'
	⚑	Koala Reserve 2.1km ↻
13.8		Broadwater
21.8	↰	River Dr 'to Empire Vale'
28.3		Empire Vale post office
34.1		catch Burns Point ferry
35.2	↱	Pacific Hwy 'to Ballina'

Cue		Continued
35.5	✳	The Big Prawn
37.1	◁	50m narrow bridge
37.9	◇↑	'to Town Centre'
38.7	↑	Ballina
41.9	↱↴	Suvla St
42.4	↱↴	Suvla St
42.6	↱↴	Shelly Beach Rd
42.7	✳	Shelly Beach
43.7	✳	Pine Ave
45.4	↰	The Coast Rd 'to Lennox Head'
64.5	●↰	Broken Head Reserve 3.6km ↻
70.3	↱↴	Browning St to Pacific Hwy'
70.5	↱↴	Jonson St
71.1		Byron Bay visitor centre

(☎ 6685 7709, Skinners Shoot Rd), with its permaculture gardens and recycled furnishings, has a great atmosphere of creative energy. A tent site costs $14; dorm beds, $24; and converted double-decker buses, $62 a double. The YHA-affiliated **J's Bay Hostel** (☎ 6685 8853, 7 Carlisle St) is spotless and well equipped, with dorm beds from $24 and doubles for $58. The stylish **Belongil Beachouse** (☎ 6685 7868, Childe St) is a great place to stay. Dorm beds cost $23, and basic doubles $55. Its cafe serves excellent healthy food with a nightly half-price special for guests.

A standard motel, the **Bay Mist** (☎ 6685 6121, 12 Bay St) overlooks the beach. Doubles start at $145. At the top end, the **Beach Hotel** (☎ 6685 6402, Bay Lane) has 1st-floor rooms with ocean views from $250 B&B (cheaper rooms start at $190).

Places to Eat A **Woolworths** supermarket (Jonson St) is close to the visitor centre.

At the last count, Byron Bay had 120 restaurants serving 22 cuisines. For cheap, interesting takeaways try the northern end of Jonson St. The **South Indian Curry House** (☎ 6685 6828, 2 Jonson St) is a little more upmarket, with mains from $10. At the southern end of the street, the **Ex Services Club** (Jonson St) has $3 lunches and evening specials. At the **Great Northern Hotel** (Jonson St) try a wood-fired pizza while sampling the local Watego's Ale.

For interesting vegetarian food head to **20,000 Cows** (Kendall St) or the **Piggery Supernatural Food Restaurant** at the Arts Factory Lodge hostel (see Places to Stay).

For an indulgence, the excellent **Misaki Byron** (☎ 6685 7966, 11 Fletcher St) has beautifully presented Japanese dishes for upwards of $18. The **Beach Cafe** (☎ 6685 7598) overlooking Clarks Beach isn't cheap either, but is just the spot for breakfast.

Day 30: Byron Bay to Murwillumbah
4–7 hours, 70.4km

This day offers a scenic ride through the north coast hinterland. The Mt Warning side trip is most worthwhile at dawn; you might consider adding a day here to allow this. Of the day's two solid climbs, the first takes advantage of the views from the lofty Coolamon Scenic Dr. (A much flatter option is to continue straight on Myocum Rd – don't turn left on Possum Shoot Rd, 9.7km.)

The second climb is through the tall forest of the **Mt Jerusalem National Park** and into the Tweed Caldera. For three million years the Mt Warning volcano pumped out lava, building a 5000-sq-km, 2000m-high shield. Twenty million years of erosion have created the southern hemisphere's largest caldera, centred on the resistant plug of **Mt Warning** (1157m; a side trip at 59.9km).

The Timber Slab Factory (24.1km) has bold, outstanding furniture crafted from salvaged rainforest timbers and feral camphor laurel. 'Mullum' (25.3km), as Mullumbimby is known, is a pleasant rural town on the Brunswick River. True Wheel Cycles (☎ 6684 1959), 107 Dalley St, is friendly and well stocked. Opposite, **Lu Lu's Cafe** is a good place for breakfast, or a lurid spirulene smoothie.

The fertile Brunswick River valley is populated by fertile families, judging by the number of schools. The road climbs steeply into the national park and then meanders down another quiet valley into Uki (55.7km), a former timber and dairy town. Its chief attraction now is the impressive **Mount Warning Hotel** (est 1914) on the western edge of town.

Side Trip: Mt Warning
12.5km

See Day 2 (p347) of the Border Loop ride in the Queensland chapter.

Murwillumbah

See Murwillumbah (p345–47) in the Border Loop ride in the Queensland chapter for information about accommodation and other services. Day 2 of the five-day **Border Loop** ride starts at Murwillumbah.

Day 31: Murwillumbah to Surfers Paradise
3–5 hours, 47.9km

From sugar-cane fields to a running mountain stream to skyscrapers – this is a short ride through a dramatically changing landscape. Many great rides head over the border to Queensland – two other routes are detailed in the Border Loop ride in the Queensland chapter.

From Murwillumbah the route suddenly heads through tall, waving sugar cane. At

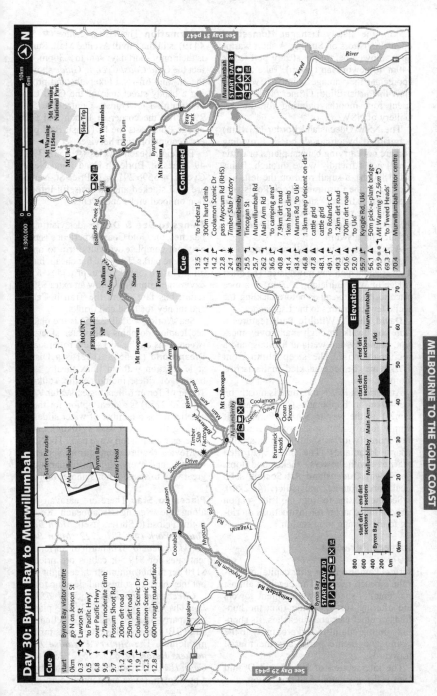

Day 30: Byron Bay to Murwillumbah

Cue

start		Byron Bay visitor centre
0km	↑	go N on Jonson St
0.3	♦↑	Lawson St
0.5	↑◄	'to Pacific Hwy'
6.8		over Pacific Hwy
9.5	◄	2.7km moderate climb
9.7	◄	Possum Shoot Rd
11.2	◄	200m dirt road
11.6	↑	250m dirt road
11.9	↑◄	Coolamon Scenic Dr
12.3	◄	Coolamon Scenic Dr
12.8	◄	600m rough road surface

Continued

Cue

13.5	↑	'to Federal'
14.2	◄	300m hard climb
14.2	◄	Coolamon Scenic Dr
22.8	◄	pass Myocum Rd (RHS)
24.7	✳	*Timber Slab Factory*
25.3		Mullumbimby
25.5	↱	Tincogan St
25.7	↰	Murwillumbah Rd
26.2	↱	Main Arm Rd
36.5	↰	'to camping area'
40.8	◄	7.9km dirt road
41.4	◄	1km hard climb
43.4	↱	Manns Rd 'to Uki'
46.8	◄	1.3km steep descent on dirt
47.8		cattle grid
48.1		cattle grid
49.1	↰	'to Rolands Ck'
49.3	◄	1.2km dirt road
50.6	◄	700m dirt road
52.0		'to Uki'
55.7	↱	Kyogle Rd, Uki
56.1	◄	50m pick-a-plank bridge
59.9	●◄	*Mt Warning 12.5km* ↰
69.1	↱	'to Tweed Heads'
70.4		Murwillumbah visitor centre

Elevation

See Day 31 p447

See Day 29 p443

MELBOURNE TO THE GOLD COAST

2.5km, the stately **Lisnagar Homestead** opens to visitors on Sunday. A short warm-up is allowed before the steady pull to the 340m Tomewin Gap (11km). Take time to appreciate the vantage point – it was this **view** that artist Elioth Gruner (1882–1938) spent four months painting for the Art Gallery of NSW.

The NSW-Queensland **border** (13.1km) is 'guarded' by a roadside booth. Providing you are not carrying banana plants or cattle you'll get a friendly wave through. Bains Rd (18.3km), a small road on the left, is a shortcut to the **Currumbin Rock Pools** side trip, but is extremely steep (otherwise, turn onto the side trip at 22.4km). By any route the pools – popular in summer holidays – are nice for a swim.

A brutally steep hill (25.4km) separates the Currumbin and Tallebudgera Valleys; taking it saves some highway travel later. The quiet village of West Burleigh (33.3km) is a nice place to take a breather before tackling the hectic few kilometres to the Esplanade.

David Fleay's Wildlife Park features a 2km boardwalk through mangrove, eucalypt, rainforest and wetland habitats, and a nocturnal house. The steep climb from 33.7km may be better tackled on the narrow footpath.

At Burleigh Heads the route is mostly on the 40km/hr Esplanade (or its various names) all the way to Surfers Paradise. It simply follows the closest road parallel to the shore (with a small detour around Miami Headland). The many patrolled **beaches** – with showers – make good stops. The **Royal Queensland Art Society** sells local works from its small gallery (45.2km).

See the Getting to/from the Ride section early in this chapter for instructions on riding to the Nerang train station.

Surfers Paradise

☎ 07

Surfers Paradise is the glitz capital of Australia's beach resorts. The beach is almost incidental – shaded by apartment towers and offering surf no better than the hundreds of other east coast beaches. Its shopping, dining, nightlife and proximity to the casino and theme parks are the tourist drawcards.

The intersection of Cavill and Orchid Aves is the epicentre of all this action.

Information The visitor centre (☎ 5538 4419) is in the Cavill Avenue Mall. Sunday is their only short day: 9am to 3.30pm. Collect the *Gold Coast Cycling Guide* showing the on- and off-road bikepaths and providing a handy street map of the Gold Coast labyrinth. The Transit Centre (☎ 5592 2911), on the corner of Beach and Cambridge Rds, hosts the In Transit Backpackers Accommodation Service.

Burleigh Beach Cycles (☎ 5535 3900), 49 James St, Burleigh Heads; and Nerang Cycles (☎ 5596 2911), 79 Price St, Nerang, are well stocked and have useful information on local clubs and events.

Things to See & Do Besides visiting the **beaches**, the Gold Coast experience is probably not complete without a trip to one of the theme parks. They are not cheap, but the all-inclusive entry price provides a full day's entertainment. Allow an extra $12 for return bus fare (from the Transit Centre) and money for food and drinks.

Sea World (☎ 5588 2205) is the place to see leaping dolphins and water skiers between spins on the corkscrew rollercoaster. **Dreamworld** (☎ 5588 1122) is a Disney-style creation with an Imax theatre and a battery of rides, including the 160km/hr Tower of Terror rollercoaster. **Water World** (☎ 5573 2255) is a great option for the energetic. It has a number of water slides, including the Twister and a 70km/hr speed slide, as well as a fun wave pool. The 'Dive-in Movies' (Saturday night from September to April, and every night in January) are a great way to spend a hot summer night.

Places to Stay There are caravan parks along the Nerang–Broadbeach Rd, but nothing close to Surfers itself. *Main Beach Tourist Park (☎ 5581 7722; Main Beach Rd, Main Beach)*, 3km north of Surfers, has tent sites for $19.50; cabins are pricey at $110 per night (minimum three-night stay), but they have en suites and sleep up to five.

Cheers Backpackers (☎ 5531 6539, 8 Pine Ave) has beds for $22. The place is very party-oriented with an excellent bar, large BBQ courtyard and vouchers for local nightclubs. The *Surfers Paradise Backpackers Resort (☎ 5592 4677, 2837 Gold Coast Hwy)*, 1km south of the centre, boasts a pool, gym, sauna and tennis court. Dorm

Day 31: Murwillumbah to Surfers Paradise

See Day 30 p445

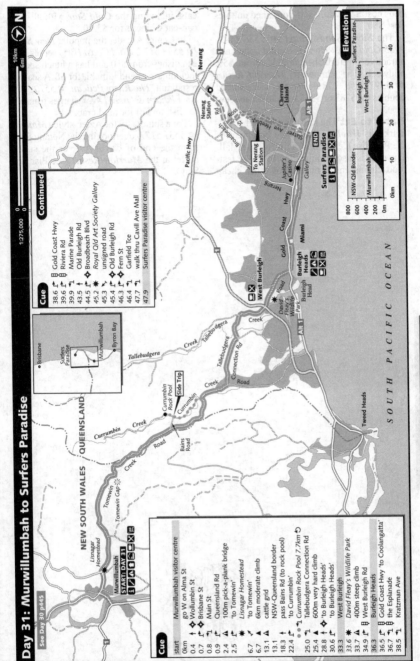

MELBOURNE TO THE GOLD COAST

Cue

start	Murwillumbah visitor centre
0km	go W on Alma St
0.4	Wollumbin St
0.7	Brisbane St
0.8	Main St
0.9	Queensland Rd
2.4	100m pick-a-plank bridge
2.5	'to Tomewin'
	Lisnagar Homestead
6.7	'to Tomewin'
6.7	6km moderate climb
13.1	cattle grid
13.1	NSW–Queensland border
18.3	pass Bains Rd (to rock pool)
22.4	'to Currumbin'
	Currumbin Rock Pool 7.7km ↻
25.0	Tallebudgera Connection Rd
25.4	600m very hard climb
28.8	'to Burleigh Heads'
30.6	'to Burleigh Heads'
33.3	West Burleigh
	David Fleay's Wildlife Park
33.6	400m steep climb
34.9	West Burleigh Rd
36.3	Burleigh Heads
36.5	Gold Coast Hwy to Coolangatta'
36.7	the Esplanade
38.5	Kratzman Ave

Cue (Continued)

38.6	Gold Coast Hwy
39.6	Riviera Rd
39.9	Marine Parade
43.5	Old Burleigh Rd
44.5	Broadbeach Blvd
45.2	*Royal Qld Art Society Gallery*
45.3	unsigned road
45.4	Old Burleigh Rd
46.3	Fern St
46.4	Garfield Tce
47.7	walk thru Cavill Ave Mall
47.9	Surfers Paradise visitor centre

beds cost $21, while self-contained doubles cost $50.

The *Silver Sands Motel* (☎ 5538 6041, 2985 Gold Coast Hwy) is a good option and attractively refurbished doubles from $59, midweek. The sumptuous *Marriott Resort* (☎ 5592 9800, 158 Ferny Ave) has standard doubles for $283 or $312 with an ocean view.

Places to Eat The most convenient supermarket is *Woolworths*, in the basement of the Paradise Centre on Cavill Avenue Mall. The mall is also populated with all the fast-food chains and a number of other cheap

eats, including the *Gold Star* with all-you-can-eat Chinese for $5.90.

In Centre Arcade, the popular *New Seoul* (☎ 5538 6177, Gold Coast Hwy) serves Korean dishes from $10 and has a lunch special, including rice and kimchi, for $8. A seafood restaurant, *The Rusty Pelican* (☎ 5570 3073, cnr Elkhorn & Orchid Ave) charges from $13 for fish to $30 for mud crab.

For a splurge try the Aztec-styled *Mango's* (☎ 5531 6177) overlooking the Nerang River from the end of Cavill Ave, or the superb buffet at the *Marriott Resort* (see Places to Stay).

Glossary

See the bicycle diagram in the Your Bicycle chapter (p81) for technical bike terms.

ACT – Australian Capital Territory
ATM – Automated Teller Machine; machine for extracting cash from a bank
Auslig – Australian Surveying & Land Information Group; national mapping agency
autumn – fall (season)

barbie, BBQ – barbecue
bathers – swimming costume, *cozzie, togs*
beanie – warm hat
beesting – almond-topped, yeasted custard bun
billabong – a pool or lagoon formed when a river's flow recedes or changes course
billy – small boiling pot; a kettle
biscuit – cookie
bitumen – tar or asphalt; surfaced road
bloke – man
bore water – water from an artesian well
bottle shop, bottleo – liquor shop
booze – alcohol
brekky – breakfast
brumby – wild horse
bungee cord – elastic strap to tie things down
bush, the – Australia's remote countryside; also native forest or wood
bushfire – fire in bushland
bush tucker – Indigenous foods found naturally in the bush
bushie – someone who lives in 'the bush'
bushranger – colonial term for a robber, usually armed, with operations based in the bush
bushwalking – hiking, tramping, walking; walking for pleasure in the bush
BYO – Bring Your Own (usually alcohol)

CALM – Department of Conservation and Land Management (Western Australia)
carbos – carbohydrates
CBD – Central Business District, downtown
chips – fries (hot) or potato crisps (packaged, cold)
come a cropper – fall (literally or metaphorically)
corrugated road – rutted dirt road
counter meal – pub meal
cozzie – swimming costume, *togs, bathers*

criterium – circuit race
crook – thief; to feel ill ('I feel crook'); something that is broken or no good
creek – stream or small river
croc – crocodile
cyclone – violent tropical storm, bringing high winds and rain to northern Australia
crayfish, cray – lobster; crawfish (USA)

damper – Australian bush bread, made of flour and water and cooked in a fire's ashes
dead horse – tomato sauce
deli – *milk bar* in SA and WA, but a delicatessen elsewhere
Devonshire tea – scones, cream and jam served with tea
dieback – microscopic soil fungus, *Phytophthora cinnamomi*, which kills various native plant species by rotting their roots
drag – main street ('the main drag'); a bore ('It's a real drag')
Dreaming (Dreamtime) – the rough European translation for the complex concept that forms the basis of Aboriginal spirituality; it incorporates the creation of the world and the spiritual energies operating around us
dunny – (outdoor) toilet

Eftpos – Electronic Funds Transfer at Point of Sale; electronic means of making retail purchases with a debit or credit card
EPA – Environment Protection Agency (includes the National Parks and Wildlife Service in Queensland)

firestick farming – technique used by Aborigines to clear land to prevent uncontrolled bushfires and attract game to the regrowth
firetrail – *4WD* track, usually in national parks, built for fire-fighting vehicles
foodies – food lovers
4WD – four-wheel drive; also 4X4
freshie – freshwater crocodile

GST – Goods & Services Tax; a Federal tax
gum tree – eucalypt tree

happy hour – period during which pubs offer cheap drinks
High Country – the Victorian and New South Wales Alps

homestead – residence of property owner (or manager) in the bush
hut – very basic building used for accommodation, mainly in national parks

jam – preserve containing fruit; jelly (USA)
jelly – cold sugary dessert; jello (USA)
jumper – sweater, pullover

knicks – padded bike shorts

lollie – sweet, candy
long weekend – three-day weekend created by a public holiday on the Friday or Monday

main – the main course of a meal
march fly – biting fly, horsefly, gadfly
midden – mound of discarded shells and bone fragments
milk bar – corner store or general store; also *deli* in SA and WA
mozzie – mosquito
MTB – mountain bike

NSW – New South Wales
NPWS – National Parks and Wildlife Service (New South Wales)
NRE – Department of National Resources and Environment (Victoria)
NRMA – New South Wales' automobile association
NT – Northern Territory

ocker – uncultivated Australian
ocky strap, octopus strap – elastic strap to tie things down, also *bungee cord*
Outback, the – remote, sparsely inhabited interior areas of Australia
Oz – Australia

paddock – fenced area of land, usually for livestock, field
petrol – motor-vehicle fuel; gas (USA)
pick-a-plank bridge – timber bridges with planks that run parallel to the road
pie floater – meat pie in a bowl of pea soup
pissed – drunk
prawn – shrimp
pub – bar or hotel
PWS – Parks and Wildlife Service (Tasmania)

Queenslander – traditional Queensland house, on stilts, with a verandah
RACQ – Royal Automobile Club of Queensland

RAC – Royal Automobile Club (Western Australia)
RACV – Royal Automobile Club of Victoria
roundabout – traffic circle

SA – South Australia
saltie – saltwater crocodile
sanger – sandwich
sclerophyllous forest – woody, evergreen forest, with small, leathery leaved plants
sealed road – surfaced road
service station – petrol (gas) station
Shellite – liquid fuel derived from petroleum and used in camp stoves
shout – (to buy) a round of drinks, as in 'it's your shout'
snow line – level below which snow seldom falls or lies on the ground
squatter – pioneer farmer who occupied land as a tenant of the government
station – large sheep or cattle farm
stinger – extremely poisonous box jellyfish found in northern Australia
stubby – 375mL bottle of beer
swag – bed roll
swimming hole – large pool on a creek or river, safe for swimming
switchback – route that follows a zigzag course up or down a steep incline

tap – faucet
tarn – small alpine lake
takeaway – takeout food; place selling takeaway food
taxi – cab
thongs – flip-flops, rubber slippers
togs – swimming costume, *bathers*, *cozzie*
Total Fire Ban – prohibition of all open flames on days of extreme fire danger
tucker – food

Unesco – United Nations Educational, Scientific and Cultural Organisation
uni – university

vego – vegetarian
vintage – the wine-grape harvest and crush period (autumn)

WA – Western Australia
waterhole – small pool or lake
Woop Woop – remote town or area
YHA – Youth Hostel Association
yabbie – small freshwater crayfish

This Book

Nicola Wells was the coordinating author of *Cycling Australia*; she wrote the introductory chapters, the Western Australia chapter and contributed to the Victoria chapter. Ian Connellan wrote the New South Wales chapter; Peter Hines wrote the Queensland chapter; Neil Irvine wrote the Tasmania chapter; Lesley Hodgson wrote most of the Victoria chapter; and Catherine Palmer wrote the South Australia chapter. Ian Connellan, Peter Hines, Lesley Hodgson and Nicola Wells contributed to the Melbourne to the Gold Coast chapter.

The Your Bicycle chapter was written by Darren Elder with contributions by Nicola Wells, Neil Irvine and Sally Dillon; the photograhs were taken by Jeff Crowe of Sport: The Library; and the illustrations were drawn by Martin Harris. The Health & Safety chapter was written by Nicola Wells, Dr Isabelle Young and Kevin Tabotta. Material from Lonely Planet's *Australia, Queensland, New South Wales, South Australia, Tasmania, Victoria* and *Western Australia* guides was used for parts of this book.

FROM THE PUBLISHER

Cycling Australia is the fourth in Lonely Planet's new series of cycling guides. The series was developed by a team from Lonely Planet's Outdoor Activities Unit in Melbourne, including Emily Coles, Sally Dillon, Teresa Donnellan, Chris Klep, Andrew Smith, Nick Tapp and series manager Darren Elder, assisted by Paul Clifton and Nicola Wells. The cover designed for this series was developed by Jamieson Gross, who also designed this book's cover.

Sally Dillon and Sonya Brooke coordinated the editing and mapping and design, respectively, of this book. Sally was assisted by Angie Phelan, Janet Brunckhorst and Nicola Wells; Darren Elder provided guidance. In mapping, Sonya was assisted by Andrew Smith, Eoin Dunlevy, Glenn van der Knijff, Paul Piaia, John Shippick, Chris Thomas and Simon Tillema; Helen Rowley completed the colour photo sections; and guidance came from Michael Blore. Layout was checked by Lindsay Brown, Glenn, Andrew Smith, Michael, and Nick Tapp. Thanks to Glenn Beanland, Annie Horner, Matt King and Brett Pascoe for helping with illustrations and images; Monique Choy for advising on the Indigenous Australia sections; and Allyson de Fraga for updating prices.

Special thanks also goes to Ron Shepherd for his invaluble historical input and Paul Farren for the loan of precious archival material; Catherine Hockey at the Melbourne Museum Infocentre and Annemarie Driver from the Australian Cycling History Resource Centre for help in sourcing archival material; Dr Irene Watson for the 'Aboriginal Culture Today' boxed text; and Roger Peterson for weather advice.

Guides by Region

Lonely Planet is known worldwide for publishing practical, reliable and no-nonsense travel information in our guides and on our Web site. The Lonely Planet list covers just about every accessible part of the world. Currently there are 16 series: Travel guides, Shoestring guides, Condensed guides, Phrasebooks, Read This First, Healthy Travel, Walking guides, Cycling guides, Watching Wildlife guides, Pisces Diving & Snorkeling guides, City Maps, Road Atlases, Out to Eat, World Food, Journeys travel literature and Pictorials.

AFRICA Africa on a shoestring • Cairo • Cairo City Map • Cape Town • Cape Town City Map • East Africa • Egypt • Egyptian Arabic phrasebook • Ethiopia, Eritrea & Djibouti • Ethiopian Amharic phrasebook • The Gambia & Senegal • Healthy Travel Africa • Kenya • Malawi • Morocco • Moroccan Arabic phrasebook • Mozambique • Read This First: Africa • South Africa, Lesotho & Swaziland • Southern Africa • Southern Africa Road Atlas • Swahili phrasebook • Tanzania, Zanzibar & Pemba • Trekking in East Africa • Tunisia • Watching Wildlife East Africa • Watching Wildlife Southern Africa • West Africa • World Food Morocco • Zimbabwe, Botswana & Namibia
Travel Literature: Mali Blues: Traveling to an African Beat • The Rainbird: A Central African Journey • Songs to an African Sunset: A Zimbabwean Story

AUSTRALIA & THE PACIFIC Auckland • Australia • Australian phrasebook • Australia Road Atlas • Cycling Australia • Cycling New Zealand • Fiji • Fijian phrasebook • Healthy Travel Australia, NZ & the Pacific • Islands of Australia's Great Barrier Reef • Melbourne • Melbourne City Map • Micronesia • New Caledonia • New South Wales • New Zealand • Northern Territory • Outback Australia • Out to Eat – Melbourne • Out to Eat – Sydney • Papua New Guinea • Pidgin phrasebook • Queensland • Rarotonga & the Cook Islands • Samoa • Solomon Islands • South Australia • South Pacific • South Pacific phrasebook • Sydney • Sydney City Map • Sydney Condensed • Tahiti & French Polynesia • Tasmania • Tonga • Tramping in New Zealand • Vanuatu • Victoria • Walking in Australia • Watching Wildlife Australia • Western Australia
Travel Literature: Islands in the Clouds: Travels in the Highlands of New Guinea • Kiwi Tracks: A New Zealand Journey • Sean & David's Long Drive

CENTRAL AMERICA & THE CARIBBEAN Bahamas, Turks & Caicos • Baja California • Belize, Guatemala & Yucatán • Bermuda • Central America on a shoestring • Costa Rica • Costa Rica Spanish phrasebook • Cuba • Dominican Republic & Haiti • Eastern Caribbean • Guatemala • Havana • Healthy Travel Central & South America • Jamaica • Mexico • Mexico City • Panama • Puerto Rico • Read This First: Central & South America • World Food Mexico • Yucatán
Travel Literature: Green Dreams: Travels in Central America

EUROPE Amsterdam • Amsterdam City Map • Amsterdam Condensed • Andalucía • Austria • Baltic States phrasebook • Barcelona • Barcelona City Map • Belgium & Luxembourg • Berlin • Berlin City Map • Britain • British phrasebook • Brussels, Bruges & Antwerp • Brussels City Map • Budapest • Budapest City Map • Canary Islands • Central Europe • Central Europe phrasebook • Copenhagen • Corfu & the Ionians • Corsica • Crete • Crete Condensed • Croatia • Cycling Britain • Cycling France • Cyprus • Czech & Slovak Republics • Denmark • Dublin • Dublin City Map • Eastern Europe • Eastern Europe phrasebook • Edinburgh • England • Estonia, Latvia & Lithuania • Europe on a shoestring • Europe phrasebook • Finland • Florence • France • Frankfurt Condensed • French phrasebook • Georgia, Armenia & Azerbaijan • Germany • German phrasebook • Greece • Greek Islands • Greek phrasebook • Hungary • Iceland, Greenland & the Faroe Islands • Ireland • Italian phrasebook • Italy • Krakow • Lisbon • The Loire • London • London City Map • London Condensed • Madrid • Malta • Mediterranean Europe • Mediterranean Europe phrasebook • Moscow • Munich • Netherlands • Normandy • Norway • Out to Eat – London • Out to Eat – Paris • Paris • Paris City Map • Paris Condensed • Poland • Polish phrasebook • Portugal • Portuguese phrasebook • Prague • Prague City Map • Provence & the Côte d'Azur • Read This First: Europe • Rhodes & the Dodecanese • Romania & Moldova • Rome • Rome City Map • Russia, Ukraine & Belarus • Russian phrasebook • Scandinavian & Baltic Europe • Scandinavian phrasebook • Scotland • Sicily • Slovenia • South-West France • Spain • Spanish phrasebook • St Petersburg • St Petersburg City Map • Sweden • Switzerland • Tuscany • Ukrainian phrasebook • Venice • Vienna • Walking in Britain • Walking in France • Walking in Ireland • Walking in Italy • Walking in Spain • Walking in Switzerland • Western Europe • World Food France • World Food Ireland • World Food Italy • World Food Spain
Travel Literature: After Yugoslavia • Love and War in the Apennines • The Olive Grove: Travels in Greece • On the Shores of the Mediterranean • Round Ireland in Low Gear • A Small Place in Italy

LONELY PLANET

Mail Order

Lonely Planet products are distributed worldwide.They are also available by mail order from Lonely Planet, so if you have difficulty finding a title please write to us. North and South American residents should write to 150 Linden St, Oakland, CA 94607, USA; European and African residents should write to 10a Spring Place, London NW5 3BH, UK; and residents of other countries to Locked Bag 1, Footscray, Victoria 3011, Australia.

INDIAN SUBCONTINENT & THE INDIAN OCEAN Bangladesh • Bengali phrasebook • Bhutan • Delhi • Goa • Healthy Travel Asia & India • Hindi & Urdu phrasebook • India • Indian Himalaya • Karakoram Highway • Kerala • Madagascar • Maldives • Mauritius, Réunion & Seychelles • Mumbai (Bombay) • Nepal • Nepali phrasebook • Pakistan • Rajasthan • Read This First: Asia & India • South India • Sri Lanka • Sri Lanka phrasebook • Tibet • Tibetan phrasebook • Trekking in the Indian Himalaya • Trekking in the Karakoram & Hindukush • Trekking in the Nepal Himalaya
Travel Literature: The Age of Kali: Indian Travels and Encounters • Hello Goodnight: A Life of Goa • In Rajasthan • Maverick in Madagascar • A Season in Heaven: True Tales from the Road to Kathmandu • Shopping for Buddhas • A Short Walk in the Hindu Kush • Slowly Down the Ganges

MIDDLE EAST & CENTRAL ASIA Bahrain, Kuwait & Qatar • Central Asia • Central Asia phrasebook • Dubai • Farsi (Persian) phrasebook • Hebrew phrasebook • Iran • Israel & the Palestinian Territories • Istanbul • Istanbul City Map • Istanbul to Cairo • Istanbul to Kathmandu • Jerusalem • Jerusalem City Map • Jordan • Lebanon • Middle East • Oman & the United Arab Emirates • Syria • Turkey • Turkish phrasebook • World Food Turkey • Yemen
Travel Literature: Black on Black: Iran Revisited • The Gates of Damascus • Kingdom of the Film Stars: Journey into Jordan

NORTH AMERICA Alaska • Boston • Boston City Map • Boston Condensed • British Columbia • California & Nevada • California Condensed • Canada • Chicago • Chicago City Map • Florida • Great Lakes • Hawaii • Hiking in Alaska • Hiking in the USA • Las Vegas • Los Angeles • Los Angeles City Map • Louisiana & the Deep South • Miami • Miami City Map • Montreal • New England • New Orleans • New York City • New York City City Map • New York City Condensed • New York, New Jersey & Pennsylvania • Oahu • Out to Eat – San Francisco • Pacific Northwest • Rocky Mountains • San Francisco • San Francisco City Map • Seattle • Southwest • Texas • Toronto • USA • USA phrasebook • Vancouver • Virginia & the Capital Region • Washington, DC • Washington, DC City Map • World Food New Orleans
Travel Literature: Caught Inside: A Surfer's Year on the California Coast • Drive Thru America

NORTH-EAST ASIA Beijing • Beijing City Map • Cantonese phrasebook • China • Hiking in Japan • Hong Kong • Hong Kong City Map • Hong Kong Condensed • Hong Kong, Macau & Guangzhou • Japan • Japanese phrasebook • Korea • Korean phrasebook • Kyoto • Mandarin phrasebook • Mongolia • Mongolian phrasebook • Seoul • Shanghai • South-West China • Taiwan • Tokyo • World Food Hong Kong
Travel Literature: In Xanadu: A Quest • Lost Japan

SOUTH AMERICA Argentina, Uruguay & Paraguay • Bolivia • Brazil • Brazilian phrasebook • Buenos Aires • Chile & Easter Island • Colombia • Ecuador & the Galapagos Islands • Healthy Travel Central & South America • Latin American Spanish phrasebook • Peru • Quechua phrasebook • Read This First: Central & South America • Rio de Janeiro • Rio de Janeiro City Map • Santiago de Chile • South America on a shoestring • Trekking in the Patagonian Andes • Venezuela
Travel Literature: Full Circle: A South American Journey

SOUTH-EAST ASIA Bali & Lombok • Bangkok • Bangkok City Map • Burmese phrasebook • Cambodia • Hanoi • Healthy Travel Asia & India • Hill Tribes phrasebook • Ho Chi Minh City • Indonesia • Indonesian phrasebook • Indonesia's Eastern Islands • Java • Lao phrasebook • Laos • Malay phrasebook • Malaysia, Singapore & Brunei • Myanmar (Burma) • Philippines • Pilipino (Tagalog) phrasebook • Read This First: Asia & India • Singapore • Singapore City Map • South-East Asia on a shoestring • South-East Asia phrasebook • Thailand • Thailand's Islands & Beaches • Thailand, Vietnam, Laos & Cambodia Road Atlas • Thai phrasebook • Vietnam • Vietnamese phrasebook • World Food Thailand • World Food Vietnam

ALSO AVAILABLE: Antarctica • The Arctic • The Blue Man: Tales of Travel, Love and Coffee • Brief Encounters: Stories of Love, Sex & Travel • Chasing Rickshaws • The Last Grain Race • Lonely Planet ... On the Edge: Adventurous Escapades from Around the World • Lonely Planet Unpacked • Not the Only Planet: Science Fiction Travel Stories • Sacred India • Travel Photography: A Guide to Taking Better Pictures • Travel with Children

LONELY PLANET

You already know that Lonely Planet produces more than this one guidebook, but you might not be aware of the other products we have on this region. Here is a selection of titles that you may want to check out as well:

Watching Wildlife Australia
ISBN 1 86450 032 8
US$19.99 • UK£12.99

Walking in Australia
ISBN 0 86442 669 0
US$21.99 • UK£13.99

Australian phrasebook
ISBN 0 86442 576 7
US$5.95 • UK£3.99

Australia
ISBN 1 86450 068 9
US$24.95 • UK£14.99

Outback Australia
ISBN 0 86442 504 X
US$21.95 • UK£13.99

Healthy Travel Australia, NZ & the Pacific
ISBN 1 86450 052 2
US$5.95 • UK£3.99

Sean & David's Long Drive
ISBN 0 86442 371 3
US$10.95 • UK£5.99

Diving & Snorkeling Australia's Great Barrier Reef
ISBN 0 86442 763 8
US$17.95 • UK£11.99

Tasmania
ISBN 0 86442 727 1
US$16.95 • UK£10.99

Australia Road Atlas
ISBN 1 86450 065 4
US$14.99 • UK£8.99

Sydney Condensed
ISBN 1 86450 045 X
US$9.95 • UK£5.99

Sydney
ISBN 0 86442 724 7
US$15.95 • UK£9.99

Available wherever books are sold

Index

Text
For a listing of rides, see the Table of Rides (pp4–5)

Bold indicates maps.

Boxed Text

ABOUT LONELY PLANET GUIDEBOOKS

Lonely Planet published its first book in 1973 in response to the numerous 'How did you do it?' questions Maureen and Tony Wheeler were asked after driving, busing, hitching, sailing and railing their way from England to Australia.

Written at a kitchen table and hand collated, trimmed and stapled, *Across Asia on the Cheap* became an instant local bestseller, inspiring thoughts of another book.

Eighteen months in South-East Asia resulted in their second guide, *South-East Asia on a shoestring*, which they put together in a backstreet Chinese hotel in Singapore in 1975. The 'yellow bible', as it quickly became known to backpackers around the world, soon became the guide to the region. It has sold well over half a million copies and is now in its 10th edition.

Today an international company with offices in Melbourne (Australia), Oakland (USA), London (UK) and Paris (France), Lonely Planet has an ever-growing list of books and other products, including: travel guides, walking guides, city maps, travel atlases, phrasebooks, diving guides, wildlife guides, healthy travel guides, restaurant guides, world food guides, first time travel guides, condensed guides, travel literature, pictorial books and, of course, cycling guides. Many of these are also published in French and various other languages.

In addition to the books, there are also videos and Lonely Planet's award winning Web site.

Some things haven't changed. The main aim is still to help make it possible for adventurous travellers to get out there – to explore and better understand the world.

At Lonely Planet we believe travellers can make a positive contribution to the countries they visit – if they respect their host communities and spend their money wisely. Since 1986 a percentage of the income from each book has been donated to aid projects and human rights campaigns.

> Lonely Planet gathers information for everyone who's curious about the planet – and especially for those who explore it first-hand. Through guidebooks, phrasebooks, activity guides, maps, literature, newsletters, image library, TV series and Web site we act as an information exchange for a worldwide community of travellers.

LONELY PLANET OFFICES

Australia
Locked Bag 1, Footscray, Victoria 3011
☎ 03 8379 8000 fax 03 8379 8111
✉ talk2us@lonelyplanet.com.au

USA
150 Linden St, Oakland, CA 94607
☎ 510 893 8555 or ☎ 800 275 8555 (toll free)
fax 510 893 8572
✉ info@lonelyplanet.com

UK
10A Spring Place, London NW5 3BH
☎ 020 7428 4800 fax 020 7428 4828
✉ go@lonelyplanet.co.uk

France
1 rue du Dahomey, 75011 Paris
☎ 01 55 25 33 00 fax 01 55 25 33 01
✉ bip@lonelyplanet.fr
🖳 www.lonelyplanet.fr

World Wide Web: 🖳 www.lonelyplanet.com *or* AOL keyword: lp
Lonely Planet Images: ✉ lpi@lonelyplanet.com.au